P9-CRA-790

THE ENDURING DEBATE

CLASSIC AND CONTEMPORARY READINGS IN AMERICAN POLITICS

Eighth Edition

THE ENDURING DEBATE

CLASSIC AND CONTEMPORARY READINGS IN AMERICAN POLITICS

Eighth Edition

Edited by
David T. Canon
John J. Coleman
Kenneth R. Mayer

W. W. NORTON & COMPANY
NEW YORK LONDON

W. W. Norton & Company has been independent since its founding in 1923, when William Warder Norton and Mary D. Herter Norton first published lectures delivered at the People's Institute, the adult education division of New York City's Cooper Union. The Nortons soon expanded their program beyond the Institute, publishing books by celebrated academics from America and abroad. By mid-century, the two major pillars of Norton's publishing program—trade books and college texts—were firmly established. In the 1950s, the Norton family transferred control of the company to its employees, and today—with a staff of 400 and a comparable number of trade, college, and professional titles published each year—W. W. Norton & Company stands as the largest and oldest publishing house owned wholly by its employees.

Printed in the United States of America

Composition: Westchester Publishing Services
Production supervisor: Elizabeth Marotta
Manufacturing by LSC Communications, Harrisonburg

Library of Congress Cataloging-in-Publication Data

Names: Canon, David T., editor. | Coleman, John J., 1959– editor. | Mayer, Kenneth R., 1960– editor.
Title: The enduring debate : classic and contemporary readings in American politics / edited by David T. Canon, John J. Coleman, Kenneth R. Mayer.
Description: Eighth edition. | New York : W. W. Norton & Company, 2017. | Includes bibliographical references.
Identifiers: LCCN 2017025060 | **ISBN 9780393283655 (pbk.)**
Subjects: LCSH: United States—Politics and government.
Classification: LCC JK21 .E53 2017 | DDC 320.473—dc23
LC record available at https://lccn.loc.gov/2017025060

W. W. Norton & Company Inc., 500 Fifth Avenue, New York, N.Y. 10110
www.wwnorton.com
W. W. Norton & Company Ltd., 15 Carlisle Street, London W1D 3BS
3 4 5 6 7 8 9 0

Contents

Preface xiii

About the Editors xv

PART I The Constitutional System

CHAPTER 1 Political Culture 3

1 "Beyond Tocqueville, Myrdal, and Hartz: The Multiple Traditions in America"—ROGERS M. SMITH 3

2 "The Three Political Cultures"—DANIEL J. ELAZAR 14

3 FROM *The Good Citizen: A History of American Civic Life* —MICHAEL SCHUDSON 26

DEBATING THE ISSUES: WHAT DOES IT MEAN TO BE AN AMERICAN? 34

4 "What It Means to Be American: Attitudes in an Increasingly Diverse America Ten Years after 9/11" —ROBERT P. JONES, DANIEL COX, E. J. DIONNE, AND WILLIAM A. GALSTON 35

5 "What Does It Mean to Be an American?"—STEVEN M. WARSHAWSKY 39

CHAPTER 2 The Founding and the Constitution 45

6 "The Nature of American Constitutionalism," FROM *The Origins of the American Constitution*—MICHAEL KAMMEN 45

7 *The Federalist*, No. 15—ALEXANDER HAMILTON 54

8 FROM *An Economic Interpretation of the Constitution of the United States* —CHARLES A. BEARD 59

DEBATING THE ISSUES: SHOULD THE CONSTITUTION BE FUNDAMENTALLY CHANGED? 65

9 "The Ratification Referendum: Sending the Constitution to a New Convention for Repair"—SANFORD LEVINSON 67

10 "Restoring the Rule of Law with States Leading the Way" —Greg Abbott 76

11 "An Article V Constitutional Convention? Wrong Idea, Wrong Time"—Walter Olson 82

CHAPTER 3 Federalism 86

12 *The Federalist*, No. 46—James Madison 86

13 from *The Price of Federalism*—Paul Peterson 91

14 "Jumping Frogs, Endangered Toads, and California's Medical-Marijuana Law"—George J. Annas 100

Debating the Issues: Immigration Reform—More Power to the States? 110

15 "Hamilton's Heirs: If He Wins a Second Term, the President-Elect Could Realistically Expel around 4 Million People in Total"—*The Economist* 111

16 "Forget Border Walls and Mass Deportations: The Real Changes in Immigration Policy are Happening in the States" —Pratheepan Gulasekaram and Karthick Ramakrishnan 114

17 "A States' Rights Approach to Immigration Reform" —Shikha Dalmia 117

CHAPTER 4 The Constitutional Framework and the Individual: Civil Liberties and Civil Rights 121

18 "Remarks by the President at the 50th Anniversary of the Selma to Montgomery Marches"—Barack Obama 121

19 "In Defense of Prejudice"—Jonathan Rauch 130

Debating the Issues: Should There Be a Religious Exemption to Nondiscrimination Laws? 138

20 "The Angry New Frontier: Gay Rights vs. Religious Liberty"—David Cole 139

21 "The Religious-Liberty War"—Tara Helfman 146

PART II Institutions

CHAPTER 5 Congress: The First Branch 155

22 FROM *Congress: The Electoral Connection*
—DAVID R. MAYHEW 155

23 "U.S. House Members in Their Constituencies: An Exploration"—RICHARD F. FENNO, Jr. 159

24 "Too Much of a Good Thing: More Representative Is Not Necessarily Better"—JOHN R. HIBBING AND ELIZABETH THEISS-MORSE 172

DEBATING THE ISSUES: CHECKS AND BALANCES—TOO MANY CHECKS, OR NOT ENOUGH BALANCE? 179

25 "America's Fragile Constitution"—YONI APPELBAUM 180

26 "Congress' Constitutional Prerogative vs. Executive Branch Overreach"—MATTHEW SPALDING 184

CHAPTER 6 The Presidency 189

27 "The Power to Persuade," FROM *Presidential Power*
—RICHARD NEUSTADT 189

28 "Perspectives on the Presidency," FROM *The Presidency in a Separated System*—CHARLES O. JONES 199

DEBATING THE ISSUES: SHOULD THE ELECTORAL COLLEGE BE REPLACED WITH A DIRECT POPULAR VOTE FOR PRESIDENT? 206

29 "Democracy Denied"—JOHN NICHOLS 207

30 "In Defense of the Electoral College"—RICHARD A. POSNER 212

31 "In Defense of the Electoral College"—ALLEN GUELZO AND JAMES HULME 215

CHAPTER 7 Bureaucracy 219

32 "The Study of Administration"—WOODROW WILSON 219

33 FROM *Bureaucracy: What Government Agencies Do and Why They Do It*—JAMES Q. WILSON 228

DEBATING THE ISSUES: SHOULD GOVERNMENT FUNCTIONS BE OUTSOURCED TO PRIVATE CONTRACTORS? 237

34 "Options for Federal Privatization and Reform Lessons from Abroad"—CHRIS EDWARDS 238

35 "*Federalist* No. 70: Where Does the Public Service Begin and End?"—JANINE R. WEDEL 248

CHAPTER 8 The Judiciary 259

36 *The Federalist,* No. 78—ALEXANDER HAMILTON 259

37 "The Court and American Life," FROM *Storm Center: The Supreme Court in American Politics*—DAVID O'BRIEN 266

38 *The Hollow Hope: Can Courts Bring About Social Change?*—GERALD N. ROSENBERG 273

DEBATING THE ISSUES: INTERPRETING THE CONSTITUTION —ORIGINALISM OR A LIVING CONSTITUTION? 279

39 "Constitutional Interpretation the Old-Fashioned Way" —ANTONIN SCALIA 280

40 "Our Democratic Constitution"—STEPHEN BREYER 288

PART III Political Behavior: Participation

CHAPTER 9 Public Opinion and the Media 303

41 "Polling the Public," FROM *Public Opinion in a Democracy*—GEORGE GALLUP 303

42 "Choice Words: If You Can't Understand Our Poll Questions, Then How Can We Understand Your Answers?" —RICHARD MORIN 311

43 "News vs. Entertainment: How Increasing Media Choice Widens Gaps in Political Knowledge and Turnout" —MARKUS PRIOR 316

DEBATING THE ISSUES: IS PARTISAN MEDIA EXPOSURE BAD FOR DEMOCRACY? 323

44 "Can Partisan Media Contribute to Healthy Politics?" —JOHN SIDES 324

45 "How Algorithms Decide the News You See" —Jihii Jolly 327

46 "Are Fox and MSNBC Polarizing America?"—Matthew Levendusky 330

CHAPTER 10 Elections and Voting 333

47 "The Voice of the People: An Echo," from *The Responsible Electorate*—V. O. Key, Jr. 333

48 "The Unpolitical Animal: How Political Science Understands Voters"—Louis Menand 339

49 "Telling Americans to Vote, or Else"—William Galston 348

Debating the Issues: Voter ID Laws—Reducing Fraud or Suppressing Votes? 352

50 "Voter Fraud: We've Got Proof It's Easy"—John Fund 353

51 "Should the Poor Be Allowed to Vote?"—Peter Beinart 356

52 "The Myth of Voter Fraud"—Lorraine C. Minnite 359

CHAPTER 11 Political Parties 362

53 "The Decline of Collective Responsibility in American Politics" —Morris P. Fiorina 362

54 "Be Careful What You Wish For: The Rise of Responsible Parties in American National Politics"—Nicol Rae 373

Debating the Issues: Should the United States Encourage Multi-Party Politics? 384

55 "Ending the Presidential-Debate Duopoly"—Larry Diamond 385

56 "A Third Party Won't Fix What's Broken in American Politics"—Ezra Klein 388

CHAPTER 12 Groups and Interests 392

57 "Political Association in the United States," from *Democracy in America*—Alexis de Tocqueville 392

58 "The Alleged Mischiefs of Faction," from *The Governmental Process*—David B. Truman 396

59 "The Logic of Collective Action," from *Rise and Decline of Nations* —Mancur Olson 404

Debating the Issues: Donor Disclosure—Is Anonynious Campaign Funding a Problem? 414

60 "Why Our Democracy Needs Disclosure"—Campaign Legal Center 415

61 "The Victims of 'Dark Money' Disclosure"—Jon Riches 420

PART IV Public Policy

CHAPTER 13 Government and the Economy 429

62 "Call for Federal Responsibility"—Franklin Roosevelt 429

63 "Against the Proposed New Deal"—Herbert Hoover 434

64 "The Rise and Fall of the GDP"—Jon Gertner 439

Debating the Issues: Is Income Inequality a Problem? 449

65 "Why Income Inequality Threatens Democracy"—Ray Williams 450

66 "How Income Inequality Benefits Everybody"—George Will 456

67 "How to Fix the Economy, and Income Inequality, the Libertarian Way"—A. Barton Hinkle 458

CHAPTER 14 Government and Society 462

68 "Providing Social Security Benefits in the Future: A Review of the Social Security System and Plans to Reform It"—David C. John 462

69 "American Business, Public Policy, Case Studies, and Political Theory"—Theodore J. Lowi 476

DEBATING THE ISSUES: SHOULD THE AFFORDABLE CARE ACT (OBAMACARE) BE REPEALED? 483

70 "United States Health Care Reform: Progress to Date and Next Steps"—BARACK OBAMA 484

71 "A Fresh Start for Health Care Reform"—EDMUND F. HAISLMAIER, ROBERT E. MOFFIT, NINA OWCHARENKO, AND ALYENE SENGER 496

CHAPTER 15 Foreign Policy and World Politics 507

72 "The Age of Open Society"—GEORGE SOROS 507

73 "Globalization Is Good for You"—RONALD BAILEY 510

DEBATING THE ISSUES: HOW DANGEROUS IS ISIS? 516

74 "The Spread of ISIS and Transnational Terrorism" —MATTHEW G. OLSEN 517

75 "Welcome to Generation War"—PAUL R. PILLAR 525

APPENDIX

The Declaration of Independence 537

The Federalist, No. 10—JAMES MADISON 541

The Constitution of the United States of America 547

Amendments to the Constitution 561

Marbury v. Madison (1803) 575

McCulloch v. Maryland (1819) 581

Brown v. Board of Education of Topeka, Kansas (1954) 587

Roe v. Wade (1973) 590

United States v. Nixon (1974) 595

United States v. Lopez (1995) 600

Obergefell v. Hodges (2015) 607

Acknowledgments 613

Preface

We compiled this reader with two goals in mind. The first was to introduce students to some of the classic works in political science, so that they could see how these historic arguments connected to the broad themes generally covered in college-level introductory courses in American government. We also introduce students to classic primary-source documents. We think there is great value in reading Richard Neustadt, David Truman, and V.O. Key, along with primary documents such as the *Federalist Papers* and a major speech by Franklin Roosevelt, among others in this book. Combining these classic readings with more modern selections is a good way to show how the main themes in American politics endure. As the title suggests, many contemporary issues are similar to what earlier generations of Americans—and the framers themselves—had to work out through existing political institutions and processes, or by changing those processes when they proved inadequate.

Our second goal was to expose students to debates on important contemporary political controversies. These debates give students examples of high-level political argumentation, showing how scholars and other expert commentators probe, analyze, and confront competing arguments. In some of the debates, authors directly challenge each other in a point/counterpoint format. In most of the debates, the authors do not directly engage each other, but rather present a range of arguments on opposing sides of issues. For example, in this edition we have added new debates on donor disclosure, ISIS, repeal of the Electoral College, and more. Our hope is that students will see the value of real argument and become discerning consumers of political information.

Finally, in addition to editing down selections to a manageable length while preserving the authors' central arguments, the book includes two pedagogical devices: the introduction to each article and debate, and discussion questions at the conclusion to each piece or cluster. The introductions provide students with the context of a given article or debate while briefly summarizing the arguments. The questions provide the basis for students to engage some of the main ideas of an article.

About the Editors

David T. Canon is professor and department chair of political science at the University of Wisconsin, Madison. His teaching and research interests focus on American political institutions, especially Congress, and racial representation. He is the author of several books, including the introductory text *American Politics Today* (with William Bianco), now in its fifth edition; *Actors, Athletes, and Astronauts: Political Amateurs in the United States Congress; Race, Redistricting, and Representation: The Unintended Consequences of Black Majority Districts* (winner of the Richard F. Fenno Prize); *The Dysfunctional Congress?* (with Kenneth Mayer); and various articles and book chapters. He served a term as the Congress editor of *Legislative Studies Quarterly*. He is an AP consultant and has taught in the University of Wisconsin AP Summer Institute for U.S. Government and Politics since 1997. Professor Canon is the recipient of a University of Wisconsin Chancellor's Distinguished Teaching Award.

John J. Coleman is dean of the College of Liberal Arts and professor of political science at the University of Minnesota. His teaching and research interests focus on political party coalitions, factions, and organizations; elections and campaign finance; and the intersection of politics and economic policy. He is the author or editor of several books, including *Party Decline in America: Policy, Politics, and the Fiscal State*, and numerous articles on topics such as political parties, legislative-executive relations, campaign finance, and the politics of economic policy. Professor Coleman is a past president of the Political Organizations and Parties section of the American Political Science Association. At the University of Wisconsin, he received a Chancellor's Distinguished Teaching Award, held a Glenn B. and Cleone Orr Hawkins Professorship, and was a Jeffrey and Susanne Lyons Family Faculty Fellow.

Kenneth R. Mayer is professor of political science at the University of Wisconsin, Madison, with research interests in the presidency, campaign finance, and election administration. He is the author of *With the Stroke of a Pen: Executive Orders and Presidential Power* (winner of the Richard E. Neustadt Award), *The Political Economy of Defense Contracting*, and *The Dysfunctional Congress? The Individual Roots of an Institutional Dilemma* (with David Canon). In 2006, he was the inaugural Fulbright-ANU Distinguished Chair in Political Science at the Australian National University and the recipient of a University of Wisconsin System teaching award.

THE
ENDURING DEBATE

CLASSIC AND CONTEMPORARY READINGS IN AMERICAN POLITICS

Eighth Edition

PART I

The Constitutional System

CHAPTER 1

Political Culture

1

"Beyond Tocqueville, Myrdal, and Hartz: The Multiple Traditions in America"

ROGERS M. SMITH

Political culture refers to the orientation of citizens toward the political system and toward themselves as actors in it. This includes the basic values, beliefs, attitudes, predispositions, and expectations that citizens bring to political life. Given the great diversity of the American population, one might expect a similarly diverse array of thought within political culture, with rival sets of political values challenging each other. However, even amidst this diversity of population, many scholars have argued that American political culture centers around commonly held beliefs, in part because of the unique characteristics of the founding of the United States. One influential interpretation is that American political life has been guided by the "liberal tradition"; the terms liberalism, liberal consensus, *and* American creed *have been used by other authors.* Liberal *here refers to its original meaning from eighteenth-century political and economic theory—a philosophy that focuses on the individual and minimizing government intervention in daily life. Within the liberal tradition, the beliefs in equality, private property, liberty, individualism, protection of religious freedom, and democracy are especially powerful. There is certainly debate over what these terms mean or how heavily to weigh one belief versus another when they are in conflict, and these clashes drive a wedge between Republicans and Democrats in the United States today. But in this interpretation, social and political movements in the United States, such as the Civil Rights and women's rights movements have generally not directly challenged these beliefs. On the contrary, most movements seek to show how their beliefs are highly consistent with these basic American principles.*

Where liberalism points to notions of equality, political scientist Rogers Smith argues that there is another, very different, tradition in American political thought that has been influential. He does not deny the significance of liberalism in American political history, as described most prominently by political scientist Louis Hartz.

Smith, however, contends that an equally significant strand of thought, "ascriptive Americanism," has been important across U.S. history. In this way of thinking, society is a hierarchy, where some groups are on top and others are below. Those on top are deemed to be deserving of the rights and benefits the liberal tradition can offer; those below are not. The most glaring examples of this disturbing pattern throughout American history have been the treatment of racial minorities, especially African Americans, and the structure of laws that denied women the same opportunities as men. Smith notes that those holding these illiberal views were not on the fringes of society but, rather, were probably the majority view at many times. We should not, Smith argues, minimize the impact of ascriptive Americanism or those who held these views. American public policy at the highest levels was influenced by its premises. Researchers at universities and other institutions aimed to show through science the inferiority of some races and groups to others. Moreover, the same individuals expended great intellectual energy to make these illiberal views seem acceptable and consistent with the liberal beliefs that they held simultaneously. American political culture, in Smith's view, combines multiple traditions of thought.

Since the nation's inception, analysts have described American political culture as the preeminent example of modern liberal democracy, of government by popular consent with respect for the equal rights of all. They have portrayed American political development as the working out of liberal democratic or republican principles, via both "liberalizing" and "democratizing" socioeconomic changes and political efforts to cope with tensions inherent in these principles. Illiberal, undemocratic beliefs and practices have usually been seen only as expressions of ignorance and prejudice, destined to marginality by their lack of rational defenses. * * *

[Alexis de] Tocqueville's thesis—that America has been most shaped by the unusually free and egalitarian ideas and material conditions that prevailed at its founding—captures important truths. Nonetheless, the purpose of this essay is to challenge that thesis by showing that its adherents fail to give due weight to inegalitarian ideologies and conditions that have shaped the participants and the substance of American politics just as deeply. For over 80% of U.S. history, its laws declared most of the world's population to be ineligible for full American citizenship solely because of their race, original nationality, or gender. For at least two-thirds of American history, the majority of the domestic adult population was also ineligible for full citizenship for the same reasons. * * *

The Tocquevillian story is thus deceptive because it is too narrow. It is centered on relationships among a minority of Americans (white men, largely of northern European ancestry) analyzed via reference to categories derived from the hierarchy of political and economic statuses men have held in Europe: monarchs and aristocrats, commercial burghers, farmers, industrial and rural laborers, and indigents. Because most European observers and British American men have regarded these categories as politically fundamental, it is understandable that they have always found the most striking fact about the new nation to be its lack of one type of ascriptive hierarchy. There was no hereditary monarchy or nobility native to British America, and the revolutionaries rejected both the authority of the British king and aristocracy and the creation of any new American substitutes. Those features of American political life made the United States appear remarkably egalitarian by comparison with Europe.

But the comparative moral, material, and political egalitarianism that prevailed at the founding among moderately propertied white men was surrounded by an array of other fixed, ascriptive systems of unequal status, all largely unchallenged by the American revolutionaries. Men were thought naturally suited to rule over women, within both the family and the polity. White northern Europeans were thought superior culturally—and probably biologically—to black Africans, bronze Native Americans, and indeed all other races and civilizations. Many British Americans also treated religion as an inherited condition and regarded Protestants as created by God to be morally and politically, as well as theologically, superior to Catholics, Jews, Muslims, and others.

These beliefs were not merely emotional prejudices or "attitudes." Over time, American intellectual and political elites elaborated distinctive justifications for these ascriptive systems, including inegalitarian scriptural readings, the scientific racism of the "American school" of ethnology, racial and sexual Darwinism, and the romantic cult of Anglo-Saxonism in American historiography. All these discourses identified the true meaning of *Americanism* with particular forms of cultural, religious, ethnic, and especially racial and gender hierarchies. Many adherents of ascriptive Americanist outlooks insisted that the nation's political and economic structures should formally reflect natural and cultural inequalities, even at the cost of violating doctrines of universal rights. Although these views never entirely prevailed, their impact has been wide and deep.

Thus to approach a truer picture of America's political culture and its characteristic conflicts, we must consider more than the familiar categories of (absent) feudalism and socialism and (pervasive) bourgeois liberalism and republicanism. The nation has also been deeply constituted by the ideologies and practices that defined the relationships of the white male minority with subordinate groups, and the relationships of these groups with each other. When these elements are kept in view, the flat plain of American egalitarianism mapped by Tocqueville and others suddenly looks quite different. We instead perceive America's initial conditions as exhibiting only a rather small, recently leveled valley of relative equality nestled amid steep mountains of hierarchy. And though we can see forces working to erode those mountains over time, broadening the valley, many of the peaks also prove to be volcanic, frequently responding to seismic pressures with outbursts that harden into substantial peaks once again.

To be sure, America's ascriptive, unequal statuses, and the ideologies by which they have been defended have always been heavily conditioned and constrained by the presence of liberal democratic values and institutions. The reverse, however, is also true. Although liberal democratic ideas and practices have been more potent in America than elsewhere, American politics is best seen as expressing the interaction of multiple political traditions, including *liberalism, republicanism*, and *ascriptive forms of Americanism*, which have collectively comprised American political culture, without any constituting it as a whole. Though Americans have often struggled over contradictions among these traditions, almost all have tried to embrace what they saw as the best features of each.

Ascriptive outlooks have had such a hold in America because they have provided something that neither liberalism nor republicanism has done so well. They have offered creditable intellectual and psychological reasons for many Americans to believe that their social roles and personal characteristics express an identity that has inherent and transcendant worth, thanks to nature, history, and God. Those rationales have obviously aided those who sat atop the nation's political, economic, and social hierarchies. But many Americans besides elites have felt that they have gained meaning, as well as material and political benefits, from their nation's traditional structures of ascribed places and destinies.

Conventional narratives, preoccupied with the absence of aristocracy and socialism, usually stress the liberal and democratic elements in the rhetoric of even America's dissenters. These accounts fail to explain how and why liberalizing efforts have frequently lost to forces favoring new forms of racial and gender hierarchy. Those forces have sometimes negated major liberal victories, especially in the half-century following Reconstruction; and the fate of that era may be finding echoes today.

My chief aim here is to persuade readers that many leading accounts of American political culture are inadequate. * * * This argument is relevant to contemporary politics in two ways. First, it raises the possibility that novel intellectual, political, and legal systems reinforcing racial, ethnic, and gender inequalities might be rebuilt in America in the years ahead. That prospect does not seem plausible if the United States has always been essentially liberal democratic, with all exceptions marginal and steadily eliminated. It seems quite real, however, if liberal democratic traditions have been but contested parts of American culture, with inegalitarian ideologies and practices often resurging even after major enhancements of liberal democracy. Second, the political implications of the view that America has never been completely liberal, and that changes have come only through difficult struggles and then have often not been sustained, are very different from the complacency—sometimes despair—engendered by beliefs that liberal democracy has always been hegemonic.

* * *

The Multiple-Traditions Thesis of American Civic Identity

It seems prudent to stress what is not proposed here. This is not a call for analysts to minimize the significance of white male political actors or their conflicts with each other. Neither is it a call for accounts that assail "Eurocentric" white male oppressors on behalf of diverse but always heroic subjugated groups. The multiple-traditions thesis holds that Americans share a *common* culture but one more complexly and multiply constituted than is usually acknowledged. Most members of all groups have shared and often helped to shape all the ideologies and institutions that have structured American life, including ascriptive ones. A few have done so while resisting all subjugating practices. But members of every group have sometimes embraced "essentialist" ideologies valorizing their own ascriptive traits and denigrating those of others, to bleak effect. Cherokees enslaved blacks, champions of women's rights disparaged blacks and immigrants, and blacks have often been hostile toward Hispanics and other new immigrants. White men, in turn, have been prominent among those combating invidious exclusions, as well as those imposing them.

Above all, recognition of the strong attractions of restrictive Americanist ideas does not imply any denial that America's liberal and democratic traditions have had great normative and political potency, even if they have not been so hegemonic as some claim. Instead, it sheds a new—and, in some respects, more flattering—light on the constitutive role of liberal democratic values in American life. Although some Americans have been willing to repudiate notions of democracy and universal rights, most have not; and though many have tried to blend those commitments with exclusionary ascriptive views, the illogic of these mixes has repeatedly proven a major resource for successful reformers. But we obscure the difficulty of those reforms (and thereby diminish their significance) if we slight the ideological and political appeal of contrary ascriptive traditions by portraying them as merely the shadowy side of a hegemonic liberal republicanism.

At its heart, the multiple-traditions thesis holds that the definitive feature of American political culture has been not its liberal, republican, or "ascriptive Americanist" elements but, rather, this more complex pattern of apparently inconsistent combinations of the traditions, accompanied by recurring conflicts. Because standard accounts neglect this pattern, they do not explore how and why Americans have tried to uphold aspects of all three of these heterogeneous traditions in combinations that are longer on political and psychological appeal than on intellectual coherency.

A focus on these questions generates an understanding of American politics that differs from Tocquevillian ones in four major respects. First, on this view, purely liberal and republican conceptions of civic identity are seen as frequently unsatisfying to many Americans, because they contain elements that threaten, rather than affirm, sincere, reputable beliefs in the propriety of the privileged positions that whites, Christianity, Anglo-Saxon traditions, and patriarchy have had in the United States. At the same time, even Americans deeply attached to those inegalitarian arrangements have also had liberal democratic values. Second, it has therefore been typical, not aberrational, for Americans to embody strikingly opposed beliefs in their institutions, such as doctrines that blacks should and should not be full and equal citizens. But though American efforts to blend aspects of opposing views have often been remarkably stable, the resulting tensions have still been important sources of change. Third, when older types of ascriptive inequality, such as slavery, have been rejected as unduly illiberal, it has been normal, not anomalous, for many Americans to embrace new doctrines and institutions that reinvigorate the hierarchies they esteem in modified form. Changes toward greater inequality and exclusion, as well as toward greater equality and inclusiveness, thus can and do occur. Finally, the dynamics of American development cannot simply be seen as a rising tide of liberalizing forces progressively submerging contrary beliefs and practices. The national course has been more serpentine. The economic, political, and moral forces propelling the United States toward liberal democracy have often been heeded by American leaders, especially since World War II. But the currents pulling toward fuller expression of alleged natural and cultural inequalities have also always won victories. In some eras they have predominated, appearing to define not only the path of safety but that of progress. In all eras, including our own, many Americans have combined their allegiance to liberal democracy with beliefs that the presence of certain groups favored by history, nature, and God has made Americans an intrinsically "special" people. Their adherents have usually regarded such beliefs as benign and intellectually well founded; yet they also have always had more or less harsh discriminatory corollaries.

To test these multiple-traditions claims, consider the United States in 1870. By then the Civil War and Reconstruction had produced dramatic advances in the liberal and democratic character of America's laws. Slavery was abolished. All persons born in the United States and subject to its jurisdiction were deemed citizens of the United States and the states in which they resided, regardless of their race, creed or gender. None could be denied voting rights on racial grounds. The civil rights of all were newly protected through an array of national statutes. The 1790 ban on naturalizing Africans had been repealed, and expatriation declared a natural right. Over the past two decades women had become more politically engaged and had begun to gain respect as political actors.

* * *

[Neither liberal or republican analyses] would have had the intellectual resources to explain what in fact occurred. Over the next fifty years, Americans did not make blacks, women, and members of other races full and equal citizens, nor did racial and gender prejudices undergo major erosion. Neither, however, were minorities and women declared to be subhuman and outside the body politic. And although white Americans engaged in extensive violence against blacks and Native Americans, those groups grew in population, and no cataclysm loomed. Instead, intellectual and political elites worked out the most elaborate theories of racial and gender hierarchy in U.S. history and partially embodied them in a staggering array of new laws governing naturalization, immigration, deportation, voting rights, electoral institutions, judicial procedures, and economic rights—but only partially. The laws retained important liberal and democratic features, and some were strengthened. They had enough purchase on the moral and material interests of most Americans to compel advocates of inequality to adopt contrived, often clumsy means to achieve their ends.

The considerable success of the proponents of inegalitarian ideas reflects the power these traditions have long had in America. But after the Civil War, * * * evolutionary theories enormously strengthened the intellectual prestige of doctrines presenting the races and sexes as naturally arrayed into what historians have termed a "raciocultural hierarchy," as well as a "hierarchy of sex." Until the end of the nineteenth century, most evolutionists * * * thought acquired characteristics could be inherited. Thus beliefs in biological differences were easily merged with the * * * historians' views that peoples were the products of historical and cultural forces. Both outlooks usually presented the current traits of the races as fixed for the foreseeable future. Few intellectuals were shy about noting the implications of these views for public policy. Anthropologist Daniel G. Brinton made typical arguments in his 1895 presidential address to the American Association for the Advancement of Science. He contended that the "black, brown and red races" each had "a peculiar mental temperament which has become hereditary," leaving them constitutionally "recreant to the codes of civilization." Brinton believed that this fact had not been adequately appreciated by American lawmakers. Henceforth, conceptions of "race, nations, tribes" had to "supply the only sure foundations for legislation; not *a priori* notions of the rights of man."

As Brinton knew, many politicians and judges had already begun to seize on such suggestions. In 1882, for example, California senator John Miller drew on the Darwinian "law of the 'survival of the fittest' " to explain that "forty centuries of Chinese life" had "ground into" the Chinese race characteristics that made them unbeatable competitors against the free white man. They were "automatic engines of flesh and blood," of "obtuse nerve," marked by degradation and demoralization, and thus far below the Anglo-Saxon, but were still a threat to the latter's livelihood in a market economy. Hence, Miller argued, the immigration of Chinese laborers must be banned. His bill prevailed, many expressing concern that these Chinese would otherwise become American citizens. The Chinese Exclusion Act was not a vestige of the past but something new, the first repudiation of America's long history of open immigration; and it was justified in terms of the postwar era's revivified racial theories.

Yet although men like Miller not only sustained but expanded Chinese exclusions until they were made virtually total in 1917 (and tight restrictions survived until 1965), they never managed to deny American citizenship to all of the "Chinese race." Until 1917 there were no restrictions on the immigration of upper-class Chinese, and in 1898 the Supreme Court declared that children born on U.S. soil to Chinese parents were American citizens (*United States* v. *Wong Kim Ark* 1898). Birthplace citizenship was a doctrine enshrined in common law, reinforced by the Fourteenth Amendment, and vital to citizenship for the children of *all* immigrant aliens. Hence it had enough legal and political support to override the Court's recognition of Congress's exclusionary desires. Even so, in other cases the Court sustained bans on Chinese immigration while admitting the racial animosities behind them, as in the "Chinese Exclusion Case" (*Chae Chan Ping* v. *United States* 1889); upheld requirements for Chinese-Americans to have certificates of citizenship not required of whites (*Fong Yue Ting* v. *United States* 1893); and permitted officials to deport even Chinese persons who had later been judged by courts to be native-born U.S. citizens (*United States* v. *Ju Toy* 1905).

The upshot, then, was the sort of none-too-coherent mix that the multiple-traditions thesis holds likely. Chinese were excluded on racial grounds, but race did not bar citizenship to those born in the United States; yet Chinese ancestry could subject some American citizens to burdens, including deportation, that others did not face. The mix was not perfect from any ideological viewpoint, but it was politically popular. It maintained a valued inclusive feature of American law (birthplace citizenship) while sharply reducing the resident Chinese population. And it most fully satisfied the increasingly powerful champions of Anglo-Saxon supremacy.

From 1887 on, academic reformers and politicians sought to restrict immigration more generally by a means that paid lip service to liberal norms even as it aimed at racist results—the literacy test. On its face, this measure expressed concern only for the intellectual merits of immigrants. But the test's true aims were spelled out in 1896 by its sponsor, Senator Henry Cabot Lodge, a Harvard Ph.D. in history and politics. Committee research, he reported, showed that the test would exclude "the Italians, Russians, Poles, Hungarians, Greeks, and Asiatics," thereby preserving "the quality of our race and citizenship." Citing "modern history" and "modern science," Thomas Carlyle and Gustave le Bon, Lodge contended that the need for racial exclusion arose from "something deeper and more fundamental than anything which concerns the intellect." Race was above all constituted by moral characteristics, the "stock of ideas, traditions, sentiments, modes of thought" that a people possessed as an "accumulation of centuries of toil and conflict." These mental and moral qualities constituted the "soul of a race," an inheritance in which its members "blindly believe," and upon which learning had no effect. But these qualities could be degraded if "a lower race mixes with a higher"; thus, exclusion by race, not reading ability, was the nation's proper goal.

When the literacy test finally passed in 1917 but proved ineffective in keeping out "lower races," Congress moved to versions of an explicitly racist national-origins quota system. It banned virtually all Asians and permitted European immigration only in ratios preserving the northern European cast of the American citizenry. Congressman Albert Johnson, chief author of the most important quota act in 1924, proclaimed that through it, "the day of indiscriminate acceptance of all races, has definitely ended." The quota system, repealed only in 1965, was a novel, elaborate monument to ideologies holding that access to American citizenship should be subject to racial and ethnic limits. It also served as the prime model for similar systems in Europe and Latin America.

* * *

But despite the new prevalence of such attitudes on the part of northern and western elites in the late nineteenth century, the Reconstruction amendments and statutes were still on the books, and surviving liberal sentiments made repealing them politically difficult. Believers in racial inequality were, moreover, undecided on just what to do about blacks. * * * "Radical" racists * * * argued that blacks, like other lower races, should be excluded from American society and looked hopefully for evidence that they were dying out. Their position was consistent with Hartz's claim that Americans could not tolerate permanent unequal statuses; persons must either be equal citizens or outsiders. But * * * "Conservatives" believed * * * that blacks and other people of color might instead have a permanent "place" in America, so long as "placeness included hierarchy." Some still thought that blacks, like the other "lower races," might one day be led by whites to fully civilized status, but no one expected progress in the near future. Thus blacks should instead be segregated, largely disfranchised, and confined to menial occupations via inferior education and discriminatory hiring practices—but not expelled, tortured, or killed. A few talented blacks might even be allowed somewhat higher stations.

* * * The result was a system closest to Conservative desires, one that kept blacks in their place, although that place was structured more repressively than most Conservatives favored. And unlike the ineffective literacy test, here racial inegalitarians achieved much of what they wanted without explicitly violating liberal legal requirements. Complex registration systems, poll taxes, and civics tests appeared race-neutral but were designed and administered to disfranchise blacks. This intent was little masked. * * * These efforts succeeded. Most dramatically, in Louisiana 95.6% of blacks were registered in 1896, and over half (130,000) voted. After disfranchising measures, black registration dropped by 90% and by 1904 totaled only 1,342. The Supreme Court found convoluted ways to close its eyes to these tactics.

By similar devices, blacks were virtually eliminated from juries in the south, where 90% of American blacks lived, sharply limiting their ability to have their personal and economic rights protected by the courts. "Separate but equal" educational and business laws and practices also stifled the capacities of blacks to participate in the nation's economy as equals, severely curtailed the occupations they could train for, and marked them—unofficially but clearly—as an inferior caste. Thus here, as elsewhere, it was evident that the nation's laws and institutions were not meant to confer the equal civic status they proclaimed for all Americans; but neither did they conform fully to doctrines favoring overt racial hierarchy. They represented another asymmetrical compromise among the multiple ideologies vying to define American political culture.

So, too, did the policies governing two groups whose civic status formally improved during these years: Native Americans and women.

* * *

This period also highlights how the influence of inegalitarian doctrines has not been confined to white male intellectuals, legislators, and judges. The leading writer of the early twentieth-century women's movement, Charlotte Perkins Gilman, was a thoroughgoing Darwinian who accepted that evolution had made women inferior to men in certain respects, although she insisted that these differences were usually exaggerated and that altered social conditions could transform them. And even as he attacked Booker T. Washington for appearing to accept the "alleged inferiority of the Negro race," W. E. B. DuBois embraced the widespread Lamarckian view that racial characteristics were socially conditioned but then inherited as the "soul" of a race. He could thus accept that most blacks were "primitive folk" in need of tutelage. * * *

The acceptance of ascriptive inegalitarian beliefs by brilliant and politically dissident female and black male intellectuals strongly suggests that these ideas had broad appeal. Writers whose interests they did not easily serve still saw them as persuasive in light of contemporary scientific theories and empirical evidence of massive inequalities. It is likely, too, that for many the vision of a meaningful natural order that these doctrines provided had the psychological and philosophical appeal that such positions have always had for human beings, grounding their status and significance in something greater and more enduring than their own lives. * * *

In sum, if we accept that ideologies and institutions of ascriptive hierarchy have shaped America in interaction with its liberal and democratic features, we can make more sense of a wide range of inegalitarian policies newly contrived after 1870 and perpetuated through much of the twentieth century. Those policies were dismantled only through great struggles, aided by international pressures during World War II and the Cold War; and it is not clear that these struggles have ended. The novelties in the policies and scientific doctrines of the Gilded Age and Progressive Era should alert us to the possibility that new intellectual systems and political forces defending racial and gender inequalities may yet gain increased power in our own time.

* * *

The achievements of Americans in building a more inclusive democracy certainly provide reasons to believe that illiberal forces will not prevail. But just as we can better explain the nation's past by recognizing how and why liberal democratic principles have been contested with frequent success, we will better understand the present and future of American politics if we do not presume they are rooted in essentially liberal or democratic values and conditions. Instead, we must analyze America as the ongoing product of often conflicting multiple traditions.

Discussion Questions

1. According to Smith, what are some examples of how Americans in the late nineteenth century simultaneously held liberal and ascriptive Americanist views?
2. How would you know if belief in ascriptive hierarchy was as widespread as Smith contends? What kind of evidence would you look for?
3. How might advocates of liberalism and ascriptive Americanism define "the public good"?

2

"The Three Political Cultures"

Daniel J. Elazar

Political scientist Daniel J. Elazar agrees with Rogers Smith that American political culture consists of competing political traditions. Elazar sees three types of value systems across the country: individualism, traditionalism, and moralism. Individualism focuses on individual rights and views governing as a set of transactions among various individuals and groups. Traditionalism attempts to use government to preserve existing social arrangements. Moralism is focused on the community and engaging in politics to do good and is similar to a thread in American political thought known as classical republicanism. Reacting to the argument that American political culture was predominantly individualistic and liberal, some historians argued that classical republicanism also played an important role in American political life and perhaps the dominant role in the revolutionary era. One's individual liberty and freedom, which are paramount in the liberal tradition, might be more subject to societal and community limits in the classical republican view. In this view, defined as moralism *by Elazar, politics is not primarily about achieving one's personal interest. Rather, the focus is on serving the community and society, and individuals are to be motivated not by self-interest but by morality and virtue. According to Elazar, these three approaches vary in their prevalence across the country, and even within states there may be variation as to which of the three predominates. Some regions have a mixture of two of these value systems, whereas other areas are more purely of one type. In large part, the uneven distribution of the three political belief systems across the country has to do with migration patterns. Once certain ethnic groups and nationalities predominated in a particular area, their political and cultural beliefs influenced government and other institutions and influenced the way politics was practiced. These habits of how institutions and politics operate have perpetuated over time because newcomers find that behaving in a manner consistent with local beliefs and culture increases one's chances of being politically successful.*

The United States is a single land of great diversity inhabited by what is now a single people of great diversity. The singleness of the country as a whole is expressed through political, cultural, and geographic unity. Conversely, the country's diversity is expressed through its states, subcultures, and sections. In this section, we will focus on the political dimensions of that diversity-in-unity—on the country's overall political culture and its subculture.

Political culture is the summation of persistent patterns of underlying political attitudes and characteristic responses to political concerns that is manifest in a particular political order. Its existence is generally unperceived by those who are part of that order, and its origins date back to the very beginnings of the particular people who share it. Political culture is an intrinsically political phenomenon. As such, it makes its own demands on the political system. For example, the definition of what is "fair" in the political arena—a direct manifestation of political culture—is likely to be different from the definition of what is fair in family or business relationships. Moreover, different political cultures will define fairness in politics differently. Political culture also affects all other questions confronting the political system. For example, many factors go into shaping public expectations regarding government services, and political culture will be significant among them. Political systems, in turn, are in some measure the products of the political cultures they serve and must remain in harmony with their political cultures if they are to maintain themselves.

* * *

Political-culture factors stand out as particularly influential in shaping the operations of the national, state, and local political systems in three ways: (1) by molding the perceptions of the political community (the citizens, the politicians, and the public officials) as to the nature and purposes of politics and its expectations of government and the political process; (2) by influencing the recruitment of specific kinds of people to become active in government and politics—as holders of elective offices, members of the bureaucracy, and active political workers; and (3) by subtly directing the actual way in which the art of government is practiced by citizens, politicians, and public officials in the light of their perceptions. In turn, the cultural components of individual and group behavior are manifested in civic behavior as dictated by conscience and internalized ethical standards, in the forms of law-abidingness (or laxity in such matters) adhered to by citizens and officials, and in the character of the positive actions of government.

* * *

The national political culture of the United States is itself a synthesis of three major political subcultures. These subcultures jointly inhabit the country, existing side by side or sometimes overlapping one another. All three are of nationwide proportions, having spread, in the course of time, from coast to coast. Yet each subculture is strongly tied to specific sections of the country, reflecting the streams and currents of migration that have carried people of different origins and backgrounds across the continent in more or less orderly patterns.

Given the central characteristics that define each of the subcultures and their centers of emphasis, the three political subcultures may be called individualistic, moralistic, and traditionalistic. Each reflects its own particular synthesis of the marketplace and the commonwealth.

It is important, however, not only to examine this description and the following ones very carefully but also to abandon the preconceptions associated with such idea-words as individualistic, moralistic, marketplace, and so on. Thus, for example, nineteenth-century individualistic conceptions of minimum intervention were oriented toward *laissez-faire*, with the role of government conceived to be that of a policeman with powers to act in certain limited fields. And in the twentieth century, the notion of what constitutes minimum intervention has been drastically expanded to include such things as government regulation of utilities, unemployment compensation, and massive subventions to maintain a stable and growing economy—all within the framework of the same political culture. The demands of manufacturers for high tariffs in 1865 and the demands of labor unions for worker's compensation in 1965 may well be based on the same theoretical justification that they are aids to the maintenance of a working marketplace. Culture is not static. It must be viewed dynamically and defined so as to include cultural change in its very nature.

The Individualistic Political Culture

The *individualistic political culture* emphasizes the conception of the democratic order as a marketplace. It is rooted in the view that government is instituted for strictly utilitarian reasons, to handle those functions demanded by the people it serves. According to this view, government need not have any direct concern with questions of the "good society" (except insofar as the government may be used to advance some common conception of the good society formulated outside the political arena, just as it serves other functions). Emphasizing the centrality of private concerns, the individualistic political culture places a premium on limiting community intervention—whether governmental or nongovernmental—into private activities, to the minimum degree necessary to keep the marketplace in proper working order. In general, government action is to be restricted to those areas, primarily in the economic realm, that encourage private initiative and widespread access to the marketplace.

The character of political participation in systems dominated by the individualistic political culture reflects the view that politics is just another means by which individuals may improve themselves socially and economically. In this sense politics is a "business," like any other that competes for talent and offers rewards to those who take it up as a career. Those individuals who choose political careers may rise by providing the governmental services demanded of them and, in return, may expect to be adequately compensated for their efforts.

Interpretation of officeholders' obligations under the individualistic political culture vary among political systems and even among individuals within a single political system. Where the standards are high, such people are expected to provide high-quality government services for the general public in the best possible manner in return for the status and economic rewards considered their due. Some who choose political careers clearly commit themselves to such norms; others believe that an office-holder's primary responsibility is to serve him- or herself and those who have supported him or her directly, favoring them at the expense of others. In some political systems, this view is accepted by the public as well as by politicians.

Political life within an individualistic political culture is based on a system of mutual obligations rooted in personal relationships. Whereas in a simple civil society those relationships can be direct ones, those with individualistic political cultures in the United States are usually too complex to maintain face-to-face ties. So the system of mutual obligation is harnessed through political parties, which serve as "business corporations" dedicated to providing the organization necessary to maintain that system. Party regularity is indispensable in the individualistic political culture because it is the means for coordinating individual enterprise in the political arena; it is also the one way of preventing individualism in politics from running wild.

In such a system, an individual can succeed politically, not by dealing with issues in some exceptional way or by accepting some concept of good government and then by striving to implement it, but by maintaining his or her place in the system of mutual obligations. A person can do this by operating according to the norms of his or her particular party, to the exclusion of other political considerations. Such a political culture encourages the maintenance of a party system that is competitive, but not overtly so, in the pursuit of office. Its politicians are interested in office as a means of controlling the distribution of the favors or rewards of government rather than as a means of exercising governmental power for programmatic ends; hence competition may prove less rewarding than accommodation in certain situations.

Since the individualistic political culture eschews ideological concerns in its "business-like" conception of politics, both politicians and citizens tend to look upon political activity as a specialized one—as essentially the province of professionals, of minimum and passing concern to laypersons, and with no place for amateurs to play an active role. Furthermore, there is a strong tendency among the public to believe that politics is a dirty—albeit necessary—business, better left to those who are willing to soil themselves by engaging in it. In practice, then, where the individualistic political culture is dominant, there is likely to be an easy attitude toward the limits of the professional's perquisites. Since a fair amount of corruption is expected in the normal course of things, there is relatively little popular excitement when any is found, unless it is of an extraordinary character. It is as if the public were willing to pay a surcharge for services rendered, rebelling only when the surcharge becomes too heavy. Of course, the judgments as to what is "normal" and what is "extraordinary" are themselves subjective and culturally conditioned.

Public officials, committed to "giving the public what it wants," are normally not willing to initiate new programs or open up new areas of government activity on their own initiative. They will do so when they perceive an overwhelming public demand for them to act, but only then. In a sense, their willingness to expand the functions of government is based on an extension of the *quid pro quo* "favors" system, which serves as the central core of their political relationships. New and better services are the reward they give the public for placing them in office. The value mix and legitimacy of change in the individualistic political culture are directly related to commercial concerns.

The individualistic political culture is ambivalent about the place of bureaucracy in the political order. In one sense, the bureaucratic method of operation flies in the face of the favor system that is central to the individualistic political process. At the same time, the virtues of organizational efficiency appear substantial to those seeking to master the market. In the end, bureaucratic organization is introduced within the framework of the favor system; large segments of the bureaucracy may be insulated from it through the merit system, but the entire organization is pulled into the political environment at crucial points through political appointment at the upper echelons and, very frequently, also through the bending of the merit system to meet political demands.

* * *

The Moralistic Political Culture

To the extent that American society is built on the principles of "commerce" (in the broadest sense) and that the marketplace provides the model for public relationships, all Americans share some of the attitudes that are of great importance in the individualistic political culture. At the same time, substantial segments of the American people operate politically within the framework of two political cultures—the moralistic and traditionalistic political cultures—whose theoretical structures and operational consequences depart significantly from the individualistic pattern at crucial points.

The *moralistic political culture* emphasizes the commonwealth conception as the basis for democratic government. Politics, to this political culture, is considered one of the great human activities: the search for the good society. True, it is a struggle for power, but it is also an effort to exercise power for the betterment of the commonwealth. Accordingly, in the moralistic political culture, both the general public and the politicians conceive of politics as a public activity centered on some notion of the public good and properly devoted to the advancement of the public interest. Good government, then, is measured by the degree to which it promotes the public good and in terms of the honesty, selflessness, and commitment to the public welfare of those who govern.

In the moralistic political culture, individualism is tempered by a general commitment to utilizing communal (preferably nongovernmental, but governmental if necessary) power to intervene in the sphere of "private" activities when it is considered necessary to do so for the public good or the well-being of the community. Accordingly, issues have an important place in the moralistic style of politics, functioning to set the tone for political concern. Government is considered a positive instrument with a responsibility to promote the general welfare, although definitions of what its positive role should be may vary considerably from era to era.

As in the case of the individualistic political culture, the change from nineteenth- to twentieth-century conceptions of what government's positive role should be has been great; for example, support for Prohibition has given way to support for wage and hour regulation. At the same time, care must be taken to distinguish between a predisposition toward communal activism and a desire for federal government activity. For example, many representatives of the moralistic political culture oppose federal aid for urban renewal without in any way opposing community responsibility for urban development. The distinction they make (implicitly, at least) is between what they consider legitimate community responsibility and what they believe to be central government encroachment; or between communitarianism, which they value, and "collectivism," which they abhor. Thus, on some public issues we find certain such representatives taking highly conservative positions despite their positive attitudes toward public activity generally. Such representatives may also prefer government intervention in the social realm—that is, censorship or screening of books and movies—over government intervention in the economy, holding that the former is necessary for the public good and the latter, harmful.

Since the moralistic political culture rests on the fundamental conception that politics exists primarily as a means for coming to grips with the issues and public concerns of civil society, it embraces the notion that politics is ideally a matter of concern for all citizens, not just those who are professionally committed to political careers. Indeed, this political culture considers it the duty of every citizen to participate in the political affairs of his or her commonwealth.

Accordingly, there is a general insistence within this political culture that government service is public service, which places moral obligations upon those who participate in government that are more demanding than the moral obligations of the marketplace. There is an equally general rejection of the notion that the field of politics is a legitimate realm for private economic enrichment. Of course, politicians may benefit economically because of their political careers, but they are not expected to *profit* from political activity; indeed, they are held suspect if they do.

Since the concept of serving the community is the core of the political relationship, politicians are expected to adhere to it even at the expense of individual loyalties and political friendships. Consequently, party regularity is not of prime importance. The political party is considered a useful political device, but it is not valued for its own sake. Regular party ties can be abandoned with relative impunity for third parties, special local parties, or nonpartisan systems if such changes are believed to be helpful in gaining larger political goals. People can even shift from party to party without sanctions if such change is justified by political belief.

In the moralistic political culture, rejection of firm party ties is not to be viewed as a rejection of politics as such. On the contrary, because politics is considered potentially good and healthy within the context of that culture, it is possible to have highly political nonpartisan systems. Certainly nonpartisanship is instituted not to eliminate politics but to improve it, by widening access to public office for those unwilling or unable to gain office through the regular party structure.

In practice, where the moralistic political culture is dominant today, there is considerably more amateur participation in politics. There is also much less of what Americans consider to be corruption in government and less tolerance of those actions considered to be corrupt. Hence politics does not have the taint it so often bears in the individualistic environment.

By virtue of its fundamental outlook, the moralistic political culture creates a greater commitment to active government intervention in the economic and social life of the community. At the same time, the strong commitment to *communitarianism* characteristic of that political culture tends to channel the interest in government intervention into highly localistic paths, such that a willingness to encourage local government intervention to set public standards does not necessarily reflect a concomitant willingness to allow outside governments equal opportunity to intervene. Not infrequently, public officials themselves will seek to initiate new government activities in an effort to come to grips with problems as yet unperceived by a majority of the citizenry. The moralistic political culture is not committed to either change or the status quo *per se* but, rather, will accept either depending upon the morally defined ends to be gained.

The major difficulty of this political culture in adjusting bureaucracy to the political order is tied to the potential conflict between communitarian principles and the necessity for large-scale organization to increase bureaucratic efficiency, a problem that could affect the attitudes of moralistic culture states toward federal activity of certain kinds. Otherwise, the notion of a politically neutral administrative system creates no problem within the moralistic value system and even offers many advantages. Where merit systems are instituted, they are rigidly maintained.

* * *

The Traditionalistic Political Culture

The *traditionalistic political culture* is rooted in an ambivalent attitude toward the marketplace coupled with a paternalistic and elitist conception of the commonwealth. It reflects an older, precommercial attitude that accepts a substantially hierarchical society as part of the ordered nature of things, authorizing and expecting those at the top of the social structure to take a special and dominant role in government. Like its moralistic counterpart, the traditionalistic political culture accepts government as an actor with a positive role in the community, but in a very limited sphere—mainly that of securing the continued maintenance of the existing social order. To do so, it functions to confine real political power to a relatively small and self-perpetuating group drawn from an established elite who often inherit their "right" to govern through family ties or social position. Accordingly, social and family ties are paramount in a traditionalistic political culture; in fact, their importance is greater than that of personal ties in the individualistic political culture, where, after all is said and done, a person's first responsibility is to him- or herself. At the same time, those who do not have a definite role to play in politics are not expected to be even minimally active as citizens. In many cases, they are not even expected to vote. In return, they are guaranteed that, outside of the limited sphere of politics, family rights (usually labeled "individual rights") are paramount, not to be taken lightly or ignored. As in the individualistic political culture, those active in politics are expected to benefit personally from their activity, though not necessarily through direct pecuniary gain.

Political parties are of minimal importance in a traditionalistic political culture, inasmuch as they encourage a degree of openness and competition that goes against the fundamental grain of an elite-oriented political order. Their major utility is to recruit people to fill the formal offices of government not desired by the established power-holders. Political competition in a traditionalistic political culture is usually conducted through factional alignments, as an extension of the personalistic politics that is characteristic of the system; hence political systems within the culture tend to have a loose one-party orientation if they have political parties at all.

Practically speaking, a traditionalistic political culture is found only in a society that retains some of the organic characteristics of the pre-industrial social order. "Good government" in the political culture involves the maintenance and encouragement of traditional patterns and, if necessary, their adjustment to changing conditions with the least possible upset. Where the traditionalistic political culture is dominant in the United States today, political leaders play conservative and custodial rather than initiatory roles unless pressed strongly from the outside.

Whereas the individualistic and moralistic political cultures may encourage the development of bureaucratic systems of organization on the grounds of "rationality" and "efficiency" in government (depending

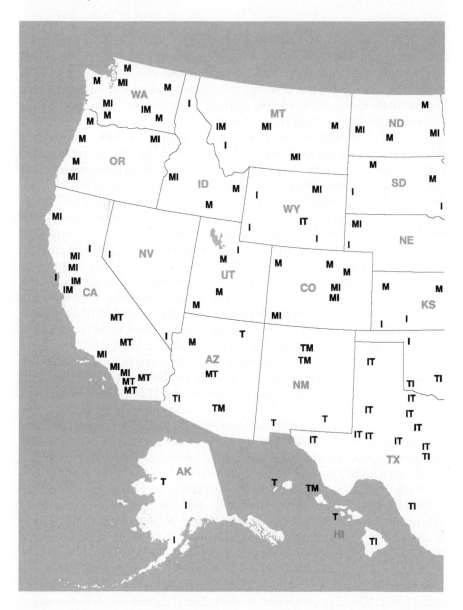

Map 1 The Regional Distribution of Political Cultures Within the States. *Source:* Daniel J. Elazar, *American Federalism: A View from the States*, 3d ed. (New York: Harper and Row Publishers, 1984), pp. 124–25. Reprinted by permission of Harper-Collins Publishers.

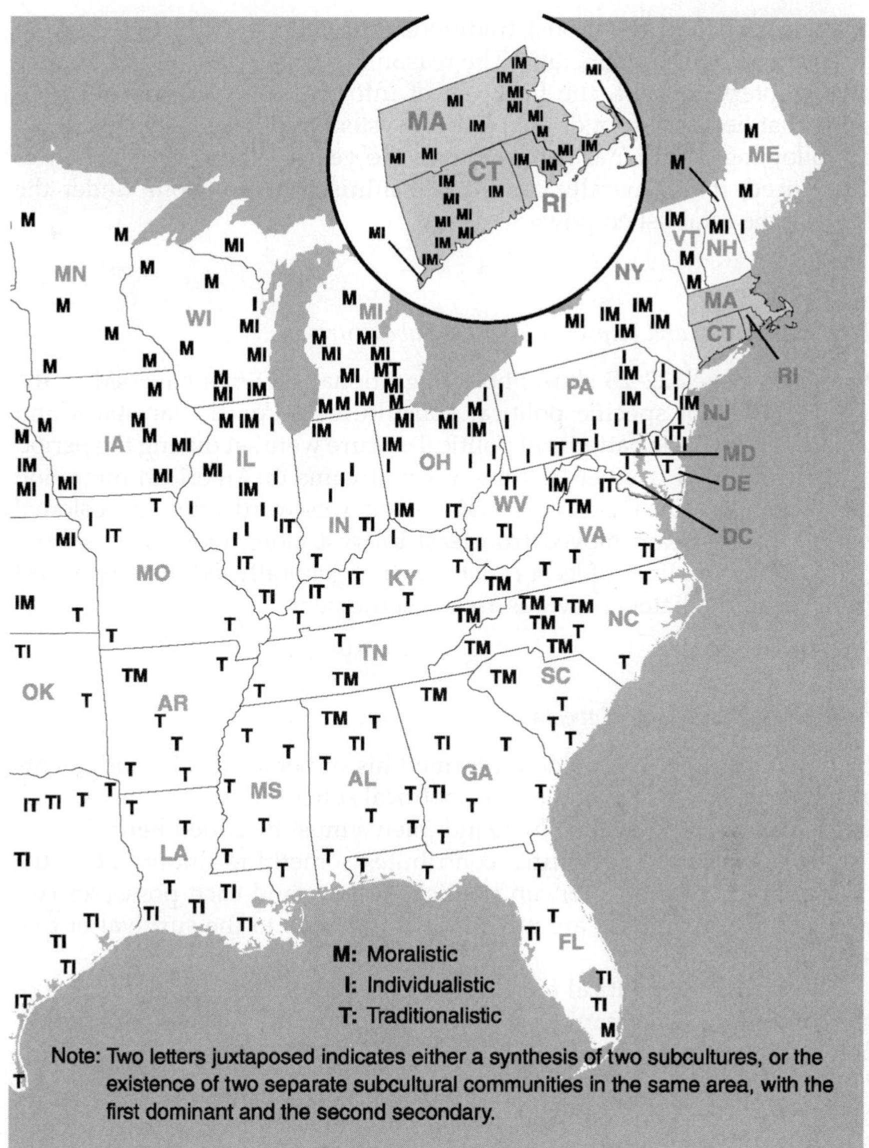
MA
CT
RI
ME
VT
NH
NY
MN
WI
MI
IA
IL
PA
NJ
MD
DE
DC
OH
IN
WV
VA
MO
KY
NC
TN
OK
AR
SC
MS
AL
GA
LA
FL
M: Moralistic
I: Individualistic
T: Traditionalistic
Note: Two letters juxtaposed indicates either a synthesis of two subcultures, or the existence of two separate subcultural communities in the same area, with the first dominant and the second secondary.

on their particular situations), traditionalistic political cultures tend to be instinctively anti-bureaucratic. The reason is that bureaucracy by its very nature interferes with the fine web of informal interpersonal relationships that lie at the root of the political system and have been developed by following traditional patterns over the years. Where bureaucracy is introduced, it is generally confined to ministerial functions under the aegis of the established power-holders.

* * *

The Distribution and Impact of Political Subcultures

Map 1 on pages 22–23 shows how migrational patterns have led to the concentration of specific political subcultures in particular states and localities. The basic patterns of political culture were set during the period of the rural-land frontier by three great streams of American migration that began on the East Coast and moved westward after the colonial period. Each stream moved from east to west along more or less fixed paths, following lines of least resistance that generally led them due west from the immediately previous area of settlement.

* * *

Political Culture: Some Caveats

By now the reader has no doubt formed his or her own value judgments as to the relative worth of the three political subcultures. For this reason a particular warning against *hasty* judgments must be added here. Each of the three political subcultures contributes something important to the configuration of the American political system, and each possesses certain characteristics that are inherently dangerous to the survival of that system.

The moralistic political culture, for example, is the primary source of the continuing American quest for the good society, yet there is a noticeable tendency toward inflexibility and narrow-mindedness among some of its representatives. The individualistic political culture is the most tolerant of out-and-out political corruption, yet it has also provided the framework for the integration of diverse groups into the mainstream of American life. When representatives of the moralistic political culture, in their striving for a better social order, try to limit individual freedom, they usually come up against representatives of the individualistic political culture, to whom individual freedom is the cornerstone of their pluralistic order, though not for any noble reasons. Conversely, of course, the moralistic political culture acts as a restraint against the tendencies of the individualistic political culture to tolerate anything as long as it is in the marketplace.

The traditionalistic political culture contributes to the search for continuity in a society whose major characteristic is change; yet in the name of continuity, its representatives have denied African Americans (as well as Native Americans and Latinos) their civil rights. When it is in proper working order, the traditionalistic culture has produced a unique group of first-rate national leaders from among its elites; but without a first-rate elite to draw upon, traditionalistic political-culture systems degenerate into oligarchies of the lowest level. Comparisons like these should induce caution in any evaluation of a subject that, by its very nature, evokes value judgments.

It is equally important to use caution in identifying individuals and groups as belonging to one cultural type or another on the basis of their public political behavior at a given moment in time. Immediate political responses to the issues of the day may reveal the political culture of the respondents, but not necessarily. Often, in fact, people will make what appear to be the same choices for different reasons—especially in public affairs, where the choices available at any given time are usually quite limited. Deeper analysis of what is behind those responses is usually needed. In other words, the names of the political cultures are not substitutes for the terms *conservative* and *liberal*, and should not be taken as such.

* * *

Discussion Questions

1. Consider the definitions Elazar presents in his analysis. What would you say are the fundamental differences and similarities among the three approaches with regard to the proper scope of government involvement in economic and social matters?

2. How important is public participation in politics across the three philosophies? Consider the role of bureaucracy as well in your response.

3. Examine Elazar's map for the part of the country where you attend school or the area you consider home. In your view, how accurately do the labels describe the politics of that area? What kinds of evidence are you considering when answering the question?

3

From *The Good Citizen: A History of American Civic Life*

MICHAEL SCHUDSON

One of the central questions in political culture is the nature of citizenship. What does citizenship entail? What obligations does it place upon the individual, and what benefits does it provide? What obligations does it place upon government, and how does government benefit from various conceptions of citizenship? These and related questions have received significant attention from scholars from multiple disciplines as well as from observers of American politics. Citizenship can be narrowly drawn to mean that one has met certain legal residency standards. Citizenship can more broadly convey access to particular rights and benefits in the political and legal spheres, and an obligation to participate energetically in those spheres. And citizenship might entail a more encompassing governmental provision of economic and social security to provide a foundation for a sense of full inclusion in national public life. Journalism scholar Michael Schudson focuses on the idea that citizenship is built upon expectations of robust participation and inclusion in American public life. He addresses the widespread concerns expressed in recent decades that American public life is in decline and that the notion of citizenship as requiring extensive participation in community and civic life has withered, imperiling the stability and legitimacy of the political system. Writing in the late 1990s, Schudson examines seven indicators of the health of citizenship and concludes that, although the indicators are mixed, the situation is not nearly as dire as some analysts would suggest.

Citizenship in the United States has not disappeared. It has not even declined. It has, inevitably, changed.

Past models of citizenship have not vanished as newer models became ascendant. The legacy of a colonial citizenship built on social hierarchy survives in the deference old families command and the traditions of public service they sometimes nurture. It endures in the trust people place in individuals who have a visible record of public service, personal integrity, charitable giving, and mentorship and sponsorship of younger leaders. It persists in the framework of our government in the ways that the constitutional machinery sifts raw opinion through deliberative legislative processes.

Similarly, the nineteenth-century citizenship of mass political participation carries on into our own day. Political parties, popular social movements, the social honor that citizens of every rank accrue for active participation in their communities, and the widespread obeisance in political rhetoric to public opinion, "the people," and majority rule all testify to the permanent contribution of mass democracy to modern politics. As for the Progressive Era ideal of the informed citizen, it, too, exerts enormous influence. It is the lamp held aloft by journalists committed to their profession, it directs civic education in and out of the schools, and it still dominates public understanding of civic obligation at election time. Even as rights-consciousness places the courtroom alongside the polling place in the practice of public life, and opens the political like a Pandora's box to cover a vastly expanded range of meanings, earlier visions of politics and citizenship survive and even prosper.

The successive coats that laminate our political ideals and practices have transformed citizenship profoundly. The United States has come from an era dominated by gentlemen to one dominated by parties, to one in which many groups and interests not only compete for political power but also contend with one another to define what powers are political. With such dramatic changes in who is free to participate in politics, what means are available for political participation, and what domains of human endeavor fall within the political, it would be remarkable if one could quickly sum up the changing quality of civic life as rise or fall. But many critics over the past two decades have made a case that the American story is, at least in the past half century, one of decline; civic life has collapsed. "By almost all the available evidence, we are witnessing a widespread turning away from public life," wrote the political philosopher Hanna Pitkin in 1981. "Public life is disappearing," the editors of *Harper's* declared in 1990, and many heartily agreed. Evidence is everywhere: the decline of parties; the fiscal impoverishment of cities strangled by suburbs; the dwindling of newspaper readership; disappearing trust in government and nearly all other major institutions; shrinking voter turnout; citizens' paltry knowledge of national and international affairs; the lack of substance in political campaigns; the decline of conversation and the informal gathering places where it is said to have flourished; the fear of street crime that keeps people behind their locked doors; the spread of scandal as a political issue—and more. The general point, it seems, has scarcely to be argued; the only question is what to do about it.

* * *

How could we know if citizenship and community are in decline? What kinds of measures might we look to, recognizing, of course, that the question is far too general to admit of any simple index?

The most familiar measure has been voter turnout—the percentage of citizens eligible to vote who do so has declined in the past generation. This is a relevant measure, indeed, in part because voting is an act not only of citizen participation but also of general faith in the political system.

Voting is an instrumental act to elect one candidate and not another, but it is also a mass ritual, and failure to engage in it suggests declining fervor for the religion of democracy. A decline in turnout is, on its face, a worrisome sign. On the other hand, high voter turnout is not necessarily a sign of civic health. An analyst would have to examine not only what percentage of the eligible electorate vote but also who is eligible to vote (the number doubled with woman's suffrage in 1920 and rose again after the Civil Rights Acts of 1964 and 1965 were passed and enforced) and what the act of voting means. The turnout decline since the 1960s is scarcely conclusive in itself. The high turnout figures of the nineteenth century, as I have argued, do not reveal that the civic health of America's party period was glowing; neither do recent low turnout figures indicate fatal illness.

A second measure would be people's expressed trust in government and other leading social institutions. Here, too, there has been a substantial decline; people are much less likely in the 1990s than in the 1960s to tell pollsters they "trust in" the president, the Congress, the medical profession, the military, the Supreme Court, business, unions, universities, or the news media. Still, as I have suggested, there can be too much trust as well as too little, and the baseline measures of trust from the 1950s and early 1960s surely reflected a moment of unusual consensus in American life held together by Cold War paranoia, middle-class complacency, postwar affluence, and the continuing denial of a voice in public life to women and minorities. Some of the skepticism about major institutions today is amply warranted. Skepticism can be healthy. Some of today's skepticism is in a grand old American tradition that distrusts all politics and politicians. Then again, some of it seems to express a deeper alienation or aimlessness, especially among the young. But in the crude measures we have, there is no distinguishing a healthy inclination to question authority from a depressed withdrawal in which it is impossible to place faith in anyone or anything.

A third plausible measure of civic health would be the stock of social capital as measured by people's membership in and connection to social groups in which they can and do participate. As Putnam has argued well, this is an important measure. Still, it is difficult to know how to weigh it against the growth of individual choice, which is its flip side. Let me offer an example. The Roman Catholic Church in America has long been a powerful institution in community-building, especially among the urban, immigrant working-class Catholics who for a century were the core of its membership. The Catholic parish was disciplined by the priest who had enormous power in prescribing norms of behavior for everyday life. His authority was exercised through a dense network of youth groups, fraternal organizations, parish sports teams, choirs, women's clubs, and, of course, parochial schools and the church itself. More than for Protestants or Jews, Catholic adherence to church was also involvement in a neighborhood. Into the 1950s, rental listings for homes and apartments in cities like Philadelphia and Chicago were categorized *by parish*. In the 1960s, the Catholic Church, like the rest of America, experienced profound changes, but more so. Pope John XXIII called the Second Vatican Council together in 1962, the first such council since 1870. The report of Vatican II, issued in 1965, declared that the church should adapt itself to modernity, dissent within the church could be tolerated, religious freedom should be prized, and the liturgy should be revised to make it more comprehensible to parishioners and more participatory. The Mass in Latin was now in English, the priest who had faced the wall and prayed silently now led the congregation in prayer; the once silent congregation now sang hymns, shook hands, and stood rather than knelt.

Vatican II was an authoritative statement that questioned authority. It had far-reaching consequences. The traditional deference of the laity to the clergy in the conduct of the church declined. As Catholics, both laity and clergy, participated actively in the civil rights movement, lay parishioners, nuns, and seminarians all were "imbued with new notions of 'rights'" and explicitly compared their lack of power or their ghettoization within the church to the condition of blacks in American society. When Vatican II was followed in 1968 by *Humanae vitae*, Pope Paul VI's encyclical that reaffirmed the prohibition on birth control, millions of Catholics were at least confused, and many of them felt betrayed, by a church they had believed was modernizing. Both clergy and laity protested, some by leaving the church or their vocations. There were 181,000 women in religious orders in 1966 and 127,000 by 1980, and the downward trend was the same for men. Even for those who remained, clerical leadership changed as lay leaders came to take a larger and larger role in church governance. The church became increasingly pluralistic: "There is no longer one way to do theology, to worship at Mass, to confess sin, or to pray. There are various ways of being Catholic, and people are choosing the style that best suits them." As Catholics moved to the suburbs, the link between parish, church, ethnicity, and personal identity did not break down, but it did to a degree break apart. Suburban Catholics are not Protestants and retain, as Andrew Greeley has argued, a distinctive Catholic "imagination," but the locus of authority about what it is to be Catholic has gravitated further from the church and closer to the household than a generation ago.

Was the old way better? Did the authoritarian structure that held together a parish community provide a stronger basis for self-fulfillment and a rich public life than the new structure that offered the individual more choice, autonomy, and power? The Catholic Church is, of course, only one example of the kind of institution that built social capital in the old days, and it is obviously an example of a particularly rigid and hierarchical cast. Yet it is one of the fundamental constituents of twentieth-century American society, the strength of its community life a major source of the strength of urban machine politics, the Democratic Party, and the union movement. Its broad influence seems much more important in this context than its atypicality, and its transformation reveals starkly that the trade-off between community and individualism is also a trade-off between hierarchy and egalitarianism, between authoritarian codes and democratic ones, between unitary, rigid ways of living and pluralistic ones, between imposition and individual choice. There are costs to the decline of traditional authority in the church, patriarchal family, party machine, and settled elites of community life. The costs are grounds for regret, nostalgia, and a variety of imaginative efforts at renewal, but few people find them grounds for turning back.

Voting, social trust, and social membership are the three most familiar measures of civic health, and the three most familiar bases on which it is argued that the present has slipped from a more desirable past. Other measures might be given consideration, too. A fourth measure is the quality of public discourse. Critics look at daytime talk shows, or listen to Howard Stern or Rush Limbaugh, or read pornography or scurrilous political gossip on the Internet, or feel assaulted by the public use of words that a generation ago could be heard only in locker rooms and not on television, or observe the reduction of political speeches to catchphrases that might win the attention of broadcast journalists committed to ever shorter sound bites. Can this be judged anything but degradation?

I do not have an answer here, but on this measure, too, there is another side of the story. The greater openness and rawness of public talk that produced raunchy talk shows also produced *All in the Family*, *Maude*, and *Ellen* in entertainment and programs like *60 Minutes* in television news. All of these programs share with their more disparaged and tasteless cousins a frank and aggressive style, a quest for transgression, and a pushing of the limits of conventional civility. Meanwhile, a serious argument can be made that ordinary Americans have better access to solid news reporting and analysis today than they did in 1960 or 1965. Journalists are less complacent in general; more individual journalists have become expert and ambitious contributors to public dialogue with magazine essays, long newspaper pieces, and nonfiction books; our leading newspapers reach many more people than ever through national editions and their own wire services (notably the *New York Times*, *Washington Post*, and *Los Angeles Times*); national network news is more sophisticated than a generation ago even if local television news is increasingly a moral desert; and in some major cities and regions there are today exponents of the best journalism the country has produced where none existed in 1960—I think of Chicago, Washington, D.C., and Los Angeles.

A fifth measure: how great is the disparity between rich and poor? Related to this: is there an economic bottom below which society by private and public efforts will not allow people to fall? Prosperity as such is no measure of civic life, nor is it apparent what level of economic inequality might endanger the public good. But there is a quality of care for the poor, lacking which a society has clearly failed. The United States remains a reluctant welfare state, never fully committed to seeing economic equality or even a baseline minimum economic subsistence as an obligation of the state. Even so, a smaller percentage of the population lives in poverty today than in 1960, although the percentage was higher in 1990 than in 1980.

One must consider quality as well as quantity in the disparity between rich and poor. It is important to know not only how great is the gap between those at the top and those at the bottom but how hopeless the world appears from the bottom. Do economic and social inequalities take on a castelike form? How well can one predict the economic or social life chances of an infant from the economic status, skin color, age, and marital status of his or her mother? If these predictions are becoming easier, then on this measure public life is getting worse.

Sixth, is the capacity of the least advantaged groups in society to make their voices heard in the political process increasing or decreasing? And what of less advantaged groups, say, blue-collar workers? If the power of unions is declining, as certainly it is, and if the Democratic Party is correspondingly less responsive to working-class concerns, has a large segment of the population lost its clearest access to political power?

Finally, is the reach of state-guaranteed rights increasing or decreasing? If it is increasing, then public life is improving in that public responsibility is growing and the range of human actions in which publicly accountable language is brought to bear is enlarging. Of course, state-guaranteed rights increase only because people believe that state or private power has violated the fundamental autonomy of individuals—the government has quartered its soldiers in your house without permission, the police have searched your house or person without a warrant, your school board has expelled you from school because your religious beliefs forbid you to salute the flag, your husband beats you, your employer threatens you for refusing sexual favors, your public transportation has not accommodated your wheelchair. If none of these things ever happened, then there would be no requirement of state-protected rights. But the existence of state-protected rights is a force for keeping these violations from happening or, at least, for calling people to account when they do. By this measure, it can scarcely be doubted that public life has improved in the past generation.

Public life can be measured by the inclusiveness of public deliberations. The more people among the total population who are eligible to shoulder the burden of public decision-making and who are equipped to do so, the better the public life of a society. By this measure, certainly, the United States after 1920 has a better public life than at any earlier time, and the United States after 1965 has a better public life than at any earlier time. To the extent that certain senseless discriminations, apart from limitations on voting, are struck down—for instance, discrimination in employment or housing on the basis of sexual orientation—this also helps to fully empower citizens to speak and participate. By this measure, American society is better since *Romer v. Evans* (1995) struck down

Colorado's anti-homosexual state constitutional amendment than it was before. To the extent that the poor and the oppressed whose voices have commonly been excluded from public deliberation today at least have institutionalized surrogates in public interest associations, law firms, foundations, and other organizations, there is progress rather than decline.

How is American public life doing today on these seven measures? Voter turnout offers troubling evidence of decline. Polling that indicates a lessening of trust in major institutions is a much more equivocal measure of civic health. We do not know what it means. How does the answer people give to an abstract question about their level of trust relate to actual behavioral indices of trust—compliance with the Internal Revenue Service or willingness to defer to the authority of a medical doctor, a government bureaucrat, a school administrator, or a court order? Nor do we know what the optimal level of trust would be. Surely it would be deeply troubling if 100 percent of the people placed "a great deal" of faith in the president, the Congress, big business, labor, medicine, universities, or the media. But is 75 percent the right level? Or 50 percent? Or 25 percent?

I do not think that trust, so far as polls are able to measure it, is an intelligible indicator of anything. What then, about social capital? Is declining membership in important civic organizations a clear sign of declining social health? I think a reasonable observer must be agnostic on this one. The decline in organizational solidarity is truly a loss, but it is also the flip side of a rise in individual freedom, which is truly a gain. Assessments of the state of public discourse must likewise reckon with its double-edged character. On the down side, public talk has clearly grown more harsh, more crude, and more uncivil over the past several decades. On the up side, however, public discourse is more honest and more inclusive of a wide range of persons and topics that the late, lamented "civility" excluded. These two measures seem to have an inherently paradoxical quality; the very social changes that give good reason for regret also give good reason for satisfaction.

As for the disparity between the most and least advantaged citizens, a straight-line trend seems hard to find. This measure seems to be very sensitive to party politics, so a society that grew more kind and just in the 1960s and 1970s became notably less so in the Reagan eighties, and only under President Bill Clinton has it begun to inch back toward decency.

Regarding the measures of political inclusion and protection for individual rights, Americans are unquestionably better off in the past quarter century than at any prior moment in our history. There are ups and downs here, too, but the 1960s and 1970s saw the emergence of a consensus that, though assaulted and even shaken, has not surrendered the field. It is, on the contrary, our new foundation.

By my count, then, there is a clear decline on one measure, clear progress on two others, a mixed verdict on three, and a judgment that one measure (trust) is thus far too faulty a concept to use. To summarize all of this as amounting to a decline in civic well-being is, to put it kindly, premature.

Of course, this is no more than a provisional thought-experiment, not a definitive assessment of the state of the nation. We do not truly know how to measure change on these seven dimensions, nor do we know how to weigh one dimension against another.

* * *

Discussion Questions

1. Schudson's argument is based on the premise that as civic life declines, the quality of citizenship declines as well. He argues that whether or not American civic life is in decline depends on where we look and how we interpret the trends. Are Schudson's seven indicators equally important, or should some be weighted more heavily than others in diagnosing the health of American civic life?
2. How might someone who views politics through the lens of moralism, individualism, or traditionalism, as explained by Daniel Elazar in the previous article, evaluate the list of indicators compiled by Schudson? Would they add or subtract any indicators?
3. Schudson, writing in the late 1990s, states that the assertions about the decline of civic life and the health of citizenship are exaggerated. With 20 years having elapsed since Schudson wrote, how well do his assessments of the seven indicators describe the present era?

Debating the Issues: What Does It Mean to Be an American?

What does it mean to be an American? This deceptively simple question is challenging to answer. Because the United States encompasses a vast array of ethnicities, religions, and cultures, it can be difficult to define "American" by reference to those criteria. The country's geography differs dramatically from region to region, and economic ways of life accordingly differ greatly as well. In many ways, diverse groups of Americans have experienced American history differently, so a common historical identity is not obviously the answer either. One popular argument is that the United States is united by a set of political ideals. As far back as the early nineteenth century, scholars have tried to identify the nature of American political culture: Is it a commitment to individualism? A belief in equality? A shared set of values about the appropriate role of government? Openness?

The events of September 11, 2001, created for most Americans a profound sense of national unity. Writing ten years later, Daniel Cox, E.J. Dionne, Robert Jones, and William Galston examine survey data and report that "Americans continue to grapple with issues of security, tolerance, religious freedom, and pluralism—matters that lie at the heart of what it means to be American." Public opinion data show the country embracing diversity and tolerance, but also divided along sharp political lines. The authors suggest that these political differences may create problems beyond the inevitable tensions that emerge in a diverse and dynamic society. In their conclusion, the authors argue that what it means to be an American has been evolving. They portray a pattern of "the classic American bargain" where new groups "become American" over a generation or two, adopting the language and culture and customs of Americans. These groups, in turn, change the nature of what it means to be an American, and later groups become American in this newly revised sense, and they themselves revise what it means to be American. In this view, the answer to "what does it mean to be an American" depends on when the question is being asked.

Steven Warshawsky argues that American identity centers around a commonly held set of ideas that can be considered the American way of life. This way of life includes beliefs in liberty, equality, property rights, religious freedom, limited government, and a common language for conducting political and economic affairs. Although America has always been a nation of immigrants, from the original European settlers to the mass immigration of the late nineteenth and early twentieth centuries, Warshawsky sees assimilation into American political culture as critical to American national identity. He also notes that America, including the scope and reach of government, has changed dramatically over time. Warshawsky asks whether these changes have also changed what it means to be an American. He argues this is a difficult question but concludes that straying too far from the principles of the Founders means "we will cease to be 'Americans' in any meaningful sense of the word."

4

"What It Means to Be American: Attitudes in an Increasingly Diverse America Ten Years after 9/11"

ROBERT P. JONES, DANIEL COX, E.J. DIONNE, AND WILLIAM A. GALSTON

Ten years after the September 11th terrorist attacks, Americans believe they are more safe but have less personal freedom and that the country is less respected in the world than it was prior to September 11, 2001. A small majority (53 percent) of Americans say that today the country is safer from terrorism than it was prior to the September 11th attacks. In contrast, nearly 8 in 10 say that Americans today have less personal freedom and nearly 7 in 10 say that America is less respected in the world today than before the terrorist attacks.

Americans strongly affirm the principles of religious freedom, religious tolerance, and separation of church and state. Nearly 9 in 10 (88 percent) Americans agree that America was founded on the idea of religious freedom for everyone, including religious groups that are unpopular. Ninety-five percent of Americans agree that all religious books should be treated with respect even if we don't share the religious beliefs of those who use them. Nearly two-thirds (66 percent) of Americans agree that we must maintain a strict separation of church and state. Americans' views of Muslims and Islam are mixed, however. As with other previously marginalized religious groups in U.S. history, Americans are grappling with the questions Islam poses to America's founding principles and way of life.

Americans who are part of the Millennial generation (ages 18–29) are twice as likely as seniors (ages 65 and older) to have daily interactions with African Americans (51 percent vs. 25 percent respectively) and Hispanics (44 percent vs. 17 percent respectively), and to speak at least occasionally to Muslims (34 percent vs. 16 percent respectively).

Nearly half (46 percent) of Americans agree that discrimination against whites has become as big a problem as discrimination against blacks and other minorities. A slim majority (51 percent) disagree.

- A slim majority of whites agree that discrimination against whites has become as big a problem as discrimination against minority groups, compared to only about 3 in 10 blacks and Hispanics who agree.
- Approximately 6 in 10 Republicans and those identifying with the Tea Party agree that discrimination against whites is as big a problem as discrimination against minority groups.
- Nearly 7 in 10 Americans who say they most trust Fox News say that discrimination against whites has become as big a problem as discrimination against blacks and other minorities. In stark contrast, less than 1 in 4 Americans who most trust public television for their news agree.

Americans are evenly divided over whether the values of Islam are at odds with American values and way of life (47 percent agree, 48 percent disagree).

- Approximately two-thirds of Republicans, Americans who identify with the Tea Party movement, and Americans who most trust Fox News agree that the values of Islam are at odds with American values. A majority of Democrats, Independents, and those who most trust CNN or public television disagree.
- Major religious groups are divided on this question. Nearly 6 in 10 white evangelical Protestants believe the values of Islam are at odds with American values, but majorities of Catholics, non-Christian religiously unaffiliated Americans, and religiously unaffiliated Americans disagree.

By a margin of 2-to-1, the general public rejects the notion that American Muslims ultimately want to establish Shari'a law as the law of the land in the United States (61 percent disagree, 30 percent agree).

- Over the last 8 months agreement with this question has increased by 7 points, from 23 percent in February 2011 to 30 percent today.
- Nearly 6 in 10 Republicans who most trust Fox News believe that American Muslims are trying to establish Shari'a law in the U.S. The attitudes of Republicans who most trust other news sources look similar to the general population.

A majority (54 percent) of the general public agree that American Muslims are an important part of the religious community in the United States, compared to 43 percent who disagree.

Nearly 8 in 10 (79 percent) Americans say people in Muslim countries have an unfavorable opinion of the United States, including 46 percent who say Muslims have a very unfavorable opinion of the United States. Among Americans who believe that people in Muslim countries have an unfavorable view of the United States, three-quarters believe that such views are not justified.

Americans employ a double standard when evaluating violence committed by self-identified Christians and Muslims. More than 8 in 10 (83 percent) Americans say that self-proclaimed Christians who commit acts of violence in the name of Christianity are not really Christians. In contrast, less than half (48 percent) of Americans say that self-proclaimed Muslims who commit acts of violence in the name of Islam are not really Muslims.

Americans hold a number of positive views about immigrants, but also have some reservations.

- Overwhelming majorities of Americans believe immigrants are hard working (87 percent) and have strong family values (80 percent), and a majority (53 percent) say newcomers from other countries strengthen American society.
- On the other hand, more than 7 in 10 (72 percent) also believe immigrants mostly keep to themselves, and a slim majority (51 percent) say they do not make an effort to learn English.

Americans are significantly more likely to say that immigrants are changing American society than their own community. A majority (53 percent) of Americans say that immigrants are changing American society and way of life a lot, compared to less than 4 in 10 (38 percent) who say immigrants are changing their community and way of life a lot. Conservatives are not more likely than liberals to say immigrants are changing their own communities a lot, but conservatives are significantly more likely than liberals to say that immigrants are changing American society a lot.

Americans' views on immigration policy are complex, but when Americans are asked to choose between a comprehensive approach to immigration reform that couples enforcement with a path to citizenship on the one hand, and an enforcement and deportation only approach on the other, Americans prefer the comprehensive approach to immigration reform over the enforcement only approach by a large margin (62 percent vs. 36 percent).

- Nearly three-quarters of Democrats and more than 6 in 10 political independents say that both securing the border and providing an earned path to citizenship is the best way to solve the illegal immigration problem. Republicans are nearly evenly divided. In contrast, nearly 6 in 10 of Americans who identify with the Tea Party movement say that securing the border and deporting all illegal immigrants is the best way to solve the illegal immigration problem.
- Majorities of every religious group say that the best way to solve the country's illegal immigration problem is to both secure the borders and provide an earned path to citizenship.

Americans express strong support for the basic tenets of the DREAM Act: allowing illegal immigrants brought to the United States as children to gain legal resident status if they join the military or go to college (57 percent favor, 40 percent oppose). And opposition to the DREAM Act is less fierce than opposition to broader reform proposals, suggesting that partial reforms based on an earned path to citizenship are likely to have a better chance of passing than broader legislation.

[These] survey findings suggest that we are in the midst of a struggle over what growing religious, racial and ethnic diversity means for American politics and society, and that partisan and ideological polarization around these questions will make them difficult to resolve. Nonetheless, this is a battle that has been waged before, and one that is likely to reach the same conclusion: New groups will—through hard work, community and an embrace of our founding values—become "American" while at the same time changing the meaning of being American in ways that, historically, have enriched the nation.

* * *

A Nation United and *Divided on Pluralism and Diversity*

Americans are a tolerant people, but we are divided by tolerance itself. We are united in our support for religious freedom, but divided over what it means. A substantial majority would like to create a path to citizenship for illegal immigrants even as—at the very same time—a small majority would also deport all illegal immigrants.

The future points to an even more tolerant and open nation because young Americans are far more comfortable with and sympathetic to ethnic, racial and religious diversity than are older Americans. But this generational divide also translates into a political divide. If conservatives and Republicans disagree sharply with liberals and Democrats on matters of taxing and spending, they also differ substantially on a broad range of issues related to immigration and to the implications of racial, religious and ethnic diversity.

Ten years after September 11, 2001, we seem far less united as a nation. As a pioneer in the struggle for religious liberty and as a nation defined by immigration, we remain an exceptionally open country. Even Americans uneasy with diversity accept it in important ways as a norm. But we are so divided across partisan, ideological and generational lines that resolving the inevitable tensions that arise in a pluralistic society may prove to be less of a challenge than settling our *political* differences over what pluralism implies, and what it requires of us. Our national motto is "Out of many, one." We find ourselves a very considerable distance from this aspiration—and politics, more than ethnicity, religion or race, is the reason why.

* * *

Conclusion: The Future of American Pluralism

It would be foolish to extrapolate the future from a single survey. But these findings do reinforce a hunch: that the country is in the midst of the kind of argument it has had again and again over diversity and immigration—and that this one will be resolved as the others have been. The American pattern has been to battle fiercely over the inclusion of new groups, to ask whether this or that new group can ever "Americanize" and whether it will push the country away from its founding principles and commitments.

And then several things happen that culminate in the classic American bargain. The new groups turn out to be, or quickly become, very committed to the underlying values and principles of our democratic republic—sometimes more passionately than those who were here earlier and may have come to take them for granted. Over a generation or two, the new arrivals work hard, build strong communities, and in the process, master the English language. They become "American." But they also change the meaning of being American in ways that, historically, have enriched the nation. And the country moves forward, still very much itself, and also transformed. Similarly, we have battled from the very beginning of our republic over the inclusion of African Americans as full citizens. Steadily, albeit with many reversals, the country has sought to live up to Martin Luther King Jr.'s insistence that the long arc of history does bend toward justice.

The generational patterns discerned in this survey suggest that while we are in for some transitional turbulence on these matters, the arc of American history will, again, bend toward inclusion.

5

"What Does It Mean to Be an American?"

STEVEN M. WARSHAWSKY

"Undocumented Americans." This is how Senate Majority Leader Harry Reid recently described the estimated 12–20 million illegal aliens living in America. What was once a Mark Steyn joke has now become the ideological orthodoxy of the Democratic Party.

Reid's comment triggered an avalanche of outrage among commentators, bloggers, and the general public. Why? Because it strikes at the heart of the American people's understanding of themselves as a nation and a civilization. Indeed, opposition to the ongoing push for "comprehensive immigration reform"—i.e., amnesty and a guest worker program—is being driven by a growing concern among millions of Americans that massive waves of legal and illegal immigration—mainly from Mexico, Latin America, and Asia—coupled with the unwillingness of our political and economic elites to mold these newcomers into red-white-and-blue Americans, is threatening to change the very character of our country. For the worse.

I share this concern. I agree with the political, economic, and cultural arguments in favor of sharply curtailing immigration into the United States, as well as refocusing our immigration efforts on admitting those foreigners who bring the greatest value to—and are most easily assimilated into—American society. * * * But this essay is not intended to rehash these arguments. Rather, I wish to explore the question that underlies this entire debate: What does it mean to be an American? This may seem like an easy question to answer, but it's not. The harder one thinks about this question, the more complex it becomes.

Clearly, Harry Reid has not given this question much thought. His implicit definition of "an American" is simply: Anyone living within the geopolitical boundaries of the United States. In other words, mere physical location on Earth determines whether or not someone is "an American." Presumably, Reid's definition is not intended to apply to tourists and other temporary visitors. Some degree of permanency—what the law in other contexts calls "residency," i.e., a subjective intention to establish one's home or domicile—is required. In Reid's view, therefore, a Mexican from Guadalajara, a Chinese from Shanghei [sic], an Indian from Delhi, or a [fill in the blank] become "Americans" as soon as they cross into U.S. territory and decide to live here permanently, legally or not. Nothing more is needed.

This is poppycock, of course. A Mexican or a Chinese or an Indian, for example, cannot transform themselves into Americans simply by moving to this country, any more than I can become a Mexican, a Chinese, or an Indian simply by moving to their countries. Yet contemporary liberals have a vested interest in believing that they can. This is not just a function of immigrant politics, which strongly favors the Democratic Party (hence the Democrats' growing support for voting rights for non-citizens). It also reflects the liberals' (and some libertarians') multicultural faith, which insists that it is morally wrong to make distinctions among different groups of people, let alone to impose a particular way of life—what heretofore has been known as the American way of life—on those who believe, speak, and act differently. Even in our own country.

In short, diversity, not Americanism, is the multicultural touchstone.

What's more, the principle of diversity, taken to its logical extreme, inevitably leads to a *rejection* of Americanism. Indeed, the ideology of multiculturalism has its roots in the radical—and anti-American—New Left and Black Power movements of the 1960s and 1970s. Thus the sorry state of U.S. history and civics education in today's schools and universities, which are dominated by adherents of this intellectual poison. Moreover, when it comes to immigration, multiculturalists actually *prefer* those immigrants who are as unlike ordinary Americans as possible. This stems from their deep-rooted opposition to traditional American society, which they hope to undermine through an influx of non-western peoples and cultures.

This, in fact, describes present U.S. immigration policy, which largely is a product of the 1965 Immigration Act (perhaps Ted Kennedy's most notorious legislative achievement). The 1965 Immigration Act eliminated the legal preferences traditionally given to European immigrants, and opened the floodgates to immigration from less-developed and non-western countries. For example, in 2006 more immigrants came to the United States from Columbia, Peru, Vietnam, and Haiti (not to mention Mexico, China, and India), than from the United Kingdom, Germany, Italy, and Greece. And once these immigrants arrive here, multiculturalists believe we should accommodate *our* society to the needs and desires of the newcomers, not the other way around. Thus, our government prints election ballots, school books, and welfare applications in foreign languages, while corporate America asks customers to "press one for English."

Patriotic Americans—those who love our country for its people, its history, its culture, and its ideals—reject the multiculturalists' denuded, and ultimately subversive, vision of what it means to be "an American." While the American identity is arguably the most "universal" of all major nationalities—as evidenced by the millions of immigrants the world over who have successfully assimilated into our country over the years—it is not an empty, meaningless concept. It has substance. Being "an American" is *not* the same thing as simply living in the United States. Nor, I would add, is it the same thing as holding U.S. citizenship. After all, a baby born on U.S. soil to an illegal alien is a citizen. This hardly guarantees that this baby will grow up to be *an American*.

So what, then, does it mean to be an American? I suspect that most of us believe, like Supreme Court Justice Potter Stewart in describing pornography, that we "know it when we see it." For example, John Wayne, Amelia Earhart, and Bill Cosby definitely are Americans. The day laborers standing on the street corner probably are not. But how do we put this inner understanding into words? It's not easy. Unlike most other nations on Earth, the American nation is not strictly defined in terms of race or ethnicity or ancestry or religion. George Washington may be the Father of Our Country (in my opinion, the greatest American who ever lived), but there have been in the past, and are today, many millions of patriotic, hardworking, upstanding Americans who are not Caucasian, or Christian, or of Western European ancestry. Yet they are undeniably as American as you or I (by the way, I am Jewish of predominantly Eastern European ancestry). Any definition of "American" that excludes such folks—let alone one that excludes me!—cannot be right.

Consequently, it is just not good enough to say, as some immigration restrictionists do, that this is a "white-majority, Western country." Yes, it is. But so are, for example, Ireland and Sweden and Portugal. Clearly, this level of abstraction does not take us very far towards understanding what it means to be "an American." Nor is it all that helpful to say that this is an English-speaking, predominately Christian country. While I think these features get us closer to the answer, there are millions of English-speaking (and non-English-speaking) Christians in the world who are not Americans, and millions of non-Christians who are. Certainly, these fundamental historical characteristics are important elements in determining who we are as a nation. Like other restrictionists, I am opposed to public policies that seek, by design or by default, to significantly alter the nation's "demographic profile." Still, it must be recognized that demography alone does not, and cannot, explain what it means to be an American.

So where does that leave us? I think the answer to our question, ultimately, must be found in the realms of ideology and culture. What distinguishes the United States from other nations, and what unites the disparate peoples who make up our country, are our unique political, economic, and social values, beliefs, and institutions. Not race, or religion, or ancestry.

Whether described as a "proposition nation" or a "creedal nation" or simply just "an idea," the United States of America is defined by *our way of life*. This way of life is rooted in the ideals proclaimed in the Declaration of Independence; in the system of personal liberty and limited government established by the Constitution; in our traditions of self-reliance, personal responsibility, and entrepreneurism; in our emphasis on private property, freedom of contract, and merit-based achievement; in our respect for the rule of law; and in our commitment to affording equal justice to all. Perhaps above all, it is marked by our abiding belief that, as Americans, we have been called to a higher duty in human history. We are the "city upon a hill." We are "the last, best hope of earth."

Many immigration restrictionists and so-called traditionalists chafe at the notion that the American people are not defined by "blood and soil." Yet the truth of the matter is, we aren't. One of the greatest patriots who ever graced this nation's history, Teddy Roosevelt, said it best: "Americanism is a matter of the spirit and of the soul." Roosevelt deplored what he called "hyphenated Americanism," which refers to citizens whose primary loyalties lie with their particular ethnic groups or ancestral lands. Such a man, Roosevelt counseled, is to be "unsparingly condemn[ed]."

But Roosevelt also recognized that "if he is heartily and singly loyal to this Republic, then no matter where he was born, he is just as good an American as anyone else." Roosevelt's words are not offered here to suggest that all foreigners are equally capable of assimilating into our country. Clearly, they aren't. Nevertheless, the appellation "American" is open to anyone who adopts our way of life and loves this country above all others.

Which brings me to the final, and most difficult, aspect of this question: How do we define the "American way of life"? This is the issue over which our nation's "culture wars" are being fought. Today the country is divided between those who maintain their allegiance to certain historically American values, beliefs, and institutions (but not all—see racial segregation), and those who want to replace them with a very different set of ideas about the role of government, the nature of political and economic liberty, and the meaning of right and wrong. Are both sides in this struggle equally "American"?

Moreover, the "American way of life" has changed over time. We no longer have the Republic that existed in TR's days. The New Deal and Great Society revolutions—enthusiastically supported, I note, by millions of white, Christian, English-speaking citizens—significantly altered the political, economic, and social foundations of this country. Did they also change what it means to be "an American"? Is being an American equally compatible, for example, with support for big government versus small government? The welfare state versus rugged individualism? Socialism versus capitalism? And so on. Plainly, this is a much harder historical and intellectual problem than at first meets the eye.

Personally, I do not think the meaning of America is nearly so malleable as today's multiculturalists assume. But neither is it quite as narrow as many restrictionists contend. Nevertheless, I am convinced that being *an American* requires something more than merely living in this country, speaking English, obeying the law, and holding a job (although this would be a very good start!). What this "something more" is, however, is not self-evident, and, indeed, is the subject of increasingly bitter debate in this country.

Yet one thing is certain: If we stray too far from the lines laid down by the Founding Fathers and the generations of great American men and women who built on their legacy, we will cease to be "Americans" in any meaningful sense of the word. As Abraham Lincoln warned during the secession era, "America will never be destroyed from the outside. If we falter and lose our freedoms, it will be because we destroyed ourselves." Today the danger is not armed rebellion, but the slow erasing of the American national character through a process of political and cultural redefinition. If this ever happens, it will be a terrible day for this country, and for the world.

Discussion Questions

1. Is it important for the United States to have a sense of shared values or not? What are the risks and benefits for individuals and the country of having a sense of shared values?

2. Political scientists and historians often refer to "American exceptionalism," or the idea that the United States was founded and grew from historically unique circumstances that gave it a distinctive political

culture, set of values, and sense of how government, the economy, society, and individuals intersect. For example, compared to other democratic countries, Americans place more emphasis on individual rights, and the United States features much greater decentralization of political power across the branches and levels of government. Do these outcomes *require* the kind of shared beliefs discussed by Warshawsky or could they also be sustained in the absence of shared beliefs?

3. Occasionally in political campaigns a candidate's beliefs or actions will be described as "un-American." What do you think people mean when they use this term? Would you describe any of the views presented in the Jones et al. survey data as un-American? If so, what makes a view un-American to you? If not, are there any beliefs that you would define as un-American?
4. A visitor from another country asks you, "What does it mean to be an American?" What do you say?

CHAPTER 2

The Founding and the Constitution

6

"The Nature of American Constitutionalism," from *The Origins of the American Constitution*

MICHAEL KAMMEN

The Constitution is a remarkably simple document that has provided a framework of governance for the United States for nearly 230 years. It establishes a shared sovereignty between the states and the federal government, a separation and checking of powers between three branches of government, qualifications for citizenship and holding office, and a delineation of the rights considered so fundamental their restriction by the government requires extensive due process and a compelling national or state concern. Yet the Constitution's simple text produces constant controversy over its interpretation and efforts to bend, twist, and nudge its application to changing economic markets, technology, social trends, and family structures. The document's durability and *flexibility amidst conflict and social change is a tribute not only to the men who drafted the Constitution in 1787, but to the American people and their willingness to embrace the challenges of self-governance at the time of the Revolution and today.*

In the following article Michael Kammen argues that in order to begin to understand the Constitution and the continuous debate surrounding its interpretation, we must look to the history of American constitutionalism. Informed by John Locke's Second Treatise of Government, *the British constitution, and a colonial experience deemed an affront to basic liberties and rights, Americans plunged into the writing of the Constitution as a means to delegate power from the sovereign people to their elected and appointed agents. It is, as Kammen notes, quite remarkable that, even before the drafting of the federal Constitution, the American states chose to draft state constitutions in the midst of a revolutionary battle for independence, rather than establish provisional governments. It is similarly remarkable that these state constitutions have grown significantly in length over the years and are so readily amended and even rewritten, in contrast to the relatively short and difficult-to-amend Constitution of the United States.*

Kammen suggests that the Constitution's simplicity and durability lies in both the historic need for compromise between conflicting interests, as well as the surprising common ground that nevertheless existed over basic principles: the need to protect personal liberty, the commitment to a republican form of government, and the importance of civic virtue for preserving citizen sovereignty. This embrace of basic governing principles could explain the deeper devotion to the U.S. Constitution, in contrast to the state documents, as well as the fear that an amended or completely altered Constitution might prove less malleable and accommodating for the governance of a diverse nation.

The Nature of American Constitutionalism

"Like the Bible, it ought to be read again and again." Franklin Delano Roosevelt made that remark about the U.S. Constitution in March 1937, during one of those cozy "fireside chats" that reached millions of Americans by radio. "It is an easy document to understand," he added. And six months later, speaking to his fellow citizens from the grounds of the Washington Monument on Constitution Day—a widely noted speech because 1937 marked the sesquicentennial of the Constitution, and because the President had provoked the nation with his controversial plan to add as many as six new justices to the Supreme Court—Roosevelt observed that the Constitution was "a layman's document, not a lawyer's contract," a theme that he reiterated several times in the course of this address.

It seems fair to say that Roosevelt's assertions were approximately half true. No one could disagree that the Constitution ought to be read and reread. Few would deny that it was meant to be comprehended by laymen, by ordinary American citizens and aspirants for citizenship. Nevertheless, we must ponder whether it is truly "an easy document to understand." Although the very language of the Constitution is neither technical nor difficult, and although it is notably succinct—one nineteenth-century expert called it "a great code in a small compass"—abundant evidence exists that vast numbers of Americans, ever since 1787, have not understood it as well as they might. Even the so-called experts (judges, lawyers, political leaders, and teachers of constitutional law) have been unable to agree in critical instances about the proper application of key provisions of the Constitution, or about the intentions of those who wrote and approved it. Moreover, we do acknowledge that the Constitution developed from a significant number of compromises, and that the document's ambiguities are, for the most part, not accidental.

Understanding the U.S. Constitution is essential for many reasons. One of the most urgent is that difficult issues are now being and will continue to be settled in accordance with past interpretations and with our jurists' sense of what the founders meant. In order to make such difficult determinations, we begin with the document itself. Quite often, however, we also seek guidance from closely related or contextual documents, such as the notes kept by participants in the Constitutional Convention held at Philadelphia in 1787, from the correspondence of delegates and other prominent leaders during the later 1780s, from *The Federalist* papers, and even from some of the Anti-Federalist tracts written in opposition to the Constitution. In doing so, we essentially scrutinize the origins of American constitutionalism.

If observers want to know what is meant by constitutionalism, they must uncover several layers of historical thought and experience in public affairs. Most obviously we look to the ideas that developed in the United States during the final quarter of the eighteenth century—unquestionably the most brilliant and creative era in the entire history of American political thought. We have in mind particularly, however, a new set of assumptions that developed after 1775 about the very nature of a constitution. Why, for example, when the colonists found themselves nearly in a political state of nature after 1775, did they promptly feel compelled to write state constitutions, many of which contained a bill of rights? The patriots were, after all, preoccupied with fighting a revolution. Why not simply set up provisional governments based upon those they already had and wait until Independence was achieved? If and when the revolution succeeded, there would be time enough to write permanent constitutions.

The revolutionaries did not regard the situation in such casual and pragmatic terms. They shared a strong interest in what they called the science of politics. They knew a reasonable amount about the history of political theory. They believed in the value of ideas applied to problematic developments, and they felt that their circumstances were possibly unique in all of human history. They knew with assurance that their circumstances were changing, and changing rapidly. They wanted self-government, obviously, but they also wanted legitimacy for their newborn governments. Hence a major reason for writing constitutions. They believed in the doctrine of the social contract (about which Jean-Jacques Rousseau had written in 1762) and they believed in government by the consent of the governed: two more reasons for devising written constitutions approved by the people or by their representatives.

The men responsible for composing and revising state constitutions in the decade following 1775 regarded constitutions as social compacts that delineated the fundamental principles upon which the newly formed polities were agreed and to which they pledged themselves. They frequently used the word "experiment" because they believed that they were making institutional innovations that were risky, for they seemed virtually unprecedented. They intended to create republican governments and assumed that to do so successfully required a fair amount of social homogeneity, a high degree of consensus regarding moral values, and a pervasive capacity for virtue, by which they meant unselfish, public-spirited behavior.

Even though they often spoke of liberty, they meant civil liberty rather than natural liberty. The latter implied unrestrained freedom—absolute liberty for the individual to do as he or she pleased. The former, by contrast, meant freedom of action so long as it was not detrimental to others and was beneficial to the common weal. When they spoke of *political* liberty they meant the freedom to be a participant, to vote and hold public office, responsible commitments that ought to be widely shared if republican institutions were to function successfully.

The colonists' experiences throughout the seventeenth and eighteenth centuries had helped to prepare them for this participatory and contractual view of the nature of government. Over and over again, as the circles of settlement expanded, colonists learned to improvise the rules by which they would be governed. They had received charters and had entered into covenants or compacts that may be described as protoconstitutional, i.e., cruder and less complete versions of the constitutional documents that would be formulated in 1776 and subsequently. These colonial charters not only described the structure of government, but frequently explained what officials (often called magistrates) could or could not do.

As a result, by the 1770s American attitudes toward constitutionalism were simultaneously derivative as well as original. On the one hand, they extravagantly admired the British constitution ("unwritten" in the sense that it was not contained in a single document) and declared it to be the ultimate achievement in the entire history of governmental development. On the other hand, as Oscar and Mary Handlin have explained, Americans no longer conceived of constitutions in general as the British had for centuries.

> In the New World the term, constitution, no longer referred to the actual organization of power developed through custom, prescription, and precedent. Instead it had come to mean a written frame of government setting fixed limits on the use of power. The American view was, of course, closely related to the rejection of the old conception that authority descended from the Crown to its officials. In the newer view—that authority was derived from the consent of the governed—the written constitution became the instrument by which the people entrusted power to their agents.

* * *

Issues, Aspirations, and Apprehensions in 1787–1788

The major problems that confronted the Constitution-makers, and the issues that separated them from their opponents, can be specified by the key words that recur so frequently in the documents that follow in this collection. The Federalists often refer to the need for much more energy, stability, and efficiency in the national government. They fear anarchy and seek a political system better suited to America's geographical expanse: "an extensive sphere" was Madison's phrase in a letter to Jefferson.

The Anti-Federalists were apprehensive about "unrestrained power" (George Mason's words), about the great risk of national "consolidation" rather than a true confederation, about the failure to include a bill of rights in the new Constitution, about the prospect of too much power in the federal judiciary, about the "tendency to aristocracy" (see the "Federal Farmer"*), about insufficient separation of powers, and a government unresponsive to the needs of diverse and widely scattered people.

Because the two sides disagreed so strongly about the nature of the proposed government—was it genuinely federal or really national?—it is all too easy to lose sight of the common ground that they shared, a common ground that made it possible for many Anti-Federalists to support the Constitution fully even before George Washington's first administration came to a close in 1793. Both sides felt an absolute commitment to republicanism and the protection of personal liberty, as we have already seen. Both sides acknowledged that a science of politics was possible and ought to be pursued, but that "our own experience" (Madison's view, though held by "Brutus"† also) ought to be heeded above all. A majority on both sides accepted the inevitable role that interests would play in public affairs and recognized that public opinion would be a powerful force. The phrase "public opinion" appears eleven times explicitly in *The Federalist* papers, and many other times implicitly or indirectly.

The desire for happiness was invoked constantly. Although admittedly a vague and elusive concept, it clearly meant much more than the safeguarding of property (though the protection of property belonged under the rubric of happiness in the minds of many). For some it simply meant personal contentment; but increasingly there were leaders, such as George Washington, who spoke of "social happiness," which referred to harmony among diverse groups. David Humphreys's "Poem on the Happiness of America" (1786) provides an indication that this notion had national as well as individual and societal connotations.

Although both sides believed that the preservation of liberty was one of the most essential ends of government, the continued existence of chattel slavery in a freedom-loving society created considerable awkwardness for the founders. In 1775–1776, when the revolutionaries had explained the reasons for their rebellion, they frequently referred to a British plot to "enslave" Americans. The constant invocation of that notion has puzzled many students because whatever the wisdom or unwisdom of imperial policy in general, there most certainly was no conspiracy in London to enslave America.

There really should be no mystery about the colonists' usage, however, because as good Lockeans they knew full well the argument in chapter four of John Locke's *Second Treatise of Government*, entitled "Of Slavery" (an argument reiterated in Rousseau's *Social Contract*). "The liberty of man in society," Locke wrote, "is to be under no other legislative power but that established by consent in the commonwealth, nor under the dominion of

*The pen name of Richard Henry Lee of Virginia, a noted Anti-Federalist [*Editors*].
†The pen name of Robert Yates, an Anti-Federalist [*Editors*].

any will or restraint of any law but what that legislative shall enact according to the trust put in it." The denial of *full* freedom quite simply meant "slavery."

Slavery and the international slave trade were discussed extensively in 1787 at the Constitutional Convention. By then, however, "slavery" was not often used as a theoretical and general synonym for unfreedom. It meant the permanent possession of one person (black) by another (white), usually for life, the slaveowner being entitled to own the children of his or her chattel as well. We must remember that the Convention met in secret session, and that the delegates agreed not to divulge information about their proceedings for fifty years. Consequently not very much was said publicly about slavery in 1787–1788 in connection with the Constitution. Not until 1840, when the U.S. government published James Madison's detailed notes on the Convention debates, did Americans learn just how much had been compromised at Philadelphia in order to placate South Carolina and Georgia. The Constitution essentially protected slavery where it existed, and remained mute about the legality of slavery in territories that might one day become additional states. Accommodation had prevailed in 1787, which meant, as it turned out, postponing for seventy-four years the moral and political crisis of the Union.

Legacies of American Constitutionalism

Although it is difficult for us fully to imagine the complexities of interest group politics, regional rivalries, and ideological differences in 1787, the instrumental achievement of that extraordinary Convention has generally been appreciated over the years. Even such a sardonic mind as H. L. Mencken's conceded as much. "The amazing thing about the Constitution," he wrote, "is that it is as good as it is—that so subtle and complete a document emerged from that long debate. Most of the Framers, obviously, were second-rate men; before and after their session they accomplished nothing in the world. Yet during that session they made an almost perfect job of the work in hand."

Their accomplishment was, indeed, remarkable. The distribution and separation of powers among three branches at the national level, and the development of federalism as a means of apportioning sovereignty between the nation and the states, have received broad recognition and the compliment of imitation by many other nations.

Equally appreciated is the fact that the U.S. Constitution is the oldest written national constitution in the world. (The Massachusetts Constitution of 1780, although amended and revised many times, is even older.) Its endurance is genuinely remarkable. We should therefore note that the framers deserve much of the credit for that endurance, not simply because they transcended their own limitations, * * * but because they contrived to restrict the ease with which the Constitution might be revised or reconsidered. There was considerable talk in 1787–1788 about holding a second convention in order to refine the product of the first. Anti-Federalists and many who were undecided wanted such a course of action. George Washington, however, regarded that idea as impractical. Hamilton, despite his dissatisfaction with many aspects of the Constitution, doubted whether a second convention could possibly be as successful as the first; and Madison feared a serious erosion of what had been accomplished in 1787.

It is easy to forget that the Philadelphia Convention vastly exceeded its authority, and that the men who met there undertook what amounted to a usurpation of legitimate authority. As [President] Franklin Delano Roosevelt pointed out on Constitution Day in 1937, contemporaries who opposed the newly drafted document "insisted that the Constitution itself was unconstitutional under the Articles of Confederation. But the ratifying conventions overruled them." The right of revolution had been explicitly invoked in 1776 and implicitly practiced in 1787. Having done their work, however, most of the delegates did not believe that it ought to be repealed or casually revised.

The complexity of changing or adding to the original document had profound implications for the subsequent history of American constitutionalism. First, it meant that in order to gain acceptance of their handiwork, the Federalists had to commit themselves, unofficially, to the formulation of a bill of rights when the first Congress met in 1789, even though many Federalists felt that such a list of protections was superfluous. They protested that a finite list of specified safeguards would imply that numerous other liberties might not be protected against encroachment by the government. The point, ultimately, is that promulgation of the U.S. Constitution required two sets of compromises rather than one: those that took place among the delegates to the Convention, and the subsequent sense that support for ratification would be rewarded by the explicit enumeration of broad civil liberties.

Next, the existence of various ambiguities in the Constitution meant that explication would subsequently be required by various authorities, such as the Supreme Court. The justices' interpretations would become part of the total "package" that we call American constitutionalism; but the justices did not always agree with one another, and the rest of the nation did not always agree with the justices. Those realities gave rise to an ongoing pattern that might be called conflict-within-consensus.

Some of those disputes and ambiguities involved very basic questions: What are the implications and limits of consent? Once we have participated in the creation of a polity and agreed to abide by its rules, then what? How are we to resolve the conflict that arises when the wishes or needs of a majority diminish the liberties or interests of a minority? This last question was the tough issue faced by the New England states in 1814, when they contemplated secession, and by South Carolina in 1828–1833 when a high tariff designed to protect northern manufacturing threatened economic distress to southern agricultural interests. And that, of course, was the thorny issue that precipitated southern secession and the greatest constitutional crisis of all in 1860–1861.

There is yet another ambiguity, or contradiction, in American constitutional thought—though it is less commonly noticed than the one described in the previous paragraph. As we have observed, the founders were not eager for a second convention, or for easy revisions or additions to their handiwork. They did provide for change; but they made the process complicated and slow. They did not believe that the fundamental law of a nation should be casually altered; and most Americans have accepted that constraint.

Nevertheless, on the *state* level Americans have amended, expanded, revised, and totally rewritten their constitutions with some frequency. A great deal of so-called positive law (i.e., legislative enactments) finds its way into state constitutions, with the result that many modern ones exceed one hundred pages in length. There is no clear explanation for this striking pattern of divergence between constitutionalism on the national and state levels. The curious pattern does suggest, however, that Americans have regarded the U.S. Constitution of 1787 as more nearly permanent than their state constitutions. Perhaps the pattern only tells us that achieving a national consensus for change in a large and diverse society is much more difficult than achieving a statewide consensus for change.

Whatever the explanation for this dualism in American constitutionalism, the paradox does not diminish the historical reality that writers of the federal as well as the first state constitutions all tried to establish charters clearly suited to the cultural assumptions and political realities of the American scene. Even though the founders explored the history of political thought in general and the history of republics in particular, they reached the commonsense conclusion that a constitution must be adapted to the character and customs of a people. Hence the debate in 1787–1788 over the relative merits of "consolidation" versus "confederation." Hence the concern about what sort of governmental system would work most effectively over a large geographical expanse. James Madison conveyed this sense of American exceptionalism several times in a letter to Thomas Jefferson (then U.S. minister to France) in 1788, when a bill of rights was under consideration.

On August 28, 1788, a month after New York became the eleventh state to ratify the Constitution, George Washington sent Alexander Hamilton a letter from his temporary retirement at Mount Vernon. The future president acknowledged that public affairs were proceeding more smoothly than he had expected. Consequently, he wrote, "I hope the political Machine may be put in motion, without much effort or hazard of miscarrying." As he soon discovered, to put the new constitutional machine in motion would require considerable effort. It did not miscarry because the "machine" had been so soundly designed. A concerted effort would be required, however, to keep the machine successfully in operation. That should not occasion surprise. The founders had assumed an involved citizenry; and the governmental system they created functions best when their assumption is validated. That is the very essence of democratic constitutionalism.

Discussion Questions

1. In your view, what would Kammen think about recent efforts to amend the Constitution to ban abortion, mandate a balanced budget, protect the flag against desecration, and protect victims' rights?
2. Although the flexibility of the Constitution helps explain its longevity, that flexibility comes at a price: ambiguity and gaps in constitutional language. What are some examples of constitutional language that is ambiguous?
3. One reason that Kammen argues it is important to understand the origins of American constitutionalism is that many judges today use their understanding of the Founders' intentions to inform their decisions. To what extent should the Founders' intentions influence modern court decisions? What are the advantages and disadvantages of this "original intent" perspective on jurisprudence?

7

The Federalist, No. 15

Alexander Hamilton

Despite the deference given the Constitution today, it did not command instant respect in 1787. The fight for ratification was bitter between the Federalists (those who supported the Constitution) and the Anti-Federalists (those who feared that the Constitution would allow the new national government to become too powerful).

The Federalist Papers, *originally written as a series of newspaper editorials intended to persuade New York to ratify the Constitution, remain the most valuable exposition of the political theory underlying the Constitution. In* The Federalist, *No. 15, reprinted below, Alexander Hamilton is at his best arguing for the necessity of a stronger central government than that established under the Articles of Confederation. He points out the practical impossibility of engaging in concerted action when each of the thirteen states retains virtual sovereignty, and the need for a strong central government to hold the new country together politically and economically.*

In the course of the preceding papers I have endeavored, my fellow-citizens, to place before you in a clear and convincing light the importance of Union to your political safety and happiness. * * * [T]he point next in order to be examined is the "insufficiency of the present Confederation to the preservation of the Union." * * * There are material imperfections in our national system and * * * something is necessary to be done to rescue us from impending anarchy. The facts that support this opinion are no longer objects of speculation. They have forced themselves upon the sensibility of the people at large, and have at length extorted . . . a reluctant confession of the reality of those defects in the scheme of our federal government which have been long pointed out and regretted by the intelligent friends of the Union.

We may indeed with propriety be said to have reached almost the last stage of national humiliation. There is scarcely anything that can wound the pride or degrade the character of an independent nation which we do not experience. Are there engagements to the performance of which we are held by every tie respectable among men? These are the subjects of constant and unblushing violation. Do we owe debts to foreigners and to our own citizens contracted in a time of imminent peril for the preservation of our political existence? These remain without any proper or satisfactory provision for their discharge. * * * Are we in a condition to resent or to repel the aggression? We have neither troops, nor treasury, nor government. * * * Is public credit an indispensable resource in time of public danger? We seem to have abandoned its cause as desperate and irretrievable. Is commerce of importance to national wealth? Ours is at the lowest point of declension. Is respectability in the eyes of foreign powers a safeguard against foreign encroachments? The imbecility of our government even forbids them to treat with us. . . . Is private credit the friend and patron of industry? That most useful kind which relates to borrowing and lending is reduced within the narrowest limits, and this still more from an opinion of insecurity than from a scarcity of money. * * *

This is the melancholy situation to which we have been brought by those very maxims and counsels which would now deter us from adopting the proposed Constitution; and which, not content with having conducted us to the brink of a precipice, seem resolved to plunge us into the abyss that awaits us below. Here, my countrymen, impelled by every motive that ought to influence an enlightened people, let us make a firm stand for our safety, our tranquility, our dignity, our reputation. Let us at last break the fatal charm which has too long seduced us from the paths of felicity and prosperity.

* * * While [opponents of the Constitution] admit that the government of the United States is destitute of energy, they contend against conferring upon it those powers which are requisite to supply that energy. * * * This renders a full display of the principal defects of the Confederation necessary in order to show that the evils we experience do not proceed from minute or partial imperfections, but from fundamental errors in the structure of the building, which cannot be amended otherwise than by an alteration in the first principles and main pillars of the fabric.

The great and radical vice in the construction of the existing Confederation is in the principle of LEGISLATION FOR STATES OR GOVERNMENTS, in their CORPORATE OR COLLECTIVE CAPACITIES, and as contradistinguished from the INDIVIDUALS of whom they consist. Though this principle does not run through all the powers delegated to the Union, yet it pervades and governs those on which the efficacy of the rest depends. Except as to the rule of apportionment, the United States have an indefinite discretion to make requisitions for men and money; but they have no authority to raise either by regulations extending to the individual citizens of America. The consequence of this is that though in theory their resolutions concerning those objects are laws constitutionally binding on the members of the Union, yet in practice they are mere recommendations which the States observe or disregard at their option. * * *

There is nothing absurd or impracticable in the idea of a league or alliance between independent nations for certain defined purposes precisely stated in a treaty regulating all the details of time, place, circumstance, and quantity, leaving nothing to future discretion, and depending for its execution on the good faith of the parties. * * *

If the particular States in this country are disposed to stand in a similar relation to each other, and to drop the project of a general DISCRETIONARY SUPERINTENDENCE, the scheme would indeed be pernicious and would entail upon us all the mischiefs which have been enumerated under the first head; but it would have the merit of being, at least, consistent and practicable. Abandoning all views towards a confederate government, this would bring us to a simple alliance offensive and defensive; and would place us in a situation to be alternate friends and enemies of each other, as our mutual jealousies and rivalships, nourished by the intrigues of foreign nations, should prescribe to us.

But if we are unwilling to be placed in this perilous situation; if we still will adhere to the design of a national government, or, which is the same thing, of a superintending power under the direction of a common council, we must resolve to incorporate into our plan those ingredients which may be considered as forming the characteristic difference between a league and a government; we must extend the authority of the Union to the persons of the citizens—the only proper objects of government.

Government implies the power of making laws. It is essential to the idea of a law that it be attended with a sanction; or, in other words, a penalty or punishment for disobedience. If there be no penalty annexed to disobedience, the resolutions or commands which pretend to be laws will, in fact, amount to nothing more than advice or recommendation. This penalty, whatever it may be, can only be inflicted in two ways: by the agency of the courts and ministers of justice, or by military force; by the COERCION of the magistracy, or by the COERCION of arms. The first kind can evidently apply only to men; the last kind must of necessity be employed against bodies politic, or communities, or States. * * * In an association where the general authority is confined to the collective bodies of the communities that compose it, every breach of the laws must involve a state of war; and military execution must become the only instrument of civil obedience. Such a state of things can certainly not deserve the name of government, nor would any prudent man choose to commit his happiness to it.

There was a time when we were told that breaches by the States of the regulations of the federal authority were not to be expected; that a sense of common interest would preside over the conduct of the respective members, and would beget a full compliance with all the constitutional requisitions of the Union. This language, at the present day, would appear as wild as a great part of what we now hear from the same quarter will be thought, when we shall have received further lessons from that best oracle of wisdom, experience. It at all times betrayed an ignorance of the true springs by which human conduct is actuated, and belied the original inducements to the establishment of civil power. Why has government been instituted at all? Because the passions of men will not conform to the dictates of reason and justice without constraint. * * *

In addition to all this * * * it happens that in every political association which is formed upon the principle of uniting in a common interest a number of lesser sovereignties, there will be found a kind of eccentric tendency in the subordinate or inferior orbs by the operation of which there will be a perpetual effort in each to fly off from the common center. This tendency is not difficult to be accounted for. It has its origin in the love of power. Power controlled or abridged is almost always the rival and enemy of that power by which it is controlled or abridged. This simple proposition will teach us how little reason there is to expect that the persons intrusted with the administration of the affairs of the particular members of a confederacy will at all times be ready with perfect good humor and an unbiased regard to the public weal to execute the resolutions or decrees of the general authority. * * *

If, therefore, the measures of the Confederacy cannot be executed without the intervention of the particular administrations, there will be little prospect of their being executed at all. * * * [Each state will evaluate every federal measure in light of its own interests] and in a spirit of interested and suspicious scrutiny, without that knowledge of national circumstances and reasons of state, which is essential to a right judgment, and with that strong predilection in favor of local objects, which can hardly fail to mislead the decision. The same process must be repeated in every member of which the body is constituted; and the execution of the plans, framed by the councils of the whole, will always fluctuate on the discretion of the ill-informed and prejudiced opinion of every part. * * *

In our case the concurrence of thirteen distinct sovereign wills is requisite under the Confederation to the complete execution of every important measure that proceeds from the Union. It has happened as was to have been foreseen. The measures of the Union have not been executed; and the delinquencies of the States have step by step matured themselves to an extreme, which has, at length, arrested all the wheels of the national government and brought them to an awful stand. Congress at this time scarcely possess the means of keeping up the forms of administration, till the States can have time to agree upon a more substantial substitute for the present shadow of a federal government. * * * Each State yielding to the persuasive voice of immediate interest or convenience has successively withdrawn its support, till the frail and tottering edifice seems ready to fall upon our heads and to crush us beneath its ruins.

PUBLIUS

DISCUSSION QUESTIONS

1. Do you think the national government is sufficiently held in check as Hamilton argues? Or is the exercise of its authority so vast as to give credence to the Anti-Federalists' fears? To put it another

way, would the framers be surprised or pleased with the balance between national and state powers today?

2. According to Hamilton, what are the weaknesses of a "league" compared to a government?
3. What is the significance of Hamilton's statement that "we must extend the authority of the Union to the persons of the citizens?"

8

From *An Economic Interpretation of the Constitution of the United States*

Charles A. Beard

One of the longest running debates over the Constitution focuses upon the motivation of the Founders in drafting the document. Was the motivation ideological, based upon beliefs of self-governance, the nature of a social contract, and the role of representation? Or was the motivation primarily economic, based upon a need to preserve economic interests that were threatened under the system of governance of the Articles of Confederation? And if the motivation was economic, what economic interests divided the Anti-Federalists from the Federalists in their opposition to or support for the Constitution?

One of the earliest and most controversial efforts to answer the question of motivation was written by Charles Beard in 1913. Beard argued that those who favored the Constitution and played the primary role in its drafting were motivated by the need to better protect their substantial "personality" interests—money, public securities, manufactures, and trade and shipping (or commerce)—in contrast to their opponents, who were primarily debtors and small farmers (with small real estate holdings). Not only was its motivation less than democratic, Beard argued, but the Constitution was ratified by only one-sixth of the male population because voting was limited to property owners.

Subsequent critiques of Beard have pointed out that there were far more economic interests than mercantilists versus farmers; that having a certain set of economic interests did not dictate the political views of the framers; and that ideas such as republicanism and liberty were more important in shaping the Constitution than the Founders' economic interests. Nonetheless, the idea that economic interests influence political outcomes resonates today.

The requirements for an economic interpretation of the formation and adoption of the Constitution may be stated in a hypothetical proposition which, although it cannot be verified absolutely from ascertainable data, will at once illustrate the problem and furnish a guide to research and generalization.

It will be admitted without controversy that the Constitution was the creation of a certain number of men, and it was opposed by a certain number of men. Now, if it were possible to have an economic biography of all those connected with its framing and adoption,—perhaps about 160,000 men altogether—the materials for scientific analysis and classification would be available. Such an economic biography would include a list of the real and personal property owned by all of these men and their families; lands and houses, with incumbrances, money at interest, slaves, capital invested in shipping and manufacturing, and in state and continental securities.

Suppose it could be shown from the classification of the men who supported and opposed the Constitution that there was no line of property division at all; that is, that men owning substantially the same amounts of the same kinds of property were equally divided on the matter of adoption or rejection—it would then become apparent that the Constitution had no ascertainable relation to economic groups or classes but was the product of some abstract causes remote from the chief business of life—gaining a livelihood.

Suppose, on the other hand, that substantially all of the merchants, money lenders, security holders, manufacturers, shippers, capitalists, and financiers and their professional associates are to be found on one side in support of the Constitution and that substantially all or the major portion of the opposition came from the non-slaveholding farmers and the debtors—would it not be pretty conclusively demonstrated that our fundamental law was not the product of an abstraction known as "the whole people," but of a group of economic interests which must have expected beneficial results from its adoption? Obviously all the facts here desired cannot be discovered, but the data presented in the following chapters bear out the latter hypothesis, and thus a reasonable presumption in favor of the theory is created.

* * *

The purpose of such an inquiry is not, of course, to show that the Constitution was made for the personal benefit of the members of the Convention. Far from it. Neither is it of any moment to discover how many hundred thousand dollars accrued to them as a result of the foundation of the new government. The only point here considered is: Did they represent distinct groups whose economic interests they understood and felt in concrete, definite form through their own personal experience with identical property rights, or were they working merely under the guidance of abstract principles of political science?

* * *

The Disfranchised

In an examination of the structure of American society in 1787, we first encounter four groups whose economic status had a definite legal expression: the slaves, the indentured servants, the mass of men who could not qualify for voting under the property tests imposed by the state constitutions and laws, and women, disfranchised and subjected to the discriminations of the common law. These groups were, therefore, not represented in the Convention which drafted the Constitution, except under the theory that representation has no relation to voting.

How extensive the disfranchisement really was cannot be determined. In some states, for instance, Pennsylvania and Georgia, propertyless mechanics in the towns could vote; but in other states the freehold qualifications certainly excluded a great number of the adult males.

In no state, apparently, had the working class developed a consciousness of a separate interest or an organization that commanded the attention of the politicians of the time. In turning over the hundreds of pages of writings left by eighteenth-century thinkers one cannot help being impressed with the fact that the existence and special problems of a working class, then already sufficiently numerous to form a considerable portion of society, were outside the realm of politics, except in so far as the future power of the proletariat was foreseen and feared.

When the question of the suffrage was before the Convention, Madison warned his colleagues against the coming industrial masses: "Viewing the subject in its merits alone, the freeholders of the Country would be the safest depositories of Republican liberty. In future times a great majority of the people will not only be without landed [property], but any other sort of property. These will either combine under the influence of their common situation; in which case, the rights of property and the public liberty will not be secure in their hands, or, which is more probable, they will become the tools of opulence and ambition; in which case there will be equal danger on another side."

* * *

It is apparent that a majority of the states placed direct property qualifications on the voters, and the other states eliminated practically all who were not taxpayers. Special safeguards for property were secured in the qualifications imposed on members of the legislatures in New Hampshire, Massachusetts, New York, New Jersey, Maryland, North Carolina, South Carolina, and Georgia. Further safeguards were added by the qualifications imposed in the case of senators in New Hampshire, Massachusetts, New Jersey, New York, Maryland, North Carolina, and South Carolina.

While these qualifications operated to exclude a large portion of the adult males from participating in elections, the wide distribution of real property created an extensive electorate and in most rural regions gave the legislatures a broad popular basis. Far from rendering to personal property that defence which was necessary to the full realization of its rights, these qualifications for electors admitted to the suffrage its most dangerous antagonists: the small farmers and many of the debtors who were the most active in all attempts to depreciate personalty [private property] by legislation. Madison with his usual acumen saw the inadequacy of such defence and pointed out in the Convention that the really serious assaults on property (having in mind of course, personalty) had come from the "freeholders."

Nevertheless, in the election of delegates to the Convention, the representatives of personalty in the legislatures were able by the sheer weight of their combined intelligence and economic power to secure delegates from the urban centres or allied with their interests. Happily for them, all the legislatures which they had to convince had not been elected on the issue of choosing delegates to a national Convention, and did not come from a populace stirred up on that question. The call for the Convention went forth on February 21, 1787, from Congress, and within a few months all the legislatures, except that of Rhode Island, had responded. Thus the heated popular discussion usually incident to such a momentous political undertaking was largely avoided, and an orderly and temperate procedure in the selection of delegates was rendered possible.

* * *

A survey of the economic interests of the members of the Convention presents certain conclusions:

A majority of the members were lawyers by profession.

Most of the members came from towns, on or near the coast, that is, from the regions in which personalty was largely concentrated.

Not one member represented in his immediate personal economic interests the small farming or mechanic classes.

The overwhelming majority of members, at least five-sixths, were immediately, directly, and personally interested in the outcome of their labors at Philadelphia, and were to a greater or less extent economic beneficiaries from the adoption of the Constitution.

1. Public security interests were extensively represented in the Convention. Of the fifty-five members who attended no less than forty appear on the Records of the Treasury Department for sums varying from a few dollars up to more than one hundred thousand dollars: * * *

It is interesting to note that, with the exception of New York, and possibly Delaware, each state had one or more prominent representatives in the Convention who held more than a negligible amount of securities, and who could therefore speak with feeling and authority on the question of providing in the new Constitution for the full discharge of the public debt: * * *

2. Personalty invested in lands for speculation was represented by at least fourteen members: * * *

3. Personalty in the form of money loaned at interest was represented by at least twenty-four members: * * *

4. Personalty in mercantile, manufacturing, and shipping lines was represented by at least eleven members: * * *

5. Personalty in slaves was represented by at least fifteen members: * * *

It cannot be said, therefore, that the members of the Convention were "disinterested." On the contrary, we are forced to accept the profoundly significant conclusion that they knew through their personal experiences in economic affairs the precise results which the new government that they were setting up was designed to attain. As a group of doctrinaires, like the Frankfurt assembly of 1848, they would have failed miserably; but as practical men they were able to build the new government upon the only foundations which could be stable: fundamental economic interests.

* * *

Conclusions

At the close of this long and arid survey—partaking of the nature of catalogue—it seems worthwhile to bring together the important conclusions for political science which the data presented appear to warrant.

[1.] The movement for the Constitution of the United States was originated and carried through principally by four groups of personalty interests which had been adversely affected under the Articles of Confederation: money, public securities, manufactures, and trade and shipping.

[2.] The first firm steps toward the formation of the Constitution were taken by a small and active group of men immediately interested through their personal possessions in the outcome of their labors.

[3.] No popular vote was taken directly or indirectly on the proposition to call the Convention which drafted the Constitution.

[4.] A large propertyless mass was, under the prevailing suffrage qualifications, excluded at the outset from participation (through representatives) in the work of framing the Constitution.

[5.] The members of the Philadelphia Convention which drafted the Constitution were, with a few exceptions, immediately, directly, and personally interested in, and derived economic advantages from, the establishment of the new system.

[6.] The Constitution was essentially an economic document based upon the concept that the fundamental private rights of property are anterior to government and morally beyond the reach of popular majorities.

[7.] The major portion of the members of the Convention are on record as recognizing the claim of property to a special and defensive position in the Constitution.

[8.] In the ratification of the Constitution, about three-fourths of the adult males failed to vote on the question, having abstained from the elections at which delegates to the state conventions were chosen, either on account of their indifference or their disfranchisement by property qualifications.

[9.] The Constitution was ratified by a vote of probably not more than one-sixth of the adult males.

[10.] It is questionable whether a majority of the voters participating in the elections for the state conventions in New York, Massachusetts, New Hampshire, Virginia, and South Carolina, actually approved the ratification of the Constitution.

[11.] The leaders who supported the Constitution in the ratifying conventions represented the same economic groups as the members of the Philadelphia Convention; and in a large number of instances they were also directly and personally interested in the outcome of their efforts.

[12.] In the ratification, it became manifest that the line of cleavage for and against the Constitution was between substantial personalty interests on the one hand and the small farming and debtor interests on the other.

[13.] The Constitution was not created by "the whole people" as the jurists have said; neither was it created by "the states" as Southern nullifiers long contended; but it was the work of a consolidated group whose interests knew no state boundaries and were truly national in their scope.

Discussion Questions

1. Do you think the framers were governed by self-interest or a commitment to principle, or some combination, when they drafted the Constitution? Explain your answer.
2. What does Beard's argument say about the use of historical evidence to support one's argument? How can historical evidence be misused and how can historians, or even readers of history, sort out what "really" happened in any specific context?
3. Think of current examples of wealthy people in politics, such as President Donald Trump. Do they tend to support positions that would enhance their own economic position? Can you think of examples of wealthy politicians who do not behave this way?

Debating the Issues: Should the Constitution Be Fundamentally Changed?

Veneration for the Constitution is a classic American value; indeed, it is often said that the essence of being an American is a set of shared values and commitments expressed within the four corners of that document, most notably equality and liberty. The Constitution is the embodiment of those values, celebrated as the first, and most enduring, written constitution in human history. We celebrate the first words of the Preamble, "We the People," salute the framers as men of historic wisdom and judgment, and honor the structures and processes of government.

We also note the practical wisdom of the framers, in their ability to reconcile competing tensions by creating a government powerful enough to function, but not at the risk of giving majorities the right to trample minority rights. Political theory at the time held that efforts to create democracies inevitably devolved into one of two end results: either mob rule, as majorities took control and used their power to oppress political minorities; or autocracy, as elites assumed control and did not give it up. The many carefully considered elements of constitutional structure—bicameralism, the balance between federal and state power, the equilibrium of checks and balances—have lasted for more than two centuries. And apart from one exceptional period of civil war, the structures have channeled political conflict peacefully.

Is that veneration truly warranted? Sanford Levinson, a professor at the University of Texas Law School, thinks not. He considers the Constitution to be a seriously flawed document in need of fundamental change. As originally written, the Constitution came nowhere near the aspirations of the Preamble, explicitly allowing slavery, and even after amendments retains several antidemocratic elements, including the Electoral College (which elected another popular vote loser to the presidency in 2016); the vastly unequal representation in the Senate, in which Wyoming (population 587,000) has the same voting power as California (population over 39 million, over sixty-five times as large); and lifetime tenure for judges. These features fail to live up to the Preamble, which Levinson considers to be the foundation of the rest of the Constitution—the whole point of the constitutional enterprise. Levinson points out that several key figures of the American Founding—Thomas Jefferson especially—believed that the Constitution would require frequent updating. This was the purpose of Article V, which sets out the process for amending the document. And, Levinson notes, many of the features of the Constitution that we venerate were not thought through but were instead the product of pure compromise, in which the framers took vastly inconsistent positions when necessary in order to secure sufficient support for ratification. So, far from being a philosophically perfect document or system, the Constitution created a cumbersome and inequitable system, one that no other democratic system has chosen to copy since.

The problem with amending the Constitution is that the features Levinson considers most offensive are very difficult or, in the case of unequal representation in the Senate, virtually impossible to change. Article V specifies that no state can be deprived of its equal representation in the Senate without its consent (something that no state could ever be expected to do). The only recourse is a constitutional convention, in which delegates would consider fundamental reform. Levinson regards this as essential in order to allow the national government to respond to the challenge of modern economic and political times.

Greg Abbott and Walter Olson weigh in on opposing sides of the wisdom of calling a constitutional convention. Abbott, the governor of Texas, hails a convention as a way to "restore the rule of law," and counters fears about a "runaway convention." He points out that the scope of a convention could be constrained by each state legislature that endorses the idea, and even if the convention ends up "throwing the entire Constitution in the trashcan," anything the convention proposes would still have to be ratified by three-fourths of the states. Abbott concludes that we cannot allow the "federal government to continue ignoring the very document that created it."

Walter Olson, a senior fellow at the libertarian Cato Institute, argues that to hold a constitutional convention would be too big a risk. Olson points out that the actual language in the Constitution about how a convention would work is very sparse. The Constitution does not say if voting power at the convention would be equally distributed (like in the Senate) or based on population (like in the House). It also does not specify the actual mechanism for triggering a convention: Does each state need to agree on the same language of the topics to be discussed at the convention? He concludes that we always should "beware of a cure that might kill the patient."

9

"The Ratification Referendum: Sending the Constitution to a New Convention for Repair"

SANFORD LEVINSON

The U.S. Constitution is radically defective in a number of important ways. Unfortunately, changing the Constitution is extremely difficult, for both political and constitutional reasons. But the difficulty of the task does not make it any less important that we first become aware of the magnitude of the deficiencies in the current Constitution and then turn our minds, as a community of concerned citizens, to figuring out potential solutions. This [reading] is organized around the conceit that Americans [should] have the opportunity to vote on the following proposal: "Shall Congress call a constitutional convention empowered to consider the adequacy of the Constitution, and, if thought necessary, to draft a new constitution that, upon completion, will be submitted to the electorate for its approval or disapproval by majority vote? Unless and until a new constitution gains popular approval, the current Constitution will continue in place."

Although such a referendum would be unprecedented with regard to the U.S. Constitution, there is certainly nothing "un-American" about such a procedure. As Professor John J. Dinan has noted in his recent comprehensive study of what he terms "the American state constitutional tradition," fourteen American states in their own constitutions explicitly give the people an opportunity "to periodically vote on whether a convention should be called." Article XIX of the New York Constitution, for example, provides that the state electorate be given the opportunity every twenty years to vote on the following question: "Shall there be a convention to revise the constitution and amend the same?" Should the majority answer in the affirmative, then the voters in each senate district will elect three delegates "at the next ensuring general election," while the statewide electorate "shall elect fifteen delegates-at-large." It should occasion no surprise that one author has described such a "mandatory referendum" as a means of "enforcing the people's right to reform their government."

It is no small matter to give people a choice with regard to the mechanisms—as well as the abstract principles—by which they are to be governed. The imagined referendum would allow "We the People of the United States of America," in whose name the document is ostensibly "ordain[ed]," to examine the fit between our national aspirations, set out in the Preamble to the Constitution, and the particular means chosen to realize those goals.

I am assuming that those reading this * * * are fellow Americans united by a deep and common concern about the future of our country. * * * I hope to convince you that, as patriotic Americans truly committed to the deepest principles of the Constitution, we should vote yes and thus trigger a new convention. My task is to persuade you that the Constitution we currently live under is grievously flawed, even in some ways a "clear and present danger" to achieving the laudable and inspiring goals to which this country professes to be committed, including republican self-government.

I believe that the best way to grasp the goals of our common enterprise is to ponder the inspiring words of the Preamble to the Constitution:

> We the People of the United States, in Order to form a more perfect Union, establish Justice, insure domestic tranquility, provide for the common defence, promote the general Welfare, and secure the Blessings of Liberty to ourselves and our Posterity, do ordain and establish this Constitution for the United States of America.

It is regrettable that law professors rarely teach and that courts rarely cite the Preamble, for it is *the single most important part* of the Constitution. The reason is simple: It announces the *point* of the entire enterprise. The 4,500 or so words that followed the Preamble in the original, unamended Constitution were all in effect merely means that were thought to be useful to achieving the great aims set out above. It is indeed the ends articulated in the Preamble that justify the means of our political institutions. And to the extent that the means turn out to be counterproductive, then we should revise them.

It takes no great effort to find elements in the original Constitution that run counter to the Preamble. It is impossible for us today to imagine how its authors squared a commitment to the "Blessings of Liberty" with the toleration and support of chattel slavery that is present in various articles of the Constitution. The most obvious example is the bar placed on Congress's ability to forbid the participation by Americans in the international slave trade until 1808. The most charitable interpretation of the framers, articulated by Frederick Douglass, is that they viewed these compromises with the acknowledged evil of slavery as temporary; the future would see its eradication through peaceful constitutional processes.

One might believe that the Preamble is incomplete because, for example, it lacks a commitment to the notion of equality. Political scientist Mark Graber has suggested that the reference to "*our* Posterity" suggests a potentially unattractive limitation of our concerns *only* to members of the American political community, with no notice taken of the posterity of other societies, whatever their plight. Even if one would prefer a more explicitly cosmopolitan Preamble, I find it hard to imagine rejecting any of the overarching values enunciated there. In any event, I am happy to endorse the Preamble as the equivalent of our creedal summary of America's civil religion.

There are two basic responses to the discovery that ongoing institutional practices are counterproductive with regard to achieving one's announced goals. One is to adjust the practices in ways that would make achievement of the aims more likely. This is, often, when we mean by the very notion of rationality: One does not persist in behaviors that are acknowledged to make more difficult the realization of one's professed hopes. Still, a second response, which has its own rationality, is to adjust the goals to the practices. Sometimes, this makes very good sense if one comes to the justified conclusion that the goals may be utopian. In such cases, it is a sign of maturity to recognize that we will inevitably fall short in our aims and that "the best may be enemy of the good" if we are tempted to throw over quite adequate, albeit imperfect, institutions in an attempt to attain the ideal.

Perhaps one might even wish to defend the framers' compromises with slavery on the ground that they were absolutely necessary to the achievement of the political union of the thirteen states. One must believe that such a union, in turn, was preferable to the likely alternative, which would have been the creation of two or three separate countries along the Atlantic coast. Political scientist David Hendrickson has demonstrated that many of the framers—and many other theorists as well—viewed history as suggesting a high probability that such separate countries would have gone to war with one another and made impossible any significant measure of "domestic tranquility." Hendrickson well describes the Constitution as a "peace pact" designed to prevent the possibility of war. If there is one thing we know, it is that unhappy compromises must often be made when negotiating such pacts. Of course, American slaves—and their descendants—could scarcely be expected to be so complacently accepting of these compromises, nor, of course, should *any* American who takes seriously the proclamation of the Pledge of Allegiance that ours is a system that takes seriously the duty to provide "liberty and justice for all."

Not only must we restrain ourselves from expecting too much of any government; we must also recognize that the Preamble sets out potentially conflicting goals. It is impossible to maximize the achievement of all of the great ends of the Constitution. To take an obvious example, providing for the "common defence" may require on occasion certain incursions into the "Blessings of Liberty." One need only refer to the military draft, which was upheld in 1918 by the Supreme Court against an attack claiming that it constituted the "involuntary servitude"—that is, slavery—prohibited by the Thirteenth Amendment. We also properly accept certain limitations on the freedom of the press with regard, say, to publishing certain information—the standard example is troop movements within a battle zone—deemed to be vital to American defense interests. The year 2005 ended with the beginning of a great national debate about the propriety of warrantless interceptions of telephone calls and other incursions on traditional civil liberties in order, ostensibly, to protect ourselves against potential terrorists.

Even if one concedes the necessity of adjusting aims in light of practical realities, it should also be readily obvious that one can easily go overboard. At the very least, one should always be vigilant in assessing such adjustments lest one find, at the end of the day, that the aims have been reduced to hollow shells. It is also necessary to ask if a rationale supporting a given adjustment that might well have been convincing at time A necessarily continues to be present at time B. Practical exigencies that required certain political compromises in 1787 no longer obtain today. We have long since realized this about slavery. It is time that we apply the same critical eye to the compromise of 1787 that granted all states an equal vote in the Senate.

To criticize that particular compromise—or any of the other features of the Constitution that I shall examine below—is not necessarily to criticize the Founders themselves. My project—and, therefore, your own vote for a new convention, should you be persuaded by what follows—requires no denigration of the Founders. They were, with some inevitable exceptions, an extraordinary group of men who performed extraordinary deeds, including drafting a Constitution that started a brand-new governmental system. By and large, they deserve the monuments that have been erected in their honor. But they themselves emphasized the importance—indeed, necessity—of learning from experience.

They were, after all, a generation that charted new paths by overturning a centuries-long notion of the British constitutional order because it no longer conformed to their own sense of possibility (and fairness). They also, as it happened, proved ruthlessly willing to ignore the limitations of America's "first constitution," the Articles of Confederation. Although Article XIII of that founding document required unanimous approval by the thirteen state legislatures before any amendment could take effect, Article VII of the Constitution drafted in Philadelphia required the approval of only nine of the thirteen states, and the approval was to be given by state conventions rather than by the legislatures.

The most important legacies handed down by the founding generation were, first, a remarkable willingness to act in bold and daring ways when they believed that the situation demanded it, coupled with the noble visions first of the Declaration of Independence and then of the Preamble. Both are as inspiring—and potentially disruptive—today as when they were written more than two centuries ago. But we should also be inspired by the copious study that Madison and others made of every available history and analysis of political systems ranging from ancient Greece to the Dutch republic and the British constitutional order. We best honor the framers by taking the task of creating a republican political order as seriously as they did and being equally willing to learn from what the history of the past 225 years, both at home and abroad, can teach us about how best to achieve and maintain such an order. At the time of its creation, we could legitimately believe that we were the only country committed to democratic self-governance. That is surely no longer the case, and we might well have lessons to learn from our co-ventures in that enterprise. To the extent that experience teaches us that the Constitution in significant aspects demeans "the consent of the governed" and has become an impediment to achieving the goals of the Preamble, we honor rather than betray the founders by correcting their handiwork.

Overcoming Veneration

* * * I suspect * * * that at least some readers might find it difficult to accept even the possibility that our Constitution is seriously deficient because they venerate the Constitution and find the notion of seriously criticizing it almost sacrilegious.

In an earlier book, *Constitutional Faith*, I noted the tension between the desire of James Madison that Americans "venerate" their Constitution and the distinctly contrasting views of his good friend Thomas Jefferson that, instead, the citizenry regularly subject it to relentless examination. Thus, whatever may have been Jefferson's insistence on respecting what he called the "chains" of the Constitution, he also emphasized that the "Creator has made the earth for the living, not the dead." It should not be surprising, then, that he wrote to Madison in 1789, "No society can make a perpetual constitution, or even a perpetual law."

Jefferson and Madison might have been good friends and political associates, but they disagreed fundamentally with regard to the wisdom of subjecting the Constitution to critical analysis. Jefferson was fully capable of writing that "[w]e may consider each generation as a distinct nation, with a right, by the will of its majority, to bind themselves, but none to bind the succeeding generation, more than the inhabitants of another country." His ultimate optimism about the Constitution lay precisely in its potential for change: "Happily for us, that when we find our constitutions defective and insufficient to secure the happiness of our people, we can assemble with all the coolness of philosophers, and set it to rights, while every other nation on earth must have recourse to arms to amend or restore their constitutions." * * *

Madison, however, would have none of this. He treated 1787 almost as a miraculous and singular event. Had he been a devotee of astrology, he might have said that the stars were peculiarly and uniquely aligned to allow the drafting of the Constitution and then its ratification. Though Madison was surely too tactful to mention this, part of the alignment was the absence of the famously contentious Jefferson and John Adams. Both were 3,000 miles across the sea, where they were serving as the first ambassadors from the new United States to Paris and London, respectively. Moreover, it certainly did not hurt that Rhode Island had refused to send any delegates at all and therefore had no opportunity to make almost inevitable mischief, not to mention being unable to vote in an institutional structure where the vote of one state could make a big difference. And, if pressed, Madison would presumably have agreed that the Constitutional Convention—and the ratifying conventions thereafter—would never have succeeded had the delegates included American slaves, Native Americans, or women in the spirit of Abigail Adams. She had famously—and altogether unsuccessfully—told her husband that leaders of the new nation should "remember the ladies." One need not see the framers in Philadelphia as an entirely homogeneous group—they were not—in order to realize that the room was devoid of those groups in America that were viewed as merely the *objects*, and not the active *subjects*, of governance.

Madison sets out his views most clearly in the *Federalist*, No. 49, where he explicitly takes issue with Jefferson's proposal for rather frequent constitutional conventions that would consider whether "alter[ation]" of the constitution might be desirable. Madison acknowledges the apparent appeal, in a system where "the people are the only legitimate fountain of power," of "appeal[ing] to the people themselves." However, "there appear to be insuperable objections against the proposed recurrence to the people." Perhaps the key objection is that *"frequent appeal to the people would carry an implication of some defect in the government [and] deprive the government of that veneration which time bestows on every thing, and without which perhaps the wisest and freest governments would not possess the requisite stability."* Only "a nation of philosophers" can forgo this emotion of veneration—and, therefore, feel free of guilt-ridden anxiety about the idea of constitutional change. However, "a nation of philosophers is as little to be expected as the philosophical race of kings wished for by Plato."

Madison is thus fearful of "disturbing the public tranquillity by interesting too strongly the public passions." The success of Americans in replacing a defective Articles of Confederation with a better Constitution does not constitute a precedent for future action. We should "recollect," he says, "that all the existing constitutions were formed in the midst of a danger which repressed the passions most unfriendly to order and concord." Moreover, the people at large possessed "an enthusiastic confidence . . . in their patriotic leaders," which, he says, fortunately "stifled the ordinary diversity of opinions on great national questions." He is extremely skeptical that the "future situations in which we must expect to be usually placed" will "present any equivalent security against the danger" of an excess of public passion, disrespect for leaders, and the full play of diverse opinions. In case there is any doubt, he writes of his fear that the *"passions*, therefore, not the *reasons*, of the public would sit in judgment."

Madison's view of his fellow Americans was far closer to that of Alexander Hamilton, with whom he had coauthored the *Federalist*. One can doubt that Madison expressed any reservations when hearing Hamilton, addressing his fellow delegates to the Philadelphia convention on June 18, 1787, denounce the conceit that "the voice of the people" is "the voice of God." On the contrary, said Hamilton: "The people are turbulent and changing; they seldom judge or determine right." Although Madison was not opposed to constitutional amendment as such, he clearly saw almost no role for a public that would engage in probing questions suggesting that there might be serious "defects" in the Constitution. Only philosophers (like himself?) or, perhaps, "patriotic leaders" could be trusted to engage in dispassionate political dialogue and reasoning. In contrast, the general public should be educated to feel only "veneration" for their Constitution rather than be encouraged to use their critical faculties and actually assess the relationship between the great ends set out in the Preamble and the instruments devised for their realization.

* * *

This is a mistake. To the extent that we continue thoughtlessly to venerate, and therefore not subject to truly critical examination, our Constitution, we are in the position of the battered wife who continues to profess the "essential goodness" of her abusive husband. To stick with the analogy for a moment, it may well be the case that the husband, when sober or not gambling, is a decent, even loving, partner. The problem is that such moments are more than counterbalanced by abusive ones, even if they are relatively rare. And he becomes especially abusive when she suggests the possibility of marital counseling and attendant change. Similarly, that there are good features of our Constitution should not be denied. But there are also significantly abusive ones, and it is time for us to face them rather than remain in a state of denial.

Trapped Inside the Article V Cage

The framers of the Constitution were under no illusion that they had created a perfect document. The best possible proof for this proposition comes from George Washington himself. As he wrote to his nephew Bushrod two months after the conclusion of the Philadelphia convention over which he had presided, *"The warmest friends and the best supporters the Constitution has do not contend that it is free from imperfections*; but they found them unavoidable and are sensible if evil is likely to arise there from, the remedy must come hereafter." Sounding a remarkably Jeffersonian note, Washington noted that the "People (for it is with them to Judge) can, as they will have the advantage of experience on their Side, decide with as much propriety on the alteration[s] and amendment[s] which are necessary." Indeed, wrote the man described as the Father of Our Country, "I do not think we are more inspired, have more wisdom, or possess more virtue, than those who will come after us."

Article V itself is evidence of the recognition of the possibility—and inevitable reality—of imperfection, else they would have adopted John Locke's suggestion in a constitution that he drafted for the Carolina colonies that would have made the document unamendable. It is an unfortunate reality, though, that Article V, practically speaking, brings us all too close to the Lockean dream (or nightmare) of changeless stasis.

As University of Houston political scientist Donald Lutz has conclusively demonstrated, the U.S. Constitution is the most difficult to amend of any constitution currently existing in the world today. Formal amendment of the U.S. Constitution generally requires the approval of two-thirds of each of the two houses of our national Congress, followed by the approval of three-quarters of the states (which today means thirty-eight of the fifty states). Article V does allow the abstract possibility that amendments could be proposed through the aegis of a constitutional convention called by Congress upon the petition of two-thirds of the states; such proposals, though, would still presumably have to be ratified by the state legislatures or, in the alternative, as was done with regard to the Twenty-first Amendment repealing the prohibition of alcohol required by the Eighteenth Amendment, by conventions in each of the states. As a practical matter, though, Article V makes it next to impossible to amend the Constitution with regard to genuinely controversial issues, even if substantial—and intense—majorities advocate amendment.

As I have written elsewhere, some significant change functionally similar to "amendment" has occurred informally, outside of the procedures set out by Article V. One scholar has aptly described this as a process of "constitutional change off-the-books." Yale law professor Bruce Ackerman has written several brilliant books detailing the process of "non-Article V" amendment, and I warmly commend them to the reader. Yet it is difficult to argue that such informal amendment has occurred, or is likely to occur, with regard to the basic *structural* aspects of the American political system with which this book is primarily concerned.

It is one thing to argue, as Ackerman has done, that the New Deal worked as a functional amendment of the Constitution by giving Congress significant new powers to regulate the national economy. Similarly, one could easily argue that the president, for good or for ill, now possesses powers over the use of armed forces that would have been inconceivable to the generation of the framers. Whatever the text of the Constitution may say about the power of Congress to "declare war" or whatever the original understanding of this clause, it is hard to deny that many presidents throughout our history have successfully chosen to take the country to war without seeking a declaration of war (or, in some cases, even prior congressional approval of any kind). Ackerman and David Golove have also persuasively argued that the Treaty Clause, which requires that two-thirds of the Senate assent to any treaty, has been transformed through the use of "executive agreements." Although such agreements are unmentioned in the text of the Constitution, presidents have frequently avoided the strictures of the Treaty Clause by labeling an "agreement" what earlier would have been viewed as a "treaty." Thus, the North American Free Trade Agreement did not have to leap the hurdles erected by the Treaty Clause; instead, it was validated by majority votes of both the House of Representatives and the Senate.

These developments are undoubtedly important, and any complete analysis of our constitutional system should take account of such flexibility. But we should not overemphasize our system's capacity to change, and it is *constitutional stasis* rather than the potential for adaptation that is my focus.

* * *

One cannot, as a practical matter, litigate the obvious inequality attached to Wyoming's having the same voting power in the Senate as California. Nor can we imagine even President George W. Bush, who has certainly not been a shrinking violet with regard to claims of presidential power, announcing that Justice John Paul Stevens—appointed in 1976 and embarking on this fourth decade of service on the Supreme Court at the age of eighty-six—is simply "too old" or has served "long enough," and that he is therefore nominating, and asking the Senate to confirm, a successor to Justice Stevens in spite of the awkward fact that the justice has not submitted his resignation.

In any event, * * * the Constitution makes it unacceptably difficult to achieve the inspiring goals of the Preamble and, therefore, warrants our disapproval. * * *

Although I am asking you to take part in a hypothetical referendum and to vote no with regard to the present Constitution, I am *not* asking you to imagine simply tearing it up and leaping into the unknown of a fanciful "state of nature." All you must commit yourself to is the proposition that the Constitution is sufficiently flawed to justify calling a new convention authorized to scrutinize all aspects of the Constitution and to suggest such changes as are felt to be desirable. The new convention would be no more able to bring its handiwork into being by fiat than were the framers in Philadelphia. All proposals would require popular approval in a further national referendum. This leaves open the possibility that, even after voting to trigger the convention, you could ultimately decide that the "devil you know" (the present Constitution) is preferable to the "devil you don't" (the proposed replacement). But the important thing, from my perspective, is to recognize that there are indeed "devilish" aspects of our present Constitution that should be confronted and, if at all possible, exorcised. To complete this metaphor, one might also remember that "the devil is in the details." * * *

10

"Restoring the Rule of Law with States Leading the Way"

GREG ABBOTT

The Constitution is increasingly eroded with each passing year. That is a tragedy given the volume of blood spilled by patriots to win our country's freedom and repeatedly defend it over the last 240 years. Moreover, the declining relevance of our Nation's governing legal document is dangerous. Thomas Hobbes's observation more than 350 years ago remains applicable today: The only thing that separates a nation from anarchy is its collective willingness to know and obey the law.

But today, most Americans have no idea what our Constitution says. According to a recent poll, one-third of Americans cannot name the three branches of government; one-third cannot name any branch; and one-third thinks that the President has the "final say" about the government's powers. Obviously, the American people cannot hold their government accountable if they do not know what the source of that accountability says.

The Constitution is not just abstract and immaterial to average Americans; it also is increasingly ignored by government officials. Members of Congress used to routinely quote the Constitution while debating whether a particular policy proposal could be squared with Congress's enumerated powers. Such debates rarely happen today. In fact, when asked to identify the source of constitutional authority for Obamacare's individual mandate, the Speaker of the House revealed all too much when she replied with anger and incredulity: *"Are you serious?"* And, while the Supreme Court continues to identify new rights protected by the Constitution's centuries-old text, it is telling that the justices frequently depart from what the document actually says and rely instead on words or concepts that are found nowhere in the document. That is why one scholar observed that "in this day and age, discussing the doctrine of enumerated powers is like discussing the redemption of Imperial Chinese bonds."

Abandoning, ignoring, and eroding the strictures of the Constitution cheapens the entire institution of law. One of the cornerstones of this country was that ours would be a Nation of laws and not of men. The Constitution is the highest such law and the font of all other laws. As long as all Americans uphold the Constitution's authority, the document will continue to provide the ultimate defense of our liberties. But once the Constitution loses its hold on American life, we also lose confidence in the ability of law to protect us. Without the rule of law the things we treasure can be taken away by an election, by whims of individual leaders, by impulsive social-media campaigns, or by collective apathy.

The Constitution provides a better way—if only we were willing to follow it. The Constitution imposes real limits on Congress and forces its members to do their jobs rather than pass the buck. The Constitution forces the President to work with Congress to accomplish his priorities rather than usurping its powers by circumventing the legislative process with executive orders and administrative fiats. And the Constitution forces the Supreme Court to confront the limits on its powers to transform the country. Although the Constitution provides no assurance that any branch of government will make policy choices you like, the Constitution offers *legitimacy* to those choices and legitimate pathways to override those choices. The people who make those choices would have to stand for election, they would have to work with others who stand for election, and crucially, they would have to play by rules that we all agree to beforehand rather than making them up as they go along.

Of course, the Constitution already does all of this. And thus it bears emphasis at the outset that *the Constitution itself is not broken*. What *is* broken is our Nation's willingness to obey the Constitution and to hold our leaders accountable to it. As explained in the following pages, all three branches of the federal government have wandered far from the roles that the Constitution sets out for them. For various reasons, "We the People" have allowed all three branches of government to get away with it. And with each power grab the next somehow seems less objectionable. When measured by how far we have strayed from the Constitution we originally agreed to, the government's flagrant and repeated violations of the rule of law amount to a wholesale abdication of the Constitution's design.

That constitutional problem calls for a constitutional solution, just as it did at our Nation's founding. Indeed, a constitutional crisis gave birth to the Constitution we have today. The Articles of Confederation, which we adopted after the Revolutionary War, proved insufficient to protect and defend our fledgling country. So the States assembled to devise what we now know as our Constitution. At that assembly, various States stepped up to offer their leadership visions for what the new Constitution should say. Virginia's delegates offered the "Virginia Plan," New Jersey's delegates offered the "New Jersey Plan," and Connecticut's delegates brokered a compromise called the "Connecticut Plan." Without those States' plans, there would be no Constitution and probably no United States of America at all.

Now it is Texas's turn. The Texas Plan is not so much a vision to alter the Constitution as it is a call to restore the rule of our current one. The problem is that we have forgotten what our Constitution means, and with that amnesia, we also have forgotten what it means to be governed by laws instead of men. The solution is to restore the rule of law by ensuring that our government abides by the Constitution's limits. Our courts are supposed to play that role, but today, we have judges who actively subvert the Constitution's original design rather than uphold it. Yet even though we can no longer rely on our Nation's leaders to enforce the Constitution that "We the People" agreed to, the Constitution provides another way forward. Acting through the States, the people can amend their Constitution to force their leaders in all three branches of government to recognize renewed limits on federal power. Without the consent of any politicians in Washington, D.C., "We the People" can rein in the federal government and restore the balance of power between the States and the United States. The Texas Plan accomplishes this by offering nine constitutional amendments:

I. Prohibit Congress from regulating activity that occurs wholly within one State.
II. Require Congress to balance its budget.
III. Prohibit administrative agencies—and the unelected bureaucrats that staff them—from creating federal law.
IV. Prohibit administrative agencies—and the unelected bureaucrats that staff them—from preempting state law.
V. Allow a two-thirds majority of the States to override a U.S. Supreme Court decision.
VI. Require a seven-justice super-majority vote for U.S. Supreme Court decisions that invalidate a democratically enacted law.
VII. Restore the balance of power between the federal and state governments by limiting the former to the powers expressly delegated to it in the Constitution.
VIII. Give state officials the power to sue in federal court when federal officials overstep their bounds.
IX. Allow a two-thirds majority of the States to override a federal law or regulation.

* * *

Objections to an Article V Convention Lack Merit

The framers intended for States to call for conventions to propose constitutional amendments when, as now, the federal government has overstepped its bounds. And over the last 200 or so years, there have been hundreds of applications calling for such a convention spread out among virtually every state legislature. Yet no application has reached the critical two-thirds threshold to require the convention.

The States' previous failures to reach the two-thirds threshold for a convention could stem from the fact that, before now, circumstances did not demand it. But it is also possible that the States' efforts have been thwarted by counterarguments that surely will surface again in response to the

Texas Plan. Whatever influence such counterarguments may have in previous contexts and other state legislatures' applications for constitutional conventions, they lack merit here.

* * *

Nor can critics credibly claim that a convention is "scary" or that it somehow threatens valuable tenets of the Constitution. That is so for at least two reasons. First, whatever happens at the convention, no amendments will be made to the Constitution unless and until they are approved by an overwhelming majority (three-fourths) of the States. That is an extraordinary super-majority requirement that ensures, in James Iredell's words, that "[i]t is highly probable that amendments agreed to in either of [Article V's] methods would be conducive to the public welfare, when so large a majority of the states consented to them." It takes only 13 States to block any measure from becoming a constitutional amendment.

* * * [It] is not as if the three-fourths approval requirement is the Constitution's only failsafe against imprudent amendments. The Constitution also leaves it to the States to limit the scope of the convention itself. In fact, four States already have applied for constitutional conventions that include some portion of the Texas Plan, and all of them limit their applications to specific issues. Likewise, the Texas Legislature can limit its application for a convention—or its participation in a convention—to the specific issues included in the Texas Plan and discussed above. To the extent the convention strayed from those issues, Texas's consent to the convention's activities would automatically dissolve. State legislatures could even command in their laws authorizing participation in a convention that the state must vote against any constitutional convention provision not authorized by the state.

Some nonetheless argue that the Constitution does not allow state legislatures to limit the scope of a convention. The critics seize on this argument to raise the specter of a "runaway convention," in which the States propose a convention to debate limited amendments, but in which the delegates end up throwing the entire Constitution in the trashcan. Even if that happened, none of the delegates' efforts would become law without approval from three-fourths of the States. But even on its own terms, the criticism lacks merit.

The specter of a "runaway convention" goes like this. First, the critics argue, the Constitution says state legislatures "shall call a Convention for proposing Amendments," not for *confirming* a pre-written amendment that the state legislatures included in their applications for a convention. That means, the critics say, that States must call general, open-ended conventions; the convention delegates then perform the work of drafting the amendments; and the States' only option is to give a thumbs-up or thumbs-down at the end of the convention process. If the framers of Article V wanted to authorize conventions limited to particular issues, the critics conclude, they would have said so.

It is true that Article V does not expressly authorize States to limit conventions to particular issues—but the problem for would-be critics of the Texas Plan is that Article V *also* does not require general and open-ended conventions. Indeed, that is by design. As noted above, the whole point of the second path for proposing amendments was to *empower* States to propose amendments to the Constitution. In adopting that second path, the framers agreed with George Mason that the States should have constitutional redress when the federal government overstepped its bounds. And nothing that Mason (or his fellow framers) said would suggest that the States were somehow limited in *how* they exercised that power to defend their prerogatives against a federal government. To the contrary, James Madison specifically noted that the Constitution was silent on the issue, and he argued that that silence was good and necessary to preserve the States' flexibility. In Madison's words, "Constitutional regulations [of such matters] ought to be as much as possible avoided."

While the Constitution's text is silent on the topic, the framers themselves were not. To take just one example, George Nicholas pointed out during Virginia's ratification debates that conventions called by the States could—indeed, *would*—be limited to particular issues: "The conventions which shall be so called will have their deliberations confined to a few points; no local interest to divert their attention; nothing but the necessary alterations." And because the States would limit their applications for conventions to particular issues, "[i]t is natural to conclude that those states who apply for calling the convention will concur in the ratification of the proposed amendments." Of course, it would not be natural to assume that the States would support the results of the convention they called if—as the critics argue—the States could have zero assurances regarding what the convention delegates would do at that convention.

The very thing that belies any allegation of radicalism in the Texas Plan—namely, the super-majority requirements for proposing and ratifying amendments—arguably undermines its efficacy as a check on federal overreach. The latter was the principal point of Patrick Henry, one of the greatest orators of the eighteenth century and a ferocious Anti-Federalist. He argued that the States' power to amend the Constitution did not go nearly far enough to protect the people from an overbearing federal government. In particular, he bemoaned Article V's super-majority requirements:

> This, Sir, is the language of democracy; that a majority of the community have a right to alter their Government when found to be oppressive: But how different is the genius of your new Constitution from this! How different from the sentiments of freemen, that a contemptible minority can prevent the good of the majority! . . . If, Sir, amendments are left to the twentieth or tenth part of the people of America, your liberty is gone forever. . . . It will be easily contrived to procure the opposition of one tenth of the people to any alteration, however judicious. The Honorable Gentleman who presides, told us, that to

> prevent abuses in our Government, we will assemble in Convention, recall our delegated powers, and punish our servants for abusing the trust reposed in them. Oh, Sir, we should have fine times indeed, if to punish tyrants, it were only sufficient to assemble the people!

Patrick Henry might be right that even an assembly of the people will be insufficient to restore the rule of law and to bring the federal government to heel. And it is true that Article V allows a minority to oppose any amendment that the overwhelming majority of Americans support.

But far from dissuading the effort to amend our Constitution, Henry's words should encourage it. The benefits of the Texas Plan are many because any change effectuated by an assembly of the people will force the federal government—whether in big ways or small—to take the Constitution seriously again. And the downsides of such an assembly are virtually nonexistent, given that any change to our Constitution's text requires such overwhelming nationwide support. The only true downside comes from doing nothing and allowing the federal government to continue ignoring the very document that created it.

11

"An Article V Constitutional Convention? Wrong Idea, Wrong Time"

Walter Olson

In his quest to catch the Road Runner, the Coyote in the old Warner Brothers cartoons would always order supplies from the ACME Corporation, but they never performed as advertised. Either they didn't work at all, or they blew up in his face.

Which brings us to the idea of a so-called Article V convention assembled for the purpose of proposing amendments to the U.S. Constitution, an idea enjoying some vogue at both ends of the political spectrum.

On the left, a group founded by liberal TV host Cenk Uygur is pushing a convention aimed at overturning the Supreme Court's hated *Citizens United* decision and declaring that from now on corporations should stop having rights, or at least not a right to spend money spreading political opinions. Four liberal states—California, Vermont, Illinois, and New Jersey—have signed on to this idea.

On the right, the longstanding proposal for a convention to draft a balanced budget amendment has at times come within striking distance of the requisite two-thirds of state legislatures needed to trigger the idea. And for the past few years, talk-show host Mark Levin has been campaigning for a convention with broader conservative goals, an idea that got a boost when Florida Senator Marco Rubio recently endorsed it, citing "Washington's refusal to place restrictions on itself."

Rubio's specifics are still sketchy—term limits for members of Congress and Supreme Court justices would be part of it—but Texas Republican Governor Greg Abbott has now jumped in with a detailed "Texas Plan" of nine constitutional amendments mostly aimed at wresting various powers back from the federal government to the states.

Some of these ideas are better than others—Governor Abbott's 92-page report is rather erudite, and lays out its arguments skillfully even if I do not find all of them sound—but every such scheme to stage an Article V convention should come with a giant ACME brand stenciled on its side. If it doesn't just sit there doing nothing, it's apt to blow up on the spot.

The detonation that skeptics most fear is what's called a runaway convention, in which the delegates called together to, say, install term limits or revamp campaign finance, decide to venture into other areas as well, and perhaps start proposing whatever new amendments they think might be a good idea. Hence [the late] Justice Antonin Scalia's brusque dismissal: "I certainly would not want a constitutional convention. Whoa! Who knows what would come out of it?"

Some respected scholars who favor a convention argue that strict instructions would deter the assembled delegates from venturing beyond the velvet rope. But if that cannot be made a legal requirement, it winds up more like an honor code. "Congress might try to limit the agenda to one amendment or to one issue, but there is no way to assure that the Convention would obey," wrote the late Chief Justice Warren Burger.

Don't believe Scalia or Burger? Go ahead and read the instruction kit for a convention, such as it is, in Article V of the U.S. Constitution. It's quite brief. Here's the full relevant text:

> The Congress, whenever two-thirds of both houses shall deem it necessary, shall propose amendments to this Constitution, or, on the application of the legislatures of two-thirds of the several states, shall call a convention for proposing amendments, which, in either case, shall be valid to all intents and purposes, as part of this Constitution, when ratified by the legislatures of three-fourths of the several states, or by conventions in three-fourths thereof, as the one or the other mode of ratification may be proposed by the Congress . . .

Note what this does *not* say. It says not a word expressly authorizing the states, Congress, or some combination of the two to confine the subject matter of a convention. It says not a word about whether Congress, in calculating whether the requisite 34 states have called for a convention, must (or must not) aggregate calls for a convention on, say, a balanced budget, with differently worded calls arising from related or perhaps even unrelated topics. It says not a word prescribing that the makeup of a convention, as many conservatives imagine, will be one-state-one-vote (as Alaska and Wyoming might hope) or whether states with larger populations should be given larger delegations (as California and New York would surely argue).

Does Congress, or perhaps the Supreme Court, get to resolve these questions—the same Congress and Supreme Court that the process is aimed at doing an end run around? If the Supreme Court resolves them, does it do so only at the very end of the process, after years of national debate have been spent in devising amendments that we find out after the fact were not generated in proper form?

Justice Burger described the whole process as "a grand waste of time." One reason is that after advocates get the process rolling by convincing two-thirds of states—or 34, itself a fairly demanding number—the amendments that emerge from a convention do not get ratified unless three-quarters of states ratify—or 38, a quite demanding number.

Put differently, it takes only 13 states to refuse to act to kill any of these ideas, bad or good, in the end. Sorry, Cenk and Marco, but so long as we have a nation fairly closely divided between Blue and Red sentiment, there will be at least 13 states skeptical of some systemic change so big that you had to go around the backs of both Congress and the Supreme Court to pull it off. If you're a progressive who thinks the populist winds blow only in your favor, reflect for a moment on the success of Donald Trump. If you're a conservative to whom radio call-ins resound as the voice of the people, consider that state legislatures confronted with the hard legal issues a convention would raise might turn for advice and assistance to elite lawyers (yikes) or even law professors (double yikes).

Finally, we shouldn't assume—as do some of Governor Abbott's co-thinkers—that most state governments are as eager as Texas to curtail the powers of the feds. One of the most significant conservative books on federalism lately, George Mason University professor Michael Greve's *The Upside-Down Constitution*, sheds light on this. Conservatives tell a campfire story of how the federal government got big by taking power away from the states. But in his (admittedly long and complicated) book, Greve argues that the truth is closer to the opposite.

Whether in spending programs, regulations, subsidies, you name it, almost every big expansion of federal power has been skillfully designed as a deal that cuts state political elites into some of the resulting flow of power and money—consider, for example, how state education, police, road, and environmental departments have come to depend on Washington's largesse. And while many states may join Texas in sincerely griping at the bad end of the deal—the endless paperwork, the unfunded mandates—that doesn't mean they'd actually join Governor Abbott in risking the connection.

Yes, the federal government has slipped its constitutional bounds, and yes, that's infuriating. Just don't confuse a plan for talking, which is what these amount to, with a plan for actually changing things, and always beware of a cure that might kill the patient.

Discussion Questions

1. Most of the time, people become critical of the Constitution when they don't get the policy results they want. When Congress fails to pass legislation because of the power of small-state senators, when the Supreme Court issues a ruling they oppose, or when the president makes a decision regarding the use of force that they oppose, the immediate impulse is to blame the system and call for change that would make their preferred policies more likely. Is this a valid reason for wanting the system to change?

2. The Constitution was written more than 230 years ago by a group of white men who had very "unmodern" views about democracy and equality. On what basis should we be bound by the decisions that they made? What would be the result if each generation were permitted to remake the rules, as Abbott suggests? Do you agree with Olson's concerns about the constitutional convention?

3. Often, opinions about the Constitution divide along philosophical lines. On one side are people who believe that the most important purpose of a constitution is to limit government size and power. On the other are people who believe that the Constitution must protect rights and promote equality, which almost always involves expanding the size and power of government. Who has the better case? Why?

CHAPTER 3

Federalism

12

The Federalist, No. 46

James Madison

Some of the most divisive and bitter political battles in our nation's history have occurred over interpretations of the constitutional principle of federalism—the division of powers and functions between the state governments and the national government. The struggle for desegregation and the civil rights of minorities, the legalization of abortion, the selective incorporation of the Bill of Rights under the Fourteenth Amendment, slavery and the Civil War all ultimately turned on the question, Who has the authority to govern: the states, or the national government? Our federal system is a delicate balance of power and shared responsibility between nation and states, each with constitutional authority to pass laws, levy taxes, and protect the interests and rights of citizens. It is a dynamic balance of power, easily destabilized by economic crises, political initiatives, and Supreme Court rulings, but often resolved in more recent years by the question, Who will pay the price for implementing and enforcing government policy?

The "double security" that James Madison discussed in The Federalist, *No. 51 did not satisfy those who feared that the national powers would encroach on state sovereignty. In* The Federalist, *No. 46, Madison went to great lengths to reassure the states that they would continue to wield a high degree of power, arguing that "the first and most natural attachment of the people will be to the governments of their respective states." While recognizing the potential for conflicts between state and federal governments, Madison concluded that the power retained by the states would be sufficient to resist arrogation by the newly established national government.*

I proceed to inquire whether the federal government or the State governments will have the advantage with regard to the predilection and support of the people. Notwithstanding the different modes in which they are appointed, we must consider both of them as substantially dependent on the great body of the citizens of the United States. * * * The federal and State governments are in fact but different agents and trustees of the people, constituted with different powers and designed for different purposes. The adversaries of the Constitution seem to have lost sight of the people altogether in their reasonings on this subject; and to have viewed these different establishments not only as mutual rivals and enemies, but as uncontrolled by any common superior in their efforts to usurp the authorities of each other. These gentlemen must here be reminded of their error. They must be told that the ultimate authority, wherever the derivative may be found, resides in the people alone, and that it will not depend merely on the comparative ambition or address of the different governments whether either, or which of them, will be able to enlarge its sphere of jurisdiction at the expense of the other. Truth, no less than decency, requires that the event in every case should be supposed to depend on the sentiments and sanction of their common constituents.

Many considerations * * * seem to place it beyond doubt that the first and most natural attachment of the people will be to the governments of their respective States. Into the administration of these a greater number of individuals will expect to rise. From the gift of these a greater number of offices and emoluments will flow. By the superintending care of these, all the more domestic and personal interests of the people will be regulated and provided for. With the affairs of these, the people will be more familiarly and minutely conversant. And with the members of these will a greater proportion of the people have the ties of personal acquaintance and friendship, and of family and party attachments; on the side of these, therefore, the popular bias may well be expected most strongly to incline.

The remaining points on which I propose to compare the federal and State governments are the disposition and the faculty they may respectively possess to resist and frustrate the measures of each other.

It has been already proved that the members of the federal will be more dependent on the members of the State governments than the latter will be on the former. It has appeared also that the prepossessions of the people, on whom both will depend, will be more on the side of the State governments than of the federal government. So far as the disposition of each towards the other may be influenced by these causes, the State governments must clearly have the advantage. But in a distinct and very important point of view, the advantage will lie on the same side. The prepossessions, which the members themselves will carry into the federal government, will generally be favorable to the States; whilst it will rarely happen that the members of the State governments will carry into the public councils a bias in favor of the general government. A local spirit will infallibly prevail much more in the members of Congress than a national spirit will prevail in the legislatures of the particular States.

* * * What is the spirit that has in general characterized the proceedings of Congress? A perusal of their journals, as well as the candid acknowledgments of such as have had a seat in that assembly, will inform us that the members have but too frequently displayed the character rather of partisans of their respective States than of impartial guardians of a common interest; that where on one occasion improper sacrifices have been made of local considerations to the aggrandizement of the federal government, the great interests of the nation have suffered on a hundred from an undue attention to the local prejudices, interests, and views of the particular States. I mean not by these reflections to insinuate that the new federal government will not embrace a more enlarged plan of policy than the existing government may have pursued; much less that its views will be as confined as those of the State legislatures; but only that it will partake sufficiently of the spirit of both to be disinclined to invade the rights of the individual States, or the prerogatives of their governments.

Were it admitted, however, that the federal government may feel an equal disposition with the State governments to extend its power beyond the due limits, the latter would still have the advantage in the means of defeating such encroachments. If an act of a particular State, though unfriendly to the national government, be generally popular in that State, and should not too grossly violate the oaths of the State officers, it is executed immediately and, of course, by means on the spot and depending on the State alone. The opposition of the federal government, or the interposition of federal officers, would but inflame the zeal of all parties on the side of the State, and the evil could not be prevented or repaired, if at all, without the employment of means which must always be resorted to with reluctance and difficulty. On the other hand, should an unwarrantable measure of the federal government be unpopular in particular States, which would seldom fail to be the case, or even a warrantable measure be so, which may sometimes be the case, the means of opposition to it are powerful and at hand. The disquietude of the people; their repugnance and, perhaps, refusal to co-operate with the officers of the Union; the frowns of the executive magistracy of the State; the embarrassments created by legislative devices, which would often be added on such occasions, would oppose, in any State, difficulties not to be despised; would form, in a large State, very serious impediments; and where the sentiments of several adjoining States happened to be in unison, would present obstructions which the federal government would hardly be willing to encounter.

But ambitious encroachments of the federal government on the authority of the State governments would not excite the opposition of a single State, or of a few States only. They would be signals of general alarm. Every government would espouse the common cause. A correspondence would be opened. Plans of resistance would be concerted. One spirit would animate and conduct the whole. The same combinations, in short, would result from an apprehension of the federal, as was produced by the dread of a foreign yoke; and unless the projected innovations should be voluntarily renounced, the same appeal to a trial of force would be made in the one case as was made in the other.

The only refuge left for those who prophesy the downfall of the State governments is the visionary supposition that the federal government may previously accumulate a military force for the projects of ambition. The reasonings contained in these papers must have been employed to little purpose indeed, if it could be necessary now to disprove the reality of this danger. That the people and the States should, for a sufficient period of time, elect an uninterrupted succession of men ready to betray both; that the traitors should, throughout this period, uniformly and systematically pursue some fixed plan for the extension of the military establishment; that the governments and the people of the States should silently and patiently behold the gathering storm and continue to supply the materials until it should be prepared to burst on their own heads must appear to everyone more like the incoherent dreams of a delirious jealousy, or the misjudged exaggerations of a counterfeit zeal, than like the sober apprehensions of genuine patriotism. Extravagant as the supposition is, let it, however, be made. Let a regular army, fully equal to the resources of the country, be formed; and let it be entirely at the devotion of the federal government: still it would not be going too far to say that the State governments with the people on their side would be able to repel the danger.

Besides the advantage of being armed, which the Americans possess over the people of almost every other nation, the existence of subordinate governments, to which the people are attached and by which the militia officers are appointed, forms a barrier against the enterprises of ambition, more insurmountable than any which a simple government of any form can admit of.

Let us not insult the free and gallant citizens of America with the suspicion that they would be less able to defend the rights of which they would be in actual possession than the debased subjects of arbitrary power would be to rescue theirs from the hands of their oppressors. Let us rather no longer insult them with the supposition that they can ever reduce themselves to the necessity of making the experiment by a blind and tame submission to the long train of insidious measures which must precede and produce it.

The argument under the present head may be put into a very concise form, which appears altogether conclusive. Either the mode in which the federal government is to be constructed will render it sufficiently dependent on the people, or it will not. On the first supposition, it will be restrained by that dependence from forming schemes obnoxious to their constituents. On the other supposition, it will not possess the confidence of the people, and its schemes of usurpation will be easily defeated by the State governments, who will be supported by the people.

On summing up the considerations stated in this and the last paper, they seem to amount to the most convincing evidence that the powers proposed to be lodged in the federal government are as little formidable to those reserved to the individual States as they are indispensably necessary to accomplish the purposes of the Union; and that all those alarms which have been sounded of a meditated and consequential annihilation of the State governments must, on the most favorable interpretation, be ascribed to the chimerical fears of the authors of them.

PUBLIUS

DISCUSSION QUESTIONS

1. Is Madison right when he states that people are more attached to their state governments than to the national government? Why or why not? If not, would it better facilitate the democratic process if they were more attached to state governments?
2. Would your answer change at all during different political times? For example, were people more attached to the national government in the wake of September 11, 2001 than they were before? Do people lose their faith in the national government during tough economic times?

13

From *The Price of Federalism*

Paul Peterson

In this concise overview of American federalism, Paul Peterson argues that both the early system and more modern system of shared sovereignty between the national government and the states have had their disadvantages. From the early period of "dual federalism" to today's system of a dominant national government, the battle over national and state government jurisdiction and power has led to bloodshed and war; the denial of political, social, and economic rights; and regional inequalities among the states.

Nevertheless, Peterson argues, there are advantages to federalism. Federalism has also facilitated capital growth and development, the creation of infrastructures, and social programs that greatly improved the quality of life for millions of Americans. Once the national government took responsibility for guaranteeing civil rights and civil liberties, the states "became the engines of economic development." Not all states are equally wealthy, but the national government has gradually diminished some of these differences by financing many social and economic programs. One battle over the proper form of federal relations involved welfare policy in the 1990s. Republicans in Congress wanted to give back to states the power to devise their own programs, whereas most Democrats and President Bill Clinton initially wanted to retain a larger degree of federal government control. However, President Clinton eventually agreed to end welfare as an entitlement and return substantial control over the program to the states. The long-term verdict on this landmark legislation is still an open question. There is considerable debate over the proper balance between federal and state funding for the state-level welfare programs.

These same debates have cropped up in more recent years in homeland security policy. Ideally, this policy would be run at the national level, and resources would be allocated to parts of the country that pose the greatest security risks. However, every state wants its share of the federal pie, so resources are not always allocated in the most efficient manner. Federalism also poses challenges for coordinating policy for "first responders" in a time of crisis: Who is responsible for coming to the aid of people in distress—local, state, or national agencies?

The Price of Early Federalism

As a principle of government, federalism has had a dubious history. It remains on the margins of political respectability even today. I was recently invited to give a presentation on metropolitan government before a United Nations conference. When I offered to discuss how the federal principle could be used to help metropolitan areas govern themselves more effectively, my sponsors politely advised me that this topic would be poorly received. The vast majority of UN members had a unified form of government, I was told, and they saw little of value in federalism. We reached a satisfactory compromise. I replaced "federal" with "two-tier form of government."

Thomas Hobbes, the founder of modern political thought, would have blessed the compromise, for he, too, had little room for federalism in his understanding of the best form of government. Hobbes said that people agreed to have a government over them only because they realized that in a state of nature, that is, when there is no government, life becomes a war of all against all. If no government exists to put malefactors in jail, everyone must become a criminal simply to avoid being a victim. Life becomes "nasty, brutish and short." To avoid the violent state of nature, people need and want rule by a single sovereign. Division of power among multiple sovereigns encourages bickering among them. Conflicts become inevitable, as each sovereign tries to expand its power (if for no other reason than to avoid becoming the prey of competing sovereigns). Government degenerates into anarchy and the world returns to the bitter state of nature from which government originally emerged.

The authors of *The Federalist* papers defended dual sovereignty by turning Hobbes's argument in favor of single sovereignty on its head. While Hobbes said that anything less than a single sovereign would lead to war of all against all, *The Federalist* argued that the best way of preserving liberty was to divide power. If power is concentrated in any one place, it can be used to crush individual liberty. Even in a democracy there can be the tyranny of the majority, the worst kind of tyranny because it is so stifling and complete. A division of power between the national and state governments reduces the possibility that any single majority will be able to control all centers of governmental power. The national government, by defending the country against foreign aggression, prevents external threats to liberty. The state governments, by denying power to any single dictator, reduce threats to liberty from within. As James Madison said in his defense of the Constitution, written on the eve of its ratification,

> The power surrendered by the people is first divided between two distinct governments, and then the portion allotted to each subdivided among distinct and separate departments. Hence a double security arises to the rights of the people. The different governments will control each other, at the same time that each will be controlled by itself. [*The Federalist*, No. 51]

Early federalism was built on the principle of dual sovereignty. The Constitution divided sovereignty between state and nation, each in control of its own sphere. Some even interpreted the Constitution to mean that state legislatures could nullify federal laws. Early federalism also gave both levels of government their own military capacity. Congress was given the power to raise an army and wage war, but states were allowed to maintain their own militia.

The major contribution of early federalism to American liberties took place within a dozen years after the signing of the Constitution. Liberty is never established in a new nation until those in authority have peacefully ceded power to a rival political faction. Those who wrote the Constitution and secured its ratification, known as the Federalists, initially captured control of the main institutions of the national government: Congress, the presidency, and the Supreme Court. Those opposed to the new constitutional order, the antifederalists, had to content themselves with an opposition role in Congress and control over a number of state governments, most notably Virginia's.

The political issues dividing the two parties were serious. The Federalist party favored a strong central government, a powerful central bank that could facilitate economic and industrial development, and a strong, independent executive branch. Federalists had also become increasingly disturbed by the direction the French Revolution had taken. They were alarmed by the execution of thousands, the confiscation of private property, and the movement of French troops across Europe. They called for the creation of a national army and reestablished close ties with Britain.

The antifederalists, who became known as Democratic-Republicans, favored keeping most governmental power in the hands of state governments. They were opposed to a national bank, a strong presidency, and industrial government. They thought the United States would remain a free country only if it remained a land of independent farmers. They bitterly opposed the creation of a national army for fear it would be used to repress political opposition. Impressed by the French Revolution's commitment to the rights of man, they excused its excesses. The greater danger, they thought, was the reassertion of British power, and they denounced the Federalists for seeming to acquiesce in the seizure of U.S. seamen by the British navy.

The conflict between the two sides intensified after George Washington retired to his home in Mount Vernon. In 1800 Thomas Jefferson, founder of the Democratic-Republican party, waged an all-out campaign to defeat Washington's Federalist successor, John Adams. In retrospect, the central issue of the election was democracy itself. Could an opposition party drive a government out of power? Would political leaders accept their defeat?

So bitter was the feud between the two parties that Representative Matthew Lyon, a Democratic-Republican, spit in the face of a Federalist on the floor of Congress. Outside the Congress, pro-French propagandists relentlessly criticized Adams. To silence the opposition, Congress, controlled by the Federalists, passed the Alien and Sedition Acts. One of the Alien Acts gave President Adams the power to deport any foreigners "concerned in any treasonable or secret machinations against the government." The

Sedition Act made it illegal to "write, print, utter, or publish . . . any false, scandalous and malicious writing . . . against . . . the Congress of the United States, or the President."

The targets of the Sedition Acts soon became clear. Newspaper editors supporting the Democratic-Republicans were quickly indicted, and ten were brought to trial and convicted by juries under the influence of Federalist judges. Matthew Lyon was sentenced to a four-month jail term for claiming, presumably falsely, that President Adams had an "unbounded thirst for ridiculous pomp, foolish adulation, and selfish avarice." Even George Washington lent his support to this political repression.

Federalism undoubtedly helped the fledgling American democracy survive this first constitutional test. When the Federalists passed the Alien and Sedition Acts, Democratic-Republicans in the Virginia and Kentucky state legislatures passed resolutions nullifying the laws. When it looked as if Jefferson's victory in the election of 1800 might be stripped away by a Federalist controlled House of Representatives, both sides realized that the Virginia state militia was at least as strong as the remnants of the Continental Army. Lacking the national army they had tried to establish, the Federalists chose not to fight. They acquiesced in their political defeat in part because their opponents had military as well as political power, and because they themselves could retreat to their own regional base of power, the state and local governments of New England and the mid-Atlantic states.

Jefferson claimed his victory was a revolution every bit as comprehensive as the one fought in 1776. The Alien and Sedition Acts were discarded, nullified not by a state legislature but by the results of a national election. President Adams returned to private life without suffering imprisonment or exile. Many years later, he and Jefferson reconciled their differences and developed through correspondence a close friendship. They died on the same day, the fiftieth anniversary of the Declaration of Independence. To both, federalism and liberty seemed closely intertwined.

The price to be paid for early federalism became more evident with the passage of time. To achieve the blessings of liberty, early federalism divided sovereign power. When Virginia and Kentucky nullified the Alien and Sedition Acts, they preserved liberties only by threatening national unity. With the election of Jefferson, the issue was temporarily rendered moot, but the doctrine remained available for use when southerners once again felt threatened by encroaching national power.

The doctrine of nullification was revived in 1830 by John C. Calhoun, sometime senator from South Carolina, who objected to high tariffs that protected northern industry at the expense of southern cotton producers. When Congress raised the tariff, South Carolina's legislature threatened to declare the law null and void. Calhoun, then serving as Andrew Jackson's vice president, argued that liberties could be trampled by national majorities unless states could nullify tyrannical acts. Andrew

Jackson, though elected on a state's rights ticket, remained committed to national supremacy. At the annual Democratic banquet honoring the memory of Thomas Jefferson, Calhoun supporters sought to trap Jackson into endorsing the doctrine. But Jackson, aware of the scheme, raised his glass in a dramatic toast to "Our federal union: it must be preserved!" Not to be outdone, Calhoun replied in kind: "The union, next to our liberty, most dear!"

A compromise was found to the overt issue, the tariff, but it was not so easy to resolve the underlying issue of slavery. In the infamous Dred Scott decision, the Supreme Court interpreted federalism to mean that boundaries could not be placed on the movements of masters and slaves. Northern territories could not free slaves that came within their boundaries; to do so deprived masters of their Fifth Amendment right not to be deprived of their property without due process of law. The decision spurred northern states to elect Abraham Lincoln president, which convinced southern whites that their liberties, most dear, were more important than federal union.

To Lincoln, as to Jackson, the union was to be preserved at all costs. Secession meant war. War meant the loss of 1 million lives, the destruction of the southern economy, the emancipation of African Americans from slavery, the demise of the doctrine of nullification, and the end to early federalism. Early federalism, with its doctrine of dual sovereignty, may have initially helped to preserve liberty, but it did so at a terrible price. As Hobbes feared, the price of dual sovereignty was war.

Since the termination of the Civil War, Americans have concluded that they can no longer trust their liberties to federalism. Sovereignty must be concentrated in the hands of the national government. Quite apart from the dangers of civil war, the powers of state and local governments have been used too often by a tyrannical majority to trample the rights of religious, racial, and political minorities. The courts now seem a more reliable institutional shelter for the nation's liberties.

But if federalism is no longer necessary or even conducive to the preservation of liberty, then what is its purpose? Is it merely a relic of an outdated past? Are the majority of the members of the United Nations correct in objecting to the very use of the word?

The Rise of Modern Federalism

The answers to these questions have been gradually articulated in the 130 years following the end of the Civil War. Although the states lost their sovereignty, they remained integral to the workings of American government. Modern federalism no longer meant dual sovereignty and shared military capacity. Modern federalism instead meant only that each level of government had its own independently elected political leaders and its own separate taxing and spending capacity. Equipped with these tools of quasi-sovereignty, each level of government could take all but the most violent of steps to defend its turf.

Although sovereignty and military capacity now rested firmly in the hands of the national government, modern federalism became more complex rather than less so. Power was no longer simply divided between the nation and its states. Cities, counties, towns, school districts, special districts, and a host of additional governmental entities, each with its own elected leaders and taxing authority, assumed new burdens and responsibilities.

Just as the blessings bestowed by early federalism were evident from its inception, so the advantages of modern federalism were clear from the onset. If states and localities were no longer the guarantors of liberty, they became the engines of economic development. By giving state and local governments the autonomy to act independently, the federal system facilitated the rapid growth of an industrial economy that eventually surpassed its European competitors. Canals and railroads were constructed, highways and sewage systems built, schools opened, parks designed, and public safety protected by cities and villages eager to make their locality a boomtown.

The price to be paid for modern federalism did not become evident until government attempted to grapple with the adverse side effects of a burgeoning capitalist economy. Out of a respect for federalism's constitutional status and political durability, social reformers first worked with and through existing components of the federal system, concentrating much of their reform effort on state and local governments. Only gradually did it become clear that state and local governments, for all their ability to work with business leaders to enhance community prosperity, had difficulty meeting the needs of the poor and the needy.

It was ultimately up to the courts to find ways of keeping the price of modern federalism within bounds. Although dual sovereignty no longer meant nullification and secession, much remained to be determined about the respective areas of responsibility of the national and state governments. At first the courts retained remnants of the doctrine of dual sovereignty in order to protect processes of industrialization from governmental intrusion. But with the advent of the New Deal, the constitutional power of the national government expanded so dramatically that the doctrine of dual sovereignty virtually lost all meaning. Court interpretations of the constitutional clauses on commerce and spending have proved to be the most significant.

According to dual sovereignty theory, article 1 of the Constitution gives Congress the power to regulate commerce "among the states," but the regulation of intrastate commerce was to be left to the states. So, for example, in 1895 the Supreme Court said that Congress could not break up a sugar monopoly that had a nationwide impact on the price of sugar, because the monopoly refined its sugar within the state of Pennsylvania. The mere fact that the sugar was to be sold nationwide was only "incidental" to its production. As late as 1935, the Supreme Court, in a 6-to-3 decision, said that Congress could not regulate the sale of poultry because the regulation took effect after the chickens arrived within the state of Illinois, not while they were in transit.

Known as the "sick chicken" case, this decision was one of a series in which the Supreme Court declared unconstitutional legislation passed in the early days of President Franklin Roosevelt's efforts to establish his New Deal programs. Seven of the "nine old men" on the Court had been appointed by Roosevelt's conservative Republican predecessors. By declaring many New Deal programs in violation of the commerce clause, the Supreme Court seemed to be substituting its political views for those of elected officials. In a case denying the federal government the right to protect workers trying to organize a union in the coal industry, the Republican views of the Court seemed to lie just barely below the surface of a technical discussion of the commerce clause. Justice George Sutherland declared, "The relation of employer and employee is a local relation . . . over which the federal government has no legislative control."

The Roosevelt Democrats were furious at decisions that seemed to deny the country's elected officials the right to govern. Not since Dred Scott* had judicial review been in such disrepute. Roosevelt decided to "pack the court" by adding six new judges over and above the nine already on the Court. Although Roosevelt's court-packing scheme did not survive the political uproar on Capitol Hill, its effect on the Supreme Court was noticeable. In the midst of the court-packing debate, Justices Charles Hughes and Owen Roberts, who had agreed with Sutherland's opinion in the coal case, changed their mind and voted to uphold the Wagner Act, a new law designed to facilitate the formation of unions. In his opinion, Hughes did not explicitly overturn the coal miner decision (for which he had voted), but he did say: "When industries organize themselves on a national scale, . . . how can it be maintained that their industrial labor relations constitute a forbidden field into which Congress may not enter?" Relations between employers and their workers, once said to be local, suddenly became part of interstate commerce.

The change of heart by Hughes and Roberts has been called "the switch in time that saved nine." The New Deal majority that emerged on the court was soon augmented by judges appointed by Roosevelt. Since the New Deal, the definition of interstate commerce has continued to expand. In 1942 a farmer raising twenty-three acres of wheat, all of which might be fed to his own livestock, was said to be in violation of the crop quotas imposed by the Agricultural Adjustment Act of 1938. Since he was feeding his cows himself, he was not buying grain on the open market, thereby

*In *Dred Scott v. Sanford* (1857), the Court declared the antislavery provision of the Missouri Compromise of 1820 to be unconstitutional [*Editors*].

depressing the worldwide price of grain. With such a definition of interstate commerce, nothing was local.

The expansion of the meaning of the commerce clause is a well-known part of American political history. The importance to federalism of court interpretations of the "spending clause" is less well known. The constitutional clause in question says that Congress has the power to collect taxes to "provide for the . . . general welfare." But how about Congress's power to collect taxes for the welfare of specific individuals or groups?

The question first arose in a 1923 case, when a childless woman said she could not be asked to pay taxes in order to finance federal grants to states for programs that helped pregnant women. Since she received no benefit from the program, she sued for return of the taxes she had paid to cover its costs. In a decision that has never been reversed, the Supreme Court said that she had suffered no measurable injury and therefore had no right to sue the government. Her taxes were being used for a wide variety of purposes. The amount being spent for this program was too small to be significant. The court's decision to leave spending issues to Congress was restated a decade later when the social security program was also challenged on the grounds that monies were being directed to the elderly, not for the general welfare. Said Justice Benjamin N. Cardozo for a court majority: "The conception of the spending power . . . [must find a point somewhere] between particular and general. . . . There is a middle ground . . . in which discretion is large. The discretion, however, is not confided to the Court. The discretion belongs to Congress, unless the choice is clearly wrong."

The courts have ever since refused to review Congress's power to spend money. They have also conceded to Congress the right to attach any regulations to any aid Congress provides. In 1987 Congress provided a grant to state governments for the maintenance of their highways, but conditioned 5 percent of the funds on state willingness to raise the drinking age from eighteen to twenty-one. The connection between the appropriation and the regulation was based on the assumption that youths under the age of twenty-one are more likely to drive after drinking than those over twenty-one. Presumably, building more roads would only encourage more inebriated young people to drive on them. Despite the fact that the connection between the appropriation and the regulation was problematic, the Supreme Court ruled that Congress could attach any reasonable conditions to its grants to the states. State sovereignty was not violated, because any state could choose not to accept the money.

In short, the courts have virtually given up the doctrine of judicial review when it comes to matters on which Congress can spend money. As a consequence, most national efforts to influence state governments come in the form of federal grants. Federal aid can also be used to influence local governments, such as counties, cities, towns, villages, and school districts. These local governments, from a constitutional point of view, are mere creatures of the state of which they are part. They have no independent sovereignty.

The Contemporary Price of Federalism

If constitutional doctrine has evolved to the point that dual sovereign theory has been put to rest, this does not mean that federalism has come to an end. Although ultimate sovereignty resides with the national government, state and local governments still have certain characteristics and capabilities that make them constituent components of a federal system. * * * Two characteristics of federalism are fundamental. First, citizens elect officials of their choice for each level of government. Unless the authority of each level of government rests in the people, it will become the agent of the other. Second, each level of government raises money through taxation from the citizens residing in the area for which it is responsible. It is hard to see how a system could be regarded as federal unless each level of government can levy taxes on its residents. Unless each level of government can raise its own fiscal resources, it cannot act independently.

Although the constitutional authority of the national government has steadily expanded, state and local governments remain of great practical significance. Almost half of all government spending for domestic (as distinct from foreign and military) purposes is paid for out of taxes raised by state and local governments.

The sharing of control over domestic policy among levels of government has many benefits, but federalism still exacts its price. It can lead to great regional inequalities. Also, the need for establishing cooperative relationships among governments can contribute to great inefficiency in the administration of government programs.

Discussion Questions

1. What is the constitutional basis for federalism?
2. How has the relationship between state governments and the national government changed since the early years of the Republic?
3. Does a federal system serve our needs today? Does the federal government have too much power relative to the states? What would be the advantages and disadvantages of a reduced federal presence in state matters?

14

"Jumping Frogs, Endangered Toads, and California's Medical-Marijuana Law"

George J. Annas

From welfare reform to health care, educational funding to inner-city development, state governments have sought more control over public policy within their borders. In the 1970s and 1980s, when this devolution of power to the states was called "New Federalism," the debate was pretty simple. Republicans favored devolution because state governments were "closer to the people" and could better determine their needs. Democrats resisted the transfer of power from Washington, fearing that many states would not adequately care for and protect minorities and poor people, or protect the environment without prodding from Washington. To the extent that the courts got involved in the debate, they tended to favor the transfer of power to the states.

The debate over devolving power from the national government to the states has grown increasingly complicated in recent years: the partisan nature of the debate shifted, the Courts have played a larger, but inconsistent role, and issues of "states' rights" increasingly tend to cut across normal ideological and partisan divisions. While Republicans continued to favor greater state control, Democratic President Bill Clinton supported devolution to the states in several areas in the 1990s, especially welfare policy. Since the mid-1990s, the Supreme Court has played a central role in the shift of power to the states, but two recent cases involving medical marijuana (Gonzales v. Raich) *and the right to die* (Gonzales v. Oregon) *show how the typical debate between national and state power can shift when a moral dimension is introduced.*

In both cases, state voters supported liberal policies (approving medical marijuana in California and the right to die in Oregon). Therefore, the "states' rights" position on federalism in these cases represented the liberal perspective, which in partisan terms means mostly Democratic, rather than the conservative positions on race, labor, market regulation, and welfare that state-centered federalism is typically associated with. What's a good liberal or conservative to do? Social liberals supported the medical marijuana law (and thus the minority in Raich*) and the right to die law in Oregon (the majority in* Gonzales*). Moral conservatives were the opposite (pro-*Raich*, anti-*Gonzales*).*

However, on the central question of federal versus state power, which has been a central ideological divide in this nation since the Federalists and Anti-Federalists battled it out at the Constitutional Convention, liberals and conservatives would have to flip their views. So a national-power liberal would have supported the Raich *decision and opposed the* Gonzales *decision (the opposite of the social liberal), whereas a state-power conservative would have opposed* Raich *and supported* Gonzales *(which is the reverse of a moral conservative's positions). That means that a national power liberal and the moral conservative would have the same views (national power would be used to regulate medical marijuana and assisted suicide), while states' rights advocates share the views of the social liberals (because voters in California approved medical marijuana and Oregon voters supported the right to die).*

Somewhat surprisingly, there was almost no consistency among the eight justices who voted on both cases (William Rehnquist was replaced by John Roberts between the two cases): only Justice Sandra Day O'Connor supported the states' rights position in both cases, and Antonin Scalia voted as a moral conservative (which runs strongly counter to his previously articulated views on national power and federalism). All of the other six justices mixed their views. The Court as a whole was inconsistent on the question of federalism as well: in the medical marijuana case, the Court upheld Congress's power to prohibit the medical use of marijuana under the Controlled Substances Act. But in the right to die case, the Court said that Congress did not give the U.S. attorney general the power under that same law to limit the drugs that doctors in Oregon could prescribe for use in an assisted suicide.

George Annas looks at the medical marijuana case (and touches on the right to die case) from the perspective of doctors. Writing in the New England Journal of Medicine, *one of the leading medical journals in the nation, Annas points out the "most interesting, and disturbing aspect of the case to physicians" is the Court's reference to "unscrupulous physicians who overprescribe when it is sufficiently profitable to do so." Annas says that such cases are rare and that the California law was narrowly written to make sure that such abuses would not occur. Twenty-eight states currently allow medical marijuana and eight states have legalized all use of marijuana, despite the fact that it is still illegal under federal law. President Obama initially said that he would not make it a priority to enforce federal law in states where marijuana was used for medical reasons. However, he later reversed course, cracking down on dispensaries that were taking advantage of state laws, indicating that the problem of unscrupulous physicians may be more widespread than Annas recognizes. It is not clear how President Trump will respond. This article is also very useful for its excellent overview of Congress's commerce clause powers and its importance in federalism cases.*

Mark Twain wasn't thinking about federalism or the structure of American government when he wrote "The Celebrated Jumping Frog of Calaveras County." Nonetheless, he would be amused to know that today, almost 150 years later, the Calaveras County Fair and Jumping Frog Jubilee not only has a jumping frog contest but also has its own Frog Welfare Policy. The policy includes a provision for the "Care of Sick or Injured Frogs" and a limitation entitled "Frogs Not Permitted to Participate," which stipulates that "under no circumstances will a frog listed on the endangered species list be permitted to participate in the Frog Jump." This fair, like medical practice, is subject to both state and federal laws. Care of the sick and injured (both frogs and people) is primarily viewed as a matter of state law, whereas protection of endangered species is primarily regulated by Congress under its authority to regulate interstate commerce.

Not to carry the analogy too far, but it is worth recalling that Twain's famous frog, Dan'l Webster, lost his one and only jumping contest because his stomach had been filled with quail shot by a competitor. The loaded-down frog just couldn't jump. Until the California medical-marijuana case, it seemed to many observers that the conservative Rehnquist Court had succeeded in filling the commerce clause with quail shot—and had effectively prevented the federal government from regulating state activities. In the medical-marijuana case, however, a new majority of justices took the lead out of the commerce clause so that the federal government could legitimately claim jurisdiction over just about any activity, including the practice of medicine. The role of the commerce clause in federalism and the implications of the Court's decision in the California medical-marijuana case for physicians are the subjects I explore in this article.

The Commerce Clause

The U.S. Constitution determines the areas over which the federal government has authority. All other areas remain, as they were before the adoption of the Constitution, under the authority of the individual states. Another way to say this is that the states retain all governmental authority they did not delegate to the federal government, including areas such as criminal law and family-law matters. These are part of the state's "police powers," usually defined as the state's sovereign authority to protect the health, safety, and welfare of its residents. Section 8 of Article I of the Constitution contains eighteen clauses specifying delegated areas (including the military, currency, postal service, and patenting) over which "Congress shall have power," and these include the commerce clause—"to regulate commerce with foreign nations, and among the several states, and with the Indian tribes."

Until the Great Depression (and the disillusionment with unregulated markets), the Supreme Court took a narrow view of federal authority that could be derived from the commerce clause by ruling consistently that it gave Congress the authority only to regulate activities that directly involved the movement of commercial products (such as pharmaceuticals) from one state to another. Since then, and at least until 1995, the Court's interpretation seemed to be going in the opposite direction: Congress was consistently held to have authority in areas that had almost any relationship at all to commerce.

Guns in Schools and Violence against Women

Under modern commerce clause doctrine, Congress has authority to regulate in three broad categories of activities: the use of the channels of interstate commerce (e.g., roads, air corridors, and waterways); the instrumentalities of interstate commerce (e.g., trains, trucks, and planes) and persons and things in interstate commerce; and "activities having a substantial relation to interstate commerce." The first two categories are easy ones in that they involve activities that cross state lines. The third category, which does not involve crossing a state line, is the controversial one. The interpretation question involves the meaning and application of the concept of "substantially affecting" interstate commerce.

In a 1937 case that the Court characterized as a "watershed case" it concluded that the real question was one of the degree of effect. Intrastate activities that "have such a close and substantial relation to interstate commerce that their control is essential or appropriate to protect that commerce from burdens and obstructions" are within the power of Congress to regulate. Later, in what has become perhaps its best-known commerce-clause case, the Court held that Congress could enforce a statute that prohibited a farmer from growing wheat on his own farm even if the wheat was never sold but was used only for the farmer's personal consumption. The Court concluded that although one farmer's personal use of homegrown wheat may be trivial (and have no effect on commerce), "taken together with that of many others similarly situated," its effect on interstate commerce (and the market price of wheat) "is far from trivial."

The 1995 case that seemed to presage a states' rights revolution (often referred to as "devolution") involved the federal Gun-Free School Zones Act of 1990, which made it a federal crime "for any individual knowingly to possess a firearm at a place that the individual knows, or has reasonable cause to believe, is a school zone." In a 5-to-4 opinion, written by the late Chief Justice William Rehnquist, the Court held that the statute exceeded Congress's authority under the commerce clause and only the individual states had authority to criminalize the possession of guns in school.

The federal government had argued (and the four justices in the minority agreed) that the costs of violent crime are spread out over the entire population and that the presence of guns in schools threatens "national productivity" by undermining the learning environment, which in turn decreases learning and leads to a less productive citizenry and thus a less productive national economy. The majority of the Court rejected these arguments primarily because they thought that accepting this line of reasoning would make it impossible to define "any limitations on federal power, even in areas such as criminal law enforcement or education, where states historically have been sovereign."

In 2000, in another 5-to-4 opinion written by Rehnquist, using the same rationale, the Court struck down a federal statute, part of the Violence against Women Act of 1994, that provided a federal civil remedy for victims of "gender-motivated violence." In the Court's words:

> Gender-motivated crimes of violence are not, in any sense of the phrase, economic activity. . . . Indeed, if Congress may regulate gender-motivated violence, it would be able to regulate murder or any other type of violence since gender-motivated violence, as a subset of all violent crime, is certain to have lesser economic impacts than the larger class of which it is a part.

The Court, specifically addressing the question of federalism, concluded that "the Constitution requires a distinction between what is truly national and what is truly local. . . . Indeed, we can think of no better example of the police power, which the Founders denied to the National Government and reposed in the States, than the suppression of violent crime and vindication of its victims."

Medical Marijuana in California

The next commerce-clause case involved physicians, albeit indirectly, and the role assigned to them in California in relation to the protection of patients who used physician-recommended marijuana from criminal prosecution. The question before the Supreme Court in the recent medical-marijuana case (*Gonzales v. Raich*) was this: Does the commerce clause give Congress the authority to outlaw the local cultivation and use of marijuana for medicine if such cultivation and use complies with the provisions of California law?

The California law creates an exemption from criminal prosecution for physicians, patients, and primary caregivers who possess or cultivate marijuana for medicinal purposes on the recommendation of a physician. Two patients for whom marijuana had been recommended brought suit to challenge enforcement of the federal Controlled Substances Act after federal Drug Enforcement Administration agents seized and destroyed all six marijuana plants that one of them had been growing for her own medical use in compliance with the California law. The Ninth Circuit Court of Appeals ruled in the plaintiffs' favor, finding that the California law applied to a separate and distinct category of activity, "the intrastate, noncommercial cultivation and possession of *cannabis* for personal medical purposes as recommended by a patient's physician pursuant to valid California state law," as opposed to what it saw as the federal law's purpose, which was to prevent "drug trafficking." In a 6-to-3 opinion, written by Justice John Paul Stevens, with Justice Rehnquist dissenting, the Court reversed the appeals court's opinion and decided that Congress, under the commerce clause, did have authority to enforce its prohibition against marijuana—even state-approved, homegrown, noncommercial marijuana, used only for medicinal purposes on a physician's recommendation.

The majority of the Court decided that the commerce clause gave Congress the same power to regulate homegrown marijuana for personal use that it had to regulate homegrown wheat. The question was whether homegrown marijuana for personal medical consumption substantially affected interstate commerce (albeit illegal commerce) when all affected patients were taken together. The Court concluded that Congress "had a rational basis for concluding that leaving home-consumed marijuana outside federal control" would affect "price and market conditions." The Court also distinguished the guns-in-school and gender-violence cases on the basis that regulation of drugs is "quintessentially economic" when economics is defined as the "production, distribution, and consumption of commodities."

This left only one real question open: Is the fact that marijuana is to be used only for medicinal purposes on the advice of a physician, as the Ninth Circuit Court had decided, sufficient for an exception to be carved out of otherwise legitimate federal authority to control drugs? The Court decided it was not, for several reasons. The first was that Congress itself had determined that marijuana is a Schedule I drug, which it defined as having "no acceptable medical use." The Court acknowledged that Congress might be wrong in this determination, but the issue in this case was not whether marijuana had possible legitimate medical uses but whether Congress had the authority to make the judgment that it had none and to ban all uses of the drug. The dissenting justices argued that personal cultivation and use of marijuana should be beyond the authority of the commerce clause. The Court majority disagreed, stating that if it accepted the dissenting justices' argument, personal cultivation for recreational use would also be beyond congressional authority. This conclusion, the majority argued, could not be sustained:

> One need not have a degree in economics to understand why a nationwide exemption for the vast quantity of marijuana (or other drugs) locally cultivated for personal use (which presumably would include use by friends, neighbors, and family members) may have a substantial impact on the interstate market for this extraordinarily popular substance. The congressional judgment that an exemption for such a significant segment of the total market would undermine the orderly enforcement of the entire [drug] regulatory scheme is entitled to a strong presumption of validity.

The other primary limit to the effect of the California law on interstate commerce is the requirement of a physician's recommendation on the basis of a medical determination that a patient has an "illness for which marijuana provides relief." And the Court's discussion of this limit may be the most interesting, and disturbing, aspect of the case to physicians. Instead of concluding that physicians should be free to use their best medical judgment and that it was up to state medical boards to decide whether specific physicians were failing to live up to reasonable medical standards—as the Court did, for example, in its cases related to restrictive abortion laws—the Court took a totally different approach. In the Court's words, the broad language of the California medical-marijuana law allows "even the most scrupulous doctor to conclude that some recreational uses would be therapeutic. And our cases have taught us that there are some unscrupulous physicians who overprescribe when it is sufficiently profitable to do so."

The California law defines the category of patients who are exempt from criminal prosecution as those suffering from cancer, anorexia, AIDS, chronic pain, spasticity, glaucoma, arthritis, migraine, and "any other chronic or persistent medical symptom that substantially limits the ability of a person to conduct one or more major life activities . . . or if not alleviated may cause serious harm to the patient's safety or physical or mental health." These limits are hardly an invitation for recreational-use recommendations. Regarding "unscrupulous physicians," the Court cited two cases that involve criminal prosecutions of physicians for acting like drug dealers, one from 1919 and the other from 1975, implying that because a few physicians might have been criminally inclined in the past, it was reasonable for Congress (and the Court), on the basis of no actual evidence, to assume that many physicians may be so inclined today. It was not only physicians that the Court found untrustworthy but sick patients and their caregivers as well:

> The exemption for cultivation by patients and caregivers [patients can possess up to 8 oz. of dried marijuana and cultivate up to 6 mature or 12 immature plants] can only increase the supply of marijuana in the California market. The likelihood that all such production will promptly terminate when patients recover or will precisely match the patients' medical needs during their convalescence seems remote; whereas the danger that excesses will satisfy some of the admittedly enormous demand for recreational use seems obvious.

Justice Sandra Day O'Connor's dissent merits comment, because it is especially relevant to the practice of medicine. She argues that the Constitution requires the Court to protect "historic spheres of state sovereignty from excessive federal encroachment" and that one of the virtues of federalism is that it permits the individual states to serve as "laboratories," should they wish, to try "novel social and economic experiments without risk to the rest of the country." Specifically, she argues that the Court's new definition of economic activity is "breathtaking" in its scope, creating exactly what the gun case rejected—a federal police power. She also rejects reliance on the wheat case, noting that under the Agricultural Adjustment Act in question in that case, Congress had exempted the planting of less than 200 bushels (about six tons), and that when Roscoe Filburn, the farmer who challenged the federal statute, himself harvested his wheat, the statute exempted plantings of less than six acres.

In O'Connor's words, the wheat case "did not extend Commerce Clause authority to something as modest as the home cook's herb garden." O'Connor is not saying that Congress cannot regulate small quantities of a product produced for personal use, only that the wheat case "did not hold or imply that small-scale production of commodities is always economic, and automatically within Congress' reach." As to potential "exploitation [of the act] by unscrupulous physicians" and patients, O'Connor finds no factual support for this assertion and rejects the conclusion that simply by "piling assertion upon assertion" one can make a case for meeting the "substantiality test" of the guns-in-school and gender-violence cases.

It is important to note that the Court was not taking a position on whether Congress was correct to place marijuana in Schedule I or a position against California's law, any more than it was taking a position in favor of guns in schools or violence against women in the earlier cases. Instead, the Court was ruling only on the question of federal authority under the commerce clause. The Court noted, for example, that California and its supporters may one day prevail by pursuing the democratic process "in the halls of Congress." This seems extremely unlikely. More important is the question not addressed in this case—whether suffering patients have a substantive due-process claim to access to drugs needed to prevent suffering or a valid medical-necessity defense should they be prosecuted for using medical marijuana on a physician's recommendation. Also not addressed was the question that will be decided during the coming year: whether Congress has delegated to the U.S. attorney general its authority to decide what a "legitimate medical use" of an approved drug is in the context of Oregon's law governing physician-assisted suicide. What is obvious from this case, however, is that Congress has the authority, under the commerce clause, to regulate both legal and illegal drugs whether or not the drugs in question actually cross state lines. It would also seem reasonable to conclude that Congress has the authority to limit the uses of approved drugs.

Federalism and Endangered Species

Because *Gonzales v. Raich* is a drug case, and because it specifically involves marijuana, the Court's final word on federalism may not yet be in. Whether the "states' rights" movement has any life left after medical marijuana may be determined in the context of the Endangered Species Act. Two U.S. Circuit Courts of Appeals, for example, have recently upheld application of the federal law to protect endangered species that, unlike the descendants of Mark Twain's jumping frog, have no commercial value. Even though the Supreme Court refused to hear appeals from both of the lower courts, the cases help us understand the contemporary reach of congressional power under the commerce clause. One case involves the protection of six tiny creatures that live in caves (the "Cave Species")—three arthropods, a spider, and two beetles—from a commercial developer. The Fifth Circuit Court of Appeals noted that the Cave Species are not themselves an object of economics or commerce, saying: "There is no market for them; any future market is conjecture. If the speculative future medicinal benefits from the Cave Species makes their regulation commercial, then almost anything would be. . . . There is no historic trade in the Cave Species, nor do tourists come to Texas to view them." Nonetheless, the court concluded that Congress had the authority, under the commerce clause, to view life as an "interdependent web" of all species; that destruction of endangered species can be aggregated, like homegrown wheat; and that the destruction of multiple species has a substantial effect on interstate commerce.

The other case, from the District of Columbia Court of Appeals, involves the arroyo southwestern toad, whose habitat was threatened by a real estate developer. In upholding the application of the Endangered Species Act to the case, the appeals court held that the commercial activity being regulated was the housing development itself, as well as the "taking" of the road by the planned commercial development. The court noted that the "company would like us to consider its challenge to the ESA [Endangered Species Act] only as applied to the arroyo toad, which it says has no 'known commercial value'—unlike, for example, Mark Twain's celebrated jumping frogs [*sic*] of Calaveras County." Instead, the court concluded that application of the Endangered Species Act, far from eroding states' rights, is consistent with "the historic power of the federal government to preserve scarce resources in one locality for the future benefit of all Americans."

On a request for a hearing by the entire appeals court, which was rejected, recently named Chief Justice John Roberts—who at the time was a member of the appeals court—wrote a dissent that was not unlike Justice O'Connor's dissent in the marijuana case. In it he argued that the court's conclusion seemed inconsistent with the guns-in-school and gender-violence cases and that there were real problems with using an analysis of the commerce clause to regulate "the taking of a hapless toad that, for reasons of its own, lives its entire life in California." The case has since been settled. The development is going ahead in a way that protects the toad's habitat.

The Future of the Commerce Clause

Twain's short story has been termed "a living American fairy tale, acted out annually in Calaveras County." In what might be termed a living American government tale, nominees to the Supreme Court are routinely asked to explain their judicial philosophy of constitutional and statutory interpretation to the Senate Judiciary Committee. Asked about his "hapless toad" opinion during the Senate confirmation hearings on his nomination to replace Rehnquist as chief justice, Roberts said: "The whole point of my argument in the dissent was that there was another way to look at this [i.e., the approach taken by the Fifth Circuit Court in the Cave Species case]. . . . I did not say that even in this case that the decision was wrong. . . . I simply said, let's look at those other grounds for decision because that doesn't present this problem." These hearings provide an opportunity for all Americans to review their understanding of our constitutional government and the manner in which it allocates power between the federal government and the fifty states. To the extent that this division of power is determined by the Court's view of the commerce clause, a return to an expansive reading of this clause seems both likely and, given the interdependence of the national and global economies, proper.

Of course, the fact that Congress has authority over a particular subject—such as whether to adopt a system of national licensure for physicians—does not mean that its authority is unlimited or even that Congress will use it. Rather, as Justice Stevens noted, cases such as the California medical-marijuana case lead to other central constitutional questions, as yet unresolved. These questions include whether patients, terminally ill or not, have a constitutional right not to suffer—at least, when their physicians know how to control their pain.

Discussion Questions

1. If you were a state legislator or a judge, how would you decide these issues? Specifically, as a matter of policy, do you think that doctors should be able to prescribe marijuana to alleviate pain? Should they be able to prescribe lethal drugs to be used by terminally ill patients? What about as a matter of law? Do you agree with the Supreme Court's decisions on these issues?
2. Do you support a state-centered or nation-centered perspective on federalism? Now go back and look at your answers to the last questions. Did you take positions that were consistent with your views on federalism or as a policy concern?
3. What does Mark Twain's jumping frog represent in Annas's article? Which Supreme Court case breathed life back into the frog? Why?

Debating the Issues: Immigration Reform—More Power to the States?

The election of Donald Trump as president would seem to indicate that a radical shift in immigration policy is imminent. He started his campaign by claiming that undocumented immigrants from Mexico were rapists and criminals, and by promising to build a wall along the entire Mexican border while making the Mexican government pay for it. Later in the campaign, Trump called for the deportation of an estimated 11–12 million undocumented workers in the first 18 months of his presidency and said that he would bar all Muslims from entering the country. After the election, there was no talk of making Mexico pay for a wall and President Trump said that deportation efforts would focus on those who had committed crimes. As the article from *The Economist* points out, this would be much like President Obama's policy.

Even with this more narrow focus, *The Economist* points out that President Trump would have a difficult time deporting 2–3 million illegal residents for two reasons. First, the federal agencies that would carry out the deportations are already facing a huge backlog of cases (more than 500,000 cases are in immigrations court) and it would be difficult to more than double their efforts. Second, states and cities are serving as "sanctuaries" by resisting deportation efforts, which would also complicate efforts to step up the pace of deportations.

While it is unlikely that the extreme measures proposed by Donald Trump during the 2016 presidential election will be implemented, it is even less likely that comprehensive immigration reform will become law any time soon. Favored by both Presidents George W. Bush and Barack Obama, comprehensive reform would have provided a "path to citizenship" for the United States' 11–12 million undocumented residents. Given the absence of significant change at the national level, Gulasekaram and Ramakrishnan argue that state and local governments will be the source of innovation in immigration policy in the next few years. They point out that while the national government still sets the main direction of immigration policy, state and local governments have a great deal of power over how those policies are implemented. These governments may choose a more restrictive approach, as pioneered in Arizona, or a more immigrant-friendly approach, as in California. Given the broad range of state-based policies, it would be difficult for the national government to impose a uniform approach.

Shikha Dalmia takes this state-based argument to the next level, proposing that states be given the power to grant work visas to meet local needs. She argues that agricultural states have been forced to shift jobs to Mexico because of a lack of workers, and the tech industry in California, Washington, and Massachusetts is losing highly skilled people because of a shortage of H-1B visas. Dalmia suggests that states be allowed to follow the lead of Canada, which allows its provinces to establish their own guest worker programs. This seems to be an immigration reform proposal that could attract bipartisan support.

15

"Hamilton's Heirs: If He Wins a Second Term, the President-Elect Could Realistically Expel around 4 Million People in Total"

The Economist

When she was seven Greisa Martinez moved illegally from Hidalgo, in Mexico, to Dallas with her parents. Now aged 28, Ms. Martinez works for United We Dream, an immigration advocacy group. Following the election of Donald Trump she has been busy. In case of an immigration raid, she instructs her charges not to open their doors to immigration officials unless they have a court-ordered warrant, and to remain silent until speaking with a lawyer. Ms. Martinez is one of around 740,000 beneficiaries of the Deferred Action for Childhood Arrivals (DACA) policy that Barack Obama implemented in 2012 by executive action. In his 100-day plan published in October, Mr. Trump vowed to reverse every one of Mr. Obama's executive actions. He could kill DACA on his first day in the Oval Office.

He could also opt to let it die a slower, gentler death by refusing to renew DACA permits, which expire every two years. Either way DACA's beneficiaries would lose their right to work legally. DACA grants undocumented immigrants who arrived in America before the age of 16, and who meet several other requirements, temporary amnesty from deportation, and eligibility to work. Applicants must not have criminal histories and they must either be enrolled in or have finished high school or have been honorably discharged from the armed forces.

In his earlier stump speeches, Mr. Trump repeatedly pledged to rid the country of all 11 million unauthorized undocumented migrants living within its borders, the bulk of whom arrived before 2004 (see [Figure 1]). He has picked the Senate's most enthusiastic deporter, Jeff Sessions, as his attorney-general. This has alarmed DACA recipients. "When we applied for DACA, we identified ourselves as undocumented. We gave our addresses. The government now has this information and can come after us or our families," says Perla Salgado from Arizona, who arrived to America at age six and has not once returned to Mexico.

Figure 1. The 9/11 Effect
United States, Adult Unauthorized Immigrants by Years of Residence

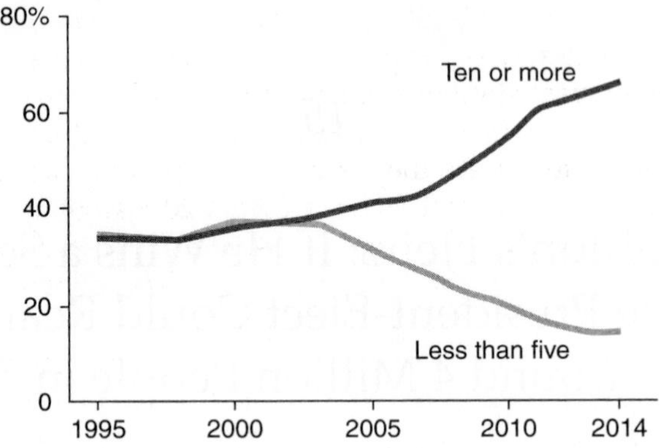

SOURCE: Pew Research Center

Since winning the election, Mr. Trump has said he will focus on illegal immigrants with criminal records—not unlike President Obama, whose administration has deported more people than any other president's. He has also made some sympathetic noises about those who arrived in the country as children. In an interview on *60 Minutes*, a television program, Mr. Trump estimated the number of criminal immigrants to be between 2 million and 3 million. The Migration Policy Institute, a think-tank, says it is closer to 820,000.

Even if Mr. Trump's administration aims for the top end of the range, it will be hard for him to keep all his campaign promises related to immigration. To gather funding for his proposed wall along America's border with Mexico, for example, Mr. Trump would need congressional approval. The president requires no such authorization to change the Department of Homeland Security's (DHS) deportation priorities, though. From his first day in the White House, Mr. Trump will have discretion over what groups should be targeted for removal. "He could easily expand the definition for what constitutes criminality to meet the 2 million to 3 million goal he set," says Ms. Martinez, the activist.

Two factors will limit the size of the deportation dragnet. The first is capacity. The federal government already spends more on enforcing immigration laws than on the FBI, Drug Enforcement Agency, U.S. Marshals service and Bureau of Alcohol, Tobacco and Firearms combined. Finding people to deport is also getting ever harder. That is partly because the number of border apprehensions has declined markedly in recent years as the flow of Mexicans into the United States has also ebbed. Immigrants captured within two weeks and 100 miles of the border are the easiest to deport because they do not have to be granted a court hearing. Those further from the country's edges do get a hearing and so are much harder to remove. Deportation hearings can take years to complete; in July, the backlog of cases in immigration court surpassed 500,000.

The second variable is cooperation from cities and states. California has been the busiest state in preparing for the Trump administration's immigration policies. Over 3 million undocumented immigrants reside in the Golden State; Texas, the second most popular home for undocumented foreigners, hosts half that number. A 2014 study by the University of Southern California estimated that workers who are in the state illegally make up 10 percent of the workforce and contribute $130 billion of California's $2.5 trillion gross domestic product.

On December 5th, California lawmakers introduced a package of bills to obstruct mass deportation. These measures include a state program to fund legal representation for immigrants in deportation hearings; a ban on immigration enforcement in public schools, in hospitals and on courthouse premises. "California will be your wall of justice," declared the president of the state senate in a statement. "We will not stand by and let the federal government use our state and local agencies to separate mothers from their children." According to a study by the University of Pennsylvania in 2015, only 37 percent of immigrants and 14 percent of detained immigrants in deportation proceedings secured lawyers to defend them in court. The same study found that immigrants with representation had five-and-a-half times better odds of avoiding deportation than their peers who represented themselves.

Some place to hide

The policies of so-called "sanctuary cities" such as Los Angeles, New York, San Francisco and Chicago will further hinder any plans Mr. Trump might have for a huge increase in the rate of deportation. There is no specific legal definition for what constitutes a sanctuary jurisdiction, but it is widely used to refer to areas that limit cooperation with federal immigration authorities. The Immigrant Legal Resource Center counted 4 states, 39 cities, and 364 counties that qualify as sanctuary jurisdictions. Some prohibit local police from asking people they arrest about their immigration status. Others refuse to obey immigration officers unless they have a warrant. Such policies can be mandated expressly by law or merely become customary. Supporters of these approaches say they help guarantee that fear of deportation does not dissuade undocumented immigrants from reporting crimes, visiting hospitals or enrolling in schools.

Scrutiny of sanctuary cities ramped up in July this year after a young American woman was killed in a touristy area of San Francisco by a man who was in the country illegally, had seven previous felony convictions, and had already been deported five times. Mr. Trump has since vowed to block federal funding to areas deemed uncooperative. Such cuts would be painful, but several mayors have cast doubt on whether they will actually happen, reasoning that it would be counterproductive to hurt the economies of America's biggest cities. Jayashri Srikantiah of Stanford Law School argues that there is case law that validates sanctuary policies and there are constitutional problems with coercing states into action with financial threats.

Even so, between 2009 and 2015 the Obama administration deported an average of about 360,000 people a year. Muzaffar Chishti, a lawyer at the Migration Policy Institute, believes that unless ample resources are poured into recruiting and training new immigration officers and expanding the pool of immigration courts, the Trump administration will struggle to remove more than half a million people a year. Over eight years that would still add up to 4 million people.

16

"Forget Border Walls and Mass Deportations: The Real Changes in Immigration Policy Are Happening in the States"

Pratheepan Gulasekaram and
Karthick Ramakrishnan

Arguments over the proper relationship between federal and state governments have been looming in the presidential campaign. The GOP candidates recently brought the issue of federalism front and center when discussing marijuana. For instance, in the second Republican primary debate, Rand Paul strongly defended the rights of states like Colorado to pass laws that legalize marijuana; Jeb Bush and Chris Christie came down on the side of strong federal enforcement.

Curiously, the candidates did not discuss the role of states in regulating immigration, which featured prominently in the 2012 election. So far, GOP presidential hopefuls have offered controversial statements and proposals for national reform that would be difficult to implement, ranging from ending birthright citizenship to building more walls and deporting millions of undocumented residents.

But these proposals for federal immigration reform face little chance of becoming law. Congress will almost certainly be strongly partisan and divided through at least 2020. Federal immigration legislation, whether permissive or restrictive, appears highly unlikely. And states and localities have stepped into the breach.

States and localities are setting immigration policy

* * * [S]tate and local immigration regulation has now become a central feature of our national policy landscape. The decade following 9/11 saw a sharp increase in state and local immigration regulation. Until 2012, the weight of that trend was restrictionist, highlighted by high profile enactments like Arizona's SB 1070 that sought to create new state-level penalties for being in the country illegally. Since 2012, however, the state and local tide has turned largely integrationist.

This reality upends the long-held notion that immigration is solely a federal responsibility. To be sure, visas, national citizenship, and deportation remain squarely under federal control, as the U.S. Supreme Court made clear in its landmark 2012 decision *Arizona v. United States*. But state and local policies affect the daily lives of immigrants profoundly on everything from access to public higher education to health insurance coverage to driver's licenses. Such state-level changes will be difficult to undo, no matter who becomes president in 2017.

For example, California, New York, and Illinois have enacted a suite of policies that confer meaningful membership to all residents, including the undocumented. The "California Package" of immigrant-friendly laws is popular in a state that accounts for a quarter of all undocumented immigrants in the United States. A few states and localities have already passed important components of the "California Package," and we can expect a widening and deepening of state and local policy adoption, especially in places with Democratic majorities and a sizeable proportion of Latino voters.

By contrast, Republican-controlled states have passed aspects of the "Arizona Package" that include penalties on employers who don't comply with e-Verify, bans on city "sanctuary laws," and denial of in-state tuition. Given this variegated state policy landscape and its strong correlation with partisanship, it will be very difficult for Congress and the president to pass federal laws that run roughshod over these state and local enactments.

The federal government relies on the states to help carry out its immigration policy

In addition, the federal government leans on state systems to administer key parts of immigration policy. For instance, the federal Priority Enforcement Program (PEP) relies on local police to send fingerprints and other information to Immigration and Customs Enforcement (ICE) so that ICE can decide who to deport. This reliance on the informational advantages available to local police continues to be critical in fashioning federal enforcement policy.

Indeed, the Secure Communities Program, the predecessor federal enforcement program to PEP, more robustly conscripted local police, with ICE issuing "detainers" or "hold requests" that directed local police to hold an individual so that ICE could pick them up. In dismantling Secure Communities and replacing it with PEP, DHS Secretary Jeh Johnson specifically noted the state and local resistance to these detainers as motivation for reimagining the way in which federal authorities would interact with them.

Similarly, federal law gives state welfare systems some control over whether noncitizens are eligible for public assistance. While some states have exercised that authority to restrict the public assistance only to those required by federal law, others have chosen to provide broader welfare coverage. Five states with high-immigrant populations—California, Illinois, Massachusetts, New York, and Washington—provide immigrant children access to health insurance regardless of legal status. Other states have expanded pregnancy and low-income health insurance coverage in ways that benefit immigrant populations.

And even when the White House declared undocumented immigrants who arrived here as children are free to stay and to work, as it did with its Deferred Action for Child Arrivals (DACA) program, states have to decide whether or not to help those recipients maximize their opportunities. The ability to attend school or seek work is meaningful only if state laws also provide in-state tuition, financial aid, driver's licenses, and access to health insurance.

Immigration is going to continue being a hot and provocative topic throughout the presidential primaries. But the heat is unlikely to come with any light. Donald Trump and others may energize some potential voters with extreme proposals, but that's not what leads to national change. For now and for the foreseeable future, the United States' most significant changes on immigration will be happening in the states. Those who want to reform immigration may well do better to push for piecemeal changes at the state level than to chase comprehensive reform federally.

17

"A States' Rights Approach to Immigration Reform"

Shikha Dalmia

Over the last decade, neither Republican president George W. Bush nor Democratic Barack Obama has succeeded in prodding Congress to enact immigration reform. That's because Congress can't find a way to balance the contradictory demands of labor, business, and talk-radio restrictionists. Meanwhile, as the economy gathers steam, industries in many states are facing a paucity of workers at all skill levels.

But there might be a way out of this logjam. How? By embracing a more federalist approach that gives states flexibility to craft their own immigration policies. This might sound radical but the under-reported story is that states have already been trying to do this and Canada did it 18 years ago. Even Sen. Jeff Sessions (R-Alabama), who has torpedoed many a reform effort, praised Canada's provincial program at a Heritage Foundation event last year as a model for America because it allows an orderly matching between foreign workers and local labor needs.

Thanks to an improving Mexican economy and aggressive immigration enforcement, net illegal migration from Mexico to America has dropped to zero, according to the Pew Hispanic Center. The upshot is crucial gaps in the construction, cleaning, landscaping, farming, crab fishing, hotel, tourism, restaurant, and many other local industries that have been relying on undocumented labor since existing visa programs for low-skilled foreign workers are either woefully inadequate or unusable.

The National Restaurant Association expects to add 1.8 million positions in the next decade—a 14 percent boost in its workforce. But the 16–24 [year-old] native-born U.S. workforce that fills these jobs isn't expected to grow at all—so either restaurants hire foreigners or the industry faces retrenchment. Similar labor shortages have forced American growers in California, Idaho and many other states to move to Mexico. Direct U.S. investment in Mexican agriculture has increased seven-fold in recent years.

Industries relying on low-skilled labor aren't the only ones suffering. A shallow STEM-worker pool is stymying high-tech companies in California and Washington. Massachusetts' start-up sector has been facing an exodus of highly qualified foreign students graduating from the Bay

State's world-class universities because they are unable to obtain H-1B visas.

To deal with the problem, Massachusetts last year implemented the ingenious Global Entrepreneur In Residence programs. Startups, where the employee is also the founder of a company, have nowhere to go for visas because H-1Bs don't apply to them. But under the GEIR program, these students are placed in participating universities where they can incubate their businesses. Universities then sponsor them for H-1B visas as university employees, something that is especially clever since they are exempt from the annual H-1B quota that other employers face.

Nor is Massachusetts alone in pushing state solutions. Fed up with Uncle Sam's insensitivity to their labor needs, lawmakers in about eight states in recent years have pushed resolutions or bills demanding permission from the federal government to craft their own immigration programs. These include not just blue states like California and New Mexico but also arch-red ones like Texas, Utah, Oklahoma, Kansas, Georgia, and even Arizona.

Utah, New Mexico, California, and Kansas have all flirted with guest worker programs for undocumented aliens to both protect mixed-status Hispanic families in their states and to avoid labor disruptions for local businesses. Utah's conservative legislature overwhelmingly approved legislation in 2011 that would allow undocumented workers who meet certain requirements to obtain a two-year guest worker visa to live in the state. The program was supposed to have been implemented two years ago but was postponed till 2017. Why? Because immigration is constitutionally a federal function and the state needs a federal waiver or permission. But the Obama administration has been dragging its feet, maybe because letting a conservative state implement pro-immigration policies won't have a political upside like unilateral executive action.

Likewise, the Texas legislature has three bills pending that would let Texas employers hire foreign workers from abroad on temporary work visas. But this program too will need federal authorization.

One way to release states from the political whims of sitting administrations would be for Congress to pass a law giving states statutory authority to create their own guest worker programs just as Canada has done through its highly successful Provincial Nominee Program (PNP).

Under the PNP, each of Canada's 13 provinces gets a quota based on its population to hand out permanent residencies or green cards, as I've written. They can sponsor foreigners for almost any reason but most use the program to fill labor gaps. Some provinces have even lured foreign techies stuck in America's green card labyrinth.

Ottawa's role is confined to conducting security or health checks on those sponsored—leaving the planning of local labor markets to the provinces. This divides central and provincial authority based on each side's primary interest, as behooves a federalist system. But the big advantage of this approach in times of heightened concern for national security is that it'll allow Uncle Sam to concentrate on conducting thorough background checks on prospective workers rather than dissipating its energy on redundant regulations.

However, notes Niskanen Center's David Bier, who has drafted a federal bill to create a pilot program along the lines of the PNP in the United States, America can begin by letting states hand out an average of 5,000 work visas—not green cards—to recruit foreign workers of their choice. These visas could be renewed indefinitely and their holders would be eventually eligible for green cards, just as H-1Bs currently are.

Although these workers would be confined to employment in the sponsoring state, they would have far more labor mobility than under the current system where visas tether them to a single employer. Moreover, it would be possible under this scheme, notes Bier, for participating states to form compacts allowing foreign workers to take jobs anywhere in the consortium.

The beauty of the program is not just that it would cut an enormous amount of red tape by letting states—instead of Uncle Sam—perform (or not) a labor certification to ensure that foreigners are not displacing native workers. By giving states more control over immigration flows, the program would change the incentive of states to treat foreigners like assets—not liabilities.

States could eschew participation if they fear a strain on their public services—eliminating a major restrictionist objection that has stymied national reform. But they'd pay an economic price as businesses—and tax revenues—moved to states with plentiful labor.

Some might worry that immigrants would use a state visa to enter the country but then relocate to another state or overstay. But immigrants have little incentive to live illegally when usable legal options are available, especially since illegals earn 22 percent less for the same job than legals, according to Princeton University's Douglas Massey's research. What's more, even though foreigners admitted through Canada's PNP are free to relocate immediately, the average three-year retention rate of provinces is close to 80 percent, as a Cato Institute study notes. The main reason is that the program allows such a granular matching between immigrant skills and local jobs that few need to leave for job opportunities elsewhere.

But to placate worries about foreigners skipping town or overstaying, Bier's proposal would set a 97 percent compliance target for participating states. States that miss this target would face a 50 percent decrease in their visa allocation for each year of non-compliance. Conversely, those that meet them would get a 10 percent increase. This would give states an incentive to enforce their own programs.

The immigration debate in America has become distressingly focused on militarizing the border and draconian interior enforcement. But a federalist solution that lets states experiment with different immigration strategies offers a realistic compromise in line with conservative principles. It is something that all Republicans—even restrictionists—should not just embrace but champion. This will turn them from cranky, naysaying obstructionists to innovative, yay-saying reformers and let them steal an issue from Democrats.

DISCUSSION QUESTIONS

1. Who do you think should control immigration policy, the national government or the states? What if the executive branch under-enforces federal laws? Should states be able to step in and enforce congressional law?
2. Do you agree with several of the authors that significant change in immigration policy at the national level is unlikely?
3. What do you see as the advantages and disadvantages of allowing states to run their own guest worker programs? Do you think this is a proposal that President Trump and the Republican Congress would support?

CHAPTER 4

The Constitutional Framework and the Individual: Civil Liberties and Civil Rights

18

"Remarks by the President at the 50th Anniversary of the Selma to Montgomery Marches"

BARACK OBAMA

On March 7, 1965, now-Congressman John Lewis led a group of about 600 people on a 50-mile march from Selma, Alabama to the state capital in Montgomery. The nonviolent march was part of a long-term attempt to register African Americans to vote and to demonstrate against Jim Crow laws. Earlier registration efforts in Selma had resulted in a violent response by authorities, arrests, beatings, and a fatal police shooting of a nonviolent protester. At one point, a local judge issued an order prohibiting any assembly of more than three people under the sponsorship of civil rights leaders, which meant that any organized effort to register African Americans to vote was illegal. After the march was announced, Governor George Wallace said that it would not be permitted, and he authorized the state police to take whatever action was necessary to prevent it.

As the marchers crossed the Edmund Pettus Bridge, they were met by police, who attacked with tear gas and clubs, continuing even after the protesters retreated. The violence, known as "Bloody Sunday" and broadcast on television, prompted public outrage and became a symbol of the injustice of Jim Crow. Two weeks later, on March 21, 1965, the Rev. Martin Luther King, Jr. led a much larger group—beginning with around 3,000 people and growing to 25,000—on the march after a federal judge ordered state police not to interfere. On the steps of the Alabama state capitol, King said "Selma, Alabama, became a shining moment in the conscience of man. If the worst in American life lurked in its dark streets, the best of American instincts arose passionately from across the nation to overcome it."

President Lyndon Johnson referred to "the outrage in Selma" when he signed the Voting Rights Act four months later, in August 1965.

On the 50th anniversary of the March 7 protest, at the Edmund Pettus Bridge, President Barack Obama spoke about the impact of the march, and about civil rights generally.

Edmund Pettus Bridge, Selma, Alabama

President and Mrs. Bush, Governor Bentley, Mayor Evans, Sewell, Reverend Strong, members of Congress, elected officials, foot soldiers, friends, fellow Americans:

[There] are places and moments in America where this nation's destiny has been decided. Many are sites of war—Concord and Lexington, Appomattox, Gettysburg. Others are sites that symbolize the daring of America's character—Independence Hall and Seneca Falls, Kitty Hawk and Cape Canaveral.

Selma is such a place. In one afternoon 50 years ago, so much of our turbulent history—the stain of slavery and anguish of civil war; the yoke of segregation and tyranny of Jim Crow; the death of four little girls in Birmingham; and the dream of a Baptist preacher—all that history met on this bridge.

It was not a clash of armies, but a clash of wills; a contest to determine the true meaning of America. And because of men and women like John Lewis, Joseph Lowery, Hosea Williams, Amelia Boynton, Diane Nash, Ralph Abernathy, C.T. Vivian, Andrew Young, Fred Shuttlesworth, Dr. Martin Luther King, Jr., and so many others, the idea of a just America and a fair America, an inclusive America, and a generous America—that idea ultimately triumphed.

As is true across the landscape of American history, we cannot examine this moment in isolation. The march on Selma was part of a broader campaign that spanned generations; the leaders that day part of a long line of heroes.

We gather here to celebrate them. We gather here to honor the courage of ordinary Americans willing to endure billy clubs and the chastening rod; tear gas and the trampling hoof; men and women who despite the gush of blood and splintered bone would stay true to their North Star and keep marching towards justice.

They did as Scripture instructed: "Rejoice in hope, be patient in tribulation, be constant in prayer." And in the days to come, they went back again and again. When the trumpet call sounded for more to join, the people came—black and white, young and old, Christian and Jew, waving the American flag and singing the same anthems full of faith and hope. A white newsman, Bill Plante, who covered the marches then and who is with us here today, quipped that the growing number of white people lowered the quality of the singing. To those who marched, though, those old gospel songs must have never sounded so sweet.

In time, their chorus would well up and reach President Johnson. And he would send them protection, and speak to the nation, echoing their call for America and the world to hear: "We shall overcome." What enormous faith these men and women had. Faith in God, but also faith in America.

The Americans who crossed this bridge, they were not physically imposing. But they gave courage to millions. They held no elected office. But they led a nation. They marched as Americans who had endured hundreds of years of brutal violence, countless daily indignities—but they didn't seek special treatment, just the equal treatment promised to them almost a century before.

What they did here will reverberate through the ages. Not because the change they won was preordained; not because their victory was complete; but because they proved that nonviolent change is possible, that love and hope can conquer hate.

As we commemorate their achievement, we are well-served to remember that at the time of the marches, many in power condemned rather than praised them. Back then, they were called Communists, or half-breeds, or outside agitators, sexual and moral degenerates, and worse—they were called everything but the name their parents gave them. Their faith was questioned. Their lives were threatened. Their patriotism challenged.

And yet, what could be more American than what happened in this place? What could more profoundly vindicate the idea of America than plain and humble people—unsung, the downtrodden, the dreamers not of high station, not born to wealth or privilege, not of one religious tradition but many, coming together to shape their country's course?

What greater expression of faith in the American experiment than this, what greater form of patriotism is there than the belief that America is not yet finished, that we are strong enough to be self-critical, that each successive generation can look upon our imperfections and decide that it is in our power to remake this nation to more closely align with our highest ideals?

That's why Selma is not some outlier in the American experience. That's why it's not a museum or a static monument to behold from a distance. It is instead the manifestation of a creed written into our founding documents: "We the People . . . in order to form a more perfect union." "We hold these truths to be self-evident, that all men are created equal."

These are not just words. They're a living thing, a call to action, a roadmap for citizenship and an insistence in the capacity of free men and women to shape our own destiny. For founders like Franklin and Jefferson, for leaders like Lincoln and FDR, the success of our experiment in self-government rested on engaging all of our citizens in this work. And that's what we celebrate here in Selma. That's what this movement was all about, one leg in our long journey toward freedom.

The American instinct that led these young men and women to pick up the torch and cross this bridge, that's the same instinct that moved patriots to choose revolution over tyranny. It's the same instinct that drew immigrants from across oceans and the Rio Grande; the same instinct that led women to reach for the ballot, workers to organize against an unjust status quo; the same instinct that led us to plant a flag at Iwo Jima and on the surface of the Moon.

It's the idea held by generations of citizens who believed that America is a constant work in progress; who believed that loving this country requires more than singing its praises or avoiding uncomfortable truths. It requires the occasional disruption, the willingness to speak out for what is right, to shake up the status quo. That's America.

That's what makes us unique. That's what cements our reputation as a beacon of opportunity. Young people behind the Iron Curtain would see Selma and eventually tear down that wall. Young people in Soweto would hear Bobby Kennedy talk about ripples of hope and eventually banish the scourge of apartheid. Young people in Burma went to prison rather than submit to military rule. They saw what John Lewis had done. From the streets of Tunis to the Maidan in Ukraine, this generation of young people can draw strength from this place, where the powerless could change the world's greatest power and push their leaders to expand the boundaries of freedom.

They saw that idea made real right here in Selma, Alabama. They saw that idea manifest itself here in America.

Because of campaigns like this, a Voting Rights Act was passed. Political and economic and social barriers came down. And the change these men and women wrought is visible here today in the presence of African Americans who run boardrooms, who sit on the bench, who serve in elected office from small towns to big cities; from the Congressional Black Caucus all the way to the Oval Office.

Because of what they did, the doors of opportunity swung open not just for black folks, but for every American. Women marched through those doors. Latinos marched through those doors. Asian Americans, gay Americans, Americans with disabilities—they all came through those doors. Their endeavors gave the entire South the chance to rise again, not by reasserting the past, but by transcending the past.

What a glorious thing, Dr. King might say. And what a solemn debt we owe. Which leads us to ask, just how might we repay that debt?

First and foremost, we have to recognize that one day's commemoration, no matter how special, is not enough. If Selma taught us anything, it's that our work is never done. The American experiment in self-government gives work and purpose to each generation.

Selma teaches us, as well, that action requires that we shed our cynicism. For when it comes to the pursuit of justice, we can afford neither complacency nor despair.

Just this week, I was asked whether I thought the Department of Justice's Ferguson report shows that, with respect to race, little has changed in this country. And I understood the question; the report's narrative was sadly familiar. It evoked the kind of abuse and disregard for citizens that spawned the Civil Rights Movement. But I rejected the notion that nothing's changed. What happened in Ferguson may not be unique, but it's no longer endemic. It's no longer sanctioned by law or by custom. And before the Civil Rights Movement, it most surely was.

We do a disservice to the cause of justice by intimating that bias and discrimination are immutable, that racial division is inherent to America. If you think nothing's changed in the past 50 years, ask somebody who lived through the Selma or Chicago or Los Angeles of the 1950s. Ask the female CEO who once might have been assigned to the secretarial pool if nothing's changed. Ask your gay friend if it's easier to be out and proud in America now than it was thirty years ago. To deny this progress, this hard-won progress—our progress—would be to rob us of our own agency, our own capacity, our responsibility to do what we can to make America better.

Of course, a more common mistake is to suggest that Ferguson is an isolated incident; that racism is banished; that the work that drew men and women to Selma is now complete, and that whatever racial tensions remain are a consequence of those seeking to play the "race card" for their own purposes. We don't need the Ferguson report to know that's not true. We just need to open our eyes, and our ears, and our hearts to know that this nation's racial history still casts its long shadow upon us.

We know the march is not yet over. We know the race is not yet won. We know that reaching that blessed destination where we are judged, all of us, by the content of our character requires admitting as much, facing up to the truth. "We are capable of bearing a great burden," James Baldwin once wrote, "once we discover that the burden is reality and arrive where reality is."

There's nothing America can't handle if we actually look squarely at the problem. And this is work for all Americans, not just some. Not just whites. Not just blacks. If we want to honor the courage of those who marched that day, then all of us are called to possess their moral imagination. All of us will need to feel as they did the fierce urgency of now. All of us need to recognize as they did that change depends on our actions, on our attitudes, the things we teach our children. And if we make such an effort, no matter how hard it may sometimes seem, laws can be passed, and consciences can be stirred, and consensus can be built.

With such an effort, we can make sure our criminal justice system serves all and not just some. Together, we can raise the level of mutual trust that policing is built on—the idea that police officers are members of the community they risk their lives to protect, and citizens in Ferguson and New York and Cleveland, they just want the same thing young people here marched for 50 years ago—the protection of the law. Together, we can address unfair sentencing and overcrowded prisons, and the stunted circumstances that rob too many boys of the chance to become men, and rob the nation of too many men who could be good dads, and good workers, and good neighbors.

With effort, we can roll back poverty and the roadblocks to opportunity. Americans don't accept a free ride for anybody, nor do we believe in equality of outcomes. But we do expect equal opportunity. And if we really mean it, if we're not just giving lip service to it, but if we really mean it and are willing to sacrifice for it, then, yes, we can make sure every child gets an education suitable to this new century, one that expands imaginations and lifts sights and gives those children the skills they need. We can make sure every person willing to work has the dignity of a job, and a fair wage, and a real voice, and sturdier rungs on that ladder into the middle class.

And with effort, we can protect the foundation stone of our democracy for which so many marched across this bridge—and that is the right to vote. Right now, in 2015, 50 years after Selma, there are laws across this country designed to make it harder for people to vote. As we speak, more of such laws are being proposed. Meanwhile, the Voting Rights Act, the culmination of so much blood, so much sweat and tears, the product of so much sacrifice in the face of wanton violence, the Voting Rights Act stands weakened, its future subject to political rancor.

How can that be? The Voting Rights Act was one of the crowning achievements of our democracy, the result of Republican and Democratic efforts. President Reagan signed its renewal when he was in office. President George W. Bush signed its renewal when he was in office. One hundred members of Congress have come here today to honor people who were willing to die for the right to protect it. If we want to honor this day, let that hundred go back to Washington and gather four hundred more, and together, pledge to make it their mission to restore that law this year. That's how we honor those on this bridge.

Of course, our democracy is not the task of Congress alone, or the courts alone, or even the President alone. If every new voter-suppression law was struck down today, we would still have, here in America, one of the lowest voting rates among free peoples. Fifty years ago, registering to vote here in Selma and much of the South meant guessing the number of jellybeans in a jar, the number of bubbles on a bar of soap. It meant risking your dignity, and sometimes, your life.

What's our excuse today for not voting? How do we so casually discard the right for which so many fought? How do we so fully give away our power, our voice, in shaping America's future? Why are we pointing to somebody else when we could take the time just to go to the polling places? We give away our power.

Fellow marchers, so much has changed in 50 years. We have endured war and we've fashioned peace. We've seen technological wonders that touch every aspect of our lives. We take for granted conveniences that our parents could have scarcely imagined. But what has not changed is the imperative of citizenship; that willingness of a 26-year-old deacon, or a Unitarian minister, or a young mother of five to decide they loved this country so much that they'd risk everything to realize its promise.

That's what it means to love America. That's what it means to believe in America. That's what it means when we say America is exceptional.

For we were born of change. We broke the old aristocracies, declaring ourselves entitled not by bloodline, but endowed by our Creator with certain inalienable rights. We secure our rights and responsibilities through a system of self-government, of and by and for the people. That's why we argue and fight with so much passion and conviction—because we know our efforts matter. We know America is what we make of it.

Look at our history. We are Lewis and Clark and Sacajawea, pioneers who braved the unfamiliar, followed by a stampede of farmers and miners, and entrepreneurs and hucksters. That's our spirit. That's who we are.

We are Sojourner Truth and Fannie Lou Hamer, women who could do as much as any man and then some. And we're Susan B. Anthony, who shook the system until the law reflected that truth. That is our character.

We're the immigrants who stowed away on ships to reach these shores, the huddled masses yearning to breathe free—Holocaust survivors, Soviet defectors, the Lost Boys of Sudan. We're the hopeful strivers who cross the Rio Grande because we want our kids to know a better life. That's how we came to be.

We're the slaves who built the White House and the economy of the South. We're the ranch hands and cowboys who opened up the West, and countless laborers who laid rail, and raised skyscrapers, and organized for workers' rights.

We're the fresh-faced GIs who fought to liberate a continent. And we're the Tuskeegee Airmen, and the Navajo code-talkers, and the Japanese Americans who fought for this country even as their own liberty had been denied.

We're the firefighters who rushed into those buildings on 9/11, the volunteers who signed up to fight in Afghanistan and Iraq. We're the gay Americans whose blood ran in the streets of San Francisco and New York, just as blood ran down this bridge.

We are storytellers, writers, poets, artists who abhor unfairness, and despise hypocrisy, and give voice to the voiceless, and tell truths that need to be told.

We're the inventors of gospel and jazz and blues, bluegrass and country, and hip-hop and rock and roll, and our very own sound with all the sweet sorrow and reckless joy of freedom.

We are Jackie Robinson, enduring scorn and spiked cleats and pitches coming straight to his head, and stealing home in the World Series anyway.

We are the people Langston Hughes wrote of who "build our temples for tomorrow, strong as we know how." We are the people Emerson wrote of, "who for truth and honor's sake stand fast and suffer long;" who are "never tired, so long as we can see far enough."

That's what America is. Not stock photos or airbrushed history, or feeble attempts to define some of us as more American than others. We respect the past, but we don't pine for the past. We don't fear the future; we grab for it. America is not some fragile thing. We are large, in the words of Whitman, containing multitudes. We are boisterous and diverse and full of energy, perpetually young in spirit. That's why someone like John Lewis at the ripe old age of 25 could lead a mighty march.

And that's what the young people here today and listening all across the country must take away from this day. You are America. Unconstrained by habit and convention. Unencumbered by what is, because you're ready to seize what ought to be.

For everywhere in this country, there are first steps to be taken, there's new ground to cover, there are more bridges to be crossed. And it is you, the young and fearless at heart, the most diverse and educated generation in our history, who the nation is waiting to follow.

Because Selma shows us that America is not the project of any one person. Because the single most powerful word in our democracy is the word "We." "We The People." "We Shall Overcome." "Yes We Can." That word is owned by no one. It belongs to everyone. Oh, what a glorious task we are given, to continually try to improve this great nation of ours.

Fifty years from Bloody Sunday, our march is not yet finished, but we're getting closer. Two hundred and thirty-nine years after this nation's founding our union is not yet perfect, but we are getting closer. Our job's easier because somebody already got us through that first mile. Somebody already got us over that bridge. When it feels the road is too hard, when the torch we've been passed feels too heavy, we will remember these early travelers, and draw strength from their example, and hold firmly the words of the prophet Isaiah: "Those who hope in the Lord will renew their strength. They will soar on [the] wings like eagles. They will run and not grow weary. They will walk and not be faint."

We honor those who walked so we could run. We must run so our children soar. And we will not grow weary. For we believe in the power of an awesome God, and we believe in this country's sacred promise.

May He bless those warriors of justice no longer with us, and bless the United States of America. Thank you, everybody.

Discussion Questions

1. A key part of the Civil Rights movement was the concept of "civil disobedience," that there were circumstances in which it was appropriate to break the law in order to demonstrate its injustice (King himself wrote a passionate defense of this strategy in his "Letter From Birmingham Jail"). Can you articulate a general rule that specifies when nonviolent law-breaking is justified?
2. Are anti-abortion advocates who block access to a clinic, environmental activists who spike trees to prevent logging, or squatters who occupy a federal building to protest government policy justified in breaking the law?

19

"In Defense of Prejudice"

JONATHAN RAUCH

Some political theorists argue that democracies must not only prevent the intrusion of government on basic liberties, but also must play a positive role in bolstering and protecting the rights of all their citizens. The challenge is admirable but difficult, as governments in practice are often faced with trade-offs between the two values. Consider free speech, a right enshrined in the First Amendment. The right to speak freely is fundamental to democratic governance. Yet it is not absolute. Is there a line where my right to speak freely impinges upon your wish not to hear what I have to say, particularly when my words are perceived as offensive, harmful, and prejudicial? What role should the government play in drawing the line, if any? Should it limit speech in order to protect others from the insult words can bring? If there is such a line, who decides where it is drawn?

In the following article Jonathan Rauch stands "in defense of prejudice" and in opposition to those who call for government regulation of speech that is insulting to or stigmatizes individuals based on their sex, race, color, handicap, religion, sexual orientation, nationality, or ethnicity. In the workplace, universities, public school curricula, the media, and criminal law, speech is increasingly regulated by codes aimed at eradicating prejudice. Rauch argues that regulating speech this way is foolish. In his view, the only way to challenge and correct prejudice is through the free flow of speech, some of which we might not want to hear. Government best protects liberty when it works to preserve rather than prevent the free flow of speech, no matter how distasteful or hurtful that speech may be.

The war on prejudice is now, in all likelihood, the most uncontroversial social movement in America. Opposition to "hate speech," formerly identified with the liberal left, has become a bipartisan piety. In the past year, groups and factions that agree on nothing else have agreed that the public expression of any and all prejudices must be forbidden. On the left, protesters and editorialists have insisted that Francis L. Lawrence resign as president of Rutgers University for describing blacks as "a disadvantaged population that doesn't have that genetic, hereditary background to have a higher average." On the other side of the ideological divide, Ralph Reed, the executive director of the Christian Coalition, responded to criticism of the religious right by calling a press conference to denounce a supposed outbreak of "name-calling, scapegoating, and religious bigotry." Craig Rogers, an evangelical Christian student at California State

University, recently filed a $2.5 million sexual-harassment suit against a lesbian professor of psychology, claiming that anti-male bias in one of her lectures violated campus rules and left him feeling "raped and trapped."

In universities and on Capitol Hill, in workplaces and newsrooms, authorities are declaring that there is no place for racism, sexism, homophobia, Christian-bashing, and other forms of prejudice in public debate or even in private thought. "Only when racism and other forms of prejudice are expunged," say the crusaders for sweetness and light, "can minorities be safe and society be fair." So sweet, this dream of a world without prejudice. But the very last thing society should do is seek to utterly eradicate racism and other forms of prejudice.

I suppose I should say, in the customary I-hope-I-don't-sound-too-defensive tone, that I am not a racist and that this is not an article favoring racism or any other particular prejudice. It is an article favoring intellectual pluralism, which permits the expression of various forms of bigotry and always will. Although we like to hope that a time will come when no one will believe that people come in types and that each type belongs with its own kind, I doubt such a day will ever arrive. By all indications, *Homo sapiens* is a tribal species for whom "us versus them" comes naturally and must be continually pushed back. Where there is genuine freedom of expression, there will be racist expression. There will also be people who believe that homosexuals are sick or threaten children or—especially among teenagers—are rightful targets of manly savagery. Homosexuality will always be incomprehensible to most people, and what is incomprehensible is feared. As for anti-Semitism, it appears to be a hardier virus than influenza. If you want pluralism, then you get racism and sexism and homophobia, and communism and fascism and xenophobia and tribalism, and that is just for a start. If you want to believe in intellectual freedom and the progress of knowledge and the advancement of science and all those other good things, then you must swallow hard and accept this: for as thickheaded and wayward an animal as us, the realistic question is how to make the best of prejudice, not how to eradicate it.

Indeed, "eradicating prejudice" is so vague a proposition as to be meaningless. Distinguishing prejudice reliably and nonpolitically from nonprejudice, or even defining it crisply, is quite hopeless. We all feel we know prejudice when we see it. But do we? At the University of Michigan, a student said in a classroom discussion that he considered homosexuality a disease treatable with therapy. He was summoned to a formal disciplinary hearing for violating the school's policy against speech that "victimizes" people based on "sexual orientation." Now, the evidence is abundant that this particular hypothesis is wrong, and any American homosexual can attest to the harm that the student's hypothesis has inflicted on many real people. But was it a statement of prejudice or of misguided belief? Hate speech or hypothesis? Many Americans who do not regard themselves as bigots or haters believe that homosexuality is a treatable disease.

They may be wrong, but are they all bigots? I am unwilling to say so, and if you are willing, beware. The line between a prejudiced belief and a merely controversial one is elusive, and the harder you look the more elusive it becomes. "God hates homosexuals" is a statement of fact, not of bias, to those who believe it; "American criminals are disproportionately black" is a statement of bias, not of fact, to those who disbelieve it.

Who is right? You may decide, and so may others, and there is no need to agree. That is the great innovation of intellectual pluralism . . . We cannot know in advance or for sure which belief is prejudice and which is truth, but to advance knowledge we don't need to know. The genius of intellectual pluralism lies not in doing away with prejudices and dogmas but in channeling them—making them socially productive by pitting prejudice against prejudice and dogma against dogma, exposing all to withering public criticism. What survives at the end of the day is our base of knowledge.

* * *

Pluralism is the principle that protects and makes a place in human company for that loneliest and most vulnerable of all minorities, the minority who is hounded and despised among blacks and whites, gays and straights, who is suspect or criminal among every tribe and in every nation of the world, and yet on whom progress depends: the dissident. I am not saying that dissent is always or even usually enlightened. Most of the time it is foolish and self-serving. No dissident has the right to be taken seriously, and the fact that Aryan Nation racists or Nation of Islam anti-Semites are unorthodox does not entitle them to respect. But what goes around comes around. As a supporter of gay marriage, for example, I reject the majority's view of family, and as a Jew I reject its view of God. I try to be civil, but the fact is that most Americans regard my views on marriage as a reckless assault on the most fundamental of all institutions, and many people are more than a little discomfited by the statement "Jesus Christ was no more divine than anybody else" (which is why so few people ever say it). Trap the racists and anti-Semites, and you lay a trap for me too. Hunt for them with eradication in your mind, and you have brought dissent itself within your sights.

The new crusade against prejudice waves aside such warnings. Like earlier crusades against antisocial ideas, the mission is fueled by good (if cocksure) intentions and a genuine sense of urgency. Some kinds of error are held to be intolerable, like pollutants that even in small traces poison the water for a whole town. Some errors are so pernicious as to damage real people's lives, so wrongheaded that no person of right mind or goodwill could support them. Like their forebears of other stripe—the Church in its campaigns against heretics, the McCarthyites in their campaigns against Communists—the modern anti-racist and anti-sexist and anti-homophobic campaigners are totalists, demanding not that misguided ideas and ugly expressions be corrected or criticized but that they be eradicated. They make war not on errors but on error, and like other totalists they act in the name of public safety—the safety, especially, of minorities.

The sweeping implications of this challenge to pluralism are not, I think, well enough understood by the public at large. Indeed, the new brand of totalism has yet even to be properly named. "Multiculturalism," for instance, is much too broad. "Political correctness" comes closer but is too trendy and snide. For lack of anything else, I will call the new antipluralism "purism," since its major tenet is that society cannot be just until the last traces of invidious prejudice have been scrubbed away. Whatever you call it, the purists' way of seeing things has spread through American intellectual life with remarkable speed, so much so that many people will blink at you uncomprehendingly or even call you a racist (or sexist or homophobe, etc.) if you suggest that expressions of racism should be tolerated or that prejudice has its part to play.

The new purism sets out, to begin with, on a campaign against words, for words are the currency of prejudice, and if prejudice is hurtful then so must be prejudiced words. "We are not safe when these violent words are among us," wrote Mari Matsuda, then a UCLA law professor. Here one imagines gangs of racist words swinging chains and smashing heads in back alleys. To suppress bigoted language seems, at first blush, reasonable, but it quickly leads to a curious result. A peculiar kind of verbal shamanism takes root, as though certain expressions, like curses or magical incantations, carry in themselves the power to hurt or heal—as though words were bigoted rather than people. "Context is everything," people have always said. The use of the word "nigger" in *Huckleberry Finn* does not make the book an "act" of hate speech—or does it? In the new view, this is no longer so clear. The very utterance of the word "nigger" (at least by a non-black) is a racist act. When a *Sacramento Bee* cartoonist put the word "nigger" mockingly in the mouth of a white supremacist, there were howls of protest and 1,400 canceled subscriptions and an editorial apology, even though the word was plainly being invoked against racists, not against blacks.

Faced with escalating demands of verbal absolutism, newspapers issue lists of forbidden words. The expressions "gyp" (derived from "Gypsy") and "Dutch treat" were among the dozens of terms stricken as "offensive" in a much-ridiculed (and later withdrawn) *Los Angeles Times* speech code. The University of Missouri journalism school issued a *Dictionary of Cautionary Words and Phrases*, which included "*Buxom*: Offensive reference to a woman's chest. Do not use. See 'Woman.' *Codger*: Offensive reference to a senior citizen."

As was bound to happen, purists soon discovered that chasing around after words like "gyp" or "buxom" hardly goes to the roots of the problem. As long as they remain bigoted, bigots will simply find other words. If they can't call you a kike then they will say Jewboy, Judas, or Hebe, and when all those are banned they will press words like "oven" and "lampshade" into their service. The vocabulary of hate is potentially as rich as your dictionary, and all you do by banning language used by cretins is to let them decide what the rest of us may say. The problem, some purists have concluded, must therefore go much deeper than laws: it must go to the deeper level of ideas. Racism, sexism, homophobia, and the rest must be built into the very structure of American society and American patterns of thought, so pervasive yet so insidious that, like water to a fish, they are both omnipresent and unseen. The mere existence of prejudice constructs a society whose very nature is prejudiced.

This line of thinking was pioneered by feminists, who argued that pornography, more than just being expressive, is an act by which men construct an oppressive society. Racial activists quickly picked up the argument. Racist expressions are themselves acts of oppression, they said. "All racist speech constructs the social reality that constrains the liberty of nonwhites because of their race," wrote Charles R. Lawrence III, then a law professor at Stanford. From the purist point of view, a society with even one racist is a racist society, because the idea itself threatens and demeans its targets. They cannot feel wholly safe or wholly welcome as long as racism is present. Pluralism says: There will always be some racists. Marginalize them, ignore them, exploit them, ridicule them, take pains to make their policies illegal, but otherwise leave them alone. Purists say: That's not enough. Society cannot be just until these pervasive and oppressive ideas are searched out and eradicated.

And so what is now under way is a growing drive to eliminate prejudice from every corner of society. I doubt that many people have noticed how far-reaching this anti-pluralist movement is becoming.

In universities: Dozens of universities have adopted codes proscribing speech or other expression that (this is from Stanford's policy, which is more or less representative) "is intended to insult or stigmatize an individual or a small number of individuals on the basis of their sex, race, color, handicap, religion, sexual orientation or national and ethnic origin." Some codes punish only persistent harassment of a targeted individual, but many, following the purist doctrine that even one racist is too many, go much further. At Penn, an administrator declared: "We at the University of Pennsylvania have guaranteed students and the community that they can live in a community free of sexism, racism, and homophobia." Here is the purism that gives "political correctness" its distinctive combination of puffy high-mindedness and authoritarian zeal.

In school curricula: "More fundamental than eliminating racial segregation has to be the removal of racist thinking, assumptions, symbols, and materials in the curriculum," writes theorist Molefi Kete Asante. In practice, the effort to "remove racist thinking" goes well beyond striking egregious references from textbooks. In many cases it becomes a kind of mental engineering in which students are encouraged to see prejudice everywhere; it includes teaching identity politics as an antidote to internalized racism; it rejects mainstream science as "white male" thinking; and it tampers with history, installing such dubious notions as that the ancient Greeks stole their culture from Africa or that an ancient carving of a bird is an example of "African experimental aeronautics."

In criminal law: Consider two crimes. In each, I am beaten brutally; in each, my jaw is smashed and my skull is split in just the same way. However, in the first crime my assailant calls me an "asshole"; in the second he calls me a "queer." In most states, in many localities, and, as of September 1994, in federal cases, these two crimes are treated differently: the crime motivated by bias—or deemed to be so motivated by prosecutors and juries—gets a stiffer punishment. "Longer prison terms for bigots," shrilled Brooklyn Democratic Congressman Charles Schumer, who introduced the federal hate-crimes legislation, and those are what the law now provides. Evidence that the assailant holds prejudiced beliefs, even if he doesn't actually express them while committing an offense, can serve to elevate the crime. Defendants in hate-crimes cases may be grilled on how many black friends they have and whether they have told racist jokes. To increase a prison sentence only because of the defendant's "prejudice" (as gauged by prosecutor and jury) is, of course, to try minds and punish beliefs. Purists say, Well, they are dangerous minds and poisonous beliefs.

In the workplace: Though government cannot constitutionally suppress bigotry directly, it is now busy doing so indirectly by requiring employers to eliminate prejudice. Since the early 1980s, courts and the Equal Employment Opportunity Commission have moved to bar workplace speech deemed to create a hostile or abusive working environment for minorities. The law, held a federal court in 1988, "does require that an employer take prompt action to prevent . . . bigots from expressing their opinions in a way that abuses or offends their co-workers," so as to achieve "the goal of eliminating prejudices and biases from our society." So it was, as UCLA law professor Eugene Volokh notes, that the EEOC charged that a manufacturer's ads using admittedly accurate depictions of samurai, kabuki, and sumo were "racist" and "offensive to people of Japanese origin"; that a Pennsylvania court found that an employer's printing Bible verses on paychecks was religious harassment of Jewish employees; that an employer had to desist using gender-based job titles like "foreman" and "draftsman" after a female employee sued.

On and on the campaign goes, darting from one outbreak of prejudice to another like a cat chasing flies. In the American Bar Association, activists demand that lawyers who express "bias or prejudice" be penalized. In the Education Department, the civil-rights office presses for a ban on computer bulletin board comments that "show hostility toward a person or group based on sex, race or color, including slurs, negative stereotypes, jokes or pranks." In its security checks for government jobs, the FBI takes to asking whether applicants are "free of biases against any class of citizens," whether, for instance, they have told racist jokes or indicated other "prejudices." Joke police! George Orwell, grasping the close relationship of jokes to dissent, said that every joke is a tiny revolution. The purists will have no such rebellions.

The purist campaign reaches, in the end, into the mind itself. In a lecture at the University of New Hampshire, a professor compared writing to sex ("You and the subject become one"); he was suspended and required to apologize, but what was most insidious was the order to undergo university-approved counseling to have his mind straightened out. At the University of Pennsylvania, a law lecturer said, "We have ex-slaves here who should know about the Thirteenth Amendment"; he was banished from campus for a year and required to make a public apology, and he, too, was compelled to attend a "sensitivity and racial awareness" session. Mandatory re-education of alleged bigots is the natural consequence of intellectual purism. Prejudice must be eliminated!

* * * "Nobody escapes," said a Rutgers University report on campus prejudice. Bias and prejudice, it found, cross every conceivable line, from sex to race to politics: "No matter who you are, no matter what the color of your skin, no matter what your gender or sexual orientation, no matter what you believe, no matter how you behave, there is somebody out there who doesn't like people of your kind." Charles Lawrence writes: "Racism is ubiquitous. We are all racists." If he means that most of us think racist thoughts of some sort at one time or another, he is right. If we are going to "eliminate prejudices and biases from our society," then the work of the prejudice police is unending. They are doomed to hunt and hunt and hunt, scour and scour and scour.

What is especially dismaying is that the purists pursue prejudice in the name of protecting minorities. In order to protect people like me (homosexual), they must pursue people like me (dissident). In order to bolster minority self-esteem, they suppress minority opinion. There are, of course, all kinds of practical and legal problems with the purists' campaign: the incursions against the First Amendment; the inevitable abuses by prosecutors and activists who define as "hateful" or "violent" whatever speech they dislike or can score points off of; the lack of any evidence that repressing prejudice eliminates rather than inflames it. But minorities, of all people, ought to remember that by definition we cannot prevail by numbers, and we generally cannot prevail by force. Against the power of ignorant mass opinion and group prejudice and superstition, we have only our voices. If you doubt that minorities' voices are powerful weapons, think of the lengths to which Southern officials went to silence the Reverend Martin Luther King, Jr. (recall that the city commissioner of Montgomery, Alabama, won a $500,000 libel suit, later overturned in *New York Times v. Sullivan* [1964], regarding an advertisement in the *Times* placed by civil-rights leaders who denounced the Montgomery police). Think of how much gay people have improved their lot over twenty-five years simply by refusing to remain silent. Recall the Michigan student who was prosecuted for saying that homosexuality is a treatable disease, and notice that he was black. Under that Michigan speech code, more than twenty blacks were charged with racist speech, while no instance of racist speech by whites was punished. In Florida, the hate-speech law was invoked against a black man who called a policeman a "white cracker"; not so surprisingly, in the first hate-crimes case to reach the Supreme Court, the victim was white and the defendant black.

In the escalating war against "prejudice," the right is already learning to play by the rules that were pioneered by the purist activists of the left. Last year leading Democrats, including the President, criticized the Republican Party for being increasingly in the thrall of the Christian right. Some of the rhetoric was harsh ("fire-breathing Christian radical right"), but it wasn't vicious or even clearly wrong. Never mind: when Democratic Representative Vic Fazio said Republicans were "being forced to the fringes by the aggressive political tactics of the religious right," the chairman of the Republican National Committee, Haley Barbour, said, "Christian-bashing" was "the left's preferred form of religious bigotry." Bigotry! Prejudice! "Christians active in politics are now on the receiving end of an extraordinary campaign of bias and prejudice," said the conservative leader William J. Bennett. One discerns, here, where the new purism leads. Eventually, any criticism of any group will be "prejudice."

Discussion Questions

1. Do you agree or disagree that some groups need to be protected against offensive or hurtful ideas or speech? How do you define "hurtful" or "offensive"? What is the basis for your position? Where is the First Amendment in this debate?

2. Would a campus newspaper be justified in rejecting a paid advertisement from (a) a group or individual that denied the Holocaust had occurred; (b) a group or individual that argued against any sort of affirmative action; or (c) an environmental group that advocated violence against the property of corporations that polluted the environment? Would you support a "speech code" that prohibited someone from making these arguments on campus? Defend your answer.

Debating the Issues: Should There Be a Religious Exemption to Nondiscrimination Laws?

The Supreme Court settled the legal debate over same-sex marriage in 2015, when in *Obergefell v. Hodges* it held that same sex-couples had a constitutional right to marry. As the readings in this section show, however, that decision did not resolve every dispute that has arisen over the issue, but rather shifted the debate to a new terrain. Now, a key question is whether a person who objects to same-sex marriage on religious grounds can be compelled to recognize or participate in it. Can a person object to a law by claiming that it burdens their religious belief? The theoretical dispute has concrete expression: in 2015, bakery owners in Oregon were fined $135,000 for refusing to bake a wedding cake for a gay couple. A Colorado bakery was ordered to provide cakes to same-sex couples, train its staff, and provide reports to a state agency showing it was complying with the order. A County Clerk in Kentucky claimed that issuing marriage licenses to gay couples violated her religious belief; she was jailed after refusing a federal judge's order to issue them.

These are the latest examples of longer debate over balancing individuals' religious freedom (which is a core constitutional right) with laws that individuals claim burden that freedom. Earlier disputes have involved Native Americans who claimed the right to take peyote as part of their religious celebrations, business owners who objected to federal law requiring them to offer birth control in their health plans, Amish who objected to a state law mandating education through the eighth grade, or a private university that cited a religious basis for its policy banning interracial dating. Sometimes the government wins these legal disputes, and sometimes the private actors win.

The legal doctrines are complicated, reflecting the fact that governments may not prohibit the free exercise of religion, but neither can they favor one religion over another, or even favor religion over non-religion.

The readings in this section approach the debate by examining Religious Freedom Restoration Acts (RFRAs) passed by the federal government and 21 states, many of them as it became clear that the *Obergefell* case was going to turn out as it did. These laws take many forms, but typically specify that the government must accommodate religious objections to laws unless the government has a "compelling interest" in an area, and has chosen the "least restrictive means" of enacting a policy. The first such law was enacted by the federal government in 1993, in part as a reaction to a 1990 Supreme Court decision that held an individual may not defy a law of "general applicability" because it burdens their religious belief.

Both authors wrote shortly before *Obergefell* was decided. Cole argues that the RFRAs are inconsistent with Supreme Court doctrine, but considers the question from a policy perspective. Should states allow religious exemptions to state anti-discrimination laws in ways that would permit a baker (or florist, or caterer) to refuse service to a same-sex wedding? While such laws are likely constitutional under current Supreme Court doctrine, Cole argues that they impose important symbolic harms by denying the dignity and equality of same-sex couples. And, in his view, they impose "a strong presumption that individual religious claims take precedence over democratically chosen collective goals," such as anti-discrimination. "The freedom to exercise one's religion," Cole concludes, "is a fundamental value, but like other values, it has its limits."

Helfman discusses the controversy of Indiana's Religious Freedom Restoration Act in March 2015. Critics insisted that the law was a thinly veiled attempt to legalize antigay discrimination (Indiana did not have a general law that prohibited discrimination on the basis of sexual orientation), and its enactment triggered widespread condemnation and boycotts.

Helfman argues that these claims are exaggerated, and that the law merely sought "to stabilize an unsteady line of judicial precedent against how judges should treat laws that impair the First Amendment right to the free exercise of religion." When religious freedom and government action conflict, she concludes that the government should face a heavy burden in justifying its laws: "The right of free exercise *is* a civil right, and the First Amendment places very real demands on government."

20

"The Angry New Frontier: Gay Rights vs. Religious Liberty"

DAVID COLE

1.

At the end of June, the Supreme Court will likely declare that the Constitution requires states to recognize same-sex marriages on the same terms that they recognize marriages between a man and a woman. If it does, the decision will mark a radical transformation in both constitutional law and public values. Twenty-five years ago, the very idea of same-sex marriage was unthinkable to most Americans; the notion that the Constitution somehow guaranteed the right to it was nothing short of delusional.

One sign of how far we have come is that the principal ground of political contention these days is not whether same-sex marriages should be recognized, but whether persons who object to such marriages on religious grounds should have the right to deny their services to couples celebrating same-sex weddings. Opponents of same-sex marriage can read the shift in public opinion as well as anyone else: a 2014 Gallup poll reported that, nationwide, 55 percent of all Americans, and nearly 80 percent of those between eighteen and twenty-nine, favor recognition of same-sex marriage. Today, same-sex couples have the right to marry in thirty-seven states and the District of Columbia. And come June, most legal experts expect the Supreme Court to require the remainder to follow suit.

Having lost that war, opponents of same-sex marriage have opened up a new battlefield—claiming that people with sincere religious objections to it should not be compelled to participate in any acts that are said to validate or celebrate same-sex marriage. There is an obvious strategic reason for this. One of the problems for opponents of same-sex marriage was that they could not credibly point to anyone who was harmed by it. Proponents, by contrast, could point to many sympathetic victims—couples who had lived in stable, committed relationships for years, but were denied the freedom to express their commitment in a state-recognized marriage, and who were therefore also denied many tangible benefits associated with marriage, including parental rights, health insurance, survivor's benefits, and hospital visitation privileges. Claims that "traditional marriage" would suffer were, by contrast, abstract and wholly unsubstantiated.

Focusing on religiously based objectors puts a human face on the opposition to same-sex marriage. Should the fundamentalist Christian florist who believes that same-sex marriage is a sin be required to sell flowers for a same-sex wedding ceremony, if she claims that to do so would violate her religious tenets? There are plenty of florists, the accommodationists argue, so surely the same-sex couple can go elsewhere, and thereby respect the florist's sincerely held religious beliefs. Should a religious nonprofit organization that makes its property available to the general public for a fee be required to rent it for a same-sex wedding? Should a religious employer be compelled to provide spousal benefits to the same-sex spouse of its employee? Should Catholic Charities' adoption service have to refer children to otherwise suitable homes of married same-sex couples? At its most general level, the question is whether religious principles justify discrimination against same-sex couples.

2.

In late March, Indiana Governor Mike Pence signed into law the Indiana Religious Freedom Restoration Act (RFRA), a state law that requires officials to exempt those with religious objections from any legal obligation that is not "essential" and the "least restrictive means" to serve "a compelling state interest." Arkansas enacted a similar law at the beginning of April. Georgia and North Carolina are considering doing so. And nineteen other states already have such laws, which could permit individuals to cite religious objections as a basis for refusing to abide by prohibitions on discrimination in public accommodations, employment, housing, and the like.

The Indiana and Arkansas laws prompted strong objections from gay rights advocates and leaders of the business community, including Apple, the NCAA, Walmart, and Eli Lilly. They see the laws as thinly veiled efforts to establish a religious excuse for discrimination against gay men and lesbians. Governor Pence initially dismissed these objections as unfounded, but as criticism mounted, Indiana legislators passed an amendment specifying that the law

> does not authorize a provider to refuse to offer or provide services, facilities, use of public accommodations, goods, employment, or housing . . . on the basis of race, color, religion, ancestry, age, national origin, disability, sex, sexual orientation, gender identity, or United States military service.

Most of the other state RFRAs, however, have no such anti-discrimination language. In Arkansas, Governor Asa Hutchinson responded to criticism by getting the legislature to tailor the law more closely to the federal Religious Freedom Restoration Act, but that law has no anti-discrimination language, and for reasons discussed below, it is far from clear that this revision will stop the law from being invoked to authorize religiously motivated discrimination.

In addition, still other state laws that have received far less attention specifically grant religious exemptions from a variety of legal obligations regarding same-sex marriage. In fact, to date every state except Delaware that has adopted same-sex marriage by legislation has included a religious exemption of some kind. They vary in their details, but among other things, they allow clergy to opt out of conducting marriage ceremonies; permit religiously affiliated nonprofit organizations to deny goods and services to same-sex weddings; and allow religiously affiliated adoption agencies freedom to deny child placements with same-sex married couples. Most were enacted as part of a political bargain, designed to ease passage of laws recognizing same-sex marriage.

At bottom, all of these laws pose the same question: How should we balance the rights of gay and lesbian couples to equal treatment with the free exercise rights of religious objectors?

Under the U.S. Constitution, the answer to this question is clear. The state violates no constitutionally protected religious liberty by imposing laws of general applicability—such as anti-discrimination mandates—on the religious and nonreligious alike. In 1990, the Supreme Court ruled, in a decision written by Justice Antonin Scalia, that being subjected to a general rule, neutrally applied to all, does not raise a valid claim under the

First Amendment's free exercise of religion clause, even if the rule burdens the exercise of one's religion.

The case, *Employment Division v. Smith*, involved a Native American tribe that sought an exemption from a criminal law banning the possession and distribution of peyote; the tribe argued that the drug was an integral part of its religious ceremonies. The Court rejected the claim. Justice Scalia reasoned that to allow religious objectors to opt out of generally applicable laws would, quoting an 1878 Supreme Court precedent, "make the professed doctrines of religious belief superior to the law of the land, and in effect . . . permit every citizen to become a law unto himself." The Court accordingly ruled that laws implicate the free exercise clause only if they specifically target or disfavor religion, not if they merely impose general obligations on all that some religiously scrupled individuals find burdensome.

Even before the Court in *Employment Division v. Smith* adopted this general rule, it rejected a claim that religious convictions should trump antidiscrimination laws. The IRS had denied tax-exempt status to Bob Jones University, a religious institution that banned interracial dating, and to Goldsboro Christian Schools, Inc., which interpreted the Bible as compelling it to admit only white students. The religious schools sued, asserting that the IRS's denial violated their free exercise rights. In *Bob Jones University v. United States*, the Court in 1983 summarily rejected that contention, asserting that the state's compelling interest in eradicating racial discrimination "outweigh[ed] whatever burden denial of tax benefits places on petitioners' exercise of their religious beliefs." If the state seeks to eradicate discrimination, the reasoning goes, it cannot simultaneously tolerate discrimination.

Under these precedents, the Constitution plainly does not compel states to grant religious exemptions to laws requiring the equal treatment of same-sex marriages. Laws recognizing same-sex marriages impose a general obligation, do not single out any religion for disfavored treatment, and in any event further the state's compelling interest in eradicating discrimination against gay men and lesbians.

But can or should states adopt such exemptions as a policy matter? In some instances, to be sure, it seems appropriate to accommodate religious scruples. Everyone agrees, for example, that a priest should not be required to perform a wedding that violates his religious tenets. But it is not at all clear that those who otherwise provide goods and services to the general public should be able to cite religion as an excuse to discriminate.

Take the fundamentalist florist. Proponents of an exemption insist that the same-sex couple denied flowers can find another florist, while the florist would either have to violate her religious tenets or lose some of her business. But this argument fails to take seriously the commitment to equality that underlies the recognition of same-sex marriage—and the harm to personal dignity inflicted by unequal treatment. Just as the eradication of race discrimination in education could not tolerate the granting of tax-exempt status to Bob Jones University, even though plenty of nondiscriminatory schools remained available, so the eradication of discrimination in the recognition of marriage cannot tolerate discrimination against same-sex marriages.

Justice Robert Jackson got the balance right when he stated, in 1944, that limits on religious freedom "begin to operate whenever [religious] activities begin to affect or collide with liberties of others or of the public." James Madison struck the same balance, noting that religion should be free of regulation only "where it does not trespass on private rights or the public peace." When a religious principle is cited to deny same-sex couples equal treatment, it collides with the liberties of others and trespasses on private rights, and should not prevail.

The fact that many of the state laws specifically single out religious objections to same-sex marriage for favorable treatment may itself pose constitutional issues under the First Amendment's clause prohibiting the establishment of religion. While states are permitted some leeway to accommodate religion, the establishment clause forbids states from favoring specific religions over others, or religion over nonreligion. And when states accommodate a religious believer by simply shifting burdens to third parties, such as when religiously motivated employers are permitted to deny benefits to same-sex spouses of their employees, the state impermissibly takes sides, favoring religion. In *Estate of Thornton v. Calder* (1984), for example, the Supreme Court held that the establishment clause invalidated a state requirement that businesses accommodate all employees' observations of the Sabbath, regardless of the impact on other workers or the business itself. State laws granting exemptions for religious objectors to same-sex marriage both give preference to religious over other conscientious objections and shift burdens to same-sex couples. Such favoritism is not only not warranted by the free exercise clause, but may be prohibited by the establishment clause.

3.

The "religious freedom restoration" laws that Indiana, Arkansas, and nineteen other states have adopted do not single out same-sex marriage as such, but they also have serious flaws. These statutes are almost certainly constitutional under existing doctrine, since they are modeled on the federal Religious Freedom Restoration Act, enacted in 1993 in response to the *Smith* decision. That's the statute the Supreme Court relied upon last year in *Burwell v. Hobby Lobby* to rule that the Department of Health and Human Services must accommodate for-profit corporations that object on religious grounds to providing insurance coverage to their employees for certain kinds of contraception. (Significantly, the Court in

Hobby Lobby found that the religious corporations' objections could be accommodated without imposing any cost on their female employees, by extending to those for-profit businesses an existing HHS accommodation that required insurance providers to provide contraception at no cost to the employees of objecting nonprofit organizations).

The federal and state RFRAs provide, as a statutory matter, what the Court refused to provide as a matter of constitutional law in the *Smith* decision. They require the government to meet a very demanding standard to justify any law, no matter how neutral and generally applicable, that imposes a "substantial burden" on anyone's exercise of religion. Because the courts are reluctant to second-guess individual religious commitments, the "substantial burden" threshold is often easily met: an individual need only articulate a plausible claim that the law requires him to do something that violates his religious principles. Religious objections could be raised to anti-discrimination laws, criminal laws, taxes, environmental and business regulations, you name it; the only limit is the creativity of religious objectors.

Once a religious objection is raised, the RFRA laws require the state to show not only that it has a "compelling" reason for denying a religious exemption, but that no more narrowly tailored way to achieve its ends is possible. This language appears to direct courts to apply the same skeptical standard—called "strict scrutiny"—applied to laws that explicitly discriminate on the basis of race, or that censor speech because of its content. This standard is so difficult to satisfy that it has been described as "strict in theory, but fatal in fact." If the RFRAs were literally enforced, many state laws would not survive that standard of review. They appear to give religious objectors what the Court in *Smith* properly refused—"a private right to ignore generally applicable laws."

Perhaps for this reason, courts have not interpreted state RFRAs literally, but have instead generally construed them to uphold laws that impose a burden on religion as long as the state has a reasonable justification for doing so. They have looked to the purpose of the RFRAs rather than to their literal language; the laws were designed, after all, to "restore" the constitutional protection of religious free exercise that existed prior to the *Smith* decision, and while the Supreme Court before *Smith* sometimes spoke in terms of compelling interests and least restrictive means, its actual application of the free exercise clause was much more measured. Thus, there have been relatively few successful RFRA lawsuits in the state or federal courts.

The courts have resisted applying strict scrutiny to religious freedom claims for good reason. Strict scrutiny is triggered by regulations of speech only where the state censors speech because of its content, such as when a state bans labor picketing or regulates political campaign advocacy. In equal protection cases, the Court applies strict scrutiny only to those rare laws that intentionally draw distinctions based on race, ethnicity, national origin, or religion, such as race-based affirmative action. By contrast, as

Justice Scalia noted in *Smith*, a religious objection can be raised to virtually any law. Applying the same scrutiny to claims of religious freedom would therefore have few meaningful limits, and would give religious objectors a presumptive veto over any law they claimed infringed their religious views.

But there is reason to believe that judicial interpretation of RFRAs may change. The Supreme Court in *Hobby Lobby* interpreted the federal RFRA to impose a much more demanding, pro-religion standard of review than had ever been imposed before. Encouraged by this development, over one hundred lawsuits have been filed under the federal RFRA challenging the Affordable Care Act's requirement that health insurance plans cover contraception. Some state courts may well follow the Supreme Court's lead and apply their state RFRAs more aggressively. And now that many states have been required by federal courts to recognize same-sex marriage, some state judges may be inclined to push back through interpretation of state RFRAs permitting religious exemptions.

When *Smith* was decided, the prohibition of the peyote ceremony seemed to many an unfair deprivation of the religious rights of Native Americans. Religious groups across the spectrum condemned the decision, and a coalition of liberals and conservatives joined together to endorse the enactment of the federal RFRA. The law was supported by the ACLU, the American Jewish Congress, and the National Association of Evangelicals, among many others; it passed the House unanimously, and passed 97–3 in the Senate. Many argued, with justification, that the Court's approach in *Smith* was insensitive to religious minorities. As the peyote case illustrated, minority religions are unlikely to have their concerns taken seriously by the majority through the ordinary democratic process. And if a generally applicable law does interfere with the exercise of religion, the bill's proponents asked, shouldn't the state bear a burden of justification?

The problem is not so much that RFRAs create a presumption in favor of religious accommodation, but that the presumption is at once so easily triggered and so difficult to overcome. Advocates for religious liberty and marriage equality might find common ground were they to support modified RFRAs that would impose a less demanding standard of justification, requiring states to show that permitting a religious exemption would undermine important collective interests or impose harm on others.

The stringent standard imposed by RFRAs, by contrast, means that anytime anyone objects on religious grounds to any law, he or she is entitled to an exemption unless the state can show that it is absolutely necessary to deny the exemption in order to further a compelling end. Because these laws impose such a heavy burden of justification, they effectively transfer a great deal of decision-making authority from the democratic process to religious objectors and the courts.

Instead of the polity deciding when to grant particular religious exemptions from a specific law, RFRAs transfer to courts the power to decide that question—subject to a strong presumption that individual religious claims take precedence over democratically chosen collective goals.

Religious liberty has an important place in American society, to be sure. Accommodation of religious practices is a sign of a tolerant multicultural society—so long as the accommodation does not simply shift burdens from one minority to another. The freedom to exercise one's religion is a fundamental value, but like other values, it has its limits. It is not a right to ignore collective obligations, nor is it a right to discriminate. Those who oppose same-sex marriage should be free to express their opposition in speech to their heart's (and religion's) content, but not to engage in acts of discrimination. As Oliver Wendell Holmes Jr. is said to have remarked: "The right to swing my fist ends where the other man's nose begins."

21

"The Religious-Liberty War"

TARA HELFMAN

When the curtain opens on Sophocles's *Antigone*, Thebes is reeling from a fratricidal war. The rivals for the crown have killed each other in battle, and the new king has ordered that no one may bury the body of the rebel leader. The play's heroine confronts a tragic choice: Should she obey divine commandment and offer her slain brother funeral rites? Or should she obey the king's command and defy the will of the gods?

The Religious Freedom Restoration Act, which became law at the federal level in 1993 and has been followed by 20 state-level versions in the decades since, attempts to shield Americans from the sort of choice Antigone had to make between the state's command and her faith's calling. In general, the RFRA statutes ensure that government cannot compel an individual to act against her faith unless (1) a compelling government interest demands it, and (2) the measure is narrowly tailored to serve those interests. But when Indiana Governor Mike Pence became the 20th governor to sign a state-level RFRA into law in March, legal tragedy degenerated into political farce as the statute became the latest staging ground in the ongoing national debate on gay rights.

Gay-rights activists charged that the Indiana law amounted to a license to discriminate on religious pretexts. The American Civil Liberties Union, originally one of the key supporters of the federal RFRA, denounced the statute as "a terrible and dangerous mistake," and Hillary Clinton, whose husband signed the original act into law in 1993, lamented on Twitter: "Sad this new Indiana law can happen in America today. We shouldn't discriminate against [people because] of who they love." Everyone from the CEO of Angie's List to the president of the NCAA had something to say about the Indiana statute, and none of it was good. When a similar backlash arose in response to the Arkansas religious-freedom bill, that state's governor, Asa Hutchinson, quickly withdrew his support, musing that his own son had signed a petition against it and stating his concerns that it would have "a negative impact on our state's image."

Lost in all this fury was the simple purpose of these RFRAs: They are designed to stabilize an unsteady line of judicial precedent regarding how judges should treat laws that impair the First Amendment right to the free exercise of religion.

The tension between the public interest and private faith is written into the very text of the Constitution, which safeguards religious liberty and guarantees the equal protection of laws. The First Amendment provides that Congress shall make no law prohibiting the free exercise of religion. But sometimes laws of general application—laws that are designed to apply equally to *all* Americans—impair the religious practice of *some* Americans.

Justice William Brennan, celebrated as a liberal lion of the Supreme Court, first formulated the test later codified by the federal RFRA in *Sherbert v. Verner.* The 1963 case involved a claim by a Seventh-Day Adventist who had been denied unemployment benefits by the state of South Carolina because she refused to work on the Sabbath. The Court held that forcing the claimant to choose between abandoning a precept of her faith and forgoing her unemployment benefits was tantamount to fining her for practicing her religion. The government would henceforth have to show that any law impairing the free exercise of religion was narrowly tailored to serve a compelling government interest. This came to be known as the Sherbert Test.

In *Wisconsin v. Yoder* (1972), the Court reaffirmed the Sherbert Test, striking down a state statute establishing compulsory eighth-grade education on the ground that it violated the First Amendment rights of Wisconsin's Amish community. In so doing, the Court was mindful of the potential danger that religious exemptions posed to the equal protection of laws. It explained:

> Although a determination of what is a "religious" belief or practice entitled to constitutional protection may present a most delicate question, the very concept of ordered liberty precludes allowing every person to make his own standards on matters of conduct in which society as a whole has important interests. Thus, if the Amish asserted their claims because of their subjective evaluation and rejection of the contemporary secular values accepted by the

majority, much as Thoreau rejected the social values of his time and isolated himself at Walden Pond, their claims would not rest on a religious basis. Thoreau's choice was philosophical and personal rather than religious, and such belief does not rise to the demands of the Religion Clauses.

In short, the Court found, faith enjoys a higher degree of protection under the Constitution than philosophy, and that is by constitutional design.

Then, in the 1989 case *Employment Division v. Smith*, the Court revisited the Sherbert Test. At issue was whether two Native Americans had been unlawfully denied unemployment benefits under Oregon law because they took peyote as part of a religious sacrament. The claimants argued they should be granted a religious exemption because state drug law placed an undue burden on their First Amendment right to free exercise of religion. Writing for the Court, Justice Antonin Scalia rejected the argument: "To make an individual's obligation to obey such a law contingent upon the law's coincidence with his religious beliefs, except where the State's interest is 'compelling'—permitting him, by virtue of his beliefs, to become a law unto himself—contradicts both constitutional tradition and common sense." The majority ruled that the answer to the problem of generally applicable laws that encroach upon religious liberty is not to carve out constitutional exemptions but for legislative bodies to carve out *statutory* exemptions.

Congress stepped into the breach. In 1993, it enacted the Religious Freedom Restoration Act, whose stated purpose was "to restore the compelling interest test as set forth in [*Sherbert* and *Yoder*] and to guarantee its application in all cases where free exercise of religion is substantially burdened." As initially enacted, the RFRA prohibited *any* government—federal, state, or local—from substantially burdening a person's exercise of religion unless the government could demonstrate that the burden furthered a compelling government interest. In a 1997 case, the Supreme Court invalidated the statute's applicability to state and local law. Congress then revised the RFRA to apply only to federal measures.

Since there were no longer protections below the federal level, states began passing their own versions of the federal RFRA, to ensure that religious liberty enjoyed the same standard of protection from state and local law as it did from federal law.

In many respects, the problems underlying the RFRA are representative of the broader challenge that the growth of government poses to the liberties enshrined in the Bill of Rights. As public regulation grows increasingly pervasive, the risk that it will encroach upon individual liberty grows correspondingly greater.

States are not passing RFRAs to protect the faithful from laws that specifically target the practices of religious groups or institutions. Such statutes are few and far between, and have been dispensed with in short order by the courts under existing First Amendment jurisprudence. Rather, RFRAs seek to protect First Amendment rights from the sort of ubiquitous regulatory creep that has come to define American government in the twenty-first century. For example, state laws requiring autopsies might conflict with the religious beliefs of the deceased and their survivors. Local zoning regulations might prevent homeowners from displaying emblems of then faith on private property. Rules establishing dress and uniform requirements might exclude Jews who wear yarmulkes from military service. And prison regulations may bar observant Muslims from having beards. It would be wrong to suggest that government lacks a compelling interest in any of these cases, all of which have been argued before courts; to take one example, the demand that there be exceptions to military dress creates a potential disciplinary hazard for the armed forces. Rather, the injury that such measures might cause to the individual's right of free exercise is all the *more* reason to require that the government show that a law's means are narrowly tailored to compelling government ends.

The judicial standards established by RFRAs are moderate and measured; the debate provoked by the Indiana law has been anything but. Presented a matter of weeks before the Supreme Court was due to hear oral arguments on the constitutionality of state bans on gay marriage, the statute unleashed a frenzy of public outcry and political posturing that has bordered at times on the surreal. Critics from Al Sharpton to the CEO of Apple Computers have denounced the Indiana law as a modern-day Jim Crow measure designed to relegate gays to a constitutional underclass. A *#boycottIndiana* campaign sprang up on social media, and Angie's List announced that it was canceling a $40-million expansion project in the state on account of the law.

The governors of Connecticut, Washington, and New York banned state-funded travel to Indiana. Connecticut Governor Dannel P. Malloy went so far as to call Indiana's law "disturbing, disgraceful, and outright discriminatory," notwithstanding the fact that his state was the first to pass its own RFRA in 1993. (In fact, the Connecticut RFRA establishes a less exacting standard for religious exemptions than Indiana's: A law must "burden" rather than "substantially burden" a person's free exercise of religion.) And New York State lawmakers denounced the law as "legalized discrimination and injustice against LGBT people."

Then, amid all the histrionics and hyperbole, a small-town pizzeria became Ground Zero in the broader culture war. When the owner of Memories Pizza in Walkerton told a local news reporter she would not cater a gay wedding because doing so would violate her religious beliefs, social media exploded with outrage. The business's Yelp page was inundated with slurs, and threats poured in via social media. The pizzeria had to shut its doors temporarily because of the outcry.

Neither the federal RFRA nor its state counterparts sanction discrimination. The Indiana RFRA, like the federal statute, requires that courts apply the very same standard to laws that impair free exercise as they do to laws that discriminate against racial minorities. What is more, RFRAs stand against a broad backdrop of federal and state anti-discrimination law, not least of which is the Civil Rights Act of 1964. Its Title II prohibits discrimination in public accommodation on the basis of race, color, religion, or national origin. Thus a restaurant owner may not invoke his religious beliefs in refusing service to an interracial couple. Nor, for that matter, could he refuse to cater an interracial wedding.

Same-sex weddings are a different matter, but this has less to do with the RFRAs than it does with the unsettled position of gay rights under state and federal law. Some states, such as New Mexico and Connecticut, have passed local variants on Title II that require businesses offering their services to the general public to do so without regard to the sex or sexual orientation of patrons. In fact, in response to the backlash over the Indiana law, that state's statute was amended to prohibit providers of public accommodations from denying goods and services to individuals on the basis of sexual orientation. Where such local anti-discrimination laws serve a compelling interest by the least restrictive means, gay rights must prevail over First Amendment claims under state RFRAs.

But where such protections are not in place, the right of free exercise of religion must prevail. The Supreme Court may well bring this debate to a close next summer, when it decides whether state prohibitions of same-sex marriage are constitutional. Whatever the outcome of that case, both state and federal courts will be bound to apply RFRAs accordingly. In the meantime, it is at best a benign mistake—at worst, cynical opportunism—to condemn RFRAs as mere pretexts for the violation of civil rights.

The right of free exercise *is* a civil right, and the First Amendment places very real demands on government. Not only do the Establishment and Free Exercise clauses require that government not interfere in religious *belief*, they also limit the government's power to burden religious *practice*. RFRAs establish a clear test against which to balance the rights of the individual and the interests of the state. If the history of religious practice in this nation is anything to go by, the constitutional debate on faith will continue long after the constitutional debate on gay marriage is settled. And for as long as that is the case, these Religious Freedom Restoration Acts are likely to be the most reliable shield individuals have against government encroachments on religious liberty. It is the shield Antigone needed.

Discussion Questions

1. What do you make of the slippery slope argument that if a business owner or local government official claims the right to refuse service to a same-sex couple (by, for example, refusing to bake a wedding cake or issue a marriage license) on the grounds that it violates their religion, could they also refuse to serve, or hire, an African American, a Muslim, a woman, a Jew, or a Born Again Christian, based on a claim of religious belief?

2. Now think about the argument from the other side. If the government can force a caterer to violate her religious belief by, say, fining her if she refuses to serve dinner at a same-sex marriage reception, what else could government mandate? Could the government punish an evangelical Christian computer programmer who refused to design a website for the Freedom from Religion Foundation? An Orthodox Jewish restaurant owner who refused to host a wedding dinner because the bride and groom insisted on having pork served? How would you draw the line?
3. Can you articulate a general rule that resolves questions of when government action should outweigh individual religious beliefs and when individual religious beliefs should prevail?

PART II

Institutions

CHAPTER 5

Congress: The First Branch

22

From *Congress: The Electoral Connection**

DAVID R. MAYHEW

Most people would like to believe that members of Congress are motivated by the desire to make good public policy that will best serve the public and national interest. Some would even support the idea that members of Congress should be willing to go against their constituents' opinions when they think it is the right thing to do. The political scientist David Mayhew argues that politicians' motivations are not so idealistic or complex. Members of Congress simply want to be re-elected, and most of their behavior—advertising, credit claiming, and position taking—is designed to make re-election easier. Further, Mayhew argues that the structure of Congress is ideally suited to facilitate the re-election pursuit. Congressional offices and staff advertise member accomplishments, committees allow for the specialization necessary to claim credit for particularistic benefits provided to the district, and the political parties in Congress do not demand loyalty when constituent interests run counter to the party line.

Mayhew's argument is not universally accepted. Many political scientists accept his underlying premise as a given: elected officials are self-interested, and this is manifest in their constant pursuit of re-election. But others disagree with the premise. Motivations, they argue, are far more complex than allowed for by such a simple statement or theory. People often act unselfishly, and members of Congress have been known to vote with their consciences even if it means losing an election. Others have pointed out that parties now put stronger constraints on congressional behavior than they did when Mayhew was writing in the early 1970s.

The organization of Congress meets remarkably well the electoral needs of its members. To put it another way, if a group of planners sat down and tried

*David Mayhew. From *Congress: The Electoral Connection* (New Haven: Yale University Press, 1974).

to design a pair of American national assemblies with the goal of serving members' electoral needs year in and year out, they would be hard pressed to improve on what exists. * * * Satisfaction of electoral needs requires remarkably little zero-sum conflict among members. That is, one member's gain is not another member's loss; to a remarkable degree members can successfully engage in electorally useful activities without denying other members the opportunity successfully to engage in them. In regard to credit claiming, this second point requires elaboration further on. Its application to advertising is perhaps obvious. The members all have different markets, so that what any one member does is not an inconvenience to any other. There are exceptions here—House members are sometimes thrown into districts together, senators have to watch the advertising of ambitious House members within their states, and senators from the same state have to keep up with each other—but the case generally holds. With position taking the point is also reasonably clear. As long as congressmen do not attack each other—and they rarely do—any member can champion the most extraordinary causes without inconveniencing any of his colleagues.

* * *

A scrutiny of the basic structural units of Congress will yield evidence to support both these * * * points. First, there are the 535 Capitol Hill *offices*, the small personal empires of the members. * * * The Hill office is a vitally important political unit, part campaign management firm and part political machine. The availability of its staff members for election work in and out of season gives it some of the properties of the former; its casework capabilities, some of the properties of the latter. And there is the franking privilege for use on office emanations. * * * A final comment on congressional offices is perhaps the most important one: office resources are given to all members regardless of party, seniority, or any other qualification. They come with the job.

Second among the structural units are the *committees*. * * * Committee membership can be electorally useful in a number of different ways. Some committees supply good platforms for position taking. The best example over the years is probably the House Un-American Activities Committee (now the Internal Security Committee), whose members have displayed hardly a trace of an interest in legislation. [Theodore] Lowi has a chart showing numbers of days devoted to HUAC public hearings in Congresses from the Eightieth through the Eighty-ninth. It can be read as a supply chart, showing biennial volume of position taking on subversion and related matters; by inference it can also be read as a measure of popular demand (the peak years were 1949–56). Senator Joseph McCarthy used the Senate Government Operations Committee as his investigative base in the Eighty-third Congress; later on in the 1960s Senators Abraham Ribicoff (D., Conn.) and William Proxmire (D., Wis.) used subcommittees of this same unit in catching public attention respectively on auto safety and defense waste. With membership on the Senate Foreign Relations Committee goes a license to make speeches on foreign policy. Some committees perhaps deserve to be designated "cause committees"; membership on them can confer an ostentatious identification with salient public causes. An example is the House Education and Labor Committee, whose members, in Fenno's analysis, have two "strategic premises": "to prosecute policy partisanship" and "to pursue one's individual policy preferences regardless of party." Committee members do a good deal of churning about on education, poverty, and similar matters. In recent years Education and Labor has attracted media-conscious members such as Shirley Chisholm (D., N.Y.), Herman Badillo (D., N.Y.), and Louise Day Hicks (D., Mass.).

Some committees traffic in particularized benefits. * * * Specifically, in giving out particularized benefits where the costs are diffuse (falling on taxpayer or consumer) and where in the long run to reward one congressman is not obviously to deprive others, the members follow a policy of universalism. That is, every member, regardless of party or seniority, has a right to his share of benefits. There is evidence of universalism in the distribution of projects on House Public Works, projects on House Interior, projects on Senate Interior, project money on House Appropriations, project money on Senate Appropriations, tax benefits on House Ways and Means, tax benefits on Senate Finance, and (by inference from the reported data) urban renewal projects on House Banking and Currency. The House Interior Committee, in Fenno's account, "takes as its major decision rule a determination to process and pass *all* requests and to do so in such a way as to maximize the chances of passage in the House. Succinctly, then, Interior's major strategic premise is: *to secure House passage of all constituency-supported, Member-sponsored bills.*"

* * *

Particularism also has its position-taking side. On occasion members capture public attention by denouncing the allocation process itself; thus in 1972 a number of liberals held up some Ways and Means "members' bills" on the House floor. But such efforts have little or no effect. Senator Douglas used to offer floor amendments to excise projects from public works appropriations bills, but he had a hard time even getting the Senate to vote on them.

Finally, and very importantly, the committee system aids congressmen simply by allowing a division of labor among members. The parceling out of legislation among small groups of congressmen by subject area has two effects. First, it creates small voting bodies in which membership may be valuable. An attentive interest group will prize more highly the favorable issue positions of members of committees pondering its fortunes than the favorable positions of the general run of congressmen. Second, it creates specialized small-group settings in which individual congressmen can make things happen and be perceived to make things happen. "I put that bill through committee." "That was my amendment." "I talked them around on that." This is the language of credit claiming. It comes easily in the committee setting and also when "expert" committee members handle bills on the floor. To attentive audiences it can be believable. Some political actors follow committee activities closely and mobilize electoral resources to support deserving members.

* * *

The other basic structural units in Congress are the *parties.* The case here will be that the parties, like the offices and committees, are tailored to suit members' electoral needs. They are more useful for what they are not than for what they are.

* * *

What is important to each congressman, and vitally so, is that he be free to take positions that serve his advantage. There is no member of either house who would not be politically injured—or at least who would not think he would be injured—by being made to toe a party line on all policies (unless of course he could determine the line). There is no congressional bloc whose members have identical position needs across all issues. Thus on the school busing issue in the Ninety-second Congress, it was vital to Detroit white liberal Democratic House members that they be free to vote one way and to Detroit black liberal Democrats that they be free to vote the other. In regard to these member needs the best service a party can supply to its congressmen is a negative one; it can leave them alone. And this in general is what the congressional parties do. Party leaders are chosen not to be program salesmen or vote mobilizers, but to be brokers, favor-doers, agenda-setters, and protectors of established institutional routines. Party "pressure" to vote one way or another is minimal. Party "whipping" hardly deserves the name. Leaders in both houses have a habit of counseling members to "vote their constituencies."

Discussion Questions

1. If members are motivated by the desire to be re-elected, is this such a bad thing? After all, shouldn't members of Congress do things that will keep the voters happy? Does the constant quest for re-election have a positive or negative impact on "representation"?
2. How could the institutions of Congress (members' offices, committees, and parties) be changed so that the collective needs of the institution would take precedence over the needs of individual members? Would there be any negative consequences for making these changes?
3. Some have argued that term limits are needed to break the neverending quest for re-election. Do you think that term limits for members of Congress are a good idea?

23

"U.S. House Members in Their Constituencies: An Exploration"

RICHARD F. FENNO, JR.

Through much of the 1970s, political scientist Richard Fenno traveled with House members in their districts, "looking over their shoulders" as the politicians met with their constituents. Fenno was interested in answering the questions, "What does an elected representative see when he or she sees a constituency? And, as a natural follow-up, what consequences do these perceptions have for his or her behavior?" This approach to research, which Fenno called "soaking and poking," gave us new insight into how House members represent their constituents.

In this excerpt from his classic book Home Style: House Members in their Districts, *Fenno argues that members perceive their districts as a set of concentric circles: the geographic, re-election, primary, and personal constituencies. The outer part of the circle is the geographic constituency, which is the entire district. At the center of the circle is the personal constituency—the inner group of advisors who are central to the member's campaign and governing operations (with the re-election and primary constituencies in between). Fenno describes how each part of the constituency has a different representational relationship with the member.*

Fenno also discusses how each member develops a distinctive "home style" in dealing with their constituency, which determines the components of district representation: the allocation of resources, the presentation of self, and explaining of Washington activity. Fenno concludes by pointing out that we have an incomplete picture of how Congress operates if we only focus on what happens in Washington. He says, ". . . the more one focuses on the home activities of its members, the more one comes to appreciate the representative strengths and possibilities of Congress. Congress is *the most representative of our national political institutions."*

Despite a voluminous literature on the subject of representative-constituency relationships, one question central to that relationship remains underdeveloped. It is: What does an elected representative see when he or she sees a constituency? And, as a natural follow-up, what consequences do these perceptions have for his or her behavior? The key problem is that of perception. And the key assumption is that the constituency a representative reacts to is the constituency he or she sees. The corollary assumption is that the rest of us cannot understand the representative-constituency relationship until we can see the constituency through the eyes of the representative. These ideas are not new. They were first articulated for students of the United States Congress by Lewis Dexter. Their importance has been widely acknowledged and frequently repeated ever since. But despite the acceptance and reiteration of Dexter's insights, we still have not developed much coherent knowledge about the perceptions members of Congress have of their constituencies.

A major reason for this neglect is that most of our research on the representative-constituency linkage gets conducted at the wrong end of that linkage. Our interest in the constituency relations of U.S. senators and representatives has typically been a derivative interest, pursued for the light it sheds on some behavior—like roll call voting—in Washington. When we talk with our national legislators about their constituencies, we typically talk to them *in Washington* and, perforce, in the Washington context. But that is a context far removed from the one in which their constituency relationships are created, nurtured, and changed. And it is a context equally far removed from the one in which we might expect their perceptions of their constituencies to be shaped, sharpened or altered. Asking constituency-related questions on Capitol Hill, when the House member is far from the constituency itself, could well produce a distortion of perspective. Researchers might tend to conceive of a separation between the representative "here in Washington" and his or her constituency "back home," whereas the representative may picture himself or herself as a part of the constituency—me *in* the constituency, rather than me *and* the constituency. As a research strategy, therefore, it makes some sense to study our representatives' perceptions of their constituencies while they are actually in their constituencies—at the constituency end of the linkage.

Since the fall of 1970, I have been traveling with some members of the House of Representatives while they were in their districts, to see if I could figure out—by looking over their shoulders—what it is they see there. These expeditions, designed to continue through the 1976 elections, have been totally open-ended and exploratory. I have tried to observe and inquire into anything and everything the members do. Rather than assume that I already know what is interesting or what questions to ask, I have been prepared to find interesting questions emerging in the course of the experience. The same with data. The research method has been largely one of soaking and poking—or, just hanging around. This paper, therefore, conveys mostly an impressionistic feel for the subject—as befits the earliest stages of exploration and mapping.

* * *

Perceptions of the Constituency

The District: The Geographical Constituency

What then do House members see when they see a constituency? One way they perceive it—the way most helpful to me so far—is as a nest of concentric circles. The largest of these circles represents the congressman's broadest view of his constituency. This is "the district" or "my district." It is the entity to which, from which, and in which he travels. It is the entity whose boundaries have been fixed by state legislative enactment or by court decision. It includes the entire population within those boundaries. Because it is a legal entity, we could refer to it as the legal constituency. It captures more of what the congressman has in mind when he conjures up "my district," however, if we label it the *geographical constituency.* We retain the idea that the district is a legally bounded space and emphasize that it is located in a particular place.

The Washington community is often described as a group of people all of whom come from somewhere else. The House of Representatives, by design, epitomizes this characteristic; and its members function with a heightened sense of their ties to place. There are, of course, constant reminders. The member's district is, after all, "the Tenth District of *California.*" Inside the chamber, he is "the gentleman from *California*"; outside the chamber he is Representative X (D. *California*). So, it is not surprising that when you ask a congressman, "What kind of district do you have?", the answer often begins with, and always includes, a geographical, space-and-place, perception. Thus, the district is seen as "the largest in the state, twenty-eight counties in the southeastern corner" or "three layers of suburbs to the west of the city, a square with the northwest corner cut out." If the boundaries have been changed by a recent redistricting, the geography of "the new district" will be compared to that of "the old district."

If one essential aspect of "the geographical constituency" is seen as its location and boundaries, another is its particular internal make-up. And House members describe their districts' internal makeup using political science's most familiar demographic and political variables—socioeconomic structure, ideology, ethnicity, residential patterns, religion, partisanship, stability, diversity, etc. Every congressman, in his mind's eye, sees his geographical constituency in terms of some special configuration of such variables. For example,

> Geographically, it covers the northern one-third of the state, from the border of (state X) to the border of (state Y), along the Z river—twenty-two counties. The basic industry is agriculture—but it's a diverse district. The city makes up one-third of the population. It is dominated by the state government and education. It's an independent-minded constituency, with a strong attachment to the work ethic. A good percentage is composed of people whose families emmigrated from Germany, Scandinavia, and Czechoslovakia. I don't exactly know the figures, but over one-half the district is German. And this goes back

> to the work ethic. They are a hardworking, independent people. They have a strong thought of 'keeping the government off my back, we'll do all right here.' That's especially true of my out-counties.

Some internal configurations are more complex than others. But, even at the broadest level, no congressman sees, within his district's boundaries, an undifferentiated glob. And we cannot talk about his relations with his "constituency" as if he did.

All of the demographic characteristics of the geographical constituency carry political implications. But as most Representatives make their first perceptual cut into "the district," political matters are usually left implicit. Sometimes, the question "what kind of district do you have?" turns up the answer "it's a Democratic district." But much more often, that comes later. It is as if they first want to sketch a prepolitical background against which they can later paint in the political refinements. We, of course, know—for many of the variables—just what those political refinements are likely to be. (Most political scientists would guess that the district just described is probably more Republican than Democratic—which it is.) There is no point to dwelling on the general political relevance of each variable. But one summary characterization does seem to have special usefulness as a background against which to understand political perceptions and their consequences. And that characteristic is the relative homogeneity or heterogeneity of the district.

As the following examples suggest, members of Congress do think in terms of the homogeneity or heterogeneity of their districts—though they may not always use the words.

> It's geographically compact. It's all suburban—no big city in the accepted sense of the word and no rural area. It's all white. There are very few blacks, maybe 2 per cent. Spanish surnamed make up about 10 per cent. Traditionally, it's been a district with a high percentage of home ownership. . . . Economically, it's above the national average in employment . . . the people of the district are employed. It's not that it's very high income. Oh, I suppose there are a few places of some wealth, but nothing very wealthy. And no great pockets of poverty either. And it's not dominated by any one industry. The X County segment has a lot of small, clean, technical industries. I consider it very homogeneous. By almost any standard, it's homogeneous.
>
> This district is a microcosm of the nation. We are geographically southern and politically northern. We have agriculture—mostly soy beans and corn. We have big business—like Union Carbide and General Electric. And we have unions. We have a city and we have small towns. We have some of the worst poverty in the country in A County. And we have some very wealthy sections, though not large. We have wealth in the city and some wealthy towns. We have urban poverty and rural poverty. Just about the only thing we don't have is a good-sized ghetto. Otherwise, everything you can have, we've got it right here.

Because it is a summary variable, the perceived homogeneity-heterogeneity characteristic is particularly hard to measure; and no metric is proposed here. Intuitively, both the number and the compatibility of significant interests within the district would seem to be involved. The greater the number of significant interests—as opposed to one dominant interest—the more likely it is that the district will be seen as heterogeneous. But if the several significant interests were viewed as having a single lowest common denominator and, therefore, quite compatible, the district might still be viewed as homogeneous. One indicator, therefore, might be the ease with which the congressman finds a lowest common denominator of interests for some large proportion of his geographical constituency. The basis for the denominator could be any of the prepolitical variables. We do not think of it, however, as a political characteristic—as the equivalent, for instance, of party registration or political safeness. The proportion of people in the district who have to be included would be a subjective judgment—"enough" so that the congressman saw his geographical constituency as more homogeneous than heterogeneous, or vice versa. All we can say is that the less actual or potential conflict he sees among district interests, the more likely he is to see his district as homogeneous. Another indicator might be the extent to which the geographical constituency is congruent with a natural community. Districts that are purely artificial (sometimes purely political) creations of districting practices, and which pay no attention to pre-existing communities of interest are more likely to be heterogeneous. Pre-existing communities or natural communities are more likely to have such homogenizing ties as common sources of communication, common organizations, and common traditions.

The Supporters: The Re-election Constituency

Within his geographical constituency, each congressman perceives a smaller, explicitly political constituency. It is composed of the people he thinks vote for him. And we shall refer to it as his *re-election constituency*. As he moves about the district, a House member continually draws the distinction between those who vote for him and those who do not. "I do well here"; "I run poorly here." "This group supports me"; "this group does not." By distinguishing supporters from nonsupporters, he articulates his baseline political perception.

House members seem to use two starting points—one cross-sectional and the other longitudinal—in shaping this perception. First, by a process of inclusion and exclusion, they come to a rough approximation of the upper and lower ranges of the re-election constituency. That is to say, there are some votes a member believes he almost always gets; there are other votes he believes he almost never gets. One of the core elements of any such distinction is the perceived partisan component of the vote—party identification as revealed in registration or poll figures and party voting. "My district registers only 37 per cent Republican. They have no place else to go. My problem is, how can I get enough Democratic votes to win the general election?" Another element is the political tendencies of various demographic groupings.

> My supporters are Democrats, farmers, labor—a DFL operation—with some academic types. . . . My opposition tends to be the main street hardware dealer. I look at that kind of guy in a stable town, where the newspaper runs the community—the typical school board member in the rural part of the district—that's the kind of guy I'll never get. At the opposite end of the scale is the country club set. I'll sure as hell never get them, either.

Starting with people he sees, very generally, as his supporters, and leaving aside people he sees, equally generally, as his nonsupporters, each congressman fashions a view of the people who give him his victories at the polls.

The second starting point for thinking about the re-election constituency is the congressman's idea of who voted for him "last time." Starting with that perception, he adds or subtracts incrementally on the basis of changes that will have taken place (or could be made by him to take place) between "last time" and "next time." It helps him to think about his re-election constituency this way because that is about the only certainty he operates with—he won last time. And the process by which his desire for re-election gets translated into his perception of a re-election constituency is filled with uncertainty. At least that is my strong impression. House members see re-election uncertainty where political scientists would fail to unearth a single objective indicator of it. For one thing, their perceptions of their supporters and nonsupporters are quite diffuse. They rarely feel certain just who did vote for them last time. And even if they do feel fairly sure about that, they may perceive population shifts that threaten established calculations. In the years of my travels, moreover, the threat of redistricting has added enormous uncertainty to the make-up of some re-election constituencies. In every district, too, there is the uncertainty which follows an unforeseen external event—recession, inflation, Watergate.

Of all the many sources of uncertainty, the most constant—and usually the greatest—involves the electoral challenger. For it is the challenger who holds the most potential for altering any calculation involving those who voted for the congressman "last time." "This time's" challenger may have very different sources of political strength from "last time's" challenger. Often, one of the major off-year uncertainties is whether or not the last challenger will try again. While it is true that House members campaign all the time, "the campaign" can be said to start only when the challenger is known. At that point, a redefinition of the re-election constituency may have to take place. If the challenger is chosen by primary, for example, the congressman may inherit support from the loser. A conservative southern Republican, waiting for the Democratic primary to determine whether his challenger would be a black or a white (both liberal), wondered about the shape of his re-election constituency:

> It depends on my opponent. Last time, my opponent (a white moderate) and I split many groups. Many business people who might have supported me, split up. If I have a liberal opponent, all the business community will support me. . . . If the black man is my opponent, I should get more Democratic votes than I got before. He can't do any better there than the man I beat before. Except for a smattering of liberals and radicals around the colleges, I will do better than last time with the whites. . . . The black vote is 20 per cent and they vote right down the line Democratic. I have to concede the black vote. There's nothing I can do about it. . . . [But] against a white liberal, I would get some of the black vote.

The shaping of perceptions proceeds under conditions of considerable uncertainty.

The Strongest Supporters: The Primary Constituency

In thinking about their political condition, House members make distinctions within their re-election constituency—thus giving us a third, still smaller concentric circle. Having distinguished between their nonsupporters and their supporters, they further distinguish between their routine or temporary supporters and their very strongest supporters. Routine supporters only vote for them, often merely following party identification; but others will support them with a special degree of intensity. Temporary supporters back them as the best available alternative; but others will support them regardless of who the challenger may be. Within each re-election constituency are nested these "others"—a constituency perceived as "my strongest supporters," "my hard core support," "my loyalists," "my true believers," "my political base." We shall think of these people as the ones each congressman believes would provide his best line of electoral defense in a primary contest, and label them *the primary constituency*. It will probably include the earliest of his supporters—those who recruited him and those who tendered identifiably strong support in his first campaign—thus, providing another reason for calculating on the basis of "last time." From its ranks will most likely come the bulk of his financial help and his volunteer workers. From its ranks will least likely come an electoral challenger.

A protected congressional seat is as much one protected from primary defeat as from general election defeat. And a primary constituency is something every congressman must have.

> Everybody needs some group which is strongly for him—especially in a primary. You can win a primary with 25,000 zealots. . . . The most exquisite case I can give you was in the very early war years. I had very strong support from the anti-war people. They were my strongest supporters and they made up about 5 per cent of the district.

The primary constituency, I would guess, draws a special measure of a congressman's interest; and it should, therefore, draw a special measure of ours. But it is not easy to delineate—for us or for them. Asked to describe his "very strongest supporters," one member replied, "That's the hardest question anyone has to answer." The primary constituency is more subtly shaded than the re-election constituency, where voting provides an objective membership test. Loyalty is not the most predictable of political qualities. And all politicians resist drawing invidious distinctions among their various supporters, as if it were borrowing trouble to begin classifying people according to fidelity. House members who have worried about or fought a primary recently may find it somewhat easier. So too may those with heterogeneous districts whose diverse elements invite differentiation. Despite some difficulty, most members—because it is politically prudent to do so—make some such distinction, in speech or in action or both. By talking to them and watching them, we can begin to understand what those distinctions are.

Here are two answers to the question, "who are your very strongest supporters?"

> My strongest supporters are the working class—the blacks and labor, organized labor. And the people who were in my state legislative district, of course. The fifth ward is low-income, working class and is my base of support. I grew up there; I have my law office there; and I still live there. The white businessmen who are supporting me now are late converts—very late. They support me as the least of two evils. They are not a strong base of support. They know it and I know it.

> I have a circle of strong labor supporters and another circle of strong business supporters. . . . They will 'fight, bleed and die' for me, but in different ways. Labor gives you the manpower and the workers up front. You need them just as much as you need the guy with the two-acre yard to hold a lawn party to raise money. The labor guy loses a day's pay on election day. The business guy gets his nice lawn tramped over and chewed up. Each makes a commitment to you in his own way. You need them both.

Each description reveals the working politician's penchant for inclusive thinking. Each tells us something about a primary constituency, but each leaves plenty of room for added refinements.

The best way to make such refinements is to observe the congressman as he comes in contact with the various elements of his re-election constituency. Both he and they act in ways that help delineate the "very strongest supporters." For example, the author of the second comment above drew a standing ovation when he was introduced at the Labor Temple. During his speech, he spoke directly to individuals in the audience. "Kenny, it's good to see you here. Ben, you be sure and keep in touch." Afterward, he lingered for an hour drinking beer and eating salami. At a businessman's annual Christmas luncheon the next day, he received neither an introduction nor applause when the main speaker acknowledged his presence, saying, "I see our congressman is here; and I use the term 'our' loosely." This congressman's "circle of strong labor supporters" appears to be larger than his "circle of strong business supporters." And the congressman, for his part, seemed much more at home with the first group than he did with the second.

Like other observers of American politics, I have found this idea of "at homeness" a useful one in helping me to map the relationship between politicians and constituents—in this case the perception of a primary constituency. House members sometimes talk in this language about the groups they encounter:

> I was born on the flat plains, and I feel a lot better in the plains area than in the mountain country. I don't know why it is. As much as I like Al [whom we had just lunched with in a mountain town], I'm still not comfortable with him. I'm no cowboy. But when I'm out there on that flat land with those ranchers and wheat farmers, standing around trading insults and jibes and telling stories, I feel better. That's the place where I click.

It is also the place where he wins elections—his primary constituency. "That's my strong area. I won by a big margin and offset my losses. If I win next time, that's where I'll win it—on the plains." Obviously, there is no one-to-one relationship between the groups with whom a congressman acts and feels most at home and his primary constituency. But it does provide a pretty good unobtrusive clue. So I found myself fashioning a highly subjective "at homeness index" to rank the degree to which each congressman seems to have support from and rapport with each group.

I recall, for example, watching a man whose constituency is dominantly Jewish participating in an afternoon installation-of-officers ceremony at a Young Men's Hebrew Association attended by about forty civic leaders of the local community. He drank some spiked punch, began the festivities by saying, "I'm probably the first tipsy installation officer you ever had," told an emotional story about his own dependence on the Jewish "Y," and traded banter with his friends in the audience throughout the proceedings. That evening as we prepared to meet with yet another and much larger (Democratic party) group, I asked where we were going. He said, "We're going to a shitty restaurant to have a shitty meal with a shitty organization and have a shitty time." And he did—from high to low on the "at homeness index." On the way home, after the meal, he talked about the group.

> Ethnically, most of them are with me. But I don't always support the party candidate, and they can't stand that. . . . This group and half the other party groups in the district are against me. But they don't want to be against me too strongly for fear I might go into a primary and beat them. So self-preservation wins out. . . . They know they can't beat me.

Both groups are Jewish. The evening group was a part of his re-election constituency, but not his primary constituency. The afternoon group was a part of both.

The Intimates: The Personal Constituency

Within the primary constituency, each member perceives still a fourth, and final, concentric circle. These are the few individuals whose relationship with him is so personal and so intimate that their relevance to him cannot be captured by their inclusion in any description of "very strongest supporters." In some cases they are his closest political advisers and confidants. In other cases, they are people from whom he draws emotional sustenance for his political work. We shall think of these people as his *personal constituency.*

One Sunday afternoon, I sat in the living room of a congressman's chief district staff assistant watching an NFL football game—with the congressman, the district aide, the state assemblyman from the congressman's home county, and the district attorney of the same county. Between plays, at halftime and over beer and cheese, the four friends discussed every aspect of the congressman's campaign, listened to and commented on his taped radio spots, analyzed several newspaper reports, discussed local and national personalities, relived old political campaigns and hijinks, discussed their respective political ambitions. Ostensibly they were watching the football game; actually the congressman was exchanging political advice, information, and perspectives with three of his six or seven oldest and closest political associates.

Another congressman begins his weekends at home by having a Saturday morning 7:30 coffee and doughnut breakfast in a cafe on the main street of his home town with a small group of old friends from the Rotary Club. The morning I was there, the congressman, a retired bank manager, a hardware store owner, a high school science teacher, a retired judge, and a past president of the city council gossiped and joked about local matters—the county historian, the library, the board of education, the churches and their lawns—for an hour. "I guess you can see what an institution this is," he said as we left. "You have no idea how invaluable these meetings are for me. They keep me in touch with my home base. If you don't keep your home base, you don't have anything."

The personal constituency is, doubtless, the most idiosyncratic of the several constituencies. Not all members will open it up to the outside observer. Nine of the seventeen did, however; and in doing so, he usually revealed a side of his personality not seen by the rest of his constituencies. "I'm really very reserved, and I don't feel at home with most groups—only with five or six friends," said the congressman after the football game. The relationship probably has both political and emotional dimensions. But beyond that, it is hard to generalize, except to say that the personal constituency needs to be identified if our understanding of the congressman's view of his constituency is to be complete.

In sum, my impression is that House members perceive four constituencies—geographical, re-election, primary, and personal—each one nesting within the previous one.

Political Support and Home Style

What, then, do these perceptions have to do with a House member's behavior? Our conventional paraphrase of this question would read: what do these perceptions have to do with behavior at the other end of the line—in Washington? But the concern that disciplines the perceptions we have been talking about is neither first nor foremost a Washington-oriented concern. It is a concern for political support at home. It is a concern for the scope of that support—which decreases as one moves from the geographical to the personal constituency. It is a concern for the stability of that support—which increases as one moves from the geographical to the personal constituency. And it ultimately issues in a concern for manipulating scopes and intensities in order to win and hold a sufficient amount of support to win elections. Representatives, and prospective representatives, think about their constituencies because they seek support there. They want to get nominated and elected, then renominated and re-elected. For most members of Congress most of the time, this electoral goal is primary. It is the prerequisite for a congressional career and, hence, for the pursuit of other goals. And the electoral goal is achieved—first and last—not in Washington but at home.

Of course, House members do many things in Washington that affect their electoral support at home. Political scientists interpret a great deal of their behavior in Washington in exactly that way—particularly their roll-call votes. Obviously, a congressman's perception of his several constituencies will affect such things as his roll-call voting, and we could, if we wished, study the effect. Indeed, that is the very direction in which our conditioned research reflexes would normally carry this investigation. But my experience has turned me in another—though not, as we shall see an unrelated—direction. I have been watching House members work to maintain or enlarge their political support at home, by going to the district and doing things there.

Our Washington-centered research has caused us systematically to underestimate the proportion of their working time House members spend in their districts. As a result, we have also underestimated its perceived importance to them. In all our studies of congressional time allocation, time spent outside of Washington is left out of the analysis. So, we end up analyzing "the average work week of a congressman" by comparing the amounts of time he spends in committee work, on the floor, doing research, handling constituent problems—but all of it in Washington. Nine of my members whose appointment and travel records I have checked carefully for the year 1973—a nonelection year—averaged 28 trips to the district and spent an average of 101 working (not traveling) days in their districts that year. A survey conducted in 419 House offices covering 1973, indicates that the average number of trips home (not counting recesses) was 35 and the number of days spent in the district during 1973 (counting recesses) was 138. No fewer than 131, nearly one-third, of the 419 members went home to their districts *every single weekend*. Obviously, the direct personal cultivation of their various constituencies takes a great deal of their time; and they must think it is worth it in terms of winning and holding political support. If it is worth *their* time to go home so much, it is worth *our* time to take a commensurate degree of interest in what they do there and why.

As they cultivate their constituencies, House members display what I shall call their *home style*. When they discuss the importance of what they are doing, they are discussing the importance of *home style* to the achievement of their electoral goal. At this stage of the research, the surest generalization one can make about home style is that there are as many varieties as there are members of Congress. "Each of us has his own formula—a truth that is true for him," said one. It will take a good deal more immersion and cogitation before I can improve upon that summary comment. At this point, however, three ingredients of home style appear to be worth looking at. They are: first, the congressman's allocation of his personal resources and those of his office; second, the congressman's presentation of self; and third, the congressman's explanation of his Washington activity. Every congressman allocates, presents, and explains. The amalgam of these three activities for any given representative constitutes (for now, at least) his home style. His home style, we expect, will be affected by his perception of his four constituencies.

* * *

It may be, that the congressman's effectiveness in Washington is vitally influenced by the pattern of support he has developed at home and by the allocational, presentational, and explanatory styles he displays there. To put the point most strongly, perhaps we cannot understand his Washington activity without first understanding his perception of his constituencies and the home style he uses to cultivate their support.

No matter how supportive of one another their Washington and home activities may be, House members still face constant tension between them. Members cannot be in two places at once. They cannot achieve legislative competence and maintain constituency contact, both to an optimal degree. The tension is not likely to abate. The legislative workload and the demand for legislative expertise are growing. And the problems of maintaining meaningful contact with their several constituencies—which may make different demands upon them—are also growing. Years ago, House members returned home for months at a time to live with their supportive constituencies, soak up the home atmosphere, absorb local problems at first hand. Today, they race home for a day, a weekend, a week at a time. The citizen demand for access, for communication, for the establishment of trust is as great as ever. The political necessity and the representational desirability of going home is as great as ever. So members of Congress go home. But the quality of their contact has deteriorated. It is harder to sustain a genuine two-way relationship—of a policy or an extra-policy sort—than it once was. They worry about it and as they do, the strain and frustration of the job increases. Many cope; others retire.

* * *

Our professional neglect of the home relationship has probably contributed to a more general neglect of the representational side of Congress's institutional capabilities. At least it does seem to be the case that the more one focuses on the home activities of its members, the more one comes to appreciate the representative strengths and possibilities of Congress. Congress *is* the most representative of our national political institutions. It mirrors much of our national diversity, and its members maintain contact with a variety of constituencies at home. While its representative strengths surely contribute to its deserved reputation as our slow institution, the same representative strengths give it the potential for acquiring a reputation as our fair institution. In a period of our national life when citizen sacrifice will be called for, what we shall be needing from our political institutions are not quick decisions, but fair decisions. * * *

Members should participate in consensus building in Washington; they should accept some responsibility for the collective performance of Congress; and they should explain to their constituents what an institution that is both collective and fair requires of its individual members.

* * *

Discussion Questions

1. Do you agree with Fenno that Congress is the most representative of our national political institutions? If so, does Fenno's argument help address Hibbing and Theiss-Morse's conclusion that Congress may be too responsive (see next article)?
2. Think about your own member of Congress. Does he or she have a strong presence in the district, or does your member seem more like a Washington politician?
3. What do you see as the relationship between how members operate in Washington and what they do in their districts? Should the two be closely tied together (as in Fenno's account of "explaining Washington activity"), or should they be more separate (as with an extensive district-based constituency service operation)?

24

"Too Much of a Good Thing: More Representative Is Not Necessarily Better"

JOHN R. HIBBING AND ELIZABETH THEISS-MORSE

David Mayhew describes an institution that should be highly responsive to voters. If members of Congress want to get re-elected, they need to do what their constituents want them to do. However, John Hibbing and Elizabeth Theiss-Morse argue that having institutions that are too representative may be "too much of a good thing." That is, it may not be in the nation's interest to always do what the public wants, especially when it comes to issues of institutional reform. On questions of reform, the public is usually convinced that the only thing preventing ideal policies is that the "people in power" are serving their own interests rather than the public's interests. According to this view, the obvious—but wrong, according to Hibbing and Theiss-Morse—solution is to weaken political institutions through "reforms" such as term limits, reducing the salaries of members of Congress, and requiring Congress to balance the federal budget every year. Hibbing and Theiss-Morse argue that these reforms might make people even more disillusioned when they discover that weakening Congress will not solve our nation's problems.

The authors also argue that the public generally does not have a very realistic understanding of the inherent nature of conflict in the political process. The public believes that there is substantial consensus on most issues and that only small "fringe" groups disagree on a broad range of issues. If this were true, frustration with Congress would certainly be understandable. But in reality, as the authors point out, the nation is deeply divided about the proper course of action. This makes conflict and compromise an inherent part of the legislative process and, at the same time, dims the prospects for simple reforms.

Reform sentiments are much in evidence on the American political scene as we approach the end of the [twentieth] century, and improving the way public opinion is represented in political institutions is often the major motivation of reformers. This is clear * * * from the activities of contemporary political elites, and from the mood of ordinary people. Gross dissatisfaction exists with the nature of representation perceived to be offered by the modern political system. People believe the political process has been commandeered by narrow special interests and by political parties whose sole aim is to contradict the other political party. Given the centrality of representation in the U.S. polity, the organizers and contributors to this symposium are to be commended. It is laudable to want to consider ways of improving the system and, thereby, making people happier with their government. Many of the ideas described in the accompanying essays have considerable merit.

We do, however, wish to raise two important cautions: one briefly and the second in greater detail. Perhaps these cautions are not needed; the authors of the accompanying pieces are almost certainly aware of them. Still, general debate often neglects these two points. Therefore, quite apart from whether it is a good idea or a bad idea, say, to reform campaign finance, enact term limits, or move toward proportional representation and away from single-member districts, it is important * * * to keep in mind that 1) "because the people want them" is not a good justification for adopting procedural reforms and 2) actual enactment of the reforms craved by the people will not necessarily leave us with a system that is more liked even by the people who asked for the reforms in the first place. We take each point in turn.

Ignoring the People's Voice on Process Matters Is Not Evil

It would be easy at this point to slip into a discussion of the political acumen possessed by the American public and, relatedly, of the extent to which elected officials and political institutions should listen to the people. But such a discussion has been going on at least since the time of Plato and it is unlikely we would add much to it here. Instead, we merely wish to point out that, whatever the overall talents of the rank and file, political change in the realm of process should *not* be as sensitive to the public's wishes as political change in the realm of policy.

It is one thing to maintain that in a democracy the people should get welfare reform if they want it. It is quite another to maintain that those same people should get term limits if they want them. Process needs to have some relative permanence, some "stickiness." This is the *definiens* of institutional processes. Without this trait, policy legitimacy would be compromised. The U.S. Constitution (like all constitutions) drives home this contention by including much on process (vetoes, impeachments, representational arrangements, terms of officials, minimum qualifications for holding particular offices, etc.) and precious little about policy. What policy proclamations *are* to be found in the Constitution have faced a strong likelihood of being reversed in subsequent actions (slavery and the Thirteenth Amendment; tax policy and the Sixteenth Amendment; Prohibition and the Twenty-First Amendment). Constitutions are written not to enshrine policy but to enshrine a system that will then make policy. These systemic structures should not be subjected lightly to popular whimsy.

The framers took great efforts to insulate processes from the momentary fancies of the people; specifically, they made amending the Constitution difficult. It is not unusual for reformers, therefore, to run up against the Constitution and its main interpreters—the courts. Witness recent decisions undermining the ability of citizens to impose legislative term limits on members of Congress save by constitutional amendment. This uphill battle to enact procedural reform is precisely what the Founders intended—and they were wise to do so.

It may be that the people's will should be reflected directly in public policy, perhaps through initiatives or, less drastically, through the actions of citizen-legislators who act as delegates rather than Burkean trustees. But this does not mean that the rules of the system themselves should change with public preferences in the same way health care policy should change with public preferences.

There may be many good reasons to change the processes of government—possibly by making government more representative—but a persuasive defense of process reforms is *not* embedded in the claim that the people are desirous of such reform. Just as the Bill of Rights does not permit a simple majority of the people to make decisions that will restrict basic rights, so the rest of the Constitution does not permit a simple majority of the people to alter willy-nilly the processes of government. There are good reasons for such arrangements.

Be Careful What You Wish For

One important reason we should be glad ordinary people are not in a position to leave their every mark on questions of political process and institutional design is the very good possibility that people will not be happy with the reforms they themselves advocate. The people generally clamor for reforms that would weaken institutions and strengthen the role of the people themselves in policy decisions. They advocate people's courts, an increased number of popular initiatives and referenda, devolution of authority to institutions "closer" to the people, term limits, staff cuts, emaciating the bureaucracy, elimination of committees, cessation of contact between interest groups and elected officials, and a weakening of political parties. These changes would clear the way for people to have greater influence on decisions, and this is what the people want, right?

Actually, our research suggests this is *not* what the people really want. The public does not desire direct democracy; it is not even clear that people desire democracy at all, although they are quite convinced they do. People want no part of a national direct democracy in which they would be asked to register their preferences, probably electronically, on important issues of the day. Proposals for such procedures are received warmly by a very small minority of citizens. Observers who notice the public's enthusiasm for virtually every populist notion sometimes go the next step of assuming the public wants direct democracy. This is simply an inaccurate assumption.

However, the public *does* want institutions to be transformed into something much closer to the people. The public sees a big disconnect between how they want representation to work and how they believe it is working. Strong support of populist government (not direct democracy) has been detected in innumerable polls conducted during the last couple of decades. That the public looks favorably upon this process agenda is beyond dispute. A national survey we conducted in 1992 found strong support for reforms that would limit the impact of the Washington scene on members of Congress. For example, seven out of 10 respondents supported a reduction in congressional salaries, eight out of 10 supported term limitations, and nine out of 10 supported a balanced-budget amendment. What ties these reforms together is the public's desire to make elected officials more like ordinary people. In focus groups we conducted at the same time as the survey, participants stated many times that elected officials in Washington had lost touch with the people. They supported reforms believed to encourage officials to start keeping in touch. Elected officials should balance the budget just like the people back home. Elected officials should live off modest salaries just like the people back home. And elected officials should face the prospect of getting a real job back home rather than staying in Washington for years and years. These reforms would force elected officials to understand the needs of their constituents rather than get swept up in the money and power that run Washington.

If these reforms were put into place, would the public suddenly love Congress? We do not think so. Certain reforms, such as campaign finance reform, may help, since they would diminish the perception that money rules politics in Washington. But the main reason the public is disgruntled with Congress and with politics in Washington is because they are dissatisfied with the processes intrinsic to the operation of a democratic political system—debates, compromises, conflicting information, inefficiency, and slowness. This argument may seem odd on its face, so in the next few paragraphs we provide our interpretation of why the public questions the need for democratic processes.

The public operates under the erroneous assumption that the majority of the American people agrees on policy matters. In focus groups we conducted in 1997, participants adamantly stated that "80 percent of the American people agree on what needs to be done [about serious societal problems], but it's the other 20 percent who have the power." This pervasive and persistent belief in the existence of popular consensus on tough policy issues is, of course, grossly mistaken. Virtually every well-worded survey question dealing with salient policy issues of the day reveals deep divisions in the American public. From welfare reform to health care; from remaining in Bosnia to the taxes-services trade-off; from a constitutional amendment on flag desecration to the situations in which abortion is believed to be properly permitted, the people are at odds with each other.

This level of popular disagreement would be quite unremarkable except for the fact that the people will not admit that the disagreement actually exists. Instead, people project their own particular views, however ill-formed, onto a clear majority of other "real" people. Those (allegedly) few people who allow it to be known that they do not hold these views are dismissed as radical and noisy fringe elements that are accorded far too much influence by polemical parties, self-serving special interests, and spineless, out-of-touch elected officials. Thus, the desire to move the locus of decision making closer to the people is based on a faulty assumption right off the bat. Many believe that if decisions emanated from the people themselves, we would get a welcome break from the fractious politics created by politicians and institutions. Pastoral, common-sensical solutions will instead quietly begin to find their way into the statute books. The artificial conflict to which we have unfortunately become accustomed will be no more and we can then begin to solve problems.

Given people's widespread belief in popular consensus, it is no wonder they despise the existing structure of governmental institutions. All that these institutions—and the people filling them—do is obscure the will of the people by making it look as though there is a great deal of divisiveness afoot. Who then can condone debate and compromise among elected officials if these processes only give disproportionate weight to nefarious fringe elements that are intent upon subverting the desires of healthy, red-blooded Americans? Who then can condone inefficiency and slowness when we all agree on what needs to be done and politicians ought just to do it? Democratic processes merely get in the way. People react positively to the idea that we ought to run government like a business—it would be efficient, frugal, and quick to respond to problems. Of course, what people tend not to realize is that it would also be undemocratic.

Too many people do not understand political conflict: they have not been taught to deal with it; they have not come to realize it is a natural part of a culture such as ours. When they are confronted with it, they conclude it is an indication something is woefully amiss and in need of correction. They jump at any solution perceived to have the potential of reducing conflict; solutions such as giving authority over to potentially autocratic and hierarchical business-like arrangements or to mythically consensual ordinary people.

Our fear is that, if the people were actually given what they want, they might soon be even more disillusioned with the political system than ever. Suppose people *were* made to feel more represented than they are now; suppose authority *were* really pushed toward the common person. The first thing people would learn is that these changes will have done nothing to eliminate political conflict. The deep policy divisions that polls now reveal among the citizenry would be of more consequence since these very views would now be more determinative of public policy. Conflict would still be pervasive. Popular discontent would not have been ameliorated. Quite likely, people would quickly grow ever more cynical about the potential for reform to accomplish what they want it to accomplish.

Instead of allowing the people to strive for the impossible—an open and inclusive democracy that is devoid of conflict—we need to educate the people about the unrealistic nature of their desires. Instead of giving the people every reform for which they agitate, we need to get them to see where their wishes, if granted, are likely to lead them. The people pay lip service to democracy but that is the extent of it. They claim to love democracy more than life itself, but they only love the concept. They do not love the actual practice of democracy because it suggests differences, because it is ponderous, because it revolves around debate (bickering) and compromise (selling out) and divisions (gridlock).

Conclusion

We hasten to point out that we are not opposed to reforms. For what it is worth, we believe the United States polity could certainly benefit from selective modifications to current institutional arrangements. But we *are* opposed to the tendency of many ordinary people to try to enact reforms intended to weaken political institutions even though these same people evince no real plan describing where that power should be transferred. It is often assumed that the people are populists and that they therefore want power in their own hands. As we have indicated, they do not in actuality want power. They only want to know that they could have this power if they wanted it. They only want to know that this power is not being exercised by those who are in a position to use it to their own advantage. They only want decisions to be made nonconflictually. And they are willing to entertain a variety of possible structures (some far from democratic) if those reforms appear to offer hope of bringing about all these somewhat contradictory desires.

Altering representational arrangements should be considered. The current system can and must be improved. The campaign finance system is an embarrassment and the dispute over drawing oddly-shaped districts for the purpose of obtaining majority-minority districts lays bare the very real problems of single member districts. But we should not jump to enact all reforms simply because people think they want them. No one said that in a democracy the people would get to shape processes however they wanted. It is not inconsistent to have democratic governmental structures that are themselves rather impervious to popular sentiments for change in those procedures. What makes the system democratic is the ability of people to influence policy, not the ability of people to influence process.

This is fortunate because the people's ideas about process are fundamentally flawed. People (understandably) think well of the American public writ large, and people (understandably) dislike conflict, so people (nonsensically) assume the two cannot go together in spite of the impressive array of factual evidence indicating that conflict and the American people—indeed any free people, as Madison so eloquently related in *Federalist* 10—go hand in hand. As a result of their misconception, the people will undoubtedly be quite dissatisfied with the actual consequences of most attempts to expand representation via campaign finance reform, term limits, or proportional representation. There may be good reasons to enact such reforms, but, we submit, neither a public likely to be suddenly pleased with the post-reform political system nor a public that is somehow deserving of a direct voice in process reform is one of them.

DISCUSSION QUESTIONS

1. In one of the more provocative claims in their article, Hibbing and Theiss-Morse say, "The public does not desire direct democracy; it is not even clear that people desire democracy at all, although they are quite convinced they do." Do you agree? What evidence do they provide to support this claim?
2. If the public had a more complex understanding of the political process, what types of reforms would it favor?
3. Is it possible to have a political system that is too responsive?

Debating the Issues: Checks and Balances—Too Many Checks, or Not Enough Balance?

For the past decade there has been a growing public perception that Congress can't govern. Battles over raising the debt ceiling, repealing Obamacare, shutting down the government, and refusing to act on President Obama's nomination of Merrick Garland to the Supreme Court in 2016 are indicators of the gridlock that has gripped Washington. President Obama responded by trying to act on his own through executive orders and the regulatory process, which produced a backlash from conservatives against "executive branch overreach."

With the election of Donald Trump and a Republican Congress, gridlock is less of a concern as unified government should allow Republicans to pass much of their policy agenda. However, fear of executive overreach is now coming from the other side of the ideological spectrum. Liberals hope that Congress will prevent some of Trump's more extreme policy proposals from the 2016 presidential campaign (such as deporting 12 million Mexican Americans, building a wall along the Mexican border, preventing all Muslims from entering the country, and starting a trade war with China). Trump's critics take great comfort in our system of checks and balances, arguing that "The Founders anticipated Trump. We can handle this," as a *Los Angeles Times* op-ed said shortly after the election.

Yoni Appelbaum isn't so sure, arguing that our Constitution is more fragile that we might think. He says that our Founders' debates over institutional structures were between those who feared legislative tyranny (the "royalists") and those who feared executive tyranny (the "parliamentarians"). Appelbaum claims the royalists won and created a "mixed monarchy" in which the president had more power than King George III. However, the fragility of our presidential system of separated powers comes from the fact that our president cannot run the show by himself. "Neither Congress nor the president has the capacity to govern alone," Appelbaum points out, "but either can refuse to compromise, and prevent the other from governing." In many other nations that have our system of government, such impasses often lead to military coups or the collapse of the political system. Indeed, the United States' longevity is unique among nations that share our constitutional form of government. Unless we recognize our system's fragility, we may not persist for another 200 years.

Matthew Spalding places the blame for our recent problems more squarely at the feet of Congress. By abdicating its law-making responsibilities, Congress has given too much authority to the bureaucratic executive—a problem that has been 100 years in the making. Congress has slowly allowed its control over lawmaking to slip away as it engages in limited oversight of the bureaucracy and allows the president to dominate through executive orders. The only solution, Spalding argues, "is for Congress to strengthen its constitutional muscles as a co-equal branch of government" by reestablishing its legislative authority and "relearn[ing] the art of lawmaking." The clear means to do this is the power of the purse, which Congress must use with more authority. While this critique was written in the context of President Obama's overreach, Spalding makes it clear that the analysis applies to the new president as well.

25

"America's Fragile Constitution"

YONI APPELBAUM

Over the past few decades, many of the unwritten rules of American political life have been discarded. Presidential appointees, once routinely confirmed by the Senate, now spend months in limbo. Signing statements have increased in frequency and scope, as presidents announce which aspects of a law they intend to enforce, and which they intend to ignore. Annual spending bills stall in Congress, requiring short-term extensions or triggering shutdowns.

The system isn't working. But even as the two parties agree on little else, both still venerate the Constitution. Politicians sing its praises. Public officials and military officers swear their allegiance. Members of Congress keep miniature copies in their pockets. The growing dysfunction of the government seems only to have increased reverence for the document; leading figures on both sides of the aisle routinely call for a return to constitutional principles.

What if this gridlock is not the result of abandoning the Constitution, but the product of flaws inherent in its design?

The history recounted in a recent book on the Constitution's origins, by Eric Nelson, a political theorist at Harvard, raises that disturbing possibility. In *The Royalist Revolution*, Nelson argues that the standard narrative of the American Revolution—overthrowing a tyrannical king and replacing him with a representative democracy—is mistaken. Many leaders of the patriot cause actually wanted George III to intervene in their disputes with parliament, to veto the bills it passed, even to assert that he alone had the right to govern the American colonies. In short, they wanted him to rule like a king. When he declined, they revolted.

As they framed their appeals to the king, Nelson demonstrates, the patriots reached back to the debate leading up to the English civil wars. In the 1620s, the Stuart monarch Charles I feuded with his parliament, which feared that he would usurp its authority to approve taxes, and reign as an absolute monarch. Both sides claimed to be working for the common good. The parliamentarians insisted that only a legislature—a miniature version of the people as a whole—could represent the people's interests. Royalists responded that legislators were mere creatures of their constituencies, bound to cater to voters' whims instead of tending to the kingdom's needs. Only a monarch, they argued, could counterbalance legislative parochialism and look to the long term.

Charles required revenues, but parliament was determined not to authorize taxes on his terms. So from 1629 to 1640, he ruled without calling parliament into session, scraping together funds by reviving moribund fines and fees, and creatively reinterpreting his royal prerogatives. The deadlock led to a series of civil wars from 1642 to 1651, to Charles's execution, and to the ultimate triumph of parliament, which absorbed almost all executive authority, leaving England's monarchs to reign in name alone.

While the wars raged, the early settlers of New England sided squarely with parliament, decrying monarchical tyranny and celebrating its replacement by parliamentary democracy. A century later, however, many of their descendants were nostalgic for Stuart royalism. By the 1760s, parliament was imposing taxes on the colonists without their consent. Patriot leaders like John Adams expressed longing for George III to restrain the legislative tyranny of parliament.

Generations of historians have largely regarded such statements as insincere rhetorical ploys—as arguments of convenience lodged and then quickly forgotten. Nelson makes a convincing case that in so doing, historians have overlooked an important part of the political philosophy that impelled the American Revolution. By citing the king's refusal to act like a king, he writes, the patriots justified taking matters into their own hands.

Once the war was over, Nelson shows, many of the patriot leaders who had previously argued for royal prerogatives proceeded to push for an executive empowered to do what George III would not. At the Constitutional Convention, the Pennsylvania delegate James Wilson stepped forward and moved "that the Executive consist of a single person." This was a loaded phrase with which to introduce a controversial idea: When, in 1649, shortly after executing Charles I, parliament abolished the monarchy, it famously declared, "The office of a King . . . shall not henceforth . . . be exercised by any one single person." Wilson was not just proposing that the United States have a president. He was attempting, in the horrified view of the Virginia delegate Edmund Randolph, to insert into the Constitution "the foetus of monarchy."

Wilson and Randolph, and their respective allies in Philadelphia, revived the old debate between the royalists and the parliamentarians:

Which posed the greater threat, legislative tyranny or monarchy? Had America revolted against a king, or against his parliament? In the end, Nelson argues persuasively, the royalists won.

In this telling, the Constitution created not a radical democracy, but a very traditional mixed monarchy. At its head stood a king—an uncrowned one called a president—with sweeping powers, whose steadying hand would hopefully check the factionalism of the Congress. The two houses of the legislature, elected by the people, would make laws, but the president—whom the Founders regarded as a third branch of the legislature—could veto them. He could also appoint his own Cabinet, command the Army, and make treaties.

The Convention placed limits on the president's powers, to be sure: Some of his actions would be contingent on approval by the Senate, or subject to overrides. But these hedges on presidential authority did not make the office a creature of Congress. Having defeated the armies of George III, the framers seized upon a most unlikely model for their nascent democracy—the very Stuart monarchy whose catastrophic failure had produced the parliamentary system—and proceeded to install an executive whose authority King George could only envy.

Since the American Revolution, many new democracies have taken inspiration from the U.S. Constitution. Around much of the world, parliamentary systems became prevalent, but some countries, particularly in Latin America, adopted the presidential model, splitting power between an executive and a legislative branch.

When, in 1985, a Yale political scientist named Juan Linz compared the records of presidential and parliamentary democracies, the results were decisive. Not every parliamentary system endured, but hardly any presidential ones proved stable. "The only presidential democracy with a long history of constitutional continuity is the United States," Linz wrote in 1990. This is quite an uncomfortable form of American exceptionalism.

Linz's findings suggest that presidential systems suffer from a large, potentially fatal flaw. In parliamentary systems, governmental deadlock is relatively rare; when prime ministers can no longer command legislative support, the impasse is generally resolved by new elections. In presidential systems, however, contending parties must eventually strike a deal. Except sometimes, they don't. Latin America's presidential democracies have tended to oscillate between authoritarianism and dysfunction.

In the 30 years since Linz published these findings, his ideas have enjoyed wide currency among political scientists and seized the imagination of pundits, but gained little purchase among U.S. politicians or the American public at large. America has, after all, defied the odds, through the rise and demise of political parties, through depressions and wars, to the present day. Why would that change? Linz's critics, moreover, suggest that trying to infer immutable laws of politics from a handful of Latin American governments is a pointless exercise.

Even if we discount the failures of other presidential democracies, though, we should not dismiss the fact that the U.S. Constitution was modeled on a system that collapsed into civil war, and that it is inherently fragile. "This is a system that requires a particular set of political norms," Eric Nelson told me, "and it can be very dangerous and dysfunctional where those norms are not present." Once those norms have been discarded, the president or either house of Congress can simply go on strike, refusing to fulfill their responsibilities. Nothing can compel them to act.

Until recently, American politicians have generally made the compromises necessary to govern. The trouble is that cultures evolve. As American politics grows increasingly polarized, the goodwill that oiled the system and helped it function smoothly disappears. In 2013, fights over the debt ceiling and funding for the Affordable Care Act very nearly produced a constitutional crisis. Congress and the president each refused to yield, and the government shut down for 16 days. In November 2014, claiming that he was "acting where Congress has failed," President Obama announced a series of executive actions on immigration. House Republicans denounced him as "threatening to unravel our system of checks and balances" and warned that they would cut off funding for the Department of Homeland Security unless Obama's actions were rolled back. For months, the two sides faced off, pledging fealty to the Constitution even as they exposed its flaws. Only at the eleventh hour did the House pull back from the edge.

Strikingly, in these and other recent crises, public opinion has tended to favor the president. As governments deadlock, executives are inclined to act unilaterally, thereby deepening crises. When parliament refused to provide Charles I with funds unless he met its demands, he moved to circumvent the legislators, and they in turn deposed him. Other presidential systems have collapsed in much the same way.

The framers do not seem to have understood this particular flaw of mixed monarchy. But then, neither did they express absolute faith in their own wisdom. "They were incredibly conscious of the fragility of what they were creating," Nelson says, "that it depends on forbearance." The Constitution was an experiment, and its signers believed that its success was contingent on the willingness of varied constituencies to work together.

When politicians today praise America's system of checks and balances, they seem to understand it as a self-correcting mechanism: When one branch pushes too hard, the other branches must push back, preserving equilibrium. That understanding actually encourages politicians to overreact, in the belief that they are playing a vital constitutional role. It also encourages complacency, because a system that rights itself requires no painful compromises to preserve.

Neither Congress nor the president has the capacity to govern alone, but either can refuse to compromise, and prevent the other from governing. If the system is thought to be indestructible, the temptation to take stands becomes overwhelming. Filibusters, shutdowns, and executive orders multiply. The veneration of the Constitution becomes its undoing.

This is the paradox of America's mixed monarchy, a system that operates best when politicians and the public remain skeptical of its ability to operate at all. Blind faith in the wisdom of the Constitution, and in its capacity to withstand the poor behavior of politicians, will eventually destroy it.

But a constant fear that the entire system will collapse absent frenzied efforts to save it might just help the country continue to defy the odds, and last another 200 years.

26

"Congress' Constitutional Prerogative vs. Executive Branch Overreach"

MATTHEW SPALDING

"In framing a government which is to be administered by men over men, the great difficulty lies in this," Madison writes in *Federalist* 51, "you must first enable the government to control the governed; and in the next place oblige it to control itself."

That meant that, in addition to performing its proper constitutional functions, there needed to be an internal check to further limit the powers of government. For that purpose, the Founders not only divided power, but also set it against itself.

This separation of powers is the defining structural mechanism of the Constitution. It divides the powers of government among three branches and vests each with independent powers and responsibilities.

"The accumulation of all powers," Madison notes in *Federalist* 47, "legislative, executive and judiciary, in the same hands, whether of one, a few, or many, and whether hereditary, self-appointed, or elective, may justly be pronounced the very definition of tyranny." Thus, for "the preservation of liberty," each branch has only those powers granted to it, and can do only what its particular grant of power authorizes it to do.

The Founders were acutely aware that each branch of government would be tempted to encroach upon the powers of the other, and sought to grant each branch of government the means to preserve its rightful powers from encroachments by the others.

The separation of powers and legislative checks and balances discourage the concentration of power and frustrate tyranny. At the same time, they require the branches of government to collaborate and cooperate, limiting conflict and strengthening consensus.

The Rise of Central Administration

The United States has been moving down the path of administrative government in fits and starts from the initial Progressive Era reforms through the New Deal's interventions in the economy. But the most significant expansion occurred more recently, under the Great Society and its progeny.

The expansion of regulatory activities on a society-wide scale in the 1960s and 1970s led to vast new centralizing authority in the federal government and a vast expansion of federal regulatory authority.

When administration is nationalized, though, it does not easily or naturally fall under the authority of one branch or another. As we've seen, bureaucracy and its control created a new source of conflict between the executive and legislative branches.

During the first part of our bureaucratic history, Congress had the upper hand. Congress, after all, had been creating these regulatory agencies to carry out its wishes and delegating its legislative powers to them in the form of broad regulatory authority.

Congress was the first to adapt to the administrative state, continuously reorganizing itself since 1970 by committees and subcommittees to oversee and interact with the day-to-day operations of the bureaucratic apparatus as it expanded.

Rather than control or diminish the bureaucracy through lawmaking or budget control, Congress has settled mostly on "oversight" of the bureaucracy.

Today, when Congress writes legislation, it uses very broad language that turns extensive power over to agencies, which are also given the authority of executing and usually adjudicating violations of their regulations in particular cases. The result is that most of the actual decisions of lawmaking and public policy—decisions previously the constitutional responsibility of elected legislators—are delegated to bureaucrats whose "rules" have the full force and effect of laws.

In 2014, about 220 pieces of legislation became law, amounting to a little more than 3,000 pages of law, while federal bureaucrats issued 79,066 pages of new and updated regulations. The modern Congress is almost exclusively a supervisory body exercising post-legislative oversight of administrative policymakers.

Modern administrative bureaucracies consolidate the powers of government by exercising the lawmaking power, executing their own rules and then judging their application in administrative courts, binding individuals not through legislative law or judicial decision, but through case-by-case rulemaking based on increasingly broad and undefined mandates, all the while less apparent and accountable to the political process and popular consent.

The consequences of the administrative state's lack of accountability have been made much more severe by Congress' current inclination to deal with every policy issue through "comprehensive" legislation.

Congress has ceased to tackle distinct problems with simple laws that can be deliberated upon and then made known to the public. Instead, for everything from health care to financial restructuring to immigration reform, Congress proposes labyrinthine bills that extend to every corner of civil society and impose an ever more complicated and expansive administrative apparatus upon a public that has no way to understand the laws it will be held accountable for.

The Affordable Care Act is a perfect example. This law transferred massive regulatory authority over most health-care decision making to a collection of more than 100 federal agencies, bureaus and commissions.

Likewise, the Dodd-Frank Wall Street Reform and Consumer Protection Act requires administrative rulemakings reaching not only to every financial institution, but well into every corner of the American economy. Its new bureaucracies, like the Consumer Financial Protection Bureau and the Financial Stability Oversight Council, operate outside of the public eye and are subject to virtually none of the traditional checks.

The Consumer Financial Protection Bureau is literally outside the rule of law. It has an independent source of revenue, insulation from legislative or executive oversight and the broad latitude and discretion to determine and enforce its own rulings.

The rise of the new imperial presidency—acting by executive orders more than legislative direction—should come as no surprise, then, given the overwhelming amount of authority that has been delegated to decision-making actors and bodies largely under executive control.

Modern executives can command the bureaucracy to implement new policies without the cooperation of Congress by abusing executive discretion, by exploiting the vagaries of poorly written laws, and by willfully neglecting and disregarding even laws that are clear and well-crafted.

By acting unilaterally without or even against the authority of Congress, the executive assumes a degree of legislative powers without legislative accountability.

Once it has been established that the president with "a pen and a phone" can govern by executive orders and regulations without Congress, it will prove difficult and perhaps impossible to prevent future executives from following this lawless path.

Rebuilding Congress

It may be a prudent option at this point to assert checks and balances through litigation.

A successful lawsuit could prevent things from getting worse, but the legislative branch's going to the judicial branch to solve its disagreements with the executive branch is not going to solve the problem.

If Congress' turning to litigation to assert its constitutional prerogative becomes the norm, it would have the perverse (and unintended) effect of further nullifying the institutional powers of Congress.

The only way to reverse the trend of a diminishing legislature and the continued expansion of the bureaucratic executive is for Congress to strengthen its constitutional muscles as a co-equal branch of government.

Thus, the first step toward restoring the structural integrity of the Constitution is for Congress to reassert its legislative authority and, as much as possible, to cease delegating what amounts to the power to make laws to administrative agencies.

Congress needs to relearn the art of lawmaking. It must regain legislative control over today's labyrinthine state through better lawmaking up front and better oversight after the fact.

Regular legislative order, especially the day-to-day, back-and-forth of authorizing, appropriating and overseeing the operations of government, will do more than anything else to restore the Article I powers of Congress and restore legislative control over today's unlimited government.

The one place where the power of Congress is not entirely lost—and where there's opportunity for gaining leverage over an unchecked executive—is Congress' power of the purse.

Used well, it would also prevent Congress from continually getting cornered in fights over incomprehensible omnibus budgets at the end of every fiscal year, the settlement of which advantages the executive.

Strategically controlling and using the budget process will turn the advantage back to Congress, forcing the executive to engage with the legislative branch and get back into the habit of executing the laws enacted by Congress.

If Congress does not act to correct the growing tilt toward executive-bureaucratic power, the structure of our government will be fundamentally—and perhaps permanently—altered.

It's still possible for Congress to restore its legislative powers, and to correct this structural imbalance. But Congress needs to act as a constitutional institution—indeed, the primary branch of constitutional government.

It must do so by putting down clear markers and drawing enforceable institutional lines before the inauguration of the next president—whoever that may be, and regardless of his or her political party.

Discussion Questions

1. If Appelbaum is correct that our constitutional system is fragile because it depends on informal norms of cooperation to work, is congressional abdication as analyzed by Spalding actually a good thing rather than something to be worried about? That is, by deferring to the bureaucracy and executive action, does Congress allow the government to function even when the president and Congress cannot agree?
2. What problems do you see with Spalding's argument about Congress reasserting its lawmaking authority? Why do you think Congress delegates so much power to the bureaucracy in the first place?
3. Do either of these authors' arguments seem to depend on whether we have unified or divided government?

CHAPTER 6

The Presidency

27

"The Power to Persuade," from *Presidential Power*

RICHARD NEUSTADT

An enduring theme in analyses of the presidency is the gap between what the public expects of the office and the president's actual powers. Neustadt, who wrote the first edition of Presidential Power *in 1960, offered a new way of looking at the office. His main point is that formal powers (the constitutional powers set out in Article II and the statutory powers that Congress grants) are not the president's most important resource. The president cannot, Neustadt concluded, expect to get his way by command—issuing orders to subordinates and other government officials with the expectation of immediate and unquestioning compliance. In a system of "separate institutions sharing power," other political actors have their own independent sources of power and therefore can refuse to comply with presidential orders. Nobody, Neustadt argues, sees things from the president's perspective (or "vantage point"). Legislators, judges, cabinet secretaries, all have their own responsibilities, constituencies, demands of office, and resources, and their interests and the president's will often differ. The key to presidential power is the power to persuade—to convince others that they should comply with the president's wishes because doing so is in their interest. Presidents persuade by bargaining: making deals, reaching compromise positions; in other words, the give and take that is part of politics.*

The limits on command suggest the structure of our government. The constitutional convention of 1787 is supposed to have created a government of "separated powers." It did nothing of the sort. Rather, it created a government of separated institutions *sharing* powers. "I am part of the legislative process," Eisenhower often said in 1959 as a reminder of his veto. Congress, the dispenser of authority and funds, is no less part of the administrative process. Federalism adds another set of separated institutions. The Bill of Rights adds others. Many public purposes can only be achieved by voluntary acts of private institutions; the press, for one, in Douglass Cater's phrase, is a "fourth branch of government." And with the coming of alliances abroad, the separate institutions of a London, or a Bonn, share in the making of American public policy.

What the Constitution separates our political parties do not combine. The parties are themselves composed of separated organizations sharing public authority. The authority consists of nominating powers. Our national parties are confederations of state and local party institutions, with a headquarters that represents the White House, more or less, if the party has a President in office. These confederacies manage presidential nominations. All other public offices depend upon electorates confined within the states. All other nominations are controlled within the states. The President and congressmen who bear one party's label are divided by dependence upon different sets of voters. The differences are sharpest at the stage of nomination. The White House has too small a share in nominating congressmen, and Congress has too little weight in nominating Presidents for party to erase their constitutional separation. Party links are stronger than is frequently supposed, but nominating processes assure the separation.

The separateness of institutions and the sharing of authority prescribe the terms on which a President persuades. When one man shares authority with another, but does not gain or lose his job upon the other's whim, his willingness to act upon the urging of the other turns on whether he conceives the action right for him. The essence of a President's persuasive task is to convince such men that what the White House wants of them is what they ought to do for their sake and on their authority.

Persuasive power, thus defined, amounts to more than charm or reasoned argument. These have their uses for a president, but these are not the whole of his resources. For the men he would induce to do what he wants done on their own responsibility will need or fear some acts by him on his responsibility. If they share his authority, he has some share in theirs. Presidential "powers" may be inconclusive when a President commands, but always remain relevant as he persuades. The status and authority inherent in his office reinforce his logic and his charm.

* * *

A president's authority and status give him great advantages in dealing with the men he would persuade. Each "power" is a vantage point for him in the degree that other men have use for his authority. From the veto to appointments, from publicity to budgeting, and so down a long list, the White House now controls the most encompassing array of vantage points in the American political system. With hardly an exception, the men who share in governing this country are aware that at some time, in some degree, the doing of *their* jobs, the furthering of *their* ambitions, may depend upon the president of the United States. Their need for presidential action, or their fear of it, is bound to be recurrent if not actually continuous. Their need or fear is his advantage.

A president's advantages are greater than mere listing of his "powers" might suggest. The men with whom he deals must deal with him until the last day of his term. Because they have continuing relationships with him, his future, while it lasts, supports his present influence. Even though there is no need or fear of him today, what he could do tomorrow may supply today's advantage. Continuing relationships may convert any "power," any aspect of his status, into vantage points in almost any case. When he induces other men to do what he wants done, a president can trade on their dependence now *and* later.

The president's advantages are checked by the advantages of others. Continuing relationships will pull in both directions. These are relationships of mutual dependence. A president depends upon the men he would persuade; he has to reckon with his need or fear of them. They too will possess status, or authority, or both, else they would be of little use to him. Their vantage points confront his own; their power tempers his.

* * *

The power to persuade is the power to bargain. Status and authority yield bargaining advantages. But in a government of "separated institutions sharing powers," they yield them to all sides. With the array of vantage points at his disposal, a President may be far more persuasive than his logic or his charm could make him. But outcomes are not guaranteed by his advantages. There remain the counter pressures those whom he would influence can bring to bear on him from vantage points at their disposal. Command has limited utility; persuasion becomes give-and-take. It is well that the White House holds the vantage points it does. In such a business any president may need them all—and more.

* * *

This view of power as akin to bargaining is one we commonly accept in the sphere of congressional relations. Every textbook states and every legislative session demonstrates that save in times like the extraordinary Hundred Days of 1933—times virtually ruled out by definition at mid-century—a president will often be unable to obtain congressional action on his terms or even to halt action he opposes. The reverse is equally accepted: Congress often is frustrated by the president. Their formal powers are so intertwined that neither will accomplish very much, for very long, without the acquiescence of the other. By the same token, though, what one demands the other can resist. The stage is set for that great game, much like collective bargaining, in which each seeks to profit from the other's needs and fears. It is a game played catch-as-catch-can, case by case. And everybody knows the game, observers and participants alike.

* * *

Like our governmental structure as a whole, the executive establishment consists of separated institutions sharing powers. The president heads one of these; Cabinet officers, agency administrators, and military commanders head others. Below the departmental level, virtually independent bureau chiefs head many more. Under mid-century conditions, Federal operations spill across dividing lines on organization charts; almost every policy entangles many agencies; almost every program calls for interagency collaboration. Everything somehow involves the president. But operating agencies owe their existence least of all to one another—and only in some part to him. Each has a separate statutory base; each has its statutes to administer; each deals with a different set of subcommittees at the Capitol. Each has its own peculiar set of clients, friends, and enemies outside the formal government. Each has a different set of specialized careerists inside its own bailiwick. Our Constitution gives the president the "take-care" clause and the appointive power. Our statutes give him central budgeting and a degree of personnel control. All agency administrators are responsible to him. But they *also* are responsible to Congress, to their clients, to their staffs, and to themselves. In short, they have five masters. Only after all of those do they owe any loyalty to each other.

"The members of the Cabinet," Charles G. Dawes used to remark, "are a President's natural enemies." Dawes had been Harding's Budget Director, Coolidge's Vice-President, and Hoover's Ambassador to London; he also had been General Pershing's chief assistant for supply in the First World War. The words are highly colored, but Dawes knew whereof he spoke. The men who have to serve so many masters cannot help but be somewhat the "enemy" of any one of them. By the same token, any master wanting service is in some degree the "enemy" of such a servant. A President is likely to want loyal support but not to relish trouble on his doorstep. Yet the more his Cabinet members cleave to him, the more they may need help from him in fending off the wrath of rival masters. Help, though, is synonymous with trouble. Many a Cabinet officer, with loyalty ill-rewarded by his lights and help withheld, has come to view the White House as innately hostile to department heads. Dawes's dictum can be turned around.

* * *

The more an officeholder's status and his "powers" stem from sources independent of the president, the stronger will be his potential pressure *on* the President. Department heads in general have more bargaining power than do most members of the White House staff; but bureau chiefs may have still more, and specialists at upper levels of established career services may have almost unlimited reserves of the enormous power which consists of sitting still. As Franklin Roosevelt once remarked:

> The Treasury is so large and far-flung and ingrained in its practices that I find it almost impossible to get the action and results I want—even with Henry [Morgenthau] there. But the Treasury is not to be compared with the State Department. You should go through the experience of trying to get any changes in the thinking, policy, and action of the career diplomats and then you'd know what a real problem was. But the Treasury and the State Department put together are nothing compared with the Na-a-vy. The admirals are really something to cope with—and I should know. To change anything in the Na-a-vy is like punching a feather bed. You punch it with your right and you punch it with your left until you are finally exhausted, and then you find the damn bed just as it was before you started punching.

* * *

There is a widely held belief in the United States that were it not for folly or for knavery, a reasonable president would need no power other than the logic of his argument. No less a personage than Eisenhower has subscribed to that belief in many a campaign speech and press conference remark. But faulty reasoning and bad intentions do not cause all quarrels with presidents. The best of reasoning and of intent cannot compose them all. For in the first place, what the president wants will rarely seem a trifle to the men he wants it from. And in the second place, they will be bound to judge it by the standard of their own responsibilities, not his. However logical his argument according to his lights, their judgment may not bring them to his view.

The men who share in governing this country frequently appear to act as though they were in business for themselves. So, in a real though not entire sense, they are and have to be. When Truman and MacArthur fell to quarreling, for example, the stakes were no less than the substance of American foreign policy, the risks of greater war or military stalemate, the prerogatives of presidents and field commanders, the pride of a proconsul and his place in history. Intertwined, inevitably, were other stakes, as well: political stakes for men and factions of both parties; power stakes for interest groups with which they were or wished to be affiliated. And every stake was raised by the apparent discontent in the American public mood. There is no reason to suppose that in such circumstances men of large but differing responsibilities will see all things through the same glasses. On the contrary, it is to be expected that their views of what ought to be done and what they then should do will vary with the differing perspectives their particular responsibilities evoke. Since their duties are not vested in a "team" or a "collegium" but in themselves, as individuals, one must expect that they will see things *for* themselves. Moreover, when they are responsible to many masters and when an event or policy turns loyalty against loyalty—a day-by-day occurrence in the nature of the case—

one must assume that those who have the duties to perform will choose the terms of reconciliation. This is the essence of their personal responsibility. When their own duties pull in opposite directions, who else but they can choose what they will do?

* * *

Outside the Executive Branch the situation is the same, except that loyalty to the President may often matter *less*. . . . And when one comes to congressmen who can do nothing for themselves (or their constituents) save as they are elected, term by term, in districts and through party structures *differing* from those on which a president depends, the case is very clear. An able Eisenhower aide with long congressional experience remarked to me in 1958: "The people on the Hill don't do what they might *like* to do, they do what they think they *have* to do in their own interest as *they* see it. . . ." This states the case precisely.

The essence of a president's persuasive task with congressmen and everybody else, *is to induce them to believe that what he wants of them is what their own appraisal of their own responsibilities requires them to do in their interest, not his*. Because men may differ in their views on public policy, because differences in outlook stem from differences in duty—duty to one's office, one's constituents, oneself—that task is bound to be more like collective bargaining than like a reasoned argument among philosopher kings. Overtly or implicitly, hard bargaining has characterized all illustrations offered up to now. This is the reason why: persuasion deals in the coin of self-interest with men who have some freedom to reject what they find counterfeit.

Let me introduce a case . . . : the European Recovery Program of 1948, the so-called Marshall Plan. This is perhaps the greatest exercise in policy *agreement* since the cold war began. When the then Secretary of State, George Catlett Marshall, spoke at the Harvard commencement in June of 1947, he launched one of the most creative, most imaginative ventures in the history of American foreign relations. What makes this policy most notable for present purposes, however, is that it became effective upon action by the 80th Congress, at the behest of Harry Truman, in the election year of 1948.

Eight months before Marshall spoke at Harvard, the Democrats had lost control of both Houses of Congress for the first time in fourteen years. Truman, whom the Secretary represented, had just finished his second troubled year as president-by-succession. Truman was regarded with so little warmth in his own party that in 1946 he had been urged *not* to participate in the congressional campaign. At the opening of Congress in January 1947, Senator Robert A. Taft, "Mr. Republican," had somewhat the attitude of a president-elect. This was a vision widely shared in Washington, with Truman relegated, thereby, to the role of caretaker-on-term. Moreover, within just two weeks of Marshall's commencement address,

Truman was to veto two prized accomplishments of Taft's congressional majority: the Taft-Hartley Act and tax reduction. Yet scarcely ten months later the Marshall Plan was under way on terms to satisfy its sponsors, its authorization completed, its first-year funds in sight, its administering agency in being: all managed by as thorough a display of executive-congressional cooperation as any we have seen since the Second World War. For any president at any time this would have been a great accomplishment. In years before mid-century it would have been enough to make the future reputation of his term. And for a Truman, at this time, enactment of the Marshall Plan appears almost miraculous.

How was the miracle accomplished? How did a President so situated bring it off? In answer, the first thing to note is that he did not do it by himself. Truman had help of a sort no less extraordinary than the outcome. Although each stands for something more complex, the names of Marshall, Vandenberg, . . . Bevin, Stalin, tell the story of that help.

In 1947, two years after V-J Day, General Marshall was something more than Secretary of State. He was a man venerated by the president as "the greatest living American," literally an embodiment of Truman's ideals. He was honored at the Pentagon as an architect of victory. He was thoroughly respected by the Secretary of the Navy, James V. Forrestal, who that year became the first Secretary of Defense. On Capitol Hill Marshall had an enormous fund of respect stemming from his war record as Army Chief of Staff, and in the country generally no officer had come out of the war with a higher reputation for judgment, intellect, and probity. Besides, as Secretary of State, he had behind him the first generation of matured foreign service officers produced by the reforms of the 1920s, and mingled with them, in the departmental service, were some of the ablest of the men drawn by the war from private life to Washington.

* * *

Taken together, these are exceptional resources for a Secretary of State. In the circumstances, they were quite as necessary as they obviously are relevant. The Marshall Plan was launched by a "lame duck" administration "scheduled" to leave office in eighteen months. Marshall's program faced a congressional leadership traditionally isolationist and currently intent upon economy. European aid was viewed with envy by a Pentagon distressed and virtually disarmed through budget cuts, and by domestic agencies intent on enlarged welfare programs. It was not viewed with liking by a Treasury intent on budget surpluses. The plan had need of every asset that could be extracted from the personal position of its nominal author and from the skills of his assistants.

Without the equally remarkable position of the senior Senator from Michigan, Arthur H. Vandenberg, it is hard to see how Marshall's assets could have been enough. Vandenberg was chairman of the Senate Foreign Relations Committee. Actually, he was much more than that. Twenty years a senator, he was the senior member of his party in the Chamber. Assiduously cultivated by F.D.R. and Truman, he was a chief Republican proponent of "bipartisanship" in foreign policy, and consciously conceived himself its living symbol to his party, to the country, and abroad. Moreover, by informal but entirely operative agreement with his colleague Taft, Vandenberg held the acknowledged lead among Senate Republicans in the whole field of international affairs. This acknowledgment meant more in 1947 than it might have meant at any other time. With confidence in the advent of a Republican administration two years hence, most of the gentlemen were in a mood to be responsive and responsible. The war was over, Roosevelt dead, Truman a caretaker, theirs the trust. That the Senator from Michigan saw matters in this light, his diaries make clear. And this was not the outlook from the Senate side alone; the attitudes of House Republicans associated with the Herter Committee and its tours abroad suggest the same mood of responsibility. Vandenberg was not the only source of help on Capitol Hill. But relatively speaking, his position there was as exceptional as Marshall's was downtown.

* * *

At Harvard, Marshall had voiced an idea in general terms. That this was turned into a hard program susceptible of presentation and support is due, in major part, to Ernest Bevin, the British Foreign Secretary. He well deserves the credit he has sometimes been assigned as, in effect, co-author of the Marshall Plan. For Bevin seized on Marshall's Harvard speech and organized a European response with promptness and concreteness beyond the State Department's expectations. What had been virtually a trial balloon to test reactions on both sides of the Atlantic was hailed in London as an invitation to the Europeans to send Washington a bill of particulars. This they promptly organized to do, and the American Administration then organized in turn for its reception without further argument internally about the pros and cons of issuing the "invitation" in the first place. But for Bevin there might have been trouble from the Secretary of the Treasury and others besides.

If Bevin's help was useful at that early stage, Stalin's was vital from first to last. In a mood of self-deprecation Truman once remarked that without Moscow's "crazy" moves "we would never have had our foreign policy . . . we never could have got a thing from Congress." George Kennan, among others, had deplored the anti-Soviet overtone of the case made for the Marshall Plan in Congress and the country, but there is no doubt that this clinched the argument for many segments of American opinion. There also is no doubt that Moscow made the crucial contributions to the case.

* * *

The crucial thing to note about this case is that despite compatibility of views on public policy, Truman got no help he did not pay for (except

Stalin's). Bevin scarcely could have seized on Marshall's words had Marshall not been plainly backed by Truman. Marshall's interest would not have comported with the exploitation of his prestige by a president who undercut him openly, or subtly, or even inadvertently, at any point. Vandenberg, presumably, could not have backed proposals by a White House which begrudged him deference and access gratifying to his fellow-partisans (and satisfying to himself). Prominent Republicans in private life would not have found it easy to promote a cause identified with Truman's claims on 1948—and neither would the prominent New Dealers then engaged in searching for a substitute.

Truman paid the price required for their services. So far as the record shows, the White House did not falter once in firm support for Marshall and the Marshall Plan. Truman backed his Secretary's gamble on an invitation to all Europe. He made the plan his own in a well-timed address to the Canadians. He lost no opportunity to widen the involvements of his own official family in the cause. Averell Harriman the Secretary of Commerce, Julius Krug the Secretary of the Interior, Edwin Nourse the Economic Council Chairman, James Webb the Director of the Budget—all were made responsible for studies and reports contributing directly to the legislative presentation. Thus these men were committed in advance. Besides, the president continually emphasized to everyone in reach that he did not have doubts, did not desire complications and would foreclose all he could. Reportedly, his emphasis was felt at the Treasury, with good effect. And Truman was at special pains to smooth the way for Vandenberg. The Senator insisted on "no politics" from the Administration side; there was none. He thought a survey of American resources and capacity essential; he got it in the Krug and Harriman reports. Vandenberg expected advance consultation; he received it, step by step, in frequent meetings with the president and weekly conferences with Marshall. He asked for an effective liaison between Congress and agencies concerned; Lovett and others gave him what he wanted. When the Senator decided on the need to change financing and administrative features of the legislation, Truman disregarded Budget Bureau grumbling and acquiesced with grace. When, finally, Vandenberg desired a Republican to head the new administering agency, his candidate, Paul Hoffman, was appointed despite the president's own preference for another. In all of these ways Truman employed the sparse advantages his "powers" and his status then accorded him to gain the sort of help he had to have.

* * *

Had Truman lacked the personal advantages his "powers" and his status gave him, or if he had been maladroit in using them, there probably would not have been a massive European aid program in 1948. * * * The President's own share in this accomplishment was vital. He made his contribution by exploiting his advantages. Truman, in effect, lent Marshall and the rest the perquisites and status of his office. In return they lent him their prestige and their own influence. The transfer multiplied *his* influence despite his limited authority in form and lack of strength politically. Without the wherewithal to make this bargain, Truman could not have contributed to European aid.

* * *

Discussion Questions

1. What examples can you identify from the administrations of recent presidents (Bush, Obama, and Trump) in which presidents were unable to get their way via "command," and had to bargain to get what they wanted? Are there examples where a command worked?
2. How should (or can) a president convince a member of Congress to support legislation that the president favors?

28

"Perspectives on the Presidency," from *The Presidency in a Separated System*

CHARLES O. JONES

Just how powerful is the president? Have the fears of some of the framers—that the president would degrade into an imperial despot—been realized, or does the separation of powers effectively check the president's ability to misuse the powers of office? Charles Jones argues that we should view the president as just one of the players in American government; the presidency exists only as one part of a set of institutions where responsibility is diffused, where the bulk of political activity takes place independent of the presidency, and where the different players and institutions learn to adjust to the others. Consider, for example, that President George W. Bush faced a Senate controlled by the Democrats for most of his first two years in office and had to work with them to achieve some of his major goals such as education reform. Or that President Barack Obama left it to Congress to work out many details of health care reform, in contrast to President Bill Clinton, who unsuccessfully attempted to get Congress to enact a major health care reform plan produced by an administration task force. Ultimately, Jones argues, the president is part of a larger "separated system," in which Congress, the courts, and the bureaucracy can shape policy.

The president is not the presidency. The presidency is not the government. Ours is not a presidential system.

I begin with these starkly negative themes as partial correctives to the more popular interpretations of the United States government as presidency-centered. Presidents themselves learn these refrains on the job, if they do not know them before. President Lyndon B. Johnson, who had impressive political advantages during the early years of his administration, reflected later on what was required to realize the potentialities of the office:

> Every President has to establish with the various sectors of the country what I call "the right to govern." Just being elected to the office does not guarantee him that right. Every President has to inspire the confidence of the people. Every President has to become a leader, and to be a leader he must attract people who are willing to follow him. Every President has to develop a moral underpinning to his power, or he soon discovers that he has no power at all.

To exercise influence, presidents must learn the setting within which it has bearing. [Then] president-elect Bill Clinton recognized the complexities of translating campaign promises into a legislative program during a news conference shortly after his election in 1992:

> It's all very well to say you want an investment tax credit, and quite another thing to make the 15 decisions that have to be made to shape the exact bill you want.
>
> It's all very well to say . . . that the working poor in this country . . . should be lifted out of poverty by increasing the refundable income tax credit for the working poor, and another thing to answer the five or six questions that define how you get that done.

For presidents, new or experienced, to recognize the limitations of office is commendable. Convincing others to do so is a challenge. Presidents become convenient labels for marking historical time: the Johnson years, the Nixon years, the Reagan years. Media coverage naturally focuses more on the president: there is just one at a time, executive organization is oriented in pyramidal fashion toward the Oval Office, Congress is too diffuse an institution to report on as such, and the Supreme Court leads primarily by indirection. Public interest, too, is directed toward the White House as a symbol of the government. As a result, expectations of a president often far exceed the individual's personal, political, institutional, or constitutional capacities for achievement. Performance seldom matches promise. Presidents who understand how it all works resist the inflated image of power born of high-stakes elections and seek to lower expectations. Politically savvy presidents know instinctively that it is precisely at the moment of great achievement that they must prepare themselves for the setback that will surely follow.

Focusing exclusively on the presidency can lead to a seriously distorted picture of how the national government does its work. The plain fact is that the United States does not have a presidential system. It has a *separated* system. It is odd that it is so commonly thought of as otherwise since schoolchildren learn about the separation of powers and checks and balances. As the author of *Federalist* 51 wrote, "Ambition must be made to counteract ambition." No one, least of all presidents, the Founders reasoned, can be entrusted with excessive authority. Human nature, being what it is, requires "auxiliary precautions" in the form of competing legitimacies.

The acceptance that this is a separated, not a presidential, system, prepares one to appraise how politics works, not to be simply reproachful and reformist. Thus, for example, divided (or split-party) government is accepted as a potential or even likely outcome of a separated system, rooted as it is in the separation of elections. Failure to acknowledge the authenticity of the split-party condition leaves one with little to study and much to reform in the post–World War II period, when the government has been divided more than 60 percent of the time.

Simply put, the role of the president in this separated system of governing varies substantially, depending on his resources, advantages, and strategic position. My strong interest is in how presidents place themselves in an ongoing government and are fitted in by other participants, notably those on Capitol Hill. The central purpose of this book is to explore these "fittings." In pursuing this interest, I have found little value in the presidency-centered, party government perspective, as I will explain below. As a substitute, I propose a separationist, diffused-responsibility perspective that I find more suited to the constitutional, institutional, political, and policy conditions associated with the American system of governing.

* * *

The Dominant Perspective

The presidency-centered perspective is consistent with a dominant and well-developed perspective that has been highly influential in evaluating the American political system. The perspective is that of party government, typically one led by a strong or aggressive president. Those advocating this perspective prefer a system in which political parties are stronger than they normally can be in a system of separated elections.

* * *

The party government perspective is best summarized in the recommendations made in 1946 by the Committee on Political Parties of the American Political Science Association.

> The party system that is needed must be democratic, responsible and effective. . . .
>
> An effective party system requires, first, that the parties are able to bring forth programs to which they commit themselves and, second, that the parties possess sufficient internal cohesion to carry out these programs. . . .
>
> The fundamental requirement of such accountability is a two-party system in which the opposition party acts as the critic of the party in power, developing, defining, and presenting the policy alternatives which are necessary for a true choice in reaching public decisions.

Note the language in this summary: party in power, opposition party, policy alternatives for choice, accountability, internal cohesion, programs to which parties commit themselves. As a whole, it forms a test that a separated system is bound to fail.

I know of very few contemporary advocates of the two-party responsibility model. But I know many analysts who rely on its criteria when judging the political system. One sees this reliance at work when reviewing how elections are interpreted and presidents are evaluated. By this standard, the good campaign and election have the following characteristics:

- Publicly visible issues that are debated by the candidates during the campaign.
- Clear differences between the candidates on the issues, preferably deriving from ideology.

- A substantial victory for the winning candidate, thus demonstrating public support for one set of issue positions.
- A party win accompanying the victory for the president, notably an increase in the presidential party's share of congressional seats and statehouses so that the president's win can be said to have had an impact on other races (the coattail effect).
- A greater than expected win for the victorious party, preferably at both ends of Pennsylvania Avenue.
- A postelection declaration of support and unity from the congressional leaders of the president's party.

The good president, by this perspective, is one who makes government work, one who has a program and uses his resources to get it enacted. The good president is an activist: he sets the agenda, is attentive to the progress being made, and willingly accepts responsibility for what happens. He can behave in this way because he has demonstrable support.

It is not in the least surprising that the real outcomes of separated elections frustrate those who prefer responsible party government. Even a cursory reading of the Constitution suggests that these demanding tests will be met only by coincidence. Even an election that gives one party control of the White House and both houses of Congress in no way guarantees a unified or responsible party outcome. And even when a president and his congressional party leaders appear to agree on policy priorities, the situation may change dramatically following midterm elections. Understandably, advocates of party government are led to propose constitutional reform.

* * *

An Alternative Perspective

The alternative perspective for understanding American national politics is bound to be anathema to party responsibility advocates. By the rendition promoted here, responsibility is not focused, it is diffused. Representation is not pure and unidirectional; it is mixed, diluted, and multidirectional. Further, the tracking of policy from inception to implementation discourages the most devoted advocate of responsibility theories. In a system of diffused responsibility, credit will be taken and blame will be avoided by both institutions and both parties. For the mature government (one that has achieved substantial involvement in social and economic life), much of the agenda will be self-generating, that is, resulting from programs already on the books. Thus the desire to propose new programs is often frustrated by demands to sustain existing programs, and substantial debt will constrain both.

Additionally there is the matter of who *should* be held accountable for what and when. This is not a novel issue by any means. It is a part of the common rhetoric of split-party government. Are the Democrats responsible for how Medicare has worked because it was a part of Lyndon Johnson's

Great Society? Or are the Republicans responsible because their presidents accepted, administered, and revised the program? Is President Carter responsible for creating a Department of Energy or President Reagan responsible for failing to abolish it, or both? The partisan rhetoric on deficits continues to blame the Democrats for supporting spending programs and the Republicans for cutting taxes. It is noteworthy that this level of debate fails to treat more fundamental issues, such as the constitutional roadblocks to defining responsibility. In preventing the tyranny of the majority, the founders also made it difficult to specify accountability.

Diffusion of responsibility, then, is not only a likely result of a separated system but may also be a fair outcome. From what was said above, one has to doubt how reasonable it is to hold one institution or one party accountable for a program that has grown incrementally through decades of single- and split-party control. Yet reforming a government program is bound to be an occasion for holding one or the other of the branches accountable for wrongs being righted. If, however, politics allows crossing the partisan threshold to place both parties on the same side, then agreements may be reached that will permit blame avoidance, credit taking, and, potentially, significant policy change. This is not to say that both sides agree from the start about what to do, in a cabal devoted to irresponsibility (though that process is not unknown). Rather it is to suggest that diffusion of responsibility may permit policy reform that would have been much less likely if one party had to absorb all of the criticism for past performance or blame should the reforms fail when implemented.

Institutional competition is an expected outcome of the constitutional arrangements that facilitate mixed representation and variable electoral horizons. In recent decades this competition has been reinforced by Republicans settling into the White House, the Democrats comfortably occupying the House of Representatives, and, in very recent times, both parties hotly contending for majority status in the Senate. Bargains struck under these conditions have the effect of perpetuating split control by denying opposition candidates (Democratic presidential challengers, Republican congressional challengers) both the issues upon which to campaign and the means for defining accountability.

The participants in this system of mixed representation and diffused responsibility naturally accommodate their political surroundings. Put otherwise, congressional Democrats and presidential Republicans learn how to do their work. Not only does each side adjust to its political circumstances, but both may also be expected to provide themselves with the resources to participate meaningfully in policy politics.

Much of the above suggests that the political and policy strategies of presidents in dealing with Congress will depend on the advantages they have available at any one time. One cannot employ a constant model of the activist president leading a party government. Conditions may encourage the president to work at the margins of president-congressional interaction (for example, where he judges that he has an advantage, as with foreign and defense issues). He may allow members of Congress to take policy initiatives, hanging back to see how the issue develops. He may certify an issue as important, propose a program to satisfy certain group demands, but fail to expend the political capital necessary to get the program enacted. The lame-duck president requires clearer explication. The last months and years of a two-term administration may be one of congressional initiative with presidential response. The point is that having been relieved of testing the system for party responsibility, one can proceed to analyze how presidents perform under variable political and policy conditions.

* * *

In a separated system of diffused responsibility, these are the expectations:

- Presidents will enter the White House with variable personal, political, and policy advantages or resources. Presidents are not equally good at comprehending their advantages or identifying how these advantages may work best for purposes of influencing the rest of the government.
- White House and cabinet organization will be quite personal in nature, reflecting the president's assessment of strengths and weaknesses, the challenges the president faces in fitting into the ongoing government, and the political and policy changes that occur during the term of office. There is no formula for organizing the presidency, though certain models can be identified.
- Public support will be an elusive variable in analyzing presidential power. At the very least, its importance for any one president must be considered alongside other advantages. "Going public" does not necessarily carry a special bonus, though presidents with limited advantages otherwise may be forced to rely on this tactic.
- The agenda will be continuous, with many issues derived from programs already being administered. The president surely plays an important role in certifying issues and setting priorities, but Congress and the bureaucracy will also be natural participants. At the very least, therefore, the president will be required to persuade other policy actors that his choices are the right ones. They will do the same with him.
- Lawmaking will vary substantially in terms of initiative, sequence, partisan and institutional interaction, and productivity. The challenge is to comprehend the variable role of the president in a government that is designed for continuity and change.
- Reform will be an especially intricate undertaking since, by constitutional design, the governmental structure is antithetical to efficient goal achievement. Yet many, if not most, reforms seek to achieve efficiency within the basic separated structure. There are not many reforms designed to facilitate the more effective working of split-party government.

Discussion Questions

1. How has the first part of the Trump administration reflected (or not) the argument Jones makes? Can a president be effective in radically reshaping that "separated system"?
2. How can Jones's view of the presidency be squared with the popular view that the president is the most powerful person in the world?

Debating the Issues: Should the Electoral College Be Replaced with a Direct Popular Vote for President?

Donald Trump won the 2016 presidential election by winning a majority of the Electoral College votes (306, 36 more than the 270 required to win), even though he lost the popular vote to Hillary Clinton by nearly 3 million votes (roughly 63 million to her 65.8 million). It was the fifth time in U.S. history, and the second in sixteen years, that a president was elected without receiving the most votes. To a modern observer of democratic systems, the election of a popular vote loser seems inconsistent with the majoritarian principle of representative government.

At the time of the Constitution's ratification, the Electoral College was a compromise designed to address concerns of small states worried about being overwhelmed by the power of large states, to respect the importance of states in a federal system, to insulate the presidential election from strong public passions, and to provide the executive a degree of independence from the legislature. It also was designed to require candidates to gain support from across the country: as Alexander Hamilton argued in *Federalist* 68, the indirect process would filter out individuals whose "talents for low intrigue, and the little arts of popularity" might be enough to win the support of one state, and would "require other talents, and a different kind of merit, to establish [an individual] in the esteem and confidence of the whole Union, or of so considerable a portion of it as would be necessary to make him a successful candidate."

But given that our concepts of representation, and the vast differences between how we think of legitimacy now and how the framers thought of it then, does the Electoral College still deserve our deference? Should it be abolished and be replaced with a simple national popular vote?

The three readings in this section provide competing perspectives. In "Democracy Denied," John Nichols, a progressive writer, argues that the Electoral College is an absurd anachronism than violates the fundamental notion that a government founded on "the will of the people" must itself be based on "the premise that the popular vote defines who wins and who loses." While we have corrected other errors in the original compromises that produced the Constitution—by adopting the direct election of Senators and abolishing slavery—he writes that "the most anti-democratic of the founding constructs—an elite Electoral College created to thwart the will of the great mass of voters—remains." Nichols supports the National Popular Vote Compact, in which states have changed their laws to award their Electoral College votes to the winner of the national popular vote, and sees reform as part of a broader move to protect voting rights nationwide.

Richard Posner, a retired federal judge, wrote in 2012 that the Electoral College has five crucial advantages: it ensures a definitive outcome, requires a candidate to have national appeal, gives swing state voters an incentive to pay close attention to candidates, gives large states due importance, and ensures that the winner has an absolute majority of votes. Posner dismisses the criticism that the Electoral College is undemocratic: "No form of representative democracy . . . is or aspires to be perfectly democratic." The entire federal judiciary, for example, (appointed to life terms) is manifestly undemocratic.

Guelzo (a professor of history) and Hulme (an attorney in Washington, D.C.) defend the Electoral College in the context of the 2016 results. They stress the importance of the institution to our federal system, and argue that "the Electoral College is preeminently both a symbol and a practical implementation of that federalism." They specifically contest the notion that the Electoral College was connected to the protection of slavery (as Nichols argues), and maintain that the claim is "more of a rhetorical posture than a serious argument."

29

"Democracy Denied"

John Nichols

In the mid-1980s, shortly after Ronald Reagan won a forty-nine-state landslide victory in his campaign for a second term, David Bowie had a top-forty hit with a haunting song from the soundtrack to the spy drama *The Falcon and the Snowman*. The song resonated with people who felt disconnected from their nation. It was titled "This Is Not America."

Sometimes, of course, an election result *is* America: a Franklin Roosevelt or a Dwight Eisenhower or a Lyndon Johnson wins so decisively that the President can claim a genuine mandate. As frustrating as it may have been for a lot of us, Ronald Reagan won big in 1984—the year George Orwell had warned about.

But what about those times when the "winner" is not the winner at all? What about those years when the finish of a long campaign is in conflict with itself?

There is always a tendency on the part of major media outlets and political insiders to suggest that the United States is defined by the prominent men and women who take office after elections. Too frequently, even those of us who dissent from the conventional wisdom of American politics fall into the trap of imagining that the headlines declaring who has won define our times. But when that is not the case, there is a duty to speak the truth: "This is not America."

Such is our circumstance today.

The Washington Post's post-election headline declared, "Trump Triumphs." The *New York Post* trumpeted, "President Trump: They Said It Couldn't Happen."

But it didn't actually happen in the way that so much of the media imagines. Trump's America is not America. In order to imagine that Trump's presidency has a triumphant mandate, or even the barest measure of democratic legitimacy, Americans must surrender to the hoax that media branding is reality.

The reality, as Michael Moore noted in caps, is that "HILLARY CLINTON WON THE POPULAR VOTE!" "If you woke up this morning thinking you live in an effed-up country, you don't," the filmmaker explained on the day after the election, stating what the headlines did not: "Your fellow Americans wanted Hillary, not Trump."

Democracies and democratic republics that take seriously the notion that governing extends from the will of the people begin with the premise that the popular vote defines who wins and who loses. In other countries that elect presidents, Hillary Clinton's popular-vote victory would have her preparing for an inauguration. In America, it had her walking her dogs on the day after her concession speech.

On election night, Clinton's win was a narrow one. But the United States has archaic systems for casting and counting ballots, which means that the tabulation process stretches out for weeks, even months, after the polls close. One week after the election, Clinton's lead had grown to more than one million votes. The Democratic advantage will just keep expanding, as the longest counts tend to be in West Coast states such as California, where Clinton is leading Trump by an almost 2-to-1 margin. Nate Cohn argues that Clinton could end up winning by two million votes and more than 1.5 percent of the total; others suggest the margin could go higher.

Even as the count progressed, Clinton's winning margin grew greater than Richard Nixon's in 1968. It was greater than John F. Kennedy's in 1960. In fact, it was greater than the winning margin in more than twenty of the presidential elections the United States has held since its founding. Of course, the elections of the distant past had smaller overall turnouts. But Kennedy and Nixon were elected in high turnout elections in relatively recent times.

And there's an even more recent election that offers an even more relevant comparison. In 2000, Democrat Al Gore beat Republican George W. Bush by 543,895 votes. At the time, that was the biggest ever popular-vote victory for someone who lost the presidency. But Hillary Clinton's popular-vote victory over Donald Trump is already dramatically greater than Gore's.

At the same time, the final 2016 count will give Trump a substantially lower percentage of the overall vote than Republican Mitt Romney received in his losing 2012 challenge to Democratic President Barack Obama.

But none of this matters, we are told, because Trump will prevail by a narrow margin in the December vote by the 538 members of the Electoral College.

So how do 538 electors trump—apologies—the choice of the more than 120,000,000 actual voters for the presidency? Because they represent a relic of the same set of founding compromises that permitted human bondage in a land where the Declaration of Independence announced "all men are created equal." The Electoral College is, constitutional scholars say, a "vestige of slavery," and was created to help protect that institution. The goal, history reminds us, was to keep the more populous northern states from overruling the South.

"It's embarrassing," argues Paul Finkelman, a law professor who has studied the institution. "I think if most Americans knew what the origins of the Electoral College is, they would be disgusted."

The Constitution has been amended frequently to correct the errors of the past. The franchise has been extended to African Americans and women; the poll tax has been banned; the voting age has been lowered. The old practice of choosing Senators via backroom deals has been replaced with an elected Senate. Yet the most anti-democratic of the founding constructs—an elite Electoral College created to thwart the will of the great mass of voters—remains.

The Electoral College warps and diminishes American democracy at every turn. As George C. Edwards III, a political science professor at Texas A&M University who edits the *Presidential Studies Quarterly*, tells us: "The Electoral College . . . has the potential to undo the people's will at many points in the long journey from the selection of electors to counting their votes in Congress."

Consider this: In Wyoming, each elector represents roughly 160,000 eligible voters, compared with the more than 600,000 eligible voters represented by an elector from California.

Often this warping and diminishment is obscured when the Electoral College's choice mirrors that of the national popular vote. The Electoral College only gets major attention when the college's choice diverges from the national popular vote.

What Americans need to recognize is that such major malfunctions are becoming more common.

For the second time in sixteen years, the national popular vote decision is going to be overridden by the Electoral College. Trump has a narrow advantage in the Electoral College (so narrow that a shift of just 57,000 votes would have made Clinton the winner in the three states she needed—Michigan,

Pennsylvania and Wisconsin—to gain the 270 electors required to prevail). But that advantage is definitional under the current system.

This is a problem.

To be fair, it is a problem that has been flagged since 1787.

The group FairVote tells us that more than 700 constitutional amendments have been proposed to modify or abolish the Electoral College, "making it the subject of more attempted reforms than any other subject." A proposal to replace the current allocation of state electors on a winner-take-all basis with a proportional electoral vote gained the endorsement of the Senate in the 1950s but failed in the House. A proposal to abolish the Electoral College won the support of the House in 1969 but was blocked by a Senate filibuster led by southern Senators who had opposed civil rights legislation.

Even Donald Trump griped that "the Electoral College is a disaster for a democracy"—but that was in 2012, not 2016.

The trouble with historic attempts to replace or reform the Electoral College is that they tended to be based on frustrations and fears extending from a particular election result, and thus absorbed in the closed circle of Congress.

The aftermath of the 2016 election, in which the Electoral College has again proven to be a disaster for democracy, can and must be different. There are many proper reactions to this election, including solidarity movements to defend those most threatened by the combination of a Trump presidency and a fiercely right-wing Congress. But if ever an election demanded a mass movement for reform, this is it.

Yes, this Congress is disinclined toward reform. But FairVote and other groups are advancing a credible vehicle for getting around Congress, and it has already gained considerable traction. Activists want state legislatures to endorse a National Popular Vote compact, which requires states to "choose to allocate their electoral votes to the candidate who wins the most popular votes in all fifty states and the District of Columbia."

Ten states and the District of Columbia—with a combined total of 165 electoral votes—have passed legislation to enter the compact. And the idea has been proposed in the legislatures of the remaining states. This is a real reform plan. But it does not need to be the only one. What is necessary now is for Americans to organize on behalf of a constitutional amendment to abolish the Electoral College, or at the least to reform it with a proportional representation plan. We can sort out the specifics later. But this moment cannot be lost to frustration at a rigged system, or hopelessness about prospects for reform.

This should be a moment of radical urgency. Activism to abolish the Electoral College should be combined with advocacy to end the corrupt practice of gerrymandering, which allows incumbent politicians and their allies to draw maps of voting districts that are skewed to prevent competition. (Since 2010, these have been used to lock in Republican control of the U.S. House of Representatives. In 2012, for instance, GOP House candidates won 49 percent of the votes and 54 percent of the seats.)

Any movement for real democracy must also address voter suppression, which played a profound role in the 2016 election. Restrictive voter ID laws, complex registration procedures, limits on early voting, and cuts in the number of polling places undermined democracy in jurisdictions across the country and, voting rights activists argue, contributed to declines in turnout that benefited Trump and his allies.

This was the first national election in fifty years that was not conducted under the full protection of the Voting Rights Act of 1965. That is a travesty, yet there is little chance that a Congress led by House Speaker Paul Ryan and Senate Majority Leader Mitch McConnell will renew the act's protections, especially under a President who has dismissed efforts to make voting easy and efficient as the "rigging" of elections.

The time really has come to embrace the proposal by Democratic Congressmen Keith Ellison of Minnesota and Mark Pocan of Wisconsin to amend the Constitution to declare: "Every citizen of the United States, who is of legal voting age, shall have the fundamental right to vote in any public election."

The same goes for the amendment proposed by Vermont Senator Bernie Sanders to overturn the U.S. Supreme Court's anti-democratic rulings in cases including the 2010 *Citizens United* decision. Only an amendment will address the flow of billionaire and corporate money into our politics, which in 2016 Senate races proved decisive.

Yes, it requires hard work to amend the Constitution. But the document has been updated twenty-seven times since 1787, often in moments as difficult and divisive and challenging as these. And the American people are ready to make the change. * * *

The anger, the frustration, the fear and loathing that extends from the 2016 presidential race is real. It will find many expressions. One of them must be a bold and unapologetic call for democracy—a call grounded in the recognition that Donald Trump did not win a mandate. He did not even win the popular vote. And a system that allows the loser to win is not sufficient for a nation that proposes to be of, by, and for the people. * * *

It will not be easy. But if the 2016 election has taught us anything, it is that radical reform is necessary. We renew ourselves not with bitterness, but with a commitment to make the change that brings democracy to the United States of America.

30

"In Defense of the Electoral College"

RICHARD A. POSNER

The Electoral College is widely regarded as an anachronism, a nondemocratic method of selecting a president that ought to be superseded by declaring the candidate who receives the most popular votes the winner. The advocates of this position are correct in arguing that the Electoral College method is not democratic in a modern sense. The Constitution provides that "Each State shall appoint, in such Manner as the Legislature thereof may direct, a Number of Electors, equal to the whole Number of Senators and Representatives to which the State may be entitled in the Congress." And it is the electors who elect the president, not the people. When you vote for a presidential candidate you're actually voting for a slate of electors.

But each party selects a slate of electors trusted to vote for the party's nominee (and that trust is rarely betrayed). Because virtually all states award all their electoral votes to the winner of the popular vote in the state, and because the Electoral College weights the less populous states more heavily along the lines of the Senate (two Senators and two Electoral College votes for every state, and then more electoral votes added for each state based on population), it is entirely possible that the winner of the electoral vote will not win the national popular vote. Yet that has happened very rarely. It happened in 2000, when Gore had more popular votes than Bush yet fewer electoral votes, but that was the first time since 1888.

There are five reasons for retaining the Electoral College despite its lack of democratic pedigree; all are practical reasons, not liberal or conservative reasons.

1) Certainty of Outcome

A dispute over the outcome of an Electoral College vote is possible—it happened in 2000—but it's less likely than a dispute over the popular vote. The reason is that the winning candidate's share of the Electoral College invariably exceeds his share of the popular vote. In last week's election, for example, Obama received 61.7 percent of the electoral vote compared to only 51.3 percent of the popular votes cast for him and Romney. (I ignore the scattering of votes not counted for either candidate.) Because almost all states award electoral votes on a winner-take-all basis, even a very slight plurality in a state creates a landslide electoral-vote victory in that state. A tie in the nationwide electoral vote is possible because the total number of votes—538—is an even number, but it is highly unlikely.

Of course a tie in the number of popular votes in a national election in which tens of millions of votes are cast is even more unlikely. But if the difference in the popular vote is small, then if the winner of the popular vote were deemed the winner of the presidential election, candidates would have an incentive to seek a recount in any state (plus the District of Columbia) in which they thought the recount would give them more additional votes than their opponent. The lawyers would go to work in state after state to have the votes recounted, and the result would be debilitating uncertainty, delay, and conflict—look at the turmoil that a dispute limited to one state, Florida, engendered in 2000.

2) Everyone's President

The Electoral College requires a presidential candidate to have transregional appeal. No region (South, Northeast, etc.) has enough electoral votes to elect a president. So a solid regional favorite, such as Romney was in the South, has no incentive to campaign heavily in those states, for he gains no electoral votes by increasing his plurality in states that he knows he will win. This is a desirable result because a candidate with only regional appeal is unlikely to be a successful president. The residents of the other regions are likely to feel disfranchised—to feel that their votes do not count, that the new president will have no regard for their interests, that he really isn't their president.

3) Swing States

The winner-take-all method of awarding electoral votes induces the candidates—as we saw in last week's election—to focus their campaign efforts on the toss-up states; that follows directly from the candidates' lack of inducement to campaign in states they are sure to win. Voters in toss-up states are more likely to pay close attention to the campaign—to really *listen* to the competing candidates—knowing that they are going to decide the election. They are likely to be the most thoughtful voters, on average (and for the further reason that they will have received the most information and attention from the candidates), and the most thoughtful voters should be the ones to decide the election.

4) Big States

The Electoral College restores some of the weight in the political balance that large states (by population) lose by virtue of the malapportionment of the Senate decreed in the Constitution. This may seem paradoxical, given that electoral votes are weighted in favor of less populous states. Wyoming, the least populous state, contains only about one-sixth of 1 percent of the U.S. population, but its three electors (of whom two are awarded only because

Wyoming has two senators like every other state) give it slightly more than one-half of 1 percent of total electoral votes. But winner-take-all makes a slight increase in the popular vote have a much bigger electoral-vote payoff in a large state than in a small one. The popular vote was very close in Florida; nevertheless Obama, who won that vote, got 29 electoral votes. A victory by the same margin in Wyoming would net the winner only 3 electoral votes. So, other things being equal, a large state gets more attention from presidential candidates in a campaign than a small states does. And since presidents and senators are often presidential candidates, large states are likely to get additional consideration in appropriations and appointments from presidents and senators before as well as during campaigns, offsetting to some extent the effects of the malapportioned Senate on the political influence of less populous states.

5) Avoid Run-Off Elections

The Electoral College avoids the problem of elections in which no candidate receives a majority of the votes cast. For example, Nixon in 1968 and Clinton in 1992 both had only a 43 percent plurality of the popular votes, while winning a majority in the Electoral College (301 and 370 electoral votes, respectively). There is pressure for run-off elections when no candidate wins a majority of the votes cast; that pressure, which would greatly complicate the presidential election process, is reduced by the Electoral College, which invariably produces a clear winner.

Against these reasons to retain the Electoral College the argument that it is undemocratic falls flat. No form of representative democracy, as distinct from direct democracy, is or aspires to be perfectly democratic. Certainly not our federal government. In the entire executive and judicial branches, only two officials are elected—the president and vice president. All the rest are appointed—federal Article III judges for life.

It can be argued that the Electoral College method of selecting the president may turn off potential voters for a candidate who has no hope of carrying their state—Democrats in Texas, for example, or Republicans in California. Knowing their vote will have no effect, they have less incentive to pay attention to the campaign than they would have if the president were picked by popular vote, for then the state of a voter's residence would be irrelevant to the weight of his vote. But of course no voter's vote swings a national election, and in spite of that, about one-half the eligible American population did vote in last week's election. Voters in presidential elections are people who want to express a political preference rather than people who think that a single vote may decide an election. Even in one-sided states, there are plenty of votes in favor of the candidate who is sure not to carry the state. So I doubt that the Electoral College has much of a turn-off effect. And if it does, that is outweighed by the reasons for retaining this seemingly archaic institution.

31

"In Defense of the Electoral College"

ALLEN GUELZO AND JAMES HULME

There is hardly anything in the Constitution harder to explain, or easier to misunderstand, than the Electoral College. And when a presidential election hands the palm to a candidate who comes in second in the popular vote but first in the Electoral College tally, something deep in our democratic viscera balks and asks why the Electoral College shouldn't be dumped as a useless relic of eighteenth-century white, gentry privilege.

Actually, there have been only five occasions when a closely divided popular vote and the electoral vote have failed to point in the same direction. No matter. After last week's results, we're hearing a litany of complaints: the Electoral College is undemocratic, the Electoral College is unnecessary, the Electoral College was invented to protect slavery—and the demand to push it down the memory hole.

All of which is strange because the Electoral College is at the core of our system of federalism. The Founders who sat in the 1787 Constitutional Convention lavished an extraordinary amount of argument on the Electoral College, and it was by no means one-sided. The great Pennsylvania jurist James Wilson believed that "if we are to establish a national Government," the president should be chosen by a direct, national vote of the people. But wise old Roger Sherman of Connecticut replied that the president ought to be elected by Congress, since he feared that direct election of presidents by the people would lead to the creation of a monarchy. "An independence of the Executive [from] the supreme Legislature, was in his opinion the very essence of tyranny if there was any such thing." Sherman was not trying to undermine the popular will, but to keep it from being distorted by a president who mistook popular election as a mandate for dictatorship.

Quarrels like this flared all through the convention, until, at almost the last minute, James Madison "took out a Pen and Paper, and sketched out a mode of Electing the President" by a "college" of "Electors . . . chosen by those of the people in each State, who shall have the Qualifications requisite."

The Founders also designed the operation of the Electoral College with unusual care. The portion of Article 2, Section 1, describing the Electoral College is longer and descends to more detail than any other single issue the Constitution addresses. More than the federal judiciary—more than the war powers—more than taxation and representation. It prescribes in precise detail how "Each State shall appoint . . . a Number of Electors, equal to the whole Number of Senators and Representatives to which the State may be entitled in the Congress"; how these electors "shall vote by Ballot" for a president and vice president; how they "shall sign and certify, and transmit sealed to the Seat of the Government of the United States, directed to the President of the Senate" the results of their balloting; how a tie vote must be resolved; what schedule the balloting should follow; and on and on.

Above all, the Electoral College had nothing to do with slavery. Some historians have branded the Electoral College this way because each state's electoral votes are based on that "whole Number of Senators and Representatives" from each State, and in 1787 the number of those representatives was calculated on the basis of the infamous 3/5ths clause. But the Electoral College merely reflected the numbers, not any bias about slavery (and in any case, the 3/5ths clause was not quite as proslavery a compromise as it seems, since Southern slaveholders wanted their slaves counted as 5/5ths for determining representation in Congress, and had to settle for a whittled-down fraction). As much as the abolitionists before the Civil War liked to talk about the "proslavery Constitution," this was more of a rhetorical posture than a serious historical argument. And the simple fact remains, from the record of the Constitutional Convention's proceedings (James Madison's famous Notes), that the discussions of the Electoral College and the method of electing a president never occur in the context of any of the convention's two climactic debates over slavery.

If anything, it was the Electoral College that made it possible to end slavery, since Abraham Lincoln earned only 39 percent of the popular vote in the election of 1860, but won a crushing victory in the Electoral College. This, in large measure, was why Southern slaveholders stampeded to secession in 1860–61. They could do the numbers as well as anyone, and realized that the Electoral College would only produce more anti-slavery Northern presidents.

Yet, even on those terms, it is hard for Americans to escape the uncomfortable sense that, by inserting an extra layer of "electors" between the people and the president, the Electoral College is something less than democratic. But even if we are a democratic nation, that is not all we are. The Constitution also makes us a federal union, and the Electoral College is preeminently both the symbol and a practical implementation of that federalism.

The states of the union existed before the Constitution, and in a practical sense, existed long before the revolution. Nothing guaranteed that, in 1776, the states would all act together, and nothing guaranteed that after the Revolution they might not go their separate and quarrelsome ways, much like the German states of the eighteenth century or the South American republics in the nineteenth century. The genius of the Constitutional Convention was its ability to entice the American states into a "more perfect union." But it was still a union of states, and we probably wouldn't have had a constitution or a country at all unless the route we took was federalism.

The Electoral College was an integral part of that federal plan. It made a place for the states as well as the people in electing the president by giving them a say at different points in a federal process and preventing big-city populations from dominating the election of a president.

Abolishing the Electoral College now might satisfy an irritated yearning for direct democracy, but it would also mean dismantling federalism. After that, there would be no sense in having a Senate (which, after all, represents the interests of the states), and further along, no sense even in having states, except as administrative departments of the central government. Those who wish to abolish the Electoral College ought to go the distance, and do away with the entire federal system and perhaps even retire the Constitution, since the federalism it was designed to embody would have disappeared.

None of that, ironically, is liable to produce a more democratic election system. There are plenty of democracies, like Great Britain, where no one ever votes directly for a head of the government. But more important, the Electoral College actually keeps presidential elections from going undemocratically awry because it makes unlikely the possibility that third-party candidates will gather enough votes to make it onto the electoral scoreboard.

Without the Electoral College, there would be no effective brake on the number of "viable" presidential candidates. Abolish it, and it would not be difficult to imagine a scenario where, in a field of a dozen micro-candidates, the "winner" only needs 10 percent of the vote, and represents less than 5 percent of the electorate. And presidents elected with smaller and smaller pluralities will only aggravate the sense that an elected president is governing without a real electoral mandate.

The Electoral College has been a major, even if poorly comprehended, mechanism for stability in a democracy, something which democracies are sometimes too flighty to appreciate. It may appear inefficient. But the Founders were not interested in efficiency; they were interested in securing "the blessings of liberty." The Electoral College is, in the end, not a bad device for securing that.

Discussion Questions

1. One other argument in favor of the Electoral College is that it "contains" electoral disputes: there is no reason for the losing candidate to contest the election in a state unless that state is pivotal in getting past the 270 vote threshold (as was the case in Florida in 2000). Is there merit in this argument? Would a national popular vote be more likely to produce a disputed result?

2. Defenders of the Electoral College often claim (as Posner, Guelzo, and Hulme do here) that it discourages multiple candidacies and third parties. But is that an advantage or a disadvantage?
3. How would a national popular vote be tabulated? There actually is no official national vote total: the result is simply the sum of all state vote totals. Would a national popular vote require a new mechanism for computing official results? How would that affect the role of states in the election system?

CHAPTER 7

Bureaucracy

32

"The Study of Administration"

Woodrow Wilson

Until the late nineteenth century, almost no one paid attention to how the government actually worked. Administrative positions were generally filled by political appointees who were supporters of elected officials, and there was little that resembled "management" in the contemporary sense. However, a great deal of money was distributed at the national level, and as scandals mounted over the manner in which the money was distributed, the demand for government accountability grew.

Reformers argued that government employees should be hired on the basis of their merit, rather than because of their political allegiance to one candidate or another. Others called for reforms in the administration of public programs. Nearly thirty years before he was president, Woodrow Wilson, then a professor at Bryn Mawr College, wrote an article for Political Science Quarterly *arguing that political scientists had neglected the study of public administration—the problems involved in managing public programs. He argued that public administration should be carried out in accordance with scientific principles of management and efficiency, an argument that would recur every few decades in demands to reform and "reinvent" government.*

It is the object of administrative study to discover, first, what government can properly and successfully do, and, secondly, how it can do these proper things with the utmost possible efficiency and at the least possible cost either of money or of energy. On both these points there is obviously much need of light among us; and only careful study can supply that light.

* * *

The science of administration is the latest fruit of that study of the science of politics which was begun some twenty-two hundred years ago. It is a birth of our own century, almost of our own generation.

Why was it so late in coming? Why did it wait till this too busy century of ours to demand attention for itself? Administration is the most obvious part of government; it is government in action; it is the executive, the operative, the most visible side of government, and is of course as old as government itself. It is government in action, and one might very naturally expect to find that government in action had arrested the attention and provoked the scrutiny of writers of politics very early in the history of systematic thought.

But such was not the case. No one wrote systematically of administration as a branch of the science of government until the present century had passed its first youth and had begun to put forth its characteristic flower of systematic knowledge. Up to our own day all the political writers whom we now read had thought, argued, dogmatized only about the *constitution* of government; about the nature of the state, the essence and seat of sovereignty, popular power and kingly prerogative; about the greatest meanings lying at the heart of government, and the high ends set before the purpose of government by man's nature and man's aims. * * * The question was always: Who shall make law, and what shall that law be? The other question, how law should be administered with enlightenment, with equity, with speed, and without fiction, was put aside as "practical detail" which clerks could arrange after doctors had agreed upon principles.

* * *

[However,] if difficulties of government action are to be seen gathering in other centuries, they are to be seen culminating in our own.

This is the reason why administrative tasks have nowadays to be so studiously and systematically adjusted to carefully tested standards of policy, the reason why we are having now what we never had before, a science of administration. The weightier debates of constitutional principle are even yet by no means concluded; but they are no longer of more immediate practical moment than questions of administration. It is getting to be harder to *run* a constitution than to frame one.

* * *

There is scarcely a single duty of government which was once simple which is not now complex; government once had but a few masters; it now has scores of masters. Majorities formerly only underwent government; they now conduct government. Where government once might follow the whims of a court, it must now follow the views of a nation.

And those views are steadily widening to new conceptions of state duty; so that at the same time that the functions of government are every day becoming more complex and difficult, they are also vastly multiplying in number. Administration is everywhere putting its hands to new undertakings. * * * Seeing every day new things which the state ought to do, the next thing is to see clearly how it ought to do them.

This is why there should be a science of administration which shall seek to straighten the paths of government, to make its business less businesslike, to strengthen and purify its organization, and to crown its dutifulness. This is one reason why there is such a science.

But where has this science grown up? Surely not on this side [of] the sea. Not much impartial scientific method is to be discerned in our administrative practices. The poisonous atmosphere of city government, the crooked secrets of state administration, the confusion, sinecurism, and corruption ever and again discovered in the bureaus at Washington forbid us to believe that any clear conceptions of what constitutes good administration are as yet very widely current in the United States.

* * *

American political history has been a history, not of administrative development, but of legislative oversight—not of progress in governmental organization, but of advance in lawmaking and political criticism. Consequently, we have reached a time when administrative study and creation are imperatively necessary to the well-being of our governments saddled with the habits of a long period of constitution-making. * * * We have reached * * * the period * * * when the people have to develop administration in accordance with the constitutions they won for themselves in a previous period of struggle with absolute power.

* * *

It is harder for democracy to organize administration than for monarchy. The very completeness of our most cherished political successes in the past embarrasses us. We have enthroned public opinion; and it is forbidden us to hope during its reign for any quick schooling of the sovereign in executive expertness or in the conditions of perfect functional balance in government. The very fact that we have realized popular rule in its fullness has made the task of *organizing* that rule just so much the more difficult. * * * An individual sovereign will adopt a simple plan and carry it out directly: he will have but one opinion, and he will embody that one opinion in one command. But this other sovereign, the people, will have a score of differing opinions. They can agree upon nothing simple: advance must be made through compromise, by a compounding of differences, by a trimming of plans and a suppression of too straightforward principles. There will be a succession of resolves running through a course of years, a dropping fire of commands running through a whole gamut of modifications.

* * *

Wherever regard for public opinion is a first principle of government, practical reform must be slow and all reform must be full of compromises. For wherever public opinion exists it must rule.

* * *

The field of administration is a field of business. It is removed from the hurry and strife of politics; it at most points stands apart even from the debatable ground of constitutional study. It is a part of political life only as the methods of the counting-house are a part of the life of society; only as machinery is part of the manufactured product. But it is, at the same time, raised very far above the dull level of mere technical detail by the fact that through its greater principles it is directly connected with the lasting maxims of political wisdom, the permanent truths of political progress.

The object of administrative study is to rescue executive methods from the confusion and costliness of empirical experiment and set them upon foundations laid deep in stable principle.

* * *

[A]dministration lies outside the proper sphere of *politics*. Administrative questions are not political questions. Although politics sets the tasks for administration, it should not be suffered to manipulate its offices.

* * *

There is another distinction which must be worked into all our conclusions, which, though but another side of that between administration and politics, is not quite so easy to keep sight of: I mean the distinction between *constitutional* and administrative questions, between those governmental adjustments which are essential to constitutional principle and those which are merely instrumental to the possibly changing purposes of a wisely adapting convenience.

* * *

A clear view of the difference between the province of constitutional law and the province of administrative function ought to leave no room for misconception; and it is possible to name some roughly definite criteria upon which such a view can be built. Public administration is detailed and systematic execution of public law. Every particular application of general law is an act of administration. The assessment and raising of taxes, for instance, the hanging of a criminal, the transportation and delivery of the mails, the equipment and recruiting of the army, and navy, etc., are all obviously acts of administration; but the general laws which direct these things to be done are as obviously outside of and above administration. The broad plans of governmental action are not administrative; the detailed execution of such plans is administrative. Constitutions, therefore, properly concern themselves only with those instrumentalities of government which are to control general law. Our federal constitution observes this principle in saying nothing of even the greatest of the purely executive offices, and speaking only of that President of the Union who was to share the legislative and policy-making functions of government, only of those judges of highest jurisdiction who were to interpret and guard its principles, and not of those who were merely to give utterance to them.

* * *

There is, [however,] one point at which administrative studies trench on constitutional ground—or at least upon what seems constitutional ground. The study of administration, philosophically viewed, is closely connected with the study of the proper distribution of constitutional authority. To be efficient it must discover the simplest arrangements by which responsibility can be unmistakably fixed upon officials; the best way of dividing authority without hampering it, and responsibility without obscuring it. And this question of the distribution of authority, when taken into the sphere of the higher, the originating functions of government, is obviously a central constitutional question.

* * *

To discover the best principle for the distribution of authority is of greater importance, possibly, under a democratic system, where officials serve many masters, than under others where they serve but a few. All sovereigns are suspicious of their servants, and the sovereign people is no exception to the rule; but how is its suspicion to be allayed by *knowledge*? If that suspicion could be clarified into wise vigilance, it would be altogether salutary; if that vigilance could be aided by the unmistakable placing of responsibility, it would be altogether beneficient. Suspicion in itself is never healthful either in the private or in the public mind. *Trust is strength* in all relations of life; and, as it is the office of the constitutional reformer to create conditions of trustfulness, so it is the office of the administrative organizer to fit administration with conditions of clearcut responsibility which shall insure trustworthiness.

And let me say that large powers and unhampered discretion seem to me the indispensable conditions of responsibility. Public attention must be easily directed, in each case of good or bad administration, to just the man deserving of praise or blame. There is no danger in power, if only it be not irresponsible. If it be divided, dealt out in shares to many, it is obscured; and if it be obscured, it is made irresponsible. But if it be centered in heads of the service and in heads of branches of the service, it is easily watched and brought to book. If to keep his office a man must achieve open and honest success, and if at the same time he feels himself intrusted with large freedom of discretion, the greater his power the less likely is he to abuse it, the more is he nerved and sobered and elevated by it. The less his power, the more safely obscure and unnoticed does he feel his position to be, and the more readily does he relapse into remissness.

Just here we manifestly emerge upon the field of that still larger question—the proper relations between public opinion and administration.

To whom is official trustworthiness to be disclosed, and by whom is it to be rewarded? Is the official to look to the public for his meed of praise and his push of promotion, or only to his superior in office? Are the people to be called in to settle administrative discipline as they are called in to settle constitutional principles? These questions evidently find their root in what is undoubtedly the fundamental problem of this whole study. That problem is: What part shall public opinion take in the conduct of administration?

The right answer seems to be, that public opinion shall play the part of authoritative critic.

But the *method* by which its authority shall be made to tell? Our peculiar American difficulty in organizing administration is not the danger of losing liberty, but the danger of not being able or willing to separate its essentials from its accidents. Our success is made doubtful by that besetting error of ours, the error of trying to do too much by vote. Self-government does not consist in having a hand in everything, any more than housekeeping consists necessarily in cooking dinner with one's own hands. The cook must be trusted with a large discretion as to the management of the fires and the ovens.

* * *

The problem is to make public opinion efficient without suffering it to be meddlesome. Directly exercised, in the oversight of the daily details and in the choice of the daily means of government, public criticism is of course a clumsy nuisance, a rustic handling delicate machinery. But as superintending the greater forces of formative policy alike in politics and administration, public criticism is altogether safe and beneficent, altogether indispensable. Let administrative study find the best means for giving public criticism this control and for shutting it out from all other interference.

But is the whole duty of administrative study done when it has taught the people what sort of administration to desire and demand, and how to get what they demand? Ought it not to go on to drill candidates for the public service?

* * *

If we are to improve public opinion, which is the motive power of government, we must prepare better officials as the *apparatus* of government. * * * It will be necessary to organize democracy by sending up to the competitive examinations for the civil service men definitely prepared for standing liberal tests as to technical knowledge. A technically schooled civil service will presently have become indispensable.

I know that a corps of civil servants prepared by a special schooling and drilled, after appointment, into a perfected organization, with appropriate hierarchy and characteristic discipline, seems to a great many very thoughtful persons to contain elements which might combine to make an offensive official class—a distinct, semi-corporate body with sympathies divorced from those of a progressive, free-spirited people, and with hearts narrowed to the meanness of a bigoted officialism.

* * *

But to fear the creation of a domineering, illiberal officialism as a result of the studies I am here proposing is to miss altogether the principle upon which I wish most to insist. That principle is, that administration in the United States must be at all points sensitive to public opinion. A body of thoroughly trained officials serving during good behavior we must have in any case: that is a plain business necessity. But the apprehension that such a body will be anything un-American clears away the moment it is asked, What is to constitute good behavior? For that question obviously carries its own answer on its face. Steady, hearty allegiance to the policy of the government they serve will constitute good behavior. That *policy* will have no taint of officialism about it. It will not be the creation of permanent officials, but of statesmen whose responsibility to public opinion will be direct and inevitable. Bureaucracy can exist only where the whole service of the state is removed from the common political life of the people, its chiefs as well as its rank and file. Its motives, its objects, its policy, its standards, must be bureaucratic.

* * *

The ideal for us is a civil service cultured and self-sufficient enough to act with sense and vigor, and yet so intimately connected with the popular thought, by means of elections and constant public counsel, as to find arbitrariness or class spirit quite out of the question.

Having thus viewed in some sort the subject-matter and the objects of this study of administration, what are we to conclude as to the methods best suited to it—the points of view most advantageous for it?

Government is so near us, so much a thing of our daily familiar handling, that we can with difficulty see the need of any philosophical study of it, or the exact point of such study, should it be undertaken. We have been on our feet too long to study now the art of walking. We are a practical people, made so apt, so adept in self-government by centuries of experimental drill that we are scarcely any longer capable of perceiving the awkwardness of the particular system we may be using, just because it is so easy for us to use any system. We do not study the art of governing: we govern. But mere unschooled genius for affairs will not save us from sad blunders in administration. Though democrats by long inheritance and repeated choice, we are still rather crude democrats. Old as democracy is, its organization on a basis of modern ideas and conditions is still an unaccomplished work. The democratic state has yet to be equipped for carrying those enormous burdens of administration which the needs of this industrial and trading age are so fast accumulating.

* * *

We can borrow the science of administration [developed elsewhere] with safety and profit if only we read all fundamental differences of condition into its essential tenets. We have only to filter it through our constitutions, only to put it over a slow fire of criticism and distil away its foreign gases.

* * *

Our own politics must be the touchstone for all theories. The principles on which to base a science of administration for America must be principles which have democratic policy very much at heart. And, to suit American habit, all general theories must, as theories, keep modestly in the background, not in open argument only, but even in our own minds—lest opinions satisfactory only to the standards of the library should be dogmatically used, as if they must be quite as satisfactory to the standards of practical politics as well. Doctrinaire devices must be postponed to tested practices. Arrangements not only sanctioned by conclusive experience elsewhere but also congenial to American habit must be preferred without hesitation to theoretical perfection. In a word, steady, practical statesmanship must come first, closet doctrine second. The cosmopolitan what-to-do must always be commanded by the American how-to-do-it.

Our duty is to supply the best possible life to a *federal* organization, to systems within systems; to make town, city, county, state, and federal governments live with a like strength and an equally assured healthfulness, keeping each unquestionably its own master and yet making all interdependent and co-operative, combining independence with mutual helpfulness. The task is great and important enough to attract the best minds.

This interlacing of local self-government with federal self-government is quite a modern conception. * * * The question for us is, how shall our series of governments within governments be so administered that it shall always be to the interest of the public officer to serve, not his superior alone but the community also, with the best efforts of his talents and the soberest service of his conscience? How shall such service be made to his commonest interest by contributing abundantly to his sustenance, to his dearest interest by furthering his ambition, and to his highest interest by advancing his honor and establishing his character? And how shall this be done alike for the local part and for the national whole?

If we solve this problem we shall again pilot the world.

Discussion Questions

1. Do you agree with Wilson's central proposition that politics and administration are separate things? Can you think of any examples where the two overlap? Is it possible, or even desirable, to separate politics and administration?
2. Should there be an expectation of neutral efficiency that separates politicians' policy views from the work of government agencies?
3. Should government officials be able to take into account whether someone supports an agency's goals when deciding whom to hire? Does your answer differ depending on whether the agency is involved in foreign policy, domestic policy, or national security?

33

From *Bureaucracy: What Government Agencies Do and Why They Do It*

JAMES Q. WILSON

Woodrow Wilson was merely the first in a long line of reformers to suggest that government might be more efficient if it ran more like a business. This sentiment persists today. Perhaps a more "businesslike" government would issue our income tax refunds more promptly, protect the environment at lower cost, and impose fewer burdens on citizens. The catch is, we want all this at low cost and minimal intrusiveness in our lives, yet we want government bureaucracies to be held strictly accountable for the authority they exercise.

James Q. Wilson argues that government will never operate like a business, nor should we expect it to. His comparison of the Watertown, Massachusetts Registry of Motor Vehicles (representing any government bureaucracy) with a nearby McDonald's (representing any private profit-seeking organization) shows that the former will most likely never service its clientele as well as the latter. The problem is not bureaucratic laziness, or any of the conventional criticisms of government agencies, but is instead due to the very different characteristics of public versus private enterprises. In order to understand "what government agencies do and why they do it," Wilson argues we must first understand that government bureaucracies operate in a political marketplace, rather than an economic one. The annual revenues and personnel resources of a government agency are determined by elected officials, not by the agency's ability to meet the demands of its customers in a cost-efficient manner. The government agency's internal structure and decision-making procedures are defined by legislation, regulation, and executive orders, whereas similar decisions in a private business are made by executive officers and management within the organization. And, perhaps most critical, a government agency's goals are often vague, difficult if not impossible to measure, and even contradictory. In business, by contrast, the task is clearer. The basic goal of a private business has always been to maximize the bottom line: profit. Although suggesting we should not approach the reform of government agencies the way we might a private bureaucracy, James Q. Wilson notes in this 1980s analysis that we should nevertheless try to make government bureaucracies operate more effectively and efficiently.

By the time the office opens at 8:45 A.M., the line of people waiting to do business at the Registry of Motor Vehicles in Watertown, Massachusetts, often will be twenty-five deep. By midday, especially if it is near the end of the month, the line may extend clear around the building. Inside, motorists wait in slow-moving rows before poorly marked windows to get a driver's license or to register an automobile. When someone gets to the head of the line, he or she is often told by the clerk that it is the wrong line: "Get an application over there and then come back," or "This is only for people getting a new license; if you want to replace one you lost, you have to go to the next window." The customers grumble impatiently. The clerks act harried and sometimes speak brusquely, even rudely. What seems to be a simple transaction may take 45 minutes or even longer. By the time people are photographed for their driver's licenses, they are often scowling. The photographer valiantly tries to get people to smile, but only occasionally succeeds.

Not far away, people also wait in line at a McDonald's fast-food restaurant. There are several lines; each is short, each moves quickly. The menu is clearly displayed on attractive signs. The workers behind the counter are invariably polite. If someone's order cannot be filled immediately, he or she is asked to step aside for a moment while the food is prepared and then is brought back to the head of the line to receive the order. The atmosphere is friendly and good-natured. The room is immaculately clean.

Many people have noticed the difference between getting a driver's license and ordering a Big Mac. Most will explain it by saying that bureaucracies are different from businesses. "Bureaucracies" behave as they do because they are run by unqualified "bureaucrats" and are enmeshed in "rules" and "red tape."

But business firms are also bureaucracies, and McDonald's is a bureaucracy that regulates virtually every detail of its employees' behavior by a complex and all-encompassing set of rules. Its operations manual is six hundred pages long and weighs four pounds. In it one learns that french fries are to be nine-thirty-seconds of an inch thick and that grill workers are to place hamburger patties on the grill from left to right, six to a row for six rows. They are then to flip the third row first, followed by the fourth, fifth, and sixth rows, and finally the first and second. The amount of sauce placed on each bun is precisely specified. Every window must be washed every day. Workers must get down on their hands and knees and pick up litter as soon as it appears. These and countless other rules designed to reduce the workers to interchangeable automata were inculcated in franchise managers at Hamburger University located in a $40 million facility. There are plenty of rules governing the Registry, but they are only a small fraction of the rules that govern every detail of every operation at McDonald's. Indeed, if the DMV manager tried to impose on his employees as demanding a set of rules as those that govern the McDonald's staff, they would probably rebel and he would lose his job.

It is just as hard to explain the differences between the two organizations by reference to the quality or compensation of their employees. The Registry workers are all adults, most with at least a high-school education; the McDonald's employees are mostly teenagers, many still in school. The Registry staff is well-paid compared to the McDonald's workers, most of whom receive only the minimum wage. When labor shortages developed in Massachusetts during the mid-1980s, many McDonald's stores began hiring older people (typically housewives) of the same sort who had long worked for the Registry. They behaved just like the teenagers they replaced.

Not only are the differences between the two organizations not to be explained by reference to "rules" or "red tape" or "incompetent workers," the differences call into question many of the most frequently mentioned complaints about how government agencies are supposed to behave. For example: "Government agencies are big spenders." The Watertown office of the Registry is in a modest building that can barely handle its clientele. The teletype machine used to check information submitted by people requesting a replacement license was antiquated and prone to errors. Three or four clerks often had to wait in line to use equipment described by the office manager as "personally signed by Thomas Edison." No computers or word processors were available to handle the preparation of licenses and registrations; any error made by a clerk while manually typing a form meant starting over again on another form.

Or: "Government agencies hire people regardless of whether they are really needed." Despite the fact that the citizens of Massachusetts probably have more contact with the Registry than with any other state agency, and despite the fact that these citizens complain more about Registry service than about that of any other bureau, the Watertown branch, like all Registry offices, was seriously understaffed. In 1981, the agency lost 400 workers—about 25 percent of its work force—despite the fact that its workload was rising.

Or: "Government agencies are imperialistic, always grasping for new functions." But there is no record of the Registry doing much grasping, even though one could imagine a case being made that the state government could usefully create at Registry offices "one-stop" multi-service centers where people could not only get drivers' licenses but also pay taxes and parking fines, obtain information, and transact other official business. The Registry seemed content to provide one service.

In short, many of the popular stereotypes about government agencies and their members are either questionable or incomplete. To explain why government agencies behave as they do, it is not enough to know that they are "bureaucracies"—that is, it is not enough to know that they are big, or complex, or have rules. What is crucial is that they are *government* bureaucracies. * * * [N]ot all government bureaucracies behave the same way or suffer from the same problems. There may even be registries of motor vehicles in other states that do a better job than the one in Massachusetts. But all government agencies have in common certain characteristics that tend to make their management far more difficult than managing a McDonald's. These common characteristics are the constraints of public agencies.

The key constraints are three in number. To a much greater extent than is true of private bureaucracies, government agencies (1) cannot lawfully retain and devote to the private benefit of their members the earnings of the organization, (2) cannot allocate the factors of production in accordance with the preferences of the organization's administrators, and (3) must serve goals not of the organization's own choosing. Control over revenues, productive factors, and agency goals is all vested to an important degree in entities external to the organization—legislatures, courts, politicians, and interest groups. Given this, agency managers must attend to the demands of these external entities. As a result, government management tends to be driven by the *constraints* on the organization, not the *tasks* of the organization. To say the same thing in other words, whereas business management focuses on the "bottom line" (that is, profits), government management focuses on the "top line" (that is, constraints). Because government managers are not as strongly motivated as private ones to define the tasks of their subordinates, these tasks are often shaped by [other] factors.

* * *

Revenues and Incentives

In the days leading up to September 30, the federal government is Cinderella, courted by legions of individuals and organizations eager to get grants and contracts from the unexpended funds still at the disposal of each agency. At midnight on September 30, the government's coach turns into a pumpkin. That is the moment—the end of the fiscal year— at which every agency, with a few exceptions, must return all unexpended funds to the Treasury Department.

Except for certain quasi-independent government corporations, such as the Tennessee Valley Authority, no agency may keep any surplus revenues (that is, the difference between the funds it received from a congressional appropriation and those it needed to operate during the year). By the same token, any agency that runs out of money before the end of the fiscal year may ask Congress for more (a "supplemental appropriation") instead of being forced to deduct the deficit from any accumulated cash reserves. Because of these fiscal rules agencies do not have a material incentive to economize: Why scrimp and save if you cannot keep the results of your frugality?

Nor can individual bureaucrats lawfully capture for their personal use any revenue surpluses. When a private firm has a good year, many of its officers and workers may receive bonuses. Even if no bonus is paid, these employees may buy stock in the firm so that they can profit from any growth in earnings (and, if they sell the stock in a timely manner, profit from a drop in earnings). Should a public bureaucrat be discovered trying to do what private bureaucrats routinely do, he or she would be charged with corruption.

We take it for granted that bureaucrats should not profit from their offices and nod approvingly when a bureaucrat who has so benefited is indicted and put on trial. But why should we take this view? Once a very different view prevailed. In the seventeenth century, a French colonel would buy his commission from the king, take the king's money to run his regiment, and pocket the profit. At one time a European tax collector was paid by keeping a percentage of the taxes he collected. In this country, some prisons were once managed by giving the warden a sum of money based on how many prisoners were under his control and letting him keep the difference between what he received and what it cost him to feed the prisoners. Such behavior today would be grounds for criminal prosecution. Why? What has changed?

Mostly we the citizenry have changed. We are creatures of the Enlightenment: We believe that the nation ought not to be the property of the sovereign; that laws are intended to rationalize society and (if possible) perfect mankind; and that public service ought to be neutral and disinterested. We worry that a prison warden paid in the old way would have a strong incentive to starve his prisoners in order to maximize his income; that a regiment supported by a greedy colonel would not be properly equipped; and that a tax collector paid on a commission basis would extort excessive taxes from us. These changes reflect our desire to eliminate moral hazards—namely, creating incentives for people to act wrongly. But why should this desire rule out more carefully designed compensation plans that would pay government managers for achieving officially approved goals and would allow efficient agencies to keep any unspent part of their budget for use next year?

Part of the answer is obvious. Often we do not know whether a manager or an agency has achieved the goals we want because either the goals are vague or inconsistent, or their attainment cannot be observed, or both. Bureau chiefs in the Department of State would have to go on welfare if their pay depended on their ability to demonstrate convincingly that they had attained their bureaus' objectives.

But many government agencies have reasonably clear goals toward which progress can be measured. The Social Security Administration, the Postal Service, and the General Services Administration all come to mind. Why not let earnings depend importantly on performance? Why not let agencies keep excess revenues?

* * *

But in part it is because we know that even government agencies with clear goals and readily observable behavior only can be evaluated by making political (and thus conflict-ridden) judgments. If the Welfare Department delivers every benefit check within 24 hours after the application is received, Senator Smith may be pleased but Senator Jones will be irritated because this speedy delivery almost surely would require that the standards of eligibility be relaxed so that many ineligible clients would get money. There is no objective standard by which the trade-off between speed and accuracy in the Welfare Department can be evaluated. Thus we have been unwilling to allow welfare employees to earn large bonuses for achieving either speed or accuracy.

The inability of public managers to capture surplus revenues for their own use alters the pattern of incentives at work in government agencies. Beyond a certain point additional effort does not produce additional earnings. (In this country, Congress from time to time has authorized higher salaries for senior bureaucrats but then put a cap on actual payments to them so that the pay increases were never received. This was done to insure that no bureaucrat would earn more than members of Congress at a time when those members were unwilling to accept the political costs of raising their own salaries. As a result, the pay differential between the top bureaucratic rank and those just below it nearly vanished.) If political constraints reduce the marginal effect of money incentives, then the relative importance of other, nonmonetary incentives will increase. . . .

That bureaucratic performance in most government agencies cannot be linked to monetary benefits is not the whole explanation for the difference between public and private management. There are many examples of private organizations whose members cannot appropriate money surpluses for their own benefit. Private schools ordinarily are run on a nonprofit basis. Neither the headmaster nor the teachers share in the profit of these schools; indeed, most such schools earn no profit at all and instead struggle to keep afloat by soliciting contributions from friends and alumni. Nevertheless, the evidence is quite clear that on the average, private schools, both secular and denominational, do a better job than public ones in educating children. Moreover, as political scientists John Chubb and Terry Moe have pointed out, they do a better job while employing fewer managers. Some other factors are at work. One is the freedom an organization has to acquire and use labor and capital.

Acquiring and Using the Factors of Production

A business firm acquires capital by retaining earnings, borrowing money, or selling shares of ownership; a government agency (with some exceptions) acquires capital by persuading a legislature to appropriate it. A business firm hires, promotes, demotes, and fires personnel with considerable though not perfect freedom; a federal government agency is told by Congress how many persons it can hire and at what rate of pay, by the Office of Personnel Management (OPM) what rules it must follow in selecting and assigning personnel, by the Office of Management and Budget (OMB) how many persons of each rank it may employ, by the Merit Systems Protection Board (MSPB) what procedures it must follow in demoting or discharging personnel, and by the courts whether it has faithfully followed the rules of Congress, OPM, OMB, and MSPB. A business firm purchases goods and services by internally defined procedures (including those that allow it to buy from someone other than the lowest bidder if a more expensive vendor seems more reliable), or to skip the bidding procedure altogether in favor of direct negotiations; a government agency must purchase much of what it uses by formally advertising for bids, accepting the lowest, and keeping the vendor at arm's length. When a business firm develops a good working relationship with a contractor, it often uses that vendor repeatedly without looking for a new one; when a government agency has a satisfactory relationship with a contractor, ordinarily it cannot use the vendor again without putting a new project out for a fresh set of bids. When a business firm finds that certain offices or factories are no longer economical it will close or combine them; when a government agency wishes to shut down a local office or military base often it must get the permission of the legislature (even when formal permission is not necessary, informal consultation is). When a business firm draws up its annual budget each expenditure item can be reviewed as a discretionary amount (except for legally mandated payments of taxes to government and interest to banks and bondholders); when a government agency makes up its budget many of the detailed expenditure items are mandated by the legislature.

All these complexities of doing business in or with the government are well-known to citizens and firms. These complexities in hiring, purchasing, contracting, and budgeting often are said to be the result of the "bureaucracy's love of red tape." But few, if any, of the rules producing this complexity would have been generated by the bureaucracy if left to its own devices, and many are as cordially disliked by the bureaucrats as by their clients. These rules have been imposed on the agencies by external actors, chiefly the legislature. They are not bureaucratic rules but *political* ones. In principle the legislature could allow the Social Security Administration, the Defense Department, or the New York City public school system to follow the same rules as IBM, General Electric, or Harvard University. In practice they could not. The reason is politics, or more precisely, democratic politics.

* * *

Public versus Private Management

What distinguishes public from private organizations is neither their size nor their desire to "plan" (that is, control) their environments but rather the rules under which they acquire and use capital and labor. General Motors acquires capital by selling shares, issuing bonds, or retaining earnings; the Department of Defense acquires it from an annual appropriation by Congress. GM opens and closes plants, subject to certain government regulations, at its own discretion; DOD opens and closes military bases under the watchful guidance of Congress. GM pays its managers with salaries it sets and bonuses tied to its earnings; DOD pays its managers with salaries set by Congress and bonuses (if any) that have no connection with organizational performance. The number of workers in GM is determined by its level of production; the number in DOD by legislation and civil-service rules.

What all this means can be seen by returning to the Registry of Motor Vehicles and McDonald's. Suppose you were just appointed head of the Watertown office of the Registry and you wanted to improve service there so that it more nearly approximated the service at McDonald's. Better service might well require spending more money (on clerks, equipment, and buildings). Why should your political superiors give you that money? It is a cost to them if it requires either higher taxes or taking funds from another agency; offsetting these real and immediate costs are dubious and postponed benefits. If lines become shorter and clients become happier, no legislator will benefit. There may be fewer complaints, but complaints are episodic and have little effect on the career of any given legislator. By contrast, shorter lines and faster service at McDonald's means more customers can be served per hour and thus more money can be earned per hour. A McDonald's manager can estimate the marginal product of the last dollar he or she spends on improving service; the Registry manager can generate no tangible return on any expenditure he or she makes and thus cannot easily justify the expenditure.

Improving service at the Registry may require replacing slow or surly workers with quick and pleasant ones. But you, the manager, can neither hire nor fire them at will. You look enviously at the McDonald's manager who regularly and with little notice replaces poor workers with better ones. Alternatively, you may wish to mount an extensive training program (perhaps creating a Registration University to match McDonald's Hamburger University) that would imbue a culture of service in your employees. But unless the Registry were so large an agency that the legislature would neither notice nor care about funds spent for this purpose—and it is not that large—you would have a tough time convincing anybody that this was not a wasteful expenditure on a frill project.

If somehow your efforts succeed in making Registry clients happier, you can take vicarious pleasure in it; in the unlikely event a client seeks you out to thank you for those efforts, you can bask in a moment's worth of glory. Your colleague at McDonald's who manages to make customers happier may also derive some vicarious satisfaction from the improvement but in addition he or she will earn more money owing to an increase in sales.

In time it will dawn on you that if you improve service too much, clients will start coming to the Watertown office instead of going to the Boston office. As a result, the lines you succeeded in shortening will become longer again. If you wish to keep complaints down, you will have to spend even more on the Watertown office. But if it was hard to persuade the legislature to do that in the past, it is impossible now. Why should the taxpayer be asked to spend more on Watertown when the Boston office, fully staffed (naturally, no one was laid off when the clients disappeared), has no lines at all? From the legislature's point of view the correct level of expenditure is not that which makes one office better than another but that which produces an equal amount of discontent in all offices.

Finally, you remember that your clients have no choice: The Registry offers a monopoly service. It and only it supplies drivers' licenses. In the long run all that matters is that there are not "too many" complaints to the legislature about service. Unlike McDonald's, the Registry need not fear that its clients will take their business to Burger King or to Wendy's. Perhaps you should just relax.

If this were all there is to public management it would be an activity that quickly and inevitably produces cynicism among its practitioners. But this is not the whole story. For one thing, public agencies differ in the kinds of problems they face. For another, many public managers try hard to do a good job even though they face these difficult constraints.

Discussion Questions

1. Wilson argues that McDonald's and the Registry of Motor Vehicles operate differently because of the inherent differences between public and private organizations. Apply his reasoning to other cases, for instance the U.S. Postal Service and FedEx, or any other area where the government and the private sector compete for business. Think about the goals of the organizations, who controls them, how you distinguish success from failure, and the consequences of failure.
2. What are the advantages and disadvantages of trying to run the government more like a business? How would you define the basic parameters of a "businesslike" government—for instance, who are the "customers"?
3. Some critics of government inefficiency argue that nearly every domestic government function—from schools to road building—could be run more efficiently if it were "privatized"—turned over to private contractors. Do you agree? Are there any government functions that do not lend themselves to privatization?

Debating the Issues: Should Government Functions Be Outsourced to Private Contractors?

Public organizations (meaning governments) have different incentives and performance measures than private organizations (meaning, in this context, private sector businesses). Another way to say this is that governments tend to be much less efficient than businesses, but this does not mean that government can be run like a business.

Nevertheless, governments today at all levels face pressure to transfer functions to the private sector, either by spinning off government functions entirely (privatization) or by contracting with private firms to provide services once provided by government employees (outsourcing). Turning over the air traffic control system or the postal service to private companies—leaving them to provide services and collect fees in a profit-making venture—would be examples of privatization. Using contractors to replace government personnel or carry out public functions—food service at national museums or military bases; private security forces instead of military personnel in Iraq—are examples of outsourcing.

Privatization has its risks. For example, in 2006, the state of Indiana sold the rights to its major highway to a Spanish and Australian consortium for $3.8 billion: in return for the rights to all tolls, the companies took the responsibility for maintenance. But lower than expected traffic and high debt led to bankruptcy in 2011, and led to a takeover by another corporation in 2015. Other private toll road operators in Alabama, California, Michigan, and Virginia have also gone through bankruptcy proceedings. Proponents of privatization argue that this process has had no impact on states, since private companies have assumed all of the risk. But critics respond that infrastructure is a basic governmental function that should not be farmed out as a profit-making enterprise.

Both outsourcing and privatization have advantages, at least as far as proponents see it: smaller government or more efficient government. Yet both practices also have some disadvantages compared to using government agencies to provide services. Compared to private firms, governments are more sensitive to problems of equity and accountability. For example, one reason the Postal Service is inefficient is that legislators created laws that require it to serve remote areas of the country and maintain post offices in small towns. A private company (say, FedEx or UPS) may not find it profitable to do the same thing, and would either not provide service or charge more for it. We would purchase efficiency at the cost of equity. Your view of whether that tradeoff is worth making probably depends heavily on whether you are a beneficiary of those inefficient services.

But disputes over whether the government does something well or not are often policy disputes about whether the government should be doing something at all. The debate here involves some of the same issues. "Options for Federal Privatization and Reform Lessons from Abroad" was written by Chris Edwards of the Cato Institute, a libertarian think-tank that supports a significantly smaller government. Here, the author proposes privatizing a wide range of government functions: the post office, air traffic control, airports, public lands, etc. He argues that privatization increases efficiency, spurs capital investment, rewards entrepreneurship, leads to more transparency, and removes "politics" from the entire process.

Not so fast, argues Janine Wedel, who is critical of contracting out government functions. Wedel argues that using contractors to provide crucial government functions—intelligence, security, information technology—has a number of negative consequences, including reduced accountability, loss of vital institutional expertise, and poor supervision. The result is that the federal government has abdicated responsibility for important functions, and has substituted profit-seeking for the more difficult (but still vital) task of allocating resources in a way that meets public demands.

34

"Options for Federal Privatization and Reform Lessons from Abroad"

CHRIS EDWARDS

A privatization revolution has swept the world since the 1980s. Governments in more than 100 countries have moved thousands of state-owned businesses and other assets to the private sector. Airports, airlines, railroads, energy companies, postal services, and other businesses valued at about $3.3 trillion have been privatized over the past three decades.

Privatization has improved government finances by raising revenues and reducing spending. More important, it has spurred economic growth and improved services because privatized businesses have cut costs, increased quality, and pursued innovation.

In a 1969 essay, management expert Peter Drucker said that politicians in the twentieth century had been "hypnotized by government . . . in love with it and saw no limits to its abilities." But he said that the love affair was coming to an end as the mismanagement of state-owned businesses was becoming more apparent everywhere. In his essay, Drucker called for a "reprivatization" of government activities, but he was a bit ahead of his time.

The privatization revolution was launched by Margaret Thatcher's government in the United Kingdom, which came to power in 1979. Prime Minister Thatcher popularized the word *privatization*, and her successful reforms were copied around the globe. She was determined to revive the stagnant British economy, and her government privatized dozens of major businesses, including British Airways, British Telecom, British Steel, and British Gas. Other nations followed the British lead because of a "disillusionment with the generally poor performance of state-owned enterprises and the desire to improve efficiency of bloated and often failing companies," noted a report on privatization by the Organisation for Economic Cooperation and Development (OECD).

Privatization swept through other developed countries in the 1980s and 1990s, with major reforms in Australia, Canada, France, Italy, New Zealand, Portugal, Spain, Sweden, and other nations. A Labour government elected in New Zealand in 1984 privatized dozens of state-owned companies, including airports, banks, energy companies, forests, and the national airline and telecommunications companies. Australia privatized dozens of companies between the mid-1990s and mid-2000s, generating proceeds of more than $100 billion. * * *

Privatization has gained support from both the political right and left. Left-of-center governments in Australia, the United Kingdom, France, Canada, and New Zealand all pursued privatization. Privatization has attracted opposition from the public in many countries, but very rarely have reforms been reversed once put in place. Privatization works, and so the reforms have lasted.

Privatization has "massively increased the size and efficiency of the world's capital markets," one finance expert found. As of 2005, the 10 largest share offerings in world history were privatizations. By 2010, about half of the global stock market capitalization outside of the United States was from companies that had been privatized in recent years. Privatization has had a huge effect on the global economy.

Today, many countries have privatized the "lowest hanging fruit." But there is much left to sell, and global privatization is continuing at a robust pace. Over the past four years, governments worldwide have sold an average $203 billion of state-owned businesses annually. China is now the largest privatizer, but Western nations continue to pursue reforms. The British government, for example, sold a majority stake in Royal Mail in 2013 and then unloaded the final block of shares in 2015.

Privatization has been a very successful reform. An OECD report reviewed the research and found "overwhelming support for the notion that privatization brings about a significant increase in the profitability, real output and efficiency of privatised companies." And a review of academic studies in the *Journal of Economic Literature* concluded that privatization "appears to improve performance measured in many different ways, in many different countries.

Despite the success of privatization, reforms have largely bypassed our own federal government. President Ronald Reagan's administration explored selling the U.S. Postal Service, Amtrak, the Tennessee Valley Authority, the air traffic control system, and federal land, but those efforts stalled. President Bill Clinton had more success. His administration oversaw the privatization of the Alaska Power Administration, the Elk Hills Naval Petroleum Reserve, the U.S. Enrichment Corporation, and Intelsat.

Little action on federal privatization has been pursued since then, but there are many federal activities that should be turned over to the private sector. The United States has a government postal system, but European countries are privatizing their systems and opening them to competition. The United States has a government air traffic control system, but Canada and the United Kingdom have privatized their systems. Our federal government owns electric utilities and a passenger rail service, but other countries have privatized those businesses.

The first section of this study examines the path-breaking British privatizations of recent decades. The second section discusses 12 advantages of privatization. The third section describes six businesses and assets that federal policymakers should privatize: the U.S. Postal Service, Amtrak, the Tennessee Valley Authority, the air traffic control system, land, and buildings. That section also highlights other businesses and assets to sell.

This study mainly uses *privatization* in a narrow sense to mean fully moving ownership of businesses and assets to the private sector. The term is often used more broadly to include government contracting, public-private partnerships, vouchers, and other forms of partial privatization. Those are all worthy reforms, but they are not the focus here.

When the next president comes into office in 2017, the time will be ripe for privatization reforms. Privatization would help spur growth in our underperforming economy and modestly reduce rising budget deficits. Privatization would also create qualitative benefits, such as increasing transparency and improving environmental stewardship.

* * *

Advantages of Privatization

* * *

1. Promotes Efficiency and Innovation

Private businesses in competitive markets have strong incentives to increase efficiency—to produce more and better products at lower costs.

Businesses seek profits, which are a measure of net value creation. If a business performs poorly, it will lose money and have to change course, or ultimately face bankruptcy or a takeover.

By contrast, government entities are usually not penalized for excess costs, misjudging public needs, or other failures. They can deliver bad results year after year and still receive funding. Government workers are rarely fired, and there is no imperative for managers to generate net value.

The superiority of private enterprise is not just a static efficiency advantage. Instead, businesses in competitive markets must pursue continuous improvements. They learn by doing and adjust to changes in society, a process called adaptive efficiency. By contrast, governments get ossified by bureaucracy and are slow to adapt.

Businesses routinely abandon low-value activities, but "the moment government undertakes anything, it becomes entrenched and permanent," noted management expert Peter Drucker. As an example, the demand for mail has plunged and the U.S. Postal Service (USPS) is losing billions of dollars a year, but Congress has blocked obvious reforms, such as ending Saturday delivery. Private businesses make such adjustments all the time as demand for their products fluctuates.

Government organizations undermine growth by keeping resources employed in low-value activities, even as tastes and technologies change. That is why Drucker said, "[T]he strongest argument for private enterprise is not the function of profit. The strongest argument is the function of loss." Losses encourage private businesses to drop less-valuable activities and move resources to more promising ones.

In the twentieth century, many economists supported government ownership because they thought that expert planners could efficiently organize production. But they ignored the dynamic role of businesses in continuously improving products and production techniques. In a *Journal of Economic Perspectives* article, Andrei Shleifer said that many economists did not foresee the "grotesque failure" of government ownership, and they did not appreciate the private-sector role in generating innovation.

* * *

[2.] Improves Capital Investment

In the private sector, businesses have incentives to maintain their facilities in good repair and to invest to meet rising demands. To fund expansions, they reinvest their profits and raise financing on debt and equity markets.

By contrast, government organizations often consume their funding on bureaucratic bloat and have little left over for repairs and upgrades. Government infrastructure is often old, congested, and poorly maintained. Capital investment falls short and tends to be misallocated. This was a common experience with British industries before they were privatized, and access to private funding to increase capital investment was an important factor in the Thatcher government's privatization drive.

The same problems of run-down public infrastructure are apparent in the United States today. The National Park Service has many poorly maintained facilities and billions of dollars of deferred maintenance. Urban subway and light rail systems across the nation have tens of billions of dollars of maintenance backlogs. Politicians enjoy launching new parks and rail systems, but they put little effort into maintaining what the government already owns.

Federal agencies cannot count on Congress for funding. Consider the air traffic control system, which is run by the Federal Aviation Administration (FAA). The system needs billions of dollars in investment to meet rising passenger demands, but the FAA has not secured stable long-term funding from Congress. Furthermore, the FAA mismanages its capital investment projects, which often experience delays and cost overruns.

Amtrak's investment budget is also mismanaged. Because of politics, the company invests in rural routes that have few passengers instead of higher-demand routes in the Northeast. In his book on Amtrak, rail expert Joseph Vranich argued, "Congressional requirements that Amtrak spend money on capital improvements to lightly used routes are outrageous. . . . Throughout Amtrak's history, it has devoted too much of its budget to where it is not needed, and not enough to where it is."

Privatization solves these sorts of problems. Privatized businesses use customer revenues and capital markets to finance upgrades. They do not have to lobby Congress to receive needed funding. And they have strong incentives to invest where the actual demand is, free from political pressures that plague government-owned businesses.

[3.] Expands Entrepreneurship and Competition

When the government produces goods and services, it tends to squelch competition, either directly by enforcing a monopoly, or indirectly by deterring entrants unwilling to compete with a subsidized government producer.

Devoid of competition, government organizations resist change and are slow to adopt better ways of doing things. The FAA runs the air traffic control system with outdated technology. The USPS is being undermined by email, but it does not have the flexibility to adapt. Airlines and intercity buses have improved their efficiencies and reduced costs under competitive pressures, but Amtrak's costs remain high.

In the economy, major innovations often come from upstarts, not industry-dominant firms. Big advances in industries, from computers to retail, have come from new firms doing things in new ways. So economic progress depends on open entry, on the ability of entrepreneurs to challenge existing providers. That is hard to do when the existing provider is the government.

Privatization abroad has often been paired with the removal of entry barriers. The European Union has urged member countries to open their markets as they privatize their airline, energy, telecommunications, transportation, and postal companies. British postal markets were opened for competition, and then Royal Mail was privatized. The privatization of British Telecom was followed by deregulation and then the rise of competitors such as Vodaphone, which is now one of the largest telecommunications firms in the world.

U.S. policymakers should use privatization as a catalyst for procompetition reforms. The government should privatize USPS, Amtrak, and other companies, and at the same time open industries to new entrants. Open entry attracts people with new ideas and encourages the dissemination of new production techniques. The best and the brightest do not want to work for moribund bureaucracies such as the USPS and Amtrak. As a result, those companies today are essentially closed to external know-how and global best practices.

The American economy is rapidly evolving, driven by globalization and new technologies. We can keep up with all the changes by making our economy as flexible and open to new ideas as possible, and privatization and competition are the best ways to do that. If America opened its postal industry to competition, there would likely be many entrepreneurs ready to revolutionize it.

[4.] Increases Transparency

Citizens have difficulty monitoring the activities of government agencies. The goals of agencies are often vague, and their finances are difficult to understand. Government officials are protected by civil service rules and can be secretive in their activities. Even members of Congress have difficulty squeezing information out of agency leaders, as we often see at congressional hearings.

By contrast, private companies have clear goals such as earning profits and expanding sales. Performance is monitored by auditors, shareholders, and creditors. And consumers monitor companies in the marketplace, giving feedback with their purchasing behavior.

Moving government activities to the private sector would make them more "public." Economist John Blundell said that, where he grew up in England, a government water facility had posted a sign, Public Property:

Keep Out. But after the facility was privatized, a new sign went up: Private Property: Public Welcome. Private businesses have an incentive to be transparent and promote good community relations.

British privatizations revealed problems that had been hidden inside government businesses, such as unknown debts, pension liabilities, and performance issues. With the privatization of the British nuclear industry, the large size of its financial problems was revealed. In preparing British Telecom for privatization, the Thatcher government found that the company "had not the faintest idea which of its activities were profitable and which were not." For British Airways, the government found undisclosed losses of hundreds of millions of British pounds as the company was being readied for privatization.

In the U.S. government, the National Park Service provides few public details about the budgets of its individual parks and sites. By contrast, the private, nonprofit Mount Vernon estate in Virginia—home of George Washington—publishes audited financial statements showing how money is raised and spent.

Or consider the USPS's accounting. The postal company provides some services in its legal monopoly and other services in competitive markets, but its financial statements make it difficult to determine how much it earns or loses on each. The company attributes a large share of costs to overhead, which hides internal cross-subsidies. Economist Robert Shapiro found that the USPS manipulates its accounting to raise prices on letters, and then uses the extra revenues to subsidize its express mail and package delivery.

Amtrak similarly hides cross-subsidies behind its opaque accounting, so it is difficult to determine the profits or losses on each of its routes. Amtrak also has a history of hiding information from investigators and of presenting unrealistic projections to Congress.

The Tennessee Valley Authority (TVA) has long been a secretive organization and immune from outside criticism, particularly with respect to its safety and environmental record. Failures at its Kingston Fossil Plant in 2008 led to the largest coal ash spill in U.S. history. The TVA had been aware of the risk but failed to take needed steps to avert it. Why? Federal auditors blamed TVA's management culture, which focuses on covering up mistakes. At the TVA, a "litigation strategy seems to have prevailed over transparency and accountability," said the auditors.

A final transparency issue is that federal agencies that operate services are often the same agencies that regulate them. The FAA operates air traffic control and regulates aviation safety. The Transportation Security Administration operates airport security and also regulates it. In such cases, privatizing the operations would eliminate the conflict of interest, and agency decisions that are now made internally would be made externally and publicly. This transparency issue is one reason the Thatcher government figured that—even if an industry had monopoly elements—

privatizing that industry would improve it because the government regulator would be split off from the entity being regulated. Privatization and transparency go hand in hand.

* * *

[5.] Enhances Customer Service

Governments are often the butt of jokes for their poor customer service. Not all government agencies provide poor service, and people have bad experiences with private companies, of course. But public polling shows that Americans have a dim view of the service they receive from federal agencies. One poll found that just one-third of the public thinks that the government gives competent service. And an annual survey of the public's "customer satisfaction" with various public and private services found that satisfaction with federal services is lower than with virtually all private services.

The problem is one of incentives. Government employees usually receive no tips, promotions, or other benefits for providing good service. Unlike sales people in private companies, they do not have to compete to find customers, so they have free rein to be unfriendly and slow.

A British Treasury study found that "most indicators of service quality have improved" in the privatized industries in that nation. When British Telecom was privatized and opened to competition, the wait time for a new phone line fell from many months to two weeks.

With British passenger rail privatization, on-time performance improved and customer satisfaction has been quite high, despite a huge increase in ridership. With Japanese rail privatization, fares dipped modestly, accident rates plunged, and ridership increased.

In the United Kingdom's privatized water industry, supply interruptions are down, the number of customers with low water pressure has fallen, and water quality has improved. Privatization is not just about efficiency, it is also about better serving public needs.

[6.] Removes Politics from Decision Making

Decisions in government organizations often reflect political factors that raise costs and misallocate spending. Comparing government and private ownership in the *Journal of Economic Perspectives*, economist Andrei Shleifer argued, "Elimination of politically motivated resource allocation has unquestionably been the principal benefit of privatization around the world."

A British finance expert said that in the years before Thatcher, "there had been frequent interference in running the nationalized industries," with politicians often making conflicting demands of companies, such as favoring higher prices one day and lower prices the next. Before Thatcher, many coal mines were kept open, not because they made economic or environmental sense, but because the coal mining unions had political power.

In America, federal businesses are unable to end unneeded spending because members of Congress defend activities in their districts. To please politicians, Amtrak runs low-value routes that lose hundreds of dollars per passenger. And Congress blocks the USPS from consolidating mail processing centers and closing low-volume post offices. The agency's least-used 4,500 rural post offices average just 4.4 customer visits a day.

The story of the FAA is similar. Politicians prevent the agency from closing unneeded air traffic control (ATC) facilities, and they prevent the elimination of jobs in FAA facilities in their districts. They have even required the FAA "to procure certain hardware and encouraged it to select certain contractors." Then there is the problem of "zombie" ATC towers:

> More than 100 U.S. airport towers and radar rooms have so few flights that they should be shut down late at night under the government's own guidelines, a move that would save taxpayers $10 million a year. Air-traffic controllers, who make a median $108,000 annual wage, have little to do overnight at those locations, which remain open because of pressure from lawmakers who control the Federal Aviation Administration's budget. Members of Congress from both parties have blocked attempts to cut tower hours or merge radar rooms, according to interviews and documents.

Such pork barrel politics make us all poorer by raising the costs of services. The environment also suffers because it is wasteful to run low-value trains and to keep open low-value ATC facilities and post offices.

* * *

Opportunities for Federal Privatization

President Ronald Reagan started a discussion on federal privatization in the 1980s. His administration explored privatizing the postal service, railroads, electric utilities, the air traffic control system, and federal land. A Reagan-appointed commission issued a major report in 1988 proposing various privatization options, but the administration's efforts mainly stalled. The administration did oversee the privatization of the National Consumer Cooperative Bank in 1981 and the freight railroad, Conrail, in 1987 for $1.7 billion. Following Reagan, President George H. W. Bush issued an executive order supporting privatization, but he made little progress on reforms.

President Bill Clinton had more success. During his administration, the Alaska Power Administration was sold in 1996 for $87 million; the Elk Hills Naval Petroleum Reserve was sold in 1998 for $3.7 billion; and the U.S. Enrichment Corporation was sold in 1998 for $3.1 billion. In 2000, Congress passed legislation putting Intelsat (owned by a consortium of governments) on the road to privatization.

The George W. Bush administration proposed partly privatizing the Social Security retirement system, but that effort was blocked in Congress. On the other side of the ledger, Bush signed into law a bill nationalizing security screening at U.S. airports.

President Barack Obama's budget for 2014 proposed privatizing the Tennessee Valley Authority. The administration also pursued the sale of excess federal buildings.

Recent decades have seen more of a focus on partial privatization. Under Presidents Bill Clinton and George W. Bush, for example, the Pentagon moved a large number of military families to 187,000 private housing units. That program has been very successful: housing quality has improved and costs are down. Also, recent administrations have encouraged private involvement in the U.S. space program, and a number of firms have won contracts to resupply the International Space Station.

Privatization will likely be on the agenda in coming years. Budget deficits are here to stay, so policymakers will be looking for ways to reduce spending and raise revenues. Policymakers will also be looking for ways to boost America's sluggish economic growth. As time passes, policymakers will be able to draw on ever more foreign privatization successes. We know that postal services, air traffic control, passenger railroads, and other activities can be successfully moved to the private sector because other countries have now done it.

Any activity that can be supported by customer charges, advertising, voluntary contributions, or other sorts of private support can be privatized. Government activities may be privatized as either for-profit businesses or nonprofit organizations, depending on the circumstances. The important thing is to move activities to the private sector, where they can grow, change, and be an organic part of society connected to the actual needs of citizens.

* * *

35

"*Federalist* No. 70: Where Does the Public Service Begin and End?"

Janine R. Wedel

Without revolution, public debate, or even much public awareness, a giant workforce has invaded Washington, D.C.—one that can undermine the public and national interest from the inside. This workforce consists of government contractors, specifically those who perform "inherently governmental" functions that the government deems so integral to its work that only federal employees should carry them out. Today, many federal government functions are conducted, and many public priorities and decisions are driven, by private companies and players instead of government agencies and officials who are duty-bound to answer to citizens and sworn to uphold the national interest.

It is hard to imagine that the founding fathers would have embraced this state of affairs. Acting as a nation—defending its security and providing for the safety of its citizens—is a bedrock concept in some of the *Federalist Papers*. For instance, John Jay writes in *Federalist* No. 2,

> As a nation we have made peace and war; as a nation we have vanquished our common enemies; as a nation we have formed alliances, and made treaties, and entered into various compacts and conventions with foreign states.
>
> A strong sense of the value and blessings of union induced the people, at a very early period, to institute a federal government to preserve and perpetuate it.

James Madison lays out a forceful case for the separation and distribution of government powers. He cautions against "a tyrannical concentration of all the powers of government in the same hands" and outlines the importance of maintaining boundaries among the divisions of government (see *Federalist* No. 47, 48, 51). I argue that the considerable contracting out of government functions is counter to the vision espoused by these statesmen. Such contracting out potentially erodes the government's ability to operate in the public and national interest. It also creates the conditions for the intertwining of state and private power and the concentration of power in just a few hands—about which Madison warned.

The Indispensable Hand

Once, government contractors primarily sold military parts, prepared food, or printed government reports. Today, contractors routinely perform "inherently governmental" functions—activities that involve "the exercise of sovereign government authority or the establishment of procedures and processes related to the oversight of monetary transactions or entitlements." The 20 "inherently governmental" functions on the books include "command of military forces, especially the leadership of military personnel who are members of the combat, combat support, or combat service support role"; "the conduct of foreign relations and the determination of foreign policy"; "the determination of agency policy, such as determining the content and application of regulations"; "the determination of Federal program priorities or budget requests"; "the direction and control of Federal employees"; "the direction and control of intelligence and counterintelligence operations; the selection or nonselection of individuals for Federal Government employment, including the interviewing of individuals for employment"; and "the approval of position descriptions and performance standards for Federal employees."

Government contractors are involved in many, if not all, of these arenas of government work. Consider, for instance, that contractors perform the following tasks:

- Run intelligence operations: Contractors from private security companies have been hired to help track and kill suspected militants in Afghanistan and Pakistan. At the National Security Agency (NSA), the number of contractor facilities approved for classified work jumped from 41 in 2002 to 1,265 in 2006. A full 95 percent of the workers at the very secret National Reconnaissance Office (one of the 16 intelligence agencies), which runs U.S. spy satellites and analyzes the information that they produce, are full-time contractors. In more than half of the 117 contracts let by three big agencies of the U.S. Department of Homeland Security (DHS)—the Coast Guard, Transportation Security Administration, and Office of Procurement Operations—the Government Accountability Office (GAO) found that contractors did inherently governmental work. One company, for instance, was awarded $42.4 million to develop budget and policies for the DHS, as well as to support its information analysis, procurement operations, and infrastructure protection.
- Manage—and more—federal taxpayer monies doled out under the stimulus plans and bailouts: The government enlisted money manager BlackRock to help advise it and manage the unsuccessful attempt to rescue Bear Stearns, as well as to save AIG and Citigroup. BlackRock also won a bid to help the Federal Reserve evaluate hard-to-price assets of Freddie Mac and Fannie Mae. * * * With regard to the $700 billion

bailout in the fall of 2008, known as the Troubled Asset Relief Program, the U.S. Treasury Department hired several contractors to set up a process to disburse the funds.

- Control crucial databases: In a mega-contract awarded by the DHS in 2004, Accenture LLP was granted up to $10 billion to supervise and enlarge a mammoth U.S. government project to track citizens of foreign countries as they enter and exit the United States. As the undersecretary for border and transportation security at the DHS at the time remarked, "I don't think you could overstate the impact of this responsibility in terms of the security of our nation."
- Choose other contractors: The Pentagon has employed contractors to counsel it on selecting other contractors. The General Services Administration enlisted CACI, a company based in Arlington, Virginia—some of whose employees were among those allegedly involved in the Abu Ghraib prisoner abuse scandal in Iraq, according to U.S. Department of the Army—to help the government suspend and debar other contractors. . . . (CACI itself later became the subject of possible suspension or debarment from federal contracts.)
- Oversee other contractors: The DHS is among the federal agencies that have hired contractors to select and supervise other contractors. Some of these contractors set policy and business goals and plan reorganizations. And, in the National Clandestine Service, an integral part of the Central Intelligence Agency (CIA), contractors are sometimes in charge of other contractors.
- Execute military and occupying operations: The Department of Defense is ever more dependent on contractors to supply a host of "mission-critical services," including "information technology systems, interpreters, intelligence analysts, as well as weapons system maintenance and base operation support." U.S. efforts in Afghanistan and Iraq illustrate this reliance. As of September 2009, U.S.-paid contractors far outnumbered U.S. military personnel in Afghanistan, composing nearly two-thirds of the combined contractor and military personnel workforce (approximately 104,000 Defense Department contractors compared with 64,000 uniformed personnel). In Iraq, contractors made up nearly half of the combined contractor and military personnel workforce (roughly 114,000 Defense Department contractors compared with 130,000 uniformed personnel). These proportions are in sharp contrast to the 1991 Persian Gulf War: The 540,000 military personnel deployed in that effort greatly outnumbered the 9,200 contractors on the scene.
- Draft official documents: Contractors have prepared congressional testimony for the secretary of energy. Websites of contractors working for the Department of Defense also have posted announcements of job openings for analysts to perform functions such as preparing the defense budget. One contractor boasted of having written the U.S. Army's Field Manual on "Contractors on the Battlefield."

In short, the outsourcing of many inherently governmental functions is now routine. The government is utterly dependent on private contractors to carry out many such functions. As the Acquisition Advisory Panel, a government-mandated, typically contractor-friendly task force made up of representatives from industry, government, and academe, acknowledged in a 2007 report that "[m]any federal agencies rely extensively on contractors in the performance of their basic missions. In some cases, contractors are solely or predominantly responsible for the performance of mission-critical functions that were traditionally performed by civil servants." This trend, the report concluded, "poses a threat to the government's long-term ability to perform its mission" and could "undermine the integrity of the government's decision making."

Contractor officials and employees are interdependent with government, involved in all aspects of governing and negotiating "over policy making, implementation, and enforcement," as one legal scholar has noted. Contractor and government employees work side by side in what has come to be called the "blended" or "embedded" workforce, often sitting next to each other in cubicles or sharing an office and doing the same or similar work (but typically with markedly different pay). When the GAO looked into the setup of Defense Department offices, its investigation established that, in some, the percentage of contractors was in the 80s.

Yet contractors' imperatives are not necessarily the same as the government's imperatives. Contractor companies are responsible for making a profit for their shareholders; government is supposedly answerable to the public in a democracy.

Amid this environment, which is complicated by mixed motives, contractors are positioned to influence policy to their liking on even the most sensitive, mission-critical government functions, such as fighting wars, guarding against terrorism, and shaping economic policy. Government investigators looking into intelligence, defense, homeland security, energy, and other arenas have raised questions about who drives policy—government or contractors—and whether government has the information, expertise, institutional memory, and personnel to manage contractors—or is it the other way around? And in three government agencies that the GAO investigated, including the DOD and DHS, the GAO found that "sensitive information is not fully safeguarded and thus may remain at risk of unauthorized disclosure or misuse." The result of all of this is that the nation's safety, security, and sovereignty may be jeopardized, along with the very core of democratic society—citizens' ability to hold their government accountable and have a say in public decisions. This seems far afield from the concept of the nation expressed by, say, John Jay.

Enabling Big Government

How did this state of affairs come to be?

Ironically, the perennial American predilection to rail against "big government" is partly to blame for the creation of still bigger government—the "shadow government" of companies, consulting firms, nonprofits, think tanks, and other nongovernmental entities that contract with the government to do so much of its work. This is government for sure, but often of a less visible and accountable kind.

The necessity of making government *look* small—or at least contained—has fueled the rise of this shadow government. In an ostensible effort to limit government, caps have been put on how many civil servants government can hire. But citizens still expect government to supply all manner of services—from Medicare and Social Security to interstate highways to national defense. To avoid this conundrum, both Democratic and Republican administrations over the years have been busily enlisting more and more contractors (who, in turn, often hire subcontractors) to do the work of government. Because they are not counted as part of the federal workforce, it can appear as if the size of government is being kept in check. Like the Potemkin village of Russia, constructed to make the ruler or the foreigner think that things are rosy, the public is led to believe they have something they do not.

* * *

Where federal employees once executed most government work, today, upwards of three-quarters of the work of federal government, measured in terms of jobs, is contracted out. Many of the most dramatic alterations have occurred since the end of the Cold War. Contracting out accelerated and assumed new incarnations during and after the Bill Clinton administration. The advent of ever more complex technologies, which gave birth to information technologies on which society now relies and which the U.S. government largely outsources, tipped the balance even further. The shadow government, which devises and implements so much policy and forms the core of governance, is the elephant in the room.

The shadow government encompasses all of the entities that swell the ranks of contractors and entire bastions of outsourcing—neighborhoods whose high-rise office buildings house an army of contractors and "Beltway Bandits." Largely out of sight except to Washington-area dwellers, contractors and the companies they work for do not appear in government phone books. They are less likely to be dragged before congressional committees for hostile questioning. They function with less visibility and scrutiny on a regular basis than government employees would face. Most important, they are not counted as government employees, and so the fiction of limited government can be upheld, while the reality is an expanding sprawl of entities that are the government in practice.

The Elephant in the Room

While it may be the elephant in the room, we know little about the nature of the beast. A key barometer of the growth of the shadow government, driven in part by an increase in demand for military, nation-building, and homeland security services after 9/11, is the number of government employees versus contractors. Government scholar Paul C. Light has compiled the most reliable figures on contractors. The number of contract workers—compared with civil servants, uniformed military personnel, and postal service employees—increased steadily over the last two decades. In 1990, roughly three out of every five employees in the total federal labor force worked indirectly for government—in jobs created by contracts and grants, as opposed to jobs performed by civil servants, uniformed military personnel, and postal service workers. By 2002, two out of every three employees in the federal labor force worked indirectly for government, and, by 2008, the number was three out of four.

In the DHS—the mega-bureaucracy established in 2003 through the merger of 180,000 employees and 22 agencies, the creation of which entailed the largest reorganization of the federal government in more than half a century—contractors are more numerous than federal employees. The DHS estimates that it employs 188,000 workers, compared with 200,000 contractors.

In some arenas of government, contractors virtually *are* the government. The DHS, which includes the Customs Service, Coast Guard, and Transportation Security Administration, has relied substantially on contractors to fill new security needs and shore up gaps. In nine cases examined by the GAO, "decisions to contract for . . . services were largely driven by the need for staff and expertise to get DHS programs and operations up and running quickly."

* * *

Meanwhile, about 70 percent of the budget of the U.S. intelligence community is devoted to contracts, according to the Office of the Director of National Intelligence, which was created in 2005 and supervises 16 federal agencies. Contract employees make up an estimated one-quarter of the country's core intelligence workforce, according to the same office. The director both heads the U.S. intelligence community and serves as the main advisor to the president on national security matters.

Contractors are plentiful in other arenas of government that directly affect national and homeland security, not only the departments of defense and homeland security. For instance, nearly 90 percent of the budgets of the Department of Energy and NASA go to contracts.

Information technology (IT), which touches practically every area of government operations, is largely contracted out. Upwards of three-quarters of governmental IT is estimated to have been outsourced even before the major Iraq War-related push to contract out. For companies in search of federal business, IT is the "the new frontier," according to Thomas Burlin, who is in charge of IBM Business Consulting Services' federal practice. With ever more complex technologies always on the horizon, the outsourcing of IT only stands to grow. Although contracting out computer network services may be unproblematic or even desirable, many IT functions cannot be separated from vital operations such as logistics that are integral to an agency's mission. * * *

Contractors are so integrated into the federal workforce that proponents of insourcing acknowledge that they face an uphill battle. Yet the proliferation of contracting widens the de facto base of government in which new forms of unaccountable governance can flourish. It makes government more vulnerable to operations that fall short of the public and national interest.

Swiss-Cheese Government

In theory, contracts and contractors are overseen by government employees who would guard against abuse. But that has become less and less true as the capacity of government oversight has diminished—a lessening that seems to flow directly from the need to maintain the facade of small government. A look at trend lines is illuminating. The number of civil servants who potentially could oversee contractors fell during the Clinton administration and continued to drop during the George W. Bush administration. The contracting business boomed under Bush, while the acquisition workforce—government workers charged with the conceptualization, design, awarding, use, or quality control of contracts and contractors—remained virtually constant. * * *

The result is that government sometimes lacks the information it needs to monitor the entities that work for it. A top GAO official reported that in many cases, government decision makers scarcely supervise the companies on their payrolls. As a result, she observed, they are unable to answer simple questions about what the firms are doing, whether they have performed well or not, and whether their performance has been cost-effective.

* * *

A paucity of oversight is one factor that has led the GAO to identify large procurement operations as "high risk" because of "their greater susceptibility to fraud, waste, abuse, and mismanagement." The list of high-risk areas has, since 1990 or 1992 (depending on the specific area), included the large procurement operations of the Departments of Defense and Energy, as well as NASA. The DHS has been on the high-risk list since its creation in 2003, and it has been faulted for a lack of oversight in procurement. As comptroller general of the United States, David M. Walker (2003) said that he is "not confident that [high-risk] agencies have the ability to effectively manage cost, quality, and performance in contracts." He added that the current challenges to contract oversight are "unprecedented."

* * *

When the number of civil servants available to supervise government contracts and contractors proportionately falls, thus decreasing the government's oversight capacity, and when crucial governmental functions are outsourced, government begins to resemble Swiss cheese—full of holes. Contractors are plugging these holes. As a consequence, contractors have become the home for much information, legitimacy, expertise, institutional memory, and leadership that once resided in government.

* * *

Concentrating Powers

Swiss-cheese government lends itself to the kind of concentration of powers that Madison warned about. Over the past decade and a half, new institutional forms of governing have gathered force as contractors perform inherently governmental functions beyond the capacity of government to manage them; as government and contractor officials interact (or do not) in the course of projects; as chains of command among contractors and the agencies they supposedly work for have become ever more convoluted; and as contractors standing in for government are not subject to the same rules that apply to government officials. The result is that new forms of governing join the state and the private, often most visibly in intelligence, defense, and homeland security enterprises, where so much has taken place since 9/11.

Incentive structures that encourage government executives (notably intelligence and military professionals) to move to the private sector, as well as new contracting practices and a limited number of government contracting firms, are among the factors that facilitate the intertwining of state and private power. With regard to the former, not only are salaries and perks for comparable jobs typically greater in the private sector, but often, so is prestige. Many government executives, retirees, and other employees follow the money by moving to the private sector. But the landing spots that supply the big bucks—and with them, influence and stature—are often those held by former government executives. Although there are rules to address the revolving door syndrome, companies with significant government contracts often are headed by former senior officials of intelligence- and defense-related government agencies. * * *

When government contractors hire former directors of intelligence- and defense-related government agencies, they are banking on "coincidences" of interest between their hires and their hires' former (government) employers. (A coincidence of interest occurs when a player crafts an array of overlapping roles across organizations to serve his own agenda—or that of his network—above that of those of the organizations for which he works.) The result of such coincidences in the intelligence arena is that "the Intelligence Community and the contractors are so tightly intertwined at the leadership level that their interests, practically speaking, are identical," as one intelligence expert said.

Also potentially facilitating the fusion of state and private power are changes in contracting practices and the dearth of competition among and consolidation of government contracting firms, which has led to government dependence on a limited number of firms. The Clinton administration transformed contracting rules with regard to oversight, competition, and transparency under the rubric of "reinventing government." As a result, small contracts often have been replaced by bigger, and frequently open-ended, multiyear, multimillion- and even billion-dollar and potentially much more lucrative contracts with a "limited pool of contractors," as the Acquisition Advisory Panel put it. Today, most federal procurement contracts are conferred either without competition or to a limited set of contractors. A Barack Obama White House memo noted the "significant increase in the dollars awarded without full and open competition" during the period 2001–2008. Moreover, industry consolidation (defense is a case in point) has produced fewer and larger firms. * * *

The routine outsourcing of government functions, the structures of incentives, and new contracting rules and practices encourage new forms of governing in which state and private power are joined. These forms seem very far afield indeed from Madison's vision of a nation in which government powers cannot be concentrated.

Reclaiming the Soul of Government

Some authorities have sounded alarm bells about the present state of affairs. In 2007, David M. Walker, the comptroller general of the United States and longtime head of the GAO, called for "a fundamental reexamination of when and under what circumstances we should use contractors versus civil servants or military personnel," And President Obama acknowledged the problem. Early in his term, Obama announced plans to "insource" certain jobs—transferring work back to the government—and expressed concern about the outsourcing of inherently governmental functions. While the administration has proposed some insourcing and efforts to push back or review the ever upward spiral of outsourcing, the current state of affairs cannot simply be rolled back.

It is not just that government is utterly dependent on private companies to do much of its work. The United States faces an entrenched problem that cannot be fixed simply by insourcing jobs or by hiring more government employees to oversee contractors, as some observers have suggested. A top-to-bottom rethinking of how government makes use of contractors is necessary. One particularly important issue that deserves attention is how to rebuild capacity that has been lost with the privatization of information, expertise, and institutional memory. Another set of challenges lies in reforming the contract laws and regulations that have been changed over the past decade and a half—and that have made the contracting system less transparent and accountable and more vulnerable to the influence of private and corporate agendas.

The changes that have taken place are so systemic and sweeping that a new system, in effect, is now in place. It is the ground on which any future changes will occur. A fundamental redesign of the system is necessary. In that redesign, we would do well to pay attention to the vision of the founding fathers regarding the security of the nation and safety of its citizens, as well as the dangers inherent in the consolidation of powers.

But reclaiming government is not merely a design challenge. Government must take its soul back. While it may be strange to mention "soul" and government in the same breath, linking the quintessentially personal with the quintessentially bureaucratic and impersonal, a government procurement lawyer described the current state of affairs as the "ebbing away of the soul of government." When an institution is drained of expertise, information, and institutional memory, it not only loses its edge, but also its essence.

* * *

Discussion Questions

1. What is an "inherently governmental function?" The current definition in federal law is "a function so intimately related to the public interest as to require performance by Federal Government employees." But this actually provides very little useful guidance, since it is a tautology: work that must be performed by federal government employees is defined as work so important that it must be performed by federal employees. Is there an alternative definition that is both meaningful and precise? What might that be?

2. One criticism is that privatization can actually *increase* costs, since private actors will require a profit which governments do not need. One common example is Medicare, which has far lower administrative expenses (around 2 percent of total costs) than private health insurance

companies (which are estimated at around 17 percent of total costs). The bankruptcies of toll road operators show what can happen when private actors can't generate sufficient profits. Is this an argument against privatization in general, in the sense that government responsibilities are by their very nature not profit-generating functions?

CHAPTER 8

The Judiciary

36

The Federalist, No. 78

Alexander Hamilton

The judiciary, Hamilton wrote in The Federalist, *No. 78, "will always be the least dangerous to the political rights of the Constitution; because it will be least in a capacity to annoy or injure them." The lack of danger Hamilton spoke of stems from the courts' lack of enforcement or policy power. Or as Hamilton more eloquently put it, the judiciary has "no influence over either the sword or the purse": it must rely on the executive branch and state governments to enforce its rulings, and depends on the legislature for its appropriations and rules governing its structure. Critics of "judicial activism" would likely disagree about the weakness of the judiciary relative to the other branches of government. But Hamilton saw an independent judiciary as an important check on the other branches' ability to assume too much power (the "bulwarks of a limited Constitution against legislative encroachments"). He also argued that the federal judiciary, as interpreter of the Constitution, would gain its power from the force of its judgments, which were rooted in the will of the people.*

To the People of the State of New York:

We proceed now to an examination of the judiciary department of the proposed government.

In unfolding the defects of the existing Confederation, the utility and necessity of a federal judicature have been clearly pointed out. It is the less necessary to recapitulate the considerations there urged, as the propriety of the institution in the abstract is not disputed; the only questions which have been raised being relative to the manner of constituting it, and to its extent. To these points, therefore, our observations shall be confined.

The manner of constituting it seems to embrace these several objects: 1st. The mode of appointing the judges. 2d. The tenure by which they are to hold their places. 3d. The partition of the judiciary authority between different courts, and their relations to each other.

First. As to the mode of appointing the judges; this is the same with that of appointing the officers of the Union in general, and has been so fully discussed in the two last numbers, that nothing can be said here which would not be useless repetition.

Second. As to the tenure by which the judges are to hold their places: this chiefly concerns their duration in office; the provisions for their support; the precautions for their responsibility.

According to the plan of the convention, all judges who may be appointed by the United States are to hold their offices *during good behavior*; which is conformable to the most approved of the State constitutions, and among the rest, to that of this State. Its propriety having been drawn into question by the adversaries of that plan, is no light symptom of the rage for objection, which disorders their imaginations and judgments. The standard of good behavior for the continuance in office of the judicial magistracy is certainly one of the most valuable of the modern improvements in the practice of government. In a monarchy it is an excellent barrier to the despotism of the prince; in a republic it is a no less excellent barrier to the encroachments and oppressions of the representative body. And it is the best expedient which can be devised in any government to secure a steady, upright, and impartial administration of the laws.

Whoever attentively considers the different departments of power must perceive, that, in a government in which they are separated from each other, the judiciary, from the nature of its functions, will always be the least dangerous to the political rights of the Constitution; because it will be least in a capacity to annoy or injure them. The Executive not only dispenses the honors, but holds the sword of the community. The legislature not only commands the purse, but prescribes the rules by which the duties and rights of every citizen are to be regulated. The judiciary, on the contrary, has no influence over either the sword or the purse; no direction either of the strength or of the wealth of the society; and can take no active resolution whatever. It may truly be said to have neither FORCE NOR WILL, but merely judgment; and must ultimately depend upon the aid of the executive arm even for the efficacy of its judgments.

This simple view of the matter suggests several important consequences. It proves incontestably that the judiciary is beyond comparison the weakest of the three departments of power that it can never attack with success either of the other two; and that all possible care is requisite to enable it to defend itself against their attacks. It equally proves that though individual oppression may now and then proceed from the courts of justice, the general liberty of the people can never be endangered from that quarter; I mean so long as the judiciary remains truly distinct from both the legislature and the Executive. For I agree, that "there is no liberty, if the power of judging be not separated from the legislative and executive powers." And it proves, in the last place, that as liberty can have nothing to fear from the judiciary alone, but would have every thing to fear from its union with either of the other departments; that as all the effects of such a union must ensue from a dependence of the former on the latter, notwithstanding a nominal and apparent separation; that as, from the natural feebleness of the judiciary it is in continual jeopardy of being overpowered, awed, or influenced by its coordinate branches; and that as nothing can contribute so much to its firmness and independence as permanency in office, this quality may therefore be justly regarded as an indispensable ingredient in its constitution, and, in a great measure, as the citadel of the public justice and the public security.

The complete independence of the courts of justice is peculiarly essential in a limited Constitution. By a limited Constitution, I understand one which contains certain specified exceptions to the legislative authority; such, for instance, as that it shall pass no bills of attainder, no *ex-post-facto* laws, and the like. Limitations of this kind can be preserved in practice no other way than through the medium of courts of justice, whose duty it must be to declare all acts contrary to the manifest tenor of the Constitution void. Without this, all the reservations of particular rights or privileges would amount to nothing.

Some perplexity respecting the rights of the courts to pronounce legislative acts void, because contrary to the constitution, has arisen from an imagination that the doctrine would imply a superiority of the judiciary to the legislative power. It is urged that the authority which can declare the acts of another void must necessarily be superior to the one whose acts may be declared void. As this doctrine is of great importance in all the American constitutions, a brief discussion of the ground on which it rests cannot be unacceptable.

There is no position which depends on clearer principles than that every act of a delegated authority, contrary to the tenor of the commission under which it is exercised, is void. No legislative act, therefore, contrary to the Constitution, can be valid. To deny this would be to affirm that the deputy is greater than his principal; that the servant is above his master; that the representatives of the people are superior to the people themselves; that men acting by virtue of powers may do not only what their powers do not authorize, but what they forbid.

If it be said that the legislative body are themselves the constitutional judges of their own powers, and that the construction they put upon them is conclusive upon the other departments, it may be answered that this cannot be the natural presumption where it is not to be collected from any particular provisions in the Constitution. It is not otherwise to be supposed that the Constitution could intend to enable the representatives of the people to substitute their *will* to that of their constituents. It is far more rational to suppose that the courts were designed to be an intermediate body between the people and the legislature, in order, among other things, to keep the latter within the limits assigned to their authority. The interpretation of the laws is the proper and peculiar province of the courts. A constitution is, in fact, and must be regarded by the judges, as a fundamental law. It therefore belongs to them to ascertain its meaning, as well as the meaning of any particular act proceeding from the legislative body. If there should happen to be an irreconcilable variance between the two, that which has the superior obligation and validity ought, of course, to be preferred; or, in other words, the Constitution ought to be preferred to the statute, the intention of the people to the intention of their agents.

Nor does this conclusion by any means suppose a superiority of the judicial to the legislative power. It only supposes that the power of the people is superior to both; and that where the will of the legislature, declared in its statutes, stands in opposition to that of the people, declared in the Constitution, the judges ought to be governed by the latter rather than the former. They ought to regulate their decisions by the fundamental laws, rather than by those which are not fundamental.

This exercise of judicial discretion, in determining between two contradictory laws, is exemplified in a familiar instance. It not uncommonly happens that there are two statutes existing at one time, clashing in whole or in part with each other, and neither of them containing any repealing clause or expression. In such a case, it is the province of the courts to liquidate and fix their meaning and operation. So far as they can, by any fair construction, be reconciled to each other, reason and law conspire to dictate that this should be done; where this is impracticable, it becomes a matter of necessity to give effect to one in exclusion of the other. The rule which has obtained in the courts for determining their relative validity is, that the last in order of time shall be preferred to the first. But this is a mere rule of construction, not derived from any positive law but from the nature and reason of the thing. It is a rule not enjoined upon the courts by legislative provision but adopted by themselves, as consonant to truth and propriety for the direction of their conduct as interpreters of the law. They thought it reasonable, that between the interfering acts of an *equal* authority, that which was the last indication of its will should have the preference.

But in regard to the interfering acts of a superior and subordinate authority, of an original and derivative power, the nature and reason of the thing indicate the converse of that rule as proper to be followed. They teach us that the prior act of a superior ought to be preferred to the subsequent act of an inferior and subordinate authority; and that accordingly, whenever a particular statute contravenes the Constitution, it will be the duty of the judicial tribunals to adhere to the latter and disregard the former.

It can be of no weight to say that the courts, on the pretence of a repugnancy, may substitute their own pleasure to the constitutional intentions of the legislature. This might as well happen in the case of two contradictory statutes; or it might as well happen in every adjudication upon any single statute. The courts must declare the sense of the law; and if they should be disposed to exercise WILL instead of JUDGMENT, the consequence would equally be the substitution of their pleasure to that of the legislative body. The observation, if it prove any thing, would prove that there ought to be no judges distinct from that body.

If, then, the courts of justice are to be considered as the bulwarks of a limited Constitution against legislative encroachments, this consideration will afford a strong argument for the permanent tenure of judicial offices, since nothing will contribute so much as this to that independent spirit in the judges which must be essential to the faithful performance of so arduous a duty.

This independence of the judges is equally requisite to guard the Constitution and the rights of individuals from the effects of those ill humors, which the arts of designing men or the influence of particular conjunctures sometimes disseminate among the people themselves; and which, though they speedily give place to better information and more deliberate reflection, have a tendency, in the meantime, to occasion dangerous innovations in the government, and serious oppressions of the minor party in the community. Though I trust the friends of the proposed Constitution will never concur with its enemies in questioning that fundamental principle of republican government, which admits the right of the people to alter or abolish the established Constitution whenever they find it inconsistent with their happiness; yet it is not to be inferred from this principle that the representatives of the people, whenever a momentary inclination happens to lay hold of a majority of their constituents, incompatible with the provisions in the existing Constitution, would, on that account, be justifiable in a violation of those provisions; or that the courts would be under a greater obligation to connive at infractions in this shape, than when they had proceeded wholly from the cabals of the representative body. Until the people have by some solemn and authoritative act annulled or changed the established form, it is binding upon themselves collectively, as well as individually; and no presumption, or even knowledge, of their sentiments, can warrant their representatives in a departure from it, prior to such an act. But it is easy to see that it would require an uncommon portion of fortitude in the judges to do their duty as faithful guardians of the Constitution, where legislative invasions of it had been instigated by the major voice of the community.

But it is not with a view to infractions of the Constitution only that the independence of the judges may be an essential safeguard against the effects of occasional ill humors in the society. These sometimes extend no farther than to the injury of the private rights of particular classes of citizens by unjust and partial laws. Here also the firmness of the judicial magistracy is of vast importance in mitigating the severity and confining the operation of such laws. It not only serves to moderate the immediate mischiefs of those which may have been passed, but it operates as a check upon the legislative body in passing them; who, perceiving that obstacles to the success of iniquitous intention are to be expected from the scruples of the courts, are in a manner compelled by the very motives of the injustice they meditate to qualify their attempts. This is a circumstance calculated to have more influence upon the character of our governments, than but few may be aware of. The benefits of the integrity and moderation of the judiciary have already been felt in more States than one; and though they may have displeased those whose sinister expectations they may have disappointed, they must have commanded the esteem and applause of all the virtuous and disinterested. Considerate men of every description ought to prize whatever will tend to beget or fortify that temper in the courts; as no man can be sure that he may not be tomorrow the victim of a spirit of injustice by which he may be a gainer today. And every man must now feel that the inevitable tendency of such a spirit is to sap the foundations of public and private confidence, and to introduce in its stead universal distrust and distress.

That inflexible and uniform adherence to the rights of the Constitution and of individuals, which we perceive to be indispensable in the courts of justice, can certainly not be expected from judges who hold their offices by a temporary commission. Periodical appointments, however regulated or by whomsoever made, would, in some way or other, be fatal to their necessary independence. If the power of making them was committed either to the Executive or legislature, there would be danger of an improper complaisance to the branch which possessed it; if to both, there would be an unwillingness to hazard the displeasure of either; if to the people or to persons chosen by them for the special purpose, there would be too great a disposition to consult popularity, to justify a reliance that nothing would be consulted but the Constitution and the laws.

There is yet a further and a weightier reason for the permanency of the judicial offices, which is deducible from the nature of the qualifications they require. It has been frequently remarked, with great propriety, that a voluminous code of laws is one of the inconveniences necessarily connected with the advantages of a free government. To avoid an arbitrary discretion in the courts, it is indispensable that they should be bound down by strict rules and precedents, which serve to define and point out their duty in every particular case that comes before them; and it will readily be conceived from the variety of controversies which grow out of the folly and wickedness of mankind, that the records of those precedents must unavoidably swell to a very considerable bulk, and must demand long and laborious study to acquire a competent knowledge of them. Hence it is, that there can be but few men in the society who will have sufficient skill in the laws to qualify them for the stations of judges. And making the proper deductions for the ordinary depravity of human nature, the number must be still smaller of those who unite the requisite integrity with the requisite knowledge. These considerations apprise us that the government can have no great option between fit character; and that a temporary duration in office, which would naturally discourage such characters from quitting a lucrative line of practice to accept a seat on the bench, would have a tendency to throw the administration of justice into hands less able, and less well qualified, to conduct it with utility and dignity. In the present circumstances of this country and in those in which it is likely to be for a long time to come, the disadvantages on this score would be greater than they may at first sight appear; but it must be confessed that they are far inferior to those which present themselves under the other aspects of the subject.

Upon the whole, there can be no room to doubt that the convention acted wisely in copying from the models of those constitutions which have established *good behavior* as the tenure of their judicial offices, in point of duration; and that so far from being blamable on this account, their plan would have been inexcusably defective if it had wanted this important feature of good government. The experience of Great Britain affords an illustrious comment on the excellence of the institution.

PUBLIUS

DISCUSSION QUESTIONS

1. Was Hamilton correct in arguing that the judiciary is the least dangerous branch of government?
2. Critics of the Supreme Court often charge that it rules on issues that should be properly decided in the legislature, while supporters claim that the Court is often the last check against the tyranny of the majority. Who has the stronger case? Can both sides be correct?
3. Hamilton argues that the "power of the people is superior to both" the legislature and the judiciary, and that judges uphold the power of the people when they support the Constitution over a statute that runs counter to the Constitution. He asserts that the people's will is reflected in the Constitution but refers to statutes as reflecting the will of the legislators. Is it legitimate to argue that the Supreme Court is supporting the will of the people, given that it is an unelected body?

"The Court and American Life," from *Storm Center: The Supreme Court in American Politics*

DAVID O'BRIEN

The "textbook" view of the federal judiciary is one in which judges sit in dispassionate review of complex legal questions, render decisions based on a careful reading of constitutional or statutory language, and expect their rulings to be adhered to strictly; the law is the law. This selection shows how unrealistic that picture is. O'Brien notes that the Supreme Court is very much a political institution, whose members pay more attention to the political cycle and public opinion than one might expect. O'Brien reviews the decision-making process in the famous case of Brown v. Board of Education of Topeka, Kansas, *in which the Court invalidated segregated public schools, as an example of how the Court fits itself into the political process. Throughout the case, justices delayed their decision, consolidated cases from around the country, and refused to set a firm timetable for implementation, relying instead on the ambiguous standard "with all deliberate speed." Far from being a purely objective arbiter of legal questions, the Court must pay close attention to its own legitimacy, and by extension the likelihood of compliance: it does no good to issue decisions that will be ignored.*

"Why does the Supreme Court pass the school desegregation case?" asked one of Chief Justice Vinson's law clerks in 1952. *Brown v. Board of Education of Topeka, Kansas* had arrived on the Court's docket in 1951, but it was carried over for oral argument the next term and then consolidated with four other cases and reargued in December 1953. The landmark ruling did not come down until May 17, 1954. "Well," Justice Frankfurter explained, "we're holding it for the election"—1952 was a presidential election year. "You're holding it for the election?" The clerk persisted in disbelief. "I thought the Supreme Court was supposed to decide cases without regard to elections." "When you have a major social political issue of this magnitude," timing and public reactions are important considerations, and, Frankfurter continued, "we do not think this is the time to decide it." Similarly, Tom Clark recalled that the Court awaited, over Douglas's dissent, additional cases from the District of Columbia and other regions, so as "to get a national coverage, rather than a sectional one." Such political considerations are by no means unique. "We often delay adjudication. It's not a question of evading at all," Clark concluded. "It's just the practicalities of life—common sense."

Denied the power of the sword or the purse, the Court must cultivate its institutional prestige. The power of the Court lies in the persuasiveness of its rulings and ultimately rests with other political institutions and public opinion. As an independent force, the Court has no chance to resolve great issues of public policy. *Dred Scott v. Sandford* (1857) and *Brown v. Board of Education* (1954) illustrate the limitations of Supreme Court policy-making. The "great folly," as Senator Henry Cabot Lodge characterized *Dred Scott*, was not the Court's interpretation of the Constitution or the unpersuasive moral position that blacks were not persons under the Constitution. Rather, "the attempt of the Court to settle the slavery question by judicial decision was simple madness." As Lodge explained:

> Slavery involved not only the great moral issue of the right of one man to hold another in bondage and to buy and sell him but it involved also the foundations of a social fabric covering half the country and caused men to feel so deeply that it finally brought them beyond the question of nullification to a point where the life of the Union was at stake and a decision could only be reached by war.

A hundred years later, political struggles within the country and, notably, presidential and congressional leadership in enforcing the Court's school desegregation ruling saved the moral appeal of *Brown* from becoming another "great folly."

Because the Court's decisions are not self-executing, public reactions inevitably weigh on the minds of the justices. Justice Stone, for one, was furious at Chief Justice Hughes's rush to hand down *Powell v. Alabama* (1932). Picketers protested the Scottsboro boys' conviction and death sentence. Stone attributed the Court's rush to judgment to Hughes's "wish to put a stop to the [public] demonstrations around the Court." Opposition to the school desegregation ruling in *Brown* led to bitter, sometimes violent confrontations. In Little Rock, Arkansas, Governor Orval Faubus encouraged disobedience by southern segregationists. The federal National Guard had to be called out to maintain order. The school board in Little Rock unsuccessfully pleaded, in *Cooper v. Aaron* (1958), for the Court's postponement of the implementation of *Brown's* mandate. In the midst of the controversy, Frankfurter worried that Chief Justice Warren's attitude had become "more like that of a fighting politician than that of a judicial statesman." In such confrontations between the Court and the country, "the transcending issue," Frankfurter reminded the brethren, remains that of preserving "the Supreme Court as the authoritative organ of what the Constitution requires." When the justices move too far or too fast in their interpretation of the Constitution, they threaten public acceptance of the Court's legitimacy.

* * *

When deciding major issues of public law and policy, justices must consider strategies for getting public acceptance of their rulings. When striking down the doctrine of "separate but equal" facilities in 1954 in *Brown v. Board of Education (Brown I),* for instance, the Warren Court waited a year before issuing, in *Brown II,* its mandate for "all deliberate speed" in ending racial segregation in public education.

Resistance to the social policy announced in *Brown I* was expected. A rigid timetable for desegregation would only intensify opposition. During oral arguments on *Brown II,* devoted to the question of what kind of decree the Court should issue to enforce *Brown,* Warren confronted the hard fact of southern resistance. The attorney for South Carolina, S. Emory Rogers, pressed for an open-ended decree—one that would not specify when and how desegregation should take place. He boldly proclaimed:

> Mr. Chief Justice, to say we will conform depends on the decree handed down. I am frank to tell you, right now [in] our district I do not think that we will send—[that] the white people of the district will send their children to the Negro schools. It would be unfair to tell the Court that we are going to do that. I do not think it is. But I do think that something can be worked out. We hope so.

"It is not a question of attitude," Warren shot back, "it is a question of conforming to the decree." Their heated exchange continued as follows:

> CHIEF JUSTICE WARREN: But you are not willing to say here that there would be an honest attempt to conform to this decree, if we did leave it to the district court [to implement]?
>
> MR. ROGERS: No, I am not. Let us get the word "honest" out of there.
>
> CHIEF JUSTICE WARREN: No, leave it in.
>
> MR. ROGERS: No, because I would have to tell you that right now we would not conform—we would not send our white children to the Negro schools.

The exchange reinforced Warren's view "that reasonable attempts to start the integration process is *[sic]* all the court can expect in view of the scope of the problem, and that an order to immediately admit all negroes in white schools would be an absurdity because impossible to obey in many areas. Thus, while total immediate integration might be a reasonable order for Kansas, it would be unreasonable for Virginia, and the district judge might decide that a grade a year or three grades a year is *[sic]* reasonable compliance in Virginia." Six law clerks were assigned to prepare a segregation research report. They summarized available studies, discussed how school districts in different regions could be desegregated, and projected the effects and reactions to various desegregation plans.

The Court's problem, as one of Reed's law clerks put it, was to frame a decree "so as to allow such divergent results without making it so broad that evasion is encouraged." The clerks agreed that there should be a simple decree but disagreed on whether there should be guidelines for its implementation. One clerk opposed any guidelines. The others thought that their absence "smacks of indecisiveness, and gives the extremists more time to operate." The problem was how precise a guideline should be established. What would constitute "good-faith" compliance? "Although we think a 12-year gradual desegregation plan permissible," they confessed, "we are not certain that the opinion should explicitly sanction it."

At conference, Warren repeated these concerns. Black and Minton thought that a simple decree, without an opinion, was enough. As Black explained, "the less we say the better off we are." The others disagreed. A short, simple opinion seemed advisable for reaffirming *Brown I* and providing guidance for dealing with the inevitable problems of compliance. Harlan wanted *Brown II* expressly to recognize that school desegregation was a local problem to be solved by local authorities. The others also insisted on making clear that school boards and lower courts had flexibility in ending segregation. In Burton's view, "neither this Court nor district courts should act as a school board or formulate the program" for desegregation.

Agreement emerged that the Court should issue a short opinion-decree. In a memorandum, Warren summarized the main points of agreement. The opinion should simply state that *Brown I* held racially segregated public schools to be unconstitutional. *Brown II* should acknowledge that the ruling created various administrative problems, but emphasize that "local school authorities have the primary responsibility for assessing and solving these problems; [and] the courts will have to consider these problems in determining whether the efforts of local school authorities" are in good-faith compliance. The cases, he concluded, should be remanded to the lower courts "for such proceedings and decree necessary and proper to carry out this Court's decision." The justices agreed, and along these lines Warren drafted the Court's short opinion-decree.

The phrase "all deliberate speed" was borrowed from Holmes's opinion in *Virginia v. West Virginia* (1911), a case dealing with how much of the state's public debt, and when, Virginia ought to receive at the time West Virginia broke off and became a state. It was inserted in the final opinion at the suggestion of Frankfurter. Forced integration might lead to a lowering of educational standards. Immediate, court-ordered desegregation, Frankfurter warned, "would make a mockery of the Constitutional adjudication designed to vindicate a claim to equal treatment to achieve 'integrated' but lower educational standards." The Court, he insisted, "does its duty if it gets effectively under way the righting of a wrong. When the wrong is deeply rooted state policy the court does its duty if it decrees measures that reverse the direction of the unconstitutional policy so as to uproot it 'with all deliberate speed.'" As much an apology for not setting precise guidelines as a recognition of the limitations of judicial power, the phrase symbolized the Court's bold moral appeal to the country.

Ten years later, after school closings, massive resistance, and continuing litigation, Black complained. "There has been entirely too much deliberation and not enough speed" in complying with *Brown*. "The time for mere 'deliberate speed' has run out." *Brown*'s moral appeal amounted to little more than an invitation for delay.

* * *

Twenty years after *Brown*, some schools remained segregated. David Mathews, secretary of the Department of Health, Education, and Welfare, reported to President Ford the results of a survey of half of the nation's primary and secondary public schools, enrolling 91 percent of all students: of these, 42 percent had an "appreciable percentage" of minority students, 16 percent had undertaken desegregation plans, while 26 percent had not, and 7 percent of the school districts remained racially segregated.

For over three decades, problems of implementing and achieving compliance with *Brown* persisted. Litigation by civil rights groups forced change, but it was piecemeal, costly, and modest. The judiciary alone could not achieve desegregation. Evasion and resistance were encouraged by the reluctance of presidents and Congress to enforce the mandate. Refusing publicly to endorse *Brown*, Eisenhower would not take steps to enforce the decision until violence erupted in Little Rock, Arkansas. He then did so "*not* to enforce integration but to prevent opposition by violence to orders of a court." Later the Kennedy and Johnson administrations lacked congressional authorization and resources to take major initiatives in enforcing school desegregation. Not until 1964, when Congress passed the Civil Rights Act, did the executive branch have such authorization.

Enforcement and implementation required the cooperation and coordination of all three branches. Little progress could be made, as Assistant Attorney General Stephen Pollock has explained, "where historically there had been slavery and a long tradition of discrimination [until] all three branches of the federal government [could] be lined up in support of a movement forward or a requirement for change." The election of Nixon in 1968 then brought changes both in the policies of the executive branch and in the composition of the Court. The simplicity and flexibility of *Brown*, moreover, invited evasion. It produced a continuing struggle over measures, such as gerrymandering school district lines and busing in the 1970s and 1980s, because the mandate itself had evolved from one of ending segregation to one of securing integration in public schools. Republican and Democratic administrations in turn differed on the means and ends of their enforcement policies in promoting integration.

Almost forty years after *Brown*, over 500 school desegregation cases remained in the lower federal courts. At issue in most was whether schools had achieved integration and become free of the vestiges of past segregation. Although lower courts split over how much proof school boards had to show to demonstrate that present *de facto* racial isolation was unrelated to past *de jure* segregation, the Court declined to review major desegregation cases from the mid-1970s to the end of the 1980s. During that time the dynamics of segregation in the country changed, as did the composition and direction of the Court.

* * *

"By itself," the political scientist Robert Dahl observed, "the Court is almost powerless to affect the course of national policy." Another political scientist, Gerald Rosenberg, goes much further in claiming that "courts can *almost never* be effective producers of significant social reform." *Brown*'s failure to achieve immediate and widespread desegregation is instructive, Rosenberg contends, in developing a model of judicial policy-making on the basis of two opposing theories of judicial power. On the theory of a "Constrained Court" three institutional factors limit judicial policy-making: "[t]he limited nature of constitutional rights"; "[t]he lack of judicial independence"; and "[t]he judiciary's lack of powers of implementation." On the other hand, a "Dynamic Court" theory emphasizes the judiciary's freedom "from electoral constraints and [other] institutional arrangements that stymie change," and thus enable the courts to take on issues that other political institutions might not or cannot. But neither theory is completely satisfactory, according to Rosenberg, because occasionally courts do bring about social change. The Court may do so when the three institutional restraints identified with the "Constrained Court" theory are absent and at least one of the following conditions exist to support judicial policy-making: when other political institutions and actors offer either (a) incentives or (b) costs to induce compliance; (c) "when judicial decisions can be implemented by the market"; or (d) when the Court's ruling serves as "a shield, cover, or excuse, for persons crucial to implementation who are *willing to act*." On the historical basis of resistance and forced compliance with *Brown*'s mandate, Rosenberg concludes that "*Brown* and its progeny stand for the proposition that courts are impotent to produce significant social reform."

Brown, nonetheless, dramatically and undeniably altered the course of American life in ways and for reasons that Rosenberg underestimates. Neither Congress nor President Eisenhower would have moved to end segregated schools in the 1950s, as their reluctance for a decade to enforce *Brown* underscores. The Court lent moral force and legitimacy to the civil rights movement and to the eventual move by Congress and President Johnson to enforce compliance with *Brown*. More importantly, to argue that the Court is impotent to bring about social change overstates the case. Neither Congress nor the president, any more than the Court, could have singlehandedly dismantled racially segregated public schools. As political scientist Richard Neustadt has argued, presidential power ultimately turns on a president's power of persuasion, the Court's power depends on the persuasiveness of its rulings and the magnitude of change in social behavior mandated. The Court raises the ante in its bid for compliance when it appeals for massive social change through a prescribed course of action, in contrast to when it simply says "no" when striking down a law. The unanimous but ambiguous ruling in *Brown* reflects the justices' awareness that their decisions are not self-enforcing, especially when they deal with highly controversial issues and their rulings depend heavily on other institutions for implementation. Moreover, the ambiguity of *Brown*'s remedial decree was the price of achieving unanimity. Unanimity appeared necessary if the Court was to preserve its institutional prestige while pursuing revolutionary change in social policy. The justices sacrificed their own policy preferences for more precise guidelines, while the Court tolerated lengthy delays in recognition of the costs of open defiance, building consensus, and gaining public acceptance. But in the ensuing decades *Brown*'s mandate was also transformed from that of a simple decree for putting an end to state-imposed segregation into the more vexing one of achieving integrated public schools. With that transformation of *Brown*'s mandate the political dynamics of the desegregation controversy evolved, along with a changing Court and country.

DISCUSSION QUESTIONS

1. In what ways does the Supreme Court take politics and public opinion into account in making decisions? Is this appropriate? What would the alternative be?
2. How does the process of appointment to the Supreme Court shape Court decisions? Should presidents make nominations based on the political views of potential justices?
3. Does O'Brien's argument confirm Hamilton's observations about the power of the Court?
4. In its 2015 decision *Obergefell v. Hodges*, the Supreme Court ruled that same-sex marriage was protected by the Constitution. Did this ruling damage the Court's public standing by ignoring the political context (a majority of the public opposed same-sex marriage in many states that had laws or constitutional amendments prohibiting same-sex marriage), or did the Court do the correct thing by supporting the basic rights of a minority group? Is there some way the Court could have finessed the issue, the way it did in *Brown*? Should it have?

38

The Hollow Hope: Can Courts Bring About Social Change?

GERALD N. ROSENBERG

Despite Alexander Hamilton's argument that the Supreme Court would be the "least dangerous branch" because it could not accomplish much without the assistance of Congress and the president, most political observers have viewed the Court as an important agent of social change. That is, in many instances when Congress and the president have not been inclined to act, the Court has pushed the nation to change important policies. In areas such as civil rights, environmental policy, women's and reproductive rights, and political reform, the standard view is of a "dynamic court" that is a "powerful, vigorous, and potent proponent of change." Proponents of this perspective see it as almost self-evident, pointing to decisions such as Brown v. Board of Education *on school desegregation,* Roe v. Wade *on abortion,* Baker v. Carr *on "one-person, one-vote," and* Obergefell v. Hodges *on same-sex marriage as examples of the Supreme Court producing important social change.*

Gerald Rosenberg says this view of the Court is simply wrong. In contrast, he presents a view of a "constrained court" that is "weak, ineffective, and powerless." Echoing Hamilton, Rosenberg points out that courts depend on political support to produce reform; that they are unlikely to produce change if they is any serious resistance because of their lack of implementation powers; and that if they lack established legal precedents they are unlikely to break new ground in a way that promotes social change. For example, following Brown v. Board of Education *there was massive resistance from southern states to implementing the ruling, so real change did not occur until Congress acted ten years later. He also argues that courts are in a weak position to change public opinion because most Americans are only vaguely aware of most landmark Supreme Court decisions.*

Rosenberg concludes that courts can only help produce significant social change when the "institutional, structural, and ideological barriers to change are weak. A court's contribution, then, is akin to officially recognizing the evolving state of affairs, more like the cutting of the ribbon on a new project than its construction."

In the last several decades movements and groups advocating what I will shortly define as significant social reform have turned increasingly to the courts. Starting with the famous cases brought by the civil rights movement and spreading to issues raised by women's groups, environmental groups, political reformers, and others, American courts seemingly have become important producers of political and social change. Cases such as *Brown* (school desegregation) and *Roe* (abortion) are heralded as having produced major change. Further, such litigation has often occurred, and appears to have been most successful, when the other branches of government have failed to act. While officious government officials and rigid, unchanging institutions represent a real social force which may frustrate popular opinion, this litigation activity suggests that courts can produce significant social reform even when the other branches of government are inactive or opposed. Indeed, for many, part of what makes American democracy exceptional is that it includes the world's most powerful court system, protecting minorities and defending liberty, in the face of opposition from the democratically elected branches. Americans look to activist courts, then, as fulfilling an important role in the American scheme. This view of the courts, although informed by recent historical experience, is essentially functional. It sees courts as powerful, vigorous, and potent proponents of change. I refer to this view of the role of the courts as the "Dynamic Court" view.

As attractive as the Dynamic Court view may be, one must guard against uncritical acceptance. Indeed, in a political system that gives sovereignty to the popular will and makes economic decisions through the market, it is not obvious why courts should have the effects it asserts. Maybe its attractiveness is based on something more than effects? Could it be that the self-understanding of the judiciary and legal profession leads to an overstatement of the role of the courts, a "mystification" of the judiciary? If judges see themselves as powerful; if the Bar views itself as influential, and insulated; if professional training in law schools inculcates students with such beliefs, might these factors inflate the self-importance of the judiciary? The Dynamic Court view may be supported, then, because it offers psychological payoffs to key actors by confirming self-images, not because it is correct. And when this "mystification" is added to a normative belief in the courts as the guardian of fundamental rights and liberties—what Scheingold (1974) calls the "myth of rights"—the allure of the Dynamic Court view may grow.

Further, for all its "obviousness," the Dynamic Court view has a well-established functional and historical competitor. In fact, there is a long tradition of legal scholarship that views the federal judiciary, in Alexander Hamilton's famous language, as the "least dangerous" branch of government. Here, too, there is something of a truism about this claim. Courts, we know, lack both budgetary and physical powers. Because, in Hamilton's words, they lack power over either the "sword or the purse," their ability to produce political and social change is limited. In contrast to the first view, the "least dangerous" branch can do little more than point out how actions have fallen short of constitutional or legislative requirements and hope that appropriate action is taken. The strength of this view, of course, is that it leaves Americans free to govern themselves without interference from non-elected officials. I refer to this view of the courts as weak, ineffective, and powerless as the "Constrained Court" view.

The Constrained Court view fully acknowledges the role of popular preferences and social and economic resources in shaping outcomes. Yet it seems to rely excessively on a formal-process understanding of how change occurs in American politics. But the formal process doesn't always work, for social and political forces may be overly responsive to unevenly distributed resources. Bureaucratic inertia, too, can derail orderly, processional change. There is room, then, for courts to effectively correct the pathologies of the political process. Perhaps accurate at the founding of the political system, the Constrained Court view may miss growth and change in the American political system.

Clearly, these two views, and the aspirations they represent, are in conflict on a number of different dimensions. They differ not only on both the desirability and the effectiveness of court action, but also on the nature of American democracy. The Dynamic Court view gives courts an important place in the American political system while the older view sees courts as much less powerful than other more "political" branches and activities. The conflict is more than one of mere definition, for each view captures a very different part of American democracy. We Americans want courts to protect minorities and defend liberties, *and* to defer to elected officials. We want a robust political life *and* one that is just. Most of the time, these two visions do not clash. American legislatures do not habitually threaten liberties, and courts do not regularly invalidate the acts of elected officials or require certain actions to be taken. But the most interesting and relevant cases, such as *Brown* and *Roe,* occur when activist courts overrule and invalidate the actions of elected officials, or order actions beyond what elected officials are willing to do. What happens then? Are courts effective producers of change, as the Dynamic Court view suggests, or do their decisions do little more than point the way to a brighter, but perhaps unobtainable future? Once again, this conflict between two deeply held views about the role of the courts in the American political system has an obvious normative dimension that is worth debating. But this book has a different aim. Relying heavily on empirical data, I ask under what conditions can courts produce political and social change? When does it make sense for individuals and groups pressing for such change to litigate? What do the answers mean about the nature of the American regime?

* * *

The findings show that, with the addition of the four conditions, the constraints derived from the Constrained Court view best capture the capacity of the courts to produce significant social reform. This is the case because, on the most fundamental level, courts depend on political support to produce such reform (Constraint II). For example, since the success of civil rights in fields such as voting and education depended on political action, political hostility doomed court contributions. With women's rights, lack of enforcement of existing laws, in addition to an unwillingness to extend legal protection, had a similar dampening effect. And with abortion and the environment, hostility from many political leaders created barriers to implementation. This finding appears clearly applicable to other fields.

Courts will also be ineffective in producing change, given any serious resistance because of their lack of implementation powers (Constraint III). The structural constraints of the Constrained Court view, built into the American judicial system, make courts virtually powerless to produce change. They must depend on the actions of others for their decisions to be implemented. With civil rights, little changed until the federal government became involved. With women's rights, we still lack a serious government effort, and stereotypes that constrain women's opportunities remain powerful. Similarly, the uneven availability of access to legal abortion demonstrates the point. Where there is local hostility to change, court orders will be ignored. Community pressure, violence or threats of violence, and lack of market response all serve to curtail actions to implement court decisions. This finding, too, appears applicable across fields.

Despite these constraints on change, in at least several of the movements examined major legal cases were won. The chief reason is that the remaining constraint, the lack of established legal precedents, was weak (Constraint I). That is, there were precedents for change and supportive movements within the broader legal culture. In civil rights, litigation in the 1930s and 1940s progressively battered the separate-but-equal standard, setting up the argument and decision in *Brown*. In women's rights, the progress of civil rights litigation, particularly in the expansion of the Fourteenth Amendment, laid the groundwork. In the area of abortion, notions of a sphere of privacy in sexual matters were first developed by the Supreme Court in 1965, broadened in 1972, and forcefully presented in several widely read law-review articles. And, by the date of the Supreme Court's abortion decisions, numerous lower courts had invalidated state abortion statutes on grounds that the Supreme Court came to enunciate. Without these precedents, which took decades to develop, it would have been years before even a legal victory could have been obtained. But legal victories do not automatically or even necessarily produce the desired change.

A quick comparison between civil rights and abortion illustrates these points. While both had legal precedents on which to construct a winning legal argument, little else was similar. With civil rights, there was a great deal of white hostility to blacks, especially in the South. On the whole, political leaders, particularly Southerners, were either supportive of segregation or unwilling to confront it as an important issue. In addition, court decisions required individuals and institutions hostile to civil rights to implement the changes. Until Congress acted a decade later, these two constraints remained and none of the conditions necessary for change were present. After congressional and executive actions were taken, the constraints were overcome and conditions for change were created, including the creation of incentives, costs, and the context in which courts could be used as cover. Only then did change occur. In contrast, at the time of the abortion decisions there was much public and elite support for abortion. There was an active reform movement in the states, and Congress was quiet, with no indication of the opposition that many of its members would later provide. Also, the presence of the market condition partially overcame the implementation constraint. To the extent that the abortion decisions had judicial effects, it is precisely because the constraints were weak and a condition necessary for change was present. Civil rights and abortion litigation, then, highlight the existence and force of the constraints and conditions.

Turning to the question of extra-judicial or indirect effects, courts are in a weak position to produce change. Only a minority of Americans know what the courts have done on important issues. Fewer still combine that knowledge with the belief in the Supreme Court's constitutional role, a combination that would enable the Court, and the lower courts, to legitimate behavior. This makes courts a particularly poor tool for changing opinions or for mobilization. As Peltason puts it, "litigation, by its complexity and technical nature and by its lack of dramatic moments, furnishes an ineffective peg around which to build a mass movement." Rally round the flag is one thing but rally round the brief (or opinion) is quite another! The evidence from the movements examined makes dubious any claim for important extra-judicial effects of court action. It strikes at the heart of the Dynamic Court view.

The cases examined show that when the constraints are overcome, and one of the four conditions is present, courts can help produce significant social reform. However, this means, by definition, that institutional, structural, and ideological barriers to change are weak. A court's contribution, then, is akin to officially recognizing the evolving state of affairs, more like the cutting of the ribbon on a new project than its construction. Without such change, the constraints reign. When Justice Jackson commented during oral argument in *Brown*, "I suppose that realistically this case is here for the reason that action couldn't be obtained from Congress", he identified a fundamental reason why the Court's action in the case would have little effect.

Given the constraints and the conditions, the Constrained Court view is the more accurate: U.S. courts can *almost never* be effective producers of significant social reform. At best, they can second the social reform acts of the other branches of government. Problems that are unsolvable in the political context can rarely be solved by courts. As Scheingold puts it, the "law can hardly transcend the conflicts of the political system in which it is embedded". Turning to courts to produce significant social reform substitutes the myth of America for its reality. It credits courts and judicial decisions with a power that they do not have.

* * *

This conclusion does not deny that courts can sometimes help social reform movements. Occasionally, though rarely, when the constraints are overcome, and one of the conditions is present, courts can make a difference. Sometimes, too, litigation can remove minor but lingering obstacles. But here litigation is often a mopping-up operation, and it is often defensive. In civil rights, for example, when opponents of the 1964 and 1965 acts went to court to invalidate them, the courts' refusal to do so allowed change to proceed. Similarly, if there had never been a *Brown* decision, a Southern school board or state wanting to avoid a federal fund cut-off in the late 1960s might have challenged its state law requiring segregation. An obliging court decision would have removed the obstacle without causing much of a stir, or wasting the scarce resources of civil rights groups. This is a very different approach to the courts than one based on using them to produce significant social reform.

Litigation can also help reform movements by providing defense services to keep the movement afloat. In civil rights, the NAACP Legal Defense and Educational Fund, Inc. (Inc. Fund) provided crucial legal service that prevented the repressive legal structures of the Southern states from totally incapacitating the movement. In springing demonstrators from jail, providing bail money, and forcing at least a semblance of due process, Inc. Fund lawyers performed crucial tasks. But again, this is a far cry from a litigation strategy for significant social reform.

* * *

American courts are not all-powerful institutions. They were designed with severe limitations and placed in a political system of divided powers. To ask them to produce significant social reform is to forget their history and ignore their constraints. It is to cloud our vision with a naive and romantic belief in the triumph of rights over politics. And while romance and even naiveté have their charms, they are not best exhibited in courtrooms.

Discussion Questions

1. Can you think of any examples of important Supreme Court decisions that may support the view that the Court can be an important agent of social change?

2. If Rosenberg is correct, does that mean that Hamilton's argument that the Court is the "least dangerous branch" is also correct? Or are there other ways that the Court exerts influence in the political system other than promoting social change?

3. Not having read the entire book, but rather just the argument and the conclusions, you are not really in a position to evaluate the evidence. What type of evidence would you have found convincing?

Debating the Issues: Interpreting the Constitution—Originalism or a Living Constitution?

Debates over the federal judiciary's role in the political process often focus on the question of how judges should interpret the Constitution. Should judges apply the document's original meaning as stated by the Framers, or should they use a framework that incorporates shifting interpretations across time? This debate intensified during Earl Warren's tenure as Chief Justice (1953–69) because of Court decisions that expanded the scope of civil liberties and criminal rights far beyond what "originalists" thought the Constitution's language authorized. The debate continues in the current, more conservative Court. The two readings in this section offer contrasting viewpoints from one sitting Supreme Court justice (Stephen Breyer) and Justice Antonin Scalia, who died in 2016.

Scalia was the intellectual force behind the conservative wing of the Court and argued that justices must be bound by the original meaning of the document, because that is the only neutral principle that allows the judiciary to function as a legal body instead of a political one. The alternative is to embrace an evolving or "Living Constitution," which Scalia criticized as allowing judges to decide cases on the basis of what seems right at the moment. He said that this "evolutionary" approach does not have any overall guiding principle and therefore "is simply not a practicable constitutional philosophy." He provided several examples of how the Living Constitution approach had produced decisions that stray from the meaning of the Constitution in the areas of abortion rights, gay rights, the right to counsel, and the right to confront one's accuser. This last example is especially provocative, given that it concerned the right of an accused child molester to confront the child who accused him of the crime. Scalia argues that there is no coherent alternative to originalism and forcefully concludes, "The worst thing about the Living Constitution is that it will destroy the Constitution."

Stephen Breyer argues for the Living Constitution approach, and places it within a broader constitutional and theoretical framework. He argues for a "consequentialist" approach that is rooted in basic constitutional purposes, the most important of which is "active liberty," which he defines as "an active and constant participation in collective power." Breyer applies this framework to a range of difficult constitutional issues, including freedom of speech in the context of campaign finance and privacy rights in the context of rapidly evolving technology. He argues that the plain language of the Constitution does not provide enough guidance to answer these difficult questions. He turns the tables on Scalia, arguing that it is the literalist or originalist position that will, ironically, lead justices to rely too heavily on their own personal views, whereas his consequentialist position is actually the view that is more likely to produce judicial restraint. Breyer goes on to criticize the originalist position as fraught with inconsistencies. It is inherently subjective, despite its attempt to emphasize the "objective" words of the Constitution. By relying on the consequentialist perspective, which emphasizes democratic participation and active liberty, justices are more likely to reach limited conclusions that apply to the facts at hand, while maximizing the positive implications for democracy.

Linda Greenhouse, an observer of the Supreme Court, summarized the debate between Scalia and Breyer in these terms: "It is a debate over text versus context. For Justice Scalia, who focuses on text, language is supreme, and the court's job is to derive and apply rules from the words chosen by the Constitution's framers or a statute's drafters. For Justice Breyer, who looks to context, language is only a starting point to an inquiry in which a law's purpose and a decision's likely consequences are the more important elements."

39

"Constitutional Interpretation the Old-Fashioned Way"

ANTONIN SCALIA

It's a pizzazzy topic: Constitutional Interpretation. It is, however, an important one. I was vividly reminded how important it was last week when the Court came out with a controversial decision in the *Roper* case. And I watched one television commentary on the case in which the host had one person defending the opinion on the ground that people should not be subjected to capital punishment for crimes they commit when they are younger than eighteen, and the other person attacked the opinion on the ground that a jury should be able to decide that a person, despite the fact he was under eighteen, given the crime, given the person involved, should be subjected to capital punishment. And it struck me how irrelevant it was, how much the point had been missed. The question wasn't whether the call was right or wrong. The important question was who should make the call. And that is essentially what I am addressing today.

I am one of a small number of judges, small number of anybody—judges, professors, lawyers—who are known as originalists. Our manner of interpreting the Constitution is to begin with the text, and to give that text the meaning that it bore when it was adopted by the people. I'm not a "strict constructionist," despite the introduction. I don't like the term "strict construction." I do not think the Constitution, or any text, should be interpreted either strictly or sloppily; it should be interpreted reasonably. Many of my interpretations do not deserve the description "strict." I do believe, however, that you give the text the meaning it had when it was adopted.

This is such a minority position in modern academia and in modern legal circles that on occasion I'm asked when I've given a talk like this a question from the back of the room—"Justice Scalia, when did you first become an originalist?"—as though it is some kind of weird affliction that seizes some people—"When did you first start eating human flesh?"

Although it is a minority view now, the reality is that, not very long ago, originalism was orthodoxy. Everybody at least *purported* to be an originalist. If you go back and read the commentaries on the Constitution by Joseph Story, he didn't think the Constitution evolved or changed. He said it means and will always mean what it meant when it was adopted.

Or consider the opinions of John Marshall in the Federal Bank case, where he says, we must not, we must always remember it is a constitution we are expounding. And since it's a constitution, he says, you have to give its provisions expansive meaning so that they will accommodate events that you do not know of which will happen in the future.

Well, if it is a constitution that changes, you wouldn't have to give it an expansive meaning. You can give it whatever meaning you want and, when future necessity arises, you simply change the meaning. But anyway, that is no longer the orthodoxy.

Oh, one other example about how not just the judges and scholars believed in originalism, but even the American people. Consider the 19th Amendment, which is the amendment that gave women the vote. It was adopted by the American people in 1920. Why did we adopt a constitutional amendment for that purpose? The Equal Protection Clause existed in 1920; it was adopted right after the Civil War. And you know that if the issue of the franchise for women came up today, we would not have to have a constitutional amendment. Someone would come to the Supreme Court and say, "Your Honors, in a democracy, what could be a greater denial of equal protection than denial of the franchise?" And the Court would say, "Yes! Even though it never meant it before, the Equal Protection Clause means that women have to have the vote." But that's not how the American people thought in 1920. In 1920, they looked at the Equal Protection Clause and said, "What does it mean?" Well, it clearly doesn't mean that you can't discriminate in the franchise—not only on the basis of sex, but on the basis of property ownership, on the basis of literacy. None of that is unconstitutional. And therefore, since it wasn't unconstitutional, and we wanted it to be, we did things the good old-fashioned way and adopted an amendment.

Now, in asserting that originalism used to be orthodoxy, I do not mean to imply that judges did not distort the Constitution now and then; of course they did. We had willful judges then, and we will have willful judges until the end of time. But the difference is that prior to the last fifty years or so, prior to the advent of the "Living Constitution," judges did their distortions the good old-fashioned way, the honest way—they lied about it. They said the Constitution means such and such, when it never meant such and such.

It's a big difference that you now no longer have to lie about it, because we are in the era of the evolving Constitution. And the judge can simply say, "Oh yes, the Constitution didn't used to mean that, but it does now." We are in the age in which not only judges, not only lawyers, but even school children have come to learn the Constitution changes. I have grammar school students come into the Court now and then, and they recite very proudly what they have been taught: "The Constitution is a living document." You know, it morphs.

Well, let me first tell you how we got to the "Living Constitution." You don't have to be a lawyer to understand it. The road is not that complicated. Initially, the Court began giving terms in the text of the Constitution a meaning they didn't have when they were adopted. For example, the First Amendment, which forbids Congress to abridge the freedom of speech. What does the freedom of speech mean? Well, it clearly did not mean that Congress or government could not impose any restrictions upon speech. Libel laws, for example, were clearly constitutional. Nobody thought the First Amendment was *carte blanche* to libel someone. But in the famous case of *New York Times v. Sullivan*, the Supreme Court said, "But the First Amendment does prevent you from suing for libel if you are a public figure and if the libel was not malicious"—that is, the person, a member of the press or otherwise, thought that what the person said was true. Well, that had never been the law. I mean, it might be a good law. And some states could amend their libel law.

It's one thing for a state to amend its libel law and say, "We think that public figures shouldn't be able to sue." That's fine. But the courts have said that the First Amendment, which never meant this before, now means that if you are a public figure, that you can't sue for libel unless it's intentional, malicious. So that's one way to do it.

Another example is the Constitution guarantees the right to be represented by counsel. That never meant the state had to pay for your counsel. But you can reinterpret it to mean that.

That was step one. Step two, I mean, that will only get you so far. There is no text in the Constitution that you could reinterpret to create a right to abortion, for example. So you need something else. The something else is called the doctrine of "Substantive Due Process." Only lawyers can walk around talking about substantive process, inasmuch as it's a contradiction in terms. If you referred to substantive process or procedural substance at a cocktail party, people would look at you funny. But, lawyers talk this way all the time.

What substantive due process is is quite simple—the Constitution has a Due Process Clause, which says that no person shall be deprived of life, liberty, or property without due process of law. Now, what does this guarantee? Does it guarantee life, liberty, or property? No, indeed! All three can be taken away. You can be fined, you can be incarcerated, you can even be executed, but not without due process of law. It's a procedural guarantee. But the Court said, and this goes way back, in the 1920s at least—in fact the first case to do it was *Dred Scott*. But it became more popular in the 1920s. The Court said there are some liberties that are so important, that no process will suffice to take them away. Hence, substantive due process.

Now, what liberties are they? The Court will tell you. Be patient. When the doctrine of substantive due process was initially announced, it was limited in this way: the Court said it embraces only those liberties that are fundamental to a democratic society and rooted in the traditions of the American people.

Then we come to step three. Step three: that limitation is eliminated. Within the last twenty years, we have found to be covered by due process the right to abortion, which was so little rooted in the traditions of the American people that it was criminal for 200 years; the right to homosexual sodomy, which was so little rooted in the traditions of the American people that it was criminal for 200 years. So it is literally true, and I don't think this is an exaggeration, that the Court has essentially liberated itself from the text of the Constitution, from the text and even from the traditions of the American people. It is up to the Court to say what is covered by substantive due process.

What are the arguments usually made in favor of the Living Constitution? As the name of it suggests, it is a very attractive philosophy, and it's hard to talk people out of it—the notion that the Constitution grows. The major argument is the Constitution is a living organism; it has to grow with the society that it governs or it will become brittle and snap.

This is the equivalent of, an anthropomorphism equivalent to, what you hear from your stockbroker, when he tells you that the stock market is resting for an assault on the 11,000 level. The stock market panting at some base camp. The stock market is not a mountain climber and the Constitution is not a living organism, for Pete's sake; it's a legal document, and like all legal documents, it says some things, and it doesn't say other things. And if you think that the aficionados of the Living Constitution want to bring you flexibility, think again.

My Constitution is a very flexible Constitution. You think the death penalty is a good idea—persuade your fellow citizens and adopt it. You think it's a bad idea—persuade them the other way and eliminate it. You want a right to abortion—create it the way most rights are created in a democratic society: persuade your fellow citizens it's a good idea and enact it. You want the opposite—persuade them the other way. That's flexibility. But to read either result into the Constitution is not to produce flexibility, it is to produce what a constitution is designed to produce—rigidity. Abortion, for example, is offstage, it is off the democratic stage; it is no use debating it; it is unconstitutional. I mean prohibiting it is unconstitutional; I mean it's no use debating it anymore—now and forever, coast to coast, I guess until we amend the Constitution, which is a difficult thing. So, for whatever reason you might like the Living Constitution, don't like it because it provides flexibility.

That's not the name of the game. Some people also seem to like it because they think it's a good liberal thing—that somehow this is a conservative/liberal battle, and conservatives like the old-fashioned originalist Constitution and liberals ought to like the Living Constitution. That's not true either. The dividing line between those who believe in the Living Constitution and those who don't is not the dividing line between conservatives and liberals.

Conservatives are willing to grow the Constitution to cover their favorite causes just as liberals are, and the best example of that is two cases we announced some years ago on the same day, the same morning. One case was *Romer v. Evans*, in which the people of Colorado had enacted an amendment to the state constitution by plebiscite, which said that neither the state nor any subdivision of the state would add to the protected statuses against which private individuals cannot discriminate. The usual ones are race, religion, age, sex, disability and so forth. Would not add sexual preference—somebody thought that was a terrible idea, and, since it was a terrible idea, it must be unconstitutional. Brought a lawsuit, it came to the Supreme Court. And the Supreme Court said, "Yes, it is unconstitutional." On the basis of—I don't know. The Sexual Preference Clause of the Bill of Rights, presumably. And the liberals loved it, and the conservatives gnashed their teeth.

The very next case we announced is a case called *BMW v. Gore*. Not the Gore you think; this is another Gore. Mr. Gore had bought a BMW, which is a car supposedly advertised at least as having a superb finish, baked seven times in ovens deep in the Alps, by dwarfs. And his BMW apparently had gotten scratched on the way over. They did not send it back to the Alps; they took a can of spray paint and fixed it. And he found out about this and was furious, and he brought a lawsuit. He got his compensatory damages, a couple of hundred dollars—the difference between a car with a better paint job and a worse paint job—plus $2 million against BMW for punitive damages for being a bad actor, which is absurd of course, so it must be unconstitutional. BMW appealed to my Court, and my Court said, "Yes, it's unconstitutional." In violation of, I assume, the Excessive Damages Clause of the Bill of Rights. And if excessive punitive damages are unconstitutional, why aren't excessive compensatory damages unconstitutional? So you have a federal question whenever you get a judgment in a civil case. Well, that one the conservatives liked, because conservatives don't like punitive damages, and the liberals gnashed their teeth.

I dissented in both cases because I say, "A pox on both their houses." It has nothing to do with what your policy preferences are; it has to do with what you think the Constitution is.

Some people are in favor of the Living Constitution because they think it always leads to greater freedom—there's just nothing to lose, the evolving Constitution will always provide greater and greater freedom, more and more rights. Why would you think that? It's a two-way street. And indeed, under the aegis of the Living Constitution, some freedoms have been taken away.

Recently, last term, we reversed a 15-year-old decision of the Court, which had held that the Confrontation Clause—which couldn't be clearer, it says, "In all criminal prosecutions, the accused shall enjoy the right . . . to be confronted with the witness against him." But a Living Constitution Court held that all that was necessary to comply with the Confrontation Clause was that the hearsay evidence which is introduced—hearsay evidence means you can't cross-examine the person who said it because he's not in the court—the hearsay evidence has to bear indicia of reliability. I'm happy to say that we reversed it last term with the votes of the two originalists on the Court. And the opinion said that the only indicium of reliability that the Confrontation Clause acknowledges is confrontation. You bring the witness in to testify and to be cross-examined. That's just one example; there are others, of eliminating liberties.

So, I think another example is the right to jury trial. In a series of cases, the Court had seemingly acknowledged that you didn't have to have trial by jury of the facts that increase your sentence. You can make the increased sentence a "sentencing factor"—you get thirty years for burglary, but if the burglary is committed with a gun, as a sentencing factor the judge can give you another ten years. And the judge will decide whether you used a gun. And he will decide it, not beyond a reasonable doubt, but whether it's more likely than not. Well, we held recently, I'm happy to say, that this violates the right to a trial by jury. The Living Constitution would not have produced that result. The Living Constitution, like the legislatures that enacted these laws, would have allowed sentencing factors to be determined by the judge because all the Living Constitution assures you is that what will happen is what the majority wants to happen. And that's not the purpose of constitutional guarantees.

Well, I've talked about some of the false virtues of the Living Constitution; let me tell you what I consider its principle vices are. Surely the greatest—you should always begin with principle—its greatest vice is its illegitimacy. The only reason federal courts sit in judgment of the constitutionality of federal legislation is not because they are explicitly authorized to do so in the Constitution. Some modern constitutions give the constitutional court explicit authority to review German legislation or French legislation for its constitutionality; our Constitution doesn't say anything like that. But John Marshall says in *Marbury v. Madison:* Look, this is lawyers' work. What you have here is an apparent conflict between the Constitution and the statute. And, all the time, lawyers and judges have to reconcile these conflicts—they try to read the two to comport with each other. If they can't, it's judges' work to decide which ones prevail. When there are two statutes, the more recent one prevails. It implicitly repeals the older one. But when the Constitution is at issue, the Constitution prevails because it is a "superstatute." I mean, that's what Marshall says: It's judges' work.

If you believe, however, that the Constitution is not a legal text, like the texts involved when judges reconcile or decide which of two statutes prevail; if you think the Constitution is some exhortation to give effect to the most fundamental values of the society as those values change from year to year; if you think that it is meant to reflect, as some of the Supreme Court cases say, particularly those involving the Eighth Amendment, if you think it is simply meant to reflect the evolving standards of decency that mark the progress of a maturing society—if that is what you think it is, then why in the world would you have it interpreted by nine lawyers? What do I know about the evolving standards of decency of American society? I'm afraid to ask.

If that is what you think the Constitution is, then *Marbury v. Madison* is wrong. It shouldn't be up to the judges, it should be up to the legislature. We should have a system like the English—whatever the legislature thinks is constitutional is constitutional. They know the evolving standards of American society, I don't. So in principle, it's incompatible with the legal regime that America has established.

Secondly, and this is the killer argument—I mean, it's the best debaters' argument—they say in politics you can't beat somebody with nobody. It's the same thing with principles of legal interpretation. If you don't believe in originalism, then you need some other principle of interpretation. Being a non-originalist is not enough. You see, I have my rules that confine me. I know what I'm looking for. When I find it—the original meaning of the Constitution—I am handcuffed. If I believe that the First Amendment meant when it was adopted that you are entitled to burn the American flag, I have to come out that way even though I don't like to come out that way. When I find that the original meaning of the jury trial guarantee is that any additional time you spend in prison which depends upon a fact must depend upon a fact found by a jury—once I find that's what the jury trial guarantee means, I am handcuffed. Though I'm a law-and-order type, I cannot do all the mean conservative things I would like to do to this society. You got me.

Now, if you're not going to control your judges that way, what other criterion are you going to place before them? What is the criterion that governs the Living Constitutional judge? What can you possibly use, besides original meaning? Think about that. Natural law? We all agree on that, don't we? The philosophy of John Rawls? That's easy. There really is nothing else. You either tell your judges, "Look, this is a law, like all laws; give it the meaning it had when it was adopted." Or, you tell your judges, "Govern us. You tell us whether people under eighteen, who committed their crimes when they were under eighteen, should be executed. You tell us whether there ought to be an unlimited right to abortion or a partial right to abortion. You make these decisions for us." I have put this question—you know I speak at law schools with some frequency just to make trouble—and I put this question to the faculty all the time, or incite the students to ask their Living Constitutional professors: "Okay professor, you are not an originalist, what is your criterion?" There is none other.

And finally, this is what I will conclude with although it is not on a happy note. The worst thing about the Living Constitution is that it will destroy the Constitution. You heard in the introduction that I was confirmed, close to nineteen years ago now, by a vote of ninety-eight to nothing. The two missing were Barry Goldwater and Jake Games, so make it one hundred. I was known at that time to be, in my political and social views, fairly conservative. But still, I was known to be a good lawyer, an honest man—somebody who could read a text and give it its fair meaning—had judicial impartiality and so forth. And so I was unanimously confirmed. Today, barely twenty years later, it is difficult to get someone confirmed to the Court of Appeals. What has happened? The American people have figured out what is going on. If we are selecting lawyers, if we are selecting people to read a text and give it the fair meaning it had when it was adopted, yes, the most important thing to do is to get a good lawyer. If on the other hand, we're picking people to draw out of their own conscience and experience a new constitution with all sorts of new values to govern our society, then we should not look principally for good lawyers. We should look principally for people who agree with us, the majority, as to whether there ought to be this right, that right and the other right. We want to pick people that would write the new constitution that we would want.

And that is why you hear in the discourse on this subject, people talking about moderate—we want moderate judges. What is a moderate interpretation of the text? Halfway between what it really means and what you'd like it to mean? There is no such thing as a moderate interpretation of the text. Would you ask a lawyer, "Draw me a moderate contract?" The only way the word has any meaning is if you are looking for someone to write a law, to write a constitution, rather than to interpret one. The moderate judge is the one who will devise the new constitution that most people would approve of. So, for example, we had a suicide case some terms ago, and the Court refused to hold that there is a constitutional right to assisted suicide. We said, "We're not yet ready to say that. Stay tuned, in a few years, the time may come, but we're not yet ready." And that was a moderate decision, because I think most people would not want—if we had gone, looked into that and created a national right to assisted suicide—that would nave been an immoderate and extremist decision.

I think the very terminology suggests where we have arrived—at the point of selecting people to write a constitution, rather than people to give us the fair meaning of one that has been democratically adopted. And when that happens, when the Senate interrogates nominees to the Supreme Court, or to the lower courts—you know, "Judge so-and-so, do you think there is a right to this in the Constitution? You don't? Well, my constituents think there ought to be, and I'm not going to appoint to the court someone who is not going to find that"—when we are in that mode, you realize, we have rendered the Constitution useless, because the Constitution will mean what the majority wants it to mean. The senators are representing the majority, and they will be selecting justices who will devise a constitution that the majority wants. And that, of course, deprives the Constitution of its principle utility. The Bill of Rights is devised to protect you and me against, who do you think? The majority. My most important function on the Supreme Court is to tell the majority to take a walk. And the notion that the justices ought to be selected because of the positions that they will take, that are favored by the majority, is a recipe for destruction of what we have had for 200 years.

To come back to the beginning, this is new—fifty years old or so—the Living Constitution stuff. We have not yet seen what the end of the road is. I think we are beginning to see. And what it is should really be troublesome to Americans who care about a Constitution that can provide protections against majoritarian rule. Thank you.

40

"Our Democratic Constitution"

STEPHEN BREYER

I shall focus upon several contemporary problems that call for governmental action and potential judicial reaction. In each instance I shall argue that, when judges interpret the Constitution, they should place greater emphasis upon the "ancient liberty," i.e., the people's right to "an active and constant participation in collective power." I believe that increased emphasis upon this active liberty will lead to better constitutional law, a law that will promote governmental solutions consistent with individual dignity and community need.

At the same time, my discussion will illustrate an approach to constitutional interpretation that places considerable weight upon consequences—consequences valued in terms of basic constitutional purposes. It disavows a contrary constitutional approach, a more "legalistic" approach that places too much weight upon language, history, tradition, and precedent alone while understating the importance of consequences. If the discussion helps to convince you that the more "consequential" approach has virtue, so much the better.

Three basic views underlie my discussion. First, the Constitution, considered as a whole, creates a framework for a certain kind of government. Its general objectives can be described abstractly as including (1) democratic self-government, (2) dispersion of power (avoiding concentration of too much power in too few hands), (3) individual dignity (through protection of individual liberties), (4) equality before the law (through equal protection of the law), and (5) the rule of law itself.

The Constitution embodies these general objectives in particular provisions. In respect to self-government, for example, Article IV guarantees a "republican Form of Government;" Article I insists that Congress meet at least once a year, that elections take place every two (or six) years, that a census take place every decade; the Fifteenth, Nineteenth, Twenty-fourth, and Twenty-sixth Amendments secure a virtually universal adult suffrage. But a general constitutional objective such as self-government plays a constitutional role beyond the interpretation of an individual provision that refers to it directly. That is because constitutional courts must consider the relation of one phrase to another. They must consider the document as a whole. And consequently the document's handful of general purposes will inform judicial interpretation of many individual provisions that do not refer directly to the general objective in question. My examples seek to show how that is so. And, as I have said, they will suggest a need for judges to pay greater attention to one of those general objectives, namely participatory democratic self-government.

Second, the Court, while always respecting language, tradition, and precedent, nonetheless has emphasized different general constitutional objectives at different periods in its history. Thus one can characterize the early nineteenth century as a period during which the Court helped to establish the authority of the federal government, including the federal judiciary. During the late nineteenth and early twentieth centuries, the Court underemphasized the Constitution's efforts to secure participation by black citizens in representative government—efforts related to the participatory "active" liberty of the ancients. At the same time, it overemphasized protection of property rights, such as an individual's freedom to contract without government interference, to the point where President Franklin Roosevelt commented that the Court's Lochner-era decisions had created a legal "no-man's land" that neither state nor federal regulatory authority had the power to enter.

The New Deal Court and the Warren Court in part reemphasized "active liberty." The former did so by dismantling various Lochner-era distinctions, thereby expanding the scope of democratic self-government. The latter did so by interpreting the Civil War Amendments in light of their purposes and to mean what they say, thereby helping African-Americans become members of the nation's community of self-governing citizens—a community that the Court expanded further in its "one person, one vote" decisions.

More recently, in my view, the Court has again underemphasized the importance of the citizen's active liberty. I will argue for a contemporary reemphasis that better combines "the liberty of the ancients" with that "freedom of governmental restraint" that Constant called "modern."

Third, the real-world consequences of a particular interpretive decision, valued in terms of basic constitutional purposes, play an important role in constitutional decision-making. To that extent, my approach differs from that of judges who would place nearly exclusive interpretive weight upon language, history, tradition and precedent. In truth, the difference is one of degree. Virtually all judges, when interpreting a constitution or a statute, refer at one time or another to language, to history, to tradition, to precedent, to purpose, and to consequences. Even those who take a more literal approach to constitutional interpretation sometimes find consequences and general purposes relevant. But the more "literalist" judge tends to ask those who cannot find an interpretive answer in language, history, tradition, and precedent alone to rethink the problem several times, before making consequences determinative. The more literal judges may hope to find in language, history, tradition, and precedent objective interpretive standards; they may seek to avoid an interpretive subjectivity that could confuse a judge's personal idea of what is good for that which the Constitution demands; and they may believe that these more "original" sources will more readily yield rules that can guide other institutions, including lower courts. These objectives are desirable, but I do not think the literal approach will achieve them, and, in any event, the constitutional price is too high. I hope that my examples will help to show you why that is so, as well as to persuade some of you why it is important to place greater weight upon constitutionally valued consequences, my consequential focus in this lecture being the effect of a court's decisions upon active liberty.

To recall the fate of Socrates is to understand that the "liberty of the ancients" is not a sufficient condition for human liberty. Nor can (or should) we replicate today the ideal represented by the Athenian agora or the New England town meeting. Nonetheless, today's citizen does participate in democratic self-governing processes. And the "active" liberty to which I refer consists of the Constitution's efforts to secure the citizen's right to do so.

To focus upon that active liberty, to understand it as one of the Constitution's handful of general objectives, will lead judges to consider the constitutionality of statutes with a certain modesty. That modesty embodies an understanding of the judges' own expertise compared, for example, with that of a legislature. It reflects the concern that a judiciary too ready to "correct" legislative error may deprive "the people" of "the political experience and the moral education that come from . . . correcting their own errors." It encompasses that doubt, caution, prudence, and concern—that state of not being "too sure" of oneself—that Learned Hand described as the "spirit of liberty." In a word, it argues for traditional "judicial restraint."

But active liberty argues for more than that. I shall suggest that increased recognition of the Constitution's general democratic participatory objectives can help courts deal more effectively with a range of specific constitutional issues. To show this I shall use examples drawn from the areas of free speech, federalism, privacy, equal protection and statutory interpretation. In each instance, I shall refer to an important modern problem of government that calls for a democratic response. I shall then describe related constitutional implications. I want to draw a picture of some of the different ways that increased judicial focus upon the Constitution's participatory objectives can have a positive effect.

* * *

I begin with free speech and campaign finance reform. The campaign finance problem arises out of the recent explosion in campaign costs along with a vast disparity among potential givers. * * * The upshot is a concern by some that the matter is out of hand—that too few individuals contribute too much money and that, even though money is not the only way to obtain influence, those who give large amounts of money do obtain, or appear to obtain, too much influence. The end result is a marked inequality of participation. That is one important reason why legislatures have sought to regulate the size of campaign contributions.

The basic constitutional question, as you all know, is not the desirability of reform legislation but whether, how, or the extent to which, the First Amendment permits the legislature to impose limitations or ceilings on the amounts individuals or organizations or parties can contribute to a campaign or the kinds of contributions they can make. * * *

One cannot (or, at least, I cannot) find an easy answer to the constitutional questions in language, history, or tradition. The First Amendment's language says that Congress shall not abridge "the freedom of speech." But it does not define "the freedom of speech" in any detail. The nation's Founders did not speak directly about campaign contributions. Madison, who decried faction, thought that members of Congress would fairly represent all their constituents, in part because the "electors" would not be the "rich" any "more than the poor." But this kind of statement, while modestly helpful to the campaign reform cause, is hardly determinative.

Neither can I find answers in purely conceptual arguments. Some argue, for example, that "money is speech"; others say "money is not speech." But neither contention helps much. Money is not speech, it is money. But the expenditure of money enables speech; and that expenditure is often necessary to communicate a message, particularly in a political context. A law that forbids the expenditure of money to convey a message could effectively suppress that communication.

Nor does it resolve the matter simply to point out that campaign contribution limits inhibit the political "speech opportunities" of those who wish to contribute more. Indeed, that is so. But the question is whether, in context, such a limitation abridges "the freedom of speech." And to announce that this kind of harm could never prove justified in a political context is simply to state an ultimate constitutional conclusion; it is not to explain the underlying reasons.

To refer to the Constitution's general participatory self-government objective, its protection of "active liberty" is far more helpful. That is because that constitutional goal indicates that the First Amendment's constitutional role is not simply one of protecting the individual's "negative" freedom from governmental restraint. The Amendment in context also forms a necessary part of a constitutional system designed to sustain that democratic self-government. The Amendment helps to sustain the democratic process both by encouraging the exchange of ideas needed to make sound electoral decisions and by encouraging an exchange of views among ordinary citizens necessary to encourage their informed participation in the electoral process. It thereby helps to maintain a form of government open to participation (in Constant's words "by all citizens without exception").

The relevance of this conceptual view lies in the fact that the campaign finance laws also seek to further the latter objective. They hope to democratize the influence that money can bring to bear upon the electoral process, thereby building public confidence in that process, broadening the base of a candidate's meaningful financial support, and encouraging greater public participation. They consequently seek to maintain the integrity of the political process—a process that itself translates political speech into governmental action. Seen in this way, campaign finance laws, despite the limits they impose, help to further the kind of open public political discussion that the First Amendment also seeks to encourage, not simply as an end, but also as a means to achieve a workable democracy.

For this reason, I have argued that a court should approach most campaign finance questions with the understanding that important First Amendment-related interests lie on both sides of the constitutional equation and that a First Amendment presumption hostile to government regulation, such as "strict scrutiny" is consequently out of place. Rather, the

Court considering the matter without benefit of presumptions, must look realistically at the legislation's impact, both its negative impact on the ability of some to engage in as much communication as they wish and the positive impact upon the public's confidence, and consequent ability to communicate through (and participate in) the electoral process.

The basic question the Court should ask is one of proportionality. Do the statutes strike a reasonable balance between their electoral speech-restricting and speech-enhancing consequences? Or do you instead impose restrictions on that speech that are disproportionate when measured against their corresponding electoral and speech-related benefits, taking into account the kind, the importance, and the extent of those benefits, as well as the need for the restrictions in order to secure them?

The judicial modesty discussed earlier suggests that, in answering these questions, courts should defer to the legislatures' own answers insofar as those answers reflect empirical matters about which the legislature is comparatively expert, for example, the extent of the campaign finance problem, a matter that directly concerns the realities of political life. But courts cannot defer when evaluating the risk that reform legislation will defeat the very objective of participatory self-government itself, for example, where laws would set limits so low that, by elevating the reputation-related or media-related advantages of incumbency to the point where they would insulate incumbents from effective challenge.

I am not saying that focus upon active liberty will automatically answer the constitutional question in particular campaign finance cases. I argue only that such focus will help courts find a proper route for arriving at an answer. The positive constitutional goal implies a systemic role for the First Amendment; and that role, in turn, suggests a legal framework, i.e., a more particular set of questions for the Court to ask. Modesty suggests where, and how, courts should defer to legislatures in doing so. The suggested inquiry is complex. But courts both here and abroad have engaged in similarly complex inquiries where the constitutionality of electoral laws is at issue. That complexity is demanded by a Constitution that provides for judicial review of the constitutionality of electoral rules while granting Congress the effective power to secure a fair electoral system.

I next turn to a different kind of example. It focuses upon current threats to the protection of privacy, defined as "the power to control what others can come to know about you." It seeks to illustrate what active liberty is like in modern America, when we seek to arrive democratically at solutions to important technologically based problems. And it suggests a need for judicial caution and humility when certain privacy matters, such as the balance between free speech and privacy, are at issue.

First, I must describe the "privacy" problem. That problem is unusually complex. It has clearly become even more so since the terrorist attacks. For one thing, those who agree that privacy is important disagree about why. Some emphasize the need to be left alone, not bothered by others, or that privacy is important because it prevents people from being judged out of context. Some emphasize the way in which relationships of love and friendship depend upon trust, which implies a sharing of information not available to all. Others find connections between privacy and individualism, in that privacy encourages non-conformity. Still others find connections between privacy and equality, in that limitations upon the availability of individualized information lead private businesses to treat all customers alike. For some, or all, of these reasons, legal rules protecting privacy help to assure an individual's dignity.

For another thing, the law protects privacy only because of the way in which technology interacts with different laws. Some laws, such as trespass, wiretapping, eavesdropping, and search-and-seizure laws, protect particular places or sites, such as homes or telephones, from searches and monitoring. Other laws protect not places, but kinds of information, for example laws that forbid the publication of certain personal information even by a person who obtained that information legally. Taken together these laws protect privacy to different degrees depending upon place, individual status, kind of intrusion, and type of information.

Further, technological advances have changed the extent to which present laws can protect privacy. Video cameras now can monitor shopping malls, schools, parks, office buildings, city streets, and other places that present law left unprotected. Scanners and interceptors can overhear virtually any electronic conversation. Thermal imaging devices can detect activities taking place within the home. Computers can record and collate information obtained in any of these ways, or others. This technology means an ability to observe, collate and permanently record a vast amount of information about individuals that the law previously may have made available for collection but which, in practice, could not easily have been recorded and collected. The nature of the current or future privacy threat depends upon how this technological/legal fact will affect differently situated individuals.

These circumstances mean that efforts to revise privacy law to take account of the new technology will involve, in different areas of human activity, the balancing of values in light of prediction about the technological future. If, for example, businesses obtain detailed consumer purchasing information, they may create individualized customer profiles. Those profiles may invade the customer's privacy. But they may also help firms provide publicly desired products at lower cost. If, for example, medical records are placed online, patient privacy may be compromised. But the ready availability of those records may lower insurance costs or help a patient carried unconscious into an operating room. If, for example, all information about an individual's genetic make-up is completely confidential, that individual's privacy is protected, but suppose a close relative, a nephew or cousin, needs the information to assess his own cancer risk?

Nor does a "consent" requirement automatically answer the dilemmas suggested, for consent forms may be signed without understanding and, in any event, a decision by one individual to release or to deny information can affect others as well.

Legal solutions to these problems will be shaped by what is technologically possible. Should video cameras be programmed to turn off? Recorded images to self-destruct? Computers instructed to delete certain kinds of information? Should cell phones be encrypted? Should web technology, making use of an individual's privacy preferences, automatically negotiate privacy rules with distant web sites as a condition of access?

The complex nature of these problems calls for resolution through a form of participatory democracy. Ideally, that participatory process does not involve legislators, administrators, or judges imposing law from above. Rather, it involves law revision that bubbles up from below. Serious complex changes in law are often made in the context of a national conversation involving, among others, scientists, engineers, businessmen and -women, the media, along with legislators, judges, and many ordinary citizens whose lives the new technology will affect. That conversation takes place through many meetings, symposia, and discussions, through journal articles and media reports, through legislative hearings and court cases. Lawyers participate fully in this discussion, translating specialized knowledge into ordinary English, defining issues, creating consensus. Typically, administrators and legislators then make decisions, with courts later resolving any constitutional issues that those decisions raise. This "conversation" is the participatory democratic process itself.

The presence of this kind of problem and this kind of democratic process helps to explain, because it suggests a need for, judicial caution or modesty. That is why, for example, the Court's decisions so far have hesitated to preempt that process. In one recent case the Court considered a cell phone conversation that an unknown private individual had intercepted with a scanner and delivered to a radio station. A statute forbid the broadcast of that conversation, even though the radio station itself had not planned or participated in the intercept. The Court had to determine the scope of the station's First Amendment right to broadcast given the privacy interests that the statute sought to protect. The Court held that the First Amendment trumped the statute, permitting the radio station to broadcast the information. But the holding was narrow. It focused upon the particular circumstances present, explicitly leaving open broadcaster liability in other, less innocent, circumstances.

The narrowness of the holding itself serves a constitutional purpose. The privacy "conversation" is ongoing. Congress could well rewrite the statute, tailoring it more finely to current technological facts, such as the widespread availability of scanners and the possibility of protecting conversations through encryption. A broader constitutional rule might itself limit legislative options in ways now unforeseeable. And doing so is particularly dangerous where statutory protection of an important personal liberty is at issue.

By way of contrast, the Court held unconstitutional police efforts to use, without a warrant, a thermal imaging device placed on a public sidewalk. The device permitted police to identify activities taking place within a private house. The case required the Court simply to ask whether the residents had a reasonable expectation that their activities within the house would not be disclosed to the public in this way—a well established Fourth Amendment principle. Hence the case asked the Court to pour new technological wine into old bottles; it did not suggest that doing so would significantly interfere with an ongoing democratic policy conversation.

The privacy example suggests more by way of caution. It warns against adopting an overly rigid method of interpreting the constitution—placing weight upon eighteenth-century details to the point where it becomes difficult for a twenty-first-century court to apply the document's underlying values. At a minimum it suggests that courts, in determining the breadth of a constitutional holding, should look to the effect of a holding on the ongoing policy process, distinguishing, as I have suggested, between the "eavesdropping" and the "thermal heat" types of cases. And it makes clear that judicial caution in such matters does not reflect the fact that judges are mitigating their legal concerns with practical considerations. Rather, the Constitution itself is a practical document—a document that authorizes the Court to proceed practically when it examines new laws in light of the Constitution's enduring, underlying values.

My fourth example concerns equal protection and voting rights, an area that has led to considerable constitutional controversy. Some believe that the Constitution prohibits virtually any legislative effort to use race as a basis for drawing electoral district boundaries—unless, for example, the effort seeks to undo earlier invidious race-based discrimination. Others believe that the Constitution does not so severely limit the instances in which a legislature can use race to create majority-minority districts. Without describing in detail the basic argument between the two positions, I wish to point out the relevance to that argument of the Constitution's democratic objective.

That objective suggests a simple, but potentially important, constitutional difference in the electoral area between invidious discrimination, penalizing members of a racial minority, and positive discrimination, assisting members of racial minorities. The Constitution's Fifteenth Amendment prohibits the former, not simply because it violates a basic Fourteenth Amendment principle, namely that the government must treat all citizens with equal respect, but also because it denies minority citizens the opportunity to participate in the self-governing democracy that the Constitution creates. By way of contrast, affirmative discrimination ordinarily seeks to enlarge minority participation in that self-governing democracy.

To that extent it is consistent with, indeed furthers, the Constitution's basic democratic objective. That consistency, along with its more benign purposes, helps to mitigate whatever lack of equal respect any such discrimination might show to any disadvantaged member of a majority group.

I am not saying that the mitigation will automatically render any particular discriminatory scheme constitutional. But the presence of this mitigating difference supports the view that courts should not apply the strong presumptions of unconstitutionality that are appropriate where invidious discrimination is at issue. My basic purpose, again, is to suggest that reference to the Constitution's "democratic" objective can help us apply a different basic objective, here that of equal protection. And in the electoral context, the reference suggests increased legislative authority to deal with multiracial issues.

The instances I have discussed encompass different areas of law—speech, federalism, privacy, equal protection, and statutory interpretation. In each instance, the discussion has focused upon a contemporary social problem—campaign finance, workplace regulation, environmental regulation, information-based technological change, race-based electoral districting, and legislative politics. In each instance, the discussion illustrates how increased focus upon the Constitution's basic democratic objective might make a difference—in refining doctrinal rules, in evaluating consequences, in applying practical cautionary principles, in interacting with other constitutional objectives, and in explicating statutory silences. In each instance, the discussion suggests how that increased focus might mean better law. And "better" in this context means both (a) better able to satisfy the Constitution's purposes and (b) better able to cope with contemporary problems. The discussion, while not proving its point purely through logic or empirical demonstration, uses example to create a pattern. The pattern suggests a need for increased judicial emphasis upon the Constitution's democratic objective.

My discussion emphasizes values underlying specific constitutional phrases, sees the Constitution itself as a single document with certain basic related objectives, and assumes that the latter can inform a judge's understanding of the former. Might that discussion persuade those who prefer to believe that the keys to constitutional interpretation instead lie in specific language, history, tradition, and precedent and who fear that a contrary approach would permit judges too often to act too subjectively?

Perhaps so, for several reasons. First, the area of interpretive disagreement is more limited than many believe. Judges can, and should, decide most cases, including constitutional cases, through the use of language, history, tradition, and precedent. Judges will often agree as to how these factors determine a provision's basic purpose and the result in a particular case. And where they differ, their differences are often differences of modest degree. Only a handful of constitutional issues—though an important handful—are as open in respect to language, history, and basic purpose as those that I have described. And even in respect to those issues, judges must find answers within the limits set by the Constitution's language. Moreover, history, tradition, and precedent remain helpful, even if not determinative.

Second, those more literalist judges who emphasize language, history, tradition, and precedent cannot justify their practices by claiming that is what the framers wanted, for the framers did not say specifically what factors judges should emphasize when seeking to interpret the Constitution's open language. Nor is it plausible to believe that those who argued about the Bill of Rights, and made clear that it did not contain an exclusive detailed list, had agreed about what school of interpretive thought should prove dominant in the centuries to come. Indeed, the Constitution itself says that the "enumeration" in the Constitution of some rights "shall not be construed to deny or disparage others retained by the people." Professor Bailyn concludes that the Framers added this language to make clear that "rights, like law itself, should never be fixed, frozen, that new dangers and needs will emerge, and that to respond to these dangers and needs, rights must be newly specified to protect the individual's integrity and inherent dignity." Instead, justification for the literalist's practice itself tends to rest upon consequences. Literalist arguments often seek to show that such an approach will have favorable results, for example, controlling judicial subjectivity.

Third, judges who reject a literalist approach deny that their decisions are subjective and point to important safeguards of objectivity. A decision that emphasizes values, no less than any other, is open to criticism based upon (1) the decision's relation to the other legal principles (precedents, rules, standards, practices, institutional understandings) that it modifies and (2) the decision's consequences, i.e., the way in which the entire bloc of decision-affected legal principles subsequently affects the world. The relevant values, by limiting interpretive possibilities and guiding interpretation, themselves constrain subjectivity, indeed the democratic values that I have emphasized themselves suggest the importance of judicial restraint. An individual constitutional judge's need for consistency over time also constrains subjectivity. That is why Justice O'Connor has explained that need in terms of a constitutional judge's initial decisions creating "footprints" that later decisions almost inevitably will follow.

Fourth, the literalist does not escape subjectivity, for his tools, language, history, and tradition, can provide little objective guidance in the comparatively small set of cases about which I have spoken. In such cases, the Constitution's language is almost always nonspecific. History and tradition are open to competing claims and rival interpretations. Nor does an emphasis upon rules embodied in precedent necessarily produce clarity, particularly in borderline areas or where rules are stated abstractly. Indeed, an emphasis upon language, history, tradition, or prior rules in such cases may simply channel subjectivity into a choice about: Which history? Which tradition? Which rules? It will then produce a decision that is no less subjective but which is far less transparent than a decision that directly addresses consequences in constitutional terms.

Finally, my examples point to offsetting consequences—at least if "literalism" tends to produce the legal doctrines (related to the First Amendment, to federalism, to statutory interpretation, to equal protection) that I have criticized. Those doctrines lead to consequences at least as harmful, from a constitutional perspective, as any increased risk of subjectivity. In the ways that I have set out, they undermine the Constitution's efforts to create a framework for democratic government—a government that, while protecting basic individual liberties, permits individual citizens to govern themselves.

To reemphasize the constitutional importance of democratic self-government may carry with it a practical bonus. We are all aware of figures that show that the public knows ever less about, and is ever less interested in, the processes of government. Foundation reports criticize the lack of high school civics education. Comedians claim that more students know the names of the Three Stooges than the three branches of government. Even law school graduates are ever less inclined to work for government—with the percentage of those entering government (or nongovernment public interest) work declining at one major law school from 12% to 3% over a generation. Indeed, polls show that, over that same period of time, the percentage of the public trusting the government declined at a similar rate.

This trend, however, is not irreversible. Indeed, trust in government has shown a remarkable rebound in response to last month's terrible tragedy [September 11]. Courts cannot maintain this upward momentum by themselves. But courts, as highly trusted government institutions, can help some, in part by explaining in terms the public can understand just what the Constitution is about. It is important that the public, trying to cope with the problems of nation, state, and local community, understand that the Constitution does not resolve, and was not intended to resolve, society's problems. Rather, the Constitution provides a framework for the creation of democratically determined solutions, which protect each individual's basic liberties and assures that individual equal respect by government, while securing a democratic form of government. We judges cannot insist that Americans participate in that government, but we can make clear that our Constitution depends upon it. Indeed, participation reinforces that "positive passion for the public good," that John Adams, like so many others, felt a necessary condition for "Republican Government" and any "real Liberty."

That is the democratic ideal. It is as relevant today as it was 200 or 2,000 years ago. Today it is embodied in our Constitution. Two thousand years ago, Thucydides, quoting Pericles, set forth a related ideal—relevant in his own time and, with some modifications, still appropriate to recall today. "We Athenians," said Pericles, "do not say that the man who fails to participate in politics is a man who minds his own business. We say that he is a man who has no business here."

DISCUSSION QUESTIONS

1. Critics of the originalist perspective often point to ambiguities in the language of the Constitution. Justice Breyer outlines several of these in his speech. What are some other examples of ambiguous language in the Constitution? (Look at the Bill of Rights as a start.) What alternative interpretations can you develop?
2. Critics of the Living Constitution, such as Justice Scalia, often argue that judges substitute their own reading of what they think the law should be for what the law is. Do you think it is possible for justices to avoid having their own views shape their decisions? How could they protect against this happening?
3. Should judges take public opinion or changing societal standards into account when ruling on the constitutionality of a statute or practice? If so, what evidence of public opinion or societal standards should matter? Surveys? Laws enacted in states? If not, what are the risks in doing so?
4. Consider Scalia's examples of when the Court has employed a Living Constitution approach. How would Breyer's approach of active liberty decide these cases? Which approach do you think leads to the better outcomes: Scalia's textualist approach or Breyer's active liberty?

PART III

Political Behavior: Participation

CHAPTER 9

Public Opinion and the Media

41

"Polling the Public," from *Public Opinion in a Democracy*

GEORGE GALLUP

Assessing public opinion in a democracy of nearly 320 million people is no easy task. George Gallup, who is largely responsible for the development of modern opinion polling, argued in his 1939 book that public opinion polls enhance the democratic process by providing elected officials with a picture of what Americans think about current events. Despite Gallup's vigorous defense of his polling techniques and the contribution of polling to democracy, the public opinion poll remains controversial. Some critics charge that public officials pay too much attention to polls, making decisions based on fluctuations in public opinion rather than on informed, independent judgment. Others say that by urging respondents to give an opinion, even if they initially respond that they have no opinion on a question, polls may exaggerate the amount of division in American society. And some critics worry that election-related polls may affect public behavior: If a potential voter hears that her candidate is trailing in the polls, perhaps she becomes demoralized and does not vote, and the poll becomes a self-fulfilling prophecy. In effect, rather than reporting on election news, the poll itself becomes the news.

We have a national election every two years only. In a world which moves as rapidly as the modern world does, it is often desirable to know the people's will on basic policies at more frequent intervals. We cannot put issues off and say "let them be decided at the next election." World events do not wait on elections. We need to know the will of the people at all times.

If we know the collective will of the people at all times the efficiency of democracy can be increased, because we can substitute specific knowledge of public opinion for blind groping and guesswork. Statesmen who know the true state of public opinion can then formulate plans with a sure knowledge of what the voting public is thinking. They can know what degree of opposition to any proposed plan exists, and what efforts are necessary to gain public acceptance for it. The responsibility for initiating action should, as always, rest with the political leaders of the country. But the collective will or attitude of the people needs to be learned without delay.

The Will of the People

How is the will of the people to be known at all times?

Before I offer an answer to this question, I would like to examine some of the principal channels by which, at the present time, public opinion is expressed.

The most important is of course a national election. An election is the only official and binding expression of the people's judgment. But, as viewed from a strictly objective point of view, elections are a confusing and imperfect way of registering national opinion. In the first place, they come only at infrequent intervals. In the second place, as [James] Bryce pointed out in *The American Commonwealth,* it is virtually impossible to separate issues from candidates. How can we tell whether the public is voting for the man or for his platform? How can we tell whether all the candidate's views are endorsed, or whether some are favored and others opposed by the voters? Because society grows more and more complex, the tendency is to have more and more issues in an election. Some may be discussed; others not. Suppose a candidate for office takes a position on a great many public issues during the campaign. If elected, he inevitably assumes that the public has endorsed all his planks, whereas this may actually not be the case.

* * *

The Role of the Elected Representative

A second method by which public opinion now expresses itself is through elected representatives. The legislator is, technically speaking, supposed to represent the interests of all voters in his constituency. But under the two-party system there is a strong temptation for him to represent, and be influenced by, only the voters of his own party. He is subject to the pressure of party discipline and of wishes of party leaders back home. His very continuance in office may depend on giving way to such pressure. Under these circumstances his behavior in Congress is likely to be governed not by what he thinks the voters of his state want, but by what he thinks the leaders of his own party in that state want.

* * *

Even in the event that an elected representative does try to perform his duty of representing the whole people, he is confronted with the problem: What is the will of the people? Shall he judge their views by the letters they write him or the telegrams they send him? Too often such expressions of opinion come only from an articulate minority. Shall the congressman judge their views by the visitors or delegations that come to him from his home district?

Pressure Groups and the Whole Nation

Legislators are constantly subject to the influence of organized lobbies and pressure groups. Senator Tydings * * * pointed out recently that the United States is the most fertile soil on earth for the activity of pressure groups. The American people represent a conglomeration of races, all with different cultural backgrounds. Sections and groups struggle with one another to fix national and international policy. And frequently in such struggles, as Senator Tydings pointed out, "self-interest and sectionalism, rather than the promotion of national welfare, dominate the contest." Senator Tydings mentions some twenty important group interests. These include labor, agriculture, veterans, pension plan advocates, chambers of commerce, racial organizations, isolationists and internationalists, high-tariff and low-tariff groups, preparedness and disarmament groups, budget balancers and spending advocates, soft-money associations and hard-money associations, transportation groups and states righters and centralizationists.

The legislator obviously owes a duty to his home district to legislate in its best interests. But he also owes a duty to legislate in the best interests of the whole nation. In order, however, to carry out this second duty he must *know* what the nation thinks. Since he doesn't always know what the voters in his own district think, it is just that much more difficult for him to learn the views of the nation. Yet if he could know those views at all times he could legislate more often in the interest of the whole country.

* * *

The Cross-Section Survey

This effort to discover public opinion has been largely responsible for the introduction of a new instrument for determining public opinion—the cross-section or sampling survey. By means of nationwide studies taken at frequent intervals, research workers are today attempting to measure and give voice to the sentiments of the whole people on vital issues of the day.

Where does this new technique fit into the scheme of things under our form of government? Is it a useful instrument of democracy? Will it prove to be vicious and harmful, or will it contribute to the efficiency of the democratic process?

The sampling referendum is simply a procedure for sounding the opinions of a relatively small number of persons, selected in such manner as to reflect with a high degree of accuracy the views of the whole voting population. In effect such surveys canvass the opinions of a miniature electorate.

Cross-section surveys do not place their chief reliance upon numbers. The technique is based on the fact that a few thousand voters correctly selected will faithfully reflect the views of an electorate of millions of voters. The key to success in this work is the cross section—the proper selection of voters included in the sample. Elaborate precautions must be taken to secure the views of members of all political parties—of rich and poor, old and young, of men and women, farmers and city dwellers, persons of all religious faiths—in short, voters of all types living in every State in the land. And all must be included in correct proportion.

* * *

Reliability of Opinion Surveys

Whether opinion surveys will prove to be a useful contribution to democracy depends largely on their reliability in measuring opinion. During the last four years [1935–39] the sampling procedure, as used in measuring public opinion, has been subjected to many tests. In general these tests indicate that present techniques can attain a high degree of accuracy, and it seems reasonable to assume that with the development of this infant science, the accuracy of its measurements will be constantly improved.

The most practical way at present to measure the accuracy of the sampling referendum is to compare forecasts of elections with election results. Such a test is by no means perfect, because a preelection survey must not only measure opinion in respect to candidates but must also predict just what groups of people will actually take the trouble to cast their ballots. Add to this the problem of measuring the effect of weather on turnout, also the activities of corrupt political machines, and it can easily be seen that election results are by no means a perfect test of the accuracy of this new technique.

* * *

Many thoughtful students of government have asked: Why shouldn't the Government itself, rather than private organizations, conduct these sampling surveys? A few political scientists have even suggested the establishment of a permanent federal bureau for sounding public opinion, arguing that if this new technique is a contribution to democracy, the government has a duty to take it over.

The danger in this proposal, as I see it, lies in the temptation it would place in the way of the party in power to conduct surveys to prove itself right and to suppress those which proved it to be wrong. A private organization, on the other hand, must stand or fall not so much on what it reports or fails to report as on the accuracy of its results, and the impartiality of its interpretations. An important requirement in a democracy is complete and reliable news reports of the activities of all branches of the government and of the views of all leaders and parties. But few persons would argue that, for this reason, the government should take over the press, and all its news gathering associations.

* * *

Cloture on Debate?

It is sometimes argued that public opinion surveys impose a cloture on debate. When the advocates of one side of an issue are shown to be in the majority, so the argument runs, the other side will lose hope and abandon their cause believing that further efforts are futile.

Again let me say that there is little evidence to support this view. Every election necessarily produces a minority. In 1936 the Republicans polled less than 40 percent of the vote. Yet the fact that the Republicans were defeated badly wasn't enough to lead them to quit the battle. They continued to fight against the New Deal with as much vigor as before. An even better example is afforded by the Socialist Party. For years the Socialist candidate for President has received but a small fraction of the total popular vote, and could count on sure defeat. Yet the Socialist Party continues as a party, and continues to poll about the same number of votes.

Sampling surveys will never impose a cloture on debate so long as it is the nature of public opinion to change. The will of the people is dynamic; opinions are constantly changing. A year ago an overwhelming majority of voters were skeptical of the prospects of the Republican Party in 1940. Today, half the voters think the GOP will win. If elections themselves do not impose cloture on debate, is it likely that opinion surveys will?

Possible Effect on Representative Government

The form of government we live under is a representative form of government. What will be the effect on representative government if the will of the people is known at all times? Will legislators become mere rubber stamps, mere puppets, and the function of representation be lost?

Under a system of frequent opinion measurement, the function of representation is not lost, for two reasons. First, it is well understood that the people have not the time or the inclination to pass on all the problems that confront their leaders. They cannot be expected to express judgment on technical questions of administration and government. They can pass judgment only on basic general policies. As society grows more complex there is a greater and greater need for experts. Once the voters have indicated their approval of a general policy or plan of action, experts are required to carry it out.

Second, it is not the province of the people to initiate legislation, but to decide which of the programs offered they like best. National policies do not spring full-blown from the common people. Leaders, knowing the general will of the people, must take the initiative in forming policies that will carry out the general will and must put them into effect.

Before the advent of the sampling referendum, legislators were not isolated from their constituencies. They read the local newspapers; they toured their districts and talked with voters; they received letters from their home State; they entertained delegations who claimed to speak for large and important blocs of voters. The change that is brought about by sampling referenda is merely one which provides these legislators with a truer measure of opinion in their districts and in the nation.

* * *

How Wise Are the Common People?

The sampling surveys of recent years have provided much evidence concerning the wisdom of the common people. Anyone is free to examine this evidence. And I think that the person who does examine it will come away believing as I do that, collectively, the American people have a remarkably high degree of common sense. These people may not be brilliant or intellectual or particularly well read, but they possess a quality of good sense which is manifested time and again in their expressions of opinion on present-day issues.

* * *

It is not difficult to understand why the conception of the stupidity of the masses has so many adherents. Talk to the first hundred persons whom you happen to meet in the street about many important issues of the day, and the chances are great that you will be struck by their lack of accurate or complete knowledge on these issues. Few of them will likely have sufficient information in this particular field to express a well founded judgment.

But fortunately a democracy does not require that every voter be well informed on every issue. In fact a democracy does not depend so much on the enlightenment of each individual, as upon the quality of the collective judgment or intelligence of thousands of individuals.

* * *

It would of course be foolish to argue that the collective views of the common people always represent the most intelligent and most accurate answer to any question. But results of sampling referenda on hundreds of issues do indicate, in my opinion, that we can place great faith in the collective judgment or intelligence of the people.

The New England Town Meeting Restored

One of the earliest and purest forms of democracy in this country was the New England town meeting. The people gathered in one room to discuss and to vote on the questions of the community. There was a free exchange of opinions in the presence of all the members. The town meeting was a simple and effective way of articulating public opinion, and the decisions made by the meeting kept close to the public will. When a democracy thus operates on a small scale it is able to express itself swiftly and with certainty.

But as communities grew, the town meeting became unwieldy. As a result the common people became less articulate, less able to debate the vital issues in the manner of their New England forefathers. Interest in politics lagged. Opinion had to express itself by the slow and cumbersome method of election, no longer facilitated by the town meeting with its frequent give and take of ideas. The indifference and apathy of voters made it possible for vicious and corrupt political machines to take over the administration of government in many states and cities.

The New England town meeting was valuable because it provided a forum for the exchange of views among all citizens of the community and for a vote on these views. Today, the New England town meeting idea has, in a sense, been restored. The wide distribution of daily newspapers reporting the views of statesmen on issues of the day, the almost universal ownership of radios which bring the whole nation within the hearing of any voice, and now the advent of the sampling referendum which provides a means of determining quickly the response of the public to debate on issues of the day, have in effect created a town meeting on a national scale.

How nearly the goal has been achieved is indicated in the following data recently gathered by the American Institute of Public Opinion. Of the 45,000,000 persons who voted in the last presidential election [1936], approximately 40,000,000 read a daily newspaper, 40,000,000 have radios, and only 2,250,000 of the entire group of voters in the nation neither have a radio nor take a daily newspaper.

This means that the nation is literally in one great room. The newspapers and the radio conduct the debate on national issues, presenting both information and argument on both sides, just as the townsfolk did in person in the old town meeting. And finally, through the process of the sampling referendum, the people, having heard the debate on both sides of every issue, can express their will. After one hundred and fifty years we return to the town meeting. This time the whole nation is within the doors.

DISCUSSION QUESTIONS

1. What are the advantages and disadvantages of modern public opinion polling for policy making and elections?
2. Setting aside the constitutional status of such a move, how would the American political system change if polls were banned?
3. Imagine you are an elected official. How would you determine when to pay attention to public opinion polls and when to ignore them? In a representative democracy, should you as an elected official *ever* ignore public opinion as revealed in polls?

42

"Choice Words: If You Can't Understand Our Poll Questions, Then How Can We Understand Your Answers?"

RICHARD MORIN

Although polls play a prominent role in contemporary politics, Richard Morin cautions that polls can be "risky." Morin, former director of polling for the Washington Post, *notes that minor differences in question wording can—and, during the impeachment of President Bill Clinton, did—result in dramatically different polling results. Other problems arise because people will answer questions "even if they don't really have an opinion or understand the question that has been asked." Ultimately, argues Morin, pollsters and the politicians who rely on them should be somewhat skeptical of the depth or significance of any particular response in the absence of additional survey data that establish a pattern.*

If his current government job ends abruptly, President Clinton might think about becoming a pollster. Anyone who ponders the meaning of the word *is* has precisely the right turn of mind to track public opinion in these mindless, mindful times.

Never has polling been so risky—or so much in demand. Never have so many of the rules of polling been bent or broken so cleanly, or so often. Pollsters are sampling public reaction just hours—sometimes minutes—after events occur. Interviewing periods, which traditionally last several days to secure a solid sample, have sometimes shrunk to just a few hours on a single night. Pollsters have been asking questions that were taboo until this past year. Is oral sex really sex? (Yes, said 76 percent of those interviewed in a *Newsweek* poll conducted barely a week after the scandal broke back in January.)

"No living pollster has ever had to poll in a situation like this," said Michael Kagay, the editor of news surveys at the *New York Times*. "We're in uncharted territory." After all, Andrew Johnson had to deal with political enemies, but not pollsters. And Richard Nixon's resignation before impeachment meant that pollsters didn't have a chance to ask whether the Senate should give him the boot.

Clinton has it about right: Words do have different meanings for different people, and these differences matter. At the same time, some seemingly common words and phrases have no meaning at all to many Americans; even on the eve of the impeachment vote last month, nearly a third of the country didn't know or didn't understand what *impeachment* meant.

Every pollster knows that questions with slightly different wording can produce different results. In the past year, survey researchers learned just how big and baffling those differences can be, particularly when words are used to capture public reaction to an arcane process that no living American—not even [then ninety-five-year-old Senator] Strom Thurmond—has witnessed in its entirety.

Fear of getting it wrong—coupled with astonishment over the persistent support for Clinton revealed in poll after poll—spawned a flood of novel tests by pollsters to determine precisely the right words to use in our questions.

Last month, less than a week before Clinton was impeached by the House, *The Washington Post* and its polling partner ABC News asked half of a random sampling of Americans whether Clinton should resign if he were impeached or should "fight the charges in the Senate." The other half of the sample was asked a slightly different question: Should Clinton resign if impeached or should he "remain in office and face trial in the Senate?"

The questions are essentially the same. The results were not. Nearly six in 10—59 percent—said Clinton should quit rather than fight impeachment charges in the Senate. But well under half—43 percent—said he should resign when the alternative was to "remain in office and stand trial in the Senate." What gives?

The difference appears to be the word *fight*. America is a peaceable kingdom; we hate it when our parents squabble and are willing to accept just about any alternative—including Clinton's resignation—to spare the country a partisan fight. But when the alternative is less overtly combative—stand trial in the Senate—Americans are less likely to scurry to the resignation option.

Such a fuss over a few words. But it is just more proof that people do not share the same understanding of terms, and that a pollster who ignores this occupational hazard may wind up looking for a new job.

Think I'm exaggerating? Then let's do another test. A month ago, [December 1998], how would you have answered this question: "If the full House votes to send impeachment articles to the Senate for a trial, then do you think it would be better for the country if Bill Clinton resigned from office, or not?"

And how would you have answered this question: "If the full House votes to impeach Bill Clinton, then do you think it would be better for the country if Bill Clinton resigned from office, or not?"

The questions (asked in a *New York Times*/CBS News poll in mid-December) seem virtually identical. But the differences in results were stunning: Forty-three percent said the president should quit if the House sends "impeachment articles to the Senate" while 60 percent said he should quit if the House "votes to impeach."

What's going on here? Kagay says he doesn't know. Neither do I, but here's a guess: Perhaps "impeach" alone was taken as "found guilty" and the phrase "send impeachment articles to the Senate for a trial" suggests that the case isn't over. If only we could do another wording test. . . .

Language problems have challenged pollsters from the very start of the Monica Lewinsky scandal. Among the first: How to describe Monica herself? *The Washington Post*'s first survey questions referred to her as a "21-year-old intern at the White House," as did questions asked by other news organizations. But noting her age was potentially biasing. Highlighting her youthfulness conjured up visions of innocence and victimhood that appeared inconsistent with her apparently aggressive and explicitly amorous conduct with Clinton. In subsequent *Post* poll questions, she became a "former White House intern" of indeterminate age.

Then came the hard part: How to describe what she and Bill were accused of doing in a way that didn't offend, overly titillate or otherwise stampede people into one position or the other? In these early days, details about who did what to whom and where were sketchy but salacious. It clearly wasn't a classic adulterous love affair; love had apparently little to do with it, at least on Clinton's part. Nor was it a one-night stand. It seemed more like the overheated fantasy of a 16-year-old boy or the musings of the White House's favorite pornographer, *Penthouse* magazine publisher Larry Flynt. Piled on top of the sex were the more complex and less easily understood issues of perjury and obstruction of justice. After various iterations, we and other organizations settled on simply "the Lewinsky matter"—nice and neutral, leaving exactly what that meant to the imaginations (or memories) of survey respondents.

One thing is clear, at least in hindsight: Results of hypothetical questions—those that ask what if?—did not hold up in the past 12 months, said political scientist Michael Traugott of the University of Michigan. Last January, pollsters posed questions asking whether Clinton should resign or be impeached if he lied under oath about having an affair with Lewinsky. Clear majorities said he should quit or be impeached.

Fast forward to the eve of the impeachment vote. Nearly everybody believed Clinton had lied under oath about his relationship with Lewinsky, but now healthy majorities said he should not be impeached—a tribute, perhaps, to the White House strategy of drawing out (dare we say stonewalling?) the investigation to allow the public to get used to the idea that their president was a sleazy weasel.

Fortunately, pollsters had time to work out the kinks in question wording. Demand for polling produced a flood of questions of all shades and flavors, and good wording drove out the bad. At times, it seemed even to pollsters that there may be too many questions about the scandal, said

Kathy Frankovic, director of surveys for CBS News. Through October [1998], more than 1,000 survey questions specifically mentioned Lewinsky's name—double the number of questions that have ever been asked about the Watergate scandal, Frankovic said.

Polling's new popularity has attracted a tonier class of critic. In the past, mostly assistant professors and aggrieved political operatives or their bosses trashed the public polls. Today, one of the fiercest critics of polling is syndicated columnist Arianna Huffington, the onetime Cambridge University debating champ, A-list socialite and New Age acolyte. A few weeks ago, Huffington revealed in her column that lots of people refuse to talk to pollsters, a problem that's not new (except, apparently, to Huffington).

Actually, I think Huffington has it backward. The real problem is that people are too willing to answer poll questions—dutifully responding to poll takers even if they don't really have an opinion or understand the question that has been asked.

A famous polling experiment illustrates the prevalence of pseudo-opinions: More than 20 years ago, a group of researchers at the University of Cincinnati asked a random sample of local residents whether the 1975 Public Affairs Act should be repealed. About half expressed a view one way or another.

Of course there never was a Public Affairs Act of 1975. Researchers made it up to see how willing people were to express opinions on things they knew absolutely nothing about.

I duplicated that experiment a few years ago in a national survey, and obtained about the same result: Forty-three percent expressed an opinion, with 24 percent saying it should be repealed and 19 percent saying it should not.

But enough about the problems. In hindsight, most experts say that the polls have held up remarkably well. Within a month of the first disclosure, the public moved quickly to this consensus, as captured by the polls: Clinton's a good president but a man of ghastly character who can stay in the White House—but stay away from my house, don't touch my daughter and don't pet the dog.

"It is so striking. The public figured this one out early on and stuck with it," said Thomas E. Mann, director of governmental studies at the Brookings Institution. "If anything, the only changes were these upward blips in support for Clinton in the face of some dramatic development that was certain to presage his collapse."

Mann and others argue that public opinion polls may never have played a more important role in American political life. "This last year illustrates the wisdom of George Gallup's optimism about the use of polls in democracy: to discipline the elites, to constrain the activists, to allow ordinary citizens to register sentiments on a matter of the greatest public importance," Mann said.

Well, hooray for us pollsters! Actually, there is evidence suggesting that all the attention in the past year may have improved the public's opinions of opinion polls and pollsters. And why shouldn't they? These polls have had something for everyone: While Democrats revel in Clinton's high job-approval ratings and otherwise bulletproof presidency, Republicans can point to the equally lopsided majority who think Clinton should be censured and formally reprimanded for his behavior.

A few weeks ago, as bombs fell in Baghdad and talk of impeachment roiled Washington, pollster Nancy Belden took a break from business to attend the annual holiday pageant at her 10-year-old son's school. As she left the auditorium, the steadfast Republican mother of one of her son's classmates approached Belden and clapped her on the shoulder. "Thank heavens for you pollsters," she said.

"I was stunned. I was delighted," Belden laughed. "I've spent many years being beat up on by people who complain that public opinion polling is somewhat thwarting the political process, as opposed to helping it. Suddenly, people are coming up to me at parties and saying thanks for doing what you do. What a relief!"

Discussion Questions

1. Morin presents striking differences in poll results when a word or a few words in a question are changed. Does this diminish the value of public opinion polls in the democratic process?
2. How might Morin respond to the arguments that George Gallup makes in "Polling the Public"?
3. Try to think of an example where subtly different wording might lead to very different polling results. Why do you think it would have that effect? As a consumer of polls, how would you try to determine what the "true" public opinion is on that issue?

43

"News vs. Entertainment: How Increasing Media Choice Widens Gaps in Political Knowledge and Turnout"

MARKUS PRIOR

Although everyone has contact with the government nearly every day—attending a public school, driving on public roads, using government-regulated electricity, and so on—few citizens have direct contact with the policymaking process. Because of this distance between the public and policymakers, the behavior of intermediaries between the government and the governed is a significant issue in a democratic polity. The media, in particular the news media, are among the most significant of these intermediaries that tell the people what the government is doing and tell the government what the people want.

In today's media environment, information is more abundant than ever, Markus Prior notes, yet participation and knowledge levels have remained stagnant. Rather than enhancing participatory democracy, as advocates of new media suggest is the norm, the onset of cable television and the Internet has worsened information and participation gaps between those individuals who like to follow the news and those who are more interested in entertainment. Prior argues that the spread of additional news choices, which sounds democratic, has had nondemocratic effects. Newshounds can dig ever deeper into the news, but other members of the public are increasingly able to ignore the news. Other critics have made a similar argument that new media tend to exacerbate public polarization because readers, viewers, and listeners gravitate to outlets presenting opinions they agree with and ignore those sources that would challenge their views.

The rise of new media has brought the question of audience fragmentation and selective exposure to the forefront of scholarly and popular debate. In one of the most widely discussed contributions to this debate. Sunstein has proposed that people's increasing ability to customize their political information will have a polarizing impact on democracy as media users become less likely to encounter information that challenges their partisan viewpoints. While this debate is far from settled, the issue which precedes it is equally important and often sidestepped: as choice between different media content increases, who continues to access *any type* of political information? Cable television and the Internet have increased media choice so much in recent decades that many Americans now live in a high-choice media environment. As media choice increases, the likelihood of "chance encounters" *with any political content* declines significantly for many people. Greater choice allows politically interested people to access more information and increase their political knowledge. Yet those who prefer nonpolitical content can more easily escape the news and therefore pick up less political information than they used to. In a high-choice environment, lack of motivation, not lack of skills or resources, poses the main obstacle to a widely informed electorate.

As media choice increases, content preferences thus become the key to understanding political learning and participation. In a high-choice environment, politics constantly competes with entertainment. Until recently, the impact of content preferences was limited because media users did not enjoy much choice between different content. Television quickly became the most popular mass medium in history, but for decades the networks' scheduling ruled out situations in which viewers had to choose between entertainment and news. Largely unexposed to entertainment competition, news had its place in the early evening and again before the late-night shows. Today, as both entertainment and news are available around the clock on numerous cable channels and web sites, people's content preferences determine more of what those with cable or Internet access watch, read, and hear.

Distinguishing between people who like news and take advantage of additional information and people who prefer other media content explains a puzzling empirical finding: despite the spectacular rise in available political information, mean levels of political knowledge in the population have essentially remained constant. Yet the fact that average knowledge levels did not change hides important trends: political knowledge has risen in some segments of the electorate, but declined in others. Greater media choice thus widens the "knowledge gap." [N]umerous studies have examined the diffusion of information in the population and the differences that emerge between more and less informed individuals. According to some of these studies, television works as a "knowledge leveler" because it presents information in less cognitively demanding ways. To reconcile this effect with the hypothesis that more television widens the knowledge gap, it is necessary to distinguish the effect of news exposure from the effect of the medium itself. In the low-choice broadcast environment, access to the medium and exposure to news were practically one and the same, as less politically interested television viewers had no choice but to watch the news from time to time. As media choice increases, exposure to the news may continue to work as a "knowledge leveler," but the distribution of news exposure itself has become more unequal. Access to the medium no longer implies exposure to the news. Television news narrows the knowledge gap *among its viewers.* For the population as a whole, more channels widen the gap.

The consequences of increasing media choice reach beyond a less equal distribution of political knowledge. Since political knowledge is an important predictor of turnout and since exposure to political information motivates turnout, the shift from a low-choice to a high-choice media environment implies changes in electoral participation as well. Those with a preference for news not only become more knowledgeable, but also vote at higher rates. Those with a stronger interest in other media content vote less.

This study casts doubt on the view that the socioeconomic dimension of the digital divide is the greatest obstacle to an informed and participating electorate. Many casual observers emphasize the great promise new technologies hold for democracy. They deplore current socioeconomic inequalities in access to new media, but predict increasing political knowledge and participation among currently disadvantaged people once these inequalities have been overcome. This ignores that greater media choice leads to greater *voluntary* segmentation of the electorate. The present study suggests that gaps based on socioeconomic status will be eclipsed by preference-based gaps once access to new media becomes cheaper and more widely available. Gaps created by unequal distribution of resources and skills often emerged due to circumstances outside of people's control. The preference-based gaps documented in this article are self-imposed as many people abandon the news for entertainment simply because they like it better. Inequality in political knowledge and turnout increases as a result of voluntary, not circumstantial, consumption decisions.

* * *

Theory

The basic premise of this analysis is that people's media environment determines the extent to which their media use is governed by content preferences. According to theories of program choice, viewers have preferences over program characteristics or program types and select the program that promises to best satisfy these preferences. The simplest models distinguish between preferences for information and entertainment. In the low-choice broadcast environment, most people watched news and learned about politics because they were reluctant to turn off the set even if the programs offered at the time did not match their preferences. One study conducted in the early 1970s showed that 40% of the respondents reported watching programs because they appeared on the channel they were already watching or because someone else wanted to see them. Audience research has proposed a two-stage model according to which people first decide to watch television and then pick the available program they like best. Klein aptly called this model the "Theory of Least Objectionable Program." If television viewers are routinely "glued to the box" and select the best available program, we can explain why so many

Americans watched television news in the 1960s and 70s despite modest political interest. Most television viewing in the broadcast era did not stem from a deliberate choice of a program, but rather was determined by convenience, availability of spare time and the decision to spend that time in front of the TV set. And since broadcast channels offered a solid block of news at the dinner hour and again after primetime, many viewers were routinely exposed to news even though they watched television primarily to be entertained.

Once exposed to television news, people learn about politics. Although a captive news audience does not exhibit the same political interest as a self-selected one and therefore may not learn as much, research on passive learning suggests that even unmotivated exposure can produce learning. Hence, even broadcast viewers who prefer entertainment programs absorb at least basic political knowledge when they happen to tune in when only news is on.

I propose that such accidental exposure should become less likely in a high-choice environment because greater horizontal diversity (the number of genres available at any particular point in time) increases the chance that viewers will find content that matches their preferences. The impact of one's preferences increases, and "indiscriminate viewing" becomes less likely. Cable subscribers' channel repertoire (the number of frequently viewed channels) is not dramatically higher than that of non-subscribers, but their repertoire reflects a set of channels that are more closely related to their genre preferences. Two-stage viewing behavior thus predicts that news audiences should decrease as more alternatives are offered on other channels. Indeed, local news audiences tend to be smaller when competing entertainment programming is scheduled. Baum and Kernell show that cable subscribers, especially the less informed among them, are less likely to watch the presidential debates than otherwise similar individuals who receive only broadcast television. According to my first hypothesis, the advent of cable TV increased the knowledge gap between people with a preference for news and people with a preference for other media content.

Internet access should contribute to an increasing knowledge gap as well. Although the two media are undoubtedly different in many respects, access to the Internet, like cable, makes media choice more efficient. Yet, while they both increase media users' content choice, cable TV and the Internet are not perfect substitutes for each other. Compared at least to dial-up Internet service, cable offers greater immediacy and more visuals. The web offers more detailed information and can be customized to a greater extent. Both media, in other words, have unique features, and access to both of them offers users the greatest flexibility. For instance, people with access to both media can watch a campaign speech on cable and then compare online how different newspapers cover the event. Depending on their needs or the issue that interests them, they can actively search a wealth of political information online or passively consume cable politics. Hence, the effects of cable TV and Internet access should be additive and the knowledge gap largest among people with access to both new media.

There are several reasons why exposure to political information increases the likelihood that an individual will cast a vote on election day. Exposure increases political knowledge, which in turn increases turnout because people know where, how, and for whom to vote. Furthermore, knowledgeable people are more likely to perceive differences between candidates and thus less likely to abstain due to indifference. Independent of learning effects, exposure to political information on cable news and political web sites is likely to increase people's campaign interest. Interest, in turn, affects turnout even when one controls for political knowledge. Entertainment fans with a cable box or Internet connection, on the other hand, will miss both the interest- and the information-based effect of broadcast news on turnout. My second hypothesis thus predicts a widening turnout gap in the current environment, as people who prefer news vote at higher rates and those with other preferences increasingly stay home from the polls.

* * *

Conclusion

When speculating about the political implications of new media, pundits and scholars tend to either praise the likely benefits for democracy in the digital age or dwell on the dangers. The optimists claim that the greater availability of political information will lead more people to learn more about politics and increase their involvement in the political process. The pessimists fear that new media will make people apolitical and provide mind-numbing entertainment that keeps citizens from fulfilling their democratic responsibilities. These two predictions are often presented as mutually exclusive. Things will either spiral upwards or spiral downwards; the circle is either virtuous or vicious. The analyses presented here show that both are true. New media do indeed increase political knowledge and involvement in the electoral process among some people, just as the optimists predict. Yet, the evidence supports the pessimists' scenario as well. Other people take advantage of greater choice and tune out of politics completely. Those with a preference for entertainment, once they gain access to new media, become less knowledgeable about politics and less likely to vote. People's media content preferences become the key to understanding the political implications of new media.

* * *

The decline in the size of news audiences over the last three decades has been identified as cause for concern by many observers who have generally interpreted it as a sign of waning political interest and a disappearing sense of civic duty. Yet changes in available content can affect news consumption and learning *even in the absence of preference changes.* People's media use may change in a modified media environment, even if their preferences (or political interest or sense of civic duty) remain constant. By this logic, the decreasing size of the news audience is not necessarily an indication of reduced political interest. Interest in politics may simply never have been as high as audience shares for evening news suggested. A combined market share for the three network newscasts of almost 90% takes on a different meaning if one considers that people had hardly any viewing alternatives. It was "politics by default," not politics by choice. Even the mediocre levels of political knowledge during the broadcast era, in other words, were partly a result of de facto restrictions of people's freedom to choose their preferred media content.

Ironically, we might have to pin our hopes of creating a reasonably evenly informed electorate on that reviled form of communication, political advertising. Large segments of the electorate in a high-choice environment do not voluntarily watch, read, or listen to political information. Their greatest chance for encounters with the political world occurs when commercials are inserted into their regular entertainment diet. And exposure to political ads can increase viewers' political knowledge. At least for the time being, before recording services like TiVo, which automatically skip the commercial breaks, or subscriber-financed premium cable channels without advertising become more widespread, political advertising is more likely than news coverage to reach these viewers.

It might seem counterintuitive that political knowledge has decreased for a substantial portion of the electorate even though the amount of political information has multiplied and is more readily available than ever before. The share of politically uninformed people has risen since we entered the so-called "information age." Television as a medium has often been denigrated as "dumb," but, helped by the features of the broadcast environment, it may have been more successful in reaching less interested segments of the population than the "encyclopedic" Internet. In contrast to the view that politics is simply too difficult and complex to understand, this study shows that motivation, not ability, is the main obstacle that stands between an abundance of political information and a well- and evenly informed public.

When differences in political knowledge and turnout arise from inequality in the distribution of resources and skills, recommendations for how to help the information have-nots are generally uncontroversial. To the extent that knowledge and turnout gaps in the new media environment arise from voluntary consumption decisions, recommendations for how to narrow them, or whether to narrow them at all, become more contestable on normative grounds. As [Anthony] Downs remarked a long time ago, "[t]he loss of freedom involved in forcing people to acquire information would probably far outweigh the benefits to be gained from a better-informed electorate." Even if a consensus emerged to reduce media choice for the public good, it would still be technically impossible, even temporarily, to put the genie back in the bottle. Avoiding politics will never again be as difficult as it was in the "golden age" of television.

* * *

Discussion Questions

1. Are you concerned by the findings in Prior's study? If not, why not? If you are, can you think of any way to overcome the problem he has identified?
2. What lessons should public officials take from Prior's study? Should they pay less attention to public opinion because of the gaps in information and interest among members of the public?
3. Do you think the sharing of news and information through social media such as Twitter and Facebook exacerbates or diminishes the trends identified by Prior?

Debating the Issues: Is Partisan Media Exposure Bad for Democracy?

From the 1960s through the 1980s, when people thought of media and news, they thought of newspapers and the broadcast television networks (ABC, CBS, NBC). Cable news soon emerged to provide an alternative (CNN, Fox, MSNBC), but one that for the most part followed the same style in their major nightly newscasts as the big networks. Late in the 1980s, talk radio, which had been around for some time, boomed in popularity and hosts such as Rush Limbaugh became household names. Hosts gleefully tweaked the mainstream media and embraced a much more aggressive, hard-hitting style that was explicitly ideological and partisan. There was, in this new forum, no pretense to being objective but, talk-radio fans would argue, the mainstream media were also not objective—they just pretended to be. News-oriented talk shows on CNN, Fox, and MSNBC followed the same pattern, as did politically oriented humor such as that offered by Jon Stewart, Stephen Colbert, and John Oliver. The rise of the Internet in the 1990s was the most recent dramatic change in communications technology. Today, Twitter receives much of the attention for breaking stories, blogs are prominent in presenting wide-ranging opinion and analysis, and Facebook provides an easy way for individuals to voice their opinions on the news.

Is it a problem for democracy if the media outlets consumed by the public are explicitly partisan and ideological? One side of this debate says that selective exposure to partisan media is good for democracy: it enhances participation in politics, influences the flow of ideas in public discourse, and potentially portrays American politics with more accuracy than the conventional "balanced" press. From another perspective, one-sided media exposure is harmful: it encourages extreme political beliefs, polarizes the electorate, creates an "echo chamber" that diminishes the ability to learn from opposing views, and leads to stalemate and gridlock in Washington.

This chapter's debate provides three perspectives on the effects of partisan media exposure. Political scientist John Sides argues that most Americans who watch news actually do so from a variety of different sources and notes that partisan media outlets do not polarize voters so much as they instead attract the already-polarized. Sides also argues that partisan media can have the positive outcome of spurring political engagement. Journalist Jihii Jolly describes a "filter bubble" (on new media platforms, prior search and reading behavior influences what articles are presented to readers as future options) that makes it easy for individuals to expose themselves selectively to one particular point of view without even knowing it. Should we worry about filter bubbles? Quoting one analyst, Jolly suggests we should, noting that even individuals visiting the same site will have a different experience and "not have a baseline to compare what is real and what is not." Political scientist Matthew Levendusky argues that partisan media has its strongest effects on those who are already at the ideological extremes, pushing them further to the extremes. But overall, this is a small group of people. At the same time, Levendusky notes that many important questions remain unanswered about the possible effects of partisan media exposure.

44

"Can Partisan Media Contribute to Healthy Politics?"

JOHN SIDES

On Monday at 5 P.M., I'm participating in a South by Southwest panel entitled "How Partisan Media Contributes to Healthy Politics." I prefer to think of this as a question: Can partisan media contribute to healthy politics? For my contribution, I want to do two things. The first is report on the available social science to show that partisan media might not be as powerful as is sometimes suggested. I think that's an important piece of context for this discussion. The second is to raise some questions about whether and how partisanship—an often maligned notion—can play a valuable role in democracy.

The Audience for Partisan News Is Not as Big as You Might Think

What percentage of Americans watches cable news for 10 minutes or more per day? Only about 10–15 percent, if you simply add up the audiences for Fox News, CNN, and MSNBC. This is based on calculations by political scientist Markus Prior, drawing on detailed data about what people actually watch and not what they report in a survey. Survey reports of news consumption are often highly inaccurate. Consider this comparison of a 2008 Pew survey to data on viewership from the Nielsen Company [see graphs on the following page].

In the survey, almost a third of Americans believe they watch one of the three cable networks "regularly." It's not quite clear what "regularly" means, of course. This is one of the problems of using survey questions to measure media exposure. But if we assume that a regular viewer should watch at least an hour per week, then in reality only about 6–7 percent of Americas meet that description.

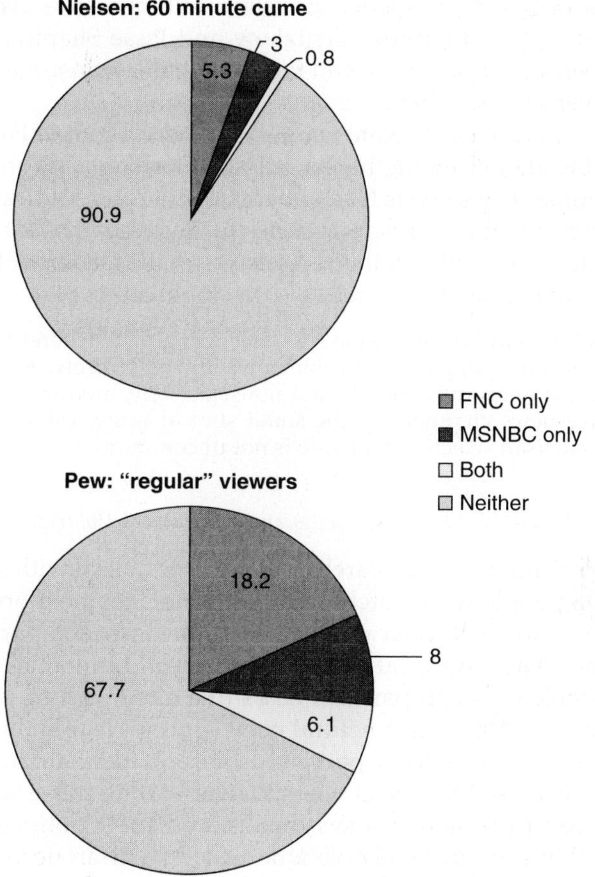

And even those numbers may be too high, because they double-count anyone who watches more than one of those channels. The seemingly inconceivable possibility that someone might watch both Fox and MSNBC leads to the next point.

Most People Are News Omnivores

Most people's "diet" of news isn't all that skewed by their partisans. There is actually a lot of overlap viewers of various cable news networks. Markus Prior reports that people who watch at least 1 minute of Fox News each week devote about 7.5 percent of their news consumption to Fox but 3.7 percent to other cable news channels. The same is true of CNN viewers. This is consistent with the research of Michael LaCour, who tracked media usage via devices that participants carried with them and that regularly recorded the ambient sounds around them. It is also consistent with the research of Matthew Gentzkow and Jesse Shapiro, who examined news consumption online and found that most consumers read ideologically diverse new outlets.

Unsurprisingly, if you isolate people who watch a lot of Fox News or a lot of MSNBC, their viewing habits reflect more skew. But this is a small group of people. The same is true of people who read political blogs: they are anything but omnivores, according to my research with Eric Lawrence and Henry Farrell, but they are also a small fraction of the public.

Prior has an excellent summary of these points:

> Automatic tracking of television viewing using two different technologies reveals that most people avoid cable news almost entirely. A large segment watches cable news infrequently and nonselectively, mixing exposure to different cable news channels. In the small slice of heavy cable news viewers, however, partisan selective exposure is not uncommon.

Partisan News May Not Polarize Partisans, but Attract Polarized Partisans

There is surprisingly little research that attempts to deal with a fundamental issue. Do people who watch partisan news become more polarized, or do people with polarized views simply like to watch partisan news? In one experiment, political scientist Matthew Levendusky randomly assigned people to watch partisan news that either did or did not share their political outlook, or to a neutral news source. He found that partisan news that reinforced subjects' political outlook made their attitudes modestly more extreme. This effect was stronger among those who said that they preferred to consume news that shared their political outlook—suggesting that even if the people who watch partisan news are already pretty partisan, partisan news will make them more so.

However, other research by Kevin Arceneaux and Martin Johnson arrives at a different conclusion. They conducted a set of experiments and allowed people to choose whether they watched their side's partisan news, the other side's news, or entertainment programming that had no news content. They found that the news shows had no effects on attitudes as long as people were allowed to choose. This suggests that, in the real world, partisan news doesn't polarize. If anything, it may be that polarization creates an audience for partisan news.

A few experiments isn't much of an evidentiary base. Much more needs to be done. But it's worth noting that we don't really know that partisan news is polarizing us, and with more evidence, we may find that it isn't.

Learning to Love Partisanship

As you can tell from the title of the panel, it was deliberately framed as a provocation. It's sometimes (often? always?) hard to like partisan news and even partisanship itself. But here is the trade-off I want to emphasize.

We want politics to involve calm, civil, rational deliberation about the common good. Partisanship doesn't necessarily facilitate that goal and can actively detract from it. But we also want politics to be full of active, eager, and engaged citizens. Partisanship does a very good job of facilitating engagement. It's one reason why voter turnout was so high in the late eighteenth century during the heyday of strong party organizations and a largely partisan press.

Indeed, if you look at partisans in the public, they look like ideal citizens in many respects. In a December 2011 YouGov poll, 65 percent of people who identified as "strong" Democrats or Republicans said they were "very much interested" in politics. Only 35 percent of those who identified as independents with no partisan leaning said that. Partisans are more likely not only to follow politics but to participate in it. Indeed, it is sort of odd to expect people to care deeply about something but then tell them they're not allowed to have strong opinions. It's like saying, "You should love baseball, but please don't actually root for a team."

I'm not suggesting that partisanship is an unalloyed good. Partisans can be misinformed if they are buying the spin their side is selling—spin that, by the way, they can usually hear in neutral news outlets doing "he said, she said" reporting, not simply in partisan news. Partisanship militates against other democratic goals, like tolerance for opposing points of view. Or compromise.

And, in any case, we've only got an hour in this panel, so we're hardly going to resolve this. I just think it's worth exploring these tensions in the folk theories we have about politics.

45

"How Algorithms Decide the News You See"

JIHII JOLLY

Homepage traffic for news sites continues to decrease. This trend is the result of an "if the news is important, it will find me" mentality that developed with the rise of social media, when people began to read links that their friends and others in their networks recommended. Thus, readers are increasingly discovering news through social media, email, and reading apps.

Publishers are well aware of this, and have tweaked their infrastructure accordingly, building algorithms that change the site experience depending on where a reader enters from.

While publishers view optimizing sites for the reading and sharing preferences of specific online audiences as a good thing, because it gets users to content they are likely to care about quickly and efficiently, that kind of catering may not be good for readers.

"We can actually act on the psychological predisposition to just expose ourselves to things that we agree with," explains Nick Diakopoulos, research fellow at the Tow Center for Digital Journalism, where he recently published a report on algorithmic accountability reporting. "And what the algorithms do is they throw gasoline on the fire."

Visitors who enter BuzzFeed via Pinterest, for instance, see a larger "Pin It" button, no Twitter share button, and a "hot on Pinterest" module. Medium, launched less than two years ago by Twitter co-founder Evan Williams, recommends content to readers via an intelligent algorithm primarily based on how long users spend reading articles. Recommended content sidebars on any news site are calculated via algorithm, and Facebook has a recommended news content block that takes into account previous clicks and offers similar links.

Diakopoulos categorizes algorithms into several categories based on the types of decisions they make. *Prioritization*, for example, ranks content to bring attention to one thing at the expense of another. *Association* marks relationships between entities, such as articles or videos that share subject matter of features. *Filtering* involves the inclusion or exclusion of certain information based on a set of criteria.

"Algorithms make it much easier not just for you to find the content that you're interested in, but for the content to find you that the algorithm thinks you're interested in," Diakopoulos says. That is, they maximize for clicks by excluding other kinds of content, helping reinforce an existing worldview by diminishing a reader's chance of encountering content outside of what they already know and believe.

This type of exclusion on the internet has become known as the filter bubble, after a 2011 book by Eli Pariser. As [Columbia Journalism Review]'s Alexis Fitts explains in a recent feature about Pariser's viral site, Upworthy:

> In Pariser's conception, the filter bubble is the world created by the shift from "human gatekeepers," such as newspaper editors who curate importance by what makes the front page, to the algorithmic ones employed by Facebook and Google, which present the content they believe a user is most likely to click on. This new digital universe is "a cozy place," Pariser writes, "populated by our favorite people and things and ideas." But it's ultimately a dangerous one. These unique universes "alter the way we'd encounter ideas and information," preventing the kind of spontaneous encounters with ideas that promote creativity and, perhaps more importantly, encouraging us to throw our attention to matters of irrelevance.
>
> "It's easy to push 'Like' and increase the visibility of a friend's post about finishing a marathon or an instructional article about how to make onion soup," writes Pariser. "It's harder to push the 'Like' button on an article titled, 'Darfur sees bloodiest month in two years.'"

These types of algorithms create a news literacy issue because if readers don't know they are influencing content, they cannot make critical decisions about what they choose to read. In the print world, partisan media was transparent about its biases, and readers could therefore select which bias they preferred. Today, readers don't necessarily know how algorithms are biased and and how nuanced the filters they receive content through really are.

"Newspapers have always been able to have an editorial voice and to possibly even affect voting patterns based on that editorial voice," says Diakopoulos. "But what we're seeing [now] is the ability to scale across a population in a much more powerful way." Facebook recently did a study that found that simply showing more news in the newsfeed affects voting decisions.

Furthermore, the algorithms that social sites use to promote content don't evaluate the validity of the content, which can and has spread misinformation.

Beyond the filter bubble, algorithmic bias extends to search engine manipulation, which refers to the process undertaken by many companies, celebrities, and public figures to ensure that favorable content rises to the top of search engine results in particular regions. Though not intuitive to the average Web user, it's actually a form of soft censorship, explains Wenke Lee, Director of the Georgia Tech Information Security Center.

After reading Pariser's book, Lee and his research team set out to test the effect of personalized search results on Google and built a tool called Bobble, a browser plug-in that runs simultaneous Google searches from different locations around the globe so users can see the difference between Google search returns for different people. They found that results differ based on several factors: Web content at any given time, the region from which a search is performed, recent search history, and how much search engine manipulation has occurred to favor a given result. Though Bobble has largely been confined to research purposes, it has been downloaded close to 10,000 times and has tremendous potential as a news literacy teaching tool.

"When we do this kind of work, there is always some pushback from people who say 'Why should people care? Why should people care about the filter bubble or biased news?' " says Lee. "But in the print media age, if somebody was to give me a manipulated version of *The New York Times*, I would be able to put my newspaper next to yours and find out that mine is different. But now? You and I can very likely see different front pages of newspapers online because they are customized for individuals, and that's pretty dangerous. Because that means I don't have a baseline to compare what is real and what is not."

For these reasons, the Center for News Literacy at Stony Brook University dedicates a portion of its curriculum to the filter bubble, covering issues of search engine manipulation and teaching how to search incognito on a Web browser—that is, without it storing your information.

Other efforts to mitigate media bias from algorithmic personalization include NewsCube, a Web service which automatically provides readers with multiple viewpoints on a given news item, and Balance, a research project at the University of Michigan that seeks to diversify the result sets provided by news aggregators (such as Google News).

Meanwhile, Diakopoulous is working on a framework for how to be transparent about algorithms, as well as processes for how they can be investigated, be it through reverse engineering by users (for which he offers methods in his report) or policy regulations on an institutional level.

"Transparency is important for the same reason why we want our newspaper editors to be transparent," he says. "If the purveyor of this very powerful media tool is honest with us about how they are using it, then at least we can be a little bit more trusting of them."

And it's also a way to give people the choice to be more media savvy—to exit the filter bubble, if they wish. "If I know your search engine works that way and I know someone else's search engine works a different way, then I can choose which one I would prefer to use."

46

"Are Fox and MSNBC Polarizing America?"

MATTHEW LEVENDUSKY

A generation ago, if ordinary Americans turned on the television at 6 P.M., they had basically one choice: to watch the evening news. They could have chosen to watch ABC, CBS, or NBC, but it wouldn't really have mattered, because they all basically gave the same news in a similar format. Today, if they did that, they would have hundreds of options, including not just the news, but also sports, movies, re-runs, and so forth. Even within news, they have a variety of choices. Not only would they have the major network news programs, but they would have many choices on cable, most notably the partisan outlets of Fox News and MSNBC (not to mention even more choices online). This choice of explicitly partisan outlets means that individuals can choose to hear messages that reinforce their beliefs, while avoiding those from alternative points of view, which some claim leads to polarization. Does this high-choice media environment, especially with its partisan outlets, polarize the public?

The evidence suggests that the media may contribute to polarization, but in a more circumscribed way than many commentators suggest. Take first the question, of choice, and in particular, whether people seek out media choices that reinforce their existing beliefs. The answer is (perhaps not surprisingly) yes: Republicans are more likely to tune in to Fox News and liberals are more likely to watch MSNBC. Researchers have also found that these effects are stronger for those who are more partisan and politically involved.

But there is perhaps an even more important type of selection at work. While the political can tune into Fox and MSNBC, those who dislike politics also have more options than ever for avoiding it. In lieu of the nightly news—or a televised presidential address—they can watch *Sports Center, Entertainment Tonight*, or a rerun of *The Big Bang Theory*. When confronted with a political option, they simply change the channel to something else that they find more agreeable. Even the most popular cable news programs get 2 to 3 million viewers on a typical evening in a country of 300 million Americans. In earlier decades, some of these individuals would have been incidentally exposed to political news and information (by, say, watching the television news at 6 o'clock, when there were no other options). Now that they can avoid news altogether, they know less about politics and are less likely to participate. So the growth of media choice strengthens the extremes while hollowing out the center, making the electorate more divided.

But what about the effects of partisan media on those who do watch these programs? While this research tradition is still relatively young, scholars have found a number of effects: on vote choice, participation, and attitudes toward bipartisanship and compromise, among others. The research looking at effects on attitudes finds that while there are effects, they are concentrated primarily among those who are already extreme. This suggests that these programs contribute to polarization not by shifting the center of the ideological distribution, but rather by lengthening the tails (i.e., moving the polarized even further away from the center).

It is vital to put these effects into context. As noted above, these programs attract a small audience, but those who watch these shows are more partisan, politically interested, and politically involved; these are the individuals who are more likely to make their voices heard in the halls of power. So to the extent that these shows matter, it is by influencing this relatively narrow audience. These programs have few direct effects on most Americans.

While scholars have learned a great deal about how media might shape polarization, there are still many questions to be answered. First, we know essentially nothing about the indirect effects of these shows: Do those who watch these shows transmit some of the effects to non-watchers through discussion in social networks? Does the Rachel Maddow fan in the cubicle next to you shape your opinions by telling you what she discussed on her show last night? Second, what is the effect of these shows on the broader media agenda, and on elites? Do the frames and issues that originate on Fox or MSNBC influence the broader media agenda? If so, that's an important finding, as it shows how these networks help to shape what a wider swath of Americans see.

In general, we understand little about how news outlets influence one another, especially in a 24-hour news cycle. Some recent work suggests that these outlets (particularly Fox) have shaped the behavior of members of Congress. The work discussed here has focused on the effects of cable TV news (with similar effects found previously for political talk radio). But there is an even broader range of material on the Internet, and few works have yet explored these effects. How the Internet—and especially social media sites like Twitter and Facebook—contributes to polarization will be an important topic in the years to come.

Discussion Questions

1. Which part or parts of the news media—newspapers, television, websites, blogs, radio, Facebook, Twitter—do you rely on most? Which would you say you trust the most? What makes these sources the most trustworthy?
2. Considering the evidence presented in these three articles, how pervasive is exposure to news coverage that is implicitly or explicitly partisan or ideological? On balance, is this exposure good or bad for American democracy? What are the strongest areas of concern? What might be the chief benefits?
3. How do you know partisan bias when you see it? Define three criteria you would use to determine whether a media outlet is catering to readers' or viewers' partisan bias.

CHAPTER 10

Elections and Voting

47

"The Voice of the People: An Echo," from *The Responsible Electorate*

V. O. KEY, JR.

The votes are cast, the tallies are in, the winning candidate claims victory and a mandate to govern—the people have spoken! But what exactly have the people said when they cast a plurality of the votes for one candidate? The political scientist V. O. Key, Jr., argues that the voice of the people is an echo of the cacophony and hubbub of candidates and parties scrambling for popular support. "Even the most discriminating popular judgment," wrote Key, "can reflect only ambiguity, uncertainty, or even foolishness if those are the qualities of the input into the echo chamber."

So what is the logic of the voting decision? Key argues that the effort among social scientists to develop theories for understanding the voting decision is important because of the ways political candidates and political leaders will respond to them. If research demonstrates that voters are influenced by "images and cultivation of style," rather than the "substance of politics," then that is what candidates will offer the voters. If the people receive only images and style as the input to the echo chamber, then eventually that is all they will come to expect. However, Key argues that contrary to the picture of voters held by many politicians and some academic research of his day, the "voters are not fools" who are easily manipulated by campaign tactics or who vote predictably according to the social groups they are in. Individual voters may behave oddly, he concedes, but "in the large, the electorate behaves about as rationally and responsibly as we should expect." His analysis of past presidential elections convinced him that the electorate made sensible decisions based upon a concern for public policy, the performance of government, and the personalities of the candidates.

In his reflective moments even the most experienced politician senses a nagging curiosity about why people vote as they do. His power and his position depend upon the outcome of the mysterious rites we perform as opposing candidates harangue the multitudes who finally march to the polls to prolong the rule of their champion, to thrust him, ungratefully, back into the void of private life, or to raise to eminence a new tribune of the people. What kinds of appeals enable a candidate to win the favor of the great god, The People? What circumstances move voters to shift their preferences in this direction or that? What clever propaganda tactic or slogan led to this result? What mannerism of oratory or style of rhetoric produced another outcome? What band of electors rallied to this candidate to save the day for him? What policy of state attracted the devotion of another bloc of voters? What action repelled a third sector of the electorate?

The victorious candidate may claim with assurance that he has the answers to all such questions. He may regard his success as vindication of his beliefs about why voters vote as they do. And he may regard the swing of the vote to him as indubitably a response to the campaign positions he took, as an indication of the acuteness of his intuitive estimates of the mood of the people, and as a ringing manifestation of the esteem in which he is held by a discriminating public. This narcissism assumes its most repulsive form among election winners who have championed intolerance, who have stirred the passions and hatreds of people, or who have advocated causes known by decent men to be outrageous or dangerous in their long-run consequences. No functionary is more repugnant or more arrogant than the unjust man who asserts, with a color of truth, that he speaks from a pedestal of popular approbation.

It thus can be a mischievous error to assume, because a candidate wins, that a majority of the electorate shares his views on public questions, approves his past actions, or has specific expectations about his future conduct. Nor does victory establish that the candidate's campaign strategy, his image, his television style, or his fearless stand against cancer and polio turned the trick. The election returns establish only that the winner attracted a majority of the votes—assuming the existence of a modicum of rectitude in election administration. They tell us precious little about why the plurality was his.

For a glaringly obvious reason, electoral victory cannot be regarded as necessarily a popular ratification of a candidate's outlook. The voice of the people is but an echo. The output of an echo chamber bears an inevitable and invariable relation to the input. As candidates and parties clamor for attention and vie for popular support, the people's verdict can be no more than a selective reflection from among the alternatives and outlooks presented to them. Even the most discriminating popular judgment can reflect only ambiguity, uncertainty, or even foolishness if those are the qualities of the input into the echo chamber. A candidate may win despite his tactics and appeals rather than because of them. If the people can choose only from among rascals, they are certain to choose a rascal.

Scholars, though they have less at stake than do politicians, also have an abiding curiosity about why voters act as they do. In the past quarter of a century [since the 1940s] they have vastly enlarged their capacity to check the hunches born of their curiosities. The invention of the sample survey—the most widely known example of which is the Gallup poll—enabled them to make fairly trustworthy estimates of the characteristics and behaviors of large human populations. This method of mass observation revolutionized the study of politics—as well as the management of political campaigns. The new technique permitted large-scale tests to check the validity of old psychological and sociological theories of human behavior. These tests led to new hunches and new theories about voting behavior, which could, in turn, be checked and which thereby contributed to the extraordinary ferment in the social sciences during recent decades.

The studies of electoral behavior by survey methods cumulate into an imposing body of knowledge which conveys a vivid impression of the variety and subtlety of factors that enter into individual voting decisions. In their first stages in the 1930s the new electoral studies chiefly lent precision and verification to the working maxims of practicing politicians and to some of the crude theories of political speculators. Thus, sample surveys established that people did, indeed, appear to vote their pocketbooks. Yet the demonstration created its embarrassments because it also established that exceptions to the rule were numerous. Not all factory workers, for example, voted alike. How was the behavior of the deviants from "group interest" to be explained? Refinement after refinement of theory and analysis added complexity to the original simple explanation. By introducing a bit of psychological theory it could be demonstrated that factory workers with optimistic expectations tended less to be governed by pocketbook considerations than did those whose outlook was gloomy. When a little social psychology was stirred into the analysis, it could be established that identifications formed early in life, such as attachments to political parties, also reinforced or resisted the pull of the interest of the moment. A sociologist, bringing to play the conceptual tools of his trade, then could show that those factory workers who associate intimately with like-minded persons on the average vote with greater solidarity than do social isolates. Inquiries conducted with great ingenuity along many such lines have enormously broadened our knowledge of the factors associated with the responses of people to the stimuli presented to them by political campaigns.

Yet, by and large, the picture of the voter that emerges from a combination of the folklore of practical politics and the findings of the new electoral studies is not a pretty one. It is not a portrait of citizens moving to considered decision as they play their solemn role of making and unmaking governments. The older tradition from practical politics may regard the voter as an erratic and irrational fellow susceptible to manipulation by skilled humbugs. One need not live through many campaigns to observe politicians, even successful politicians, who act as though they regarded the people as manageable fools. Nor does a heroic conception of the voter emerge from the new analyses of electoral behavior. They can be added up to a conception of voting not as a civic decision but as an almost purely deterministic act. Given knowledge of certain characteristics of a voter—his occupation, his residence, his religion, his national origin, and perhaps certain of his attitudes—one can predict with a high probability the direction of his vote. The actions of persons are made to appear to be only predictable and automatic responses to campaign stimuli.

* * *

Conceptions and theories of the way voters behave do not raise solely arcane problems to be disputed among the democratic and antidemocratic theorists or questions to be settled by the elegant techniques of the analysts of electoral behavior. Rather, they touch upon profound issues at the heart of the problem of the nature and workability of systems of popular government. Obviously the perceptions of the behavior of the electorate held by political leaders, agitators, and activists condition, if they do not fix, the types of appeals politicians employ as they seek popular support. These perceptions—or theories—affect the nature of the input to the echo chamber, if we may revert to our earlier figure, and thereby control its output. They may govern, too, the kinds of actions that governments take as they look forward to the next election. If politicians perceive the electorate as responsive to father images, they will give it father images. If they see voters as most certainly responsive to nonsense, they will give them nonsense. If they see voters as susceptible to delusion, they will delude them. If they see an electorate receptive to the cold, hard realities, they will give it the cold, hard realities.

In short, theories of how voters behave acquire importance not because of their effects on voters, who may proceed blithely unaware of them. They gain significance because of their effects, both potentially and in reality, on candidates and other political leaders. If leaders believe the route to victory is by projection of images and cultivation of styles rather than by advocacy of policies to cope with the problems of the country, they will project images and cultivate styles to the neglect of the substance of politics. They will abdicate their prime function in a democratic system, which amounts, in essence, to the assumption of the risk of trying to persuade us to lift ourselves by our bootstraps.

Among the literary experts on politics there are those who contend that, because of the development of tricks for the manipulation of the masses, practices of political leadership in the management of voters have moved far toward the conversion of election campaigns into obscene parodies of the models set up by democratic idealists. They point to the good old days when politicians were deep thinkers, eloquent orators, and far-sighted statesmen. Such estimates of the course of change in social institutions must be regarded with reserve. They may be only manifestations of the inverted optimism of aged and melancholy men who, estopped from hope for the future, see in the past a satisfaction of their yearning for greatness in our political life.

Whatever the trends may have been, the perceptions that leadership elements of democracies hold of the modes of response of the electorate must always be a matter of fundamental significance. Those perceptions determine the nature of the voice of the people, for they determine the character of the input into the echo chamber. While the output may be governed by the nature of the input, over the longer run the properties of the echo chamber may themselves be altered. Fed a steady diet of buncombe [bunkum], the people may come to expect and to respond with highest predictability to buncombe. And those leaders most skilled in the propagation of buncombe may gain lasting advantage in the recurring struggles for popular favor.

The perverse and unorthodox argument of this little book is that voters are not fools. To be sure, many individual voters act in odd ways indeed; yet in the large the electorate behaves about as rationally and responsibly as we should expect, given the clarity of the alternatives presented to it and the character of the information available to it. In American presidential campaigns of recent decades the portrait of the American electorate that develops from the data is not one of an electorate straitjacketed by social determinants or moved by subconscious urges triggered by devilishly skillful propagandists. It is rather one of an electorate moved by concern about central and relevant questions of public policy, of governmental performance, and of executive personality. Propositions so uncompromisingly stated inevitably represent overstatements. Yet to the extent that they can be shown to resemble the reality, they are propositions of basic importance for both the theory and the practice of democracy.

To check the validity of this broad interpretation of the behavior of voters, attention will center on the movements of voters across party lines as they reacted to the issues, events, and candidates of presidential campaigns between 1936 and 1960. Some Democratic voters of one election turned Republican at the next; others stood pat. Some Republicans of one presidential season voted Democratic four years later; others remained loyal Republicans. What motivated these shifts, sometimes large and sometimes small, in voter affection? How did the standpatters differ from the switchers? What led them to stand firmly by their party preference of four years earlier? Were these actions governed by images, moods, and other irrelevancies; or were they expressions of judgments about the sorts of questions that, hopefully, voters will weigh as they responsibly cast their ballots? On these matters evidence is available that is impressive in volume, if not always so complete or so precisely relevant as hindsight would wish. If one perseveres through the analysis of this extensive body of information, the proposition that the voter is not so irrational a fellow after all may become credible.

DISCUSSION QUESTIONS

1. When you cast your vote, how do you decide whom to vote for? Is your decision process affected by the nature of the political campaign that has just been completed, or does the campaign have little effect?
2. Does the 2016 presidential election support Key's view of the electoral process? What kinds of information would you want to have in order to answer this question?

48

"The Unpolitical Animal: How Political Science Understands Voters"

LOUIS MENAND

How well do Americans measure up to the ideal of highly informed, engaged, attentive, involved citizens? V. O. Key argued that Americans, on the whole, do reasonably well in making sound collective judgments. Writing around the same time as Key, another political scientist, Philip Converse, reached a gloomier conclusion. Most Americans couldn't be "ideal" citizens because most had minimal and inconsistent political belief systems. To a large degree, he concluded, Americans had many top-of-the-head opinions that had no strong connection to a set of principles. Louis Menand revisits the question addressed by V. O. Key: do elections represent the will of the people? Menand reviews Converse's conclusions and then discusses three theories that attempt to make some sense of Americans' failure to behave as ideal citizens. One theory declares that elections are more or less random events in which a large bloc of voters responds to "slogans, misinformation, 'fire alarms' (sensational news), 'October surprises' (last-minute sensational news), random personal associations, and 'gotchas.'" Another theory posits that voter decisions are guided not simply by random events and information, but by elite opinion. Elites do understand the issues and work within ideological frameworks and they find ways to pitch ideas to voters so they gain a governing majority. Elections are thus primarily about the interests and beliefs of rival elite factions. The third theory in part rescues the voter from these unflattering portraits. Here, voters use information shortcuts, especially but not only political party labels, to render verdicts that are substantively meaningful. "People use shortcuts—the social-scientific term is 'heuristics'—to reach judgments about political candidates, and, on the whole, these shortcuts are as good as the long and winding road of reading party platforms, listening to candidate debates, and all the other elements of civic duty." Menand concludes in this 2004 article that voter decisions may be based on shortcuts that make sense to them—such as which candidate is more optimistic—rather than the weighing and balancing of principles and policy positions that ideologues would prefer.

In every presidential-election year, there are news stories about undecided voters, people who say that they are perplexed about which candidate's positions make the most sense. They tell reporters things like "I'd like to know more about Bush's plan for education," or "I'm worried that Kerry's ideas about Social Security don't add up." They say that they are thinking about issues like "trust," and whether the candidate cares about people like them. To voters who identify strongly with a political party, the undecided voter is almost an alien life form. For them, a vote for Bush is a vote for a whole philosophy of governance and a vote for Kerry is a vote for a distinctly different philosophy. The difference is obvious to them, and they don't understand how others can't see it, or can decide whom to vote for on the basis of a candidate's personal traits or whether his or her position on a particular issue "makes sense." To an undecided voter, on the other hand, the person who always votes for the Democrat or the Republican, no matter what, must seem like a dangerous fanatic. Which voter is behaving more rationally and responsibly?

If you look to the political professionals, the people whose job it is to know what makes the fish bite, it is clear that, in their view, political philosophy is not the fattest worm. *Winning Elections: Political Campaign Management, Strategy & Tactics* . . . is a collection of articles drawn from the pages of *Campaigns & Elections: The Magazine for People in Politics.* The advice [of] the political professionals is: Don't assume that your candidate's positions are going to make the difference. "In a competitive political climate," as one article explains, "informed citizens may vote for a candidate based on issues. However, uninformed or undecided voters will often choose the candidate whose name and packaging are most memorable. To make sure your candidate has that 'top-of-mind' voter awareness, a powerful logo is the best place to start." You want to present your candidate in language that voters will understand. They understand colors. "Blue is a positive color for men, signaling authority and control," another article advises. "But it's a negative color for women, who perceive it as distant, cold and aloof. Red is a warm, sentimental color for women—and a sign of danger or anger to men. If you use the wrong colors to the wrong audience, you're sending a mixed message."

It can't be the case, though, that electoral outcomes turn on things like the color of the buttons. Can it? When citizens stand in the privacy of the booth and contemplate the list of those who bid to serve, do they really think, That's the guy with the red logo. A lot of anger there. I'll take my chances with the other one? In Civics 101, the model voter is a citizen vested with the ability to understand the consequences of his or her choice; when these individual rational choices are added up, we know the will of the people. How accurate is this picture?

Skepticism about the competence of the masses to govern themselves is as old as mass self-government. Even so, when that competence began to be measured statistically, around the end of the Second World War, the numbers startled almost everyone. The data were interpreted most powerfully by the political scientist Philip Converse, in an article on "The Nature of Belief Systems in Mass Publics," published in 1964. Forty years later, Converse's conclusions are still the bones at which the science of voting behavior picks.

Converse claimed that only around ten percent of the public has what can be called, even generously, a political belief system. He named these people "ideologues," by which he meant not that they are fanatics but that they have a reasonable grasp of "what goes with what"—of how a set of opinions adds up to a coherent political philosophy. Non-ideologues may use terms like "liberal" and "conservative," but Converse thought that they basically don't know what they're talking about, and that their beliefs are characterized by what he termed a lack of "constraint": they can't see how one opinion (that taxes should be lower, for example) logically ought to rule out other opinions (such as the belief that there should be more government programs). About forty-two percent of voters, according to Converse's interpretation of surveys of the 1956 electorate, vote on the basis not of ideology but of perceived self-interest. The rest form political preferences either from their sense of whether times are good or bad (about twenty-five percent) or from factors that have no discernible "issue content" whatever. Converse put twenty-two percent of the electorate in this last category. In other words, about twice as many people have no political views as have a coherent political belief system.

Just because someone's opinions don't square with what a political scientist recognizes as a political ideology doesn't mean that those opinions aren't coherent by the lights of some more personal system of beliefs. But Converse found reason to doubt this possibility. When pollsters ask people for their opinion about an issue, people generally feel obliged to have one. Their answer is duly recorded, and it becomes a datum in a report on "public opinion." But, after analyzing the results of surveys conducted over time, in which people tended to give different and randomly inconsistent answers to the same questions, Converse concluded that "very substantial portions of the public" hold opinions that are essentially meaningless—off-the-top-of-the-head responses to questions they have never thought about, derived from no underlying set of principles. These people might as well base their political choices on the weather. And, in fact, many of them do.

Findings about the influence of the weather on voter behavior are among the many surveys and studies that confirm Converse's sense of the inattention of the American electorate. In election years from 1952 to 2000, when people were asked whether they cared who won the presidential election, between twenty-two and forty-four percent answered "don't care" or "don't know." In 2000, eighteen percent said that they decided which presidential candidate to vote for only in the last two weeks of the campaign; five percent, enough to swing most elections, decided the day they voted.

Seventy percent of Americans cannot name their senators or their congressman. Forty-nine percent believe that the President has the power to suspend the Constitution. Only about thirty percent name an issue when they explain why they voted the way they did, and only a fifth hold consistent opinions on issues over time. Rephrasing poll questions reveals that many people don't understand the issues that they have just offered an opinion on. According to polls conducted in 1987 and 1989, for example, between twenty and twenty-five percent of the public thinks that too little is being spent on welfare, and between sixty-three and sixty-five percent feels that too little is being spent on assistance to the poor. And voters apparently do punish politicians for acts of God. In a paper written in 2004, the Princeton political scientists Christopher Achen and Larry Bartels estimate that "2.8 million people voted against Al Gore in 2000 because their states were too dry or too wet" as a consequence of that year's weather patterns. Achen and Bartels think that these voters cost Gore seven states, any one of which would have given him the election.

All political systems make their claim to legitimacy by some theory, whether it's the divine right of kings or the iron law of history. Divine rights and iron laws are not subject to empirical confirmation, which is one reason that democracy's claims have always seemed superior. What polls and surveys suggest, though, is that the belief that elections express the true preferences of the people may be nearly as imaginary. When you move downward through what Converse called the public's "belief strata," candidates are quickly separated from ideology and issues, and they become attached, in voters' minds, to idiosyncratic clusters of ideas and attitudes. The most widely known fact about George H. W. Bush in the 1992 election was that he hated broccoli. Eighty-six percent of likely voters in that election knew that the Bushes' dog's name was Millie; only fifteen percent knew that Bush and Clinton both favored the death penalty. It's not that people know nothing. It's just that politics is not what they know.

In the face of this evidence, three theories have arisen. The first is that electoral outcomes, as far as "the will of the people" is concerned, are essentially arbitrary. The fraction of the electorate that responds to substantive political arguments is hugely outweighed by the fraction that responds to slogans, misinformation, "fire alarms" (sensational news), "October surprises" (last-minute sensational news), random personal associations, and "gotchas." Even when people think that they are thinking in political terms, even when they believe that they are analyzing candidates on the basis of their positions on issues, they are usually operating behind a veil of political ignorance. They simply don't understand, as a practical matter, what it means to be "fiscally conservative," or to have "faith in the private sector," or to pursue an "interventionist foreign policy." They can't hook up positions with policies. From the point of view of democratic theory, American political history is just a random walk through a series of electoral options. Some years, things turn up red; some years, they turn up blue.

A second theory is that although people may not be working with a full deck of information and beliefs, their preferences are dictated by something, and that something is elite opinion. Political campaigns, on this theory, are essentially struggles among the elite, the fraction of a fraction of voters who have the knowledge and the ideological chops to understand the substantive differences between the candidates and to argue their policy implications. These voters communicate their preferences to the rest of the electorate by various cues, low-content phrases and images (warm colors, for instance) to which voters can relate, and these cues determine the outcome of the race. Democracies are really oligarchies with a populist face.

The third theory of democratic politics is the theory that the cues to which most voters respond are, in fact, adequate bases on which to form political preferences. People use shortcuts—the social-scientific term is "heuristics"—to reach judgments about political candidates, and, on the whole, these shortcuts are as good as the long and winding road of reading party platforms, listening to candidate debates, and all the other elements of civic duty. Voters use what Samuel Popkin, one of the proponents of this third theory, calls "low-information rationality"—in other words, gut reasoning—to reach political decisions; and this intuitive form of judgment proves a good enough substitute for its high-information counterpart in reflecting what people want.

An analogy (though one that Popkin is careful to dissociate himself from) would be to buying an expensive item like a house or a stereo system. A tiny fraction of consumers has the knowledge to discriminate among the entire range of available stereo components, and to make an informed choice based on assessments of cost and performance. Most of us rely on the advice of two or three friends who have recently made serious stereo-system purchases, possibly some online screen shopping, and the pitch of the salesman at J&R Music World. We eyeball the product, associate idiosyncratically with the brand name, and choose from the gut. When we ask "experts" for their wisdom, mostly we are hoping for an "objective" ratification of our instinctive desire to buy the coolest-looking stuff. Usually, we're O.K. Our tacit calculation is that the marginal utility of more research is smaller than the benefit of immediate ownership.

On the theory of heuristics, it's roughly the same with candidates: voters don't have the time or the inclination to assess them in depth, so they rely on the advice of experts—television commentators, political activists, Uncle Charlie—combined with their own hunches, to reach a decision. Usually (they feel), they're O.K. If they had spent the time needed for a top-to-toe vetting, they would probably not have chosen differently. Some voters might get it wrong in one direction, choosing the liberal candidate when they in fact preferred a conservative one, but their error is cancelled out by the voters who mistakenly choose the conservative. The will of the people may not be terribly articulate, but it comes out in the wash.

This theory is the most attractive of the three, since it does the most to salvage democratic values from the electoral wreckage Converse described.

It gives the mass of voters credit for their decisions by suggesting not only that they can interpret the cues given by the campaigns and the elite opinion-makers but that the other heuristics they use—the candidate seems likable, times are not as good as they were—are actually defensible replacements for informed, logical reasoning. Popkin begins his well-regarded book on the subject, *The Reasoning Voter,* with an example from Gerald Ford's primary campaign against Ronald Reagan in 1976. Visiting a Mexican-American community in Texas, Ford (never a gaffe-free politician) made the mistake of trying to eat a tamale with the corn husk, in which it is traditionally served, still on it. This ethnic misprision made the papers, and when he was asked, after losing to Jimmy Carter in the general election, what the lesson of his defeat was, Ford answered, "Always shuck your tamales." Popkin argues that although familiarity with Mexican-American cuisine is not a prerequisite for favoring policies friendly to Mexican-Americans, Mexican-Americans were justified in concluding that a man who did not know how to eat a tamale was not a man predisposed to put their needs high on his list. The reasoning is illogical: Ford was not running for chef, and it was possible to extrapolate, from his positions, the real difference it would make for Mexican-Americans if he were President rather than Reagan or Carter. But Mexican-Americans, and their sympathizers, felt "in their gut" that Ford was not their man, and that was enough.

The principal shortcut that people use in deciding which candidates to vote for is, of course, the political party. The party is the ultimate Uncle Charlie in American politics. Even elite voters use it when they are confronted, in the voting booth, with candidates whose names they have never seen before. There is nothing in the Constitution requiring candidates to be listed on the ballot with their party affiliations, and, if you think about it, the custom of doing so is vaguely undemocratic. It makes elections a monopoly of the major parties, by giving their candidates an enormous advantage—the advantage of an endorsement right there on the ballot—over everyone else who runs. It is easy to imagine a constitutional challenge to the practice of identifying candidates by party, but it is also easy to imagine how wild the effects would be if voters were confronted by a simple list of names with no identifying tags. Every election would be like an election for student-body president: pure name recognition.

Any time information is lacking or uncertain, a shortcut is generally better than nothing. But the shortcut itself is not a faster way of doing the math; it's a way of skipping the math altogether. My hunch that the coolest-looking stereo component is the best value simply does not reflect an intuitive grasp of electronics. My interest in a stereo is best served if I choose the finest sound for the money, as my interest in an election is best served if I choose the candidate whose policies are most likely to benefit me or the people I care about. But almost no one calculates in so abstract a fashion. Even voters who supported Michael Dukakis in 1988 agreed that he looked ridiculous wearing a weird helmet when he went for a ride in a tank, and a lot of those people felt that, taken together with other evidence of his manner and style of self-expression, the image was not irrelevant to the substance of his campaign. George H. W. Bush underwent a similar moment in 1992, when he was caught showing astonishment at the existence of scanners at supermarket checkout counters. Ideologues opposed to Bush were pleased to propose this as what psychologists call a "fast and frugal" means of assessing the likely effects of his economic policies.

When political scientists interpret these seat-of-the-pants responses as signs that voters are choosing rationally, and that representative government therefore really does reflect the will of the people, they are, in effect, making a heuristic of heuristics. They are not doing the math. Doing the math would mean demonstrating that the voters' intuitive judgments are roughly what they would get if they analyzed the likely effects of candidates' policies, and this is a difficult calculation to perform. One shortcut that voters take, and that generally receives approval from the elite, is pocketbook voting. If they are feeling flush, they vote for the incumbent; if they are feeling strapped, they vote for a change. But, as Larry Bartels, the co-author of the paper on Gore and the weather, has pointed out, pocketbook voting would be rational only if it could be shown that replacing the incumbent did lead, on average, to better economic times. Without such a demonstration, a vote based on the condition of one's pocketbook is no more rational than a vote based on the condition of one's lawn. It's a hunch.

Bartels has also found that when people do focus on specific policies they are often unable to distinguish their own interests. His work, which he summed up in a recent article for *The American Prospect,* concerned public opinion about the estate tax. When people are asked whether they favor Bush's policy of repealing the estate tax, two-thirds say yes—even though the estate tax affects only the wealthiest one or two percent of the population. Ninety-eight percent of Americans do not leave estates large enough for the tax to kick in. But people have some notion—Bartels refers to it as "unenlightened self-interest"—that they will be better off if the tax is repealed. What is most remarkable about this opinion is that it is unconstrained by other beliefs. Repeal is supported by sixty-six percent of people who believe that the income gap between the richest and the poorest Americans has increased in recent decades, and that this is a bad thing. And it's supported by sixty-eight percent of people who say that the rich pay too little in taxes. Most Americans simply do not make a connection between tax policy and the overall economic condition of the country. Whatever heuristic they are using, it is definitely not doing the math for them. This helps make sense of the fact that the world's greatest democracy has an electorate that continually "chooses" to transfer more and more wealth to a smaller and smaller fraction of itself.

But who *ever* does the math? As Popkin points out, everybody uses heuristics, including the elite. Most of the debate among opinion-makers is conducted in shorthand, and even well-informed voters rely on endorsements and party affiliations to make their choices. The very essence of being an ideologue lies in trusting the label—liberal or conservative, Republican or Democrat. Those are "bundling" terms: they pull together a dozen positions on individual issues under a single handy rubric. They do the work of assessment for you.

It is widely assumed that the upcoming [2004] Presidential election will be decided by an electorate that is far more ideological than has historically been the case. Polls indicate much less volatility than usual, supporting the view that the public is divided into starkly antagonistic camps—the "red state-blue state" paradigm. If this is so, it suggests that we have at last moved past Converse's picture of an electoral iceberg, in which ninety percent of the population is politically underwater. But Morris Fiorina, a political scientist at Stanford, thinks that it is not so, and that the polarized electorate is a product of elite opinion. "The simple truth is that there is no culture war in the United States—no battle for the soul of America rages, at least none that most Americans are aware of," he says in his short book *Culture War? The Myth of a Polarized America*. . . . Public-opinion polls, he argues, show that on most hot-button issues voters in so-called red states do not differ significantly from voters in so-called blue states. Most people identify themselves as moderates, and their responses to survey questions seem to substantiate this self-description. What has become polarized, Fiorina argues, is the elite. The chatter—among political activists, commentators, lobbyists, movie stars, and so on—has become highly ideological. It's a non-stop *Crossfire*, and this means that the candidates themselves come wrapped in more extreme ideological coloring. But Fiorina points out that the ideological position of a candidate is not identical to the position of the people who vote for him or her. He suggests that people generally vote for the candidate whose views strike them as closest to their own, and "closest" is a relative term. With any two candidates, no matter how far out, one will always be "closer" than the other.

Of course, if Converse is correct, and most voters really don't have meaningful political beliefs, even ideological "closeness" is an artifact of survey anxiety, of people's felt need, when they are asked for an opinion, to have one. This absence of "real opinions" is not from lack of brains; it's from lack of interest. "The typical citizen drops down to a lower level of mental performance as soon as he enters the political field," the economic theorist Joseph Schumpeter wrote, in 1942. "He argues and analyzes in a way which he would readily recognize as infantile within the sphere of his real interests. He becomes a primitive again. His thinking is associative and affective." And Fiorina quotes a passage from the political scientist Robert Putnam: "Most men are not political animals. The world of public affairs is not their world. It is alien to them—possibly benevolent, more probably threatening, but nearly always alien. Most men are not interested in politics. Most do not participate in politics."

Man may not be a political animal, but he is certainly a social animal. Voters do respond to the cues of commentators and campaigners, but only when they can match those cues up with the buzz of their own social group. Individual voters are not rational calculators of self-interest (nobody truly is), and may not be very consistent users of heuristic shortcuts, either. But they are not just random particles bouncing off the walls of the voting booth. Voters go into the booth carrying the imprint of the hopes and fears, the prejudices and assumptions of their family, their friends, and their neighbors. For most people, voting may be more meaningful and more understandable as a social act than as a political act.

That it is hard to persuade some people with ideological arguments does not mean that those people cannot be persuaded, but the things that help to convince them are likely to make ideologues sick—things like which candidate is more optimistic. For many liberals, it may have been dismaying to listen to John Kerry and John Edwards, in their speeches at the Democratic National Convention, utter impassioned bromides about how "the sun is rising" and "our best days are still to come." But that is what a very large number of voters want to hear. If they believe it, then Kerry and Edwards will get their votes. The ideas won't matter, and neither will the color of the buttons.

Discussion Questions

1. What information shortcuts do you think would be reasonable to use when making voting decisions?
2. Menand is concerned that voters' heuristics might not be reliable if voters actually "did the math." What heuristics do you think might be particularly unreliable guides to voting choices?
3. What, if any, risks are posed to the American political system if voters base their decisions on information shortcuts? Which of the three theories discussed by Menand would be the most troubling for democracy, in your view?

49

"Telling Americans to Vote, or Else"

William Galston

Observers of American politics have long lamented the relatively low rate of election turnout in the United States. Nationally, turnout in presidential elections dropped gradually after 1960 before ticking up in 2004 and 2008. Depending on the measure used, the rate in those two elections ranged from about 55 percent to 62 percent—higher in some states, lower in others. Turnout dropped in 2012 and stayed near the 2012 level in 2016. Midterm congressional races and most state-level elections and local contests see even lower turnout. Many propositions have been put forward to explain low turnout, and more have been offered as ways to increase turnout. Among others, these include making voter registration easier, allowing registration on the day of the election, offering more absentee voting or early in-person voting options, extending voting hours on Election Day, and making Election Day a national holiday. William Galston contends that another option should be considered: mandatory voting. Galston reports that mandatory voting is employed in over thirty countries, about half with an enforcement mechanism such as a small fine. The results on turnout, he states, have been positive and significant. Writing in 2011, he argues that mandatory voting has three advantages: it would strengthen the concept of citizenship by reminding citizens that there are responsibilities that go along with rights; it would reduce the skews in turnout across groups, so that the electorate on Election Day better reflected the composition of the population; and it would reduce polarization in American politics by enticing middle-of-the-road voters back to the voting booth. Despite the advantages he claims for mandatory voting, Galston recognizes that America's individualistic and libertarian ways of thinking make the concept a difficult one to sell in the United States.

Jury duty is mandatory; why not voting? The idea seems vaguely un-American. Maybe so, but it's neither unusual nor undemocratic. And it would ease the intense partisan polarization that weakens our capacity for self-government and public trust in our governing institutions.

Thirty-one countries have some form of mandatory voting, according to the International Institute for Democracy and Electoral Assistance. The list includes nine members of the Organization for Economic Cooperation and Development and two-thirds of the Latin American nations. More than half back up the legal requirement with an enforcement mechanism, while the rest are content to rely on the moral force of the law.

Despite the prevalence of mandatory voting in so many democracies, it's easy to dismiss the practice as a form of statism that couldn't work in America's individualistic and libertarian political culture. But consider Australia, whose political culture is closer to that of the United States than that of any other English-speaking country. Alarmed by a decline in voter turnout to less than 60 percent in 1922, Australia adopted mandatory voting in 1924, backed by small fines (roughly the size of traffic tickets) for nonvoting, rising with repeated acts of nonparticipation. The law established permissible reasons for not voting, like illness and foreign travel, and allows citizens who faced fines for not voting to defend themselves.

The results were remarkable. In the 1925 election, the first held under the new law, turnout soared to 91 percent. In recent elections, it has hovered around 95 percent. The law also changed civic norms. Australians are more likely than before to see voting as an obligation. The negative side effects many feared did not materialize. For example, the percentage of ballots intentionally spoiled or completed randomly as acts of resistance remained on the order of 2 to 3 percent.

Proponents offer three reasons in favor of mandatory voting. The first is straightforwardly civic. A democracy can't be strong if its citizenship is weak. And right now American citizenship is attenuated—strong on rights, weak on responsibilities. There is less and less that being a citizen requires of us, especially after the abolition of the draft. Requiring people to vote in national elections once every two years would reinforce the principle of reciprocity at the heart of citizenship.

The second argument for mandatory voting is democratic. Ideally, a democracy will take into account the interests and views of all citizens. But if some regularly vote while others don't, officials are likely to give greater weight to participants. This might not matter much if nonparticipants were evenly distributed through the population. But political scientists have long known that they aren't. People with lower levels of income and education are less likely to vote, as are young adults and recent first-generation immigrants.

Changes in our political system have magnified these disparities. During the 1950s and '60s, when turnout rates were much higher, political parties reached out to citizens year-round. At the local level these parties, which reformers often criticized as "machines," connected even citizens of modest means and limited education with neighborhood institutions and gave them a sense of participation in national politics as well. (In its heyday, organized labor reinforced these effects.) But in the absence of these more organic forms of political mobilization, the second-best option is a top-down mechanism of universal mobilization.

Mandatory voting would tend to even out disparities stemming from income, education and age, enhancing our system's inclusiveness. It is true, as some object, that an enforcement mechanism would impose greater burdens on those with fewer resources. But this makes it all the more likely that these citizens would respond by going to the polls, and they would stand to gain far more than the cost of a traffic ticket.

The third argument for mandatory voting goes to the heart of our current ills. Our low turnout rate pushes American politics toward increased polarization. The reason is that hardcore partisans are more likely to dominate lower-turnout elections, while those who are less fervent about specific issues and less attached to political organizations tend not to participate at levels proportional to their share of the electorate.

A distinctive feature of our constitutional system—elections that are quadrennial for president but biennial for the House of Representatives—magnifies these effects. It's bad enough that only three-fifths of the electorate turns out to determine the next president, but much worse that only two-fifths of our citizens vote in House elections two years later. If events combine to energize one part of the political spectrum and dishearten the other, a relatively small portion of the electorate can shift the system out of all proportion to its numbers.

Some observers are comfortable with this asymmetry. But if you think that today's intensely polarized politics impedes governance and exacerbates mistrust—and that is what most Americans firmly (and in my view rightly) believe—then you should be willing to consider reforms that would strengthen the forces of conciliation.

Imagine our politics with laws and civic norms that yield near-universal voting. Campaigns could devote far less money to costly, labor-intensive get-out-the-vote efforts. Media gurus wouldn't have the same incentive to drive down turnout with negative advertising. Candidates would know that they must do more than mobilize their bases with red-meat rhetoric on hot-button issues. Such a system would improve not only electoral politics but also the legislative process. Rather than focusing on symbolic gestures whose major purpose is to agitate partisans, Congress might actually roll up its sleeves and tackle the serious, complex issues it ignores.

The United States is not Australia, of course, and there's no guarantee that the similarity of our political cultures would produce equivalent political results. For example, reforms of general elections would leave untouched the distortions generated by party primaries in which small numbers of voters can shape the choices for the entire electorate. And the United States Constitution gives the states enormous power over voting procedures. Mandating voting nationwide would go counter to our traditions (and perhaps our Constitution) and would encounter strong state opposition. Instead, a half-dozen states from parts of the country with different civic traditions should experiment with the practice, and observers—journalists, social scientists, citizens' groups and elected officials—would monitor the consequences.

We don't know what the outcome would be. But one thing is clear: If we do nothing and allow a politics of passion to define the bounds of the electorate, as it has for much of the last four decades, the prospect for a less polarized, more effective political system that enjoys the trust and confidence of the people is not bright.

Discussion Questions

1. How convinced are you that mandatory voting would have the benefits identified by Galston? Are there other benefits that might result?
2. Would mandatory voting create problems? If so, what might these be?
3. Should voting be considered a responsibility in the same sense that jury duty is considered a responsibility?

Debating the Issues: Voter ID Laws—Reducing Fraud or Suppressing Votes?

Recent national elections have raised many concerns about the voting system and the standards for administering elections in the United States. Charges of impropriety in voting procedures and vote counting, as well as complaints that certain voting technologies were systematically likely to produce more voter error or not accurately record voter choices, were legion. Massive voter mobilization campaigns on both the political left and right registered millions of new voters. Huge sums were poured into campaign advertising, further stoking the interest of these newly registered voters and the public in general. In such a charged political environment, concerns about the integrity of the voting process have taken on a particular urgency. One issue on which battle lines are frequently drawn is voter identification, especially the requirement that voters show a photo ID. Heading into the 2016 election, 32 states required voters to show some form of identification, with eight of those states requiring photo ID and eight requesting that voters provide a photo ID. During 2016 federal courts struck down in whole or in part voter ID laws in several states, concluding that the laws had a disparate impact that deterred minority and low-income voters.

The readings in this debate explore the issue of voter identification laws from three perspectives. John Fund points to examples where individuals posed undercover to commit voter fraud and were successful in their efforts. The gist of Fund's argument is that the claim that fraud is rare, often advanced by opponents of voter ID laws, ignores the ease by which fraud can actually occur and the difficulty in detecting it. To Fund, opposition to voter ID is rooted in the willingness of Democratic party officials to tolerate or benefit from individuals voting fraudulently. Peter Beinart does not take a position on the prevalence of voter fraud, but instead argues that voter ID laws are a modern-day equivalent of a poll tax. Before being declared unconstitutional, poll taxes were fees charged in some states for the ability to register to vote. He sees voter ID laws as imposing similar financial burdens on low-income voters and suggests that the main intent of the laws is to suppress minority and low-income voter turnout to the benefit of Republican party candidates. One possible implication of Beinart's argument is that even if fraud were frequent, voter ID might not be a desirable remedy due to its drawbacks. Finally, Lorraine Minnite argues that when there is fraud, it is likely party operatives, election officials, or politicians who commit it, not individual voters. Why, then, do states adopt voter ID laws? Minnite sees these laws as racially motivated and a stark continuation of attempts to thwart racial equality and inclusion by adopting voter regulations that disproportionately deter minority voters.

50

"Voter Fraud: We've Got Proof It's Easy"

John Fund

Liberals who oppose efforts to prevent voter fraud claim that there is no fraud—or at least not any that involves voting in person at the polls.

But New York City's watchdog Department of Investigations has just provided the latest evidence of how easy it is to commit voter fraud that is almost undetectable. DOI undercover agents showed up at 63 polling places last fall and pretended to be voters who should have been turned away by election officials; the agents assumed the names of individuals who had died or moved out of town, or who were sitting in jail. In 61 instances, or 97 percent of the time, the testers were allowed to vote. Those who did vote cast only a write-in vote for a "John Test" so as to not affect the outcome of any contest. DOI published its findings two weeks ago in a searing 70-page report accusing the city's Board of Elections of incompetence, waste, nepotism, and lax procedures.

The Board of Elections, which has a $750-million annual budget and a work force of 350 people, reacted in classic bureaucratic fashion, which prompted one city paper to deride it as "a 21st-century survivor of Boss Tweed–style politics." The Board approved a resolution referring the DOI's investigators for prosecution. It also asked the state's attorney general to determine whether DOI had violated the civil rights of voters who had moved or are felons, and it sent a letter of complaint to Mayor Bill de Blasio. Normally, I wouldn't think de Blasio would give the BOE the time of day, but New York's new mayor has long been a close ally of former leaders of ACORN, the now-disgraced "community organizing" group that saw its employees convicted of voter-registration fraud all over the country during and after the 2008 election.

Greg Soumas, president of New York's BOE, offered a justification for calling in the prosecutors: "If something was done in an untoward fashion, it was only done by DOI. We [are] unaware of any color of authority on the part of [DOI] to vote in the identity of any person other than themselves—and our reading of the election law is that such an act constitutes a felony." The Board is bipartisan, and all but two of its members voted with Soumas. The sole exceptions were Democrat Jose Araujo, who abstained because the DOI report implicated him in hiring his wife and sister-in-law for Board jobs, and Republican Simon Shamoun.

Good-government groups are gobsmacked at Soumas's refusal to smell the stench of corruption in his patronage-riddled empire. "They should focus not on assigning blame to others, but on taking responsibility for solving the problems themselves," Dick Dadey of the watchdog group Citizens Union told the *Daily News*. "It's a case of the Board of Elections passing the buck." DOI officials respond that the use of undercover agents is routine in anti-corruption probes and that people should carefully read the 70-page report they've filed before criticizing it. They are surprised how little media attention their report has received.

You'd think more media outlets would have been interested, because the sloppiness revealed in the DOI report is mind-boggling. Young undercover agents were able to vote using the names of people three times their age, people who in fact were dead. In one example, a 24-year-old female agent gave the name of someone who had died in 2012 at age 87; the workers at the Manhattan polling site gave her a ballot, no questions asked. Even the two cases where poll workers turned away an investigator raise eyebrows. In the first case, a poll worker on Staten Island walked outside with the undercover investigator who had just been refused a ballot; the "voter" was advised to go to the polling place near where he used to live and "play dumb" in order to vote. In the second case, the investigator was stopped from voting only because the felon whose name he was using was the son of the election official at the polling place.

Shooting the messenger has been a typical reaction in other states when people have demonstrated just how easy it is to commit voter fraud. Guerrilla videographer James O'Keefe had three of his assistants visit precincts during New Hampshire's January 2012 presidential primary. They asked poll workers whether their books listed the names of several voters, all deceased individuals still listed on voter-registration rolls. Poll workers handed out ten ballots, never once asking for a photo ID. O'Keefe's team immediately gave back the ballots, unmarked, to precinct workers. Debbie Lane, a ballot inspector at one of the Manchester polling sites, later said: "I wasn't sure what I was allowed to do. . . . I can't tell someone not to vote, I suppose." The only precinct in which O'Keefe or his crew did *not* obtain a ballot was one in which the local precinct officer had personally known the dead "voter."

New Hampshire's Democratic governor, John Lynch, sputtered when asked about O'Keefe's video, and he condemned the effort to test the election system even though no actual votes were cast. "They should be prosecuted to the fullest extent of the law, if in fact they're found guilty of some criminal act," he roared. But cooler heads eventually prevailed, and the GOP state legislature later approved a voter-ID bill, with enough votes to override the governor's veto. Despite an exhaustive and intrusive investigation, no charges were ever filed against any of O'Keefe's associates.

Later in 2012, in Washington, D.C., one of O'Keefe's assistants was able to obtain Attorney General Eric Holder's ballot even though Holder is

62 years old and bears no resemblance to the 22-year-old white man who obtained it merely by asking if Eric Holder was on the rolls. But the Department of Justice, which is currently suing Texas to block that state's photo-ID law, dismissed the Holder ballot incident as "manufactured." The irony was lost on the DOJ that Holder, a staunch opponent of voter-ID laws, could have himself been disenfranchised by a white man because Washington, D.C., has no voter-ID law. Polls consistently show that more than 70 percent of Americans—including clear majorities of African Americans and Hispanics—support such laws.

Liberals who oppose ballot-security measures claim that there are few prosecutions for voter fraud, which they take to mean that fraud doesn't happen. But as the New York DOI report demonstrates, it is comically easy, given the sloppy-voter registration records often kept in America, to commit voter fraud in person. (A 2012 study by the Pew Research Center found that nationwide, at least 1.8 million deceased voters are still registered to vote.) And unless someone confesses, in-person voter fraud is very difficult to detect—or stop. New York's Gothamist news service reported last September that four poll workers in Brooklyn reported they believed people were trying to vote in the name of other registered voters. Police officers observed the problems but did nothing because voter fraud isn't under the police department's purview.

What the DOI investigators were able to do was eerily similar to actual fraud that has occurred in New York before. In 1984, Brooklyn's Democratic district attorney, Elizabeth Holtzman, released a state grand-jury report on a successful 14-year conspiracy that cast thousands of fraudulent votes in local, state, and congressional elections. Just like the DOI undercover operatives, the conspirators cast votes at precincts in the names of dead, moved, and bogus voters. The grand jury recommended voter ID, a basic election-integrity measure that New York has steadfastly refused to implement.

In states where non-photo ID is required, it's also all too easy to manufacture records that allow people to vote. In 2012, the son of Congressman Jim Moran, the Democrat who represents Virginia's Washington suburbs, had to resign as field director for his father's campaign after it became clear that he had encouraged voter fraud. Patrick Moran was caught advising an O'Keefe videographer on how to commit in-person voter fraud. The scheme involved using a personal computer to forge utility bills that would satisfy Virginia's voter-ID law and then relying on the assistance of Democratic lawyers stationed at the polls to make sure the fraudulent votes were counted. Last year, Virginia tightened its voter-ID law and ruled that showing a utility bill was no longer sufficient to obtain a ballot.

Given that someone who is dead, is in jail, or has moved isn't likely to complain if someone votes in his name, how do we know that voter fraud at the polls isn't a problem? An ounce of prevention—in the form of voter ID and better training of poll workers—should be among the minimum precautions taken to prevent an electoral miscarriage or meltdown in a close race.

After all, even a small number of votes can have sweeping consequences. Al Franken's 312-vote victory in 2008 over Minnesota senator Norm Coleman gave Democrats a filibuster-proof Senate majority of 60 votes, which allowed them to pass Obamacare. Months after the Obamacare vote, a conservative group called Minnesota Majority finished comparing criminal records with voting rolls and identified 1,099 felons—all ineligible to vote—who had voted in the Franken–Coleman race. Fox News's random interviews with ten of those felons found that nine had voted for Franken, backing up national academic studies that show felons tend to vote strongly for Democrats.

Minnesota Majority took its findings to prosecutors across the state, but very few showed any interest in pursuing the issue. Some did, though, and 177 people have been convicted as of mid-2012—not just "accused" but actually *convicted*—of voting fraudulently in the Senate race. Probably the only reason the number of convictions isn't higher is that the standard for convicting someone of voter fraud in Minnesota is that the person must have been both ineligible and must have "knowingly" voted unlawfully. Anyone accused of fraud is apt to get off by claiming he didn't know he'd done anything wrong.

Given that we now know for certain how easy it is to commit undetectable voter fraud and how serious the consequences can be, it's truly bizarre to have officials at the New York City Board of Elections and elsewhere savage those who shine a light on the fact that their modus operandi invites fraud. One might even think that they're covering up their incompetence or that they don't want to pay attention to what crimes could be occurring behind the curtains at their polling places. Or both.

51

"Should the Poor Be Allowed to Vote?"

PETER BEINART

If Hong Kong's pro-democracy protesters succeed in booting C.Y. Leung from power, the city's unelected chief executive should consider coming to the United States. He might fit in well in the Republican Party.

In an interview Monday with *The New York Times* and other foreign newspapers, Leung explained that Beijing cannot permit the direct election of Hong Kong's leaders because doing so would empower "the people in Hong Kong who earn less than $1,800 a month." Leung instead defended the current plan to have a committee of roughly 1,200 eminent citizens vet potential contenders because doing so, in the *Times'* words, "would insulate candidates from popular pressure to create a welfare state, and would allow the city government to follow more business-friendly policies."

If that sounds vaguely familiar, it should. Leung's views about the proper relationship between democracy and economic policy represent a more extreme version of the views supported by many in today's GOP.

Start with Mitt Romney. In 2012, at a fundraiser with ultra-wealthy donors, the Republican nominee famously denigrated the "47 percent" of Americans who "believe that government has a responsibility to care for them, who believe that they are entitled to health care, to food, to housing"—to a welfare state. Because these self-appointed "victims" were voting in order to get things from government, Romney argued, their motives were inferior to the potential Romney voters who "take personal responsibility and care for their lives."

In distinguishing between Americans whose economic independence permits them to make reasoned political choices and those who because of their poverty cannot, Romney was channeling a hoary American tradition. In 1776, John Adams argued that men (let alone women) "who are wholly destitute of Property" were "too dependent upon other Men to have a Will of their own." In 1800, only three states allowed property-less white men to vote. For most of the twentieth century, southern states imposed "poll taxes" that effectively barred not only African Americans from voting but some poor whites as well.

Romney didn't suggest that the 47 percent be denied the right to vote, of course. But other Republicans have flirted with the idea. In 2010, Tea Party Nation President Judson Phillips observed that "The Founding Fathers . . . put certain restrictions on who gets the right to vote . . . one of those was you had to be a property owner. And that makes a lot of sense, because if you're a property owner you actually have a vested stake in the community." In 2011, Iowa Representative Steve King made a similar observation, noting approvingly, "There was a time in American history when you had to be a male property owner in order to vote. The reason for that was, because [the Founding Fathers] wanted the people who voted—that set the public policy, that decided on the taxes and the spending—to have some skin in the game. Now we have data out there that shows that 47 percent of American households don't pay taxes . . . But many of them are voting. And when they vote, they vote for more government benefits." In 2012, Florida House candidate Ted Yoho remarked, "I've had some radical ideas about voting and it's probably not a good time to tell them, but you used to have to be a property owner to vote." Yoho went on to win the election.

Philips, King, and Yoho are outliers. Most prominent Republicans would never propose that poor people be denied the franchise. But they support policies that do just that. When GOP legislatures make it harder to vote—either by restricting early voting, limiting the hours that polls remain open, requiring voter identification or disenfranchising ex-felons—the press usually focuses on the disproportionate impact on racial minorities and Democrats. But the most profound impact may be on the poor.

Voter-identification laws, in particular, act as a new form of poll tax. After Texas passed its voter-ID law, a study found that Texans who earned less than $20,000 per year were more than 10 times more likely to lack the necessary identification than Texans who earned more than $150,000. On the surface, this discrepancy might seem possible to remedy, since courts have generally demanded that the states that require voter identification provide some form of ID for free. But there's a catch. Acquiring that free ID requires showing another form of identification—and those cost money. In the states with voter-ID laws, notes a report by the Brennan Center for Justice at NYU Law School, "Birth certificates can cost between $8 and $25. Marriage licenses, required for married women whose birth certificates include a maiden name, can cost between $8 and $20. By comparison, the notorious poll tax—outlawed during the civil rights era—cost $10.64 in current dollars."

To make matters worse, roughly half a million people without access to a car live more than 10 miles from the nearest office that regularly issues IDs. And the states that require IDs, which just happen to be mostly in the south, also just happen to have some of the worst public transportation in the country.

Not surprisingly, a 2007 study by researchers at Washington University and Cal Tech found that, "registered voters with low levels of educational attainment or lower levels of income are less likely to vote the more restrictive the voter identification regime." Barring former felons from voting has an even more dramatic impact on the poor, since almost half of state prison inmates earned less than $10,000 in the year before their incarceration.

Obviously, the United States is not Hong Kong. But there's a reason some of the city's demonstrators have adopted the label "Occupy." Like the Americans who assembled in Zuccotti Park in 2011, they are fighting a system in which political exclusion and economic exclusion reinforce each other. Hong Kong's chief oligarch is named C.Y. Leung. But here in the United States, we have ours too.

52

"The Myth of Voter Fraud"

Lorraine C. Minnite

When there has been election fraud in American elections, it has usually been committed by politicians, party operatives, and election officials who have something at stake in electoral outcomes. Voters rarely commit fraud because for them, it is a motiveless crime, the individual benefits to the fraudulent voter are immaterial, while the costs are prohibitive.

The most important illustration of outright corruption of elections is the century-long success of white supremacists in the American South stripping African Americans of their right to vote. Elites and party bosses in the urban North followed the Southern example, using some of the same tricks to manipulate electoral outcomes and to disfranchise immigrants and the poor.

From this perspective, the impact of election fraud on American elections has been massive. It was only with the rise of the Black Freedom Movement and passage of the Voting Rights Act in 1965 that the tricks and political chicanery were halted. In fact, according to political historian J. Morgan Kousser, the Voting Rights Act is the most important fraud-prevention legislation ever passed.

In response to these victories, a reactionary movement arose to push back against progress in civil rights and to counter the thrust toward a more equal society. Over the last 40 years, that movement has made important gains, especially in the courts, where a conservative Supreme Court, in a 2013 case called *Shelby County v. Holder,* gutted one of the most effective features of the Voting Rights Act—the "preclearance" formula which forced states and localities with the most egregious histories of vote denial to obtain permission from the Justice Department before putting new election rules in place.

Prior to the contested 2000 presidential election, only 14 states either requested or required that voters show some form of identification at the polls. Since then, the number of states requiring ID to vote has doubled and the forms of acceptable identification have narrowed. In what is likely no coincidence, the rate at which states have adopted tougher photo identification requirements accelerated with the election of the nation's first black president and the demise of legally mandated federal oversight in the *Shelby* case.

In rapid succession, partisan lawmakers in state after state have pushed through the new rules, claiming tougher identity checks are necessary to staunch or prevent voter fraud. And yet, in no state adopting a photo ID requirement has any lawmaker or anyone else, for that matter, presented a credible showing of a problem with voters corrupting the electoral process. In other words, if the claimed reason of preventing voter fraud is taken at face value, there is no rational basis for the policy intervention. So what is actually going on?

I think the phony claims and renewed political chicanery are a reflection of the fact that a century and a half after the Civil War, and 50 years after the signing of the Voting Rights Act, a deeper struggle for democracy, equality, and inclusion continues. Beneath the skirmish over arcane voting rules is a fraught tension between our ideals and our fears, between what we profess to believe about the "sanctity" of the ballot, and racialized and class-based notions of worthiness embedded in the question of who is to be a citizen in the United States.

The myth of voter fraud persists because it is a racialized weapon in a power struggle over the soul of American democracy. To see this, we must set our current politics in a historical context. Long-standing fears about unworthy citizens polluting and distorting electoral outcomes are the underside of the usual celebratory story we like to tell ourselves of a progressive struggle for voting rights. In fact, the struggle has not unfolded in a linear fashion. Each successive advance has generated counter-movements rooted in alternative and reactionary histories aimed at "taking back" at least a part of what has been lost. In our own time, from the moment blacks began exercising their newly (re-)won right to vote, that right was undermined in ways that constrained its power to deliver social justice. The question of who is to be a citizen in our racially divided and injured society remains unresolved.

Discussion Questions

1. Would you approve of a proposal that all voters be required to show photo identification at polling places? Do you think it would decrease turnout? If so, is this a reasonable cost to pay to ensure that people cannot vote using another person's name or cannot vote without proving that they live in the voting district? Or should turnout be prioritized and the risk that some people will vote inappropriately be accepted as a reasonable risk?

2. What are the advantages and drawbacks of using the kinds of evidence pointed to by Fund when crafting voter ID laws or public policy in general? How do you, or can you, distinguish between something that an undercover operation shows could happen and something that in fact happens regularly?

3. As a general matter, do you believe there is a trade-off between maximizing turnout and minimizing voter fraud? Or are these goals compatible? Why?
4. If photo IDs were provided free of charge and mailed to all potential voters, would that adequately address the concerns raised by Beinart and Minnite?

CHAPTER 11

Political Parties

53

"The Decline of Collective Responsibility in American Politics"

MORRIS P. FIORINA

For more than three decades, political scientists have studied the changing status of American political parties. Morris Fiorina suggests that political parties provide many benefits for American democracy, in particular by clarifying policy alternatives and letting citizens know whom to hold accountable when they are dissatisfied with government performance. Writing in the early 1980s, he sees decline in all the key areas of political-party activity: in the electorate, in government, and in party organizations. He argues that the decline eliminates the motivation for elected members of the parties to define broad policy objectives, leading to diminished political participation and a rise in alienation. Policies are aimed at serving the narrow interests of the various single-issue groups that dominate politics rather than the broad constituencies represented by parties. Without strong political parties to provide electoral accountability, American politics has suffered a "decline in collective responsibility" in Fiorina's view. In the effort to reform the often-corrupt political parties of the late 1800s—commonly referred to as "machines" led by "bosses"—Fiorina asks us to consider whether Americans have overly weakened the best institutional device available to hold elected officials accountable at the ballot box.

Though the Founding Fathers believed in the necessity of establishing a genuinely national government, they took great pains to design one that could not lightly do things *to* its citizens; what government might do *for* its citizens was to be limited to the functions of what we know now as the "watchman state."

* * *

Given the historical record faced by the Founders, their emphasis on constraining government is understandable. But we face a later historical record, one that shows two hundred years of increasing demands for government to act positively. Moreover, developments unforeseen by the Founders increasingly raise the likelihood that the uncoordinated actions of individuals and groups will inflict serious damage on the nation as a whole. The by-products of the industrial and technological revolutions impose physical risks not only on us, but on future generations as well. Resource shortages and international cartels raise the spectre of economic ruin. And the simple proliferation of special interests with their intense, particularistic demands threatens to render us politically incapable of taking actions that might either advance the state of society or prevent foreseeable deteriorations in that state. None of this is to suggest that we should forget about what government can do *to* us—the contemporary concern with the proper scope and methods of government intervention in the social and economic orders is long overdue. But the modern age demands as well that we worry about our ability to make government work *for* us. The problem is that we are gradually losing that ability, and a principal reason for this loss is the steady erosion of *responsibility* in American politics.

* * *

Unfortunately, the importance of responsibility in a democracy is matched by the difficulty of attaining it. In an autocracy, individual responsibility suffices; the location of power in a single individual locates responsibility in that individual as well. But individual responsibility is insufficient whenever more than one person shares governmental authority. We can hold a particular congressman individually responsible for a personal transgression such as bribe-taking. We can even hold a president individually responsible for military moves where he presents Congress and the citizenry with a *fait accompli*. But on most national issues individual responsibility is difficult to assess. If one were to go to Washington, randomly accost a Democratic congressman, and berate him about a 20-percent rate of inflation, imagine the response. More than likely it would run, "Don't blame me. If 'they' had done what I've advocated for *x* years, things would be fine today."

* * *

American institutional structure makes this kind of game-playing all too easy. In order to overcome it we must lay the credit or blame for national conditions on all those who had any hand in bringing them about: some form of *collective responsibility* is essential.

The only way collective responsibility has ever existed, and can exist given our institutions, is through the agency of the political party; in American politics, responsibility requires cohesive parties. This is an old claim to be sure, but its age does not detract from its present relevance. In fact, the continuing decline in public esteem for the parties and continuing efforts to "reform" them out of the political process suggest that old arguments for party responsibility have not been made often enough or, at least, convincingly enough, so I will make these arguments once again in this essay.

A strong political party can generate collective responsibility by creating incentive for leaders, followers, and popular supporters to think and act in collective terms. First, by providing party leaders with the capability (e.g., control of institutional patronage, nominations, and so on) to discipline party members, genuine leadership becomes possible. Legislative output is less likely to be a least common denominator—a residue of myriad conflicting proposals—and more likely to consist of a program actually intended to solve a problem or move the nation in a particular direction. Second, the subordination of individual officeholders to the party lessens their ability to separate themselves from party actions. Like it or not, their performance becomes identified with the performance of the collectivity to which they belong. Third, with individual candidate variation greatly reduced, voters have less incentive to support individuals and more incentive to support or oppose the party as a whole. And fourth, the circle closes as party-line voting in the electorate provides party leaders with the incentive to propose policies that will earn the support of a national majority, and party back-benchers* with the personal incentive to cooperate with leaders in the attempt to compile a good record for the party as a whole.

In the American context, strong parties have traditionally clarified politics in two ways. First, they allow citizens to assess responsibility easily, at least when the government is unified, which it more often was in earlier eras when party meant more than it does today. Citizens need only evaluate the social, economic, and international conditions they observe and make a simple decision for or against change. They do not need to decide whether the energy, inflation, urban, and defense policies advocated by their congressman would be superior to those advocated by [the president]—were any of them to be enacted!

The second way in which strong parties clarify American politics follows from the first. When citizens assess responsibility on the party as a whole, party members have personal incentives to see the party evaluated favorably. They have little to gain from gutting their president's program one day and attacking him for lack of leadership the next, since they share in the president's fate when voters do not differentiate within the party. Put simply, party responsibility provides party members with a personal stake in their collective performance.

*Back-benchers are junior members of the British Parliament, who sit in the rear benches of the House of Commons. Here, the term refers to junior members of political parties [*Editors*].

Admittedly, party responsibility is a blunt instrument. The objection immediately arises that party responsibility condemns junior Democratic representatives to suffer electorally for an inflation they could do little to affect. An unhappy situation, true, but unless we accept it, Congress as a whole escapes electoral retribution for an inflation they *could* have done something to affect. Responsibility requires acceptance of both conditions. The choice is between a blunt instrument or none at all.

* * *

In earlier times, when citizens voted for the party, not the person, parties had incentives to nominate good candidates, because poor ones could have harmful fallout on the ticket as a whole. In particular, the existence of presidential coattails (positive and negative) provided an inducement to avoid the nomination of narrowly based candidates, no matter how committed their supporters. And, once in office, the existence of party voting in the electorate provided party members with the incentive to compile a good *party* record. In particular, the tendency of national midterm elections to serve as referenda on the performance of the president provided a clear inducement for congressmen to do what they could to see that their president was perceived as a solid performer. By stimulating electoral phenomena such as coattail effects and mid-term referenda, party transformed some degree of personal ambition into concern with collective performance.

* * *

The Continuing Decline of Party in the United States

Party Organizations

In the United States, party organization has traditionally meant state and local party organization. The national party generally has been a loose confederacy of subnational units that swings into action for a brief period every four years. This characterization remains true today, despite the somewhat greater influence and augmented functions of the national organizations. Though such things are difficult to measure precisely, there is general agreement that the formal party organizations have undergone a secular decline since their peak at the end of the nineteenth century. The prototype of the old-style organization was the urban machine, a form approximated today only in Chicago.

* * *

[*Fiorina discusses the reforms of the late nineteenth and early twentieth century.*]

In the 1970s two series of reforms further weakened the influence of organized parties in American national politics. The first was a series of legal changes deliberately intended to lessen organized party influence in the presidential nominating process. In the Democratic party, "New

Politics" activists captured the national party apparatus and imposed a series of rules changes designed to "open up" the politics of presidential nominations. The Republican party—long more amateur and open than the Democratic party—adopted weaker versions of the Democratic rules changes. In addition, modifications of state electoral laws to conform to the Democratic rules changes (enforced by the federal courts) stimulated Republican rules changes as well.

* * *

A second series of 1970s reforms lessened the role of formal party organizations in the conduct of political campaigns. These are financing regulations growing out of the Federal Election Campaign Act of 1971 as amended in 1974 and 1976. In this case the reforms were aimed at cleaning up corruption in the financing of campaigns; their effects on the parties were a by-product, though many individuals accurately predicted its nature. Serious presidential candidates are now publicly financed. Though the law permits the national party to spend two cents per eligible voter on behalf of the nominee, it also obliges the candidate to set up a finance committee separate from the national party. Between this legally mandated separation and fear of violating spending limits or accounting regulations, for example, the law has the effect of encouraging the candidate to keep his party at arm's length.

* * *

The ultimate results of such reforms are easy to predict. A lesser party role in the nominating and financing of candidates encourages candidates to organize and conduct independent campaigns, which further weakens the role of parties. . . . [I]f parties do not grant nominations, fund their choices, and work for them, why should those choices feel any commitment to their party?

Party in the Electorate

In the citizenry at large, party takes the form of a psychological attachment. The typical American traditionally has been likely to identify with one or the other of the two major parties. Such identifications are transmitted across generations to some degree, and within the individual they tend to be fairly stable. But there is mounting evidence that the basis of identification lies in the individual's experiences (direct and vicarious, through family and social groups) with the parties in the past. Our current party system, of course, is based on the dislocations of the Depression period and the New Deal attempts to alleviate them. Though only a small proportion of those who experienced the Depression directly are active voters today, the general outlines of citizen party identifications much resemble those established at that time.

Again, there is reason to believe that the extent of citizen attachments to parties has undergone a long-term decline from a nineteenth-century high. And again, the New Deal appears to have been a period during which the decline was arrested, even temporarily reversed. But again, the decline of party has reasserted itself in the 1970s.

* * *

As the 1960s wore on, the heretofore stable distribution of citizen party identifications began to change in the general direction of weakened attachments to the parties. Between 1960 and 1976, independents, broadly defined, increased from less than a quarter to more than a third of the voting-age population. Strong identifiers declined from slightly more than a third to about a quarter of the population.

* * *

Indisputably, party in the electorate has declined in recent years. Why? To some extent the electoral decline results from the organizational decline. Few party organizations any longer have the tangible incentives to turn out the faithful and assure their loyalty. Candidates run independent campaigns and deemphasize their partisan ties whenever they see any short-term electoral gain in doing so. If party is increasingly less important in the nomination and election of candidates, it is not surprising that such diminished importance is reflected in the attitudes and behavior of the voter.

Certain long-term sociological and technological trends also appear to work against party in the electorate. The population is younger, and younger citizens traditionally are less attached to the parties than their elders. The population is more highly educated; fewer voters need some means of simplifying the choices they face in the political arena, and party, of course, has been the principal means of simplification. And the media revolution has vastly expanded the amount of information easily available to the citizenry. Candidates would have little incentive to operate campaigns independent of the parties if there were no means to apprise the citizenry of their independence. The media provide the means.

Finally, our present party system is an old one. For increasing numbers of citizens, party attachments based on the Great Depression seem lacking in relevance to the problems of the late twentieth century. Beginning with the racial issue in the 1960s, proceeding to the social issue of the 1970s, and to the energy, environment, and inflation issues of today, the parties have been rent by internal dissension. Sometimes they failed to take stands, at other times they took the wrong ones from the standpoint of the rank and file, and at most times they have failed to solve the new problems in any genuine sense. Since 1965 the parties have done little or nothing to earn the loyalties of modern Americans.

Party in Government

If the organizational capabilities of the parties have weakened, and their psychological ties to the voters have loosened, one would expect predictable consequences for the party in government. In particular, one would expect to see an increasing degree of split party control within and across the levels of American government. The evidence on this point is overwhelming.

* * *

The increased fragmentation of the party in government makes it more difficult for government officeholders to work together than in times past (not that it has ever been terribly easy). Voters meanwhile have a more difficult time attributing responsibility for government performance, and this only further fragments party control. The result is lessened collective responsibility in the system.

What has taken up the slack left by the weakening of the traditional [party] determinants of congressional voting? It appears that a variety of personal and local influences now play a major role in citizen evaluations of their representatives. Along with the expansion of the federal presence in American life, the traditional role of the congressman as an all-purpose ombudsman has greatly expanded. Tens of millions of citizens now are directly affected by federal decisions. Myriad programs provide opportunities to profit from government largesse, and myriad regulations impose costs and/or constraints on citizen activities. And, whether seeking to gain profit or avoid costs, citizens seek the aid of their congressmen. When a court imposes a desegregation plan on an urban school board, the congressional offices immediately are contacted for aid in safeguarding existing sources of funding and in determining eligibility for new ones. When a major employer announces plans to quit an area, the congressional offices immediately are contacted to explore possibilities for using federal programs to persuade the employer to reconsider. Contractors appreciate a good congressional word with DOD [Department of Defense] procurement officers. Local artistic groups cannot survive without NEA [National Endowment for the Arts] funding. And, of course, there are the major individual programs such as social security and veterans' benefits that create a steady demand for congressional information and aid services. Such activities are nonpartisan, nonideological, and, most important, noncontroversial. Moreover, the contribution of the congressman in the realm of district service appears considerably greater than the impact of his or her single vote on major national issues. Constituents respond rationally to this modern state of affairs by weighing nonprogrammatic constituency service heavily when casting their congressional votes. And this emphasis on the part of constituents provides the means for incumbents to solidify their hold on the office. Even if elected by a narrow margin, diligent service activities enable a congressman to neutralize or even convert a portion of those who would otherwise oppose him on policy or ideological grounds. Emphasis on local, nonpartisan factors in congressional voting enables the modern congressman to withstand national swings, whereas yesteryear's uninsulated congressmen were more dependent on preventing the occurrence of the swings.

* * *

[*The result is the insulation of the modern congressional member from national forces altogether.*]

The withering away of the party organizations and the weakening of party in the electorate have begun to show up as disarray in the party in government. As the electoral fates of congressmen and the president have diverged, their incentives to cooperate have diverged as well. Congressmen have little personal incentive to bear any risk in their president's behalf, since they no longer expect to gain much from his successes or suffer much from his failures. Only those who personally agree with the president's program and/or those who find that program well suited for their particular district support the president. And there are not enough of these to construct the coalitions necessary for action on the major issues now facing the country. By holding only the president responsible for national conditions, the electorate enables officialdom as a whole to escape responsibility. This situation lies at the root of many of the problems that now plague American public life.

Some Consequences of the Decline of Collective Responsibility

The weakening of party has contributed directly to the severity of several of the important problems the nation faces. For some of these, such as the government's inability to deal with inflation and energy, the connections are obvious. But for other problems, such as the growing importance of single-issue politics and the growing alienation of the American citizenry, the connections are more subtle.

Immobilism

As the electoral interdependence of the party in government declines, its ability to act also declines. If responsibility can be shifted to another level or to another officeholder, there is less incentive to stick one's neck out in an attempt to solve a given problem. Leadership becomes more difficult, the ever-present bias toward the short-term solution becomes more pronounced, and the possibility of solving any given problem lessens.

. . . [P]olitical inability to take actions that entail short-run costs ordinarily will result in much higher costs in the long run—we cannot continually depend on the technological fix. So the present American immobilism cannot be dismissed lightly. The sad thing is that the American people appear to understand the depth of our present problems and, at least in principle, appear prepared to sacrifice in furtherance of the long-run good. But they will not have an opportunity to choose between two or more such long-term plans. Although both parties promise tough, equitable policies, in the present state of our politics, neither can deliver.

Single-Issue Politics

In recent years both political analysts and politicians have decried the increased importance of single-issue groups in American politics. Some in fact would claim that the present immobilism in our politics owes more to the rise of single-issue groups than to the decline of party. A little thought, however, should reveal that the two trends are connected. Is single-issue politics a recent phenomenon? The contention is doubtful; such groups have always been active participants in American politics. The gun lobby already was a classic example at the time of President Kennedy's assassination. And however impressive the antiabortionists appear today, remember the temperance movement, which succeeded in getting its constitutional amendment. American history contains numerous forerunners of today's groups, from anti-Masons to abolitionists to the Klan—singularity of purpose is by no means a modern phenomenon. Why, then, do we hear all the contemporary hoopla about single-issue groups? Probably because politicians fear them now more than before and thus allow them to play a larger role in our politics. Why should this be so? Simply because the parties are too weak to protect their members and thus to contain single-issue politics.

In earlier times single-issue groups were under greater pressures to reach accommodations with the parties. After all, the parties nominated candidates, financed candidates, worked for candidates, and, perhaps most important, party voting protected candidates. When a contemporary single-issue group threatens to "get" an officeholder, the threat must be taken seriously.

* * *

Not only did the party organization have greater ability to resist single-issue pressures at the electoral level, but the party in government had greater ability to control the agenda, and thereby contain single-issue pressures at the policy-making level. Today we seem condemned to go through an annual agony over federal abortion funding. There is little doubt that politicians on both sides would prefer to reach some reasonable compromise at the committee level and settle the issue. But in today's decentralized Congress there is no way to put the lid on. In contrast, historians tell us that in the late nineteenth century a large portion of the Republican constituency was far less interested in the tariff and other questions of national economic development than in whether German immigrants should be permitted to teach their native language in their local schools, and whether Catholics and "liturgical Protestants" should be permitted to consume alcohol. Interestingly, however, the national agenda of the period is devoid of such issues. And when they do show up on the state level, the exceptions prove the rule; they produce party splits and striking defeats for the party that allowed them to surface.

In sum, a strong party that is held accountable for the government of a nation-state has both the ability and the incentive to contain particularistic pressures. It controls nominations, elections, and the agenda, and it collectively realizes that small minorities are small minorities no matter how intense they are. But as the parties decline they lose control over nominations and campaigns, they lose the loyalty of the voters, and they lose control of the agenda. Party officeholders cease to be held collectively accountable for party performance, but they become individually exposed to the political pressure of myriad interest groups. The decline of party permits interest groups to wield greater influence, their success encourages the formation of still more interest groups, politics becomes increasingly fragmented, and collective responsibility becomes still more elusive.

Popular Alienation from Government

For at least a decade political analysts have pondered the significance of survey data indicative of a steady increase in the alienation of the American public from the political process. . . . The American public is in a nasty mood, a cynical, distrusting, and resentful mood. The question is, Why?

If the same national problems not only persist but worsen while ever-greater amounts of revenue are directed at them, why shouldn't the typical citizen conclude that most of the money must be wasted by incompetent officials? If narrowly based interest groups increasingly affect our politics, why shouldn't citizens increasingly conclude that the interests run the government? For fifteen years the citizenry has listened to a steady stream of promises but has seen very little in the way of follow-through. An increasing proportion of the electorate does not believe that elections make a difference, a fact that largely explains the much-discussed post-1960 decline in voting turnout.

Continued public disillusionment with the political process poses several real dangers. For one thing, disillusionment begets further disillusionment. Leadership becomes more difficult if citizens do not trust their leaders and will not give them the benefit of a doubt. Policy failure becomes more likely if citizens expect the policy to fail. Waste increases and government competence decreases as citizens' disrespect for politics encourages a lesser breed of person to make careers in government. And "government by a few big interests" becomes more than a cliché if citizens increasingly decide the cliché is true and cease participating for that reason.

Finally, there is the real danger that continued disappointment with particular government officials ultimately metamorphoses into disillusionment with government per se. Increasing numbers of citizens believe that government is not simply overextended but perhaps incapable of any further bettering of the world. Yes, government is overextended, inefficiency is pervasive, and ineffectiveness is all too common. But government is one of the few instruments of collective action we have, and even those committed to selective pruning of government programs cannot blithely allow the concept of an activist government to fall into disrepute.

Of late, however, some political commentators have begun to wonder whether contemporary thought places sufficient emphasis on government *for* the people. In stressing participation have we lost sight of *accountability*? Surely, we should be as concerned with what government produces as with how many participate. What good is participation if the citizenry is unable to determine who merits their support?

Participation and responsibility are not logically incompatible, but there is a degree of tension between the two, and the quest for either may be carried to extremes. Participation maximizers find themselves involved with quotas and virtual representation schemes, while responsibility maximizers can find themselves with a closed shop under boss rule. Moreover, both qualities can weaken the democracy they supposedly underpin. Unfettered participation produces Hyde Amendments* and immobilism. Responsible parties can use agenda power to thwart democratic decision—for more than a century the Democratic party used what power it had to suppress the racial issue. Neither participation nor responsibility should be pursued at the expense of all other values, but that is what has happened with participation over the course of the past two decades, and we now reap the consequences in our politics.

Discussion Questions

1. How do political parties provide "collective responsibility" and improve the quality of democracy? Do you believe the complaints raised by Fiorina thirty-five years ago remain persuasive?
2. Are strong parties in the interest of individual politicians? What might be some reasons that members of Congress would agree to strong parties? What would make them distance themselves from their party's leadership?
3. President Donald Trump won the Republican Party nomination in 2016 despite opposition from many party leaders and elected officials. Is his electoral success in 2016 a confirmation of Fiorina's concerns or a rejection of them?

*The Hyde Amendment, passed in 1976 (three years after *Roe v. Wade*), prohibited using Medicaid funds for abortion [*Editors*].

54

"Be Careful What You Wish For: The Rise of Responsible Parties in American National Politics"

NICOL RAE

Writing about twenty-five years after Morris Fiorina, Nicol Rae sees significant changes in American political parties. To Rae, American parties had developed in the ways preferred by many reformers who wanted parties to be more cohesive, policy-focused, determined to implement their agendas, and active in elections. Parties in Congress have become more unified and more determined to exercise their authority. The party national committees have become highly involved in candidate recruitment and training, fundraising, and advertising. Presidential nomination rules—notwithstanding the success of Donald Trump in 2016—have been adjusted to make it more difficult for outsider candidates to triumph over those preferred by party insiders. The nomination system works to produce candidates satisfactory to the middle of the party rather than the middle of the nation. Among voters, partisanship appeared to be on the rise and the proportion of split-ticket voters was decreasing. Rae's diagnosis is that "American national parties appear very healthy in all aspects compared to their condition thirty years ago."

The results, he suggests, have not been as beneficial for democracy as many scholars assumed they would be. Pointing to partisan conflict, especially in Congress, he writes that "it is hard to argue that the strengthening of America's parties has improved the governmental process and enhanced the quality of America's representative democracy." Rae argues that the parties have increasingly become defined by interests that attach themselves to one party or the other rather than truly straddling the two parties. The parties, in turn, must become more vigilant in defending those interests that attach to them, leaving little room to work with members of the other party to solve problems.

Despite all these changes, Rae concludes that American parties have not become "responsible parties" in the sense advocated by many reformers. They may be doing a better job of pursuing coherent agendas—though not to the degree seen in other countries—but the nature of the U.S. system of separated, divided, and federal powers makes truly responsible parties highly unlikely. Responsible parties would be able to implement their promises and agendas without obstruction from the other party, a situation that Rae argues appears only rarely in American politics.

In the comparative study of political parties in twentieth-century advanced democracies, the United States has always been something of a problematic outlier owing to the absence of organized, disciplined, and ideological mass political parties. Almost all other advanced democracies are parliamentary political systems characterized by what [political scientist J. Austin] Ranney termed "responsible party government," in which a party or coalition of parties forms a cabinet responsible to the lower house of the legislature. Legislators from the governing party or coalition thus have powerful incentives in terms of re-election, career, and policy goals to sustain the government in office, and at election time the government is ultimately held accountable as voters vote for or against the candidates of the governing party (or parties).

From its very beginning, however, the U.S. political system has remained conspicuously resistant to strong mass political parties, and responsible party government has found little enthusiasm among Americans outside the academy. The framers of the U.S. Constitution equated parties with interest groups ("factions"), which they regarded as the greatest danger to republican virtue and future government stability in the United States. The constitutional separation of the branches of the federal government—with separated elections and staggered terms for the executive and legislatures—places formidable obstacles in the way of responsible party government by comparison with parliamentary systems where the two branches are fused by cabinet governments. American federalism—with significant governmental powers reserved to the states—has also presented a barrier to responsible party government. Beyond the constitutional impediments to party government, the notion of strong, centralized governing parties is also antithetical to America's political culture. The individualism and suspicion of government ingrained in the American political psyche since colonial times has militated against large concentrations of private power with influence over government. Finally, unlike in Europe, mass political parties failed to develop in the United States, and so the American parties never developed the mass ideological loyalty and organizational apparatus necessary for them to serve as channels of accountability in a responsible party government model.

The United States has nevertheless had national political parties of a sort and party conflict since the 1790s, and no representative democracy of any significance has been able to operate without them. Without such intermediary political institutions to structure political choices, mass representative democracy would surely be rendered meaningless. So although Americans have never had much love for national political parties, they have not been able to devise a political system in which parties do not play a significant role. The 1950 APSA [American Political Science Association] report reflected the consensus among American political scientists of the New Deal generation that the American parties were too weak to perform their necessary role in channeling democratic choices for Americans and suggested a number of methods by which they might be strengthened and made more nearly "responsible" on the European model.

In America, by comparison, the parties were too outdated and ramshackle to play what the party scholars saw as their appropriate role in the world's leading representative democracy. This was seen as an issue that needed to be addressed by the political science profession as a whole—hence the APSA committee on the state of the parties, headed by the most distinguished American parties scholar of the day—E.E. Schattschneider. The Foreword succinctly summarized the consensus among contemporary American party scholars:

> Historical and other factors have caused the American two-party system to operate as two loose associations of state and local organizations, with very little national machinery and very little national cohesion. As a result, either major party, when in power, is ill-equipped to organize its members in the legislative and executive branches into a government held together and guided by a party program. Party responsibility at the polls thus tends to vanish. This is a very serious matter, for it affects the very heartbeat of American democracy.

Part I of the report developed the argument for greater party responsibility and illustrated how the contemporary American national parties were simply not living up to the role. Part II consisted of a set of concrete proposals by the committee to make the parties more responsible, e.g., enhance the role of the national party committees; create an elite 50-member national party body or "party council" to coordinate the national state and local party organizations, draft the platform, and generally set party policy; strengthen the party organizations in Congress; encourage intraparty participation (particularly in the presidential nominating process), including the creation of a formal "party membership"; and, finally, expand the research capacity of the parties.

* * *

If the Parties Are Dead, How Did American Politics Get to Be So Partisan?

Thirty years on, a contemporary analysis of American politics would not regard the weakness of the political parties as primarily responsible for the ills of the political system. There does now appear to be some real evidence that in several important aspects the parties are beginning to resemble those advocated by the 1950 APSA report, yet it is by no means clear that the quality of American democracy has been enhanced by this development in the manner envisaged by the party theorists. If anything, it is the apparent strength and ideological coherence of the parties and the apparent polarization between them that is now seen as problematic. Moreover, the rise of partisanship and polarization in a separated system of government appears only to have enhanced policy gridlock and increased popular frustration with government. This might seem to imply that the prescriptions of the "responsible party government" theorists were always flawed in their application to the American context. * * *

Some signs of party revival in the United States were already evident during the 1970s, but it took some time for party scholars to recognize the trend. The area where political scientists first began to notice party renewal was the new role of the national party committees. Traditionally, the national party committees had no control over the state parties, and their duties were largely confined to organizing the quadrennial national party nominating convention and conducting presidential election campaigns. The Democrats' reform of the presidential nominating process after 1968 gave the Democratic National Committee sovereignty over the state parties in issues regarding presidential delegate selection. This authority was confirmed by the 1975 Supreme Court decision in the case of *Cousins v. Wigoda*.

Perhaps more significant, however, was the transformation of the Republican National Committee following the Watergate debacle. Under a series of national chairmen beginning with William Brock (1977–1981), the committee began to transform itself into a major fundraising and campaign service organization for GOP candidates right down to the state legislative level. The Republican National Committee developed a formidable national small-donor fundraising base, established training programs for candidates and campaign managers at all levels, played a greater role in candidate recruitment, and coordinated national Republican media campaigns in election years. The Democratic National Committee began to play a similar role in the 1980s and 1990s, although their fundraising prowess has lagged behind that of their Republican counterparts. This evolution of what Aldrich has termed "the party in service" has greatly heightened the visibility and electoral role of national party committees and helped create a genuine national party identity. To the extent that the national parties have worked with Republican and Democratic candidates, their heightened level of activity—combined with the increasing ideological homogeneity of party candidates—has surely enhanced national party solidarity since the APSA report was issued.

Congress provides the clearest example of the revival of party in the United States over the past quarter century. Congressional scholars first became aware of what was happening when they noticed that party unity scores in Congress had risen significantly during the 1980s and early 1990s. [David] Rohde noted that southern Democrats, traditionally at least as conservative as Republicans in their voting, were now voting much more in line with their liberal national party colleagues. The 1960s civil rights revolution had finally unraveled the ideologically incoherent parties of the post–New Deal era that had so exasperated President Roosevelt. With southern blacks enfranchised and voting Democratic, southern

Democratic candidates now had to pay attention to their political demands, which did not differ greatly from those of their liberal northern counterparts. Similarly, genuinely conservative southern whites now found a more ideologically congenial home in the rising southern GOP. Liberal Democratic and conservative Republican growth in the South paralleled each other, and the effect on the national Republican and Democratic parties was to make them more broadly conservative and liberal (respectively) in the ideological sense. This process was already under way during the 1970s but was generally overlooked in the general consensus of pessimism regarding the future of the parties. The decline in the number and influence of conservative Democrats as the Republican Party grew in the South was also paralleled by a decline in the number of liberal or progressive Republicans as the Democrats gradually grew stronger in the Northeastern states. In retrospect, then, the civil rights revolution was an absolutely critical development in the emergence of modern American political parties.

Rohde and [Barbara] Sinclair also noted that the growth in party coherence and unity on Capitol Hill was accompanied by dramatic growth in the power of the party leadership in both chambers of Congress. During the 1970s, the growing number of northern liberal Democrats in the House Democratic caucus finally revolted against the dominance of largely southern conservative Democratic committee chairs. The Democrats introduced new rules providing for elections of committee chairs and reduced the chairs' control over committee personnel and agendas. At the same time, they empowered the party caucus and the party leadership. Party leaders gained a much greater role in committee assignments and, since the Speaker gained control over the membership of the powerful House Rules committee, de facto control over the schedule of legislation.

Commentary on these rules changes initially focused on the great power given to subcommittees and individual members by the reductions in chairs' powers, but the most important long-term effect was the dramatic strengthening of the congressional party leadership that occurred once party leaders started to take advantage of the new opportunities provided by the reforms. With more ideologically homogeneous congressional parties, it is logical to expect that individual members would seek to empower the party leadership to ensure implementation of common policy goals. In what Sinclair describes as a "principal-agent" relationship, members have indeed empowered leaders to perform legislative tasks in line with those goals. [John] Aldrich and Rohde go further, describing the emergence of a system of "conditional party government" in Congress: If there is a sufficient consensus on policy objectives within the majority party, members will empower party leaders to deliver those objectives. The ideological congressional party realignment engendered by the civil rights revolution has, according to Aldrich and Rohde, created the perfect environment for stronger partisanship and party leadership on Capitol Hill. The accuracy of this analysis is also borne out by the experience of the U.S. Senate, where, despite the absence of such explicit reforms as in the House, the same pattern of growing party unity and enhanced leadership influence can be observed.

While the Democrats were acting like a more coherent majority party during the 1980s, the Republican minority arguably went even farther in an ideological and partisan direction. The reassertion of control by the Democratic Party leadership led to a loss of influence on the part of the Republican minority—particularly in the House of Representatives. During the era of the conservative coalition, the Republicans had considerable leverage over legislation through their alliance with the conservative southern Democrats, both on the House and Senate floors and in committee. In the postreform House of the 1980s, the Republicans found themselves shut out of the policy-making process by a reassertive Democratic leadership. In reaction, the Republican minority became increasingly vocal, ideological, and partisan, as demonstrated by the rise of the Georgia firebrand Newt Gingrich to a position of party leadership by the late 1980s.

In presidential politics the case for party revival appears somewhat less evident. Even before the establishment of the primary nominating system, candidate organizations and the news media were becoming more important players in nominating politics at the expense of traditional state and local party bosses. The primary system confirmed this development and rendered the national party conventions purely ceremonial occasions to ratify the winners of the primary election campaign. Performance in early caucuses and primary contests (particularly in the relatively small states of Iowa and New Hampshire), fundraising ability, and the impact of media expectations and coverage have become the crucial determinants of presidential success, with no significant role for party officeholders in the process. Indeed, the reformed process allowed rank outsiders who would never have gained the support of traditional party leaders—such as George McGovern and Jimmy Carter—to secure presidential nominations.

Although the fundamentals of the nominating system have not changed in the decades since, modifications in the primary calendar have diluted the chances of outsider candidates and to some extent increased the influence of party elites. The tendency toward "frontloading" of the primary calendar, with more and more major states with large numbers of delegates voting at an earlier stage in the process, has considerably diluted the potential impact of an outsider candidate's unexpectedly strong showing in Iowa and New Hampshire. In a frontloaded calendar, with more than 50 percent of the delegates being chosen in a one-month period and dozens of simultaneous campaigns in some of the country's biggest and most expensive media markets, the advantages of nationally known candidates able to raise large sums of money have increased considerably. These are likely to be candidates "anointed" by the contemporary party "establishment"—large fundraisers and leaders of political action committees, or 527 committees. Though not on the ideological fringe of either party, these elites are not going to back candidates who are outside the mainstream of national party ideology; after all, that ideology is largely determined by the very interest groups that provide the money for the party. All presidential nominees since 1984 have been the candidates closest to this fundraising party establishment. In a clear example of the advantages of the present system, Arizona Senator John McCain won the New Hampshire primary easily in 2000, but because he lacked support among the Republican allied interests and fundraisers, McCain was overtaken by the establishment favorite George W. Bush, whose fundraising and organizational prowess proved decisive in the multistate primaries that followed shortly thereafter.

The impact of money and organization on presidential nominating politics thus also has the effect of driving the candidates toward the ideological center of the party rather than that of the nation. Interest groups and large donors contribute to the candidate who holds issue positions that they approve of but who they also bet can defeat the other party's candidate in the general election. The outcome in primary politics is to drive candidates toward their party's ideological agenda and single-issue interest group supporters. The overall effect is a polarization of party candidates that mirrors the increased partisanship in Congress. Informally, the donors of primary campaign money have become a de facto party elite, although far removed from the background and motivation of traditional party bosses.

We must finally consider the evidence of party revival in the electorate. The 1970s theory of dealignment was based on the apparent alienation of the American electorate from the major political parties. This was evident in declining levels of partisan affiliation, growth in the number of self-described independents in the electorate, increased electoral volatility, declining turnout, and increased levels of split-ticket voting. All of these phenomena were more pronounced among the younger voters of the baby boom generation, who came of age politically during the 1960s. It was their electoral disaffection from the parties that provided the strongest evidence of dealignment, with some scholars tracing a long-term pattern of electoral disaggregation set in train by the reforms of the progressive era.

In the succeeding decades, however, the worst fears of the dealignment theorists have not been borne out. The surge toward independent affiliation appears to have crested in the 1970s, and partisanship in the electorate has experienced something of a revivial. Partisans have held their own and there is evidence that the intensity of partisanship has increased. The 2004 election, the most partisan election in recent history, also witnessed marked increases in voter turnout. The electoral volatility of the 1960s and 1970s appears to have been a temporary phenomenon; recent American elections have been exceedingly close and competitive, with relatively small margins separating the parties' national totals in both presidential and congressional races, and a markedly stable pattern in the geographic distribution of the vote. Finally, split-ticket voting, which peaked in the 1970s, has also gone into a marked decline, with far fewer split party outcomes between presidential and congressional candidates at the state and district levels. In fact, the 2004 election had the fewest in decades.

In summary, American national parties appear very healthy in all aspects compared to their condition thirty years ago. They are more ideologically coherent, maintain viable and significant national organizations, are much stronger in Congress, and enjoy a stronger and more committed mass base of support. It would appear that the parties have gone at least some way toward the model envisaged by the authors of the 1950 report. Yet this enhanced partisanship has not produced entirely positive results. On the contrary, it is argued today that the country is too partisan and too polarized, and that this polarization and partisanship has led to an unhealthy degree of bitterness and invective in national political debate. Party polarization in Congress and between Congress and the White House has also impeded the smooth working of a legislative process devised by the framers to generate compromise. In short, it is hard to argue that the strengthening of America's parties has improved the governmental process and enhanced the quality of America's representative democracy.

* * *

American Parties in the Twenty-First Century

What are we to make of American parties at the dawn of the twenty-first century? Certainly American parties today look more like political parties in other democracies than they did when Duverger was writing in the late 1940s. The impact of the 1960s civil rights revolution has been to create two more ideologically coherent parties: a generally liberal or center-left party and a conservative party. The national party organizations, though not in direct control of the party machinery in the states and locales as in other democratic systems, now play a major part in electoral campaigning at all levels. Party unity and the power of the party leadership in Congress is at its highest levels since the Gilded Age. In presidential politics, the new party elite of fundraisers, political action committees, and 527 organizations uses the frontloaded nominating system to nominate established political figures in the ideological mainstream of the party rather than mavericks. Finally, the electorate is more inclined to behave in a partisan fashion than it was in the 1960s and 1970s. We can say conclusively that dealignment is over and that American parties are more serious political institutions and more significant in the governing process than they were 30 years ago, or even when the APSA committee issued its report in 1950.

* * *

Contemporary American parties are alliances of interest groups. In some sense they always have been, although in the traditional party these interests were defined geographically or locally. In modern America, interests are primarily national in scope. Very few national interests today are genuinely bipartisan, and most associate with one political party or the other—labor, teachers, environmentalists, trial lawyers, the entertainment industry, and national organizations that campaign on behalf of women, minorities, and gays tend to cleave to the Democratic party, while the Republicans are supported by corporate and financial interests, conservative religious organizations, and gun owners. Dislike of the opposing coalition is the glue that keeps each interest alliance together. These groups fund the party campaigns at all levels and provide the activists and other critical resources. Their endorsements are eagerly sought by party candidates, and they generally play a critical role in primary elections. Of course this means that successful candidates must adhere closely to the groups' positions to get nominated. Once in office, their political objectives are logically in line with those of the groups that support them. Since groups on opposite sides of the party divide generally hold opposing positions on issues, the overall effect has been to pull both parties away from the center ground on most issues and closer to the positions of their interest group allies.

Several other factors operate to maximize the influence of the interest group activists over party politics. One of the most obvious is legislative redistricting. In recent decades, the cumulative effect of state legislatures drawing electoral district boundaries for themselves—and for the U.S. House—combined with post–1965 federal voting rights legislation, federal court rulings, and modern computer technology has been to create legislative districts that are usually "safe" for one major party or the other. With the overwhelming majority of legislative districts now being deliberately configured to produce a partisan outcome, the key contest becomes the primary election—invariably low in turnout and with an electorate disproportionately composed of the most committed interest group and party activists. The overall effect has been to homogenize party candidates' ideology, increase party unity, and bolster the party leadership as the agent that has to produce legislative outcomes satisfactory to the groups that support the party and thereby help insure incumbents' re-election.

The nature of contemporary news media also encourages the more polarized tone of American politics. Cable news media and radio talk shows are the province of the party activists and tend to cover politics in an adversarial fashion. The further "narrowcasting" created by the Internet has tended to encourage discussions among the like-minded rather than a nuanced consideration of the issues. All these news sources tend to encourage partisanship and adversarial politics. It certainly cannot be argued—as it was in the 1950 report—that the contemporary American voter is denied a debate between clear-cut choices on the issues.

Conclusion

None of the factors encouraging polarization seems likely to change in the short term. Although mass party development or responsible party government still seem highly unlikely, there has undoubtedly been a revival of parties and partisanship in the United States in the past quarter century, primarily due to three factors: (*a*) the civil rights revolution; (*b*) the capture of the party labels by coalitions of single-issue and ideological elite interests who see those labels as instruments to achieve their ends; and (*c*) the development of political communications media that encourage rhetorical and political conflict.

Despite these changes, American political parties are likely to remain outliers in the study of comparative parties because America itself is an outlier on so many political indices. Relative to European parties, the American parties are still generally less ideological, far less well-organized, less cohesive, less centralized, and less critical to the day-to-day business of government. * * * Despite the wishes of the APSA committee, the U.S. Constitution and American political culture effectively preclude responsible party government from developing in the United States except during intermittent periods when one party controls all the branches of the federal government.

* * *

The party scholars behind the 1950 report would certainly be pleased to see the development of more coherent and effective parties in the United States and the end of the organizationally ramshackle and ideologically incoherent parties of the post–New Deal era. Whether they would be pleased by the degree of polarization and conflict in contemporary American party politics is a different matter. Implicit in the concept of responsible party government was the notion that in addition to presenting distinct choices to the electorate and enabling voters to hold the government to account at election time, political parties were also the most effective agents for containing and resolving conflict in society. The assumption was that party elites would have sufficient consensus on the fundamentals of political debate to prevent political conflict from getting out of hand. If parties are merely vehicles of polarized political elites, however, they are more likely to magnify such conflict than to contain it.

The irony may be that having finally witnessed the development of ideologically coherent parties that make sense to external observers, political scientists have also become more aware of the potentially unhealthy side effects—partisan rancor, political polarization, policy stasis in a separated national governing system—that may attend such a development.

Discussion questions

1. Is it more of a problem for American democracy that parties have become more cohesive, unified, and determined to implement their views, or is it more of a problem that the structure of American government makes it difficult for parties to implement their plans? Or is neither of these much of a problem for American democracy?
2. Rae details several ways in which American parties have changed. Are all of these changes for the worse in your view? If so, explain why. If not, explain which changes you see as positive and which you see as problems.

Debating the Issues: Should the United States Encourage Multi-Party Politics?

The American political system is dominated by the Republican and Democratic parties. Other political parties run candidates and occasionally win, but the electoral record of "third" or "minor" parties is generally quite poor. Political scientists point to a number of behavioral and structural reasons for this pattern.

As for behavior, most Americans sense that the two-party system is what is "normal" in American politics, and any other choices can seem risky. Voters are often reluctant to "waste" their vote for a candidate they believe has no chance to win, especially if they also believe that casting such a vote would increase the chances that a candidate they strongly dislike would win. Liberal Democrats faced this dilemma in 2000 when deciding whether to vote for Ralph Nader, the Green Party candidate for president, or Al Gore, the Democrat. When Gore lost by 537 votes in Florida, sealing the victory for Republican candidate George W. Bush, many of the more than 97,000 Floridians who voted for Ralph Nader no doubt wondered if they had made a mistake. In 2016, Libertarian Party candidate Gary Johnson and Green Party candidate Jill Stein created similar dilemmas for some Republicans and Democrats. The percentage of votes won by Johnson exceeded the margin of votes between Donald Trump and Hillary Clinton in nine of the ten closest states. Stein and other minor party candidates won additional votes in these states.

And as for structure, third parties face the need to raise substantial financial resources; the time and expense of getting on the ballot in all the states, which often involves lawsuits; and the relative lack of attention from news media. In addition, most electoral districts in the United States—for elections to the U.S. House or a state legislature, for example—elect a single person to an office, so that means the candidate with the highest number of votes will win. Because of this arrangement, potential smaller parties have an incentive to join forces with one of the larger parties, and skilled candidates are more likely to want to run on the ticket of one of those larger parties. It is certainly not impossible for more than two parties to have a solid, durable presence in such a system—the British system has a similar system of district-based elections and has two major parties and a competitive third party—but it is difficult. The most successful third party in American history, the Republican party, was not a "third" party for long, as it quickly replaced the collapsing Whig Party.

Despite these electoral struggles, political scientists and other supporters of multi-party politics point out other contributions that minor parties can make. Minor party candidates can raise issues that neither major party candidate is likely to raise. They can provide an alternative to voters who believe the major parties have become too extreme or have become too alike. Voters may sometimes support a third-party candidate before moving their support from one major party to another, giving these voters a means by which to shift their voting habits.

Should the United States encourage multi-party politics? Larry Diamond says yes. Americans are dissatisfied with their politics and their politicians. Diamond argues that the electoral system is rigid and slow to adapt, and this rigidity has consequences for addressing health, education, and other concerns. Although a majority of Americans voice support in public opinion surveys for having the option to vote for a minor party candidate—presumably, survey respondents mean voting for a candidate with a possibility of winning, since there are usually numerous minor party options on the ballot in most states for presidential elections—structural constraints make it hard for minor party candidates to be visible to voters. Diamond advocates for one specific change: making it easier for third-party candidates to participate in the presidential debates conducted by the Commission on Presidential Debates during the general election campaign. Ezra Klein takes a more pessimistic view toward third parties. While third parties might well introduce new issues into public discussion, Klein fears that in practice a third-party president would find himself or herself with two major parties unwilling to promote the president's agenda and determined to defeat it. And a Congress with third-party members would be unlikely to grant those newcomers any institutional power because to do so would mean reducing the influence of members of the major parties. In Klein's view, third parties are unlikely to reduce the frustrations that voters express about American politics.

55

"Ending the Presidential-Debate Duopoly"

Larry Diamond

The Democratic and Republican parties—which cannot seem to agree on anything else these days—have conspired to construct and defend a duopoly that closes competition to all other political alternatives. As a result, every current state governor and every one of the 535 members of Congress (save Maine Senator Angus King and Vermont Senator Bernie Sanders) was elected on one of the two party tickets. Governance in Washington is increasingly deadlocked between two parties that are being dragged to the extremes, while new alternatives that might fashion creative policy options and broader governing coalitions are stifled from competing. The political parties have become rigid and resistant to change, and have lost their capacity to find necessary and imaginative solutions to major problems.

Is it any wonder, then, that the polls show unprecedented disaffection among the American public? Sixty-two percent of Americans do not think the federal government has the consent of the governed, and 86 percent feel the political system is broken and does not serve the interests of the American people.

In *The Economist*'s 2013 democracy index, the United States is looking mediocre by international standards. It ranks only 19th in the quality of democracy. Americans should care about the quality and openness of their democracy for its own sake.

But there are also strong connections between the adaptability and competitiveness of its political institutions and the outcomes they produce. Globally, the United States ranks 14th in education, 19th in quality of infrastructure, 26th in child well-being, 26th in life expectancy, 33rd in Internet download speeds, and 44th in healthcare efficiency, but first in one thing—the rate of incarceration.

Nowhere is openness, innovation, and competition more sorely needed than in presidential politics. If competition is good for the economy, why shouldn't it be good for the political system as well? If economic markets thrive when there are low barriers to entry, why shouldn't the political marketplace—democracy—benefit from the same principle?

Two-thirds of Americans say they wish they had the option to vote for an independent candidate for president. But any alternative to the 162-year-old duopoly of Democrats and Republicans is blocked by the system the two parties have created. Leave aside the huge hurdles of organization and funding that independents must scale to collect enough signatures to qualify for the ballot across the states. Even more formidable is the obstacle imposed by a crucial but little known and unaccountable gatekeeper, the Commission on Presidential Debates (CPD). Members of this unelected and unaccountable commission have established a rule that makes it impossible for an independent, nonpartisan, or third-party ticket to gain access to the general-election debates. In the contemporary era, these debates have become such a dominant focus of political attention that no candidate (and particularly not a third one) can become president without participating.

Even if a third-party candidate does not manage to use the debate as a springboard to the Oval Office, his or her presence on the stage might reshape the conversation. With a third-party candidate in the race, both Democrats and Republicans would have a strong incentive to speak to the issues propelling that candidacy.

The CPD requires candidates for president to average over 15 percent in five polls (which they reserve the right to select, and which are open to manipulation) taken in September, just days before the debates. Since 1960 not one American who had not participated in a major-party primary has ever polled over 15 percent less than two weeks before the debates. (Ross Perot was polling in the single digits when he was permitted into the debates under an old rule.) For a candidate who has not run the gauntlet of the two major-party primaries, new research demonstrates that getting to that level of support in the polls by mid-September might require an expenditure of nearly $270 million. No independent campaign has ever spent, or ever will spend, that kind of money without knowing that its presidential and vice-presidential candidates can stand on the stage of the debates in the fall with a fair chance to compete.

In January, 49 prominent Republicans, Democrats, and independents—including current and former governors, members of Congress, cabinet members, academics, military leaders, and me—wrote to the CPD, asking it to change the rule and open up the debates to an independent voice. (Atlantic Media chairman David Bradley is also a signatory to the letter.) The letter proposed a different (or at least supplementary) means for earning a third spot on the debate stage: If one or more alternative candidates or parties qualified for the presidential ballot in states with enough electoral votes to win the election, then whichever one gathered the most signatures as part of the ballot-access process would be invited to participate in the debates. It urged that this decision be made by April 30 of the election year, to allow enough time for the candidate to mount a serious national campaign—and to be tested and scrutinized by the media. And it invited the CPD to propose other means by which an alternative ticket could reasonably qualify to enter the debates.

When a Petition for Rulemaking was filed with the FEC and posted for public comment in December, all but one of the 1,252 public comments endorsed the request for a new rule. Only the CPD claimed there was no need for a change. Despite this overwhelming backing, the CPD has stonewalled. In fact, the 17-member board has refused even to meet with the four dozen signers of the Change the Rule letter.

For more than two centuries, the United States has been a beacon of hope for democracy worldwide. For the last century, the United States has been the world's most successful and powerful democracy. But both of these elements of global leadership are now rapidly eroding. Making the election for America's highest office more open and competitive might renew the vigor and promise of its democracy.

56

"A Third Party Won't Fix What's Broken in American Politics"

Ezra Klein

The question I get more than any other about American politics is: The Democratic Party and the Republican Party both suck. Don't we need a third party to fix this?

Well, to paraphrase Bill Clinton, it depends what the meaning of "this" is.

If you think the problem with American politics is that there are ideas that are popular among voters but suppressed by the two major parties, then a third party could potentially help a lot.

But if you think the problem with American politics is that Congress is gridlocked, the president seems powerless to do anything about it, and Americans are increasingly frustrated, then a third party might well make things worse.

The Case for a Third Party

Political scientist Ronald Rapaport wrote the book on third parties. Literally. It's called *Three's a Crowd,* because of course it is. And the key thing he found about third parties is that "they need some sort of unique agenda. There has to be a reason why you're going to support a third party."

Third parties are a political weapon: they force the system to confront issues it might otherwise prefer to ignore. Take Ross Perot, the most successful leader of a third party in recent American history. "People like to think of Perot as being centrist. But he was not," says Rapoport. "He was extreme on the issues he cared about. And with Perot, it was economic nationalism and balancing the budget."

It's worth stopping on that point a moment. In Washington, the yearning for a third party is often by elites—and for elites. It's for the third party of Unity08, or No Labels, or Mike Bloomberg, or Simpson-Bowles. It's a third party of technocrats: fiscally moderate, socially permissive. A third party of sober moderates. A third party *of things people in Washington already care about.*

That third party won't work. The space for a third political party—if it exists—isn't in Washington's zone of elite agreement. It's in the zones of popular agreement that elites have little patience for. America's unaffiliated voters aren't moderates. They are, by Washington's standards, extremists—they're just extreme in a way that blithely crosses left and right lines, then doubles back on itself again. They support single-payer health care and tax cuts. Or they're against gay marriage but for a living wage. Or they're for open borders and cuts to social spending. Or they want a smaller military and sharp restrictions on abortions.

Perot's enthusiasts were a good example, Rapoport says. "His supporters, on issues like choice, were very pro-choice. On affirmative action, they were very against affirmative action."

Third parties like Perot's can force issues to the fore. But, typically, they get co-opted. Bill Clinton was much more intent on reducing the deficit because Perot showed the issue's power. Newt Gingrich's Contract With America echoed Perot's United We Stand. By 1996 there wasn't much left for Perot and his party to do.

Rapoport quotes historian Eric Hofstadter's famous line on American third parties: They're like bees. Once they've stung, they die.

The Problem with a Third-Party President

America's two-party duopoly has been going on a long time. What's new is the world where even the duopoly's favored ideas are stymied. Today, the chances of infrastructure investment or immigration reform aren't much better than the chances of single-payer health care. What's changed isn't that Washington is closed to new ideas. It's that it's closed to any ideas.

Could a third party break that deadlock? Probably not. In fact, it might well make it worse.

Imagine a third party that actually elects a new president. Right now, the basic problem in American politics is that one of the two major political parties has an interest in destroying the president. As incoming Senate Majority Leader Mitch McConnell said in 2010, "the single most important thing we want to achieve is for President Obama to be a one-term president."

The statement is often used to paint McConnell as uniquely Machiavellian, but in truth, it's banal: the single most important thing any minority political party wants to achieve is becoming the majority party. That's not because they're evil; it's because they believe being in the majority is the best way for them to do good. But the way for them to get there is to destroy the incumbent. Hence, the gridlock we see today.

A third-party president would change this in one big way: now *both* major political parties would have a direct incentive to destroy the president.

"The reason congressional parties work with the president from their party is that they share policy goals *and* because they share electoral goals," says Sarah Binder, a congressional scholar at the Brookings Institution. "You put a Michael Bloomberg at the top and maybe they still share policy goals but they don't share electoral goals. So you sever that electoral incentive."

In fact, the perverse reality of a third party is that the major party that agrees with it the most is also the most threatened by its existence. Think of Ralph Nader acting as a spoiler for Al Gore. So the fact of sharing policy goals often means they're directly opposed on electoral goals. No one in Congress is going to want to help an executive whose success is a threat to their chance of ever being in the majority again.

The Problem with a Third Party in Congress

Arguably, a third party could attack congressional gridlock at its source: by winning seats in Congress and then doing . . . something . . . to fix the chamber. But that something is hard to imagine.

I asked Binder for the rosiest possible scenario for a congressional third party. But she couldn't come up with much. "I can't even quite wrap my head around the politics, the electoral politics, the institutional politics, that would ever lead a third party to be in a position to make a difference in Congress," she said. "Everything in Congress is structured by the parties. If you want committee assignments, it's the parties that control committee assignments. Unless you can displace a major party I don't see how you get the toehold that gives you institutional power."

Rapoport didn't have much more of an answer. Third parties, he said, "are bad at process." They tend to be structured around a charismatic founder or a particular issue but, if they get far enough to actually wield power, they're ground to death by the byzantine institutions of American politics.

You can see that in Congress now, in fact. There are a number of third-party candidates serving in the Senate. Maine's Angus King, Vermont's Bernie Sanders, and Alaska's Lisa Murkowski were all elected as third-party candidates (Murkowski ran as a Republican write-in after losing the Republican primary). But in order to wield any power they've allied themselves with one of the two major parties. Sanders and King caucus with the Democratic Party and vote like typical Democrats—indeed, Sanders is thinking about running for president as a Democrat. Murkowski caucuses with the Republican Party and votes like a Republican. Even when Congress has three parties, it really only has two.

If a third party did win seats in Congress and accepted less institutional power for more party coherence, it's hard to say what problems it would solve. Congress is riven by disagreement and an inability to compromise. A third party would simply add another set of disagreements and another group who could potentially block action to the mix.

Which is all to say that the perverse incentives and byzantine structures that are causing so many problems for our two-party system would end up causing just as many problems, if not more, for a multi-party system.

A third party might change the ideas Washington takes seriously. But it's hard to see it fixing the fact that Washington can't do much with the ideas it already does take seriously.

Discussion Questions

1. Imagine that it is a presidential election year and you are living in a closely contested "battleground" state. Each of the major parties believes its candidate can win your state, and each will need your state in order to win a majority of the Electoral College votes and the election. Public opinion surveys indicate the election to be essentially tied between the two major party candidates. A third party candidate that you have strongly supported throughout the election year is also running. Supporters of one of the major party candidates urge you to forget about voting for the third party candidate because she cannot win. Even worse, because you are not voting for their candidate, you are in effect helping the other major party win, and you dislike that candidate most of all. Do you vote for the third party candidate, the major party candidate, or not vote at all? Why?
2. While voters have more options with multi-party elections, the likelihood increases that the winning candidate will not receive a majority of the vote. And as Klein argues, successful third-party candidates will face many roadblocks once they are in office. Considering these trade-offs, would American democracy be better off or worse off with more than two major parties?
3. The national presidential debates are the most-viewed events of the general election campaign and the most extended exposure most voters will have to the candidates. Given this information, do you support Diamond's proposal? Why or why not?

CHAPTER 12

Groups and Interests

57

"Political Association in the United States," from *Democracy in America*

ALEXIS DE TOCQUEVILLE

The right of political association—joining together—has long been a cornerstone of American democracy. Alexis de Tocqueville, a French citizen who studied early nineteenth-century American society, argued that the right to associate provides an important check on a majority's power to suppress a political minority. Tocqueville pointed out that allowing citizens to associate in a variety of groups with a variety of interests provides a political outlet for all types of political perspectives to be heard. It also enables compromises to be reached as each interest group attempts to build support among shifting coalitions on individual issues. "There is a place for individual independence," Tocqueville argued, in the American system of government. "[A]s in society, all the members are advancing at the same time toward the same goal, but they are not obliged to follow exactly the same path."

Better use has been made of association and this powerful instrument of action has been applied to more varied aims in America than anywhere else in the world.

* * *

The inhabitant of the United States learns from birth that he must rely on himself to combat the ills and trials of life; he is restless and defiant in his outlook toward the authority of society and appeals to its power only when he cannot do without it. The beginnings of this attitude first appear at school, where the children, even in their games, submit to rules settled by themselves and punish offenses which they have defined themselves. The same attitude turns up again in all the affairs of social life. If some obstacle blocks the public road halting the circulation of traffic, the neighbors at once form a deliberative body; this improvised assembly produces an executive authority which remedies the trouble before anyone has thought of the possibility of some previously constituted authority beyond that of those concerned. Where enjoyment is concerned, people associate to make festivities grander and more orderly. Finally, associations are formed to combat exclusively moral troubles: intemperance is fought in common. Public security, trade and industry, and morals and religion all provide the aims for associations in the United States. There is no end which the human will despairs of attaining by the free action of the collective power of individuals.

* * *

The right of association being recognized, citizens can use it in different ways. An association simply consists in the public and formal support of specific doctrines by a certain number of individuals who have undertaken to cooperate in a stated way in order to make these doctrines prevail. Thus the right of association can almost be identified with freedom to write, but already associations are more powerful than the press. When some view is represented by an association, it must take clearer and more precise shape. It counts its supporters and involves them in its cause; these supporters get to know one another, and numbers increase zeal. An association unites the energies of divergent minds and vigorously directs them toward a clearly indicated goal.

Freedom of assembly marks the second stage in the use made of the right of association. When a political association is allowed to form centers of action at certain important places in the country, its activity becomes greater and its influence more widespread. There men meet, active measures are planned, and opinions are expressed with that strength and warmth which the written word can never attain.

But the final stage is the use of association in the sphere of politics. The supporters of an agreed view may meet in electoral colleges and appoint mandatories to represent them in a central assembly. That is, properly speaking, the application of the representative system to one party.

* * *

In our own day freedom of association has become a necessary guarantee against the tyranny of the majority. In the United States, once a party has become predominant, all public power passes into its hands; its close supporters occupy all offices and have control of all organized forces. The most distinguished men of the opposite party, unable to cross the barrier keeping them from power, must be able to establish themselves outside it; the minority must use the whole of its moral authority to oppose the physical power oppressing it. Thus the one danger has to be balanced against a more formidable one.

The omnipotence of the majority seems to me such a danger to the American republics that the dangerous expedient used to curb it is actually something good.

Here I would repeat something which I have put in other words when speaking of municipal freedom: no countries need associations more—to prevent either despotism of parties or the arbitrary rule of a prince—than those with a democratic social state. In aristocratic nations secondary bodies form natural associations which hold abuses of power in check. In countries where such associations do not exist, if private people did not artificially and temporarily create something like them, I see no other dike to hold back tyranny of whatever sort, and a great nation might with impunity be oppressed by some tiny faction or by a single man.

* * *

In America the citizens who form the minority associate in the first place to show their numbers and to lessen the moral authority of the majority, and secondly, by stimulating competition, to discover the arguments most likely to make an impression on the majority, for they always hope to draw the majority over to their side and then to exercise power in its name.

Political associations in the United States are therefore peaceful in their objects and legal in the means used; and when they say that they only wish to prevail legally, in general they are telling the truth.

* * *

The Americans * * * have provided a form of government within their associations, but it is, if I may put it so, a civil government. There is a place for individual independence there; as in society, all the members are advancing at the same time toward the same goal, but they are not obliged to follow exactly the same path. There has been no sacrifice of will or of reason, but rather will and reason are applied to bring success to a common enterprise.

Discussion Questions

1. Tocqueville argues that "freedom of association has become a necessary guarantee against the tyranny of the majority." Although freedom of association is a central part of any free society, would you place limits on this freedom? What if an American sought to offer nonviolent assistance to a foreign terrorist group? In your view, what activities would be acceptable and which would be unacceptable for this individual?

2. The Constitution guarantees the people the right to assemble and to petition government regarding their grievances. It also guarantees freedom of speech. All these are the essence of interest-group activity.

Nonetheless, many Americans are uneasy with the influence wielded by organized interest groups. What, if any, restrictions on interest-group activity would you be comfortable with? Would you support limits on what interest groups could spend to lobby government officials? To communicate with the public? To run advertisements that support or criticize candidates? How, if at all, can these restrictions be made consistent with the constitutional guarantee of freedom to associate, organize, and petition government, and the guarantee of free speech?

58

"The Alleged Mischiefs of Faction," from *The Governmental Process*

David B. Truman

At various times in U.S. history, the public has become especially concerned with the power of interest groups in politics and seeks to limit their activities. One political scientist refers to this as the "ideals vs. institutions" gap—there are times when "what is" is so different from what Americans believe "should be," that pressure mounts to reform lobbying laws, campaign regulations, business practices, and so on. Going back to James Madison in his famous Federalist 10, *however, the argument that competition between interests should be encouraged has also been powerful in American political thought. The claim in this school of thought, known as pluralist theory, is that the competition among groups in society for political power produces the best approximation of the overall public good. In the following excerpt from* The Governmental Process, *David Truman argues that such groups have been a common and inevitable feature of American politics. Groups form to give individuals a means of self-expression and to help them find security in an uncertain world. In fact, the uncertainty of the social environment, and the resulting threat to one's interests, is a chief motivation for groups to form, and "taming" this environment is a central concern for group members. Rather than leading to a system rigidly ruled by a few dominant powers, Truman, writing in the 1950s, suggests the reality is more dynamic. What critics of group influence fail to recognize is the fact that people have "multiple or overlapping membership" in groups so that "no tolerably normal person is totally absorbed in any group in which he participates." There is balance, in other words, to the views any one member brings to the organization and ultimately to the political process. Further, the potential for a group to form is always present, and "[s]ometimes it may be this possibility of organization that alone gives the potential group a minimum of influence in the political process." These features of the interest group system push toward compromise and balance in public policy.*

Most accounts of American legislative sessions—national, state, or local—are full of references to the maneuverings and iniquities of various organized groups. Newspaper stories report that a legislative proposal is being promoted by groups of business men or school teachers or farmers or consumers or labor unions or other aggregations of citizens. Cartoonists picture the legislature as completely under the control of sinister, portly, cigar-smoking individuals labeled "special interests," while a diminutive John Q. Public is pushed aside to sulk in futile anger and pathetic frustrations. A member of the legislature rises in righteous anger on the floor of the house or in a press conference to declare that the bill under discussion is being forced through by the "interests," by the most unscrupulous high-pressure "lobby" he has seen in all his years of public life. An investigating committee denounces the activities of a group as deceptive, immoral, and destructive of our constitutional methods and ideals. A chief executive attacks a "lobby" or "pressure group" as the agency responsible for obstructing or emasculating a piece of legislation that he has recommended "in the public interest."

* * *

Such events are familiar even to the casual student of day-to-day politics, if only because they make diverting reading and appear to give the citizen the "low-down" on his government. He tends, along with many of his more sophisticated fellow citizens, to take these things more or less for granted, possibly because they merely confirm his conviction that "as everybody knows, politics is a dirty business." Yet at the same time he is likely to regard the activities of organized groups in political life as somehow outside the proper and normal processes of government, as the lapses of his weak contemporaries whose moral fiber is insufficient to prevent their defaulting on the great traditions of the Founding Fathers. These events appear to be a modern pathology.

Group Pressure and the Founding Fathers

Group pressures, whatever we may wish to call them, are not new in America. One of the earliest pieces of testimony to this effect is essay number 10 of *The Federalist,* which contains James Madison's classic statement of the impact of divergent groups upon government and the reasons for their development. He was arguing the virtues of the proposed Union as a means to "break and control the violence of faction," having in mind, no doubt, the groups involved in such actions of the debtor or propertyless segment of the population as Shays's Rebellion. He defined faction in broader terms, however, as "a number of citizens, whether amounting to a majority or minority of the whole, who are united and actuated by some common impulse of passion, or of interest. . . ."

* * *

[Madison's] analysis is not just the brilliant generalization of an armchair philosopher or pamphleteer; it represents as well the distillation from Madison's years of acquaintance with contemporary politics as a member of the Virginia Assembly and of [the Continental] Congress. Using the words "party" and "faction" almost interchangeably, since the political party as we know it had not yet developed, he saw the struggles of such groups as the essence of the political process. One need not concur in all his judgments to agree that the process he described had strong similarities to that of our own day.

The entire effort of which *The Federalist* was a part was one of the most skillful and important examples of pressure group activity in American history. The State ratifying conventions were handled by the Federalists with a skill that might well be the envy of a modern lobbyist. It is easy to overlook the fact that "unless the Federalists had been shrewd in manipulation as they were sound in theory, their arguments could not have prevailed."

* * *

Alexis de Tocqueville, perhaps the keenest foreign student ever to write on American institutions, noted as one of the most striking characteristics of the nation the penchant for promoting a bewildering array of projects through organized societies, among them those using political means. "In no country in the world," he observed, "has the principle of association been more successfully used or applied to a greater multitude of objects than in America." Tocqueville was impressed by the organization of such groups and by their tendency to operate sometimes upon and sometimes parallel to the formal institutions of government. Speaking of the similarity between the representatives of such groups and the members of legislatures, he stated: "It is true that they [delegates of these societies] have not the right, like the others, of making the laws; but they have the power of attacking those which are in force and of drawing up beforehand those which ought to be enacted."

Since the modern political party was, in the Jackson period, just taking the form that we would recognize today, Tocqueville does not always distinguish sharply between it and other types of political interest groups. In his discussion of "political associations," however, he gives an account of the antitariff convention held in Philadelphia in October of 1831, the form of which might well have come from the proceedings of a group meeting in an American city today:

> Its debates were public, and they at once assumed a legislative character; the extent of the powers of Congress, the theories of free trade, and the different provisions of the tariff were discussed. At the end of ten days the Convention broke up, having drawn up an address to the American people in which it declared: (1) that Congress had not the right of making a tariff, and that the existing tariff was unconstitutional; (2) that the prohibition of free trade was prejudicial to the interests of any nation, and to those of the American people especially.

Additional evidence might be cited from many quarters to illustrate the long history of group politics in this country. Organized pressures supporting or attacking the charter of the Bank of the United States in

Jackson's administration, the peculations surrounding Pendleton's "Palace of Fortune" in the pre–Civil War period, the operations of the railroads and other interests in both national and state legislatures in the latter half of the last century, the political activities of farm groups such as the Grange in the same period—these and others indicate that at no time have the activities of organized political interests not been a part of American politics. Whether they indicate pathology or not, they are certainly not new.

* * *

The political interest group is neither a fleeting, transitory newcomer to the political arena nor a localized phenomenon peculiar to one member of the family of nations. The persistence and the dispersion of such organizations indicate rather that we are dealing with a characteristic aspect of our society. That such groups are receiving an increasing measure of popular and technical attention suggests the hypothesis that they are appreciably more significant in the complex and interdependent society of our own day than they were in the simpler, less highly developed community for which our constitutional arrangements were originally designed.

Many people are quite willing to acknowledge the accuracy of these propositions about political groups, but they are worried nevertheless. They are still concerned over the meaning of what they see and read of the activities of such organizations. They observe, for example, that certain farm groups apparently can induce the Government to spend hundreds of millions of dollars to maintain the price of food and to take "surplus" agricultural produce off the market while any urban residents are encountering painful difficulty in stretching their food budgets to provide adequately for their families. They observe that various labor organizations seem to be able to prevent the introduction of cheaper methods into building codes, although the cost of new housing is already beyond the reach of many. Real estate and contractors' trade associations apparently have the power to obstruct various governmental projects for slum clearance and low-cost housing. Veterans' organizations seem able to secure and protect increases in pensions and other benefits almost at will. A church apparently can prevent the appropriation of Federal funds to public schools unless such funds are also given to the schools it operates in competition with the public systems. The Government has declared that stable and friendly European governments cannot be maintained unless Americans buy more goods and services abroad. Yet American shipowners and seamen's unions can secure a statutory requirement that a large proportion of the goods purchased by European countries under the Marshall Plan* must be carried in American ships. Other industries

*The Marshall Plan was the U.S. European Recovery Plan after World War II [*Editors*].

and trade associations can prevent the revision of tariff rates and customs regulations that restrict imports from abroad.

In all these situations the fairly observant citizen sees various groups slugging it out with one another in pursuit of advantages from the Government. Or he sees some of them co-operating with one another to their mutual benefit. He reads of "swarms" of lobbyists "putting pressure on" congressmen and administrators. He has the impression that any group can get what it wants in Washington by deluging officials with mail and telegrams. He may then begin to wonder whether a governmental system like this can survive, whether it can carry its responsibilities in the world and meet the challenges presented by a ruthless dictatorship. He wants to see these external threats effectively met. The sentimental nonsense of the commercial advertisements aside, he values free speech, free elections, representative government, and all that these imply. He fears and resents practices and privileges that seem to place these values in jeopardy.

A common reaction to revelations concerning the more lurid activities of political groups is one of righteous indignation. Such indignation is entirely natural. It is likely, however, to be more comforting than constructive. What we seek are correctives, protections, or controls that will strengthen the practices essential in what we call democracy and that will weaken or eliminate those that really threaten that system. Uncritical anger may do little to achieve that objective, largely because it is likely to be based upon a picture of the governmental process that is a composite of myth and fiction as well as of fact. We shall not begin to achieve control until we have arrived at a conception of politics that adequately accounts for the operations of political groups. We need to know what regular patterns are shown by group politics before we can predict its consequences and prescribe for its lapses. We need to re-examine our notions of how representative government operates in the United States before we can be confident of our statements about the effects of group activities upon it. Just as we should not know how to protect a farm house from lightning unless we knew something of the behavior of electricity, so we cannot hope to protect a governmental system from the results of group organization unless we have an adequate understanding of the political process of which these groups are a part.

* * *

There are two elements in this conception of the political process in the United States that are of crucial significance and that require special emphasis. These are, first, the notion of multiple or overlapping membership and, second, the function of unorganized interests, or potential interest groups.

The idea of overlapping membership stems from the conception of a group as a standardized pattern of interactions rather than as a collection of human units. Although the former may appear to be a rather misty abstraction, it is actually far closer to complex reality than the latter notion. The view of a group as an aggregation of individuals abstracts from the observable fact that in any society, and especially a complex one, no single group affiliation accounts for all of the attitudes or interests of any individual except a fanatic or a compulsive neurotic. No tolerably normal person is totally absorbed in any group in which he participates. The diversity of an individual's activities and his attendant interests involve him in a variety of actual and potential groups. Moreover, the fact that the genetic experiences of no two individuals are identical and the consequent fact that the spectra of their attitudes are in varying degrees dissimilar means that the members of a single group will perceive the group's claims in terms of a diversity of frames of reference. Such heterogeneity may be of little significance until such time as these multiple memberships conflict. Then the cohesion and influence of the affected group depend upon the incorporation or accommodation of the conflicting loyalties of any significant segment of the group, an accommodation that may result in altering the original claims. Thus the leaders of a Parent-Teacher Association must take some account of the fact that their proposals must be acceptable to members who also belong to the local taxpayers' league, to the local chamber of commerce, and to the Catholic Church.

* * *

We cannot account of an established American political system without the second crucial element in our conception of the political process, the concept of the unorganized interest, or potential interest group. Despite the tremendous number of interest groups existing in the United States, not all interests are organized. If we recall the definition of an interest as a shared attitude, it becomes obvious that continuing interaction resulting in claims upon other groups does not take place on the basis of all such attitudes. One of the commonest interest groups forms, the association, emerges out of severe or prolonged disturbances in the expected relationships of individuals in similar institutionalized groups. An association continues to function as long as it succeeds in ordering these disturbed relationships, as a labor union orders the relationships between management and workers. Not all such expected relationships are simultaneously or in a given short period sufficiently disturbed to produce organization. Therefore only a portion of the interests or attitudes involved in such expectations are represented by organized groups. Similarly, many organized groups—families, businesses, or churches, for example—do not operate continuously as interest groups or as political interest groups.

Any mutual interest, however, any shared attitude, is a potential group. A disturbance in established relationships and expectations anywhere in the society may produce new patterns of interaction aimed at restricting or eliminating the disturbance. Sometimes it may be this possibility of organization that alone gives the potential group a minimum of influence in the political process. Thus . . . the Delta planters in Mississippi "must speak for their Negroes in such programs as health and education," although the latter are virtually unorganized and are denied the means of active political participation.*

* * *

Obstacles to the development of organized groups from potential ones may be presented by inertia or by the activities of opposed groups, but the possibility that severe disturbances will be created if these submerged, potential interests should organize necessitates some recognition of the existence of these interests and gives them at least a minimum of influence.

More important for present purposes than the potential groups representing separate minority elements are those interests or expectations that are so widely held in the society and are so reflected in the behavior of almost all citizens that they are, so to speak, taken for granted. Such "majority" interests are significant not only because they may become the basis for organized interest groups overlaps extensively the memberships of the various organized interest groups. The resolution of conflicts between the claims of such unorganized interests and those of organized interest groups must grant recognition to the former not only because affected individuals may feel strongly attached to them but even more certainly because these interests are widely shared and are a part of many established patterns of behavior the disturbance of which would be difficult and painful. They are likely to be highly valued.

* * *

It is thus multiple memberships in potential groups based on widely held and accepted interests that serve as a balance wheel in a going political system like that of the United States. To some people this observation may appear to be a truism and to others a somewhat mystical notion. It is neither. In the first place, neglect of this function of multiple memberships in most discussions of organized interest groups indicates that the observation is not altogether commonplace. Secondly, the statement has no mystical quality; the effective operation of these widely held interests is to be inferred directly from verbal and other behavior in the political sphere. Without the notion of multiple memberships in potential groups it is literally impossible to account for the existence of a viable polity such as that in the United States or to develop a coherent conception of the political process. The strength of these widely held but largely unorganized interests explains the vigor with which propagandists for organized groups

*Until the 1960s, most Southern blacks were denied the right to vote [*Editors*].

attempt to change other attitudes by invoking such interests. Their importance is further evidenced in the recognized function of the means of mass communication, notably the press, in reinforcing widely accepted norms of "public morality."

* * *

Thus it is only as the effects of overlapping memberships and the functions of unorganized interests and potential groups are included in the equation that it is accurate to speak of governmental activity as the product or resultant of interest group activity. As [political scientist Arthur F.] Bentley has put it:

> There are limits to the technique of the struggle, this involving also limits to the group demands, all of which is solely a matter of empirical observation. . . . Or, in other words, when the struggle proceeds too harshly at any point there will become insistent in the society a group more powerful than either of those involved which tends to suppress the extreme and annoying methods of the groups in the primary struggle. It is within the embrace of these great lines of activity that the smaller struggles proceed, and the very word struggle has meaning only with reference to its limitations.

To assert that the organization and activity of powerful interest groups constitutes a threat to representative government without measuring their relation to and effects upon the widespread potential groups is to generalize from insufficient data and upon an incomplete conception of the political process. Such an analysis would be as faulty as one that ignoring differences in national systems, predicted identical responses to a given technological change in the United States, Japan, and the Soviet Union.

Discussion Questions

1. Even if you are not a member of an organized interest group, can you think of any such groups that speak for you? What would it take for you to become a member of or involved in the group?

2. Is Truman right that new organizations emerge in important policy debates, leaving most views well represented? Can you think of instances in which, counter to Truman's viewpoint, a new organization did not emerge, leaving a group unrepresented?

3. Among the many forms of interest group activity, campaign contributions seem to provoke some of the harshest criticisms. Is this reasonable? Is there any reason to be more concerned about campaign contributions than about lobbying, lawsuits, funding research, or any other activities groups employ to pursue their cause? How would Truman answer this question?

59

"The Logic of Collective Action," from *Rise and Decline of Nations**

MANCUR OLSON

Americans organize at a tremendous rate to pursue common interests in the political arena. Yet not all groups are created equal, and some types of political organizations are much more common than others. In particular, it is far easier to organize groups around narrow economic interests than it is to organize around broad "public goods" interests. Why do some groups organize while others do not?

The nature of collective goods, according to the economist Mancur Olson, explains this phenomenon. When a collective good is provided to a group, no member of the group can be denied the benefits of the good. For example, if Congress passes a law that offers subsidies for a new kind of energy technology, any company that produces that technology will benefit from the subsidy. The catch is, any company will benefit even if they did not participate in the collective effort to win the subsidy. Olson argues that "the larger the number of individuals or firms that would benefit from a collective good, the smaller the share of the gains . . . that will accrue to the individual or firm." Hence, the less likely any one member of the group will contribute to the collective effort to secure the collective benefit. For smaller groups, any one member's share of the collective good is larger and more meaningful; thus it is more likely any one member of the group will be willing to make an individual sacrifice to provide a benefit shared by the entire group. An additional distinction is that in a large group, there is often a tendency to assume someone else will take care of the problem—this is known as the "free rider" problem or, as Olson puts it, "let George do it." This is less likely to happen in smaller groups.

The logic helps to explain the greater difficulty so-called "public interest groups" have in organizing and staying organized to pursue such collective goods as air pollution control and consumer product safety. These goods benefit large numbers of people, but the benefit to any one person, Olson would argue, is not sufficient for them to sacrifice time or money for the effort to succeed, especially if the individual believes that he or she will benefit from the collective good even if they do not contribute. Olson identifies "selective incentives" as one way in which these larger groups are able to overcome the incentive for individuals to free ride.

*Mancur Olson. "The Logic of Collective Action," from *Rise and Decline of Nations* (New Haven: Yale University Press, 1982).

The Logic

The argument of this book begins with a paradox in the behavior of groups. It has often been taken for granted that if everyone in a group of individuals or firms had some interest in common, then there would be a tendency for the group to seek to further this interest. Thus many students of politics in the United States for a long time supposed that citizens with a common political interest would organize and lobby to serve that interest. Each individual in the population would be in one or more groups and the vector of pressures of these competing groups explained the outcomes of the political process. Similarly, it was often supposed that if workers, farmers, or consumers faced monopolies harmful to their interests, they would eventually attain countervailing power through organizations such as labor unions or farm organizations that obtained market power and protective government action. On a larger scale, huge social classes are often expected to act in the interest of their members; the unalloyed form of this belief is, of course, the Marxian contention that in capitalist societies the bourgeois class runs the government to serve its own interests, and that once the exploitation of the proletariat goes far enough and "false consciousness" has disappeared, the working class will in its own interest revolt and establish a dictatorship of the proletariat. In general, if the individuals in some category or class had a sufficient degree of self-interest and if they all agreed on some common interest, then the group would to some extent also act in a self-interested or group-interested manner.

If we ponder the logic of the familiar assumption described in the preceding paragraph, we can see that it is fundamentally and indisputably faulty. Consider those consumers who agree that they pay higher prices for a product because of some objectionable monopoly or tariff, or those workers who agree that their skill deserves a higher wage. Let us now ask what would be the expedient course of action for an individual consumer who would like to see a boycott to combat a monopoly or a lobby to repeal the tariff, or for an individual worker who would like a strike threat or a minimum wage law that could bring higher wages. If the consumer or worker contributes a few days and a few dollars to organize a boycott or a union or to lobby for favorable legislation, he or she will have sacrificed time and money. What will this sacrifice obtain? The individual will at best succeed in advancing the cause to a small (often imperceptible) degree. In any case he will get only a minute share of the gain from his action. The very fact that the objective or interest is common to or shared by the group entails that the gain from any sacrifice an individual makes to serve this common purpose is shared with everyone in the group. The successful boycott or strike or lobbying action will bring the better price or wage for everyone in the relevant category, so the individual in any large group with a common interest will reap only a minute share of the gains from whatever sacrifices the individual makes to achieve this common interest. Since any gain goes to everyone in the group, those who contribute nothing to the effort will get just as much as those who made a contribution. It pays to "let George do it," but George has little or no incentive to do anything in the group interest either, so (in the absence of factors that are completely left out of the conceptions mentioned in the first paragraph) there will be little, if any, group action. The paradox, then, is that (in the absence of special arrangements or circumstances to which we shall turn later) large groups, at least if they are composed of rational individuals, will *not* act in their group interest.

This paradox is elaborated and set out in a way that lets the reader check every step of the logic in a book I wrote entitled *The Logic of Collective Action*.

* * *

Organizations that provide collective goods to their client groups through political or market action * * * are * * * not supported because of the collective goods they provide, but rather because they have been fortunate enough to find what I have called *selective incentives.* A selective incentive is one that applies selectively to the individuals depending on whether they do or do not contribute to the provision of the collective good.

A selective incentive can be either negative or positive; it can, for example, be a loss or punishment imposed only on those who do *not* help provide the collective good. Tax payments are, of course, obtained with the help of negative selective incentives, since those who are found not to have paid their taxes must then suffer both taxes and penalties. The best-known type of organized interest group in modern democratic societies, the labor union, is also usually supported, in part, through negative selective incentives. Most of the dues in strong unions are obtained through union shop, closed shop, or agency shop arrangements which make dues paying more or less compulsory and automatic. There are often also informal arrangements with the same effect; David McDonald, former president of the United Steel Workers of America, describes one of these arrangements used in the early history of that union. It was, he writes, a technique

> which we called . . . visual education, which was a high-sounding label for a practice much more accurately described as dues picketing. It worked very simply. A group of dues-paying members, selected by the district director (usually more for their size than their tact) would stand at the plant gate with pick handles or baseball bats in hand and confront each worker as he arrived for his shift.

As McDonald's "dues picketing" analogy suggests, picketing during strikes is another negative selective incentive that unions sometimes need; although picketing in industries with established and stable unions is usually peaceful, this is because the union's capacity to close down an enterprise against which it has called a strike is clear to all; the early phase of unionization often involves a great deal of violence on the part of both unions and anti-union employers and scabs.

* * *

Positive selective incentives, although easily overlooked, are also commonplace, as diverse examples in *The Logic* demonstrate. American farm organizations offer prototypical examples. Many of the members of the stronger American farm organizations are members because their dues payments are automatically deducted from the "patronage dividends" of farm cooperatives or are included in the insurance premiums paid to mutual insurance companies associated with the farm organizations. Any number of organizations with urban clients also provide similar positive selective incentives in the form of insurance policies, publications, group air fares, and other private goods made available only to members. The grievance procedures of labor unions usually also offer selective incentives, since the grievances of active members often get most of the attention. The symbiosis between the political power of a lobbying organization and the business institutions associated with it often yields tax or other advantages for the business institution, and the publicity and other information flowing out of the political arm of a movement often generates patterns of preference or trust that make the business activities of the movement more remunerative. The surpluses obtained in such ways in turn provide positive selective incentives that recruit participants for the lobbying efforts.

Small groups, or occasionally large "federal" groups that are made up of many small groups of socially interactive members, have an additional source of both negative and positive selective incentives. Clearly most people value the companionship and respect of those with whom they interact. In modern societies solitary confinement is, apart from the rare death penalty, the harshest legal punishment. The censure or even ostracism of those who fail to bear a share of the burdens of collective action can sometimes be an important selective incentive. An extreme example of this occurs when British unionists refuse to speak to uncooperative colleagues, that is, "send them to Coventry." Similarly, those in a socially interactive group seeking a collective good can give special respect or honor to those who distinguish themselves by their sacrifices in the interest of the group and thereby offer them a positive selective incentive. Since most people apparently prefer relatively like-minded or agreeable and respectable company, and often prefer to associate with those whom they especially admire, they may find it costless to shun those who shirk the collective action and to favor those who over-subscribe.

Social selective incentives can be powerful and inexpensive, but they are available only in certain situations. As I have already indicated, they have little applicability to large groups, except in those cases in which the large groups can be federations of small groups that are capable of social interaction. It also is not possible to organize most large groups in need of a collective good into small, socially interactive subgroups, since most individuals do not have the time needed to maintain a huge number of friends and acquaintances.

The availability of social selective incentives is also limited by the social heterogeneity of some of the groups or categories that would benefit from a collective good. Everyday observation reveals that most socially interactive groups are fairly homogeneous and that many people resist extensive social interaction with those they deem to have lower status or greatly different tastes. Even Bohemian or other nonconformist groups often are made up of individuals who are similar to one another, however much they differ from the rest of society. Since some of the categories of individuals who would benefit from a collective good are socially heterogeneous, the social interaction needed for selective incentives sometimes cannot be arranged even when the number of individuals involved is small.

* * *

In short, the political entrepreneurs who attempt to organize collective action will accordingly be more likely to succeed if they strive to organize relatively homogeneous groups. The political managers whose task it is to maintain organized or collusive action similarly will be motivated to use indoctrination and selective recruitment to increase the homogeneity of their client groups. This is true in part because social selective incentives are more likely to be available to the more nearly homogeneous groups, and in part because homogeneity will help achieve consensus.

Information and calculation about a collective good is often itself a collective good. Consider a typical member of a large organization who is deciding how much time to devote to studying the policies or leadership of the organization. The more time the member devotes to this matter, the greater the likelihood that his or her voting and advocacy will favor effective policies and leadership for the organization. This typical member will, however, get only a small share of the gain from the more effective policies and leadership: in the aggregate, the other members will get almost all the gains, so that the individual member does not have an incentive to devote nearly as much time to fact-finding and thinking about the organization as would be in the group interest. Each of the members of the group would be better off if they all could be coerced into spending more time finding out how to vote to make the organization best further their interests. This is dramatically evident in the case of the typical voter in a national election in a large country. The gain to such a voter from studying issues and candidates until it is clear what vote is truly in his or her interest is given by the difference in the value to the individual of the "right" election outcome as compared with the "wrong" outcome, *multiplied by the probability a change in the individual's vote will alter the outcome of the election.* Since the probability that a typical voter will change the outcome of the election is vanishingly small, the typical citizen is usually "rationally ignorant" about public affairs. Often, information about public affairs is so interesting or entertaining that it pays to acquire it for these reasons alone—this appears to be the single most important source of exceptions to the generalization that *typical* citizens are rationally ignorant about public affairs.

Individuals in a few special vocations can receive considerable rewards in private goods if they acquire exceptional knowledge of public goods. Politicians, lobbyists, journalists, and social scientists, for example, may earn more money, power, or prestige from knowledge of this or that public business. Occasionally, exceptional knowledge of public policy can generate exceptional profits in stock exchanges or other markets. Withal, the typical citizen will find that his or her income and life chances will not be improved by zealous study of public affairs, or even of any single collective good.

The limited knowledge of public affairs is in turn necessary to explain the effectiveness of lobbying. If all citizens had obtained and digested all pertinent information, they could not then be swayed by advertising or other persuasion. With perfectly informed citizens, elected officials would not be subject to the blandishments of lobbyists, since the constituents would then know if their interests were betrayed and defeat the unfaithful representative at the next election. Just as lobbies provide collective goods to special-interest groups, so their effectiveness is explained by the imperfect knowledge of citizens, and this in turn is due mainly to the fact that information and calculation about collective goods is also a collective good.

* * *

The fact that the typical individual does not have an incentive to spend much time studying many of his choices concerning collective goods also helps to explain some otherwise inexplicable individual contributions toward the provision of collective goods. The logic of collective action that has been described in this chapter is not immediately apparent to those who have never studied it; if it were, there would be nothing paradoxical in the argument with which this chapter opened, and students to whom the argument is explained would not react with initial skepticism. No doubt the practical implications of this logic for the individual's own choices were often discerned before the logic was ever set out in print, but this does not mean that they were always understood even at the intuitive and practical level. In particular, when the costs of individual contributions to collective action are very small, the individual has little incentive to investigate whether or not to make a contribution or even to exercise intuition. If the individual knows the costs of a contribution to collective action in the interest of a group of which he is a part are trivially small, he may rationally not take the trouble to consider whether the gains are smaller still. This is particularly the case since the size of these gains and the policies that would maximize them are matters about which it is usually not rational for him to investigate.

This consideration of the costs and benefits of calculation about public goods leads to the testable prediction that voluntary contributions toward the provision of collective goods for large groups without selective incentives will often occur when the costs of the individual contributions are negligible, but that they will *not* often occur when the costs of the individual contributions are considerable. In other words, when the costs of individual action to help to obtain a desired collective good are small enough, the result is indeterminate and sometimes goes one way and sometimes the other, but when the costs get larger this indeterminacy disappears. We should accordingly find that more than a few people are willing to take the moment of time needed to sign petitions for causes they support, or to express their opinions in the course of discussion, or to vote for the candidate or party they prefer. Similarly, if the argument here is correct, we should not find many instances where individuals voluntarily contribute substantial sums of resources year after year for the purpose of obtaining some collective good for some large group of which they are a part. Before parting with a large amount of money or time, and particularly before doing so repeatedly, the rational individual will reflect on what this considerable sacrifice will accomplish. If the individual is a typical individual in a large group that would benefit from a collective good, his contribution will not make a perceptible difference in the amount that is provided. The theory here predicts that such contributions become less likely the larger the contribution at issue.

Even when contributions are costly enough to elicit rational calculation, there is still one set of circumstances in which collective action can occur without selective incentives. This set of circumstances becomes evident the moment we think of situations in which there are only a few individuals or firms that would benefit from collective action. Suppose there are two firms of equal size in an industry and no other firms can enter the industry. It still will be the case that a higher price for the industry's product will benefit both firms and that legislation favorable to the industry will help both firms. The higher price and the favorable legislation are then collective goods to this "oligopolistic" industry, even though there are only two in the group that benefit from the collective goods. Obviously, each of the oligopolists is in a situation in which if it restricts output to raise the industry price, or lobbies for favorable legislation for the industry, it will tend to get half of the benefit. And the cost-benefit ratio of action in the common interest easily could be so favorable that, even though a firm bears the whole cost of its action and gets only half the benefit of this action, it could still profit from acting in the common interest. Thus if the group that would benefit from collective action is sufficiently small and the cost-benefit ratio of collective action for the group sufficiently favorable, there may well be calculated action in the collective interest even without selective incentives.

* * *

Untypical as my example of equal-sized firms may be, it makes the general point intuitively obvious: other things being equal, *the larger the number of individuals or firms that would benefit from a collective good, the smaller the share of the gains from action in the group interest that will accrue to the individual or firm that undertakes the action. Thus, in the absence of selective incentives, the incentive for group action diminishes as group size increases, so that large groups are less able to act in their common interest than small ones.* If an additional individual or firm that would value the collective good enters the scene, then the share of the gains from group-oriented action that anyone already in the group might take must diminish. This holds true whatever the relative sizes or valuations of the collective good in the group.

* * *

The significance of the logic that has just been set out can best be seen by comparing groups that would have the same net gain from collective action, if they could engage in it, but that vary in size. Suppose there are a million individuals who would gain a thousand dollars each, or a billion in the aggregate, if they were to organize effectively and engage in collective action that had a total cost of a hundred million. If the logic set out above is right, they could not organize or engage in effective collective action without selective incentives. Now suppose that, although the total gain of a billion dollars from collective action and the aggregate cost of a hundred million remain the same, the group is composed instead of five big corporations or five organized municipalities, each of which would gain two hundred million. Collective action is not an absolute certainty even in this case, since each of the five could conceivably expect others to put up the hundred million and hope to gain the collective good worth two hundred million at no cost at all. Yet collective action, perhaps after some delays due to bargaining, seems very likely indeed. In this case any one of the five would gain a hundred million from providing the collective good even if it had to pay the whole cost itself; and the costs of bargaining among five would not be great, so they would sooner or later probably work out an agreement providing for the collective action. The numbers in this example are arbitrary, but roughly similar situations occur often in reality, and the contrast between "small" and "large" groups could be illustrated with an infinite number of diverse examples.

The significance of this argument shows up in a second way if one compares the operations of lobbies or cartels within jurisdictions of vastly different scale, such as a modest municipality on the one hand and a big country on the other. Within the town, the mayor or city council may be influenced by, say, a score of petitioners or a lobbying budget of a thousand dollars. A particular line of business may be in the hands of only a few firms, and if the town is distant enough from other markets only these few would need to agree to create a cartel. In a big country, the resources needed to influence the national government are likely to be much more substantial, and unless the firms are (as they sometimes are) gigantic, many of them would have to cooperate to create an effective cartel. Now suppose that the million individuals in our large group in the previous paragraph were spread out over a hundred thousand towns or jurisdictions, so that each jurisdiction had ten of them, along with the same proportion of citizens in other categories as before. Suppose also that the cost-benefit ratios remained the same, so that there was still a billion dollars to gain across all jurisdictions or ten thousand in each, and that it would still cost a hundred million dollars across all jurisdictions or a thousand in each. It no longer seems out of the question that in many jurisdictions the groups of ten, or subsets of them, would put up the thousand-dollar total needed to get the thousand for each individual. Thus we see that, if all else were equal, small jurisdictions would have more collective action per capita than large ones.

Differences in intensities of preference generate a third type of illustration of the logic at issue. A small number of zealots anxious for a particular collective good are more likely to act collectively to obtain that good than a larger number with the same aggregate willingness to pay. Suppose there are twenty-five individuals, each of whom finds a given collective good worth a thousand dollars in one case, whereas in another there are five thousand, each of whom finds the collective good worth five dollars. Obviously, the argument indicates that there would be a greater likelihood of collective action in the former case than in the latter, even though the aggregate demand for the collective good is the same in both. The great historical significance of small groups of fanatics no doubt owes something to this consideration.

The argument in this chapter predicts that those groups that have access to selective incentives will be more likely to act collectively to obtain collective goods than those that do not, and that smaller groups will have a greater likelihood of engaging in collective action than larger ones. The empirical portions of *The Logic* show that this prediction has been correct for the United States.

* * *

Discussion Questions

1. Besides the size of a group, what other considerations do you think would play a role in people's decision to join a collective endeavor? Are you convinced that the size of a group is as important as Olson argues?
2. Think of your own decisions to join or not join a group. Have you ever been a "free rider?" For example, have there been protests against tuition increases at your school that you supported but did not participate in? If so, what would it have taken to get you to join?
3. If Olson is right, would Tocqueville's view (see article 57 in this book) about the role of groups in overcoming the potential tyranny of the majority need to be modified?

Debating the Issues: Donor Disclosure—Is Anonymous Campaign Funding a Problem?

The First Amendment of the U.S. Constitution says that "Congress shall make no law . . . abridging the freedom of speech." The Supreme Court must define the boundaries of what that broad prohibition means. Does it apply to pornography? To commercial speech? To speech that advocates the overthrow of the government or incites violence? Political advertising and campaign spending similarly generate a difficult set of questions. In its rulings, the Court has equated the use of money in campaigns with speech. In other words, money facilitates the making and spreading of messages. Supporting a candidate with a contribution is making a statement, and is thus speech, and the money itself helps the candidate speak through advertisements and other means. Spending independently to promote a candidate or message and not giving the money directly to a candidate is similarly a kind of speech—spending the money allows you to distribute the message. The Court has recognized a government interest in promoting fair elections that are free from corruption, so it has determined that some regulation of campaign finance is warranted. But the question is where to draw the line between activity that is permissible and that which is prohibited.

In its January 2010 decision in *Citizens United v. Federal Election Commission* (FEC), the Supreme Court decided that the First Amendment protects the right of non-profit and for-profit corporations and labor unions to spend directly to run ads calling for the election or defeat of a candidate in political campaigns, rather than having to set up political action committees (PACs). Political action committees must raise donations that they then either contribute directly to candidates and parties or spend independently to send a campaign message. The Court decision said that corporations and unions could bypass PACs and spend directly from their treasuries to speak on matters of interest to their organizations, including who they believe would be preferable candidates to elect. The amounts they could spend to support these messages, so long as they were not giving the money directly to a candidate or party, were not limited. The premise in the Court's decision was that the risk of the corrupting influence of money is most powerful when the money is going directly to a candidate or party's campaign coffers, not when an organization is spending money to transmit a message independently. *Citizens United* and subsequent lower court rulings and Federal Election Commission decisions also paved the way for so-called Suped PACs, which can collect unlimited donations so long as they spend the money independently—for example, on TV ads—and did not contribute it to a candidate or party. For the most part, donors, including to Super PACs, must be named and submitted in federal campaign finance reports.

In the years since these decisions, debate has flared over campaign donations and spending that do not require disclosure of those spending or contributing the funds. Proponents of disclosure such as the Campaign Legal Center in this chapter note that although most funding must be disclosed, the amount that is undisclosed, often referred to as "dark money," is also significant. Their chief arguments are that voters have a right to know who is speaking through these funds and that non-disclosure increases the risk of corrupt activity and influence. Proponents of anonymous (un-disclosed) speech, such as Jon Riches of the Goldwater Institute in this chapter, who believe anonymous speech (including the provision of funds in campaigns) should be protected, say the issue is simple: we should care more about the message than who is delivering it. Supporters of this view note the prevalence of anonymous speech during the American Revolution. Better for democracy that the ideas be heard and voters can then decide. Moreover, it can sometimes be risky if one's support for particular causes is revealed. They point to Brendan Eich, the widely respected inventor of Javascript, who resigned under pressure as CEO of Mozilla in 2014 for a $1,000 donation he had made eight years earlier supporting California's Proposition 8, which prohibited same-sex marriage. Supporters of anonymous speech say that because government officials take actions and make decisions that affect the livelihood of organizations and individuals, these organizations and individuals must be able to spend funds in campaigns—maybe even to defeat these officials—without fear of reprisal. They worry that disclosure databases, rather than being of everyday use to voters, provide a tool for government officials and other powerful political figures to monitor their supporters and opponents.

60

"Why Our Democracy Needs Disclosure"

Campaign Legal Center

The disclosure of political spending has become a hot-button issue as many of those seeking to buy influence and sway election results with million-dollar checks would prefer to do it anonymously. The individuals and corporations writing the checks know they're doing it and so do the politicians that benefit. Only the public is left in the dark in this equation and that is a serious threat to our democracy. The amount of misinformation out there about disclosure is staggering, so the Legal Center has produced a primer on the topic to help separate the fact from the fiction.

Q: Why is disclosure of election-related fundraising and spending important?

A: Disclosure of money raised spent in elections has been the bedrock of our political system for many years, usually supported by all political parties. Voters deserve to know who is funding political communications in order to evaluate the full context of the message. Citizens need to know who has spent money to elect or defeat officials in order to hold those officeholders accountable and prevent corruption.

Justice Kennedy, in the only portion of last year's *Citizens United* opinion that had the support of eight of the nine Justices, noted the importance of disclosing the sources of campaign spending. He wrote that disclosure "provide[s] the electorate with information," makes sure "that voters are fully informed about the person or group who is speaking," and ensures people are "able to evaluate the arguments to which they are being subjected."

Justice Kennedy explained further: "The First Amendment protects political speech, and disclosure permits citizens and shareholders to react to the speech of corporate entities in a proper way. The transparency enables the electorate to make informed decisions and give proper weight to different speakers and messages." He also went on to say: "With the advent of the Internet, prompt disclosure of expenditures can provide shareholders and citizens with the information needed to hold corporations and elected officials accountable for their positions and supporters. Shareholders can determine whether their corporation's political speech advances the corporation's interest in making profits, and citizens can see whether elected officials are 'in the pocket' of so-called moneyed interests."

Justice Kennedy presumed that disclosure would serve as a check on potential misuse of independent expenditures, saying "[i]f elected officials succumb to improper influences from independent expenditures; if they surrender their best judgment; and if they put expediency before principle, then surely there is cause for concern."

Justice Scalia also made a forceful defense of election-related disclosure last year in a concurring opinion in *Doe v. Reed*. In that case, which upheld disclosure requirements for petition signers for ballot measures, Justice Scalia wrote: "Requiring people to stand up in public for their political acts fosters civic courage, without which democracy is doomed."

Q: What do you mean when you say disclosure?

A: Disclosure means shining a light on the money that is raised and spent to influence our elections. It should be clear who is paying for a TV advertisement or a piece of mail and where their money comes from. Already, candidates for federal office have to file reports detailing how much money they raised, where it came from, and what they spent it on. When they run an ad on TV or on the radio, the candidate has to personally state that they approved the message in the ad. Tens of millions of dollars were spent in 2010 on ads paid for by groups that reveal nothing about their donors. Far more of this undisclosed spending is anticipated in 2012.

Q: Why worry about disclosure? I thought most donations come from small donors.

A: Even in 2008, when more individuals donated to campaigns than ever before, only 12 percent of the money in congressional candidates' coffers came from small donations from individuals. That figure represents only a fraction of the total money spent on federal elections. The floodgates that the Supreme Court opened in *Citizens United* allow unlimited corporate and union money to drown out the voices of individual donors like never before. And without robust disclosure laws, the powerful interests behind that money remain in the shadows. Some groups have admitted receiving donations of tens of millions of dollars from one source—and many other large donations to elect or defeat candidates through these "outside" groups are completely hidden.

Q: Does disclosure really provide voters with useful information?

A: Full disclosure of the money in politics provides voters with information that is critical to holding representatives accountable through elections. In order to make that accountability meaningful, voters need to know if their elected officials will answer to them or to corporations, unions, and wealthy donors who pay for the advertisements that flood the airways. When special interest groups can spend large amounts of money while hidden in the shadows, it becomes easier for them to threaten political retribution to lawmakers who don't vote their way. Stronger disclosure laws will make clear the role that special interests play in our elections and will ensure that voters have all of the facts when they go to the polls.

It is also important for voters to know who is paying for the ads bombarding them, because voters will find some sources more "trustworthy" than others. Members of the NRA or the Brady Campaign to Prevent Gun Violence, or any citizen, will have different views about the reliability of an ad if they know that a pro- or anti-gun group paid for it. Ads about cigarette taxes may be seen as more or less reliable if you know they were paid for by tobacco companies or anti-smoking groups.

Q: I thought the Citizens United *decision means corporations and labor unions can spend what they want on elections without disclosing where the money comes from.*

A: No—in fact, *Citizens United* said the opposite. Eight Justices agreed that organizations attempting to influence our elections should be required to disclose their spending and contributors, and agreed that disclosure should include the funder of communications that discuss candidates in the midst of an election, and not merely those that expressly advocate for a candidate's election or defeat.

Q: So if Congress passed landmark campaign finance legislation ten years ago, and the Supreme Court has upheld disclosure requirements by an 8–1 margin, why don't we have effective disclosure now?

A: Simple—the Federal Election Commission (FEC) subverted the disclosure law that Congress wrote and that the Supreme Court upheld with a little-noticed "interpretation of law" that virtually gutted the its effectiveness.

The McCain-Feingold campaign finance law passed by Congress and signed by President Bush in 2002 specified that disclosure is required of *all* persons who contributed $1,000 or more to groups running "electioneering communications"—the ads that flood the airwaves in the weeks before an election. But the FEC's interpretation required disclosure only of persons who contributed $1,000 or more expressly "for the purpose of furthering electioneering communications." The agency explained that disclosure is only required if the contribution is "*specifically designated* for [electioneering communications] by the donor." In other words, a donor can evade disclosure simply by contributing to the organization for general purposes and refraining from designating their money for political ads.

Q: Why is it a problem if only contributions designated for election activity have to be disclosed? Wouldn't that mean all contributions used to fund these new ads are reported?

A: Unfortunately, the FEC's enforcement of its own "interpretation of law," described above, has made it *even easier* for groups to keep the source of their campaign funds hidden in the shadows. Just a few months after the Supreme Court's overwhelming affirmance of disclosure requirements in *Citizens United*, the FEC ignored the recommendation of its general counsel and dismissed a complaint that a group called "Freedom's Watch" had violated the law when it spent more than $125,000 on a political ad without disclosing donors. In dismissing the complaint, the three Republican Commissioners narrowed the interpretation of the disclosure law even further—to require disclosure of contributions only if the donor specifies that their money should go to a *particular ad*. Since it is almost never the case that someone donates money to fund a specific ad—indeed, generally the ads are not created until after the money is raised—the FEC has neutered the disclosure law passed by Congress in 2002.

Q: What sort of secret spending is occurring?

A: Although candidates and some political organizations have to disclose information about their contributors and spending, many groups that work to influence elections do not. Corporations, unions, and non-profits can spend millions of dollars to support or oppose a candidate and the public will never know where that money is coming from. The newest and most troubling vehicles for this secret money are the new organizations with deliberately nondescript names like "Crossroads GPS" and "Priorities USA." They accept unlimited amounts of money from business corporations, labor unions, and the über-wealthy without ever disclosing their donors. The public has no way of knowing who really is spending money to influence their vote.

Q: Does disclosure violate the First Amendment?

A: Absolutely not. To the contrary, the Supreme Court has held that disclosure advances the public's First Amendment right to information. Disclosure empowers Americans to evaluate the people and organizations that are trying to influence their vote and to exercise that vote effectively.

Q: Some say that disclosure stifles free speech—is that true?

A: The Supreme Court has consistently upheld as constitutional candidate election-related disclosure laws, except where someone has shown specific evidence that disclosure of their name will result in *threats, harassment, or reprisals.* As recently as *Citizens United,* the Court held that the challenged federal disclosure requirement did not "impose a chill on speech or expression."

In the landmark 1976 case *Buckley v. Valeo,* the Supreme Court upheld blanket disclosure requirements and suggested that if contributors could give courts facts that show, for example, "specific evidence of past or present harassment," or a "pattern of threats or specific manifestations of public hostility," they might qualify for an exemption from disclosure requirements. But the Court has granted those exemptions when the facts of a case show that a speaker has been threatened with bodily harm. For example, in separate Supreme Court cases, the NAACP and the Socialist Workers Party were exempted from disclosure requirements after proving to the courts that their members would be subject to serious threats and bodily harm. The FEC has a similar procedure in place to exempt groups that can show that disclosure presents a personal risk.

Q: What about a right to anonymous speech?

A: There is no right to anonymous speech when an organization is trying to influence the outcome of a candidate's election. The Supreme Court has explicitly rejected "[t]he existence of a generalized right of anonymity in speech." After all, as Justice Stevens wrote for the Supreme Court in *City of Ladue v. Gilleo,* "the identity of the speaker is an important component of many attempts to persuade." In order for citizens to make informed choices when they go to the polls, they should know who has been trying to persuade them to vote one way or the other.

Q: Is campaign finance disclosure a partisan issue?

A: It should not be. Campaign finance reforms have historically passed with bipartisan support. Requiring disclosure of contributors to 527 organizations passed with overwhelming bipartisan support in 2000 when our elections were threatened with huge waves of secret spending. Congressional leaders like Speaker John Boehner, House Majority Leader Eric Cantor, and even Senate Majority Leader Mitch McConnell have in the past voiced their support for increased transparency and disclosure of political contributions. However, in the last Congress, the DISCLOSE Act became a partisan issue, with Republicans claiming they were kept out of the drafting and that the bill contained provisions that favored Democrats and unions. Democrats said they could not find Republican members willing to participate in drafting the bill.

Q: Why is support for disclosure so critical now?

A: We are at a unique moment in the relationship of money and politics. The FEC, created after the Watergate scandal and tasked with enforcing campaign finance laws, has become deadlocked and unable to perform its functions and ensure disclosure of money spent in federal elections. At the same time, the *Citizens United* decision has unleashed a torrent of unidentifiable but generously funded spending on our elections. The opponents of disclosure have been emboldened by victories on other campaign finance issues and are launching an assault on the decades-old disclosure laws that safeguard our elections. The basic principle that voters should have the information they need to make an informed choice in the voting booth is under attack by wealthy special interests.

61

"The Victims of 'Dark Money' Disclosure"

JON RICHES

The Dangers of Disclosure

Proponents of government-mandated disclosure have set forth several arguments for compelling private charitable organizations to disclose their donors. Those arguments range from the wrong but perhaps well-intentioned to the nefarious. In any event, the strongest arguments for government reporting are easily eclipsed by the dangers of disclosure. On the soft end of the spectrum are those government reporting advocates who claim they are not seeking to prevent speech, but only to inform the public of who is speaking. On the hard end of the spectrum are partisan political operatives who wish to use disclosure mandates to silence opposing views. As Arshad Hasan, executive director of the anti-privacy group ProgressNow put it, "The next step for us is to take down this network of institutions that are state-based in each and every one of our states." A similar sentiment was echoed by the sponsor of the DISCLOSE Act, the federal bill that would have mandated greater disclosure by nonprofit organizations, when he candidly proclaimed," the deterrent effect on [political speech] should not be underestimated." Regardless of motive, the dangers of disclosure are far outweighed by any putative benefits.

Private association is a fundamental part of our nation's history and underpins a free society. Mandatory disclosure undermines core values that are essential for free speech and thus representative democracy. Specifically, mandatory disclosure: (1) prevents public discourse from focusing on the message, rather than the messenger; (2) allows for retaliation against speakers by those who disagree, particularly for minority opinions or when speaking truth to power; and (3) muddles regulations so that no one knows what speech is permitted and what is not, thus further chilling speech. Even assuming mandatory disclosure achieves its ostensible goals, an assumption that research does not appear to support, the costs of disclosure are simply too high.

Anonymous Speech Keeps Marketplace of Ideas Focused on the Message

Anonymous speech is an essential component of free speech, which is an essential component of representative democracy. One of the most important features of anonymous speech is that it focuses the dialogue on the message and issue, rather than the speaker. This is invaluable and irreplaceable in literary, social, and political dialogue. As the U.S. Supreme Court recognized in *Talley v. California*, "Anonymous pamphlets, leaflets, brochures and even books have played an important role in the progress of mankind."

Indeed, the ratification debate of our own Constitution was argued primarily under the pseudonym "Publius." The actual authors, Alexander Hamilton, James Madison, and John Jay, feared that their arguments would be eclipsed by *ad hominem* attacks had the papers not been published anonymously. At the time of ratification, Alexander Hamilton in particular was subject to personal attacks because of his foreign birth and perceived links to the British Crown. As one author noted, "Hamilton's anonymity meant to avoid prejudice and preclude obfuscation of his message, and these interests are still compelling justifications for speaking anonymously." Similarly, although a less controversial character, given the regional rivalries of the time, James Madison's Virginian roots would have made New Yorkers suspicious of his arguments had they been penned in his own name. Given these realities, an objective assessment of the U.S. Constitution would have been much less likely had it not been for anonymous political speech in the *Federalist Papers*. Put simply, the Constitution may never have been ratified had it not been for anonymous political speech.

The *Federalist Papers* are also instructive for another reason. In *Citizens United v. FCC*, writing for the majority, Justice Kennedy cited to James Madison's *Federalist* 10 in observing that factions will necessarily exist in our republic, "but the remedy of destroying the liberty of some factions is worse than the disease." Justice Kennedy went on to observe, "Factions should be checked by permitting them all to speak . . . and by entrusting the people to judge what is true and what is false." In our republic, citizens should be trusted to judge the value of the speech, irrespective of the speaker. Competing arguments ought to be weighed on their merits. Indeed, even under the most ideal circumstances, the value of government reporting mandates is negligible when the *content* of the speech, rather than its *source*, is the primary consideration in evaluating the strength of competing arguments, particularly in the political context. How many Americans are tired of *ad hominem* attacks on and by political actors, divorced from their positions on political issues? How worn is the country by character assassinations perpetrated by political campaigns? Is there not a yearning for dialogue that is above the caliber of gossip columns? Unfortunately, disclosure mandates drive political dialogue in the opposite direction. The result, as Madison and Justice Kennedy observed, is a "remedy" worse than the "disease" and an affront to the sensibilities of free people who should be entrusted to weigh the value of free speech.

The value of anonymous speech is not limited to purely political dialogue. Authors of literary works as well as editorials and news articles have long published anonymously or under assumed names. Lewis Carroll published anonymously to maintain his privacy. George Orwell wrote under a pen name because he was embarrassed of his early poverty. Both Charlotte and Emily Brontë published their classics under pseudonyms to avoid the significant gender biases of the time. Other authors may do so out of fear of economic or social retaliation. As the U.S. Supreme Court recognized in *McIntyre*, "Whatever the motivation may be, at least in the field of literary endeavor, the interest in having anonymous works enter the marketplace of ideas unquestionably outweighs any public interest in requiring disclosure as a condition of entry."

The same is true of the news media. Reporters routinely rely on anonymous sources to reveal major and significant newsworthy events. For example, the identity of Bob Woodward's and Carl Bernstein's primary source, Deep Throat, who provided information on the Nixon Administration's involvement in the Watergate scandal was not revealed until

2005—over 30 years after President Nixon resigned. Indeed, reporters have faced incarceration for refusing to reveal their anonymous sources, even during national security investigations. These reporters reason, correctly, that anonymous speech often encourages truthful reporting, particularly from those who fear retaliation or retribution for speaking.

In addition to news reporting, every major newspaper in the country continues to publish anonymous editorials and commentary pieces. It can hardly be argued that media reports and truth in reporting are not tremendously important public values. But imagine a law that compelled the disclosure of news sources who choose to be anonymous or mandated that every newspaper editorial include a byline—and the names of every stockholder in the media corporation that owns the newspaper. The outrage would be swift and justified. The same should be true in the context of donor disclosure to nonprofit organizations—and for the same reasons. The real value of free speech is in the message, not the messenger, and the dangers of disclosure far outweigh any supposed benefits. One of the most significant such dangers is preventing retaliation against speakers who choose to be anonymous by those who disagree, particularly when speaking truth to power.

Anonymous Speech Prevents Retaliation, Especially When Speaking Truth to Power

Writing for the majority in *Talley v. California*, Justice Black wrote, "Persecuted groups and sects from time to time throughout history have been able to criticize oppressive practices and laws either anonymously or not at all." Political actors have routinely sought the identities of speakers with whom they disagree in order to harass, humiliate, and ultimately silence them.

During the Civil Rights era, for example, the Alabama attorney general sought to compel the National Association for the Advancement of Colored People ("NAACP") to turn over the names and addresses of all of its members to the state. This act of force and intimidation was fortunately rebuffed by the U.S. Supreme Court as a violation of the NAACP's and its members' First Amendment rights.

Even staunch advocates for free speech, such as John Adams, could not help using the power of government to silence critics, when, in 1798, he signed the Sedition Act. That statute made it a federal crime to "write, print, utter or publish . . . any false, scandalous and malicious writing or writings against the government of the United States." Of course, Adams punished such criminal acts only if their "scandalous" writings "pertained to him or his allies." Unfortunately, judicial review had yet to be established in 1798. Had it been, perhaps Mr. Adams would have received an admonishment from the Supreme Court, such as the one that echoed over two centuries later in *Citizens United*:

> When Government seeks to use its full power, including the criminal law, to command where a person may get his or her information or what distrusted source he or she may not hear, it uses censorship to control thought. This is unlawful. The First Amendment confirms the freedom to think for ourselves.

Unfortunately, efforts to compel disclosure in order to silence critics continue today. These include threats from government bureaucrats, like we saw when Dina Galassini tried to organize some friends and neighbors to oppose a local bond measure in Fountain Hills, Arizona. They include threats from other citizens, such as when Margie Christoffersen lost her job as a restaurant manager after her $100 donation to the campaign to ban gay marriage in California became public. And perhaps most ominously, these include threats from those wielding law enforcement authority, like the controversial Arizona sheriff, Joe Arpaio, who has jailed journalists critical of his office as well as political opponents. As the U.S. Supreme Court has long recognized, public disclosure of donations undoubtedly discourages political participation and exposes contributors to harassment and retaliation. Anonymous speech protected by the First Amendment has been the one barrier to prevent these abuses.

Regulatory Labyrinths Chill Free Speech

In order for opportunities for robust and free speech to be open to every speaker—not just the sophisticated or well-connected—the rules of the road must be simple and clear. Citizens and citizens groups must know what is permissible and what is impermissible, so they can steer their conduct accordingly. This is, in fact, a constitutional precept that negates vague and overbroad laws, particularly in the context of the First Amendment. Unfortunately, in the area of campaign finance law and mandatory donor disclosure, the rules of the road can be anything but simple and clear. Regulations are so often muddled that the average speaker does not know what is permissible and what is not. The unfortunate and inevitable result is less speech.

The U.S. Supreme Court in *Citizens United* recognized the importance of simplicity and clarity in the context of campaign finance speech restrictions:

> The First Amendment does not permit laws that force speakers to retain a campaign finance attorney, conduct demographic marketing research, or seek declaratory rulings before discussing the most salient political issues of our day. Prolix laws chill speech for the same reason that vague laws chill speech: People of common intelligence must necessarily guess at [the law's] meaning and differ as to its application.

A recent law review article provided one example of a small group of concerned citizens in a rural county who wanted to run a message about an environmental policy to illustrate how average Americans might get caught in the morass of campaign finance restrictions. The authors estimated that in order to form a political action committee to comply with federal election law, an average issue group would likely have to spend $9,000 in legal fees and ongoing compliance costs of $2,800. This expense alone makes political advocacy for most Americans cost-prohibitive.

Even more dangerous is the possibility that citizens who do choose to speak will get ensnared in the complexities of campaign finance restrictions. Dina Galassini had firsthand experience with this when Fountain Hills labeled her efforts to e-mail friends and organize a street protest a "political committee." The predictable result was that Ms. Galassini was scared her grassroots efforts were illegal, and she ceased her communications. As the U.S. Supreme Court observed, "As a practical matter . . . given the complexity of the regulations and the deference courts show to administrative determinations, a speaker who wants to avoid threats of criminal liability and the heavy costs of defending against FEC enforcement must ask a governmental agency for prior permission to speak." This acts as a prior-restraint on communication, the effect of which is to prevent speech—an outcome that is anathema to the First Amendment. Moreover, as the Court forecast in a FEC enforcement case, "Faced with the need to assume a more sophisticated organizational form, to adopt specific accounting procedures, to file periodic detailed reports . . . it would not be surprising if at least some groups decided that the contemplated political activity was simply not worth it."

In this sense, mandatory disclosure laws have the precise effect they were intended to have by many government reporting advocates—they silence opposing views. In his concurring opinion in *Citizens United*, Justice Thomas observed that the intimidation tactics by government reporting advocates have spurred a "cottage industry that uses forcibly disclosed donor information to preempt citizens' exercise of their First Amendment rights." Justice Thomas then cited a *New York Times* article that described a new nonprofit group formed in the run-up to the 2008 elections that "plann[ed] to confront donors to conservative groups, hoping to create a chilling effect that will dry up contributions . . . [by exposing donors to] legal trouble, public exposure, and watchdog groups digging through their lives." This organization's leader described his donor disclosure efforts simply as "going for the jugular."

Cloaked as advocates of greater information and transparency, the enemies of free speech are at the gate. Defenders of the First Amendment must be ready to identify the dangers of donor disclosure and challenge efforts to compel government reporting wherever they occur. The courts should be one such battleground.

DISCUSSION QUESTIONS

1. Supporters of anonymous speech worry about reprisals from government officials or from others who might oppose the political views of a donor. How heavily do you weigh this concern in deciding whether or to what degree to require disclosure of campaign funding?
2. Imagine you hear a campaign advertisement that you fully agree with, but you then find that the major donors sponsoring the ad support many causes that you strongly oppose. Would you be more likely to dismiss the message or to reevaluate your view of the donor? Does your answer affect your views on the value of disclosure?
3. What kinds of disclosure in support of political causes or candidates would you support? All campaign-related funds? Or are there limits you would support? For example, currently donations to federal candidates under $200 do not have to be disclosed. Do you support this threshold? Should it be higher? Lower?
4. There are no disclosure requirements on social media posts, hours spent volunteering, and other ways in which individuals and groups can support a candidate and the issue positions the candidate supports. Campaign funding to support candidates and issues does have extensive, though not complete, disclosure requirements. Is campaign funding inherently different from other forms of political support, or should additional forms of campaign support have mandatory disclosure? Or should none of these activities require disclosure?

PART IV

Public Policy

CHAPTER 13

Government and the Economy

62

"Call for Federal Responsibility"

FRANKLIN ROOSEVELT

The national government has always played a role in the economy. Since the late 1700s, the government has provided property for private development, enforced contracts and prohibited the theft of private property, provided subsidies to encourage the growth of particular industries, developed the infrastructure of the growing country, and regulated trade. The question that commands the attention of political leaders and citizens alike today is what the limits of government involvement in the economy ought to be. To what extent should the free market make most economic decisions to maximize efficiency and productivity? Should the government regulate markets in the pursuit of other goals, such as equality, and to address market failures, such as monopolies and public goods that are underprovided by the market (such as education and environmental protection)?

This debate reached a peak during the Great Depression, as the nation struggled to define the government's role in reviving the economy, and played a critical role in the 1932 presidential election between the Democratic candidate, Franklin Roosevelt, and the Republican president, Herbert Hoover. In the campaign speech printed here, FDR argued that the federal government should play a role in unemployment insurance, housing for the poor, and public-works programs to compensate for the hardship of the Great Depression. Hoover, on the other hand, was very much opposed to altering the relationship between government and the private sector, which was "builded up by 150 years of toil of our fathers." It was the extension of freedom and the exercise of individual initiative, Hoover claimed, that made the American economic system strong and that would gradually bring about economic recovery. Roosevelt prevailed, and the resulting New Deal changed the face of government. Although the federal government adopted a much more active role in regulating the economy and providing social safety, the central issues discussed by Roosevelt and Hoover are still being debated today as President Trump and the Republican Congress attempt to reduce regulations, especially environmental regulations, to promote economic efficiency.

The first principle I would lay down is that the primary duty rests on the community, through local government and private agencies, to take care of the relief of unemployment. But we then come to a situation where there are so many people out of work that local funds are insufficient.

It seems clear to me that the organized society known as the State comes into the picture at this point. In other words, the obligation of government is extended to the next higher unit.

I [practice] what I preach. In 1930 the state of New York greatly increased its employment service and kept in close touch with the ability of localities to take care of their own unemployed. But by the summer of 1931 it became apparent to me that actual state funds and a state-supervised system were imperative.

I called a special session of the legislature, and they appropriated a fund of $20 million for unemployment relief, this fund to be reimbursed to the state through the doubling of our income taxes. Thus the state of New York became the first among all the states to accept the definite obligation of supplementing local funds where these local funds were insufficient.

The administration of this great work has become a model for the rest of the country. Without setting up any complex machinery or any large overhead, the state of New York is working successfully through local agencies, and, in spite of the fact that over a million people are out of work and in need of aid in this one state alone, we have so far met at least the bare necessities of the case.

This past spring the legislature appropriated another $5 million, and on November 8 the voters will pass on a $30 million bond issue to tide us over this winter and at least up to next summer.

* * *

I am very certain that the obligation extends beyond the states and to the federal government itself, if and when it becomes apparent that states and communities are unable to take care of the necessary relief work.

It may interest you to have me read a short quotation from my message to the legislature in 1931:

> What is the State? It is the duly constituted representative of an organized society of human beings, created by them for their mutual protection and well-being. One of the duties of the State is that of caring for those of its citizens who find themselves the victims of such adverse circumstances as make them unable to obtain even the necessities of mere existence without the aid of others.
>
> In broad terms, I assert that modern society, acting through its government, owes the definite obligation to prevent the starvation or the dire want of any of its fellowmen and women who try to maintain themselves but cannot. To these unfortunate citizens aid must be extended by the government, not as a matter of charity but as a matter of social duty.

That principle which I laid down in 1931, I reaffirm. I not only reaffirm it, I go a step further and say that where the State itself is unable successfully to fulfill this obligation which lies upon it, it then becomes the positive duty of the federal government to step in to help.

In the words of our Democratic national platform, the federal government has a "continuous responsibility for human welfare, especially for the protection of children." That duty and responsibility the federal government should carry out promptly, fearlessly, and generously.

It took the present Republican administration in Washington almost three years to recognize this principle. I have recounted to you in other speeches, and it is a matter of general information, that for at least two years after the crash, the only efforts made by the national administration to cope with the distress of unemployment were to deny its existence.

When, finally, this year, after attempts at concealment and minimizing had failed, it was at last forced to recognize the fact of suffering among millions of unemployed, appropriations of federal funds for assistance to states were finally made.

I think it is fair to point out that a complete program of unemployment relief was on my recommendation actually under way in the state of New York over a year ago; and that in Washington relief funds in any large volume were not provided until this summer, and at that they were pushed through at the demand of Congress rather than through the leadership of the President of the United States.

At the same time, I have constantly reiterated my conviction that the expenditures of cities, states, and the federal government must be reduced in the interest of the nation as a whole. I believe that there are many ways in which such reduction of expenditures can take place, but I am utterly unwilling that economy should be practised at the expense of starving people.

We must economize in other ways, but it shall never be said that the American people have refused to provide the necessities of life for those who, through no fault of their own, are unable to feed, clothe, and house themselves. The first obligation of government is the protection of the welfare and well-being, indeed the very existence, of its citizens.

* * *

The next question asks my attitude toward appropriations for public works as an aid to unemployment. I am perfectly clear as to the principles involved in this case also.

From the long-range point of view it would be advisable for governments of all kinds to set up in times of prosperity what might be called a nest egg to be used for public works in times of depression. That is a policy which we should initiate when we get back to good times.

But there is the immediate possibility of helping the emergency through appropriations for public works. One question, however, must be answered first because of the simple fact that these public works cost money.

We all know that government treasuries, whether local or state or federal, are hard put to it to keep their budgets balanced; and, in the case of the federal Treasury, thoroughly unsound financial policies have made its situation not exactly desperate but at least threatening to future stability if the policies of the present administration are continued.

All public works, including federal, must be considered from the point of view of the ability of the government Treasury to pay for them. There are two ways of paying for public works. One is by the sale of bonds. In principle, such bonds should be issued only to pay for self-sustaining projects or for structures which will without question have a useful life over a long period of years. The other method of payment is from current revenues, which in these days means in most cases added taxes. We all know that there is a very definite limit to the increase of taxes above the present level.

From this point, therefore, I can go on and say that, if funds can be properly provided by the federal government for increased appropriations for public works, we must examine the character of these public works. I have already spoken of that type which is self-sustaining. These should be greatly encouraged. The other type is that of public works which are honestly essential to the community. Each case must rest on its own merits.

It is impossible, for example, to say that all parks or all playgrounds are essential. One may be and another may not be. If a school, for instance, has no playground, it is obvious that the furnishing of a playground is a necessity to the community. But if the school already has a playground and some people seek merely to enlarge it, there may be a very definite question as to how necessary that enlargement is.

Let me cite another example. I am much interested in providing better housing accommodations for the poor in our great cities. If a slum area can be torn down and new modern buildings put up, I should call that almost a human necessity; but, on the other hand, the mere erection of new buildings in some other part of the city while allowing the slums to remain raises at once a question of necessity. I am confident that the federal government working in cooperation with states and cities can do much to carry on increased public works and along lines which are sound from the economic and financial point of view.

Now I come to another question. I am asked whether I favor a system of unemployment insurance reserves made compulsory by the states, supplemented by a system of federally coordinated state employment offices to facilitate the reemployment of jobless workers.

The first part of the question is directly answered by the Democratic platform which advocates unemployment insurance under state laws.

This is no new policy for me. I have advocated unemployment insurance in my own state for some time, and, indeed, last year six Eastern governors were my guests at a conference which resulted in the drawing up of what might be called an idea plan of unemployment insurance.

This type of insurance is not a cure-all but it provides at least a cushion to mitigate unemployment in times of depression. It is sound if, after starting it, we stick to the principle of sound insurance financing. It is only where governments, as in some European countries, have failed to live up to these sound principles that unemployment insurance has been an economic failure.

As to the coordinated employment offices, I can only tell you that I was for the bills sponsored by Senator Wagner of my own state and passed by the Congress. They created a nationally coordinated system of employment offices operated by the individual states with the advisory cooperation of joint boards of employers and employees.

To my very great regret this measure was vetoed by the President of the United States. I am certain that the federal government can, by furnishing leadership, stimulate the various states to set up and coordinate practical, useful systems.

Discussion Questions

1. Franklin Roosevelt's call for a New Deal and the importance of government investment in "public works" as a way of helping the economy get out of the Great Depression and get people back to work sounds very similar to President Trump's call for more investment in the nation's infrastructure. What is the proper role of the government in helping people get jobs? Should this be left to the private sector, or should the national government invest more in building highways, bridges, and airports to get more people back to work?

2. FDR's famous line from this speech is, "The first obligation of every government is the protection of the welfare and well-being, indeed the very existence, of its citizens." Do you agree? If so, how do you define the limits of that obligation?

63

"Against the Proposed New Deal"

HERBERT HOOVER

This campaign is more than a contest between two men. It is more than a contest between two parties. It is a contest between two philosophies of government.

We are told by the opposition that we must have a change, that we must have a new deal. It is not the change that comes from normal development of national life to which I object but the proposal to alter the whole foundations of our national life which have been builded through generations of testing and struggle, and of the principles upon which we have builded the nation. The expressions our opponents use must refer to important changes in our economic and social system and our system of government, otherwise they are nothing but vacuous words. And I realize that in this time of distress many of our people are asking whether our social and economic system is incapable of that great primary function of providing security and comfort of life to all of the firesides of our 25 million homes in America, whether our social system provides for the fundamental development and progress of our people, whether our form of government is capable of originating and sustaining that security and progress.

This question is the basis upon which our opponents are appealing to the people in their fears and distress. They are proposing changes and so-called new deals which would destroy the very foundations of our American system.

Our people should consider the primary facts before they come to the judgment—not merely through political agitation, the glitter of promise, and the discouragement of temporary hardships—whether they will support changes which radically affect the whole system which has been builded up by 150 years of the toil of our fathers. They should not approach the question in the despair with which our opponents would clothe it.

Our economic system has received abnormal shocks during the past three years, which temporarily dislocated its normal functioning. These shocks have in a large sense come from without our borders, but I say to you that our system of government has enabled us to take such strong action as to prevent the disaster which would otherwise have come to our nation. It has enabled us further to develop measures and programs which are now demonstrating their ability to bring about restoration and progress.

We must go deeper than platitudes and emotional appeals of the public platform in the campaign if we will penetrate to the full significance of the changes which our opponents are attempting to float upon the wave of distress and discontent from the difficulties we are passing through. We can find what our opponents would do after searching the record of their appeals to discontent, group and sectional interest. We must search for them in the legislative acts which they sponsored and passed in the Democratic-controlled House of Representatives in the last session of Congress. We must look into measures for which they voted and which were defeated. We must inquire whether or not the presidential and vice-presidential candidates have disavowed these acts. If they have not, we must conclude that they form a portion and are a substantial indication of the profound changes proposed.

And we must look still further than this as to what revolutionary changes have been proposed by the candidates themselves.

We must look into the type of leaders who are campaigning for the Democratic ticket, whose philosophies have been well known all their lives, whose demands for a change in the American system are frank and forceful. I can respect the sincerity of these men in their desire to change our form of government and our social and economic system, though I shall do my best tonight to prove they are wrong. I refer particularly to Senator Norris, Senator La Follette, Senator Cutting, Senator Huey Long, Senator Wheeler, William R. Hearst and other exponents of a social philosophy different from the traditional American one. Unless these men feel assurance of support to their ideas, they certainly would not be supporting these candidates and the Democratic Party. The seal of these men indicates that they have sure confidence that they will have voice in the administration of our government.

I may say at once that the changes proposed from all these Democratic principals and allies are of the most profound and penetrating character. If they are brought about, this will not be the America which we have known in the past.

Let us pause for a moment and examine the American system of government, of social and economic life, which it is now proposed that we should alter. Our system is the product of our race and of our experience in building a nation to heights unparalleled in the whole history of the world. It is a system peculiar to the American people. It differs essentially from all others in the world. It is an American system.

It is founded on the conception that only through ordered liberty, through freedom to the individual, and equal opportunity to the individual will his initiative and enterprise be summoned to spur the march of progress.

It is by the maintenance of equality of opportunity and therefore of a society absolutely fluid in freedom of the movement of its human particles that our individualism departs from the individualism of Europe. We resent class distinction because there can be no rise for the individual through the frozen strata of classes, and no stratification of classes can take place in a mass livened by the free rise of its particles. Thus in our ideals the able and ambitious are able to rise constantly from the bottom to leadership in the community.

This freedom of the individual creates of itself the necessity and the cheerful willingness of men to act cooperatively in a thousand ways and for every purpose as occasion arises; and it permits such voluntary cooperations to be dissolved as soon as they have served their purpose, to be replaced by new voluntary associations for new purposes.

There has thus grown within us, to gigantic importance, a new conception. That is, this voluntary cooperation within the community. Cooperation to perfect the social organization; cooperation for the care of those in distress; cooperation for the advancement of knowledge, of scientific research, of education; for cooperative action in the advancement of many phases of economic life. This is self-government by the people outside of government; it is the most powerful development of individual freedom and equal opportunity that has taken place in the century and a half since our fundamental institutions were founded.

It is in the further development of this cooperation and a sense of its responsibility that we should find solution for many of our complex problems, and not by the extension of government into our economic and social life. The greatest function of government is to build up that cooperation, and its most resolute action should be to deny the extension of bureaucracy. We have developed great agencies of cooperation by the assistance of the government which promote and protect the interests of individuals and the smaller units of business. The Federal Reserve System, in its strengthening and support of the smaller banks; the Farm Board, in its strengthening and support of the farm cooperatives; the Home Loan Banks, in the mobilizing of building and loan associations and savings banks; the Federal Land Banks, in giving independence and strength to land mortgage associations; the great mobilization of relief to distress, the mobilization of business and industry in measures of recovery, and a score of other activities are not socialism—they are the essence of protection to the development of free men.

The primary conception of this whole American system is not the regimentation of men but the cooperation of free men. It is founded upon the conception of responsibility of the individual to the community, of the responsibility of local government to the state, of the state to the national government.

It is founded on a peculiar conception of self-government designed to maintain this equal opportunity to the individual, and through decentralization it brings about and maintains these responsibilities. The centralization of government will undermine responsibilities and will destroy the system.

Our government differs from all previous conceptions, not only in this decentralization but also in the separation of functions between the legislative, executive, and judicial arms of government, in which the independence of the judicial arm is the keystone of the whole structure.

It is founded on a conception that in times of emergency, when forces are running beyond control of individuals or other cooperative action, beyond the control of local communities and of states, then the great reserve powers of the federal government shall be brought into action to protect the community. But when these forces have ceased, there must be a return of state, local, and individual responsibility.

The implacable march of scientific discovery with its train of new inventions presents every year new problems to government and new problems to the social order. Questions often arise whether, in the face of the growth of these new and gigantic tools, democracy can remain master in its own house, can preserve the fundamentals of our American system. I contend that it can; and I contend that this American system of ours has demonstrated its validity and superiority over any other system yet invented by human mind.

It has demonstrated it in the face of the greatest test of our history—that is the emergency which we have faced in the past three years.

When the political and economic weakness of many nations of Europe, the result of the World War and its aftermath, finally culminated in collapse of their institutions, the delicate adjustment of our economic and social life received a shock unparalleled in our history. No one knows that better than you of New York. No one knows its causes better than you. That the crisis was so great that many of the leading banks sought directly or indirectly to convert their assets into gold or its equivalent with the result that they practically ceased to function as credit institutions; that many of our citizens sought flight for their capital to other countries; that many of them attempted to hoard gold in large amounts. These were but indications of the flight of confidence and of the belief that our government could not overcome these forces.

Yet these forces were overcome—perhaps by narrow margins—and this action demonstrates what the courage of a nation can accomplish under the resolute leadership in the Republican Party. And I say the Republican Party, because our opponents before and during the crisis, proposed no constructive program; though some of their members patriotically supported ours. Later on the Democratic House of Representatives did develop the real thought and ideas of the Democratic Party, but it was so destructive that it had to be defeated, for it would have destroyed, not healed.

In spite of all these obstructions, we did succeed. Our form of government did prove itself equal to the task. We saved this nation from a quarter of a century of chaos and degeneration, and we preserved the savings, the insurance policies, gave a fighting chance to men to hold their homes. We saved the integrity of our government and the honesty of the American dollar. And we installed measures which today are bringing back recovery. Employment, agriculture, business—all of these show the steady, if slow, healing of our enormous wound.

I therefore contend that the problem of today is to continue these measures and policies to restore this American system to its normal functioning, to repair the wounds it has received, to correct the weaknesses and evils which would defeat that system. To enter upon a series of deep changes, to embark upon this inchoate new deal which has been propounded in this campaign, would be to undermine and destroy our American system.

DISCUSSION QUESTIONS

1. State governments have always played a role in regulating the economy, from consumer protection to using tax breaks as a way to attract business investment within a state's borders. What kind of economic activities are best regulated at the state level? When should the federal government play a role?
2. Which of the activities that the government performs do you consider essential? Why?
3. Hoover's arguments against government bureaucracy and in favor of individual and community responsibility resonate today with the Freedom Caucus in Congress and other conservative Republicans. What similarities do you see between Hoover's arguments and the current opponents of big government?

64

"The Rise and Fall of the GDP"

JON GERTNER

"Gross Domestic Product," or GDP, is a familiar economic term: It is a standard measure of overall economic activity, the amount of money that is spent during a particular period of time. Politicians are quick to take credit when the GDP grows, for growth is a sign of economic expansion. And when communities are concerned about the environmental or quality-of-life impact of a new development or industrial site, community and business leaders reassure them by pointing to the economic growth that will result.

But is all growth good growth? Jon Gertner argues that GDP is an inaccurate measure of overall economic well-being. Higher GDP does not necessarily mean we are better off, because it includes all types of spending—even spending that results from waste (gasoline burned by cars sitting in traffic jams), unhealthy activities (consumption of cholesterol-laden foods and the cardiologists' bills that often result), or high-spending consumerism (buying a new car every few years or the newest electricity-hog appliances). By comparing "high GDP man" and "low GDP man," Gertner makes it clear that the person spending more and contributing more to the economy may not be acting in the nation's best interests. He also uses the analogy of a car dashboard that tells the driver only how fast she is going and conveys no other information about how the car is functioning. Political leaders would be better served by a "human development index" that would reveal the nation's performance according to measures of health, education, the environment, employment, material well-being, interpersonal connectedness, and political engagement, rather than simply growth.

Whatever you may think progress looks like—a rebounding stock market, a new house, a good raise—the governments of the world have long held the view that only one statistic, the measure of gross domestic product, can really show whether things seem to be getting better or getting worse. GDP is an index of a country's entire economic output—a tally of, among many other things, manufacturers' shipments, farmers' harvests, retail sales and construction spending. It's a figure that compresses the immensity of a national economy into a single data point of surpassing density. The conventional feeling about GDP is that the more it grows, the better a country and its citizens are doing. In the United States, economic activity plummeted at the start of 2009 and only started moving up during the second half of the year. Apparently things are moving in that direction still. In the first quarter of this year, the economy again expanded, this time by an annual rate of about 3.2 percent.

All the same, it has been a difficult few years for GDP. For decades, academics and gadflies have been critical of the measure, suggesting that it is an inaccurate and misleading gauge of prosperity. What has changed more recently is that GDP has been actively challenged by a variety of world leaders, especially in Europe, as well as by a number of international groups, like the Organization for Economic Cooperation and Development. The GDP, according to arguments I heard from economists as far afield as Italy, France, and Canada, has not only failed to capture the well-being of a twenty-first century society but has also skewed global political objectives toward the single-minded pursuit of economic growth. "The economists messed everything up," Alex Michalos, a former chancellor at the University of Northern British Columbia, told me recently when I was in Toronto to hear his presentation on the Canadian Index of Well-Being. The index is making its debut this year as a counterweight to the monolithic gross domestic product numbers. "The main barrier to getting progress has been that statistical agencies around the world are run by economists and statisticians," Michalos said. "And they are not people who are comfortable with human beings." The fundamental national measure they employ, he added, tells us a good deal about the economy but almost nothing about the specific things in our lives that really matter.

In the United States, one challenge to the GDP is coming not from a single new index, or even a dozen new measures, but from several hundred new measures—accessible free online for anyone to see, all updated regularly. Such a system of national measurements, known as State of the USA, will go live online this summer [see www.stateoftheusa.org]. Its arrival comes at an opportune moment, but it has been a long time in the works. In 2003, a government official named Chris Hoenig was working at the U.S. Government Accountability Office, the investigative arm of Congress, and running a group that was researching ways to evaluate national progress. Since 2007, when the project became independent and took the name State of the USA, Hoenig has been guided by the advice of the National Academy of Sciences, an all-star board from the academic and business worlds and a number of former leaders of federal statistical agencies. Some of the country's elite philanthropies—including the Hewlett, MacArthur and Rockefeller foundations—have provided grants to help get the project started.

* * *

Those involved with the self-defined indicators movement—people like Hoenig, as well as supporters around the world who would like to dethrone GDP—argue that achieving a sustainable economy, and a sustainable society, may prove impossible without new ways to evaluate national progress. Left unanswered, however, is the question of which indicators are the most suitable replacements for, or most suitable enhancements to, GDP. Should they measure educational attainment or employment? Should they account for carbon emissions or happiness? As Hoenig himself is inclined to say, and not without some enthusiasm, a new panel of national measures won't necessarily settle such arguments. On the contrary, it will have a tendency to start them.

High-GDP Man vs. Low-GDP Man

For now at least, GDP holds almost unassailable sway, not only as the key national indicator for the economic health of the United States but also for that of the rest of the world's developed countries, which employ a standardized methodology—there's actually a handbook—to calculate their economic outputs. And, as it happens, there are some good reasons that everyone has depended on it for so long. "If you want to know why GDP matters, you can just put yourself back in the 1930 period, where we had no idea what was happening to our economy," William Nordhaus, a Yale economist who has spent a distinguished career thinking about economic measurement, told me recently. "There were people then who said things were fine and others who said things weren't fine. But we had no comprehensive measures, so we looked at things like boxcar loadings." If you compare the crisis of 1930 with the crisis of 2008, Nordhaus added, it has made an enormous difference to track what's happening in the economy through indexes like GDP. Such knowledge can enable a quick and informed policy response, which in the past year took shape as a big stimulus package, for example. To Nordhaus, in fact, the GDP—the antecedents of which were developed in the early 1930s by an economist named Simon Kuznets at the federal government's request—is one of the greatest inventions of the twentieth century. "It's not a machine or a computer," he says, "and it's not the way you usually think of an invention. But it's an awesome thing."

* * *

For years, economists critical of the measure have enjoyed spinning narratives to illustrate its logical flaws and limitations. Consider, for example, the lives of two people—let's call them High-GDP Man and Low-GDP Man. High-GDP Man has a long commute to work and drives an automobile that gets poor gas mileage, forcing him to spend a lot on fuel. The morning traffic and its stresses aren't too good for his car (which he replaces every few years) or his cardiovascular health (which he treats with expensive pharmaceuticals and medical procedures). High-GDP Man works hard, spends hard. He loves going to bars and restaurants, likes his flat-screen televisions and adores his big house, which he keeps at 71 degrees year round and protects with a state-of-the-art security system. High-GDP Man and his wife pay for a sitter (for their kids) and a nursing home (for their aging parents). They don't have time for housework, so they employ a full-time housekeeper. They don't have time to cook much, so they usually order in. They're too busy to take long vacations.

As it happens, all those things—cooking, cleaning, home care, three-week vacations and so forth—are the kind of activity that keep Low-GDP Man and his wife busy. High-GDP Man likes his washer and dryer; Low-GDP Man doesn't mind hanging his laundry on the clothesline. High-GDP Man buys bags of prewashed salad at the grocery store; Low-GDP Man grows vegetables in his garden. When High-GDP Man wants a book, he buys it; Low-GDP Man checks it out of the library. When High-GDP Man wants to get in shape, he joins a gym; Low-GDP Man digs out an old pair of Nikes and runs through the neighborhood. On his morning commute, High-GDP Man drives past Low-GDP Man, who is walking to work in wrinkled khakis.

By economic measures, there's no doubt High-GDP Man is superior to Low-GDP Man. His salary is higher, his expenditures are greater, his economic activity is more robust. You can even say that by modern standards High-GDP Man is a bigger boon to his country. What we can't really say for sure is whether his life is any better. In fact, there seem to be subtle indications that various "goods" that High-GDP Man consumes should, as some economists put it, be characterized as "bads." His alarm system at home probably isn't such a good indicator of his personal security; given all the medical tests, his health care expenditures seem to be excessive. Moreover, the pollution from the traffic jams near his home, which signals that business is good at the local gas stations and auto shops, is very likely contributing to social and environmental ills. And we don't know if High-GDP Man is living beyond his means, so we can't predict his future quality of life. For all we know, he could be living on borrowed time, just like a wildly overleveraged bank.

GDP vs. Human Development Index

* * *

Most criticisms of GDP have tended to fall into two distinct camps. The first group maintains that GDP itself needs to be fixed. High-GDP Man and Low-GDP Man have to become one, in effect. This might entail, for starters, placing an economic value on work done in the home, like housekeeping and child care. Activities that are currently unaccounted for, like cooking dinner at your own stove, could also be treated the same as activities that are now factored into GDP, like food prepared in a restaurant. Another fix might be to cease giving only positive values to events that actually detract from a country's well-being, like hurricanes and floods; both boost GDP through construction costs.

The second group of critics, meanwhile, has sought to recast the criticism of GDP from an accounting debate to a philosophical one. Here things get far more complicated. The argument goes like this: Even if GDP was revised as a more modern, logical GDP 2.0, our reliance on such a measure suggests that we may still be equating economic growth with progress on a planet that is possibly overburdened already by human consumption and pollution. The only way to repair such an imbalance would be to institutionalize other national indicators (environmental, say, or health-related) to reflect the true complexity of human progress. Just how many indicators are required to assess societal health—3? 30? 300, à la State of the USA?—is something economists have been struggling with for years as well.

So far only one measure has succeeded in challenging the hegemony of growth-centric thinking. This is known as the Human Development Index, which turns 20 this year. The HDI is a ranking that incorporates a nation's GDP and two other modifying factors: its citizens' education, based on adult literacy and school-enrollment data, and its citizens' health, based on life-expectancy statistics. The HDI, which happens to be used by the United Nations, has plenty of critics. For example, its three-part weightings are frequently criticized for being arbitrary; another problem is that minor variations in the literacy rates of developed nations, for example, can yield significant differences in how countries rank.

One economist who helped create the Human Development Index was Amartya Sen, a Nobel laureate in economics who teaches at Harvard. * * * Sen joined the Nobel laureate Joseph Stiglitz and the French economist Jean-Paul Fitoussi on a commission established by President Nicolas Sarkozy of France to consider alternatives to GDP. * * * [T]he commission endorsed both main criticisms of the GDP: the economic measure itself should be fixed to better represent individuals' circumstances today, and every country should also apply other indicators to capture what is happening economically, socially and environmentally. The commission sought a metaphor to explain what it meant. Eventually it settled on an automobile.

Suppose you're driving, Stiglitz told me. You would like to know how the vehicle is functioning, but when you check the dashboard there is only one gauge. (It's a peculiar car.) That single dial conveys one piece of important information: how fast you're moving. It's not a bad comparison to the current GDP, but it doesn't tell you many other things: How much fuel do you have left? How far can you go? How many miles have you gone already? So what you want is a car, or a country, with a big dashboard—but not so big that you can't take in all of its information.

The question is: How many measures beyond GDP—how many dials on a new dashboard—will you need? Stiglitz and his fellow academics ultimately concluded that assessing a population's quality of life will require metrics from at least seven categories: health, education, environment, employment, material well-being, interpersonal connectedness and political engagement. They also decided that any nation that was serious about progress should start measuring its "equity"—that is, the distribution of material wealth and other social goods—as well as its economic and environmental sustainability. "Too often, particularly I think in an American context, everybody says, 'We want policies that reflect our values,' but nobody says what those values are," Stiglitz told me. The opportunity to choose a new set of indicators, he added, is tantamount to saying that we should not only have a conversation about recasting GDP. We should also, in the aftermath of an extraordinary economic collapse, talk about what the goals of a society really are.

Taking the Environment Into Account

The report from the Stiglitz-Sen-Fitoussi commission isn't a blueprint, exactly—it's more like open-source software, posted online for anyone to download, discuss and modify. It doesn't tell countries how they should measure progress. It tells them how they should think about measuring progress. One challenge here—something that the commission's members well understood—is that recommending new indicators and actually implementing them are very different endeavors. Almost everyone I spoke with in the indicators movement, including Chris Hoenig at State of the USA, seems to agree that at the moment our reach exceeds our grasp. When I met with Rebecca Blank, the undersecretary of commerce for economic affairs, whose job it is to oversee the data agencies that put together GDP, she noted that new national measures depend on more than a government's willingness; they also necessitate additional financing, interagency cooperation and great leaps in the science of statistical analysis. Blank wasn't averse to some of the commission's recommendations—indeed, she recently endorsed the idea, proposed by Steve Landefeld at the Bureau of Economic Analysis, that our national accounts add a "household perspective" that represents individuals' economic circumstances better than GDP. "But some of the constraint is we don't have the money to do it," she told me, referring to various new measures. "Some of the constraint is we know how to do it, but we need to collect additional data that we don't currently have. And some of the constraint is that we don't really know how to do it quite yet."

Environmental and sustainability indicators offer a few good examples of how big the challenge is. A relatively easy first step, several members of the Stiglitz commission told me, would be to build in a "depletion charge" to GDP for the natural resources—oil, gas, timber and even fisheries—that a country transforms into dollars. At the moment, we don't do this; it's as if these commodities have no value until they are extracted and sold. A charge for resource depletion might not affect GDP in the United States all that much; the country is too big and too thoroughly based on knowledge and technology industries for the depletion costs of things like coal mining and oil drilling to make much of an impact. On the other hand, in countries like Saudi Arabia and China, GDP might look different (that is to say, lower) if such a charge were subtracted from their economic outputs. Geoffrey Heal, a professor at Columbia who worked on the environmental aspects of the commission's report, told me that including resource depletion in the national accounts—something the United States considered in the early 1990s and then abandoned for political reasons—could be implemented within a year if the world's developed nations agreed to do it. After that, he suggests, a next step might be to subtract from GDP the cost of the health problems—asthma and early deaths, for instance—caused by air pollutants like sulfur dioxide.

But environmental accounting gets more difficult. "We can put monetary values on mineral stocks, fisheries and even forests, perhaps," Heal says. "But it's hard to put a monetary value on alteration of the climate system, loss of species and the consequences that might come from those." On the other hand, Heal points out, you have to decide to measure something difficult before you can come up with a technique for measuring it. That was the case when the United States decided to create national accounts on economic production during the Great Depression. What the Stiglitz commission ultimately concluded was that it's necessary to make a few sustainability dials on the dashboard simply raw data—registering things like a country's carbon footprint or species extinctions—until we figure out how to give the effects approximate monetary values. Maybe in 10 years, Heal guesses, economists would be able to do that.

To Heal, making a real and rapid effort at calculating these costs and then posting the information is imperative. According to Heal, we have no sense of how much "natural capital"—our stocks of clean air and water and our various ecosystems—we need to conserve to maintain our economy and our quality of life. "If you push the world's natural capital below a certain level," Heal asks, "do you so radically alter the system that it has a long-term impact on human welfare?" He doesn't know the answer. Yet, he adds, if we were to pass that point—and at present we have no dials to indicate whether we have—then we couldn't compensate for our error through technological innovation or energy breakthroughs. Because by then it would be too late.

Putting a Number on Happiness

As difficult as it might be to compile sustainability indicators, it's equally challenging to create measures that describe our social and emotional lives. In this area, there's a fair amount of skepticism from the academic establishment about putting happiness onto a national dashboard of well-being. William Nordhaus of Yale told me that some of the measurements are "absurd." Amartya Sen, too, told me that he has reservations about the worth of statistics that purport to describe human happiness.

Stiglitz and his colleagues nevertheless concluded that such research was becoming sufficiently rigorous to warrant its possible inclusion. At first the connection to GDP can be puzzling. One explanation, however, is that while our current economic measures can't capture the larger effects of unemployment or chronic depression, providing policy makers with that information may influence their actions. "You might say, If we have unemployment, don't worry, we'll just compensate the person," Stiglitz told me. "But that doesn't fully compensate them." Stiglitz pointed to the work of the Harvard professor Robert Putnam, who served on the Stiglitz-Sen-Fitoussi commission, which suggests that losing a job can have repercussions that affect a person's social connections (one main driver of human happiness, regardless of country) for many years afterward.

When I caught up with Putnam, he said that the "damage to this country's social fabric from this economic crisis must have been huge, huge, huge." And yet, he noted, "We have plenty of numbers about the economic consequences but none of the numbers about the social consequences." Over the past decade, Putnam has been working on measures—having to do with church attendance, community involvement and the like—to quantify our various social links; just recently, the U.S. Census Bureau agreed to include questions of his in some of its monthly surveys. Still, his efforts are a work in progress. When I asked Putnam whether government should be in the business of fostering social connections, he replied, "I don't think we should have a government Department of Friendship that introduces people to one another." But he argued that just as registering the social toll of joblessness would add a dimension of urgency to the unemployment issue, it seemed possible that measuring social connections, and putting those measures on a national dashboard, could be in society's best interests. As it happens, the Canadian Index of Well-Being will contain precisely such a measure; and it's very likely that a related measure of "social capital," as it's often called, will become a State of the USA indicator too. "People will get sick and die, because they don't know their neighbors," Putnam told me. "And the health effects of social isolation are of the same magnitude as people smoking. If we can care about people smoking, because that reduces their life expectancy, then why not think about social isolation too?"

It seems conceivable, in fact, that including various measures of emotional well-being on a national dashboard could lead to policies quite different from what we have now. "There's an enormous inequality of suffering in society," Daniel Kahneman told me recently. By his estimate, "if you look at the 10 percent of people who spend the most time suffering, they account for almost half of the total amount of suffering." Kahneman suggested that tremendous social and economic gains could therefore be made by dealing with the mental-health problems—depression, say—of a relatively small fraction of the population. At the same time, he added, new measures of emotional well-being that he has been working on might soon give us a more enlightened perspective on the complex relationship between money and happiness.

Currently, research suggests that increased wealth leads us to report increased feelings of satisfaction with our lives—a validation, in effect, that higher GDP increases the well-being in a country. But Kahneman told me that his most recent studies, conducted with the Princeton economist Angus Deaton, suggest that money doesn't necessarily make much of a difference in our moment-to-moment happiness, which is distinct from our feelings of satisfaction. According to their work, income over about $70,000 does nothing to improve how much we enjoy our activities on a typical day. And that raises some intriguing questions. Do we want government to help us increase our sense of satisfaction? Or do we want it to help us get through our days without feeling misery? The two questions lead toward two very different policy options. Is national progress a matter of making an increasing number of people very rich? Or is it about getting as many people as possible into the middle class?

The Political Resistance

* * *

As for the effects of such changes, Stiglitz told me, "What we measure affects what we do, and better measurement will lead to better decisions, or at least different decisions." But until the developed nations of the world actually move beyond GDP—a big if—this remains a reasoned hypothesis only. A lingering question is whether some government officials, perceiving dangers in a new measurement system, might conclude that such an overhaul would wreak political havoc and therefore ought to be avoided. A heightened focus on environmental indicators, for starters, could give environmental legislation a far greater urgency. And a revision of economic measures presents other potential policy complications.

It has long been the case, for example, that the GDP of the United States outpaces that of European countries with higher taxes and greater government spending; it has thus seemed reasonable to view our economic growth as a vindication of a national emphasis on free markets and entrepreneurship. But things look different if you see the measure itself as flawed or inadequate. We take shorter vacations than Europeans, for instance, which is one reason their GDP is lower than ours—but that could change if our indicators start putting a value on leisure time. Some of the disparity, meanwhile, between the United States and various European countries, Stiglitz argued, is a statistical bias resulting from the way GDP formulas account for public-sector benefits. In other words, the services received from the government in a country like Sweden—in public education, health care and child care, among other things—are likely undervalued. Rejiggering the measures of prosperity would almost certainly challenge our self-perceptions, Stiglitz said, perhaps so much so that in the United States we might begin to ask, Is our system working as well for most people as we think it has been?

* * *

DISCUSSION QUESTIONS

1. If all growth (increases in spending) is not necessarily good growth, how can we distinguish between "good" growth and "bad" growth? Of the criteria mentioned for the "human development index," which would be the most difficult to measure? Do you think other things should be included in the measure?
2. In public policy debates, analysts often distinguish "economic" indicators—inflation, unemployment, consumer spending—from "social" indicators, such as crime, divorce, school dropout rates, and teen pregnancies. In light of Gertner's argument, is this separation appropriate? Why or why not?
3. Do you think the Stiglitz-Sen-Fitoussi Commission will make any headway with political leaders (in terms of getting their index implemented)? What political obstacles would they face?

Debating the Issues: Is Income Inequality a Problem?

By any measure, income and wealth are distributed unequally in the United States. That may not come as a surprise, but the degree to which wealth and income are concentrated might be. According to recent Census figures, the top 1 percent of adults earned $1.3 million in 2014 compared to $428,000 in 1980 (in constant 2014 dollars), an increase of more than threefold. In contrast, the average income of the bottom 50 percent has stagnated at $16,000 per adult over this 34-year period. The concentration of wealth is even more pronounced than income inequality, with the richest 14,000 families in the United States (the top .01 percent) owning more than five times as much as the bottom 90 percent, or over 133 million families.

The fact of income inequality is indisputable. Whether that inequality has negative effects (and what to do about it) is a more complicated question. To many, high levels of income inequality signify gross failure of basic norms of fairness, and have harmful consequences for cohesion, civil life, and ultimately, even political stability. In this view, income inequality is both a cause and a consequence of political inequality, as the rich are better equipped to rig the system in their favor through favorable tax laws and regulations that further protect and concentrate wealth. Those who aren't wealthy wind up with the scraps: underfunded public schools, dangerous neighborhoods, crumbling infrastructure, inadequate services, and on and on. Others maintain that inequality is not a serious problem, and that even if it were, the alternative—draconian policies that forcefully redistribute wealth—is even worse. Moreover, since nobody can say what distribution of income would be fair, any attempt to achieve balance is arbitrary.

In the 2016 presidential campaign, income inequality was the centerpiece of Bernie Sanders's campaign in the primaries. Hillary Clinton emphasized the issue as well, but Donald Trump emerged as the favorite of white working class voters with his theme of "making America great again." The direction of Trump's economic policies are still unclear at the time of this writing, but income inequality remains a central concern.

Ray Williams makes the case that income inequality threatens democracy. He begins with an almost mind-numbing set of statistics on income and wealth inequality and argues that high-income inequality is associated with "more crime, less happiness, poorer mental and physical health, less racial harmony, and less civic and political participation." One of the more interesting studies cited by Williams found that Americans greatly underestimate the degree of wealth inequality in our nation and would prefer a more equal distribution, like Sweden's. George Will counters that "income inequality in a capitalist system is truly beautiful" because it is the engine of economic growth. Will argues that people like Mark Zuckerberg, Michael Dell, Bill Gates, Jeff Bezos, and Steve Jobs become wealthy because they have great ideas that produce innovative products. In turn, these ideas create thousands of jobs and create innovations that keep consumer prices down. The secret to creating economic growth is allowing the wealthy to keep their wealth to create jobs.

Barton Hinkle provides the angle that is likely to get the most sympathetic hearing from the Trump administration: we should tackle inequality by easing regulations that impede economic growth. This libertarian perspective of relying on the free market to create growth and wealth has moved into the mainstream in the past several decades. Airlines, trucking, telecommunications, and utilities industries were all deregulated in the past thirty years. However, according to Hinkle there are still some "low-hanging fruit" of inefficient regulations that are holding back growth and contributing to inequality. Copyrights and patents, immigration policies, especially for high-skilled workers, occupational licensing, and zoning all should be modified to encourage more entrepreneurship and job creation. Hinkle's suggestion on immigration policy may be resisted by the Trump administration, but small-government, pro-free market Republicans in Congress should be sympathetic to his agenda.

65

"Why Income Inequality Threatens Democracy"

RAY WILLIAMS

Rising economic inequality is threatening not only economic progress but also the democratic political system in the United States.

Emerging from the 2008–09 financial crisis, the global economy is strengthening. Yet around the world, prosperity evades most people. Increasingly the biggest benefits of economic prosperity are being accrued by a tiny elite. We live in a world where a small number of the richest people own half of the world's wealth.

In the United States, the increase in the income share of the top one percent is at its highest level since the eve of the Great Depression. In India, the number of billionaires has increased tenfold in the past decade. In Europe, poor people struggle with post-recovery austerity policies while moneyed investors benefit from bank bailouts. Africa has had a resource boom in the last decade but most people there still struggle daily for food, clean water, and healthcare.

Many economic and political experts have argued that extreme concentrations of wealth are not just morally questionable but that concentration in the hands of a few stunts long-term economic growth, too, making it more difficult to reduce poverty. What must now be admitted is that extreme income inequality also is undermining democracy.

Let's take a look at the evidence for increasing income inequality and its negative impact in the United States:

- The poorest half of the Earth's population owns 1 percent of the Earth's wealth. The richest 1 percent of the Earth's population owns 46 percent. The poorest half of the U.S. population owns 2.5 percent of the country's wealth. The top 1 percent owns 35 percent of it;
- The United States is the most economically stratified society in the western world. As *The Wall Street Journal* reported, a recent study found that the top .01 percent or 14,000 American families hold 22.2 percent of wealth, and the bottom 90 percent, or over 133 million families, just 4 percent of the nation's wealth;
- The U.S. Census Bureau and the World Wealth Report 2010 both report increases for the top 5 percent of households even during the recent recession. Based on Internal Revenue Service figures, the richest 1 percent has tripled their cut of America's income pie in one generation;
- In 81 percent of American counties, the median family income, about $52,000, is less than it was 15 years ago. This is despite the fact that the economy has grown 83 percent in the past quarter-century and corporate profits have doubled. American workers produce twice the amount of goods and services as 25 years ago, but get less of the pie;
- The amount of money that was given out in bonuses on Wall Street last year is twice the amount workers earned in the country combined;
- The wealthiest 85 people on the planet have more money that the poorest 3.5 billion people combined;
- The median wealth per adult number is only about $39,000, placing the United States about 27th among the world's nations, behind Australia, most of Europe, and even small countries like New Zealand, Ireland and Kuwait;
- The top 1 percent of America owns 50 percent of investment assets (stocks, bonds, mutual funds). The poorest half of America owns just .5 percent of the investments;
- The poorest Americans do come out ahead in one statistic: the bottom 90 percent of America owns 73 percent of the debt;
- Since 1990, CEO compensation has increased by 300 percent. Corporate profits have doubled. The average worker's salary has increased 4 percent. Adjusted for inflation, the minimum wage has actually decreased. CEOs

in 1965 earned about 24 times the amount of the average worker. In 1980 they earned 42 times as much. Today, CEOs earn 325 times the average worker:

- In a study of 34 developed countries, the United States had the second highest level of income inequality, ahead of only Chile;
- Young people in the United States are getting poorer. The median wealth of people under 35 has dropped 68 percent since 1984. The median wealth of older Americans has increased 42 percent in the same period;
- Four hundred Americans have wealth equal to the GDP of Russia.
- In 1946, a child born into poverty had about a 50-percent chance of scaling the income ladder into the middle class. In 1980, the chances were 40 percent. A child born today has about a 33-percent chance.
- Twenty-five of the largest corporations in America in 2010 paid their CEOs more money than they paid in taxes that year.
- Some hedge fund mangers made $4 billion annually, enough to pay the salaries of every public school teacher in New York City, according to Paul Buchheit of DePaul University.

Robert Reich, former Secretary of Labor under President Bill Clinton, recently cited a *Forbes* story that reported "only twice before in American history has so much been held by so few, and the gap between them and the great majority been a chasm—in the late 1920s and in the era of the robber barons in the 1880s."

Dominic Barton, Managing Director of McKinsey and Co., argues, "Few would disagree that unchecked increases in inequality will be costly for capitalism in the long run—due to the divisions that it creates within society and the strain that it puts on social safety nets."

The Pew Foundation study, reported in the *New York Times,* concluded, "The chance that children of the poor or middle class will climb up the income ladder, has not changed significantly over the last three decades." *The Economist*'s special report, *Inequality in America,* concluded, "The fruits of productivity gains have been skewed towards the highest earners and towards companies whose profits have reached record levels as a share of GDP."

A joint effort by the Russell Sage Foundation, the Carnegie Corporation, and the Lyle Spencer Foundation has released several reports based on research on the issue of income inequality. They have concluded that over the past three decades, the United States has experienced a slow rise in economic inequality and as a result, the fruits of economic growth have gone largely to the wealthy; median incomes have stagnated; and the poor have increasingly been left behind.

In their book, *Winner-Take-All Politics: How Washington Made The Rich Richer—And Turned Its Back On The Middle Class,* Jacob Hacker and Paul Pearson argue that since the late 1970s, an intense campaign of anti-democracy policy changes have resulted in an intense concentration of wealth and income to very few individuals and corporations in the United States.

Many people believe it is only the recession that has had a negative impact on the economic welfare of people in the United States, but wealthy individuals and corporations have fared well during tough economic times.

According to Richard Wolff, professor of Economics at the University of Massachusetts, U.S. corporations, particularly the large ones, "have avoided taxes as effectively as they have controlled government expenditures to benefit them." Wolff points out that during the Depression and World War II, federal income tax receipts from individuals and corporations were fairly equal, but by 1980, individual income taxes were four times higher than corporate taxes. "Since World War II, corporations have shifted much of the federal tax burden for themselves to the public—and especially onto the middle class," Wolff says.

The most comprehensive recent study of corporate taxes by professors at Duke, MIT, and the University of California concluded, "We find a significant percent of firms that appear to be successfully avoiding large portions of the corporate income over a sustained period of time." For example, the *New York Times* reported that GE's total tax was 14.3 percent over the last 5 years, while in 2009 receiving a $140-billion bailout guarantee of its debt from the federal government.

What happens to societies where there are large and growing gaps in wealth? Significant social problems, and declining indicators of well-being and happiness, recent research seems to suggest.

British epidemiologists Richard Wilkinson and Kate Pickett, authors of *The Spirit Level: Why Greater Equality Makes Societies Stronger,* argue that almost every indicator of social health in wealthy societies is related to its level of economic equality. The authors, using data from the United States and other developed nations, contend that GDP and overall wealth are less significant than the gap between the rich and the poor, which is the worst in the United States among developed nations. "In more unequal societies, people are more out for themselves, their involvement in community life drops away," Wilkinson says. If you live in a state or country where level of income is more equal, "you will be less likely to have mental illness and other social problems," he argues.

A University of Leicester psychologist, Adrian White, has produced the first ever "world map of happiness," based on over 100 studies of more than 80,000 people and by analyzing data from the CIA, UNESCO, The New Economics Foundation, the World Health Organization, and European databases. The well-being index that was produced was based on the prediction variables of health, wealth, and education. According to this study, Denmark was ranked first, Switzerland second, Canada tenth and the United States twenty-third.

A study published in *Psychological Science* by Mike Morrison, Louis Tay, and Ed Diener, which is based on the Gallup World Poll of 128 countries and 130,000 people, found that the more satisfied people are with their country, the better they feel about themselves. Recent surveys in the United States show a significant percentage of Americans who are unhappy about their country. According to the World Values Survey of over 80 countries, the United States ranks only 16th, behind such countries such as Switzerland, the Netherlands, Sweden, and Canada, with Denmark ranked first.

Linda McQuaig and Neil Brooks, authors of *The Trouble with Billionaires*, argue that increasing poverty due to economic inequality in the United States and Canada has detrimental effects on health and social conditions and undermines democracy. They cite the fact that while the United States has the most billionaires in the world; it ranks poorly in the Western world in terms of infant mortality, life expectancy, crime levels—particularly violent crime—and electoral participation.

Between 1983 and 1999, men's life expectancy decreased in more than 50 U.S. counties, according to a study by Majid Ezzati, associate professor of International health at the Harvard School of Public Health. For women, the news was even worse: life expectancy decreased in more than 900 counties—more than a quarter of the total. The United States no longer boasts anywhere near the world's longest life expectancy. It doesn't even make the top 40. In this and many other ways, the richest nation on earth is not the healthiest.

Ezzati's results are one example. There is also evidence that living in a society with wide disparities—in health, in wealth, in education—is worse for all the society's members, even the well off. Life-expectancy statistics hint at this. People at the top of the U.S. income spectrum "live a very long time," says Lisa Berkman, Director of Harvard University's Center Population and Development Studies, "but people at the top in some other countries live a lot longer."

A meta-analysis published by the *British Medical Journal* shows a link between income inequality and mortality and health. The researchers concluded that people living in regions with high-income inequality had an increased risk of premature death, independent of their individual socioeconomic status, age, or gender. While it is logical to assume the lowest-income citizens would be at greater health risk, the study concluded that income inequality is "detrimental to the more affluent members of society, since these citizens experience psychosocial stress from the inequality and loss of social cohesion."

Often popular media portrays the image of everyone favoring and wanting to be wealthy, but that may be deceiving.

Recent neuroscience research reveals that the brain rejects inequality and prefers equitable balance—physiological, emotional, social, and psychological. E. Tricomi and colleagues advanced this argument, published in the journal *Nature*. They contend the human brain dislikes inequality when it comes to money. And other behavioral and anthropological evidence shows that humans dislike social inequality and unfair distribution of outcomes. Researchers at the California Institute of Technology and Trinity College in Ireland have identified reward centers in the brain that are sensitive to inequality. This research shows a dislike of unfairness and inequality is more than just a social convention. On a physiological level, people may not be as selfish as once believed. Other studies have shown that many wealthy people want to restore equality and balance by charitable donations to assuage their guilt and decrease their own discomfort over having more than other people.

Research indicates that high inequality reverberates through societies on multiple levels, correlating with, if not causing, more crime, less happiness, poorer mental and physical health, less racial harmony, and less civic and political participation. Tax policy and social-welfare programs, then, take on importance far beyond determining how much income people hold onto.

In their report, "Building A Better America—One Wealth Quintile at a Time," Dan Ariely of Duke University and Michael I. Norton of Harvard Business School showed that across ideological, economic, and gender groups, Americans thought the richest 20 percent of American society controlled about 59 percent of the country's wealth, while the real number is actually 84 percent. At the same time, the survey respondents believed that the top 20 percent should own only 32 percent of the wealth. In contrast, in Sweden, a country with significantly greater economic equality, 20 percent of the richest people there control only 36 percent of the wealth of the country. In the American survey, 92 percent of the respondents said they'd rather live in a country with Sweden's wealth distribution. They concluded that a majority of Americans they surveyed "dramatically underestimated the current level of inequality," and "respondents constructed ideal wealth distributions that were far more equitable even than their immensely low estimates of the actual distribution." They contend that all demographic groups, including conservatives like Republicans and the wealthy, "desired more equal distribution of wealth than the status quo."

In an article in the *New York Times* Eduardo Porter argues, "Comparisons across countries suggest a fairly strong, negative link between the level of inequality and the odds of advancement across the generations. And the United States appears at extreme ends along both of these dimensions—with some of the highest inequality and lowest mobility in the industrial world." He goes on to say,

> If the very rich can use the political system to slow or stop the ascent of the rest, the United States could become a hereditary plutocracy under the trappings of liberal democracy.
>
> One doesn't have to believe in equality to be concerned about these trends. Once inequality becomes very acute, it breeds resentment and political instability, eroding the legitimacy of democratic institutions. It can produce political polarization and gridlock, splitting the political system between haves and have-nots, making it more difficult for governments to address imbalances

and respond to brewing crises. That too can undermine economic growth, let alone democracy.

Frederick Soft, writing in the *American Journal of Political Science* provides an analysis of economic inequality and democratic political engagement, concluding "higher levels of income inequality powerfully depress political interest, the frequency of political discussion and participation in elections among all but the most affluent citizens, providing compelling evidence that greater economic inequality yields greater political inequality."

So while income inequality is a growing serious problem for the economic and social health of the U.S. population, it's fair to say it's also a threat to its democratic system.

66

"How Income Inequality Benefits Everybody"

George Will

Every day the Chinese go to work, Americans get a raise: Chinese workers, many earning each day about what Americans spend on a Starbucks latte, produce apparel, appliances, and other stuff cheaply, thereby enlarging Americans' disposable income. Americans similarly get a raise when they shop at the stores that made Sam Walton a billionaire.

The ranks of billionaires are constantly churned. Most of the people on the original Forbes 400 list of richest Americans in 1982 were off the list in 2013. Mark Zuckerberg, Facebook's chief executive, was not born until 1984. America needs more billionaires like him, Michael Dell, Bill Gates, Jeff Bezos, and Steve Jobs. With the iPod, iPhone and iPad, unique products when introduced, Jobs's Apple created monopolies. But instead of raising their prices, Apple has cut them because "profits attract imitators and innovators." Which is one reason why monopolies come and go. When John D. Rockefeller began selling kerosene in 1870, he had approximately 4 percent of the market. By 1890, he had 85 percent. Did he use this market dominance to gouge consumers? Kerosene prices fell from 30 cents a gallon in 1869 to 6 cents in 1897. And in the process of being branded a menacing monopoly, Rockefeller's Standard Oil made gasoline so cheap that Ford found a mass market for Model T's.

Monopoly profits are social blessings when they "signal to the ambitious the wealth they can earn by entering previously unknown markets." So "when the wealth gap widens, the lifestyle gap *shrinks*." Hence, "income inequality in a capitalist system is truly beautiful" because "it provides the incentive for creative people to gamble on new ideas, and it turns luxuries into common goods." Since 2000, the price of a 50-inch plasma TV has fallen from $20,000 to $550.

Henry Ford doubled his employees' basic wage in 1914, supposedly to enable them to buy Fords. Actually, he did it because in 1913 annual worker turnover was 370 percent. He *lowered* labor costs by reducing turnover and the expense of constantly training new hires.

All these thoughts are from John Tamny, a one-man antidote to economic obfuscation and mystification. Thomas Carlyle (1795–1881), who called economics "the dismal science," never read Tamny, a *Forbes* editor, editor of RealClearMarkets and now author of the cheerful, mind-opening book, *Popular Economics: What the Rolling Stones,* Downton Abbey, *and LeBron James Can Teach You About Economics.*

In the early 1970s, when the Rolling Stones were coining money and Britain's top tax rate was 83 percent, Keith Richards, guitarist and social philosopher, said: "That's the same as being told to leave the country." The Stones decamped to France, leaving Britain, Tamny notes, to collect 83 percent of nothing.

Americans execrate "outsourcing," which supposedly involves sending "American jobs" overseas. Well. Nike employs 40 times more manufacturing workers in Vietnam than in the United States, but it could not afford as many American workers as it has without the efficiencies of outsourcing. Tamny cities Enrico Moretti, an economist at the University of California at Berkeley, who says that when Americans buy an iPhone online, it is shipped from China and the only American who touches it is the UPS delivery person. Is it regrettable that Americans are not doing the assembly jobs for which Chinese are paid the "latte wage"?

Actually, Americans incessantly "outsource" here at home by, for example, having Iowans grow their corn and dentists take care of their teeth, jobs at which Iowans and dentists excel and the rest of us do not. LeBron James could be an adequate NFL tight end, but why subtract time from being a superb basketball player? The lesson, says Tamny, is that individuals—and nations—should do what they do better than others and let others do other things.

Millions of jobs, he says, would be created if we banned computers, ATMs, and tractors. The mechanization of agriculture destroyed millions of jobs performed with hoes and scythes. Was Cyrus McCormick—founder of what would later become the International Harvester Co.—a curse?

The best way to (in Barack Obama's 2008 words to Joe the Plumber) "spread the wealth around," is, Tamny argues, "to leave it in the hands of the wealthy." Personal consumption absorbs a small portion of their money and the remainder is not idle. It is invested by them, using the skill that earned it. Will it be more beneficially employed by the political class of a confiscatory government?

"Nothing," Tamny demonstrates, "is easier to understand than economics. It is everywhere you look." Readers of his book will subsequently look at things differently.

67

"How to Fix the Economy, and Income Inequality, the Libertarian Way"

A. BARTON HINKLE

Conservatives want to get the economy roaring again. Republican presidential candidate Jeb Bush, for instance, wants to bring back 4-percent growth. Liberals want to reduce economic inequality. Hence the surging support for Bernie Sanders. The two goals often seem to work at cross purposes. But what if there were an idea that could do both? Brink Lindsey, a scholar at the Cato Institute, has written a paper that identifies not just one such idea, but four. Each of them addresses what he terms "regressive regulations": government rules that "redistribute income and wealth up the socioeconomic scale." Those rules have two other common features: They impede economic progress, and they have few disinterested defenders anywhere along the political spectrum. Nearly the only people who support them are the moneyed interests that benefit from them. They are, therefore, "low-hanging fruit guarded by dragons." Tackle them, and you can do a great deal of good.

Lindsey's ideas address:

1. Overly Restrictive Copyrights and Excessive Patents

Copyrights and patents are supposed to incentivize innovation by protecting property rights. Lindsey argues they have gone too far. A 1998 extension of copyright protection, for instance, was retroactive—even though "it is impossible to change incentives with respect to works that are already created. Retroactive extension thus amounted to a straight-up wealth transfer from consumers—and would-be adapters and remixers—to copyright holders."

Patents have exploded, from 61,620 in 1983 to more than 300,000 today—even though research and development outlays, as well as the rate of technological breakthroughs, have remained steady. Now you can patent such nebulous things as "methods of doing business."

The proliferation of patents has fed an army of "patent trolls," who buy patents on the cheap from distressed companies. As the Electronic Frontier Foundation explains, "the Patent Office has a habit of issuing patents for ideas that are neither new nor revolutionary, and these patents can be very broad. . . . (T)he troll will then send out threatening letters to those they argue infringe their patent(s)," demanding exorbitant licensing fees as the price of staying out of court—and in business.

Indeed, the majority of patent infringement suits today are "brought by firms that make no products . . . and whose chief activity is to prevent other companies" from making any. Result: the stifling of innovation, often by struggling entrepreneurs.

2. Too-tight Immigration Policies, Especially for High-skilled Workers

"The most straightforward way to increase economic output," Lindsey notes, "is simply to add more inputs used in production—namely, capital and labor." He recaps reams of research showing that immigrants "are disproportionately entrepreneurial and innovative."

One-fourth of Silicon Valley companies have at least one founder born abroad, for instance, even though immigrants make up less than 13 percent of the U.S. population. Others have reported that immigrants are now twice as likely to start a business as native-born Americans, and in 2011 created one out of every four new businesses in the United States.

Immigrants might be poorer than the typical American when they arrive here, but many don't stay that way, and those who climb the economic ladder bring many native-born Americans with them: immigrant-owned businesses have created 4 million jobs here. Unfortunately, only 7 percent of permanent resident visas go to "individuals who qualify on the basis of their work skills or other economic value," Lindsey writes.

3. Occupational Licensing

Nearly one-third of American occupations now require a permission slip from the government—up from 10 percent in 1970—including makeup artists, auctioneers, bartenders, florists, and ballroom dance instructors.

This causes harm in several ways. It acts as a drag on employment, which impedes economic growth. It raises prices for consumers, sometimes by as much as one-third, which hits the poor the hardest. It erects barriers to entry for the less educated: Thirty-two percent of Americans have a college degree, but 43 percent of people in licensed jobs are required to have one.

And for what? Not for health or safety. Lindsey points out that if health and safety were the principal drivers of licensing, then most states would license the same basket of occupations. That's not the case. Moreover, as Matthew Yglesias notes, in a Vox article on how the Obama administration is encouraging states to rethink excessive occupational licensing: "You can tell from the enormous state-to-state variation that rules are often going well beyond what's needed for safety." Alaska requires three days of training for manicurists; Alabama, 163.

Yglesias adds another point: "Licensing has in some cases become a cudgel with which to punish the already disadvantaged. Over a dozen states have rules that can make nonpayment of student loans into grounds for license revocation—turning state licensing boards into debt collectors. And rules barring people with felony convictions from obtaining licenses are widespread, which tends to exacerbate all the problems with racial and socioeconomic disparities in the criminal justice system."

4. Zoning

From 1950 to 1970, housing prices moved in tandem with construction costs. Then prices began to outstrip costs, and the trend "has been especially dramatic in America's big coastal cities."

Density might explain that—maybe some cities are just filling up—except that home prices do not correlate highly with density. However, prices do apparently correlate with "the progressive tightening of land-use restrictions." This "regulatory tax" can add as much as 50 percent to the cost of a dwelling.

Zoning, Lindsey says, exists "to protect homeowners' property values at the expense of housing for everybody else . . . and accomplishes its objectives by keeping poor people away from rich people." Not surprisingly, zoning "controls tend to be strictest in the cities with the highest per capita incomes."

As a result, and contrary to historical trends, people are moving away from big coastal cities—which are, by the way, "the country's most productive places," the ones that have "incubated the greatest productivity gains."

High prices caused by zoning are forcing people—non-rich people—to move to less productive regions, which hurts both their own economic prospects and the economy overall. (Lindsey cites a writer for *The Economist* who terms the phenomenon "moving to stagnation.")

It's customary in contemporary political discourse to pit economic liberty against economic equality: A laissez-faire economy supposedly brutalizes the weak, while a controlled economy slowly chokes to death on its own red tape. Lindsey has done the country a service by reminding everyone this dichotomy is too simplistic. Sometimes the best way to give the poor a hand up is simply to take government's boot off their neck.

Discussion Questions

1. If Williams is right and people really do want a more equal distribution of income and wealth, why haven't policies been changed to reflect those desires?
2. If Will is right and income and wealth inequality is good for the economy, why have the incomes of the bottom half been stagnant for the past three decades, while the income of the top 1 percent has tripled? Is there some way to create more jobs while also allowing incomes at the bottom to grow?
3. Which of Hinkle's suggestions make the most sense to you? Which of the regulations may be important to protect other social goals?

CHAPTER 14

Government and Society

68

"Providing Social Security Benefits in the Future: A Review of the Social Security System and Plans to Reform It"

DAVID C. JOHN

There is wide agreement that Social Security requires major reforms if it is to continue to provide economic security to retirees. The baby boom generation has begun retiring, and the amount of money paid out in benefits exceeds the amount paid into the system in payroll taxes. Very soon, the program will start drawing down a Trust Fund that has been funded by surplus contributions over previous decades, although paying off the obligations in that fund will require additional revenues, since the Trust Fund is made up of special Treasury securities that the government, in effect, owes to itself. By 2035, the Trust Fund will be exhausted, at which point payroll tax revenues will only be enough to pay 79 percent of scheduled benefits.

Clearly, something must change. At the heart of the debate over what to do are two contrasting perspectives of what the Social Security system should accomplish, both deeply rooted in American political culture. Should we view Social Security as a national guarantee of basic income for retirees, no matter what? Or should Social Security be an individualistic program that permits people to succeed—or fail—based on the choices that they make? Put another way, is Social Security a social welfare program or an investment program? David C. John of the Heritage Foundation, writing about the proposals in 2004, weighs into this debate by outlining some principles for what Social Security reform should look like from a conservative perspective. John is a strong proponent of Personal Retirement Accounts (PRA), which would allow workers to invest a portion of their Social Security taxes in individual accounts that they alone would control. However, as he notes, none of the proposed reforms address the "transition problem." That is, because Social Security is a "pay as you go" program—the payroll taxes paid by today's workers fund the Social Security benefits of today's retirees—if today's workers are allowed to take a portion of their payroll taxes and put it in a PRA, it means there will be even less money to pay for the current obligations for today's retirees than under the current system, at least for the next several decades. John writes, "neither the current system nor any of the proposed reforms comes close to closing the gap."

Social Security is the best-loved American government program, but how it works and is financed is almost completely unknown. Most Americans have a vague idea that they pay taxes for their benefits and that their benefits are linked somehow to their earnings. Many also know that the program is in trouble and needs to be "fixed" sometime soon to deal with the retirement of the baby boomers. Beyond this, their knowledge of the facts is severely limited and often colored by rumors and stories.

Most politicians exploit this lack of knowledge and limit their statements on Social Security to platitudes and vague promises. To make matters worse, reformers tend either to be content with similar platitudes or to speak in such detail that few outside the policy world can understand what they are saying. The simple fact is that today's Social Security is extremely complex, and any reform plan that is more than fine words will be similarly complex.

This paper attempts to simplify the reform debate by comparing various plans (including the current system) side by side. Each of the six sections of this paper compares how the current system and the reform plans handle a specific subject. Only reform plans that have been scored by Social Security's Office of the Chief Actuary are included in this comparison, using numbers contained in the 2003 Report of the Social Security Trustees. * * *

While looking at just one or two sections of special interest may be tempting, this approach would probably be misleading. For the best effect, each section should be considered together with the other sections in order to form a complete picture of the plan. Using simply one section by itself to judge an entire plan will not yield an accurate result.

Seven Important Rules for Real Social Security Reform

Information in this side-by-side comparison is based on Social Security's scoring memos for each plan and conclusions that can be drawn from information contained in those memos. While there are many good points in the reform plans examined in this analysis, this is not an endorsement of any proposal by the author or The Heritage Foundation. Instead, this comparison provides details of specific plans. However, it would be wise for reformers to follow a set of general principles to ensure that any

Social Security reform both resolves Social Security's problems and provides workers with greater retirement security. Those principles are listed below.

This comparison of plans makes no effort to examine whether the Social Security reform plans included in it meet or violate any or all of the principles.

Principles for Social Security Reform

- **The benefits of current retirees and those close to retirement must not be reduced.** The government has a moral contract with those who currently receive Social Security retirement benefits, as well as with those who are so close to retirement that they have no other options for building a retirement nest egg. If the benefits of younger workers cannot be maintained given the need to curb the burgeoning cost of the program, then they should have the opportunity to make up the difference by investing a portion of their Social Security taxes in a personal retirement account.
- **The rate of return on a worker's Social Security taxes must be improved.** Today's workers receive very poor returns on their Social Security payroll taxes. As a general rule, the younger a worker is or the lower his or her income, the lower his or her rate of return will be. Reform must provide a better retirement income to future retirees without increasing Social Security taxes. The best way to do this is to allow workers to divert a portion of their existing Social Security taxes into a personal retirement account that can earn significantly more than Social Security can pay.
- **Americans must be able to use Social Security to build a nest egg for the future.** A well-designed retirement system includes three elements: regular monthly retirement income, dependent's insurance, and the ability to save for retirement. Today's Social Security system provides a stable level of retirement income and does provide benefits for dependents. But it does not allow workers to accumulate cash savings to fulfill their own retirement goals or to pass on to their heirs. Workers should be able to use Social Security to build a cash nest egg that can be used to increase their retirement income or to build a better economic future for their families. The best way to do this is to establish, within the framework of Social Security, a system of personal retirement accounts.
- **Personal retirement accounts must guarantee an adequate minimum income.** Seniors must be able to count on a reasonable and predictable minimum level of monthly income, regardless of what happens in the investment markets.
- **Workers should be allowed to fund their Social Security personal retirement accounts by allocating some of their existing payroll tax dollars to them.** Workers should not be required to pay twice for their

benefits—once through existing payroll taxes and again through additional income taxes or contributions used to fund a personal retirement account. Moreover, many working Americans can save little after paying existing payroll taxes and so cannot be expected to make additional contributions to a personal account. Thus Congress should allow Americans to divert a portion of the taxes that they currently pay for Social Security retirement benefits into personal retirement accounts.

- **For currently employed workers, participation in the new accounts must be voluntary.** No one should be forced into a system of personal retirement accounts. Instead, currently employed workers must be allowed to choose between today's Social Security and one that offers personal retirement accounts.
- **Any Social Security reform plan must be realistic, cost-effective, and reduce the unfunded liabilities of the current system.** True Social Security reform will provide an improved total retirement benefit. But it should also reduce Social Security's huge unfunded liabilities by a greater level than the "transition" cost needed to finance benefits for retirees during the reform. Like paying points to obtain a better mortgage, Social Security reform should lead to a net reduction in liabilities.

The Social Security System and Plans for Reform

The Current System

Social Security currently pays an inflation-indexed monthly retirement and survivors' benefit, based on a worker's highest 35 years of earnings. Past earnings are indexed for average wage growth in the economy before calculating the benefit. The benefit formula is progressive, meaning that lower-income workers receive a benefit equal to a higher proportion of their average income than upper-income workers receive. The program is expected to continue to collect more in payroll taxes than it pays out in benefits until about 2018.

Unused payroll taxes are borrowed by the federal government and replaced by special-issue Treasury bonds. After the system begins to pay out more than it receives, the federal government will cover the resulting cash flow deficits by repaying the special-issue Treasury bonds out of general revenues. When the bonds run out in about 2042, Social Security benefits will automatically be reduced to a level equal to incoming revenue. This is projected to require a 27-percent reduction in 2042, with greater reductions after that.

The DeMint Plan

Representative Jim DeMint (R-SC) has introduced a voluntary personal retirement account (PRA) plan that would establish progressively funded voluntary individual accounts for workers under age 55 on January 1, 2005.

The amount that goes into each worker's account would vary according to income, with lower-income workers able to save a higher percentage. For average-income workers, the account would equal about 5.1 percent of income.

The government would pay the difference between the monthly benefit that can be financed from an annuity paid for by using all or some of the PRA and the amount that the current system promises. The sum of the annuity and the government-paid portion of Social Security would be guaranteed at least to equal benefits promised under the current system, and 35 percent of PRA assets would be invested in government bonds to help pay for any Social Security cash flow deficits. This proportion would be reduced gradually in the future. General revenue money would be used to pay for additional cash flow deficits.

The Graham Plan

Senator Lindsay Graham (R-SC) has proposed a plan that would give workers under age 55 (in 2004) three options. (Workers above the age of 55 would be required to remain in the current system and would receive full benefits.)

Under *Option 1,* workers would establish PRAs funded with part of their existing payroll taxes, equal to 4 percent of pay up to a maximum of $1,300 per year. Workers' benefits would be reduced by changing the benefit indexing formula from the current wage growth index to one based on consumer prices. Over time, this change would reduce benefits for workers at all income levels, but the effect on lower-income workers would be eased by a mandated minimum benefit of at least 120 percent of the poverty level for workers with a 35-year work history. The government-paid monthly benefit would be further reduced to reflect the value of the PRA. This reduction would be calculated using the average earnings of government bonds so that, if the PRA earned more than government bonds, the total monthly benefit would be higher. Option 1 also raises survivor benefits to 75 percent of the couple's benefit for many survivors.

Option 2 is essentially the same as Option 1, but without PRAs. The government would pay all benefits for workers who choose this option. Option 2 includes both the basic benefit reduction and the minimum benefit requirement.

Option 3 pays the same level of benefits promised under current law, but workers who select this option would pay higher payroll taxes in return. Initially, the payroll tax rate for retirement and survivors benefits would increase from 12.4 percent of income to 14.4 percent of income (counting both the worker's and the employer's shares of the tax). In subsequent years, the tax rate would continue to climb in 0.25 percent increments.

The Smith Plan

Representative Nick Smith (R–MI) has proposed a voluntary PRA plan that would create personal retirement savings accounts funded with an amount equal to 2.5 percent of income, paid out of existing payroll taxes. This would increase to 2.75 percent of income in 2025 and could become larger after 2038 if Social Security has surplus cash flows. Retirement and survivors' benefits would be reduced by an amount equal to the value of lifetime account contributions plus a specified interest rate.

The Smith plan would also make many changes in Social Security's benefit formula, mainly affecting middle-income and upper-income workers. These changes would eventually result in most workers receiving a flat monthly benefit of about $550 in 2004 dollars. It would also gradually increase the retirement age for full benefits and require that all newly hired local and state workers be covered by Social Security. The Smith plan transfers $866 billion from general revenues to Social Security between 2007 and 2013 to help cover cash flow deficits and allows additional general revenue transfers when needed after that.

The Ferrara Plan

Peter Ferrara, Director of the International Center for Law and Economics, has proposed a plan that would create voluntary PRAs that would be funded according to a progressive formula that allows lower-income workers to save a higher proportion of their payroll taxes than upper-income workers. Average-income workers could save about 6.4 percent of their income. Workers would be guaranteed that the total of their PRA-generated benefits and government-paid monthly benefits would at least equal the benefits promised under the current system.

Any Social Security cash flow deficits that remain would be financed through general revenue transfers equal to a 1 percent reduction in the growth rate of all government spending for eight years, the corporate income taxes deemed to result from the investment of personal account contributions, and issuing about $1.4 trillion in "off-budget" bonds. Under the Ferrara plan, these bonds would be considered a replacement for the existing system's unfunded liability and thus would not increase the federal debt.

The Orszag-Diamond Plan

Peter Orszag, Senior Fellow at the Brookings Institution,* and Peter Diamond, Institute Professor of Economics at the Massachusetts Institute of Technology, have developed a plan that does not include any form of

*Peter Orszag was President Obama's Budget Director at the Office of Management and Budget until July 2010. He now is at the Council on Foreign Relations [*Editors*].

PRA or government investment of Social Security trust fund money in private markets. Instead, it gradually changes the benefit formula to reduce benefits for moderate-income and upper-income workers and requires that all state and local government workers come under Social Security. It would also gradually reduce benefits by raising the age at which workers could receive full benefits. Workers could still retire earlier, but at lower benefits. Benefits would increase for lower-income workers, widows, and the disabled.

In addition, the plan would gradually increase the payroll tax for all workers from the current 12.4 percent of income to 15.36 percent of income in 2078. It would also raise the earnings threshold on Social Security taxes—thus requiring higher-income workers to pay additional payroll taxes—and impose a new 3 percent tax on income above the earnings threshold. Workers would not receive any credit toward benefits for income covered by this new tax.

* * *

1. Personal Retirement Accounts

What Is This, and Why Is It Important?

Allowing workers to invest a portion of their Social Security taxes is the only alternative to raising Social Security taxes or reducing Social Security benefits. However, personal retirement accounts are not all equal. The money that goes into the PRAs could come from diverting a portion of existing Social Security taxes or from some other source.

Similarly, the size of the accounts (usually expressed as a percentage of the worker's pay) is important. While larger accounts would temporarily increase the amount of additional funds required to pay benefits to retirees, they would also accumulate a pool of money faster than smaller accounts and finance a greater portion of benefits in future years. This can reduce the amount of additional tax dollars needed in future decades.

Finally, how the PRAs are invested is important. Even though they show steady growth over time stocks and commercial bonds are generally more volatile than government bonds. Investing a portion of the PRAs in government bonds makes the accounts slightly less volatile while providing some of the additional dollars needed to pay benefits to current retirees.

2. Retirement and Survivors Benefits

What Is This, and Why Is It Important?

Other than creating personal retirement accounts that allow workers to self-fund all or a portion of their Social Security retirement benefits, most reform plans deal with the program's coming deficits by either changing the level of retirement benefits promised or finding ways to increase program revenues. This section examines how various reform plans treat promised retirement benefits.

Social Security uses a complex formula to calculate an individual worker's retirement benefits. Subtle changes in this formula can cause a large change in benefits over time. For instance, changing how past income is indexed to a constant purchasing power will have only a minor impact for the first several years. However, the effect is cumulative and after several decades will result in major changes in benefits.

Similarly, seemingly minor changes in "bend points" or other aspects of the benefit formula can, over the long term, cause major changes in benefits for upper-income and/or moderate-income workers. It is even possible to use the benefit formula to approximate an increase in the full retirement age without actually raising it. Thus, a plan could still allow workers to quality for "full retirement benefits" at 65, 66, or 67 but award them full retirement benefits (as defined under the current system) only if they wait to retire until a later age.

The first question that any plan must answer is whether it would pay the full level of benefits promised under the current system. If so, it must deal with how to pay the cost, since the current system cannot afford to pay for all of the promised benefits. Other important questions include whether the plan proposes benefit changes (usually reductions) if workers do not choose to have a personal retirement account, protects lower-income workers (who more often have an interrupted work history) by instituting some sort of minimum benefit level, and/or addresses the low benefits for certain lower-income, widowed, and disabled workers under the current system.

3. Payroll Taxes

What Is This, and Why Is It Important?

Increasing Social Security payroll taxes would be one way to pay projected cash flow deficits. This method is closer to the self-funding that has characterized the system so far, but raising payroll taxes has significant drawbacks. Alternatives to payroll tax increases include instituting some form of personal retirement account to increase the return on taxes, reducing benefits, and using significant amounts of general revenue money to cover Social Security's cash flow deficits.

Currently, all workers pay 5.3 percent of their income to pay for Social Security retirement and survivors benefits. In 2004, this tax will be paid on the first $87,700 of an employee's income.* Employers match this tax for a total of 10.6 percent of each worker's income. In addition, both employer and employee pay an additional 0.9 percent of the worker's income (1.8

*This threshold is indexed and changes every year. It was $127,200 in 2017 [*Editors*].

percent total) for Social Security disability benefits. Thus, the employer and employee pay a total Social Security payroll tax of 12.4 percent.

Additional payroll taxes could be collected in three ways:

- The overall tax rate could be increased. However, this imposes higher taxes on all income groups and could reduce employment in the economy by making it more expensive to hire additional workers.
- The tax could be imposed on income levels above the threshold, currently at $87,700. In the short run, this would increase revenues, but since retirement benefits are paid on all income taxed for Social Security, it would also eventually increase the amount of benefits the system would have to pay each year and offset the amount raised through the higher taxes.
- Payroll taxes could be disconnected from the benefit formula. This could take the form of a new tax paid on income above the current $87,700 earnings threshold, collecting taxes on income up to the $87,700 level but counting only income up to $60,000 or some other level toward benefits, or some combination of the two. In either case, this type of tax would break the link between taxes and income that has existed since Social Security began in 1935. To date, neither the right nor the left has been willing to break this link for fear that it would be the first step toward turning Social Security into a welfare system. Both sides have worried that such a move—or even the perception of such a move—would undermine the program's widespread support among the American people.

4. Social Security's Unfunded Liability

What Is This, and Why Is It Important?

Both the current Social Security system and every plan to reform it will require significant amounts of general revenue money in addition to the amount collected through payroll taxes. This additional money is necessary to reduce the difference between what Social Security currently owes and what it will be able to pay.

In the reform plans, the transition cost represents a major reduction from the unfunded liability of the current program. Even though the reform plans are expensive, all of them would require less additional money than the current system. However, both the amount and the timing of this additional money would vary depending on the plan.

The amount of additional money that is needed can be measured according to two different systems. Both measurements give valuable information.

Present value reflects the idea that a dollar today has more value to a person than that same dollar has sometime in the future. It gives an idea of when the additional money is needed by giving greater weight to money needed in the near future than to an equal amount needed further in the future. In addition to showing the amount of money needed, a higher present value number indicates that money is needed sooner rather than later. [The present value of the unfunded liability ranges from $929 billion in the Orszag-Diamond plan to $7.6 trillion in the Ferrara plan.]

The *sum of the deficits* indicates the total amount of additional money that will be needed. This measure gives $100 needed today the same weight as $100 needed in 15 years. This measure adds up only the future cash flow deficits; it does not include cash flow surpluses because the government does not have any way to save or invest that money for future use. Using both of these measurements gives a better picture of the situation than using just one. [The sum of the deficits of the unfunded liability ranges from $7.1 trillion in the Graham plan to $16.4 trillion in the Ferrara plan.]

Paying for the current system or any of the reform plans will require Congress to balance Social Security's needs against those of the rest of the economy. In general, as more additional dollars are needed for the current system or a reform plan, less money will be available for other government programs and the private sector.

As this burden on the general federal budget increases and persists, Congress would find it increasingly more difficult to come up with that money, and it would become increasingly less likely that such a plan would really be paid for on schedule. This is especially true for the current system, which will incur the massive deficits to pay all of the promised benefits.

* * *

5. Paying for Social Security's Unfunded Liability

What Is This, and Why Is It Important?

Both the current Social Security program and all of the proposed reform plans will require large amounts of general revenue money to cover the annual cash flow deficits. Exactly when that money is first needed, how many years it will be needed, and the total amount that will be needed varies from plan to plan. Avoiding use of general revenue money would require either reducing Social Security benefits enough to eliminate the annual deficits or imposing new taxes to generate sufficient revenue. Neither the current system nor any of the proposed reform plans comes close to closing the gap.

Some plans do specify sources for the needed general revenues, but these are handicapped by the fact that no Congress can bind the hands of a future Congress. Thus, even if Congress did pass a plan that specified the source of the needed general revenues, a future Congress could change the plan by a majority vote. The only way to avoid this uncertainty would be for Congress to pass and the states to ratify the plan as a constitutional amendment—which would be prohibitively difficult.

In short, both the current system and all known reform plans would have to find the necessary general revenues from some combination of four sources: borrowing additional money collecting more taxes than needed to fund the rest of the government, reducing other government spending, or reducing Social Security benefits more than is called for under either current law or any of the reform plans.

The most important thing to remember is that the existing Social Security system and the reform plans all face this problem. This is not a weakness that is limited to PRA plans or any other reform plan. The only question is when the cash flow deficits begin and how large they will be.

Current Law

Current law makes no provision for funding Social Security's unfunded liability. The program has no credit line with the U.S. Treasury, and when its trust fund promises are exhausted, current law will require it to reduce benefits.

The DeMint Plan

While some press releases connected with Representative DeMint's plan suggest that some of its general revenue needs could be generated by reducing the growth of federal spending, no language specifying where the general revenues would come from is included in his legislation.

The Graham Plan

Senator Graham's plan includes a commission that would recommend reductions in corporate welfare and redirect the savings to reduce his plan's unfunded liability. At best, a reduction in corporate welfare would generate only part of the needed general revenue. The commission would produce a legislative proposal that would then be considered by Congress.

Because the commission would be created by the same legislation that implements Graham's Social Security reforms, its recommendations could not even be considered until after the plan is enacted. As a result, passage of the Graham plan does not guarantee that these revenues would be available. Regardless of what the commission recommended, a future Congress could reject the proposed cuts in corporate welfare. In that case, Congress would have to come up with another method to raise the needed revenue.

The Smith Plan

Other than the proposed benefit changes that would partially reduce Social Security's unfunded liability, the Smith plan does not specify how it would pay cash flow deficits.

The Ferrara Plan

The Ferrara plan includes three mechanisms designed to create the needed general revenues.

First, it would mandate a 1 percent reduction in the growth of all federal spending (including entitlements such as Social Security) for at least eight years and redirect that revenue to Social Security. Since Congress cannot legally force a subsequent Congress to follow a set course of action, the only enforcement mechanism available is a constitutional amendment. As a result, the Ferrara plan simply appropriates to Social Security the amount of revenue that would result if Congress were to reduce spending growth. In practice, a future Congress could choose not to reduce spending growth and, instead, just let the deficit grow larger or generate the necessary revenue in some other way.

Second, the Ferrara plan would transfer to Social Security the amount of corporate income taxes that could potentially result from the investment of personal accounts in corporate stocks and bonds. This is not a new or higher tax. This transfer is intended to reflect the taxes that would be paid at the current 35 percent corporate tax rate. Since SSA does not conduct dynamic scoring, this transfer is based on the static assumption that two-thirds of the stocks and bonds held through personal accounts reflect domestic corporate investment.

Third, the Ferrara plan would borrow about $1.4 trillion in special off-budget bonds. However, there is no practical way to create off-budget bonds that would not count against the federal debt. Even if there were, such a move would reduce the amount of transparency in the federal budget.

The Orszag-Diamond Plan

While the Orszag-Diamond plan includes both some benefit reductions and benefit increases for widows, the disabled, and low-income workers, the two elements of the plan are roughly equal. It reduces Social Security's unfunded liability using tax increases contained in the plan, including an increase in the payroll tax rate, a gradual increase in the amount of income subject to Social Security taxes, and a new 3 percent tax on any salary income not subject to Social Security taxes.

6. Making Social Security a Better Deal for Workers

What Is This, and Why Is It Important?

In the long run, a reform plan should do more than just preserve the current Social Security system with its many flaws. While a key requirement of any reform plan is to provide a stable, guaranteed, and adequate level of benefits at an affordable cost, it should do more.

The current system fails to allow workers to build any form of nest egg for the future. Instead, it is the highest single tax for about 80 percent of workers. In return, each worker receives a life annuity that ends with the death(s) of the worker, the surviving spouse (if there is one), or young children (if any). In today's world, where two-earner families are increasingly the norm, the current system even limits survivor benefits to the higher of either the deceased spouses benefits or the surviving spouse's benefits. Whichever account is lower, no matter how long that spouse worked, is marked paid in full and extinguished.

At a minimum, a reform plan should allow workers to pass on some of what they earned and paid in Social Security taxes to improve their spouse's retirement benefits. It should also allow workers the flexibility to use their entire account for retirement benefits or take a smaller retirement benefit and use the balance to pay for a grandchild's college education, start a small business, or pass on money to a later generation.

In judging whether each proposed reform would be better for America's workers, readers may differ sharply. However, while most summaries and studies examine Social Security reform from the viewpoint of federal budget impact, tax rates, and the survivability of the system, few consider the overall impact of reform on the workers it was designed to benefit in the first place. Social Security should not be reformed or "saved" for its own sake, but only if it more effectively provides the benefits workers need at a price they can afford.

Discussion Questions

1. The payroll tax of 6.2 percent that workers pay into Social Security is only applied to the first $127,200 of income in 2017, and increases each year based on inflation. This makes the payroll tax regressive, since someone making $20,000 a year pays a larger percentage of their income (6.2 percent) than someone making $200,000 a year (3.9 percent, since only the first $127,200 is taxed). Is this a valid reason for raising the payroll cap, or even eliminating it altogether?

2. Are the broad objectives initially established for Social Security—income security for old age, risk sharing across the population and across generations—still appropriate today? Are individuals better

able to plan for and manage their retirement today than in the 1930s or even the 1990s? What do you see as the major advantages and disadvantages of the current Social Security system and proposals for partial privatization?

69

"American Business, Public Policy, Case Studies, and Political Theory"

THEODORE J. LOWI

Before Lowi's article appeared in 1964, many social scientists analyzed public policy through case studies that focused on one particular policy and its implementation. Lowi argued that what the social sciences lacked was a means to cumulate, compare, and contrast the diverse findings of these studies. We needed, in other words, a typology of policy making. In the article below, Lowi argues that different types of public policies produce different patterns of participation. Public policies can be classified as distributive, regulatory, or redistributive, each with its own distinctive "arena of power." For example, public policies that provide benefits to a single congressional district, group, or company can be classified as distributive. In the distributive arena of power, policy beneficiaries are active in seeking to expand or extend their benefits, but there is no real opposition. Rather, legislators build coalitions premised upon "mutual non-interference" interests, and their representatives seek particular benefits, such as a research and development contract, a new highway, or a farm subsidy, but they do not oppose the similar requests of others. The regulatory and redistributive policy arenas also display distinctive dynamics and roles that participants in the process play. Lowi's work was important not only for providing a classification scheme by which social scientists could think more systematically about different public policies, but for proposing that we study "politics" as a consequence of different types of public policy. Traditionally, social scientists have studied politics to see what kinds of policies are produced.

What is needed is a basis for cumulating, comparing, and contrasting diverse findings. Such a framework or interpretative scheme would bring the diverse cases and findings into a more consistent relation to each other and would begin to suggest generalizations sufficiently close to the data to be relevant and sufficiently abstract to be subject to more broadly theoretical treatment.

* * *

The scheme is based upon the following argument: (1) The types of relationships to be found among people are determined by their expectations—by what they hope to achieve or get from relating to others. (2) In politics, expectations are determined by governmental outputs or policies. (3) Therefore, a political relationship is determined by the type of policy at stake, so that for every type of policy there is likely to be a distinctive type of political relationship. If power is defined as a share in the making of policy, or authoritative allocations, then the political relationship in question is a power relationship or, over time, a power structure.

* * *

There are three major categories of public policies in the scheme: distribution, regulation, and redistribution. These types are historically as well as functionally distinct, distribution being almost the exclusive type of national domestic policy from 1789 until virtually 1890. Agitation for regulatory and redistributive policies began at about the same time, but regulation had become an established fact before any headway at all was made in redistribution.

These categories are not mere contrivances for purposes of simplification. They are meant to correspond to real phenomena—so much so that the major hypotheses of the scheme follow directly from the categories and their definitions. Thus, *these areas of policy or government activity constitute real arenas of power.* Each arena tends to develop its own characteristic political structure, political process, elites, and group relations. What remains is to identify these arenas, to formulate hypotheses about the attributes of each, and to test the scheme by how many empirical relationships it can anticipate and explain.

Areas of Policy Defined

(1) In the long run, all governmental policies may be considered redistributive, because in the long run some people pay in taxes more than they receive in services. Or, all may be thought regulatory because, in the long run, a governmental decision on the use of resources can only displace a private decision about the same resource or at least reduce private alternatives about the resource. But politics works in the short run, and in the short run certain kinds of government decisions can be made without regard to limited resources. Policies of this kind are called "distributive," a term first coined for nineteenth-century land policies, but easily extended to include most contemporary public land and resource policies; rivers and harbors ("pork barrel") programs; defense procurement and R & D [research and development]; labor, business, and agricultural "clientele" services; and the traditional tariff. Distributive policies are characterized by the ease with which they can be disaggregated and dispensed unit by small unit, each unit more or less in isolation from other units and from any general rule. "Patronage" in the fullest meaning of the word can be taken as a synonym for "distributive." These are policies that are virtually not policies at all but are highly individualized decisions that only by accumulation can be called a policy. They are policies in which

the indulged and the deprived, the loser and the recipient, need never come into direct confrontation. Indeed, in many instances of distributive policy, the deprived cannot as a class be identified, because the most influential among them can be accommodated by further disaggregation of the stakes.

(2) Regulatory policies are also specific and individual in their impact, but they are not capable of the almost infinite amount of disaggregation typical of distributive policies. Although the laws are stated in general terms ("Arrange the transportation system artistically." "Thou shalt not show favoritism in pricing."), the impact of regulatory decisions is clearly one of directly raising costs and/or reducing or expanding the alternatives of private individuals ("Get off the grass!" "Produce kosher if you advertise kosher!"). Regulatory policies are distinguishable from distributive in that in the short run the regulatory decision involves a direct choice as to who will be indulged and who deprived. Not all applicants for a single television channel or an overseas air route can be propitiated. Enforcement of an unfair labor practice on the part of management weakens management in its dealings with labor. So, while implementation is firm-by-firm and case-by-case, policies cannot be disaggregated to the level of the individual or the single firm (as in distribution), because individual decisions must be made by application of a general rule and therefore become interrelated within the broader standards of law. Decisions cumulate among all individuals affected by the law in roughly the same way. Since the most stable lines of perceived common impact are the basic sectors of the economy, regulatory decisions are cumulative largely along sectoral lines; regulatory policies are usually disaggregable only down to the sector level.

(3) Redistributive policies are like regulatory policies in the sense that relations among broad categories of private individuals are involved and, hence, individual decisions must be interrelated. But on all other counts there are great differences in the nature of impact. The categories of impact are much broader, approaching social classes. They are, crudely speaking, haves and have-nots, bigness and smallness, bourgeoisie and proletariat. The aim involved is not use of property but property itself, not equal treatment but equal possession, not behavior but being. The fact that our income tax is in reality only mildly redistributive does not alter the fact of the aims and the stakes involved in income tax policies. The same goes for our various "welfare state" programs, which are redistributive only for those who entered retirement or unemployment rolls without having contributed at all. The nature of a redistributive issue is not determined by the outcome of a battle over how redistributive a policy is going to be. Expectations about what it *can* be, what it threatens to be, are determinative.

Arenas of Power

Once one posits the general tendency of these areas of policy or governmental activity to develop characteristic political structures, a number of hypotheses become compelling. And when the various hypotheses are accumulated, the general contours of each of the three arenas begin quickly to resemble, respectively, the three "general" theories of political process identified earlier. The arena that develops around distributive policies is best characterized in the terms of [E. E.] Schattschneider's findings. The regulatory arena corresponds to the pluralist school, and the school's general notions are found to be limited pretty much to this one arena. The redistributive arena most closely approximates, with some adaptation, an elitist view of the political process.

(1) The distributive arena can be identified in considerable detail from Schattschneider's case study alone. What he and his pluralist successors did not see was that the traditional structure of tariff politics is also in largest part the structure of politics of all those diverse policies identified earlier as distributive. The arena is "pluralistic" only in the sense that a large number of small, intensely organized interests are operating. In fact, there is even greater multiplicity of participants here than the pressure-group model can account for, because essentially it is a politics of every man for himself. The single person and the single firm are the major activists.

* * *

When a billion-dollar issue can be disaggregated into many millions of nickel-dime items and each item can be dealt with without regard to the others, multiplication of interests and of access is inevitable, and so is reduction of conflict. All of this has the greatest of bearing on the relations among participants and, therefore, the "power structure." Indeed, coalitions must be built to pass legislation and "make policy," but what of the nature and basis of the coalitions? In the distributive arena, political relationships approximate what Schattschneider called "mutual non-interference"—"a mutuality under which it is proper for each to seek duties [indulgences] for himself but improper and unfair to oppose duties [indulgences] sought by others." In the area of rivers and harbors, references are made to "pork barrel" and "log-rolling," but these colloquialisms have not been taken sufficiently seriously. A log-rolling coalition is not one forged of conflict, compromise, and tangential interest but, on the contrary, one composed of members who have absolutely nothing in common; and this is possible because the "pork barrel" is a container for unrelated items. This is the typical form of relationship in the distributive arena.

The structure of these log-rolling relationships leads typically, though not always, to Congress; and the structure is relatively stable because all who have access of any sort usually support whoever are the leaders. And there tend to be "elites" of a peculiar sort in the Congressional committees whose jurisdictions include the subject matter in question. Until recently, for instance, on tariff matters the House Ways and Means Committee was virtually the government. Much the same can be said for Public Works on rivers and harbors. It is a broker leadership, but "policy" is best understood as cooptation rather than conflict and compromise.

* * *

(2) The regulatory arena could hardly be better identified than in the thousands of pages written for the whole polity by the pluralists. But, unfortunately, some translation is necessary to accommodate pluralism to its more limited universe. The regulatory arena appears to be composed of a multiplicity of groups organized around tangential relations. . . . Within this narrower context of regulatory decisions, one can even go so far as to accept the most extreme pluralist statement that policy tends to be a residue of the interplay of group conflict. This statement can be severely criticized only by use of examples drawn from non-regulatory decisions.

As I argued before, there is no way for regulatory policies to be disaggregated into very large numbers of unrelated items. Because individual regulatory decisions involve direct confrontations of indulged and deprived, the typical political coalition is born of conflict and compromise among tangential interests that usually involve a total sector of the economy. Thus, while the typical basis for coalition in distributive politics is uncommon interests (log-rolling), an entirely different basis is typical in regulatory politics. The pluralist went wrong only in assuming the regulatory type of coalition is *the* coalition.

* * *

What this suggests is that the typical power structure in regulatory politics is far less stable than that in the distributive arena. Since coalitions form around shared interests, the coalitions will shift as the interests change or as conflicts of interest emerge. With such group-based and shifting patterns of conflict built into every regulatory issue, it is in most cases impossible for a Congressional committee, an administrative agency, a peak association governing board, or a social elite to contain all the participants long enough to establish a stable power elite. Policy outcomes seem inevitably to be the residue remaining after all the reductions of demands by all participants have been made in order to extend support to majority size. But a majority-sized coalition of shared interests on one issue could not possibly be entirely appropriate for some other issue. In regulatory decision-making, relationships among group leadership elements and between them on any one or more points of governmental access are too unstable to form a single policy-making elite. As a consequence, decision-making tends to pass from administrative agencies and Congressional committees to Congress, the place where uncertainties in the policy process have always been settled. Congress as an institution is the last resort for breakdowns in bargaining over policy, just as in the case of parties the primary is a last resort for breakdowns in bargaining over nominations. No one leadership group can contain the conflict by an almost infinite subdivision and distribution of the stakes. In the regulatory political process, Congress and the "balance of power" seem to play the classic role attributed to them by the pluralists.

* * *

(3) Issues that involve redistribution cut closer than any others along class lines and activate interests in what are roughly class terms. If there is ever any cohesion within the peak associations, it occurs on redistributive issues, and their rhetoric suggests that they occupy themselves most of the time with these. In a ten-year period just before and after, but not including, the war years [World War II], the Manufacturers' Association of Connecticut, for example, expressed itself overwhelmingly more often on redistributive than on any other types of issues.

* * *

Where the peak associations, led by elements of Mr. Mills's power elite,* have reality, their resources and access are bound to affect power relations. Owing to their stability and the impasse (or equilibrium) in relations among broad classes of the entire society, the political structure of the redistributive arena seems to be highly stabilized, virtually institutionalized. Its stability, unlike that of the distributive arena, derives from shared interests. But in contrast to the regulatory arena, these shared interests are sufficiently stable and clear and consistent to provide the foundation for ideologies.

* * *

Finally, just as the nature of redistributive policies influences politics towards the centralization and stabilization of conflict, so does it further influence the removal of decision-making from Congress. A decentralized and bargaining Congress can cumulate but it cannot balance, and redistributive policies require complex balancing on a very large scale. What [William] Riker has said of budget-making applies here: ". . . legislative governments cannot endure a budget. Its finances must be totted up by party leaders in the legislature itself. In a complex fiscal system, however, haphazard legislative judgments cannot bring revenue into even rough alignment with supply. So budgeting is introduced—which transfers financial control to the budget maker. . . ." Congress can provide exceptions to principles and it can implement those principles with elaborate standards of implementation as a condition for the concessions that money-providers will make. But the makers of principles of redistribution seem to be the holders of the "command posts."

*According to C. Wright Mills, a small network of individuals, which he called the "power elite," controls the economy, the political system, and the military [*Editors*].

None of this suggests a power elite such as Mills would have had us believe existed, but it does suggest a type of stable and continual conflict that can only be understood in class terms. The foundation upon which the social-stratification and power-elite school rested, especially when dealing with national power, was so conceptually weak and empirically unsupported that its critics were led to err in the opposite direction by denying the direct relevance of social and institutional positions and the probability of stable decision-making elites. But the relevance of that approach becomes stronger as the scope of its application is reduced and as the standards for identifying the scope are clarified. But this is equally true of the pluralist school and of those approaches based on a "politics of this-or-that policy."

* * *

DISCUSSION QUESTIONS

1. Provide examples of each type of policy that Lowi discusses (distributive, regulatory, and redistributive).
2. If you were a member of Congress, which type of policy would you try to emphasize if your main interest was in getting re-elected?
3. Are there any types of policies that do not seem to fit Lowi's framework? Do some policies fit more than one category?

Debating the Issues: Should the Affordable Care Act (Obamacare) Be Repealed?

The Affordable Care Act ("Obamacare") was the most significant domestic legislation enacted in the United States since the 1960s, and also one of the most controversial. Its supporters lauded its regulation of the health insurance industry, its cost controls, and its expansion of programs and subsidies that increased the number of people with health insurance. Its critics attacked the "individual mandate" requiring everyone to purchase health insurance, and its taxes on certain categories of medical equipment. Opposition to the law spurred the rise of the Tea Party and played a central role in the Republican Party's gains in the House and Senate in the 2010 midterm elections. Donald Trump made "repeal and replace" a central part of his successful presidential campaign.

The three pillars of the ACA are (a) prohibiting health insurers from denying coverage to individuals based on pre-existing conditions; (b) a requirement that all individuals have health insurance, either through employers, government programs like Medicare or Medicaid, or on the private insurance market; and (c) income-based subsidies to help with the affordability of coverage.

According to President Obama's article in the *Journal of the American Medical Association*, the law has succeeded: it has reduced the rate of uninsured Americans from 16 percent to 9 percent, allowing 20 million previously uninsured to obtain coverage. It has expanded access to basic preventive services. It has slowed the rate of growth of health care costs, reducing increases in the cost of private insurance and actually *lowering* costs in Medicare and Medicaid. And it has improved outcomes, lowering hospital readmission rates and the frequency of hospital-acquired infections. Because of the ACA, argues Obama, "Americans can now count on access to health coverage throughout their lives, and the federal government has an array of tools to bring the rise of health care costs under control."

Nonsense, responds Haislmaier and his co-authors, contesting nearly every claim about the ACA's success. Millions of people lost insurance they liked, and many people had their relationships with doctors disrupted as insurers narrowed provider networks. The costs of insurance grew, with premiums for many plans increasing by more than 10 percent a year, in part by imposing inflexible rules that prevent people from buying the kind of coverage they want, rather than what the federal government says they need. The ACA increased taxes, including those on middle class families, by $770 billion over 10 years. And the "widely despised" individual mandate takes away any element of individual choice. These authors propose an alternative reform that uses "market-based" reforms reliant on competition tax changes, and state-level regulation to improve efficiency and lower costs.

If there is one place in which the two readings agree, it is that health care reform will continue to be a controversial and contested policy.

70

"United States Health Care Reform: Progress to Date and Next Steps"

BARACK OBAMA

Health care costs affect the economy, the federal budget and virtually every American family's financial well-being. Health insurance enables children to excel at school, adults to work more productively, and Americans of all ages to live longer, healthier lives. When I took office, health care costs had risen rapidly for decades, and tens of millions of Americans were uninsured. Regardless of the political difficulties, I concluded comprehensive reform was necessary.

The result of that effort, the Affordable Care Act (ACA), has made substantial progress in addressing these challenges. Americans can now count on access to health coverage throughout their lives, and the federal government has an array of tools to bring the rise of health care costs under control. However, the work toward a high-quality, affordable, accessible health care system is not over.

In this Special Communication, I assess the progress the ACA has made toward improving the U.S. health care system and discuss how policy makers can build on that progress in the years ahead. I close with reflections on what my administration's experience with the ACA can teach about the potential for positive change in health policy in particular and public policy generally.

Impetus for Health Reform

In my first days in office, I confronted an array of immediate challenges associated with the Great Recession. I also had to deal with one of the nation's most intractable and long-standing problems, a health care system that fell far short of its potential. In 2008, the United States devoted 16 percent of the economy to health care, an increase of almost one-quarter since 1998 (when 13 percent of the economy was spent on health care), yet much of that spending did not translate into better outcomes for patients. The health care system also fell short on quality of care, too often failing to keep patients safe, waiting to treat patients when they were sick rather than focusing on keeping them healthy, and delivering fragmented, poorly coordinated care.

Moreover, the U.S. system left more than 1 in 7 Americans without health insurance coverage in 2008. Despite successful efforts in the 1980s and 1990s to expand coverage for specific populations, like children, the United States had not seen a large, sustained reduction in the uninsured rate since Medicare and Medicaid began (Figure 1). The United States' high uninsured rate had negative consequences for uninsured Americans, who experienced greater financial insecurity, barriers to care, and odds of poor health and preventable death; for the health care system, which was burdened with billions of dollars in uncompensated care; and for the U.S. economy, which suffered, for example, because workers were concerned about joining the ranks of the uninsured if they sought additional education or started a business. Beyond these statistics were the countless, heartbreaking stories of Americans who struggled to access care because of a broken health insurance system. These included people like Natoma Canfield, who had overcome cancer once but had to discontinue her coverage due to rapidly escalating premiums and found herself facing a new cancer diagnosis uninsured.

Figure 1. Percentage of Individuals in the United States without Health Insurance, 1963–2015

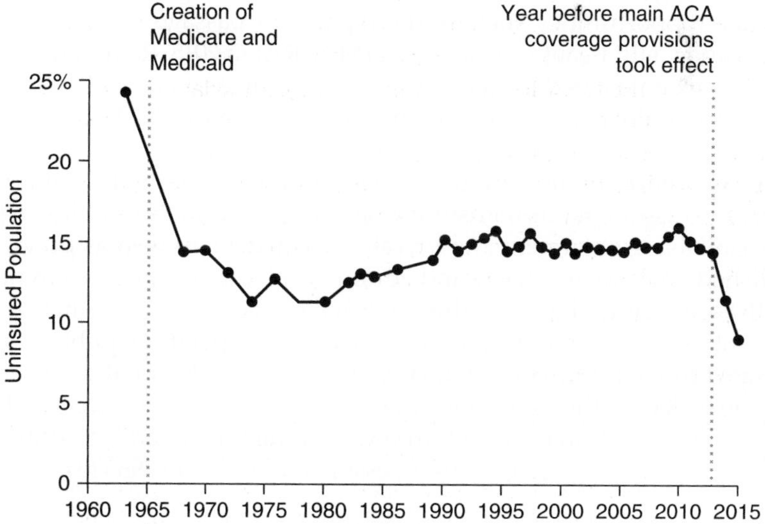

SOURCE: Data are derived from the National Health Interview Survey and for years prior to 1982, supplementary information from other survey sources and administrative records. For years 1989 and later, data are annual. For prior years, data are generally but not always biannual. ACA indicates Affordable Care Act.

In 2009, during my first month in office, I extended the Children's Health Insurance Program and soon thereafter signed the American Recovery and Reinvestment Act, which included temporary support to sustain Medicaid coverage as well as investments in health information technology, prevention, and health research to improve the system in the long run. In the summer of 2009, I signed the Tobacco Control Act, which has contributed to a rapid decline in the rate of smoking among teens, from 19.5 percent in 2009 to 10.8 percent in 2015, with substantial declines among adults as well.

Beyond these initial actions, I decided to prioritize comprehensive health reform not only because of the gravity of these challenges but also because of the possibility for progress. Massachusetts had recently implemented bipartisan legislation to expand health insurance coverage to all its residents. Leaders in Congress had recognized that expanding coverage, reducing the level and growth of health care costs, and improving quality was an urgent national priority. At the same time, a broad array of health care organizations and professionals, business leaders, consumer groups, and others agreed that the time had come to press ahead with reform. Those elements contributed to my decision, along with my deeply held belief that health care is not a privilege for a few, but a right for all. After a long debate with well-documented twists and turns, I signed the ACA on March 23, 2010.

Progress Under the ACA

The years following the ACA's passage included intense implementation efforts, changes in direction because of actions in Congress and the courts, and new opportunities such as the bipartisan passage of the Medicare Access and CHIP Reauthorization Act (MACRA) in 2015. Rather than detail every development in the intervening years, I provide an overall assessment of how the health care system has changed between the ACA's passage and today.

The evidence underlying this assessment was obtained from several sources. To assess trends in insurance coverage, this analysis relies on publicly available government and private survey data, as well as previously published analyses of survey and administrative data. To assess trends in health care costs and quality, this analysis relies on publicly available government estimates and projections of health care spending; publicly available government and private survey data; data on hospital readmission rates provided by the Centers for Medicare & Medicaid Services; and previously published analyses of survey, administrative, and clinical data. The dates of the data used in this assessment range from 1963 to early 2016.

Expanding and Improving Coverage

The ACA has succeeded in sharply increasing insurance coverage. Since the ACA became law, the uninsured rate has declined by 43 percent, from

16.0 percent in 2010 to 9.1 percent in 2015, with most of that decline occurring after the law's main coverage provisions took effect in 2014 (Figure 1). The number of uninsured individuals in the United States has declined from 49 million in 2010 to 29 million in 2015. This is by far the largest decline in the uninsured rate since the creation of Medicare and Medicaid 5 decades ago. Recent analyses have concluded these gains are primarily because of the ACA, rather than other factors such as the ongoing economic recovery. Adjusting for economic and demographic changes and other underlying trends, the Department of Health and Human Services estimated that 20 million more people had health insurance in early 2016 because of the law.

Each of the law's major coverage provisions—comprehensive reforms in the health insurance market combined with financial assistance for low- and moderate-income individuals to purchase coverage, generous federal support for states that expand their Medicaid programs to cover more low-income adults, and improvements in existing insurance coverage—has contributed to these gains. States that decided to expand their Medicaid programs saw larger reductions in their uninsured rates from 2013 to 2015, especially when those states had large uninsured populations to start with (Figure 2). However, even states that have not adopted Medicaid expansion have seen substantial reductions in their uninsured rates, indicating that

Figure 2. Decline in Adult Uninsured Rate from 2013 to 2015 vs. 2013 Uninsured Rate by State

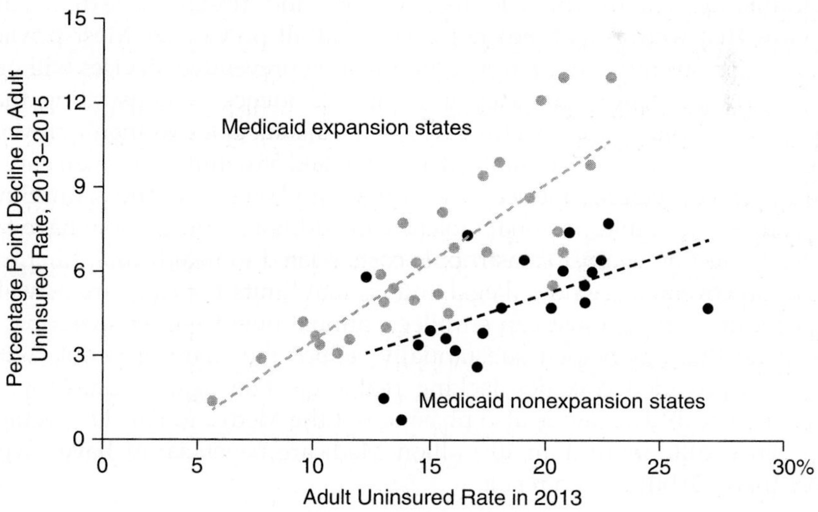

SOURCE: Data are derived from the Gallup-Healthways Well-Being Index and reflect uninsured rates for individuals 18 years or older. Dashed lines reflect the result of an ordinary least squares regression relating the change in the uninsured rate from 2013 to 2015 to the level of the uninsured rate in 2013, run separately for each group of states. The 29 states in which expanded coverage took effect before the end of 2015 were categorized as Medicaid expansion states, and the remaining 21 states were categorized as Medicaid nonexpansion states.

the ACA's other reforms are increasing insurance coverage. The law's provision allowing young adults to stay on a parent's plan until age 26 years has also played a contributing role, covering an estimated 2.3 million people after it took effect in late 2010.

Early evidence indicates that expanded coverage is improving access to treatment, financial security, and health for the newly insured. Following the expansion through early 2015, nonelderly adults experienced substantial improvements in the share of individuals who have a personal physician (increase of 3.5 percentage points) and easy access to medicine (increase of 2.4 percentage points) and substantial decreases in the share who are unable to afford care (decrease of 5.5 percentage points) and reporting fair or poor health (decrease of 3.4 percentage points) relative to the pre-ACA trend. Similarly, research has found that Medicaid expansion improves the financial security of the newly insured (for example, by reducing the amount of debt sent to a collection agency by an estimated \$600–\$1000 per person gaining Medicaid coverage). Greater insurance coverage appears to have been achieved without negative effects on the labor market, despite widespread predictions that the law would be a "job killer." Private-sector employment has increased in every month since the ACA became law, and rigorous comparisons of Medicaid expansion and nonexpansion states show no negative effects on employment in expansion states.

The law has also greatly improved health insurance coverage for people who already had it. Coverage offered on the individual market or to small businesses must now include a core set of health care services, including maternity care and treatment for mental health and substance use disorders, services that were sometimes not covered at all previously. Most private insurance plans must now cover recommended preventive services without cost-sharing, an important step in light of evidence demonstrating that many preventive services were underused. This includes women's preventive services, which has guaranteed an estimated 55.6 million women coverage of services such as contraceptive coverage and screening and counseling for domestic and interpersonal violence. In addition, families now have far better protection against catastrophic costs related to health care. Lifetime limits on coverage are now illegal and annual limits typically are as well. Instead, most plans must cap enrollees' annual out-of-pocket spending, a provision that has helped substantially reduce the share of people with employer-provided coverage lacking real protection against catastrophic costs (Figure 3). The law is also phasing out the Medicare Part D coverage gap. Since 2010, more than 10 million Medicare beneficiaries have saved more than \$20 billion as a result.

Reforming the Health Care Delivery System

Before the ACA, the health care system was dominated by "fee-for-service" payment systems, which often penalized health care organizations and health care professionals who find ways to deliver care more efficiently, while failing to reward those who improve the quality of care. The ACA has changed the health care payment system in several important ways. The law modified rates paid to many that provide Medicare services and Medicare Advantage plans to better align them with the actual costs of providing care. Research on how past changes in Medicare payment rates have affected private payment rates implies that these changes in Medicare payment policy are helping decrease prices in the private sector as well. The ACA also included numerous policies to detect and prevent health care fraud, including increased scrutiny prior to enrollment in Medicare and Medicaid for health care entities that pose a high risk of fraud, stronger penalties for crimes involving losses in excess of $1 million, and additional funding for antifraud efforts. The ACA has also widely deployed "value-based payment" systems in Medicare that tie fee-for-service payments to the quality and efficiency of the care delivered by health care organizations and health care professionals. In parallel with these efforts, my administration has worked to foster a more competitive market by increasing transparency around the prices charged and the quality of care delivered.

Most importantly over the long run, the ACA is moving the health care system toward "alternative payment models" that hold health care entities accountable for outcomes. These models include bundled payment models

Figure 3. Percentage of Workers with Employer-Based Single Coverage without an Annual Limit on Out-of-pocket Spending

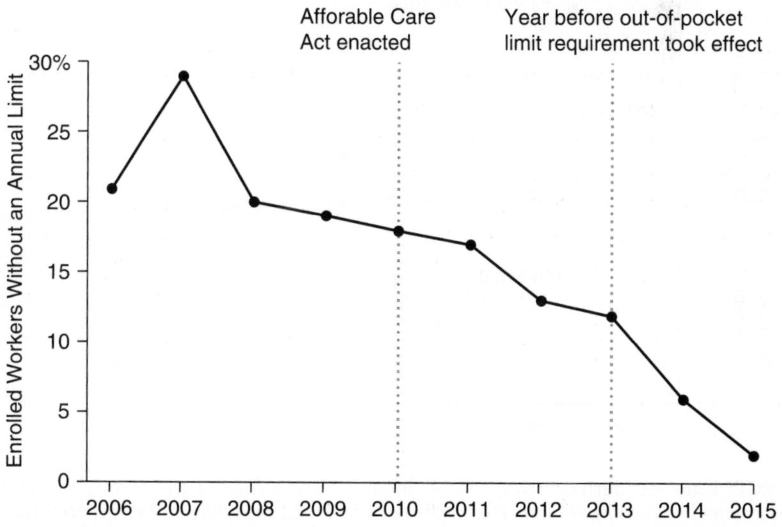

SOURCE: Data from the Kaiser Family Foundation/Health Research and Education Trust Employer Health Benefits Survey.

that make a single payment for all of the services provided during a clinical episode and population-based models like accountable care organizations (ACOs) that base payment on the results health care organizations and health care professionals achieve for all of their patients' care. The law created the Center for Medicare and Medicaid Innovation (CMMI) to test alternative payment models and bring them to scale if they are successful, as well as a permanent ACO program in Medicare. Today, an estimated 30 percent of traditional Medicare payments flow through alternative payment models that broaden the focus of payment beyond individual services or a particular entity, up from essentially none in 2010. These models are also spreading rapidly in the private sector, and their spread will likely be accelerated by the physician payment reforms in MACRA.

Trends in health care costs and quality under the ACA have been promising (Figure 4). From 2010 through 2014, mean annual growth in real per-enrollee Medicare spending has actually been *negative*, down from a mean of 4.7 percent per year from 2000 through 2005 and 2.4 percent per year from 2006 to 2010 (growth from 2005 to 2006 is omitted to avoid including the rapid growth associated with the creation of Medicare Part D). Similarly, mean real per-enrollee growth in private insurance spending has been 1.1 percent per year since 2010, compared with a mean of 6.5 percent from 2000 through 2005 and 3.4 percent from 2005 to 2010.

Figure 4. Rate of Change in Real per-Enrollee Spending by Payer

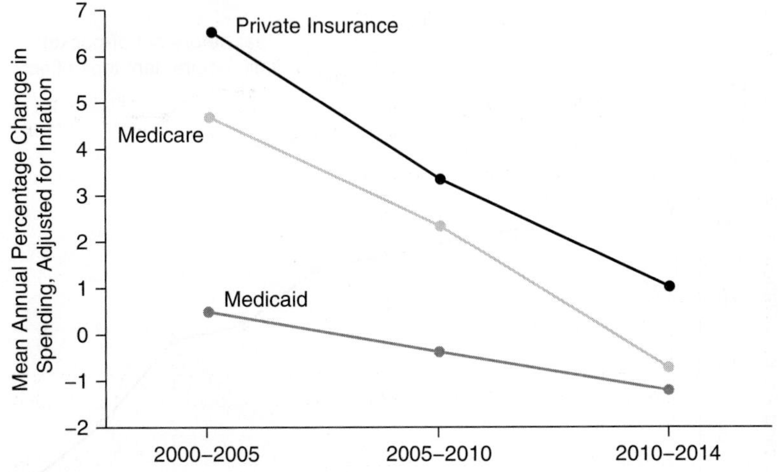

SOURCE: Data are derived from the National Health Expenditure Accounts. Inflation adjustments use the Gross Domestic Product Price Index reported in the National Income and Product Accounts. The mean growth rate for Medicare spending reported for 2005 through 2010 omits growth from 2005 to 2006 to exclude the effect of the creation of Medicare Part D.

As a result, health care spending is likely to be far lower than expected. For example, relative to the projections the Congressional Budget Office (CBO) issued just before I took office, CBO now projects Medicare to spend 20 percent, or about $160 billion, less in 2019 alone. The implications for families' budgets of slower growth in premiums have been equally striking. Had premiums increased since 2010 at the same mean rate as the preceding decade, the mean family premium for employer-based coverage would have been almost $2,600 higher in 2015. Employees receive much of those savings through lower premium costs, and economists generally agree that those employees will receive the remainder as higher wages in the long run. Furthermore, while deductibles have increased in recent years, they have increased no faster than in the years preceding 2010. Multiple sources also indicate that the overall share of health care costs that enrollees in employer coverage pay out of pocket has been close to flat since 2010 (Figure 5), most likely because the continued increase in deductibles has been canceled out by a decline in co-payments.

At the same time, the United States has seen important improvements in the quality of care. The rate of hospital-acquired conditions (such as adverse drug events, infections, and pressure ulcers) has declined by

Figure 5. Out-of-pocket Spending as a Percentage of Total Health Care Spending for Individuals Enrolled in Employer-Based Coverage

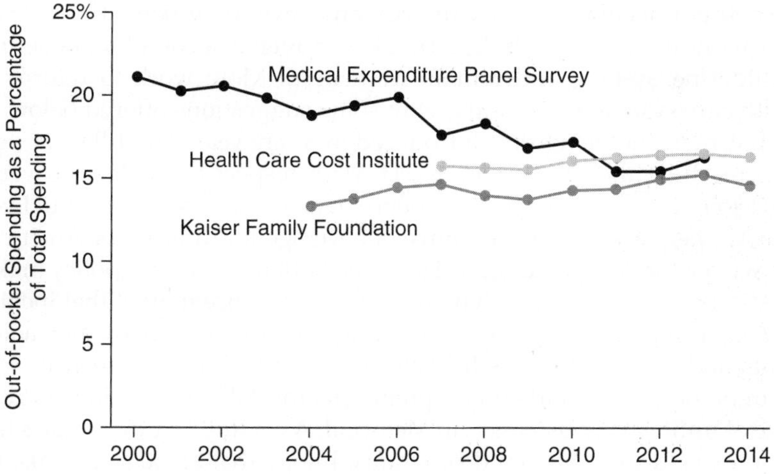

SOURCE: Data for the series labeled Medical Expenditure Panel Survey (MEPS) were derived from MEPS Household Component and reflect the ratio of out-of-pocket expenditures to total expenditures for nonelderly individuals reporting full-year employer coverage. Data for the series labeled Health Care Cost Institute (HCCI) were derived from the analysis of the HCCI claims database; to capture data revisions, the most recent value reported for each year was used. Data for the series labeled Kaiser Family Foundation were derived from the analyses of the Trueven Marketscan claims database reported by KFF in 2016.

17 percent, from 145 per 1000 discharges in 2010 to 121 per 1000 discharges in 2014. Using prior research on the relationship between hospital-acquired conditions and mortality, the Agency for Healthcare Research and Quality has estimated that this decline in the rate of hospital-acquired conditions has prevented a cumulative 87,000 deaths over 4 years. The rate at which Medicare patients are readmitted to the hospital within 30 days after discharge has also decreased sharply, from a mean of 19.1 percent during 2010 to a mean of 17.8 percent during 2015 (Figure 6; written communication; March 2016; Office of Enterprise Data and Analytics, Centers for Medicare & Medicaid Services). The Department of Health and Human Services has estimated that lower hospital readmission rates resulted in 565,000 fewer total readmissions from April 2010 through May 2015.

While the Great Recession and other factors played a role in recent trends, the Council of Economic Advisers has found evidence that the reforms introduced by the ACA helped both slow health care cost growth and drive improvements in the quality of care. The contribution of the ACA's reforms is likely to increase in the years ahead as its tools are used more fully and as the models already deployed under the ACA continue to mature.

Building on Progress to Date

I am proud of the policy changes in the ACA and the progress that has been made toward a more affordable, high-quality, and accessible health care system. Despite this progress, too many Americans still strain to pay for their physician visits and prescriptions, cover their deductibles, or pay their monthly insurance bills; struggle to navigate a complex, sometimes bewildering system; and remain uninsured. More work to reform the health care system is necessary, with some suggestions offered below.

First, many of the reforms introduced in recent years are still some years from reaching their maximum effect. With respect to the law's coverage provisions, these early years' experience demonstrate that the Health Insurance Marketplace is a viable source of coverage for millions of Americans and will be for decades to come. However, both insurers and policy makers are still learning about the dynamics of an insurance market that includes all people regardless of any preexisting conditions, and further adjustments and recalibrations will likely be needed, as can be seen in some insurers' proposed Marketplace premiums for 2017. In addition, a critical piece of unfinished business is in Medicaid. As of July 1, 2016, 19 states have yet to expand their Medicaid programs. I hope that all 50 states take this option and expand coverage for their citizens in the coming years, as they did in the years following the creation of Medicaid and CHIP.

* * *

Second, while the ACA has greatly improved the affordability of health insurance coverage, surveys indicate that many of the remaining

Figure 6. Medicare 30-Day, All-Condition Hospital Readmission Rate

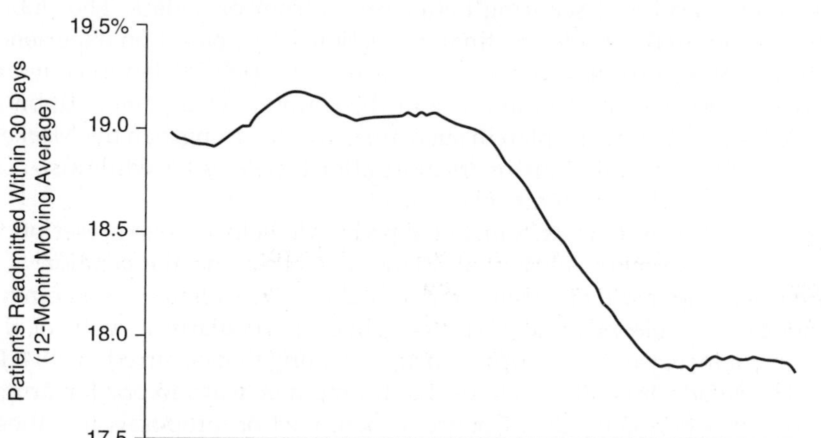

SOURCE: Data were provided by the Centers for Medicare & Medicaid Services (written communication; March 2016). The plotted series reflects a 12-month moving average of the hospital readmission rates reported for discharges occurring in each month.

uninsured individuals want coverage but still report being unable to afford it. Some of these individuals may be unaware of the financial assistance available under current law, whereas others would benefit from congressional action to increase financial assistance to purchase coverage, which would also help middle-class families who have coverage but still struggle with premiums. The steady-state cost of the ACA's coverage provisions is currently projected to be 28 percent below CBO's original projections, due in significant part to lower-than-expected Marketplace premiums, so increased financial assistance could make coverage even more affordable while still keeping federal costs below initial estimates.

Third, more can and should be done to enhance competition in the Marketplaces. For most Americans in most places, the Marketplaces are working. The ACA supports competition and has encouraged the entry of hospital-based plans, Medicaid managed care plans, and other plans into new areas. As a result, the majority of the country has benefited from competition in the Marketplaces, with 88 percent of enrollees living in counties with at least 3 issuers in 2016, which helps keep costs in these areas low. However, the remaining 12 percent of enrollees live in areas with only 1 or 2 issuers. Some parts of the country have struggled with limited insurance market competition for many years, which is one reason that, in the original debate over health reform. Congress considered and I supported including a Medicare-like public plan. Public programs like

Medicare often deliver care more cost-effectively by curtailing administrative overhead and securing better prices from providers. The public plan did not make it into the final legislation. Now, based on experience with the ACA, I think Congress should revisit a public plan to compete alongside private insurers in areas of the country where competition is limited. Adding a public plan in such areas would strengthen the Marketplace approach, giving consumers more affordable options while also creating savings for the federal government.

Fourth, although the ACA included policies to help address prescription drug costs, like more substantial Medicaid rebates and the creation of a pathway for approval of biosimilar drugs, those costs remain a concern for Americans, employers, and taxpayers alike—particularly in light of the 12 percent increase in prescription drug spending that occurred in 2014. In addition to administrative actions like testing new ways to pay for drugs, legislative action is needed. Congress should act on proposals like those included in my fiscal year 2017 budget to increase transparency around manufacturers' actual production and development costs, to increase the rebates manufacturers are required to pay for drugs prescribed to certain Medicare and Medicaid beneficiaries, and to give the federal government the authority to negotiate prices for certain high-priced drugs.

* * *

Lessons for Future Policy Makers

While historians will draw their own conclusions about the broader implications of the ACA, I have my own. These lessons learned are not just for posterity: I have put them into practice in both health care policy and other areas of public policy throughout my presidency.

The first lesson is that any change is difficult, but it is especially difficult in the face of hyperpartisanship. Republicans reversed course and rejected their own ideas once they appeared in the text of a bill that I supported. For example, they supported a fully funded risk-corridor program and a public plan fallback in the Medicare drug benefit in 2003 but opposed them in the ACA. They supported the individual mandate in Massachusetts in 2006 but opposed it in the ACA. They supported the employer mandate in California in 2007 but opposed it in the ACA—and then opposed the administration's decision to delay it. Moreover, through inadequate funding, opposition to routine technical corrections, excessive oversight, and relentless litigation, Republicans undermined ACA implementation efforts. We could have covered more ground more quickly with cooperation rather than obstruction. It is not obvious that this strategy has paid political dividends for Republicans, but it has clearly come at a cost for the country, most notably for the estimated 4 million Americans left uninsured because they live in GOP-led states that have yet to expand Medicaid.

The second lesson is that special interests pose a continued obstacle to change. We worked successfully with some health care organizations and groups, such as major hospital associations, to redirect excessive Medicare payments to federal subsidies for the uninsured. Yet others, like the pharmaceutical industry, oppose any change to drug pricing, no matter how justifiable and modest, because they believe it threatens their profits. We need to continue to tackle special interest dollars in politics. But we also need to reinforce the sense of mission in health care that brought us an affordable polio vaccine and widely available penicillin.

The third lesson is the importance of pragmatism in both legislation and implementation. Simpler approaches to addressing our health care problems exist at both ends of the political spectrum: the single-payer model vs government vouchers for all. Yet the nation typically reaches its greatest heights when we find common ground between the public and private good and adjust along the way. That was my approach with the ACA. We engaged with Congress to identify the combination of proven health reform ideas that could pass and have continued to adapt them since. This includes abandoning parts that do not work, like the voluntary long-term care program included in the law. It also means shutting down and restarting a process when it fails. When HealthCare.gov did not work on day one, we brought in reinforcements, were brutally honest in assessing problems, and worked relentlessly to get it operating. Both the process and the website were successful, and we created a playbook we are applying to technology projects across the government.

While the lessons enumerated above may seem daunting, the ACA experience nevertheless makes me optimistic about this country's capacity to make meaningful progress on even the biggest public policy challenges. Many moments serve as reminders that a broken status quo is not the nation's destiny. I often think of a letter I received from Brent Brown of Wisconsin. He did not vote for me and he opposed "ObamaCare." but Brent changed his mind when he became ill, needed care, and got it thanks to the law. Or take Governor John Kasich's explanation for expanding Medicaid: "For those that live in the shadows of life, those who are the least among us. I will not accept the fact that the most vulnerable in our state should be ignored. We can help them." Or look at the actions of countless health care providers who have made our health system more coordinated, quality-oriented, and patient-centered. I will repeat what I said 4 years ago when the Supreme Court upheld the ACA: I am as confident as ever that looking back 20 years from now, the nation will be better off because of having the courage to pass this law and persevere. As this progress with health care reform in the United States demonstrates, faith in responsibility, belief in opportunity, and ability to unite around common values are what makes this nation great.

71

"A Fresh Start for Health Care Reform"

EDMUND F. HAISLMAIER, ROBERT E. MOFFIT,
NINA OWCHARENKO, AND ALYENE SENGER

Despite President Barack Obama's insistence that the national health care debate is over, and that he will not "re-litigate" the misnamed Patient Protection and Affordable Care Act (PPACA), the practical concerns, aggravated by implementation glitches and policy failures, guarantee that the debate over the PPACA is far from over.

In the next phase of the health care debate, supporters of the PPACA will undoubtedly attempt to fix or tweak the weaknesses and failures of the law. Such an approach would be based on preserving and expanding the government's role in health care. Indeed, some analysts have already proposed policies that would further strengthen the government's hand in managing and regulating the health care system.

Those who reject the notion of increasing government control in health care can pursue an alternative path—a path based on the principles of patient-centered, market-based health care reforms. That alternative path not only gives individuals greater choice, but also empowers them to make their own health care decisions.

Better Solutions

The need for health care reform has never been questioned by health care policy analysts on either side of the political spectrum. Furthermore, the broad goals of controlling costs, improving quality, and expanding access are widely shared. Yet, while both sides agree that reform is necessary, their policy solutions differ dramatically, most importantly on the question of who controls the key decisions in health care.

For the Obama Administration and defenders of the PPACA, the common conviction is that for major issues in health care, government officials should be the key decision makers. Those government decisions are imposed through detailed federal rules and regulations. The PPACA epitomizes this approach, and the course of its regulatory implementation—strewn with the broken promises of the President—provides an excellent guide to the consequences and inherent challenges of such an approach.

In contrast, those who believe in a patient-centered, market-based approach to reform trust individuals, not the government, to be the key decision makers in the financing of health care. To achieve this goal, Congress should embark on a reform agenda that is grounded in the following policy cornerstones: (1) reforming the tax treatment of health insurance so that individuals choose the health care coverage that best fits their needs (not the government's dictates); (2) restoring commonsense regulation of health insurance by devolving it back to the states; and modernizing (3) Medicare and (4) Medicaid by adopting policies that harness the powerful free-market forces of choice and competition.

The PPACA: Broken Promises

During the public campaign in support of President Obama's health plan, the President made numerous promises to the American people about the law's effect on everyday Americans. Four years into its implementation, it is growing ever more apparent that these promises have all but vanished.

Promise #1: If you like your health care plan, you'll be able to keep your health care plan, period."

Reality: Millions of Americans have already lost, and more will likely lose, their coverage due to the PPACA. The PPACA has significantly disrupted the market for those who buy coverage on their own by imposing new coverage and benefit mandates, causing a reported 4.7 million health insurance cancelations in 32 states in 2013.

The same is true for those with employer-sponsored insurance. During the first half of 2014, Heritage Foundation analysis of the market enrollment data found that net enrollment in employer-group coverage declined by almost 4 million individuals, offsetting the gains in individual-purchased coverage by 61 percent.

Promise #2: "If you like your doctor, you will be able to keep your doctor, period."

Reality: Many Americans have not been able to keep their doctors as insurers try to offset the added costs of the PPACA by limiting the number of providers in their networks. In many of the PPACA's exchange plans, access to providers is limited; nationwide, 48 percent of all exchange plan provider networks are deemed to be "narrowed" and of those narrowed networks, nearly 40 percent are classified as "ultra-narrow." Likewise, due to significant payment reductions in the PPACA, some seniors with Medicare Advantage plans are being forced to find new doctors. UnitedHealth, the largest provider of these plans, has recently reduced its provider networks in at least 14 states.

In addition to these network access issues, there is the impact of the PPACA on the health care workforce, in particular its effects on workforce shortages and greater administrative burdens.

Promise #3: "In an Obama Administration, we'll lower premiums by up to $2,500 for a typical family per year."

Reality: Premiums for those who purchase coverage in the individual market have significantly increased in a majority of states, and premiums in the group market also continue to rise. In 2014, PPACA coverage in the exchanges was more expensive than comparable 2013 coverage in the pre-PPACA individual market in 42 states. For Americans with employer-sponsored coverage, premium costs also continue to increase. Family premiums for employer-sponsored coverage have increased by an average of $3,459 since 2009.

Although 2015 premium rates have not been finalized, an initial analysis of 19 states with available data shows that 28 percent of Silver-level exchange plans will have premium increases greater than 10 percent, while only 14 percent of Silver-level exchange plans will have rate decreases of more than 10 percent.

Promise #4: "Under my plan, no family making less than $250,000 a year will see any form of tax increase."

Reality: The PPACA contains 18 separate tax increases, fees, and penalties, many of which heavily impact the middle class. Altogether, the PPACA's taxes and penalties will collect more than $770 billion in new federal government revenues over 10 years. The individual mandate, the medical device tax, the federal health insurer tax, and new penalties and limits on health savings accounts and flexible spending accounts are just a few of the taxes that affect middle class Americans.

Promise #5: "I will protect Medicare."

Reality: The PPACA cuts Medicare to offset new health care spending. The PPACA makes unprecedented and unrealistic payment reductions to Medicare providers and Medicare Advantage plans in order to finance the law's new spending on subsidized coverage for the non-Medicare population. The cuts amount to over $700 billion from 2013 to 2022. If these draconian reductions take place as scheduled, they will significantly impact seniors' ability to access treatments and the quality of their care.

With such a lackluster record, it is not surprising that public opposition to the law remains strong and consistent. As a matter of fact, when all polls are averaged, the level of public opposition to the PPACA has always been higher than the level of public support.

Principles of Patient-Centered, Market-Based Health Care Reform

Traditionally, terms such as "patient-centered" or "market-based" have been used to contrast an alternative approach to greater government control in health care. However, the vocabulary of health care policy is often elastic, and different people sometimes use the same terms to express significantly different concepts. For example, the Obama Administration recently changed its description of the government-run health exchange to "marketplace."

The linguistic elasticity adds to the general confusion among the public and policymakers that seems to plague this already complex area of public policy. Consequentially, clarifying the rationale, objectives, and principles of patient-centered health care reform is important for properly understanding the concepts and implications of this approach. Specifically, truly patient-centered, market-based health reform means that:

- **Individuals are the key decision makers in the health care system.** That would be a major departure from most current arrangements under which governments or employers determine the type and scope of health care benefits and how those benefits are financed. In normal markets, consumers drive the system through their choices of products and services, reflecting their personal needs and preferences. In response, the providers of goods and services compete to meet consumer demands and preferences by supplying products that offer consumers better value in terms of price, quality, and features. The only way to achieve the same results in health care is by putting basic decision-making authority into the hands of consumers and patients.
- **Individuals buy and own their own health insurance coverage.** In a normal market, when individuals exchange money for a good or service, they acquire a property right in that good or service, but in today's system, individuals and families rarely have property rights in their health insurance coverage. The policy is owned and controlled by a third party—either the employer or government bureaucrats. In a reformed system, individuals would own their health insurance, just as they own virtually every other type of insurance or virtually any other product in other sectors of the economy.
- **Individuals are able to choose from a wide range of options.** Individuals, not employers or government officials, would choose their own health plan and level of coverage. Having a choice among health plans is particularly important because, of necessity, it incorporates a whole set of other implicit choices—such as what the plan will pay for versus what the consumer will purchase directly from providers, how and from whom the patient will receive care, and any informational tools or services the plan provides to assist patients in deciding among competing providers and treatment options. The corollary is that suppliers of medical goods and services, including health plans, must have the necessary flexibility to offer consumers and patients innovative and better-value solutions. That means that government rules and regulations should be limited to those that are necessary to ensure safety and a level playing field. Laws and regulations that favor particular providers, suppliers, business models, or

plan designs over others, or that create unreasonable barriers to market entry by new competitors, are inherently anti-consumer.

The challenge for policymakers is to undertake the reforms needed to transform the present system into one that rewards the search for and creation of better value. As other economic sectors show, health care need not be a zero-sum game in which costs can be controlled only by limiting benefits and benefits can be expanded only by increasing costs. Rather, a value-maximizing system would simultaneously demand and reward continuous benefit improvements accompanied by continuous cost reductions.

Such a value-maximizing result can be achieved in health care only if the system is restructured to make the consumer the key decision maker. When individual consumers decide how the money is spent, either directly for medical care or indirectly through their health insurance choices, the incentives will be aligned throughout the system to generate better value—in other words, to produce more for less.

A Fresh Start to Health Care Reform: The Right Policy

As it stands, the PPACA is burdened by practical infirmities that render it unworkable and unfair. Its policy prescriptions are unaffordable. This combination of bad policy and inherently flawed management has had, and will have, consequences that render the law persistently unpopular.

Congress should start fresh. It should repeal the PPACA and focus on the fundamentals: reform of the tax treatment of health care; devolving health insurance regulation back to the states; and reform of the major health care entitlement programs of Medicare and Medicaid.

Time to Reform the Tax Treatment of Health Care

The current tax treatment of health insurance is largely a relic of World War II wage and price controls. While those laws regulated cash wages, they exempted "insurance and pension benefits" of a "reasonable amount" from the definition of "wages" and "salaries," to which the controls were applied. Faced with labor shortages (as working-age men joined the armed forces) employers used that loophole to effectively skirt the wage controls by offering increased compensation in the form of employer-paid health insurance.

This distinction between cash wages and certain non-cash employee benefits also raised the issue of how the value of such benefits should be treated for tax purposes. When Congress enacted a major revision of the federal tax code in 1954 it explicitly excluded from the calculation of gross income any employer payments for a worker's medical care or health insurance. Moreover, this exclusion applies to both federal income and payroll (Social Security and Medicare) taxes. Thus, the tax exclusion for employer-sponsored health insurance meant that working families could fund their medical care with income that was completely tax-free.

Furthermore, unlike the case with most other tax breaks, Congress did not set a limit on the amount of income that could be diverted into paying for employer-sponsored health benefits on a pre-tax basis. Thus, having more of their compensation paid in the form of tax-free health benefits, and less in the form of taxable wages, became particularly attractive to workers in periods of higher inflation and higher marginal tax rates, such as during the 1970s.

The aggregate value of this federal tax preference in 2014 is about $250 billion per year, with reductions in federal personal income tax accounting for about $175 billion of that figure and reductions in payroll taxes accounting for the other $75 billion.

The principal effect of this policy was the widespread adoption of employer-sponsored health benefits as the dominant form of health coverage for American workers and their families. The share of the non-elderly population covered by employer-sponsored health insurance peaked at an estimated 71.4 percent in 1980. Even though the share has gradually declined since then, in 2012, an estimated 58.5 percent of the non-elderly population was still covered under such plans.

Yet that decline reveals some of the major drawbacks of this tax policy. Back in the 1950s and 1960s, it was fairly common for a worker to spend his entire career with the same employer. Yet the American workforce has become far more mobile since then. For instance, a Department of Labor survey of workers born between 1957 and 1964, found that they had an average of 11 jobs between the ages of 18 and 46. Obviously, a tax policy that links health insurance to the place of work means that each time a worker changes employers, he must change his health plan.

This tax policy also produces what economists call "horizontal inequity," meaning that if two individuals have the same income, but one has employer-sponsored health benefits while the other buys his own health insurance, the first individual receives a larger tax break than the second. At the same time, this tax policy also creates "vertical inequity." If two individuals work for the same employer and participate in the same health plan with the same cost, but have different incomes, the tax benefit each receives will vary based on their different marginal tax rates. That is so because the value of the tax exclusion for employer-sponsored coverage is equal to an individual's combined marginal tax rates for both income and payroll taxes, with the consequence that the size of the tax relief provided by the tax exclusion varies according to the different marginal tax rates imposed at different income levels.

Yet, the biggest problem with the tax exclusion from the health policy perspective is that while it offers workers substantial tax relief, it does so only if the workers let their employers decide how that portion of their compensation is spent. That translates to less choice and competition in health insurance, reduced consumer awareness of the true costs and value of medical care, and incentives to tailor health plans more toward meeting the interests of employers than to the preferences of the workers and their families.

The PPACA and the Tax Treatment of Health Care

Not only does the PPACA fail to correct these flaws in long-standing health care tax policy, it layers new complexity and distortions onto the existing system. It provides new, and substantial, subsidies for buying health insurance, but only to those individuals who have incomes between 100 percent and 400 percent of the federal poverty level (FPL) and purchase their coverage through government-run exchanges. Furthermore, it denies those new subsidies to individuals with access to employer-sponsored coverage, while at the same time imposing fines on employers with 50 or more full-time workers if they do not offer coverage.

Indeed, the only helpful change to health care tax policy that the PPACA makes is to limit the amount of employer-provided coverage that may be excluded from taxation. However, Congress did even that in a convoluted fashion. Rather than simply setting a limit—as Congress previously did with the tax exclusion for contributions to retirement plans—the PPACA imposes a punitive excise tax on any employer health plan whose value exceeds specified amounts.

A Better Approach

The proper goals for a true reform of the tax treatment of health insurance should be to make the system simpler and fairer for individuals, while also ensuring that it is neutral both with respect to how an individual obtains coverage (whether directly or through an employer or an association) as well as with respect to an individual's choice of plan design (such as a health-maintenance organization (HMO), a preferred-provider organization (PPO), a high-deductible plan, or another arrangement).

Various proposals for health care tax reform have been offered over the years. Most would repeal the tax exclusion and replace it with a new, universal tax deduction or tax credit for health expenses.

Replacing the current tax treatment of health benefits with a new design for health care tax relief that is both revenue and budget neutral (based on pre-PPACA levels) is the first step in transforming the American health system into one that is more patient-centered, market-based, and value-focused. No amount of government regulation or micromanagement of the system—such as tinkering with provider reimbursement rates or payment arrangements—can produce better value. That desired result will only be achieved by giving consumers more control over how to spend their health care dollars, thus forcing health insurers and medical providers to respond to consumer demand by offering better quality and prices for their products and services.

Even so, there is the practical concern that simply replacing the tax exclusion with a new design for health care tax relief would be an abrupt and major change in tax policy—resulting in further dislocation, at least initially, to the existing health care financing arrangements of millions of Americans. One way to avoid that problem is by including a transitional mechanism in the design, as follows:

First, instead of eliminating the tax exclusion, convert the existing limitation on high-cost employer health plans into a straightforward cap on the value of the exclusion.

Second, replace all the other narrower health care tax breaks (such as the tax deduction for coverage purchased by the self-employed, the Trade Adjustment Assistance health care tax credit for dislocated workers, and the itemized deduction for medical expenses) with an alternative health care tax relief option available to all taxpayers, regardless of income or source of coverage.

Third, permit individuals with access to employer-sponsored coverage to choose whether the tax exclusion, or the new tax relief option, should be applied to the value of their employer-sponsored benefits. Each worker would simply instruct his employer, on his W-4 form, which type of health care tax relief to apply in calculating his tax withholding.

Fourth, index the cap on the amount of the exclusion to decrease as needed in future years, so as to maintain at a baseline level the aggregate amount of tax relief provided by both the new option and the exclusion. For years in which the combined aggregate amount of tax relief provided by the alternative tax relief option and the exclusion exceeded the baseline level, the Treasury Department would be required to apply the indexing adjustment to lower the exclusion cap for the following year to make up the difference.

Under this approach there would be no abrupt dislocation of existing coverage arrangements. Those with employer-sponsored coverage could stay in their plans. The only difference would be that each worker could choose the form of the tax treatment to be applied. In general, most lower-wage workers would likely benefit more under the new tax option than the exclusion, while most higher-wage workers would likely find that they are better off continuing to claim the tax exclusion.

This arrangement would not only avoid the PPACA's problem of creating incentives for employers to discontinue coverage, but might actually result in more lower-wage workers enrolling in employer-sponsored coverage. That is because employer coverage would become more affordable to those workers if they opted to apply the new tax relief option, instead of the tax exclusion, to that coverage.

Over time, the indexing of the cap on the exclusion would eventually bring the value of the tax exclusion into parity with the value of the new tax relief option. However, that would occur gradually—not abruptly—and as a byproduct of individual workers exercising their personal preferences.

Commonsense Insurance-Market Reforms

Beyond reforming health care tax policy, the next step in creating a more patient-centered, market-based health system is to reform the regulation of health insurance to make coverage more competitive and value-focused. It is necessary not only for consumers to have incentives to seek better value, but also for insurers to have sufficient scope to innovate in offering better value products.

America's private health insurance market consists of two basic subgroups: the employer-group market, and the individual insurance market. Plans purchased from commercial insurers—whether individual or employer-group policies—are primarily regulated by state insurance laws.

There are, however, instances where federal regulations apply. The Employee Retirement and Income Security Act (ERISA), for example, establishes federal protections for the arrangements that an employer makes for providing benefits to his workers. The state, however, still regulates the commercial products that the employer might choose to purchase.

In 1996, Congress enacted the Health Insurance Portability and Accountability Act (HIPAA). That act, among other policy changes, set in place basic market rules for employer-group coverage and individual-market coverage. For employer plans, HIPAA included policies on a number of issues relating to guarantee issue, guarantee renewability, limitations on pre-exclusions, and prohibition on discrimination based on health status. For individual plans, HIPAA was limited to guarantee renewability and rules in the case of workers who lost their group coverage.

The PPACA and Insurance Regulation

While there were certainly some problems with insurance market regulation prior to the PPACA, those relatively modest problems could easily have been remedied with a few thoughtful and limited reforms. Instead, Congress enacted in the PPACA a raft of new regulations on insurers and health plans that standardize coverage, restrict innovation in plan design, and increase premiums for many Americans. Consequently, many of the new requirements imposed on insurers by the PPACA—such as the new federal benefit mandates that standardize coverage and the rating rules that artificially increase premiums for younger adults—are counterproductive and lead to the need for the widely despised individual mandate to offset their destabilizing effects.

A Better Approach

State governments have performed the basic function of regulating insurance reasonably well for over a century, and there is no need for the federal government to supplant these efforts as it is now doing under the

PPACA. Therefore, Congress should immediately devolve the regulation of health insurance back to the states.

From there, states should initiate a policy agenda that aims to stabilize the market while expanding choice and competition by reducing burdensome and costly rating rules and benefit mandates. State lawmakers should also pursue policies to achieve greater harmonization among the states. For instance, reciprocity agreements between states would permit residents in one state to buy coverage that is issued and regulated in another state. In 2011, Maine included such a reciprocity provision in its broader health insurance reform law. Enacting such policies would expand the choices available to consumers, increase competition among insurers, and help clear the way for potential federal interstate purchase legislation. Finally, states should advance medical liability reforms to help improve access and bring down the cost of practicing medicine.

To address the outstanding concern over protections for those individuals with pre-existing conditions, Congress could solve this issue in a relatively simple fashion without resorting to the kind of sweeping and complex regulation enacted in the PPACA.

Dating back to the 1996 HIPAA law, Congress enacted a set of modest and reasonable rules for employer-group coverage that specified that individuals switching from one group plan to another (or from group coverage to an individual plan) could not be denied new coverage, be subjected to preexisting-condition exclusions, or be charged higher premiums because of their health status. Thus, in the group market, pre-existing-condition exclusions could only be applied to those without prior coverage, or to those who wait until they need medical care to enroll in their employer's plan. Furthermore, there were limits even in those cases. Such individuals could still obtain the group coverage, and any pre-existing medical condition could not be excluded from that coverage for more than 12 months.

Under these employer group rules, individuals who received and kept coverage are rewarded, and individuals who wait until they are sick to enroll in coverage are penalized, but the penalties were neither unreasonable nor severe. That was also why those rules worked without needing to mandate that individuals purchase coverage, as required by the PPACA.

The problem, however, is that the same kind of rules did not apply to the individual market. Thus, an individual could have purchased nongroup health insurance for many years, and still be denied coverage or face pre-existing-condition exclusions when he needed or wanted to pick a different plan. Not only was that unfair to those individuals who had bought insurance while they were healthy, it also did little to encourage other healthy individuals to purchase coverage before they needed it.

Thus, the obvious, modest, and sensible reform would be to apply a set of rules to the individual-health-insurance market similar to the ones that already govern the employer-group-coverage market.

* * *

Opportunity for a Fresh Start

The debate over reforming America's health care system is far from over. The ongoing implementation and technical problems plaguing the PPACA, combined with consistent opposition to the law as a whole, will necessitate another debate over health care reform. That will offer opportunities for Congress to advance a much better alternative. The alternative is one that does not reinforce greater government control as does the PPACA, but rather provides a fresh approach based on patient-centered, market-based principles. Such an approach would address the ongoing challenges associated with the tax treatment of health insurance, the over-regulation of insurance markets, and the pressing need for serious reforms to health care entitlements.

Discussion Questions

1. Critics of the "market-based" reform theory argue that health care cannot be understood as a market. People are not sensitive to costs, and are rarely in a position to shop around to find bargains (if you go to the ER with symptoms of a heart attack or appendicitis, you probably won't have much interest in comparison pricing or choosing which treatment to have based on cost). If market forces do not exist, can a market-based reform ever work?
2. One common way of conceptualizing health care reform is to think of the system in terms of three things: advanced care, universal access, and affordability. You can choose two. Which ones are most important?
3. What are the challenges involved in repealing and replacing the Affordable Care Act, something that both congressional Republicans and President Trump support? The first attempt to do so failed in 2017 because it proved difficult to satisfy both conservative Republicans who favored complete repeal and moderate Republicans who wanted to keep Medicare funding and maintain coverage levels. What are the challenges in coming up with a replacement?
4. Should health care be a "right," in the sense that individuals ought to be guaranteed access to health services by government? What would the consequences of such a right be? Does not recognizing health care as a right mean that some individuals might be unable to get access to health care, even that they might die as a result?

CHAPTER 15

Foreign Policy and World Politics

72

"The Age of Open Society"

GEORGE SOROS

"Globalization" refers, generally speaking, to the diffusion of interests and ideologies across national borders. Proponents of globalization point to the hope that it will encourage global economic development and foster universal human rights that are not dependent on where someone happens to live. Critics fall into two camps. One consists of those who fear that globalization will undermine national sovereignty and lead to a "one world" government that leaves everyone at the mercy of distant bureaucrats and officials. The other camp consists of those who see globalization as a smokescreen for corporate hegemony, where multinational corporations exploit workers in countries with low wages, few job protections, and lax environmental regulations, all in the name of higher profits.

George Soros, an investor who made billions of dollars in currency speculation and is now a philanthropist who promotes democracy, believes that economic globalization and political globalization are out of sync: although capital and markets move freely across national boundaries, political institutions do not. A global "open society" would, in his view, insure that the political and social needs of all countries are met (not simply the needs of industrialized nations, whose interests tend to dominate international markets), and would foster the development of stable political and financial institutions. This would require a broad international organization, either as part of the United Nations or as an independent institution. It would have to be based on the idea that certain interests transcend questions of national sovereignty.

Global politics and global economics are dangerously out of sync. Although we live in a global economy characterized by free trade and the free movement of capital, our politics are still based on the sovereignty of the state. International institutions exist, but their powers are limited by how much authority states are willing to confer on them. At the same time, the powers of the state are limited by the freedom of capital to escape taxation and regulation by moving elsewhere. This is particularly true of the countries at the periphery of the global capitalist system, whose economic destiny depends on what happens at the center.

This state of affairs would be sustainable if the market mechanism could be trusted to satisfy social needs. But that is not the case.

We need to find international political arrangements that can meet the requirements of an increasingly interdependent world. These arrangements ought to be built on the principles of open society. A perfect society is beyond our reach. We must content ourselves with the next best thing: a society that holds itself open to improvement. We need institutions that allow people of different views, interests, and backgrounds to live together in peace. These institutions should assure the greatest degree of freedom compatible with the common interest. Many mature democracies come close to qualifying as open societies. But they refuse to accept openness as a universal principle.

How could this principle of openness be translated into practice? By the open societies of the world forming an alliance for this purpose. The alliance would have two distinct but interrelated goals: to foster the development of open society within individual countries; and to establish international laws, rules of conduct, and institutions to implement these norms.

It is contrary to the principles of open society to dictate from the outside how a society should govern itself. Yet the matter cannot be left entirely to the state, either. The state can be an instrument of oppression. To the extent possible, outside help should take the form of incentives; the evolution of open society requires aid for economic and institutional development. Punitive measures, though sometimes unavoidable, tend to be counterproductive.

Unfortunately, positive intervention is out of favor because of an excessive faith in the magic of the marketplace. There is an alliance of democratic countries, NATO, capable of military intervention, but there is no similar alliance to engage in constructive intervention. This open-society alliance ought to have a much broader membership than NATO, and it must include nongovernmental members as well as heads of state. As former U.S. Secretary of State Henry Kissinger points out, states have interests but no principles; we cannot rely on them to implement the principle of openness.

Democratic governments are, however, responsive to the wishes of their electorates. Therefore, the impulse for the alliance has to come from the people, not from their leaders. Citizens living in open societies must recognize a global open society as something worth sacrifice. This responsibility rests in particular with the United States, the sole surviving superpower and the dominant force in the global capitalist system. There can be no global open society without its leadership. But the United States has become carried away by its success and fails to see why it should subordinate its self-interest to some nebulous common principle. The United States jealously guards its sovereignty and behaves as if it ought to be the sole arbiter of right and wrong. Washington will have to undergo a significant change of heart before it is ready to lead an open-society alliance.

The alliance, if it comes to pass, must not lose sight of its own fallibity. Foreign aid, though very valuable, is notoriously inefficient. Rule-based incentives are more promising. The international financial architecture needs to be redesigned to help give underdeveloped countries a leg up. Incentives would be conditional on each country's success in establishing open political and financial institutions.

The alliance could act within the United Nations, or it could go it alone. But a commitment to such an alliance would offer an opportunity to reform the United Nations. The noble intentions enunciated in the preamble of the U.N. Charter can never be attained as long as the United Nations remains a rigid association of sovereign states. But there is ample room for improvement, and an open-society alliance would be a start. Perhaps one day, then, historians will look back at these years to come as the Age of Open Society.

Discussion Questions

1. Is Soros's suggestion about an open society practical? Do you think there are circumstances under which nations would agree to such a proposal?

2. How, if at all, will globalization change notions about national identity? Do you think that, twenty-five or fifty years from now, being a U.S. citizen—or a citizen of any other country—will have the same meaning as it does now?

73

"Globalization Is Good for You"

Ronald Bailey

Trade—particularly the domestic consequences of trade—was a central part of the 2016 presidential election. Republican Donald Trump railed against trade agreements like the North American Free Trade Agreement (NAFTA) and the Trans Pacific Partnership (TPP), calling them "horrible" deals that destroyed American jobs and allowed other countries to take advantage of the United States by exporting far more to the United States than they take as imports. Lower labor costs, looser environmental standards, and less regulation in other countries mean that companies have an incentive to shift jobs overseas. The result is economic dislocation in regions that see massive job losses, and the overall economic benefits of these deals are of little comfort to those workers and communities who see their livelihoods disappear.

Yet free trade has been a centerpiece of global economic policy for decades, and supporters argue that efforts to protect domestic producers through trade barriers—chiefly tariffs, or taxes paid when a good is imported—wind up increasing the costs of goods, creating inefficiencies, and reducing overall wealth.

In this selection, Ronald Bailey summarizes recent research on overall effects of the increasingly free movement of goods, capital, and even people, across borders. On just about every dimension one can think of—individual income, overall wealth, economic growth, life expectancy, gender equality, child labor, environmental protection, even the likelihood of military conflict—free trade and globalization have positive effects. "All of this open movement of people and stuff across borders pays off in many measurable ways," argues Bailey, "some obvious, some more surprising."

How important is the open exchange of goods to the spreading of prosperity? This important: Since 1950, world trade in goods has expanded from $600 billion (in 2015 dollars) to $18.9 trillion in 2013. That's a more than 30-fold increase, during a period in which global population grew less than threefold.

This massive increase in trade was kicked off in 1948 by the General Agreement on Tariffs and Trade, which began the liberalization process of lowering tariff and non-tariff barriers. As a result, autarkic national economies became more integrated and intertwined with one another. The World Bank reports that openness to trade—the ratio of a country's trade (exports plus imports) to its gross domestic product (GDP)—has more than doubled on average since 1950.

Immigration has also contributed significantly to economic growth and higher wages. Today some 200 million people, about 3 percent of the world's population, live outside their countries of birth. According to the Partnership for a New American Economy, 28 percent of all U.S. companies started in 2011 had immigrant founders—despite immigrants comprising roughly 13 percent of the population. In addition, some 40 percent of Fortune 500 firms were founded by immigrants or their children.

All of this open movement of people and stuff across borders pays off in many measurable ways, some obvious, some more surprising.

Longer, Healthier Lives

A 2010 study in *World Development*, titled "Good For Living? On the Relationship between Globalization and Life Expectancy," looked at data from 92 countries and found that economic globalization significantly boosts life expectancy, especially in developing countries. The two Swedish economists behind the study, Andreas Bergh and Therese Nilsson, noted that as Uganda's economic globalization index rose from 22 to 46 points (almost two standard deviations) over the 1970–2005 period, average life expectancy increased by two to three years.

Similarly, a 2014 conference paper titled "The long-run relationship between trade and population health: evidence from five decades," by Helmut Schmidt University economist Dierk Herzer, concluded, after examining the relationship between economic openness and population health for 74 countries between 1960 and 2010, that "international trade in general has a robust positive long-run effect on health, as measured by life expectancy and infant mortality."

Women's Liberation

A 2012 working paper by University of Konstantz economist Heinrich Ursprung and University of Munich economist Niklas Potrafke analyzed how women fare by comparing globalization trends with changes in the Social Institutions and Gender Index (SIGI), which was developed by the Organisation for Economic Co-operation and Development (OECD). SIGI takes several aspects of gender relations into account, including family law codes, civil liberties, physical integrity, son preference, and ownership rights. It's an index of deprivation that captures causes of gender inequality rather than measuring outcomes.

"Observing the progress of globalization for almost one hundred developing countries at ten-year intervals starting in 1970," Ursprung and Potrafke concluded, "we find that economic and social globalization exert a decidedly positive influence on the social institutions that reduce female subjugation and promote gender equality." They further noted that since globalization tends to liberate women from traditional social and political orders, "social globalization is demonized, by the established local ruling class, and by western apologists who, for reasons of ideological objections to markets, join in opposing globalization."

Less Child Labor

A 2005 *World Development* study, "Trade Openness, Foreign Direct Investment and Child Labor," by Eric Neumayer of the London School of Economics and Indra de Soysa of the Norwegian University of Science and Technology, looked at the effects of trade openness and globalization on child labor in poor countries. Their analysis refuted the claims made by anti-globalization proponents that free trade induces a "race to the bottom," encouraging the exploitation of children as cheap laborers. Instead the researchers found that the more open a country is to international trade and foreign investment, the lower the incidence of exploitation. "Globalization is associated with less, not more, child labor," they concluded.

Faster Economic Growth

A 2008 World Bank study, "Trade Liberalization and Growth: New Evidence," by the Stanford University economists Romain Wacziarg and Karen Horn Welch, found that trade openness and liberalization significantly boost a country's rate of economic growth.

The authors noted that in 1960, just 22 percent of countries representing 21 percent of the global population had open trade policies. This rose to 73 percent of countries representing 46 percent of world population by the year 2000. The study compared growth rates of countries before and after trade liberalization, finding that "over the 1950–98 period, countries that liberalized their trade regimes experienced average annual growth rates that were about 1.5 percentage points higher than before liberalization" and that "investment rates by rose 1.5–2.0 percentage points."

Higher Incomes

Trade openness boosts economic growth, but how does it affect per-capita incomes? A 2009 Rutgers University-Newark working paper, "Trade Openness and Income—a Re-examination," by economists Vlad Manole and Mariana Spatareanu, calculated the trade restrictiveness indices for 131 developed and developing countries between 1990 and 2004. Its conclusion: A "lower level of trade protection is associated with higher per-capita income."

Less Poverty

A 2011 Research Institute of Industrial Economics working paper—"Globalization and Absolute Poverty—A Panel Data Study," by the Swedish economists Bergh and Nilsson—analyzed the effects of globalization and trade openness on levels of absolute poverty (defined as incomes of less than $1 per day) in 100 developing countries. The authors found "a robust negative correlation between globalization and poverty."

Interestingly, most of the reduction in absolute poverty results from better information flows—e.g., access to cellphones—that improve the functioning of markets and lead to the liberalization of trade. For example, the globalization index score for Bangladesh increased from 8 points in 1980 to 30 points in 2000, which yielded a reduction in absolute poverty of 12 percentage points.

More Trees

A number of studies have found that trade openness tends to improve environmental quality in rich countries while increasing pollution and deforestation in poor countries. For example, a 2009 *Journal of Environmental Economics and Management* study by three Japanese researchers, titled "Does Trade Openness Improve Environmental Quality?", found that air and water pollution decline among rich-country members of the OECD, whereas it increases in poor countries as they liberalize and embark on the process of economic development.

But as poor countries become rich, they flip from getting dirtier to becoming cleaner. A 2012 *Canadian Journal of Agricultural Economics* study, "Deforestation and the Environmental Kuznets Curve in Developing Countries: A Panel Smooth Transition Regression Approach," explored the relationship between deforestation and real income for 52 developing countries during the 1972–2003 period. The study found that deforestation reverses when average incomes reach a bit more than $3,000 per year.

These studies basically confirm the Environmental Kuznets Curve hypothesis, in which various indicators of environmental degradation tend to get worse during the early stages of economic growth, but when average income reaches a certain point, subsequent economic growth leads to environmental improvement. Since trade openness and globalization boost economic growth and incomes, this suggests that opposing them slows down eventual environmental improvement in poor countries.

Peace

In 1943, Otto T. Mallery wrote, "If soldiers are not to cross international boundaries, goods must do so. Unless the shackles can be dropped from trade, bombs will be dropped from the sky." This insight was bolstered by a 2011 working paper, "Does Trade Integration Contribute to Peace?", by the University of California, Davis researcher Ju Hyun Pyun and the Korea University researcher Jong-Wha Lee. The two evaluated the effects of bilateral trade and global openness on the probability of conflict between countries from 1950 to 2000, and concluded that "an increase in bilateral trade interdependence significantly promotes peace." They added, "More importantly, we find that not only bilateral trade but global trade openness also significantly promotes peace."

More Productive Workers

The economic gains from unfettered immigration are vastly more enormous than those that would result from the elimination of remaining trade restrictions. Total factor productivity (TFP) is the portion of output not explained by the amount of inputs used in production. Its level is determined by how efficiently and intensely the inputs are utilized in production. In other words, it is all those factors—technology, honest government, a stable currency, etc.—that enable people to work "smarter" and not just harder.

A 2012 working paper titled "Open Borders," by the University of Wisconsin economist John Kennan, found that if all workers moved immediately to places with higher total factor productivity, it would produce the equivalent of doubling the world's supply of laborers. Using U.S. TFP as a benchmark, the world's workers right now are the equivalent of 750 million Americans, but allowing migration to high TFP regions would boost that to the equivalent of 1.5 billion American workers.

Think of it this way: A worker in Somalia can produce only one-tenth the economic value of a worker in the United States. But as soon as she trades the hellhole of Mogadishu for the comparative paradise of Minneapolis, she can immediately take advantage of the higher American TFP to produce vastly more. Multiply that by the hundreds of millions still stuck in low-productivity countries.

Assuming everybody moved immediately, Kennan calculated that it would temporarily depress the average wages of the host countries' natives by 20 percent. If emigration were more gradual, there would be essentially no effects on native-born wages.

In a 2011 working paper for the Center for Global Development, "Economics and Emigration: Trillion Dollar Bills on the Sidewalk?", Michael Clemens reviewed the literature on the relationship between economic growth and migration. He concluded that removing mobility barriers could plausibly produce overall gains of 20–60 percent of global GDP. Since world GDP is about $78 trillion now, that suggests that opening borders alone could boost global GDP to between $94 and $125 trillion.

Better Job Prospects

A 2013 University of Munich working paper on immigration and economic growth by the University of Auvergne economist Ekrame Boubtane and her colleagues analyzed data from 22 OECD countries between 1987 and 2009. It found that "migration inflows contribute to host country economic prosperity (positive impact on GDP per capita and total unemployment rate)." The authors concluded that "immigration flows do not harm the employment prospects of residents, native- or foreign-born. Hence, OECD countries may adjust immigration policies to labor market needs, and can receive more migrants, without worrying about a potential negative impact on growth and employment."

In a 2009 National Bureau of Economic Research study, "The Effect of Immigration on Productivity: Evidence from U.S. States," the University of California, Davis economist Giovanni Peri looked at the effects of differential rates of immigration to various American states in the 1990s and 2000s. Peri found that "an increase in employment in a U.S. state of 1 percent due to immigrants produced an increase in income per worker of 0.5 percent in that state." In other words, more immigrants meant higher average wages for all workers.

Discussion Questions

1. The positive effects of free trade are of little comfort to factory workers who lose their jobs because their employer moved production to a country with lower labor costs. How do you make the case for free trade to those who bear the brunt of the costs? What happens when the "rising tide" of economic growth doesn't lift all boats?
2. Many critics of globalization argue that allowing goods and capital to move freely across borders only moves jobs to countries with the cheapest and most exploitable labor forces, where job protections are minimal (or nonexistent). Supporters respond that these jobs, even though they might not pay much by Western standards, still provide much better opportunities for people in developing nations than would otherwise be the case. Who do you think has the better case?
3. What is the alternative to globalization? What costs are associated with, for example, trying to protect domestic jobs from being exported? What are the benefits of such efforts?

Debating the Issues: How Dangerous Is ISIS?

The Islamic State has emerged as the most significant terror group of the past decade, easily supplanting the Taliban and Al Qaeda. It has sponsored terrorism all over the world, and claimed responsibility for or inspired attacks in San Bernardino, CA (December 2015, 14 dead), Orlando, FL (June 2016, 49 dead), and Ft. Hood, Texas (November 2009, 13 dead).

ISIS, in the words of Matthew Olsen, former Director of the National Counterterrorism Center, constitutes "the most urgent threat to our security in the world today." He argues that ISIS has become more sophisticated even as it loses territory, and that its ability to communicate to and inspire followers anywhere in the world makes it a significant risk to global stability. He advocates a combined response of military action, increased surveillance and intelligence action, and communication efforts that combat the radicalization of people inside the United States.

Pillar takes a broader view, arguing that proposed action against ISIS must be understood in the larger context of the history of the American military abroad. Until World War II, Americans had a record of unbroken military success, combined with infrequent wars. In recent decades, military intervention has become more common and less successful, and "an entire generation of Americans has come of age with its country perpetually at war." This has led to the impulse that military action is the first option in dealing with any threat, even when it was an initial military response that caused the threat, and when the continued application of force (through, for example, drone strikes) is a continuing cause of radicalization.

The main reason ISIS exists is the Iraq War and the chaos and power vacuum in the region that resulted. The urge to fight the group with military force merely repeats the initial error, and plays into ISIS's hands. Even "toppling the ISIS command structure" would not eliminate the threat; it would take hundreds of thousands of U.S. troops, and would result in another lengthy and unsuccessful war.

The questions both authors address—even as they come to very different conclusions—are how to understand the threats to the United States, and, once those threats are identified, how to fight them.

74

"The Spread of ISIS and Transnational Terrorism"

MATTHEW G. OLSEN

Thank you Chairman Corker, Ranking Member Cardin, and distinguished members of the Committee. I am honored to have this opportunity to appear before you to discuss the spread of the Islamic State in Iraq and Syria and the threat from transnational terrorism.

We meet this morning in the wake of the horrific attacks in Brussels last month and the recent attacks in Paris and in San Bernardino late last year. These massacres serve both as a sobering reminder of the complexity of the threats we face from terrorist groups of global reach and as a call for action in the ongoing struggle against terrorism. Indeed, these attacks give this hearing added significance, as you convene to examine the threat to the United States and our interests around the world and the steps we should take to counter terrorist groups both at home and abroad.

By any measure, ISIS presents the most urgent threat to our security in the world today. The group has exploited the conflict in Syria and sectarian tensions in Iraq to entrench itself in both countries, now spanning the geographic center of the Middle East. Using both terrorist and insurgent tactics, the group has seized and is governing territory, while at the same time securing the allegiance of allied terrorist groups across the Middle East and North Africa. ISIS's sanctuary enables it to recruit, train, and execute external attacks, as we have now seen in Europe, and to incite assailants around the world. It has recruited thousands of militants to join its fight in the region and uses its propaganda campaign to radicalize countless others in the West. And at the same time, we continue to face an enduring threat from Al Qaeda and its affiliates, who maintain the intent and capacity to carry out attacks in the West.

In my remarks today, I will focus first on the nature of the terrorist threat from transnational terrorist groups, focusing on ISIS and Al Qaeda. I then will address some of the key elements of the strategy to degrade and defeat these groups, as well as the challenges we face ahead.

The Spread of ISIS

Let me begin with the spread of ISIS from its roots in Iraq. ISIS traces its origin to the veteran Sunni terrorist, Abu Mus'ab al-Zarqawi, who founded the group in 2004 and pledged his allegiance to bin Laden. Al Qaeda in Iraq, as it was then known, targeted U.S. forces and civilians to pressure the United States and other countries to leave Iraq and gained a reputation for brutality and tyranny.

In 2007, the group's continued targeting and repression of Sunni civilians in Iraq caused a widespread backlash—often referred to as the Sunni Awakening—against the group. This coincided with a surge in U.S. and coalition forces and Iraq counterterrorism operations that ultimately denied ISIS safe haven and led to a sharp decrease in its attack tempo. Then in 2011, the group began to reconstitute itself amid growing Sunni discontent and the civil war in Syria. In 2012, ISIS conducted an average of 5–10 suicide attacks in Iraq per month, an attack tempo that grew to 30–40 attacks per month in 2013.

While gaining strength in Iraq, ISIS exploited the conflict and chaos in Syria to expand its operations across the border. The group established the al-Nusrah Front as a cover for its activities in Syria, and in April 2013, the group publicly declared its presence in Syria under the ISIS name. Al-Nusrah leaders immediately rejected ISIS's announcement and publicly pledged allegiance to Al Qaeda. And by February 2014, Al Qaeda declared that ISIS was no longer a branch of the group.

At the same time, ISIS accelerated its efforts to remove Iraqi and Syrian government control of key portions of their respective territories, seizing control of Raqqa, Syria, and Fallujah, Iraq, in January 2014. The group marched from its safe haven in Syria, across the border into northern Iraq, slaughtering thousands of Iraqi Muslims, Sunni and Shia alike, on its way to seizing Mosul in June 2014. Through these battlefield victories, the group gained weapons, equipment, and territory, as well as an extensive war chest. In the summer of 2014, ISIS declared the establishment of an Islamic caliphate under the name the "Islamic State" and called for all Muslims to pledge support to the group and its leader, Abu Bakr al-Baghdadi.

Three overarching factors account for the rise and rapid success of ISIS over the past three years.

First, ISIS has exploited the civil war in Syria and the lack of security in northern Iraq to establish a safe haven. At the same time, Assad's brutal suppression of the Syrian people acted as a magnet for extremists and foreign fighters. In western Iraq, the withdrawal of security forces during the initial military engagements with ISIS left swaths of territory ungoverned. ISIS has used these areas to establish sanctuaries in Syria and Iraq from where the group could amass and coordinate fighters and resources with little interference. With virtually no security forces along the Iraq-Syria border, ISIS was able to move personnel and supplies with ease within its held territories.

Second, ISIS has proven to be an effective fighting force. Its battlefield strategy employs a mix of terrorist operations, hit-and-run tactics, and paramilitary assaults to enable the group's rapid gains. These battlefield advances, in turn, sparked other Sunni insurgents into action, and they have helped the group hold and administer territory. Disaffected Sunnis have had few alternatives in Iraq or Syria. The leadership in both countries has pushed them to the sidelines in the political process for years, failing to address their grievances. ISIS has been recruiting these young Sunnis to fight. Since September 2014, the U.S.-led military coalition has halted ISIS's momentum and reversed the group's territorial gains, but ISIS has sought to adapt its tactics in the face of coalition air strikes.

Third, ISIS views itself as the new leader of the global jihad. The group has developed an unprecedented ability to communicate with its followers worldwide. It operates the most sophisticated propaganda machine of any terrorist group. ISIS disseminates timely, high-quality media content on multiple platforms, including on social media, designed to secure a widespread following for the group. ISIS uses a range of media to tout its military capabilities, executions of captured soldiers, and battlefield victories.

ISIS's media campaign also is aimed at drawing foreign fighters to the group, including many from Western countries. The media campaign also allows ISIS to recruit new fighters to conduct independent or inspired attacks in the West. ISIS's propaganda outlets include multiple websites, active Twitter feeds, YouTube channels, and online chat rooms. ISIS uses these platforms to radicalize and mobilize potential operatives in the United States and elsewhere. The group's supporters have sustained this momentum on social media by encouraging attacks in the United States and against U.S. interests in retaliation for our airstrikes. As a result, ISIS threatens to outpace Al Qaeda as the dominant voice of influence in the global extremist movement.

The Threat from ISIS Today

Today, ISIS reportedly has between 20,000 and 25,000 fighters in Iraq and Syria, an overall decrease from the number of fighters in 2014. ISIS controls much of the Tigris-Euphrates basin. Significantly, however, ISIS's frontlines in parts of northern and central Iraq and northern Syria have been pushed back, according to the Defense Department, and ISIS probably can no longer operate openly in approximately 25 to 30 percent of populated areas in Iraq and Syria that it dominated in August 2014.

ISIS also has branched out, taking advantage of the chaos and lack of security in countries like Yemen to Libya to expand to new territory and enlist new followers. ISIS can now claim formal alliances with eight affiliated groups across an arc of instability and unrest stretching from the Middle East across North Africa.

Libya is the most prominent example of the expansion of ISIS. There, ISIS's forces include as many as 6,500 fighters, who have captured the town of Sirte and 150 miles of coastline over the past year. This provides ISIS with a relatively safe base from which to attract new recruits and execute attacks elsewhere, including on Libya's oil facilities. In addition,

ISIS has proven its ability to conduct operations in western Libya, including a suicide bombing at a police training, which killed at least 60 people earlier this year.

From this position, ISIS poses a multi-faceted threat to Europe and to the United States. The strategic goal of ISIS remains to establish an Islamic caliphate through armed conflict with governments it considers apostate—including European nations and the United States. In early 2014, ISIS's leader Abu Bakr al-Baghdadi warned that the United States will soon "be in direct conflict" with the group. In September 2014, the group's spokesperson Abu Muhammad al-Adnani released a speech instructing supporters to kill disbelievers in Western countries "in any manner or way," without traveling to Syria or waiting for direction.

ISIS has established an external operations organization under Adnani's leadership. This unit reportedly is a distinct body inside ISIS responsible for identifying recruits, supplying training and cash, and arranging for the delivery of weapons. The unit's main focus has been Europe, but it also has directed deadly attacks outside Europe, including in Turkey, Egypt, Tunisia, and Lebanon.

A recent *New York Times* report attributes 1,200 deaths to ISIS outside Iraq and Syria, and about half of the dead have been local civilians in Arab countries, many killed in attacks on mosques and government offices. In the past two years ISIS reportedly has directed or inspired more than 80 external attacks in as many as 20 nations. And ISIS has carried out or inspired at least 29 deadly assaults targeting Westerners around the world, killing more than 650 people.

Most concerning, the recent attacks in Brussels and Paris demonstrate that ISIS now has both the intent and capability to direct and execute sophisticated attacks in Western Europe. These attacks reflect an alarming trend. Over the past year, ISIS has increased the complexity, severity, and pace of its external attacks. The Brussels and Paris attacks were not simply inspired by ISIS, but rather they were ISIS-planned and directed. And they were conducted as part of a coordinated effort to maximize casualties by striking some of the most vulnerable targets in the West: a train station and airport in Brussels, and a nightclub, cafe, and sporting arena in Paris. Further, recent reports that ISIS has used chemical weapons in Syria, and that it conducted surveillance of Belgium nuclear facilities, raise the specter that the group is intent on using weapons of mass destruction.

In the United States, the threat from ISIS is on a smaller scale but persistent. We have experienced attacks that ISIS has inspired—including the attacks in San Bernardino and in Garland, Texas—and there has been an overall uptick over the past year in the number of moderate-to-small scale plots. Lone actors or insular groups—often self-directed or inspired by overseas groups, like ISIS—pose the most serious threat to carry out attacks here. Homegrown violent extremists will likely continue gravitating to simpler plots that do not require advanced skills, outside training, or communication with others. The online environment serves a critical role in radicalizing and mobilizing homegrown extremists towards violence. Highlighting the challenge this presents, the FBI Director said last year that the FBI has homegrown violent extremist cases, totaling about 900, in every state. Most of these cases are connected to ISIS.

Several factors are driving this trend toward the increasing pace and scale of terrorist-related violence. First, the sheer number of Europeans and other Westerners who have gone to Syria to fight in the conflict and to join ISIS is supplying a steady flow of operatives to the group. Reports indicate that more than 6,000 Europeans—including many French, German, British, and Belgian nationals—have travelled to Syria to join the fight. This is part of the total of approximately 40,000 foreign fighters in the region. Among the Europeans who have left for Syria, several hundred fighters have returned to their home countries, typically battle-hardened, trained, and further radicalized. The number of Americans who have travelled to Syria or Iraq, or have tried to, exceeds 250.

As such, we should not underestimate the potential of an ISIS-directed attack in the United States. While the principal threat from ISIS in the United States is from homegrown, ISIS-inspired actors, the fact that so many Americans have travelled to Syria and Iraq to fight, along with thousands more from visa waiver countries in Europe, raises the real concern that these individuals could be deployed here to conduct attacks similar to the attacks in Paris and Brussels.

Second, ISIS has developed more advanced tactics in planning and executing these attacks. In both Brussels and Paris, the operatives staged coordinated attacks at multiple sites, effectively hampering police responses. The militants exploited weaknesses in Europe's border controls in order to move relatively freely from Syria to France and Belgium. The group has also moved away from previous efforts to attack symbolically significant targets—such as the 2014 attack on a Jewish museum in Brussels—and appears to have adopted the guidance of a senior ISIS operative in the group's online magazine, who directed followers "to stop looking for specific targets" and to "hit everyone and everything." Further, the explosives used in Paris and likely in Brussels indicate the terrorists have achieved a level of proficiency in bomb making. The use of TATP in Paris and the discovery of the material in raids in Brussels suggest that the operatives have received sophisticated explosives training, possibly in Syria.

Third, existing networks of extremists in Europe are providing the infrastructure to support the execution of attacks there. The investigations of the Paris and Belgium attacks have revealed embedded radical networks that supply foreign fighters to ISIS in Syria and operatives and logistical support for the terrorist attacks in those cities. While such entrenched and isolated networks are not present in the United States, ISIS continues to target Americans for recruitment, including through the use of focused social media, in order to identify and mobilize operatives here.

Looking more broadly, the rise of ISIS should be viewed as a manifestation of the transformation of the global jihadist movement over the past several years. We have seen this movement diversify and expand in the aftermath of the upheaval and political chaos in the Arab world since 2010. Instability and unrest in large parts of the Middle East and North Africa have led to a lack of security, border control, and effective governance. In the last few years, four states—Iraq, Syria, Libya, and Yemen—have effectively collapsed. ISIS and other terrorist groups exploit these conditions to expand their reach and establish safe havens. As a result, the threat now comes from a decentralized array of organizations and networks, with ISIS being the group that presents the most urgent threat today.

Specifically, Al Qaeda core continues to support attacking the West and is vying with ISIS to be the recognized leader of the global jihad. There is no doubt that sustained U.S. counterterrorism pressure has led to the steady elimination of Al Qaeda's senior leaders and limited the group's ability to operate, train, and recruit operatives. At the same time, the core leadership of Al Qaeda continues to wield substantial influence over affiliated and allied groups, such as Yemen-based Al Qaeda in the Arabian Peninsula. On three occasions over the past several years, AQAP has sought to bring down an airliner bound for the United States. And there is reason to believe it still harbors the intent and substantial capability to carry out such a plot.

In Syria, veteran Al Qaeda fighters have traveled from Pakistan to take advantage of the permissive operating environment and access to foreign fighters. They are focused on plotting against the West. Al-Shabaab also maintains a safe haven in Somalia and threatens U.S. interests in the region, asserting the aim of creating a caliphate across east Africa. The group has reportedly increased its recruitment in Kenya and aims to destabilize parts of Kenya. Finally, AQIM (and its splinter groups) and Boko Haram—now an official branch of ISIS—continue to maintain their base of operations in North and West Africa and have demonstrated sustained capabilities to carry out deadly attacks against civilian targets.

The Strategy To Defeat ISIS

Against this backdrop, I will briefly address the current strategy to confront and ultimately defeat ISIS. As formidable as ISIS has become, the group is vulnerable. Indeed, the U.S.-led military campaign has killed thousands of ISIS fighters and rolled back ISIS's territorial gains in parts of Iraq and Syria. ISIS has not had any major strategic military victories in Iraq or Syria for almost a year. As ISIS loses its hold on territory, its claim that it has established the "caliphate" will be eroded, and the group will lose its central appeal.

On the military front, a coalition of twelve nations has conducted more than 8,700 airstrikes in Syria and Iraq, according to the Defense Department. These strikes have taken out a range of targets, including ISIS vehicles, weaponry, training camps, oil infrastructure, and artillery positions. In addition, several nations have joined the United States in deploying military personnel to assist the Iraqi government, training more than 17,000 Iraqi security forces.

The military effort also has included the successful targeting of ISIS leaders. United States special operations forces have gone into Syria to support the fight against ISIS, bringing a unique set of capabilities, such as intelligence gathering, enabling local forces, and targeting high-value ISIS operatives and leaders.

From a counterterrorism perspective, the United States is pursuing multiple lines of effort. First, the United States is focusing on stemming the flow of foreign fighters to Syria, and disrupting ISIS's financial networks. The government reports that at least 50 countries plus the United Nations now contribute foreign terrorist fighter profiles to INTERPOL, and the United States has bilateral arrangements with 40 international partners for sharing terrorist travel information. In 2015, the U.S. government sanctioned more than 30 ISIS-linked senior leaders, financiers, foreign terrorist facilitators, and organizations, helping isolate ISIS from the international financial system. In addition, since 2014, the FBI has arrested approximately 65 individuals in ISIS-related criminal matters.

Second, to counter ISIS propaganda, the United States is strengthening its efforts to prevent ISIS from radicalizing and mobilizing recruits. The White House recently announced the creation of an interagency countering violent extremism (CVE) task force under the leadership of the Department of Homeland Security and the Department of Justice, with additional staffing from the FBI and National Counterterrorism Center. The CVE task force is charged with integrating whole-of-government programs and activities and establishing new CVE efforts. As part of this initiative, the DHS Office for Community Partnerships is developing innovative ways to support communities that seek to discourage violent extremism and to undercut terrorist narratives.

Third, and more broadly, the United States continues to lead the international diplomatic effort to resolve the underlying conflicts in the region. This includes working toward a negotiated political transition that removes Bashar al-Asad from power and ultimately leads to an inclusive government that is responsive to the needs of all Syrians. This effort also includes supporting the Iraqi government's progress toward effective and inclusive governance, stabilization efforts, and reconciliation.

To augment this strategy, there are a number of initiatives that merit consideration.

One is a surge in our intelligence capabilities. Such a surge should include enhancing our technical surveillance capabilities, providing additional resources for the development of sources to penetrate ISIS, and fostering closer relationships with intelligence services in the region. This focus on intelligence collection would help address the fact that our law enforcement and intelligence agencies have found it increasingly difficult to collect specific intelligence on terrorist intentions and plots. This intelligence gap is due in part to the widespread availability and adoption of encrypted communication technology. Indeed, ISIS has released a how-to manual to its followers on the use of encryption to avoid detection. The gap also is the result of the illegal disclosures of our intelligence collection methods and techniques. These disclosures have provided terrorists with a roadmap on how to evade our surveillance. Therefore, rebuilding our intelligence capabilities should be an imperative.

Next, the United States should continue to work in concert with European partners and support Europe's effort to break down barriers to information sharing among agencies and among nations and to strengthen border controls. Today, European nations do not always alert each other when they encounter a terrorism suspect at a border. Europe should incorporate the lessons we learned after 9/11 and adopt structural changes that enable sharing of information between law enforcement and intelligence agencies and that support watchlisting of suspected terrorists.

Finally, the United States should redouble its efforts to counter ISIS on the ideological front. This begins with a recognition that the United States, along with nations in Europe, must build and maintain trust and strong relationships with Muslim communities who are on the front lines of the fight against radicalization. This also means we must reject unambiguously the hateful rhetoric that erodes that trust. The U.S. strategy should focus on empowering Muslim American communities to confront extremist ideology, working to galvanize and amplify networks of people, both in the government and private sector, to confront ISIS's ideology of oppression and violence. While the government has made strides in this direction, the pace and scale of the effort has not matched the threat.

Conclusion

In the wake of the terrorist attacks in Europe and here in the United States, our continued focus on ISIS and transnational terrorist threats is absolutely warranted. We should not underestimate the capacity of ISIS and other groups to adapt and evade our defenses and to carry out acts of violence, both here at home and around the world.

But no terrorist group is invincible. The enduring lessons of 9/11 are that we can overcome and defeat the threat of terrorism through strength, unity, and adherence to our founding values, and that American leadership is indispensible to this fight.

75

"Welcome to Generation War"*

Paul R. Pillar

Since World War II—the largest military effort ever by the United States, and one ending with clear victory—the use of U.S. military force overseas has exhibited two patterns. One is the increasing frequency and duration of the application of force. This trend has become especially noticeable since the turn of the twenty-first century, with the United States fighting its two longest major military campaigns, in Afghanistan and Iraq. Simultaneously, Washington has conducted combat operations in Libya, and Syria, and elsewhere, all under the indeterminate rubric of "war on terror." An entire generation of Americans has come of age with its country perpetually at war.

This state of permanent warfare is hard to explain in terms of national self-image. Americans have traditionally seen themselves as peace-loving folks who strike back only when someone else picks a fight. In the words of John Quincy Adams, they tend not to seek out "monsters to destroy." The United States has not been a latter-day Sparta, defining its virtue in terms of martial spirit.

The second pattern makes the first even more difficult to comprehend: the overall results of all this fighting overseas have been poor. Uncle Sam has regularly cried "uncle." The Korean War ended in a draw. The only major U.S. war since then to register a win was Operation Desert Storm, the expulsion of Iraqi forces from Kuwait in 1991. The other large U.S. military campaigns of the last sixty years fall on the opposite side of the ledger. They include the Vietnam and Iraq fiascos, as well as a war in Afghanistan that has gone on for fourteen years and shows no sign of ending. More modestly sized uses of air power have brought only mixed results: some success in the Balkans in the 1990s, but extremist-infested chaos in Libya after the intervention in 2011. Smaller U.S. operations on the ground also have had mixed outcomes, ranging from achievement of some modest objectives in the Caribbean to significant U.S. casualties in, and an embarrassing withdrawal from, Lebanon in the early 1980s.

The United States has been employing military force overseas more than what prudent pursuit of its interests would call for. Yet it keeps coming

*Paul R. Pillar. "Welcome to Generation War," *The National Interest*, July/August 2016. Reprinted by permission of The National Interest.

back for more. An impulse for more foreign military expeditions, despite its poor record, is reflected not only in the two-decade trend toward permanent warfare but also in current pressure in American public debate to do still more militarily in the Middle East. This impulse is not just a matter of policymakers misunderstanding foreign conflicts. More fundamental elements of American thinking are at work and are affecting today's debates about military force in Syria, Iraq, and Afghanistan.

One possible way to explain the trend toward permanent U.S. engagement in warfare concerns long-term changes in the international system and the position of the United States in it. There is some validity to this approach. The United States evolved into a superpower with the increased opportunities and responsibilities that come with it. But the ability to project military power across the globe does not imply that it is prudent to do so, particularly given the United States' string of poor results. Political scientist Barry Posen explains that although the unmatched ability to project military power gives the United States command of the global commons (e.g., sea lanes and international air space), it does not give Washington the ability to control events wherever it wants. The expansion of U.S. military capabilities has prompted excessive applications of force, much as a person who owns a nifty hammer tends to perceive nails everywhere.

Theories elevating terrorism to a new and systemic threat wield little explanatory power. Granted, the September 11, 2001 terrorist attacks did trigger an abrupt change in the American public mood. But international terrorism has been around for centuries and has been shaping U.S. interests for many decades. America's recent military misadventures cannot be sufficiently explained by the rise of terrorism. The costly expedition into Iraq had nothing to do with terrorism, notwithstanding contorted efforts by the promoters of that war to capitalize on the martial post–9/11 public mood.

A traditional explanation for resorting to arms focuses on the vested interests of particular stakeholders. In the United States, this thesis has been most popular on the left, but has had a wider cachet ever since Dwight Eisenhower spoke about a military industrial complex. Of course institutional biases exist, but the attitudes expressed by the U.S. institution most involved in the use of force—the military—do not support the thesis. The military tends to favor full application of resources to assigned missions, not the undertaking of new missions. It was a civilian policymaker, Madeleine Albright, who asked the nation's top military officer, Colin Powell, "What's the point of having this superb military that you're always talking about if we can't use it?" Today's senior military officers are exhibiting some of the same caution that Powell did. In a recent hearing of the Senate Armed Services Committee that addressed the possibility of establishing a no-fly zone in Syria, the vice chairman of the Joint Chiefs of Staff, Gen. Paul Selva, remarked that "we have the military capacity to impose a no-fly zone," but "the potential for miscalculation and loss of American life in the air" render the idea unwise. The hawkish and disappointed committee chairman, John

McCain, referred to this testimony as "one of the more embarrassing statements I have ever heard from a uniformed military officer."

The infrequent use of military force in America's earlier history informs today's frequent use. Blessed with physical separation from foreign threats, Americans adopted the non-Clausewitzian habit of thinking about military means and political ends as two separate realms. They thought about war as the last resort, sallying forth abroad to eliminate whatever threat was sufficiently serious to justify such an expedition. Unlike the Europeans living with continuous threats at close quarters, Americans did not have to develop ways of thinking about security and military force that were more balanced and sustainable over the long term even with more permanent and intense engagement with the outside world.

But after World War II, the American superpower *did* become permanently and intensely engaged with the rest of the world. It was the sort of engagement that Americans were used to associating solely with wars, some "colder" than others. Thus an irony of American history is that the infrequency of wars in the nineteenth century helped to shape a national outlook that, combined with requirements of America's global involvement in the twenty-first century, has brought Americans close to believing themselves to be in perpetual war. The belief has helped foster the reality.

The optimism that post–World War II Americans have exhibited as to what can be accomplished through force is rooted in the remarkable success that the United States enjoyed while rising to a position of unparalleled power. After all, military force produced an impressive winning streak through World War II. Even the one earlier war that should be scored as a draw—the War of 1812—was perceived by many Americans at the time as a win because combat ended with a smashing American victory at New Orleans. Even the Civil War that tore the nation apart later in the nineteenth century was ultimately a successful application of arms: a rebellion was quelled, the union was preserved and the country emerged freer than before.

America's military successes have been so obvious, so long-standing and so deeply embedded in American culture and lore that they still shape current discourse on the use of force. That history, ingrained in American habits of thought, impedes the learning of lessons from more recent and less successful uses of force. The history is part of what lies behind McCain's belief that it should not be too hard for "the most powerful nation on Earth" to set up a no-fly zone or to "take out" the so-called Islamic State.

Most of the wars the United States fought while still on a winning streak did not confront it directly with the nationalism-soaked problems that U.S. military interventions have encountered since the streak ended. The United States got its first real taste of such problems dealing with a stubborn insurgency in the Philippines after taking the islands from Spain following an easy win in the Spanish-American War. The lessons from that experience were not fully applied to a bigger insurgency elsewhere in Southeast Asia half a century later. Robert McNamara, the U.S. secretary of defense during the first half of the Vietnam War, wrote many years afterward with insight and anguish:

> We underestimated the power of nationalism to motivate a people (in this case, the North Vietnamese and Vietcong) to fight and die for their beliefs and values—and we continue to do so today in many parts of the world.

In many of America's more recent foreign expeditions, resistance to applications of U.S. military power stems not only from such strong nationalist sentiment but also from widespread perceptions of U.S. power as threatening rather than helpful. The difficulty most Americans have had in recognizing such perceptions and the problems they pose for U.S. military campaigns emanates from the benign American exceptionalist self-image. It also has historical roots in the geographic isolation that gave citizens of a younger and weaker United States the luxury of not having to think much about how someone else's projected power can feel threatening.

What should have been sobering lessons from the more recent and less successful military interventions have tended to be swept aside in favor of the historically based optimism about the utility of force. The "Vietnam War syndrome"—a public hesitance about such interventions after the nation got so badly burned in that war—was largely blown away by the inspiring success of Desert Storm. Although the Iraq War is deeply relevant to the ISIS situation, the lessons of that costly expedition have been compartmentalized and largely lost.

Some who supported that war explain it away as all about a mistake, not to be repeated, concerning nonexistent weapons of mass destruction. Donald Trump has tried to inoculate himself by claiming, with some exaggeration, always to have opposed the Iraq War, but such opposition has not deterred him from calling on Washington to "bomb the sh-t" out of ISIS. Ted Cruz's attempt to do something similar with his criticisms of neocons has not stopped him from calling for carpet bombing in Syria. Many Republican opponents of Barack Obama cling to the myth that the president snatched defeat from the jaws of victory by implementing the troop withdrawal agreement negotiated by the Bush administration—a myth that disregards both the substantial pace at which the Iraqi civil war was still being fought at the time and the failure of earlier military efforts to resolve the political conflicts that underlie instability in Iraq today.

Beyond all of this is a frequent admonition not to "overreact" to the bad experience of the Iraq War, an admonition voiced so frequently that it has become an overreaction about overreaction. Coupled with that theme are efforts to depict any proposals for more military intervention in the Middle East as much different in cost and duration from the quagmire that the Iraq War became. Typical is the urging by James Jeffrey, ambassador in Baghdad and a White House policy adviser in the George W. Bush administration, to initiate a U.S. ground war against ISIS, which he assures us would be a "short," "crisp," "rapid takedown" of the group. Similar spin comes from columnist Richard Cohen, who is more interested in using force against the Assad regime than against ISIS and says that a no-fly zone and "maybe taking a shot to two at a key government installation" would do the job. The relevance of lessons from the Iraq War simply gets defined away with unrealistically sanguine images of what the next war would look like.

Certain other rhetorical dynamics of current debates about the use of force in Syria and Iraq add to the historically based bias in favor of using it. One is the American habit of discussing almost any serious issue overseas as a problem that the United States can and should solve. A related rhetorical asymmetry is the greater appeal of positive, confident-sounding calls for the United States to do just that, compared with the lesser appeal of caution or skepticism about whether the United States really *can* solve other people's civil wars. Saying anything that sounds like, "that's a nasty problem, but given the downsides of our available options, we'll have to live with it" does not win American political leaders votes.

The public and political appetite for action usually means specifically visible, forceful action. That means that military responses have greater appeal than less visible policy tools, such as behind-closed-doors diplomacy. Amid today's Middle East security issues, the "war on terror" concept continues to weigh heavily on American debate and foreign-policy discourse. It is a metaphor that has shaped reality. It has led to the false syllogism that if a problem is serious then America is at war, and if America is at war then it needs to use military force to solve the problem. The influence of this line of thinking is heard in the frequent declarations from Republican presidential candidates and others that "we are at war," notwithstanding the absence of a congressional declaration of war.

A related pseudologic equates leadership with toughness, and toughness with military force. Barack Obama has been especially vulnerable to criticism of his leadership along these lines, given his image as a pedantic law professor who came into office eager to withdraw from existing wars and whose administration has been said to "lead from behind." The lack of appeal, emotionally as well as politically, of this presidential style has led commentators not normally hostile to Democrats to complain about Obama's unwillingness to amp up his rhetoric. Dana Milbank of the *Washington Post* calls him "President Oh-bummer" and says although tough talk won't defeat terrorists "it will rally a nation." Milbank's *Post* colleague Richard Cohen says Obama's approach leaves him "empty and cold." Cohen observes that Obama "is a cautious man who fears his rhetoric running away from him"—an accurate statement about the president's concerns that also points to an actual process of rhetoric pushing policy, another reason that the use of military force has gone beyond what is in the nation's best interests.

Other dynamics compound this trend in Washington's approach to the Middle East. One is the luxury that political opponents have, and incumbent policymakers do not, of sounding appealing themes without having to voice less appealing cautions about long-term complications and consequences. Amid fears of terrorist groups and a presidential election, the rhetorical energy drives predominantly in the direction of more rather than less reliance on military force.

Another factor is the universal human tendency to treat sunk costs as investments. This tendency has especially affected American discourse about Iraq, and all the more so given propagation of the myth that the United States was on the verge of a victory there in 2009. Politicians and military veterans alike relate news about the latest fighting in Iraqi cities to sacrifices that U.S. troops made in the same locales during an earlier phase of the war. Such connections are drawn even though sunk costs really *are* sunk and past ill-advised expenditures have not bought any current opportunities.

At some level of consciousness the Pottery Barn rule—if you break it, you buy it—has affected American thinking about troublesome military expeditions, adding to the impetus to escalate and extend rather than to retrench and curtail. By itself the rule is laudable and teaches responsibility. The trouble is that the rule tends to get applied only after breakage has occurred. And with Americans thinking of themselves as builders rather than breakers, some commitments have been made with insufficient advance thought about what was likely to be broken.

All of the aforementioned factors have contributed to Washington's current state of unending warfare and of perpetuating the costly pattern of using military force beyond what careful consideration of U.S. interests would dictate. Among recent military expeditions, the invasion of Iraq remains a glaring example of how not to apply force—blind to the troubles that would spill out once Iraqi pottery got broken and with unrealistically rosy assumptions about how liberalism and democracy would fall into place after a dictator's ouster. But that war was an extreme case, given the extraordinary absence of any policy process to consider whether launching the war was a good idea and thus insufficient opportunity within the government to question the rosy assumptions and to consider all the possible costs and consequences.

Perhaps more illustrative of the general point about the American bias toward war have been the policies of, and pressures upon, Obama, who by contrast has deliberated meticulously ("dithering," to some) about applications of military force. He has tried to resist demands to expand the unproductive record of unending warfare. He has succeeded in resisting some, but has succumbed enough to disappoint followers who wanted a president who would be getting Americans out of wars rather than keeping the nation immersed in them. The political pressures from those followers have been much weaker than pressures coming from the opposite direction. Obama has had to deal with a Congress in which one chamber for most of his presidency, and both chambers for his final two years, have been controlled by an opposition party whose foreign policies have been dominated by neoconservatism. His first secretary of state and aspiring successor is more hawkish than he and is part of an element in his own party that favors armed intervention on humanitarian grounds, which was the rationale for the operation in Libya. The perceived trait that Obama, fairly or unfairly, continually has had to counteract is wimpiness, not recklessness.

The administration's first test was the war in Afghanistan. Long before President Obama entered office, the United States had failed to find an off-ramp. Once the Taliban had been ousted from Kabul and Al Qaeda rousted from its haven, the United States could have opted for an honorable conclusion to its justified military response to a major terrorist attack, before the operation morphed into a nation-building exercise in the graveyard of empires. The more time that passed after the successful ousting and rousting in the first few months of Operation Enduring Freedom, the less honorable any exit would have seemed. Moreover, for Obama in particular, Afghanistan was the "good" war in contrast to the "bad" war in Iraq, which to his credit he had opposed from the beginning. So a complete exit while Afghan factions continued to wage their civil war was not in the cards. The policy response included a surge that always made more domestic political sense than military sense, being too small and quick to accomplish much on the ground. The administration's response also has come to include a scotching of any idea of an exit in the foreseeable future, an apparent acceptance of indefinite extension of what already is America's longest war. All this in a country that, notwithstanding the association with 9/11, has taken its place in modern history because of an insurgency more than three decades ago against a client regime of the Soviets. Afghanistan is not inherently destined to be enmeshed in international terrorism, and whatever strategic significance it has is incommensurate with the longest ever U.S. war.

Some of the same psychological and political tendencies in the American approach to countering terrorism have been apparent in the use of unmanned aerial vehicles, or drones, to kill suspected terrorists. Lethal operations with drones began in 2002 under George W. Bush, and the Obama administration has increased their pace. The appeal of drones is partly as another splendid hammer that cries out for nails to be struck. More significantly and defensibly, drone strikes have been the only practical way to reach some suspected terrorists in remote places. Adding to their appeal is the same attraction that gives any other use of armed force an advantage over less kinetic tools of statecraft: it brings direct, immediate, tangible results, in this case in the form of dead terrorists. More indirect and intangible are the negative effects, including resentment and radicalization stimulated by collateral damage from the operations. The asymmetry that favors more attention to the first effect than the second—even though the longer-term radicalizing impact may ultimately shape terrorist threats against the United States more than any number of bad guys the drones kill—probably already has pushed the drone strikes past a point of diminishing returns. The results have not been encouraging in, for example, Yemen, where the number of violent radicals has increased during the same period that drone strikes have, even before the effects of the current civil war there began to be felt.

The most intense debates about the use of U.S. armed force are now centered on ISIS and its enclaves in Iraq and Syria, where the ISIS problem is superimposed on a complicated civil war in which a mélange of other opposition groups are also fighting against the Assad regime. Given that ISIS has supplanted Al Qaeda in American perceptions as the embodiment of international terrorism, discussion of what to do about ISIS is heavily weighed down by the baggage of 9/11 and the "war on terror." Among the consequences are the presumption that military force is the primary tool to wage this "war" and an assumption that if ISIS is not dispatched in the Middle East then it is very likely to harm Americans. A tone of urgency has infused calls to destroy ISIS before it conducts a major terrorist attack in the United States.

More sober consideration would begin by recalling what should be one of leading lessons from the Iraq War: that ISIS did not exist before that war, and that the group (originally Al Qaeda in Iraq) came into existence as a direct result of the civil war that the U.S. invasion and overthrow of Saddam Hussein ignited. Careful consideration of the problem would note that ISIS, unlike the main Al Qaeda organization from which it openly split, rejected the "far enemy" strategy of Osama bin Laden and Ayman al-Zawahiri. ISIS has focused instead on building and defending its so-called caliphate (from the "near enemy"), with any terrorism against the West fulfilling the secondary goals of revenge, recruitment, diversion, and deterrence.

Amid the sense of urgency about destroying ISIS's enclave, little is said publicly about exactly what difference a group's control of that kind of distant real estate makes for counterterrorism in the United States and the West. Even if some such real estate makes a difference, there is nothing sacred about the ground that ISIS has been occupying in Iraq and Syria. The broader history of Al Qaeda suggests that if there is going to be any base of operations for anti-Western terrorism, it is as likely to be somewhere on the periphery (such as Yemen), as in the group's original sanctuary. More fundamental is the question of how a terrorist group's control of *any* piece of territory affects the West. Experience indicates that such territorial control is neither necessary nor sufficient for significant international terrorist operations. Most of the preparation for 9/11 took place in apartments and flight schools in the West, and in cyberspace, rather than in the Afghan haven. Looking at counterterrorism through a war-tinted lens leads naturally to the equating of progress against ISIS with the movement of front lines on a map, as in conventional war.

What happens in ISIS's caliphate does affect the group's ability to inspire violent acts in the West. But these inspirational links may well be a matter of already radicalized individuals looking for a prominent brand in whose name they might commit violent acts they would have committed anyway. The mass shooting in San Bernardino, California in December 2015, which played a major role in stimulating the sense of urgency and alarm about possible ISIS-related attacks in the United States, is instructive. Although the shooters invoked the ISIS name, no evidence has emerged of any organizational connection with ISIS itself. Reportedly, the male half of the shooting pair had sought contact with different extremist groups, including Jabhat al-Nusra and al-Shabaab.

Of the two countries where ISIS has established its enclave, Iraq carries for Americans the baggage of the Iraq War and associated attitudes about sunk costs, but Syria is nonetheless the more complicated situation because of the uprising against the Assad regime. The revolt has regime-change juices flowing, stimulating an American itch to weigh in militarily, rather like what happened with Libya. This itch has spread to the Syrian regime itself, even though the Assads have ruled in Damascus for nearly half a century, so there would not seem to be a reason for urgency in toppling their regime. The impulse to use military force against the regime nonetheless has been strong, as suggested by how much American domestic opponents criticized the Obama administration for making use of a peaceful channel brokered by Russia to dispose of the Syrian regime's chemical weapons rather than going to war over the issue.

Much of the urging to do more militarily in Syria constitutes inchoate expressions of toughness by politicians or of displeasure with the Syrian mess by others who assume this is yet another problem the United States ought to be able to solve if it applies its power. The relative priorities of confronting the Syrian regime and of dealing with ISIS are often left unclear, as are details of exactly what sort of additional military action the United States might take. The closest things to specificity have been mentions of a no-fly zone and calls for initiation of a ground war against ISIS. For the latter purpose, for example, McCain and former Republican presidential candidate Lindsey Graham have talked about deploying ten thousand U.S. combat troops each to Syria and Iraq.

The idea of a no-fly zone—embraced by, among others, Hillary Clinton—has the attraction of being responsive to the urge to apply more U.S. military force in Syria while sounding less costly than another quagmire on the ground. But although such a zone can be useful where (as with Iraqi Kurdistan in the past) a friendly and well-established authority on the ground could use protection from a hostile force with air power, that is not the situation in Syria. Left unanswered in most calls for a no-fly zone are questions about who controls the ground underneath the prohibited airspace and who will do the fighting to ensure the control stays the way America wants it. Moreover, even just the air component entails a much bigger military commitment—i.e., initiating direct hostilities with the Syrian regime—than those suggesting the idea seem to realize. (Given that ISIS has no air force, a no-fly zone would be useless against that group.) Enforcement of the zone would probably include attacks against Syrian air-defense capabilities and would entail significant risk of direct combat with Russian aircraft flying missions in support of the Syrian regime.

Proposals for U.S. ground operations against ISIS are based on the false premise that "taking out" the group with a quick assault on its positions would be the end of the task. It would not. It would mark the beginning of a new phase of the war characterized by guerrilla attacks, terrorism, and other asymmetric operations. Chaos and instability left where the self-styled caliphate once stood would be a fertile garden for additional violent extremism, whether it bore the ISIS name or some other label. There would be no more justification for declaring "mission accomplished" after toppling the ISIS command structure than there was for declaring it in Iraq after toppling Saddam Hussein's regime. Political scientists Stephen Biddle and Jacob Shapiro assess that taking and holding ISIS's territory would require not ten or twenty thousand U.S. troops but instead one hundred thousand. In other words, it would be another large, costly, and, perhaps, interminable counterinsurgency and nation-building effort.

For the United States to plunge into the Syrian war would play into ISIS's hands. It would confirm the group's narratives about it leading Muslim defenses against a predatory West and about apocalypse between itself and the leader of the West. The inevitable collateral damage from increased lethal operations would foster the sort of resentment that aids terrorist recruitment.

Barack Obama, when pressed to do more militarily, has explained the situations in Syria and Iraq in terms that indicate he understands well the aforementioned costs and risks. In his last year in office, he has resisted the pressures to go beyond to go beyond the approximately four thousand U.S. troops he has reinserted in Iraq, a very small ground presence in Syria and anti-ISIS air operations in both countries. His successor, however, is likely to be someone who will not only have more hawkish views but also, as a first-term president, be more easily moved by the urges and impulses that have pushed the United States into its state of perpetual warfare.

Those urges and impulses are deeply rooted in American history and, thus, in American habits of thinking. Occasionally, as after the Vietnam War, the sheer magnitude of the costs has led to a temporary departure from those habits.

Given the nature of the current debate, such a departure does not appear forthcoming. Quite the contrary. The United States appears destined, for reasons related to what makes it exceptional, to continue using military force beyond what serves its interests. It will take exceptional leadership to limit the resulting damage.

Discussion Questions

1. Those who insist that the threat ISIS poses in the United States is overblown often compare the number of people killed in terror attacks inside the United States (an average of about 25 per year since 2010, although the number varies depending on what is defined as a terror attack) to the number killed by automobiles or guns (about 33,000 per year), drownings (about 3,500), or any number of other causes. Is this a meaningful argument? Is it right to argue that we should not worry about terrorism because—today—there are other things that pose a higher risk of harm?

2. Is there any common ground between Olson and Pillar? Is it possible to address the threat that ISIS poses without committing to major military action in Syria and Iraq?

Appendix

The Declaration of Independence

In Congress, July 4, 1776

When in the course of human events, it becomes necessary for one people to dissolve the political bands which have connected them with another, and to assume among the Powers of the earth, the separate and equal station to which the Laws of Nature and of Nature's God entitle them, a decent respect to the opinions of mankind requires that they should declare the causes which impel them to the separation.

We hold these truths to be self-evident, that all men are created equal, that they are endowed by their Creator with certain unalienable rights, that among these are Life, Liberty and the pursuit of Happiness. That to secure these rights, Governments are instituted among Men, deriving their just powers from the consent of the governed. That whenever any Form of Government becomes destructive of these ends, it is the Right of the People to alter or to abolish it, and to institute new Government, laying its foundation on such principles and organizing its powers in such form, as to them shall seem most likely to effect their Safety and Happiness. Prudence, indeed, will dictate that Governments long established should not be changed for light and transient causes; and accordingly all experience hath shown, that mankind are more disposed to suffer, while evils are sufferable, than to right themselves by abolishing the forms to which they are accustomed. But when a long train of abuses and usurpations, pursuing invariably the same Object evinces a design to reduce them under absolute Despotism, it is their right, it is their duty, to throw off such Government, and to provide new Guards for their future security.—Such has been the patient sufferance of these Colonies; and such is now the necessity which constrains them to alter their former Systems of Government. The history of the present King of Great Britain is a history of repeated injuries and usurpations, all having in direct object the establishment of an absolute Tyranny over these States. To prove this, let Facts be submitted to a candid world.

He has refused his Assent to Laws, the most wholesome and necessary for the public good.

He has forbidden his Governors to pass Laws of immediate and pressing importance, unless suspended in their operation till his Assent should be obtained; and when so suspended, he has utterly neglected to attend to them.

He has refused to pass other Laws for the accommodation of large districts of people, unless those people would relinquish the right of Representation in the Legislature, a right inestimable to them and formidable to tyrants only.

He has called together legislative bodies at places unusual, uncomfortable, and distant from the depository of their public Records, for the sole purpose of fatiguing them into compliance with his measures.

He has dissolved Representative Houses repeatedly, for opposing with manly firmness his invasions on the rights of the people.

He has refused for a long time, after such dissolutions, to cause others to be elected; whereby the Legislative powers, incapable of Annihilation, have returned to the People at large for their exercise; the State remaining in the mean time exposed to all the dangers of invasion from without, and convulsions within.

He has endeavoured to prevent the population of these States; for that purpose obstructing the Laws for Naturalization of Foreigners; refusing to pass others to encourage their migrations hither, and raising the conditions of new Appropriations of Lands.

He has obstructed the Administration of Justice, by refusing his Assent to Laws for establishing Judiciary Powers.

He has made Judges dependent on his Will alone, for the tenure of their offices, and the amount and payment of their salaries.

He has erected a multitude of New Offices, and sent hither swarms of Officers to harrass our People, and eat out their substance.

He has kept among us, in times of peace, Standing Armies without the Consent of our legislature.

He has affected to render the Military independent of and superior to the Civil Power.

He has combined with others to subject us to a jurisdiction foreign to our constitution, and unacknowledged by our laws; giving his Assent to their Acts of pretended Legislation:

For quartering large bodies of armed troops among us:

For protecting them, by a mock Trial, from Punishment for any Murders which they should commit on the Inhabitants of these States:

For cutting off our Trade with all parts of the world:

For imposing Taxes on us without our Consent:

For depriving us in many cases, of the benefits of Trial by jury:

For transporting us beyond Seas to be tried for pretended offences:

For abolishing the free System of English Laws in a neighbouring Province, establishing therein an Arbitrary government, and enlarging its

Boundaries so as to render it at once an example and fit instrument for introducing the same absolute rule into these Colonies:

For taking away our Charters, abolishing our most valuable Laws, and altering fundamentally the Forms of our Governments:

For suspending our own Legislatures, and declaring themselves invested with Power to legislate for us in all cases whatsoever.

He has abdicated Government here, by declaring us out of his Protection and waging War against us.

He has plundered our seas, ravaged our Coasts, burnt our towns, and destroyed the lives of our people.

He is at this time transporting large armies of foreign mercenaries to compleat the works of death, desolation and tyranny, already begun with circumstances of Cruelty & perfidy scarcely paralleled in the most barbarous ages, and totally unworthy the Head of a civilized nation.

He has constrained our fellow Citizens taken Captive on the high Seas to bear Arms against their Country, to become the executioners of their friends and Brethren, or to fall themselves by their Hands.

He has excited domestic insurrections amongst us, and has endeavored to bring on the inhabitants of our frontiers, the merciless Indian Savages, whose known rule of warfare, is an undistinguished destruction of all ages, sexes, and conditions.

In every stage of these Oppressions we have Petitioned for Redress in the most humble terms: Our repeated Petitions have been answered only by repeated injury. A Prince, whose character is thus marked by every act which may define a Tyrant, is unfit to be the ruler of a free people.

Nor have we been wanting in attention to our British brethren. We have warned them from time to time of attempts by their legislature to extend an unwarrantable jurisdiction over us. We have reminded them of the circumstances of our emigration and settlement here. We have appealed to their native justice and magnanimity, and we have conjured them by the ties of our common kindred to disavow these usurpations, which, would inevitably interrupt our connections and correspondence. They too must have been deaf to the voice of justice and of consanguinity. We must, therefore, acquiesce in the necessity, which denounces our Separation, and hold them, as we hold the rest of mankind, Enemies in War, in Peace Friends.

WE, THEREFORE, the Representatives of the UNITED STATES OF AMERICA, in General Congress, Assembled, appealing to the Supreme Judge of the world for the rectitude of our intentions, do, in the Name, and by Authority of the good People of these Colonies, solemnly publish and declare, That these United Colonies are, and of Right ought to be FREE AND INDEPENDENT STATES; that they are Absolved from all Allegiance to the British Crown, and that all political connection between them and the State of Great Britain, is and ought to be totally dissolved; and that as Free and Independent States, they have full Power to levy War, conclude Peace, contract Alliances, establish Commerce, and to do all other Acts and Things which Independent States may of right do. And for the support of this Declaration, with a firm reliance on the protection of Divine Providence, we mutually pledge to each other our Lives, our Fortunes and our sacred Honor.

The foregoing Declaration was, by order of Congress, engrossed, and signed by the following members:

John Hancock

NEW HAMPSHIRE
Josiah Bartlett
William Whipple
Matthew Thornton

MASSACHUSETTS BAY
Samuel Adams
John Adams
Robert Treat Paine
Elbridge Gerry

RHODE ISLAND
Stephen Hopkins
William Ellery

CONNECTICUT
Roger Sherman
Samuel Huntington
William Williams
Oliver Wolcott

NEW YORK
William Floyd
Philip Livingston
Francis Lewis
Lewis Morris

NEW JERSEY
Richard Stockton
John Witherspoon
Francis Hopkinson
John Hart
Abraham Clark

PENNSYLVANIA
Robert Morris
Benjamin Rush
Benjamin Franklin
John Morton
George Clymer
James Smith
George Taylor
James Wilson
George Ross

DELAWARE
Caesar Rodney
George Read
Thomas M'Kean

MARYLAND
Samuel Chase
William Paca
Thomas Stone
Charles Carroll, of Carrollton

VIRGINIA
George Wythe
Richard Henry Lee
Thomas Jefferson
Benjamin Harrison
Thomas Nelson, Jr.
Francis Lightfoot Lee
Carter Braxton

NORTH CAROLINA
William Hooper
Joseph Hewes
John Penn

SOUTH CAROLINA
Edward Rutledge
Thomas Heyward, Jr.
Thomas Lynch, Jr.
Arthur Middleton

GEORGIA
Button Gwinnett
Lyman Hall
George Walton

Resolved, That copies of the Declaration be sent to the several assemblies, conventions, and committees, or councils of safety, and to the several commanding officers of the continental troops; that it be proclaimed in each of the United States, at the head of the army.

The Federalist, No. 10

James Madison

To the People of the State of New York:

Among the numerous advantages promised by a well-constructed Union, none deserves to be more accurately developed than its tendency to break and control the violence of faction. The friend of popular governments never finds himself so much alarmed for their character and fate, as when he contemplates their propensity to this dangerous vice. He will not fail, therefore, to set a due value on any plan which, without violating the principles to which he is attached, provides a proper cure for it. The instability, injustice, and confusion introduced into the public councils, have, in truth, been the mortal diseases under which popular governments have everywhere perished; as they continue to be the favorite and fruitful topics from which the adversaries to liberty derive their most specious declamations. The valuable improvements made by the American constitutions on the popular models, both ancient and modern, cannot certainly be too much admired; but it would be an unwarrantable partiality, to contend that they have as effectually obviated the danger on this side, as was wished and expected. Complaints are everywhere heard from our most considerate and virtuous citizens, equally the friends of public and private faith, and of public and personal liberty, that our governments are too unstable; that the public good is disregarded in the conflicts of rival parties; and that measures are too often decided, not according to the rules of justice and the rights of the minor party, but by the superior force of an interested and overbearing majority. However anxiously we may wish that these complaints had no foundation, the evidence of known facts will not permit us to deny that they are in some degree true. It will be found, indeed, on a candid review of our situation, that some of the distresses under which we labor have been erroneously charged on the operation of our governments; but it will be found, at the same time, that other causes will not alone account for many of our heaviest misfortunes; and, particularly, for that prevailing and increasing distrust of public engagements, and alarm for private rights, which are echoed from one end of the continent to the other. These must be chiefly, if not wholly, effects of the unsteadiness and injustice with which a factious spirit has tainted our public administrations.

By a faction, I understand a number of citizens, whether amounting to a majority or minority of the whole, who are united and actuated by some common impulse of passion, or of interest, adverse to the rights of other citizens, or to the permanent and aggregate interests of the community.

There are two methods of curing the mischiefs of faction: the one, by removing its causes; the other, by controlling its effects.

There are again two methods of removing the causes of faction: the one, by destroying the liberty which is essential to its existence; the other, by giving to every citizen the same opinions, the same passions, and the same interests.

It could never be more truly said than of the first remedy, that it is worse than the disease. Liberty is to faction what air is to fire, an aliment without which it instantly expires. But it could not be less folly to abolish liberty, which is essential to political life, because it nourishes faction, than it would be to wish the annihilation of air, which is essential to animal life, because it imparts to fire its destructive agency.

The second expedient is as impracticable as the first would be unwise. As long as the reason of man continues fallible, and he is at liberty to exercise it, different opinions will be formed. As long as the connection subsits between his reason and his self-love, his opinions and his passions will have a reciprocal influence on each other; and the former will be objects to which the latter will attach themselves. The diversity in the faculties of men, from which the rights of property originate, is not less an insuperable obstacle to a uniformity of interests. The protection of these faculties is the first object of government. From the protection of different and unequal faculties of acquiring property, the possession of different degrees and kinds of property immediately results; and from the influence of these on the sentiments and views of the respective proprietors, ensues a division of the society into different interests and parties.

The latent causes of faction are thus sown in the nature of man; and we see them everywhere brought into different degrees of activity, according to the different circumstances of civil society. A zeal for different opinions concerning religion, concerning government, and many other points, as well of speculation as of practice; an attachment to different leaders ambitiously contending for pre-eminence and power; or to persons of other descriptions whose fortunes have been interesting to the human passions, have, in turn, divided mankind into parties, inflamed them with mutual animosity, and rendered them much more disposed to vex and oppress each other than to co-operate for their common good. So strong is this propensity of mankind to fall into mutual animosities, that where no substantial occasion presents itself, the most frivolous and fanciful distinctions have been sufficient to kindle their unfriendly passions and excite their most violent conflicts. But the most common and durable source of factions has been the various and unequal distribution of property. Those who hold and those who are without property have ever formed distinct interests in society. Those who are creditors, and those who are debtors, fall under a like discrimination. A landed interest, a manufacturing interest, a mercantile interest, a moneyed interest, with many lesser interests, grow up of necessity in civilized nations, and divide them into different classes, actuated by different sentiments and views. The regulation of these various and interfering interests forms the principal task of modern legislation, and involves the spirit of party and faction in the necessary and ordinary operations of the government.

No man is allowed to be a judge in his own cause, because his interest would certainly bias his judgment, and, not improbably, corrupt his integrity. With equal, nay with greater reason, a body of men are unfit to be both judges and parties at the same time; yet what are many of the most important acts of legislation, but so many judicial determinations, not indeed concerning the rights of single persons, but concerning the rights of large bodies of citizens? and what are the different classes of legislators but advocates and parties to the causes which they determine? Is a law proposed concerning private debts? It is a question to which the creditors are parties on one side and the debtors on the other. Justice ought to hold the balance between them. Yet the parties are, and must be, themselves the judges; and the most numerous party, or, in other words, the most powerful faction must be expected to prevail. Shall domestic manufactures be encouraged, and in what degree, by restrictions on foreign manufactures? are questions which would be differently decided by the landed and the manufacturing classes, and probably by neither with a sole regard to justice and the public good. The apportionment of taxes on the various descriptions of property is an act which seems to require the most exact impartiality; yet there is, perhaps, no legislative act in which greater opportunity and temptation are given to a predominant party to trample on the rules of justice. Every shilling with which they overburden the inferior number is a shilling saved to their own pockets.

It is in vain to say that enlightened statesmen will be able to adjust these clashing interests and render them all subservient to the public good. Enlightened statesmen will not always be at the helm. Nor, in many cases, can such an adjustment be made at all without taking into view indirect and remote considerations, which will rarely prevail over the immediate interest which one party may find in disregarding the rights of another or the good of the whole.

The inference to which we are brought is, that the *causes* of faction cannot be removed, and that relief is only to be sought in the means of controlling its *effects*.

If a faction consists of less than a majority, relief is supplied by the republican principle, which enables the majority to defeat its sinister views by regular vote. It may clog the administration, it may convulse the society;

but it will be unable to execute and mask its violence under the forms of the Constitution. When a majority is included in a faction, the form of popular government, on the other hand, enables it to sacrifice to its ruling passion or interest both the public good and the rights of other citizens. To secure the public good and private rights against the danger of such a faction, and at the same time to preserve the spirit and the form of popular government, is then the great object to which our inquiries are directed. Let me add that it is the great desideratum [desire] by which this form of government can be rescued from the opprobrium under which it has so long labored, and be recommended to the esteem and adoption of mankind.

By what means is this object attainable? Evidently by one of two only. Either the existence of the same passion or interest in a majority at the same time must be prevented, or the majority, having such coexistent passion or interest, must be rendered by their number and local situation unable to concert and carry into effect schemes of oppression. If the impulse and the opportunity be suffered to coincide, we well know that neither moral nor religious motives can be relied on as an adequate control. They are not found to be such on the injustice and violence of individuals, and lose their efficacy in proportion to the number combined together, that is, in proportion as their efficacy becomes needful.

From this view of the subject it may be concluded that a pure democracy, by which I mean a society consisting of a small number of citizens, who assemble and administer the government in person, can admit of no cure for the mischiefs of faction. A common passion or interest will, in almost every case, be felt by a majority of the whole; a communication and concert result from the form of government itself; and there is nothing to check the inducements to sacrifice the weaker party or an obnoxious individual. Hence it is that such democracies have ever been spectacles of turbulence and contention; have ever been found incompatible with personal security or the rights of property; and have in general been as short in their lives as they have been violent in their deaths. Theoretic politicians, who have patronized this species of government, have erroneously supposed that by reducing mankind to a perfect equality in their political rights, they would, at the same time, be perfectly equalized and assimilated in their possessions, their opinions, and their passions.

A republic, by which I mean a government in which the scheme of representation takes place, opens a different prospect, and promises the cure for which we are seeking. Let us examine the points in which it varies from pure democracy, and we shall comprehend both the nature of the cure and the efficacy which it must derive from the Union.

The two great points of difference between a democracy and a republic are: first, the delegation of the government in the latter to a small number of citizens elected by the rest; secondly, the greater number of citizens and greater sphere of country over which the latter may be extended.

The effect of the first difference is, on the one hand, to refine and enlarge the public views, by passing them through the medium of a chosen body of citizens, whose wisdom may best discern the true interest of their country, and whose patriotism and love of justice will be least likely to sacrifice it to temporary or partial considerations. Under such a regulation, it may well happen that the public voice, pronounced by the representatives of the people, will be more consonant to the public good than if pronounced by the people themselves, convened for the purpose. On the other hand, the effect may be inverted. Men of factious tempers, of local prejudices, or of sinister designs, may by intrigue, by corruption, or by other means, first obtain the suffrages, and then betray the interests of the people. The question resulting is, whether small or extensive republics are more favorable to the election of proper guardians of the public weal; and it is clearly decided in favor of the latter by two obvious considerations.

In the first place, it is to be remarked that, however small the republic may be, the representatives must be raised to a certain number in order to guard against the cabals of a few; and that, however large it may be, they must be limited to a certain number in order to guard against the confusion of a multitude. Hence, the number of representatives in the two cases not being in proportion to that of the two constituents, and being proportionally greater in the small republic, it follows that, if the proportion of fit characters be not less in the large than in the small republic, the former will present a greater option and consequently a greater probability of a fit choice.

In the next place, as each representative will be chosen by a greater number of citizens in the large than in the small republic, it will be more difficult for unworthy candidates to practise with success the vicious arts by which elections are too often carried; and the suffrages of the people being more free, will be more likely to centre in men who possess the most attractive merit and the most diffusive and established characters.

It must be confessed that in this, as in most other cases, there is a mean, on both sides of which inconveniences will be found to lie. By enlarging too much the number of electors, you render the representative too little acquainted with all their local circumstances and lesser interests: as by reducing it too much, you render him unduly attached to these, and too little fit to comprehend and pursue great and national objects. The federal Constitution forms a happy combination in this respect; the great and aggregate interests being referred to the national, the local and particular to the State legislatures.

The other point of difference is, the greater number of citizens and extent of territory which may be brought within the compass of republican than of democratic government; and it is this circumstance principally which renders factious combinations less to be dreaded in the former than in the latter. The smaller the society, the fewer probably will be the distinct parties and interests composing it; the fewer the distinct parties and interests, the more frequently will a majority be found of the same party; and the smaller the number of individuals composing a majority, and the smaller the compass within which they are placed, the more easily will they concert and execute their plans of oppression. Extend the sphere, and you take in a greater variety of parties and interests; you make it less probable that a majority of the whole will have a common motive to invade the rights of other citizens; or if such a common motive exists, it will be more difficult for all who feel it to discover their own strength and to act in unison with each other. Besides other impediments, it may be remarked that, where there is a consciousness of unjust or dishonorable purposes, communication is always checked by distrust in proportion to the number whose concurrence is necessary.

Hence, it clearly appears that the same advantage which a republic has over a democracy in controlling the effects of faction is enjoyed by a large over a small republic,—is enjoyed by the Union over the States composing it. Does the advantage consist in the substitution of representatives whose enlightened views and virtuous sentiments render them superior to local prejudices and to schemes of injustice? It will not be denied that the representation of the Union will be most likely to possess these requisite endowments. Does it consist in the greater security afforded by a greater variety of parties, against the event of any one party being able to outnumber and oppress the rest? In an equal degree does the increased variety of parties comprised within the Union, increase this security. Does it, in fine, consist in the greater obstacles opposed to the concert and accomplishment of the secret wishes of an unjust and interested majority? Here, again, the extent of the Union gives it the most palpable advantage.

The influence of factious leaders may kindle a flame within their particular States, but will be unable to spread a general conflagration through the other States. A religious sect may degenerate into a political faction in a part of the Confederacy; but the variety of sects dispersed over the entire face of it must secure the national councils against any danger from that source. A rage for paper money, for an abolition of debts, for an equal division of property, or for any other improper or wicked project, will be less apt to pervade the whole body of the Union than a particular member of it; in the same proportion as such a malady is more likely to taint a particular county or district, than an entire State.

In the extent and proper structure of the Union, therefore, we behold a republican remedy for the diseases most incident to republican government. And according to the degree of pleasure and pride we feel in being republicans, ought to be our zeal in cherishing the spirit and supporting the character of Federalists.

Publius

The Constitution of the United States of America

Federalist Paper Number and Author

Annotated with references to the Federalist Papers; *bracketed material is by the editors of this volume.*

[PREAMBLE]

We the People of the United States, in Order to form a more per-
84 (Hamilton) fect Union, establish Justice, insure domestic Tranquility, provide
for the common defence, promote the general Welfare, and secure
the Blessings of Liberty to ourselves and our Posterity, do ordain
and establish this Constitution for the United States of America.

ARTICLE I

Section 1

[LEGISLATURE POWERS]

All legislative Powers herein granted shall be vested in a Con-
10, 45 (Madison) gress of the United States, which shall consist of a Senate and
House of Representatives.

Section 2

[HOUSE OF REPRESENTATIVES, HOW CONSTITUTED, POWER OF IMPEACHMENT]

39 (Madison) The House of Representatives shall be composed of Members
45 (Madison) chosen every second Year by the People of the several States, and
the Electors in each State shall have the Qualifications requisite
52–53, 57 (Madison) for Electors of the most numerous Branch of the State Legislature.

No Person shall be a Representative who shall not have attained
52 (Madison), to the Age of twenty five Years, and been seven Years a Citizen of
60 (Hamilton) the United States, and who shall not, when elected, be an Inhabitant of that State in which he shall be chosen.

54 (Madison) Representatives and *direct Taxes** shall be apportioned among
the several States which may be included within this Union,

* [Modified by Sixteenth Amendment.]

according to their respective Numbers, *which shall be determined*
by adding to the whole Number of free Persons, including those bound to
54 *Service for a Term of Years,* and excluding Indians not taxed, *three-*
(Madison) *fifths of all other Persons.** The actual Enumeration shall be made
within three Years after the first Meeting of the Congress of the
58 (Madison) United States, and within every subsequent Term of ten Years, in
such Manner as they shall by Law direct. The Number of Repre-
55–56 sentatives shall not exceed one for every thirty Thousand, but
(Madison) each State shall have at Least one Representative; *and until such*
enumeration shall be made, the State of New Hampshire shall be entitled
to chuse three, Massachusetts eight, Rhode Island and Providence Plan-
tations one, Connecticut five, New-York six, New Jersey four, Pennsyl-
vania eight, Delaware one, Maryland six, Virginia ten, North Carolina
five, South Carolina five and Georgia three.†

When vacancies happen in the Representation from any State, the Executive Authority thereof shall issue Writs of Election to fill such Vacancies.

79 The House of Representatives shall chuse their Speaker and
(Hamilton) other Officers; and shall have the sole Power of Impeachment.

Section 3

[THE SENATE, HOW CONSTITUTED, IMPEACHMENT TRIALS]

39, 45 The Senate of the United States shall be composed of two Sena-
(Madison), 60 tors from each State, *chosen by the Legislature thereof,*‡ for six Years;
(Hamilton), and each Senator shall have one Vote.

62–63 Immediately after they shall be assembled in Consequence of
(Madison) 59 the first Election, they shall be divided as equally as may be into
(Hamilton) three Classes. The Seats of the Senators of the first Class shall be
vacated at the Expiration of the second Year, of the second Class
at the Expiration of the fourth Year, and of the third Class at the
68 Expiration of the sixth Year, so that one third may be chosen every
(Hamilton) second Year: *and if Vacancies happen by Resignation, or otherwise,*
during the Recess of the Legislature of any State, the Executive thereof
may make temporary Appointments until the next Meeting of the Legis-
lature, which shall then fill such Vacancies.§

62 No person shall be a Senator who shall not have attained to the
(Madison), 64 (Jay) Age of thirty Years, and been nine Years a Citizen of the United
States, and who shall not, when elected, be an Inhabitant of that
State for which he shall be chosen.

* [Modified by Fourteenth Amendment.]
† [Temporary provision.]
‡ [Modified by Seventeenth Amendment.]
§ [Modified by Seventeenth Amendment.]

The Vice-President of the United States shall be President of the Senate, but shall have no Vote, unless they be equally divided.

39 (Madison), 65–67, 79 (Hamilton) The Senate shall chuse their other Officers, and also a President pro tempore, in the Absence of the Vice-President, or when he shall exercise the Office of President of the United States.

65 (Hamilton) The Senate shall have the sole Power to try all Impeachments.
84 (Hamilton) When sitting for that Purpose, they shall be on Oath or Affirmation. When the President of the United States is tried, the Chief Justice shall preside: And no Person shall be convicted without the Concurrence of two thirds of the Members present.

Judgment in Cases of Impeachment shall not extend further than to removal from Office, and disqualification to hold and enjoy any Office of honor, Trust or Profit under the United States: but the Party convicted shall nevertheless be liable and subject to Indictment, Trial, Judgment and Punishment, according to Law.

Section 4

[ELECTION OF SENATORS AND REPRESENTATIVES]

59–61 (Hamilton) The Times, Places and Manner of holding Elections for Senators and Representatives, shall be prescribed in each State by the Legislature thereof; but the Congress may at any time by Law make or alter such Regulations, except as to the Place of Chusing Senators.

*The Congress shall assemble at least once in every Year, and such Meeting shall be on the first Monday in December, unless they shall by Law appoint a different Day.**

Section 5

[QUORUM, JOURNALS, MEETINGS, ADJOURNMENTS]

Each House shall be the Judge of the Elections, Returns and Qualifications of its own Members, and a Majority of each shall constitute a Quorum to do Business; but a smaller Number may adjourn from day to day, and may be authorized to compel the Attendance of absent Members, in such Manner, and under such Penalties as each House may provide.

Each House may determine the Rules of its Proceedings, punish its Members for disorderly Behavior, and, with the Concurrence of two-thirds, expel a Member.

Each House shall keep a Journal of its Proceedings, and from time to time publish the same, excepting such Parts as may in their Judgment require Secrecy; and the Yeas and Nays of the

*[Modified by Twentieth Amendment.]

Members of either House on any question shall, at the Desire of one-fifth of those Present, be entered on the Journal.

Neither House, during the Session of Congress, shall, without the Consent of the other, adjourn for more than three days, nor to any other Place than that in which the two Houses shall be sitting.

Section 6

[COMPENSATION, PRIVILEGES, DISABILITIES]

The Senators and Representatives shall receive a Compensation for their Services, to be ascertained by Law, and paid out of the Treasury of the United States. They shall in all Cases, except Treason, Felony and Breach of the Peace, be privileged from Arrest during their Attendance at the Session of their respective Houses, and in going to and returning from the same; and for any Speech or Debate in either House, they shall not be questioned in any other Place.

55 (Madison), 76 (Hamilton) No Senator or Representative shall, during the Time for which he was elected, be appointed to any civil Office under the authority of the United States, which shall have been created, or the Emoluments whereof shall have been increased during such time; and no Person holding any Office under the United States, shall be a Member of either House during his Continuance in Office.

Section 7

[PROCEDURE IN PASSING BILLS AND RESOLUTIONS]

66 (Hamilton) All bills for raising Revenue shall originate in the House of Representatives; but the Senate may propose or concur with Amendments as on other Bills.

69, 73 (Hamilton) Every Bill which shall have passed the House of Representatives and the Senate, shall, before it become a Law, be presented to the President of the United States; If he approve he shall sign it, but if not he shall return it, with his Objections to that House in which it shall have originated, who shall enter the Objections at large on their Journal, and proceed to reconsider it. If after such Reconsideration two-thirds of that House shall agree to pass the Bill, it shall be sent, together with the Objections, to the other House, by which it shall likewise be reconsidered, and if approved by two-thirds of that House it shall become a Law. But in all such Cases the Votes of both Houses shall be determined by Yeas and Nays, and the Names of the Persons voting for and against the Bill shall be entered on the Journal of each House respectively. If

any Bill shall not be returned by the President within ten Days (Sundays excepted) after it shall have been presented to him, the
69, 73 Same shall be a Law, in like Manner as if he had signed it, unless
(Hamilton) the Congress by their Adjournment prevent its Return, in which Case it shall not be a Law.

Every Order, Resolution, or Vote to which the Concurrence of the Senate and House of Representatives may be necessary (except on a question of Adjournment) shall be presented to the President of the United States; and before the Same shall take Effect, shall be approved by him, or being disapproved by him, shall be repassed by two-thirds of the Senate and House of Representatives, according to the Rules and Limitations prescribed in the Case of a Bill.

Section 8

[POWERS OF CONGRESS]

The Congress shall have Power

30–36 (Hamilton), 41 (Madison) To lay and collect Taxes, Duties, Imposts and Excises, to pay the Debts and provide for the common Defence and general Welfare of the United States; but all Duties, Imposts and Excises shall be uniform throughout the United States;

56 (Madison) To borrow money on the Credit of the United States;

42, 45, 56 (Madison) To regulate Commerce with foreign Nations, and among the several States, and with the Indian Tribes;

32 (Hamilton), To establish an uniform Rule of Naturalization, and uniform Laws on the subject of Bankruptcies throughout the United States;

42 (Madison) To coin Money, regulate the Value thereof, and of foreign Coin, and fix the Standard of Weights and Measures;

42 (Madison) To provide for the Punishment of counterfeiting the Securities and current Coin of the United States;

42 (Madison) To establish Post Offices and Post Roads;

42 (Madison) To promote the Progress of Science and useful Arts, by secur-
43 (Madison) ing for limited Times to Authors and Inventors the exclusive Right to their respective Writings and Discoveries;

81 (Hamilton) To constitute Tribunals inferior to the supreme Court;

42 (Madison) To define and Punish Piracies and Felonies committed on the high Seas, and Offenses against the Law of Nations;

41 (Madison) To declare War, grant Letters of Marque and Reprisal, and make Rules concerning Captures on Land and Water;

23, 24, 26 (Hamilton), To raise and support Armies, but no Appropriation of Money to that Use shall be for a longer Term than two Years;

41 (Madison) To provide and maintain a Navy;

To make Rules for the Government and Regulation of the land and naval forces;

29 (Hamilton) To provide for calling forth the Militia to execute the Laws of the Union, suppress Insurrections and repel Invasions;

29 (Hamilton), To provide for organizing, arming, and disciplining the Militia, and for governing such Part of them as may be employed
56 (Madison) in the Service of the United States, reserving to the States respectively, the Appointment of the Officers, and the Authority of training the Militia according to the discipline prescribed by Congress;

32 (Hamilton), 43 (Madison) To exercise exclusive Legislation in all Cases whatsoever, over such District (not exceeding ten Miles square) as may, by Cession of particular States, and the Acceptance of Congress, become the Seat of the Government of the United States, and to exercise like Authority over all Places purchased by the Consent of the
43 (Madison) Legislature of the State in which the Same shall be, for the Erection of Forts, Magazines, Arsenals, dock-Yards, and other needful Buildings;—And

To make all Laws which shall be necessary and proper for
29, 33 (Hamilton) carrying into Execution the foregoing Powers, and all other Powers vested by this Constitution in the Government of the United
44 (Madison) States, or in any Department or Officer thereof.

Section 9

[SOME RESTRICTIONS ON FEDERAL POWER]

42 (Madison) *The Migration or Importation of such Persons as any of the States now existing shall think proper to admit, shall not be prohibited by the Congress prior to the Year one thousand eight hundred and eight, but a tax or duty may be imposed on such Importation, not exceeding ten dollars for each Person.**

83, 84 (Hamilton) The privilege of the Writ of *Habeas Corpus* shall not be suspended, unless when in Cases of Rebellion or Invasion the public Safety may require it.

84 (Hamilton) No Bill of Attainder or ex post facto Law shall be passed.

No Capitation, or other direct, Tax shall be laid, unless in Proportion to the Census or Enumeration herein before directed to be taken.†

No Tax or Duty shall be laid on Articles exported from any State.

32 (Hamilton) No Preference shall be given by any Regulation of Commerce or Revenue to the Ports of one State over those of another: nor shall Vessels bound to, or from, one State, be obliged to enter, clear, or pay Duties in another.

No Money shall be drawn from the Treasury, but in Consequence of Appropriations made by Law; and a regular Statement

* [Temporary provision.]
† [Modified by Sixteenth Amendment.]

and Account of the Receipts and Expenditures of all public Money shall be published from time to time.

No Title of Nobility shall be granted by the United States: And
39 (Madison), no Person holding any Office of Profit or Trust under them, shall,
84 (Hamilton) without the Consent of the Congress, accept of any present, Emolument, Office, or Title, of any kind whatever, from any King, Prince or foreign State.

Section 10

[RESTRICTIONS UPON POWERS OF STATES]

33 (Hamilton), No State shall enter into any Treaty, Alliance, or Confederation; grant Letters of Marque and Reprisal; coin Money; emit Bills
44 (Madison) of Credit; make any Thing but gold and silver Coin a Tender in Payment of Debts; pass any Bill of Attainder, ex post facto Law, or Law impairing the Obligation of Contracts, or grant any Title of Nobility.

32 (Hamilton), No State shall, without the Consent of the Congress, lay any
Imposts or Duties on Imports or Exports, except what may be
44 (Madison) absolutely necessary for executing its inspection Laws: and the net Produce of all Duties and Imposts, laid by any State on Imports or Exports, shall be for the Use of the Treasury of the United States; and all such Laws shall be subject to the Revision and Controul of the Congress.

No State shall, without the Consent of Congress, lay any duty of Tonnage, keep Troops, or Ships of War in time of Peace, enter into any Agreement or Compact with another State, or with a foreign Power, or engage in War, unless actually invaded, or in such imminent Danger as will not admit of Delay.

ARTICLE II

Section 1

[EXECUTIVE POWER, ELECTION, QUALIFICATIONS OF THE PRESIDENT]

39 (Madison), The executive Power shall be vested in a President of the
70, 71, 84 (Hamilton) United States of America. *He shall hold his Office during the Term of four years, and, together with the Vice-President, chosen for the same Term, be elected, as follows:**

69, 71 (Hamilton) Each State shall appoint, in such Manner as the Legislature
thereof may direct, a Number of Electors, equal to the whole
39, 45 (Madison), Number of Senators and Representatives to which the State may be entitled in the Congress: but no Senator or Representative, or

* [Number of terms limited to two by Twenty-second Amendment.]

Person holding an Office of Trust or Profit under the United
68, 77 (Hamilton) States, shall be appointed an Elector.

The electors shall meet in their respective States, and vote by ballot for two Persons, of whom one at least shall not be an Inhabitant of the same State with themselves. And they shall make a List of all the Persons voted for, and of the Number of Votes for each; which List they shall sign and certify, and transmit sealed to the Seat of the Government of the
66 (Hamilton) *United States, directed to the President of the Senate. The President of the Senate shall, in the Presence of the Senate and House of Representatives, open all the Certificates, and the Votes shall then be counted. The Person having the greatest Number of Votes shall be the President, if such Number be a Majority of the whole Number of Electors appointed; and if there be more than one who have such Majority, and have an equal Number of Votes, then the House of Representatives shall immediately chuse by Ballot one of them for President; and if no Person have a Majority, then from the five highest on the List the said House shall in like Manner chuse the President. But in chusing the President, the Votes shall be taken by States, the Representation from each State having one Vote; a quorum for this Purpose shall consist of a Member or Members from two-thirds of the States, and a Majority of all the States shall be necessary to a Choice. In every Case, after the Choice of the President, the Person having the greatest Number of Votes of the Electors shall be the Vice-President. But if there should remain two or more who have equal Votes, the Senate shall chuse from them by Ballot the Vice-President.**

The Congress may determine the Time of chusing the Electors, and the Day on which they shall give their Votes; which Day shall be the same throughout the United States.

No Person except a natural born Citizen, or a Citizen of the United States, at the time of the Adoption of this Constitution, shall be eligible to the Office of President; neither shall any Person be eligible to that Office who shall not have attained to the Age of
64 (Jay) thirty-five Years, and been fourteen Years a Resident within the United States.

In Case of the Removal of the President from Office, or his Death, Resignation, or Inability to discharge the Powers and Duties of the said Office, the same shall devolve on the Vice-President, and the Congress may by Law provide for the Case of Removal, Death, Resignation or Inability, both of the President and Vice-President, declaring what Officer shall then act as President, and such Officer shall act accordingly, until the Disability be removed, or a President shall be elected.

The President shall, at stated Times, receive for his Services, a
73, 79 (Hamilton) Compensation, which shall neither be encreased nor diminished

* [Modified by Twelfth and Twentieth Amendment.]

during the Period for which he shall have been elected, and he shall not receive within that Period any other Emolument from the United States, or any of them.

Before he enter on the Execution of his Office, he shall take the following Oath or Affirmation:—"I do solemnly swear (or affirm) that I will faithfully execute the Office of President of the United States, and will to the best of my Ability, preserve, protect and defend the Constitution of the United States."

Section 2

[POWERS OF THE PRESIDENT]

69, 74 The President shall be Commander in Chief of the Army and
(Hamilton) Navy of the United States, and of the Militia of the several States,
when called into the actual Service of the United States; he may
require the Opinion, in writing, of the principal Officer in each of
the executive Departments, upon any Subject relating to the
74 Duties of their respective Offices, and he shall have Power to
(Hamilton) 69 Grant Reprieves and Pardons for Offenses against the United
(Hamilton) States, except in Cases of Impeachment.

74 (Hamilton) He shall have Power, by and with the Advice and Consent of
42 the Senate, to make Treaties, provided two thirds of the Senators
(Madison) 64 (Jay), present concur; and he shall nominate, and by and with the
66 Advice and Consent of the Senate, shall appoint Ambassadors,
(Hamilton) other public Ministers and Consuls, Judges of the Supreme
42 Court, and all other Officers of the United States, whose Appoint-
(Madison), ments are not herein otherwise provided for, and which shall be
established by Law: but the Congress may by Law vest the
66, 69, 76, 77 Appointment of such inferior Officers, as they think proper, in
(Hamilton) the President alone, in the Courts of Law, or in the Heads of
67, 76 Departments.

(Hamilton) The President shall have Power to fill up all Vacancies that may happen during the Recess of the Senate, by granting Commissions which shall expire at the End of their next Session.

Section 3

77 (Hamilton) [POWERS AND DUTIES OF THE PRESIDENT]

69, 77 He shall from time to time give to the Congress Information of
(Hamilton) the State of the Union, and recommend to their Consideration
77 such Measures as he shall judge necessary and expedient; he may,
(Hamilton) 69, 77 on extraordinary Occasions, convene both Houses, or either of
(Hamilton) 42 them, and in Case of Disagreement between them, with Respect
(Madison), to the Time of Adjournment, he may adjourn them to such Time
69, 77 (Hamilton) as he shall think proper; he shall receive Ambassadors and other
public Ministers; he shall take Care that the Laws be faithfully

78 (Hamilton) executed, and shall Commission all the Officers of the United States.

Section 4

[IMPEACHMENT]

39 (Madison), The President, Vice-President and all civil Officers of the United States, shall be removed from Office on Impeachment
69 (Hamilton) for, and Conviction of, Treason, Bribery, or other high Crimes and Misdemeanors.

Article III

Section 1

[JUDICIAL POWER, TENURE OR OFFICE]

81, 82 (Hamilton) The judicial Power of the United States, shall be vested in one
65 Supreme Court, and in such inferior Courts as the Congress may
(Hamilton) from time to time ordain and establish. The Judges, both of the
78, 79 (Hamilton) supreme and inferior Courts, shall hold their Offices during good Behavior, and shall, at stated Times, receive for their Services a Compensation, which shall not be diminished during their Continuance in Office.

Section 2

[JURISDICTION]

80 (Hamilton) The judicial Power shall extend to all Cases, in Law and Equity, arising under this Constitution, the Laws of the United States, and Treaties made, or which shall be made, under their Authority;—to all Cases affecting Ambassadors, other public Ministers and Consuls;—to all Cases of admiralty and maritime Jurisdiction;—to Controversies to which the United States shall be a party;—to Controversies between two or more States;—*between a State and Citizens of another State;*—between Citizens of different States,—between Citizens of the same State claiming Lands under Grants of different States, *and between a State*, or the Citizens thereof, *and foreign States, Citizens or Subjects.**

81 (Hamilton) In all Cases affecting Ambassadors, other public Ministers and Consuls, and those in which a State shall be Party, the supreme Court shall have original Jurisdiction. In all the other Cases before mentioned, the Supreme Court shall have appellate Jurisdiction, both as to Law and Fact, with such Exceptions, and under such Regulations as the Congress shall make.

* [Modified by the Eleventh Amendment.]

83, 84 (Hamilton) The Trial of all Crimes, except in Cases of Impeachment, shall be by Jury; and such Trial shall be held in the State where the said Crimes shall have been committed; but when not committed within any State, the Trial shall be at such Place or Places as the Congress may by Law have directed.

Section 3

[TREASON, PROOF, AND PUNISHMENT]

43 (Madison), 98 (Hamilton) Treason against the United States, shall consist only in levying War against them, or in adhering to their Enemies, giving them Aid and Comfort. No Person shall be convicted of Treason unless on the Testimony of two Witnesses to the same overt Act, or on Confession in open Court.

43 (Madison), 84 (Hamilton) The Congress shall have Power to declare the Punishment of Treason, but no Attainder of Treason shall work Corruption of Blood, or Forfeiture except during the Life of the Person attained.

ARTICLE IV

Section 1

[FAITH AND CREDIT AMONG STATES]

42 (Madison) Full Faith and Credit shall be given in each State to the public Acts, Records, and judicial Proceedings of every other State. And the Congress may by general Laws prescribe the Manner in which such Acts, Records and Proceedings shall be proved, and the Effect thereof.

Section 2

[PRIVILEGES AND IMMUNITIES, FUGITIVES]

80 (Hamilton) The Citizens of each State shall be entitled to all Privileges and Immunities of Citizens in the several States.

A Person charged in any State with Treason, Felony, or other Crime, who shall flee from Justice, and be found in another State, shall on demand of the executive Authority of the State from which he fled, be delivered up, to be removed to the State having Jurisdiction of the Crime.

*No Person held to Service or Labour in one State, under the Laws thereof, escaping into another, shall, in Consequence of any Law or Regulation therein, be discharged from such Service or Labour, but shall be delivered up on Claim of the Party to whom such Service or Labour may be due.**

* [Repealed by the Thirteenth Amendment.]

Section 3

[ADMISSION OF NEW STATES]

43 (Madison) New States may be admitted by the Congress into this Union; but no new States shall be formed or erected within the Jurisdiction of any other State; nor any State be formed by the Junction of two or more States, or Parts of States, without the Consent of the Legislatures of the States concerned as well as of the Congress.

43 (Madison) The Congress shall have Power to dispose of and make all needful Rules and Regulations respecting the Territory or other Property belonging to the United States; and nothing in this Constitution shall be so construed as to Prejudice any Claims of the United States, or of any particular State.

Section 4

[GUARANTEE OF REPUBLICAN GOVERNMENT]

39, 43 (Madison) The United States shall guarantee to every State in this Union a Republican Form of Government, and shall protect each of them against Invasion; and on Application of the Legislature, or of the Executive (when the Legislature cannot be convened) against domestic Violence.

ARTICLE V

[AMENDMENT OF THE CONSTITUTION]

39, 43 (Madison) 85 (Hamilton) The Congress, whenever two-thirds of both Houses shall deem it necessary, shall propose Amendments to this Constitution, or, on the Application of the Legislatures of two-thirds of the several States, shall call a Convention for proposing Amendments, which, in either Case, shall be valid to all Intents and Purposes, as Part of this Constitution, when ratified by the Legislatures of three-fourths of the several States, or by Conventions in three-fourths thereof, as the one or the other Mode of Ratification may be proposed by the Congress; *Provided that no Amendment which may be made prior to the Year One thousand eight hundred and eight shall in any Manner affect the first and fourth Clauses in the Ninth Section of the first Article;** and that no State,
43 without its Consent, shall be deprived of its equal Suffrage in
(Madison) the Senate.

* [Temporary provision.]

ARTICLE VI

[DEBTS, SUPREMACY, OATH]

43 All Debts contracted and Engagements entered into, before the
(Madison) Adoption of this Constitution, shall be as valid against the United
States under this Constitution, as under the Confederation.

This Constitution, and the Laws of the United States which
shall be made in Pursuance thereof; and all Treaties made, or
27, 33 which shall be made, under the Authority of the United States,
(Hamilton), 39, 44 shall be the supreme Law of the Land; and the Judges in every
(Madison) State shall be bound thereby, any Thing in the Constitution or
Laws of any State to the Contrary notwithstanding.

The Senators and Representatives before mentioned, and the
Members of the several State Legislatures, and all executive and
27 judicial Officers, both of the United States and of the several States,
(Hamilton), 44 shall be bound by Oath or Affirmation, to support this Constitu-
(Madison) tion; but no religious Test shall ever be required as a Qualification
to any Office or public Trust under the United States.

ARTICLE VII

[RATIFICATION AND ESTABLISHMENT]

39, 40, 43 The Ratification of the Conventions of nine States, shall be suf-
(Madison) ficient for the Establishment of this Constitution between the
States so ratifying the Same.*

Done in Convention by the Unanimous Consent of the States present the Seventeenth Day of September in the Year of our Lord one thousand seven hundred and Eighty seven and of the Independence of the United States of America the Twelfth. *In Witness* whereof We have hereunto subscribed our Names,

G:º WASHINGTON—
Presidt, and Deputy
from Virginia

* [The Constitution was submitted on September 17, 1787, by the Constitutional Convention, was ratified by the conventions of several states at various dates up to May 29, 1790, and became effective on March 4, 1789.]

New Hampshire	John Langdon Nicholas Gilman	Delaware	Geo Read Gunning Bedfor Jun John Dickinson Richard Bassett Jaco: Broom
Massachusetts	Nathaniel Gorham Rufus King		
Connecticut	Wm Saml Johnson Roger Sherman	Maryland	James McHenry Dan of St Thos. Jenifer Danl Carroll
New York	Alexander Hamilton		
New Jersey	Wil: Livingston David Brearley Wm Paterson Jona: Dayton	Virginia	John Blair— James Madison Jr.
		North Carolina	Wm Blount Richd Dobbs Spaight Hu Williamson
Pennsylvania	B Franklin Thomas Mifflin Robt Morris Geo. Clymer Thos. FitzSimons Jared Ingersoll James Wilson Gouv Morris	South Carolina	J. Rutledge Charles Cotesworth Pinckney Charles Pinckney Pierce Butler
		Georgia	William Few Abr Baldwin

Amendments to the Constitution

Proposed by Congress and Ratified
by the Legislatures of the Several States,
Pursuant to Article V of the Original Constitution.

Amendments I–X, known as the Bill of Rights, were proposed by Congress on September 25, 1789, and ratified on December 15, 1791. Federalist Papers comments, mainly in opposition to a Bill of Rights, can be found in #84 (Hamilton).

Amendment I

[FREEDOM OF RELIGION, OF SPEECH, AND OF THE PRESS]

Congress shall make no law respecting an establishment of religion, or prohibiting the free exercise thereof; or abridging the freedom of speech, or of the press; or the right of the people peaceably to assemble, and to petition the Government for a redress of grievances.

Amendment II

[RIGHT TO KEEP AND BEAR ARMS]

A well regulated Militia, being necessary to the security of a free State, the right of the people to keep and bear Arms, shall not be infringed.

Amendment III

[QUARTERING OF SOLDIERS]

No Soldier shall, in time of peace be quartered in any house, without the consent of the Owner, nor in time of war, but in a manner to be prescribed by law.

AMENDMENT IV

[SECURITY FROM UNWARRANTABLE SEARCH AND SEIZURE]

The right of the people to be secure in their persons, houses, papers, and effects, against unreasonable searches and seizures, shall not be violated, and no Warrants shall issue, but upon probable cause, supported by Oath or affirmation, and particularly describing the place to be searched, and the persons or things to be seized.

AMENDMENT V

[RIGHTS OF ACCUSED PERSONS IN CRIMINAL PROCEEDINGS]

No person shall be held to answer for a capital, or otherwise infamous crime, unless on a presentment or indictment of a Grand Jury, except in cases arising in the land or naval forces, or in the Militia, when in actual service in time of War or public danger; nor shall any person be subject for the same offence to be twice put in jeopardy of life or limb; nor shall be compelled in any Criminal Case to be a witness against himself, nor be deprived of life, liberty, or property, without due process of law; nor shall private property be taken for public use, without just compensation.

AMENDMENT VI

[RIGHT TO SPEEDY TRIAL, WITNESSES, ETC.]

In all criminal prosecutions, the accused shall enjoy the right to a speedy and public trial, by an impartial jury of the State and district wherein the crime shall have been committed, which district shall have been previously ascertained by law, and to be informed of the nature and cause of the accusation; to be confronted with the witnesses against him; to have compulsory process for obtaining Witnesses in his favor, and to have the Assistance of Counsel for his defence.

AMENDMENT VII

[TRIAL BY JURY IN CIVIL CASES]

In suits at common law, where the value in controversy shall exceed twenty dollars, the right of trial by jury shall be preserved, and no fact tried by a jury shall be otherwise re-examined in any Court of the United States, than according to the rules of the common law.

AMENDMENT VIII

[BAILS, FINES, PUNISHMENTS]

Excessive bail shall not be required, nor excessive fines imposed, nor cruel and unusual punishments inflicted.

AMENDMENT IX

[RESERVATION OF RIGHTS OF PEOPLE]

The enumeration in the Constitution, of certain rights, shall not be construed to deny or disparage others retained by the people.

AMENDMENT X

[POWERS RESERVED TO STATES OR PEOPLE]

The powers not delegated to the United States by the Constitution, nor prohibited by it to the States, are reserved to the States respectively, or to the people.

AMENDMENT XI

[Proposed by Congress on March 4, 1794; declared ratified on January 8, 1798.]

[RESTRICTION OF JUDICIAL POWER]

The Judicial power of the United States shall not be construed to extend to any suit in law or equity, commenced or prosecuted against one of the United States by Citizens of another State, or by Citizens or Subjects of any foreign State.

AMENDMENT XII

[Proposed by Congress on December 9, 1803; declared ratified on September 25, 1804.]

[ELECTION OF PRESIDENT AND VICE-PRESIDENT]

The Electors shall meet in their respective states, and vote by ballot for President and Vice-President, one of whom, at least, shall not be an inhabitant of the same state with themselves; they shall name in their ballots the person voted for as President, and in distinct ballots the person voted for as Vice-President, and they shall make distinct lists of all persons voted for as President, and of all persons voted for as Vice-President, and of the number of votes for each, which lists they shall sign and certify, and transmit sealed to the seat of the government of the United States, directed to the President of the Senate;—The President of the Senate shall, in presence of the Senate and House of Representatives, open all the certificates and the votes shall then be counted;—The person having the greatest number of votes for President, shall be the President, if such number be a majority of the whole number of Electors appointed; and if no person have such majority, then from the persons having the highest numbers not exceeding three on the list of those voted for as President, the House of Representatives shall choose immediately, by ballot, the President. But in choosing the President, the votes shall be taken by states, the representation from each state having one vote; a quorum for this purpose shall consist of a member or members from two-thirds of the states, and a majority of all the states shall be necessary to a choice. And if the House of Representatives shall not choose a President whenever the right of choice shall devolve upon them, before the fourth day of March next following, then the Vice-President shall act as President, as in the case of the death or other constitutional disability of the President. The person having the greatest number of votes as Vice-President, shall be the Vice-President, if such number be a majority of the whole number of Electors appointed, and if no person have a majority, then from the two highest numbers on the list, the Senate shall choose the Vice-President; a quorum for the purpose shall consist of two-thirds of the whole number of Senators, and a majority of the whole number shall be necessary to a choice. But no person constitutionally ineligible to the office of President shall be eligible to that of Vice-President of the United States.

AMENDMENT XIII

[Proposed by Congress on January 31, 1865; declared ratified on December 18, 1865.]

Section 1

[ABOLITION OF SLAVERY]

Neither slavery nor involuntary servitude, except as a punishment for crime whereof the party shall have been duly convicted, shall exist within the United States, or any place subject to their jurisdiction.

Section 2

[POWER TO ENFORCE THIS ARTICLE]

Congress shall have power to enforce this article by appropriate legislation.

AMENDMENT XIV

[Proposed by Congress on June 13, 1866, declared ratified on July 28, 1868.]

Section 1

[CITIZENSHIP RIGHTS NOT TO BE ABRIDGED BY STATES]

All persons born or naturalized in the United States, and subject to the jurisdiction thereof, are citizens of the United States and of the State wherein they reside. No state shall make or enforce any law which shall abridge the privileges or immunities of citizens of the United States; nor shall any State deprive any person of life, liberty, or property, without due process of law; nor deny to any person within its jurisdiction the equal protection of the laws.

Section 2

[APPORTIONMENT OF REPRESENTATIVES IN CONGRESS]

Representatives shall be apportioned among the several States according to their respective numbers, counting the whole number of persons in each State, excluding Indians not taxed. But when the right to vote at any election for the choice of electors for President and Vice-President of the United States, Representatives in Congress, the Executive and Judicial officers of a State, or the members of the Legislature thereof, is denied to any of the male inhabitants of such State, being twenty-one years of age, and citizens of the United States, or in any way abridged, except for participation in rebellion, or other crime, the basis of representation therein shall be reduced in the proportion which the number of such male citizens shall bear to the whole number of male citizens twenty-one years of age in such State.

Section 3

[PERSONS DISQUALIFIED FROM HOLDING OFFICE]

No person shall be a Senator or Representative in Congress, or elector of President and Vice-President, or hold any office, civil or military, under the United States, or under any State, who, having previously taken an oath, as a member of Congress, or as an officer of the United States, or as a member of any State legislature, or as an executive or judicial officer of any State, to support the Constitution of the United States, shall have engaged in insurrection or rebellion against the same, or given aid or comfort to the enemies thereof. But Congress may by a vote of two-thirds of each House, remove such disability.

Section 4

[WHAT PUBLIC DEBTS ARE VALID]

The validity of the public debt of the United States, authorized by law, including debts incurred for payment of pensions and bounties for services in suppressing insurrection or rebellion, shall not be questioned. But neither the United States nor any State shall assume or pay any debt or obligation incurred in aid of insurrection or rebellion against the United States, or any claim for the loss or emancipation of any slave; but all such debts, obligations and claims shall be held illegal and void.

Section 5

[POWER TO ENFORCE THIS ARTICLE]

The Congress shall have power to enforce, by appropriate legislation, the provisions of this article.

AMENDMENT XV

[Proposed by Congress on February 26, 1869; declared ratified on March 30, 1870.]

Section 1

[BLACK SUFFRAGE]

The right of citizens of the United States to vote shall not be denied or abridged by the United States or by any State on account of race, color, or previous condition of servitude.

Section 2

[POWER TO ENFORCE THIS ARTICLE]

The Congress shall have power to enforce this article by appropriate legislation.

AMENDMENT XVI

[Proposed by Congress on July 12, 1909; declared ratified on February 25, 1913.]

[AUTHORIZING INCOME TAXES]

The Congress shall have power to lay and collect taxes on incomes, from whatever source derived, without apportionment among the several States, and without regard to any census or enumeration.

AMENDMENT XVII

[Proposed by Congress on May 13, 1912; declared ratified on May 31, 1913.]

[POPULAR ELECTION OF SENATORS]

The Senate of the United States shall be composed of two Senators from each State, elected by the people thereof, for six years; and each Senator shall have one vote. The electors in each State shall have the qualifications requisite for electors of the most numerous branch of the State Legislature.

When vacancies happen in the representation of any State in the Senate, the executive authority of such State shall issue writs of election to fill such vacancies: Provided, That the Legislature of any State may empower the executive thereof to make temporary appointments until the people fill the vacancies by election as the Legislature may direct.

This amendment shall not be so construed as to affect the election or term of any Senator chosen before it becomes valid as part of the Constitution.

AMENDMENT XVIII

[Proposed by Congress December 18, 1917; declared ratified on January 29, 1919.]

Section 1

[NATIONAL LIQUOR PROHIBITION]

After one year from the ratification of this article, the manufacture, sale, or transportation of intoxicating liquors within, the importation thereof into, or the exportation thereof from the United States and all territory subject to the jurisdiction thereof for beverage purposes is hereby prohibited.

Section 2

[POWER TO ENFORCE THIS ARTICLE]

Congress and the several states shall have concurrent power to enforce this article by appropriate legislation.

Section 3

[RATIFICATION WITHIN SEVEN YEARS]

*This article shall be inoperative unless it shall have been ratified as an amendment to the Constitution by the legislatures of the several states, as provided in the Constitution, within seven years from the date of the submission hereof to the states by Congress.**

AMENDMENT XIX

[Proposed by Congress on June 4, 1919; declared ratified on August 26, 1920.]

[FEMALE SUFFRAGE]

The right of the citizens of the United States to vote shall not be denied or abridged by the United States or by any state on account of sex.

Congress shall have power, by appropriate legislation, to enforce this article by appropriate legislation.

AMENDMENT XX

[Proposed by Congress on March 2, 1932; declared ratified on February 6, 1933.]

Section 1

[TERMS OF OFFICE]

The terms of the President and Vice-President shall end at noon on the 20th day of January, and the terms of Senators and Representatives at noon on the 3rd day of January, of the years in which such terms would have ended if this article had not been ratified; and the terms of their successors shall then begin.

* [Repealed by the Twenty-first Amendment.]

Section 2

[TIME OF CONVENING CONGRESS]

The Congress shall assemble at least once in every year, and such meeting shall begin at noon on the 3rd day of January, unless they shall by law appoint a different day.

Section 3

[DEATH OF PRESIDENT-ELECT]

If, at the time fixed for the beginning of the term of the President, the President-elect shall have died, the Vice-President-elect shall become President. If a President shall not have been chosen before the time fixed for the beginning of his term, or if the President-elect shall have failed to qualify, then the Vice-President-elect shall act as President until a President shall have qualified; and the Congress may by law provide for the case wherein neither a President-elect nor a Vice-President-elect shall have qualified, declaring who shall then act as President, or the manner in which one who is to act shall be selected, and such person shall act accordingly until a President or Vice-President shall have qualified.

Section 4

[ELECTION OF THE PRESIDENT]

The Congress may by law provide for the case of the death of any of the persons from whom the House of Representatives may choose a President whenever the right of choice shall have devolved upon them, and for the case of the death of any of the persons from whom the Senate may choose a Vice-President whenever the right of choice shall have devolved upon them.

Section 5

[AMENDMENT TAKES EFFECT]

Sections 1 and 2 shall take effect on the 15th day of October following ratification of this article.

Section 6

[RATIFICATION WITHIN SEVEN YEARS]

This article shall be inoperative unless it shall have been ratified as an amendment to the Constitution by the legislatures of three-fourths of the several States within seven years from the date of its submission.

AMENDMENT XXI

[Proposed by Congress on February 20, 1933; declared ratified on December 5, 1933.]

Section 1

[NATIONAL LIQUOR PROHIBITION REPEALED]

The eighteenth article of amendment to the Constitution of the United States is hereby repealed.

Section 2

[TRANSPORTATION OF LIQUOR INTO "DRY" STATES]

The transportation or importation into any State, Territory, or Possession of the United States for delivery or use therein of intoxicating liquors, in violation of the laws thereof, is hereby prohibited.

Section 3

[RATIFICATION WITHIN SEVEN YEARS]

The article shall be inoperative unless it shall have been ratified as an amendment to the Constitution by conventions in the several States, as provided in the Constitution, within seven years from the date of the submission hereof to the States by the Congress.

AMENDMENT XXII

[Proposed by Congress on March 21, 1947; declared ratified on February 26, 1951.]

Section 1

[TENURE OF PRESIDENT LIMITED]

No person shall be elected to the office of the President more than twice, and no person who has held the office of President or acted as President for more than two years of a term to which some other person was elected President shall be elected to the Office of the President more than once. But this Article shall not apply to any person holding the office of President when this Article was proposed by the Congress, and shall not prevent any person who may be holding the office of President, or acting as President, during the term within which this Article becomes operative from holding the office of President or acting as President during the remainder of such term.

Section 2

[RATIFICATION WITHIN SEVEN YEARS]

This Article shall be inoperative unless it shall have been ratified as an amendment to the Constitution by the legislatures of three-fourths of the several states within seven years from the date of its submission to the States by the Congress.

AMENDMENT XXIII

[Proposed by Congress on June 21, 1960; declared ratified on March 29, 1961.]

Section 1

[ELECTORAL COLLEGE VOTES FOR THE DISTRICT OF COLUMBIA]

The District constituting the seat of Government of the United States shall appoint in such manner as the Congress may direct:

A number of electors of President and Vice-President equal to the whole number of Senators and Representatives in Congress to which the District would be entitled if it were a State, but in no event more than the least populous State; they shall be in addition to those appointed by the States, but they shall be considered, for the purposes of the election of President and Vice-President, to be electors appointed by a State; and they shall meet in the District and perform such duties as provided by the twelfth article of amendment.

Section 2

[POWER TO ENFORCE THIS ARTICLE]

The Congress shall have power to enforce this article by appropriate legislation.

AMENDMENT XXIV

[Proposed by Congress on August 27, 1963; declared ratified on January 23, 1964.]

Section 1

[ANTI-POLL TAX]

The right of citizens of the United States to vote in any primary or other election for President or Vice-President, for electors for President or Vice-President, or for Senator or Representative in Congress, shall not be denied or abridged by the United States or any State by reason of failure to pay any poll tax or other tax.

Section 2

[POWER TO ENFORCE THIS ARTICLE]

The Congress shall have power to enforce this article by appropriate legislation.

AMENDMENT XXV

[Proposed by Congress on July 7, 1965; declared ratified on February 10, 1967.]

Section 1

[VICE-PRESIDENT TO BECOME PRESIDENT]

In case of the removal of the President from office or his death or resignation, the Vice-President shall become President.

Section 2

[CHOICE OF A NEW VICE-PRESIDENT]

Whenever there is a vacancy in the office of the Vice-President, the President shall nominate a Vice-President who shall take office upon confirmation by a majority vote of both houses of Congress.

Section 3

[PRESIDENT MAY DECLARE OWN DISABILITY]

Whenever the President transmits to the President pro tempore of the Senate and the Speaker of the House of Representatives his written declaration that he is unable to discharge the powers and duties of his office, and until he transmits to them a written declaration to the contrary, such powers and duties shall be discharged by the Vice-President as Acting President.

Section 4

[ALTERNATE PROCEDURES TO DECLARE AND TO END PRESIDENTIAL DISABILITY]

Whenever the Vice-President and a majority of either the principal officers of the executive departments or of such other body as Congress may by law provide, transmit to the President pro tempore of the Senate and the Speaker of the House of Representatives their written declaration that the President is unable to discharge the powers and duties of his office, the Vice-President shall immediately assume the powers and duties of the office as Acting President.

Thereafter, when the President transmits to the President pro tempore of the Senate and the Speaker of the House of Representatives his written declaration that no inability exists, he shall resume the powers and duties of his office unless the Vice-President and a majority of either the principal officers of the executive department or of such other body as Congress may by law provide, transmit within four days to the President pro tempore of the Senate and the Speaker of the House of Representatives their written declaration that the President is unable to discharge the powers and duties of his office. Thereupon Congress shall decide the issue, assembling within 48 hours for that purpose if not in session. If the Congress, within 21 days after receipt of the latter written declaration, or, if Congress is not in session, within 21 days after Congress is required to assemble, determines by two-thirds vote of both houses that the President is unable to discharge the powers and duties of his office, the Vice-President shall continue to discharge the same as Acting President; otherwise, the President shall resume the powers and duties of his office.

AMENDMENT XXVI

[Proposed by Congress on March 23, 1971; declared ratified on June 30, 1971.]

Section 1

[EIGHTEEN-YEAR-OLD SUFFRAGE]

The right of citizens of the United States, who are eighteen years of age or older, to vote shall not be denied or abridged by the United States or by any State on account of age.

Section 2

[POWER TO ENFORCE THIS ARTICLE]

The Congress shall have power to enforce this article by appropriate legislation.

AMENDMENT XXVII

[LIMITING CONGRESSIONAL PAY CHANGES]

[Proposed by Congress on September 25, 1789; ratified on May 7, 1992.]

No law varying the compensation for the services of the Senators and Representatives shall take effect until an election of Representatives shall have intervened.

Marbury v. Madison (1803)

The power of judicial review—the authority of the federal courts to determine the constitutionality of state and federal legislative acts—was established early in the nation's history in the case of Marbury v. Madison *(1803). While the doctrine of judicial review is now firmly entrenched in the American judicial process, the outcome of* Marbury *was by no means a sure thing. The doctrine had been outlined in* The Federalist, *No. 78, and had been relied on implicitly in earlier, lower federal court cases, but there were certainly sentiments among some of the Founders to suggest that only Congress ought to be able to judge the constitutionality of its acts.*

The facts leading up to the decision in Marbury v. Madison *tell an intensely political story. Efforts to reform the federal judiciary had been ongoing with the Federalist administration of President Adams. Following the defeat of the Federalist party in 1800 and the election of Thomas Jefferson as president, the Federalist Congress passed an act reforming the judiciary. The act gave the outgoing president Adams authority to appoint several Federalist justices of the peace before Jefferson's term as president began. This would have enabled the Federalist party to retain a large measure of power.*

Marbury was appointed to be a justice of the peace by President Adams, but his commission, signed by the president and sealed by the secretary of state, without which he could not assume office, was not delivered to him before President Jefferson took office March 4, 1803. Jefferson refused to order James Madison, his secretary of state, to deliver the commission. Marbury, in turn, filed an action in the U.S. Supreme Court seeking an order—called a writ of mandamus—directing the secretary of state to compel the delivery of the commission.

The Constitution grants the Supreme Court original jurisdiction in only a limited number of cases—those involving ambassadors, public ministers, and those in which a state is a party; in the remaining cases, the Court has authority only as an appellate court. When it acts according to its original jurisdiction, the Court exercises initial authority over a controversy, just like a trial court, as distinguished from the more limited authority it exercises when a case is presented as an appeal from a lower court's decision.

In 1789, Congress passed legislation setting up the federal courts, called the Judiciary Act of 1789. That legislation gave the Supreme Court the original authority to "issue writs of mandamus in cases warranted by the principles and usage of law. . . ." Thus, the ultimate question in Marbury v. Madison *was whether Congress could, by statute, enlarge the original jurisdiction of the Court.*

The Court first considered whether Marbury's appointment was complete—and therefore irrevocable—before Jefferson took office. Under the law, the appointment was deemed complete when the president signed the commission and the secretary of state sealed it; the appointment was a completed fact at that time, and was not dependent upon delivery. Therefore, the Court found that Marbury was entitled to his commission. The Court then decided that by withholding the commission, Secretary of State Madison was violating Marbury's legal rights. The remaining question was whether the Supreme Court could issue an order compelling the delivery of the commission.

CHIEF JUSTICE MARSHALL delivered the opinion of the Court.

. . . It is, then, the opinion of the Court,

1st. That by signing the commission of Mr. Marbury, the President of the United States appointed him a justice of peace for the county of Washington, in the District of Columbia; and that the seal of the United States, affixed thereto by the Secretary of State, is conclusive testimony of the verity of the signature, and of the completion of the appointment, and that the appointment conferred on him a legal right to the office for the space of five years.

2d. That, having this legal title to the office, he has a consequent right to the commission; a refusal to deliver which is a plain violation of that right, for which the laws of his country afford him a remedy.

It remains to be inquired whether,

3d. He is entitled to the remedy for which he applies. This depends on,

1st. The nature of the writ applied for; and,

2d. The power of this court.

* * *

This . . . is a plain case for a mandamus, either to deliver the commission, or a copy of it from the record; and it only remains to be inquired,

Whether it can issue from this court.

The act to establish the judicial courts of the United States authorizes the Supreme Court "to issue writs of mandamus in cases warranted by the principles and usages of law, to any courts appointed, or persons holding office, under the authority of the United States."

The Secretary of State, being a person holding an office under the authority of the United States, is precisely within the letter of the description, and if this court is not authorized to issue a writ of mandamus to such an officer, it must be because the law is unconstitutional, and therefore absolutely incapable of conferring the authority, and assigning the duties which its words purport to confer and assign.

The constitution vests the whole judicial power of the United States in one Supreme Court, and such inferior courts as congress shall, from time to time, ordain and establish. This power is expressly extended to all cases arising under the laws of the United States; and, consequently, in some form, may be exercised over the present case; because the right claimed is given by a law of the United States.

In the distribution of this power it is declared that "the Supreme Court shall have original jurisdiction in all cases affecting ambassadors, other public ministers and consuls, and those in which a state shall be a party. In all other cases, the Supreme Court shall have appellate jurisdiction."

* * *

To enable this court, then, to issue a mandamus, it must be shown to be an exercise of appellate jurisdiction, or to be necessary to enable them to exercise appellate jurisdiction.

* * *

It is the essential criterion of appellate jurisdiction, that it revises and corrects the proceedings in a cause already instituted, and does not create that cause. . . . [Y]et to issue such a writ to an officer for the delivery of a paper, is in effect the same as to sustain an original action for that paper, and, therefore, seems not to belong to appellate, but to original jurisdiction.

The authority, therefore, given to the Supreme Court, by the act establishing the judicial courts of the United States, to issue writs of mandamus to public officers, appears not to be warranted by the constitution; and it becomes necessary to inquire whether a jurisdiction so conferred can be exercised.

The question, whether an act, repugnant to the constitution, can become the law of the land, is a question deeply interesting to the United States; but, happily, not of an intricacy proportioned to its interest. It seems only necessary to recognize certain principles, supposed to have been long and well established, to decide it.

That the people have an original right to establish, for their future government, such principles, as, in their opinion, shall most conduce to their own happiness is the basis on which the whole American fabric has been erected. The exercise of this original right is a very great exertion; nor can it, nor ought it, to be frequently repeated. The principles, therefore, so established, are deemed fundamental. And as the authority from which they proceed is supreme, and can seldom act, they are designed to be permanent.

This original and supreme will organizes the government, and assigns to different departments their respective powers. It may either stop here, or establish certain limits not to be transcended by those departments.

The government of the United States is of the latter description. The powers of the legislature are defined and limited; and that those limits may not be mistaken, or forgotten, the constitution is written. To what purpose are powers limited, and to what purpose is that limitation committed to writing, if these limits may, at any time, be passed by those intended to be restrained? The distinction between a government with limited and unlimited powers is abolished, if those limits do not confine the persons on whom they are imposed, and if acts prohibited and acts allowed, are of equal obligation. It is a proposition too plain to be contested, that the constitution controls any legislative act repugnant to it; or, that the legislature may alter the constitution by an ordinary act.

Between these alternatives there is no middle ground. The constitution is either a superior paramount law, unchangeable by ordinary means, or it is on a level with ordinary legislative acts, and, like other acts, is alterable when the legislature shall please to alter it.

If the former part of the alternative be true, then a legislative act contrary to the constitution is not law: if the latter part be true, then written constitutions are absurd attempts, on the part of the people, to limit a power in its own nature illimitable.

Certainly all those who have framed written constitutions contemplate them as forming the fundamental and paramount law of the nation, and, consequently, the theory of every such government must be, that an act of the legislature, repugnant to the constitution, is void.

This theory is essentially attached to a written constitution, and, is consequently, to be considered, by this court, as one of the fundamental principles of our society. It is not therefore to be lost sight of in the further consideration of this subject.

If an act of the legislature, repugnant to the constitution, is void, does it, notwithstanding its invalidity, bind the courts, and oblige them to give it effect? Or, in other words, though it be not law, does it constitute a rule as operative as if it was a law? This would be to overthrow in fact what was established in theory; and would seem, at first view, an absurdity too gross to be insisted on.

* * *

It is emphatically the province and duty of the judicial department to say what the law is. Those who apply the rule to particular cases, must of necessity expound and interpret that rule. If two laws conflict with each other, the courts must decide on the operation of each.

So if a law be in opposition to the constitution; if both the law and the constitution apply to a particular case, so that the court must either decide that case conformably to the law, disregarding the constitution; or conformably to the constitution, disregarding the law; the court must determine which of these conflicting rules governs the case. This is of the very essence of judicial duty.

If, then, the courts are to regard the constitution, and the constitution is superior to any ordinary act of the legislature, the constitution, and not such ordinary act, must govern the case to which they both apply.

Those, then, who controvert the principle that the constitution is to be considered, in court, as a paramount law, are reduced to the necessity of maintaining that courts must close their eyes on the constitution, and see only the law.

This doctrine would subvert the very foundation of all written constitutions. It would declare that an act which, according to the principles and theory of our government, is entirely void, is yet, in practice, completely obligatory. It would declare that if the legislature shall do what is expressly forbidden, such act, notwithstanding the express prohibition, is in reality effectual. It would be giving to the legislature a practical and real omnipotence, with the same breath which professes to restrict their powers within narrow limits. It is prescribing limits, and declaring that those limits may be passed at pleasure.

That it thus reduces to nothing what we have deemed the greatest improvement on political institutions, a written constitution, would of itself be sufficient, in America, where written constitutions have been viewed with so much reverence, for rejecting the construction. But the peculiar expressions of the constitution of the United States furnish additional arguments in favour of its rejection.

The judicial power of the United States is extended to all cases arising under the constitution.

Could it be the intention of those who gave this power, to say that in using it the constitution should not be looked into? That a case arising under the constitution should be decided without examining the instrument under which it arises?

This is too extravagant to be maintained.

In some cases, then, the constitution must be looked into by the judges.

. . . [I]t is apparent, that the framers of the constitution contemplated that instrument as a rule for the government of courts, as well as of the legislature.

Why otherwise does it direct the judges to take an oath to support it? This oath certainly applies in an especial manner, to their conduct in their official character. How immoral to impose it on them, if they were to be used as the instruments, and the knowing instruments, for violating what they swear to support!

The oath of office, too, imposed by the legislature, is completely demonstrative of the legislative opinion on this subject.

* * *

Why does a judge swear to discharge his duties agreeably to the constitution of the United States, if that constitution forms no rule for his government? If it is closed upon him, and cannot be inspected by him?

If such be the real state of things, this is worse than solemn mockery. To prescribe, or to take this oath, becomes equally a crime.

It is also not entirely unworthy of observation, that in declaring what shall be the supreme law of the land, the constitution itself is first mentioned;

and not the laws of the United States generally, but those only which shall be made in pursuance of the constitution, have that rank.

Thus, the particular phraseology of the constitution of the United States confirms and strengthens the principle, supposed to be essential to all written constitutions, that a law repugnant to the constitution is void; and that courts, as well as other departments, are bound by that instrument.

McCulloch v. Maryland (1819)

Early in the nation's history, the U.S. Supreme Court interpreted the powers of the national government expansively. The first Supreme Court case to directly address the scope of federal authority under the Constitution was McCulloch v. Maryland *(1819). The facts were straightforward: Congress created the Bank of the United States—to the dismay of many states that viewed the creation of a national bank as a threat to the operation of banks within their own state borders. As a result, when a branch of the Bank of the United States was opened in Maryland, that state attempted to limit the bank's ability to do business under a law that imposed taxes on all banks not chartered by the state.*

In an opinion authored by Chief Justice Marshall, the Court considered two questions: whether Congress had the authority to create a national bank; and whether Maryland could in turn tax it. Marshall's answer to these two questions defends an expansive theory of implied powers for the national government and propounds the principle of national supremacy with an eloquence rarely found in judicial decisions.

CHIEF JUSTICE JOHN MARSHALL delivered the opinion of the Court.

The first question made in the cause is, has Congress power to incorporate a bank? The power now contested was exercised by the first Congress elected under the present constitution. The bill for incorporating the Bank of the United States did not steal upon an unsuspecting legislature, and pass unobserved. Its principle was completely understood, and was opposed with equal zeal and ability. . . . In discussing this question, the counsel for the state of Maryland have deemed it of some importance, in the construction of the constitution, to consider that instrument not as emanating from the people, but as the act of sovereign and independent states. The powers of the general government, it has been said, are delegated by the states, who alone are truly sovereign; and must be exercised in subordination to the states, who alone possess supreme dominion. . . . No political dreamer was ever wild enough to think of breaking down the lines which separate the states, and of compounding the American people into one common mass. Of consequence, when they act, they act in their states. But the measures they adopt do not, on that account, cease to be the measures of the people themselves, or become the measures of the state governments.

From these conventions the constitution derives its whole authority. The government proceeds directly from the people; is "ordained and established" in the name of the people; and is declared to be ordained, "in order to form a more perfect union, establish justice, insure domestic tranquility, and secure the blessings of liberty to themselves and to their posterity." The assent of the states, in their sovereign capacity, is implied in calling a convention, and thus submitting that instrument to the people. But the people were at perfect liberty to accept or reject it; and their act was final. It required not the affirmance, and could not be negatived, by the state governments. The constitution, when thus adopted, was of complete obligation, and bound the state sovereignties.

The government of the Union, then (whatever may be the influence of this fact on the case), is, emphatically, and truly, a government of the people. In form and in substance it emanates from them. Its powers are granted by them, and are to be exercised directly on them, and for their benefit.

This government is acknowledged by all to be one of enumerated powers. The principle, that it can exercise only the powers granted to it, is now universally admitted. But the question respecting the extent of the powers actually granted, is perpetually arising, and will probably continue to arise, as long as our system shall exist. The government of the United States though limited in its powers, is supreme; and its laws, when made in pursuance of the constitution, form the supreme law of the land, "anything in the constitution or laws of any state to the contrary notwithstanding."

* * *

A constitution, to contain an accurate detail of all the subdivisions of which its great powers will admit, and of all the means by which they may be carried into execution, would partake of the prolixity of a legal code, and could scarcely be embraced by the human mind. It would probably never be understood by the public. Its nature, therefore, requires, that only its great outlines should be marked, its important objects designated, and the minor ingredients which compose those objects be deduced from the nature of the objects themselves. . . . in considering this question, then, we must never forget, that it is a constitution we are expounding.

Although, among the enumerated powers of government, we do not find the word "bank" or "incorporation," we find the great powers to lay and collect taxes; to borrow money; to regulate commerce; to declare and conduct a war; and to raise and support armies and navies. The sword and the purse, all the external relations, and no inconsiderable portion of the industry of the nation, are entrusted to its government. . . . [I]t may with great reason be contended, that a government, entrusted with such ample powers, on the due execution of which the happiness and prosperity of the nation so vitally depends, must also be entrusted with ample means for their execution. The power being given, it is the interest of the nation to facilitate its execution. It can never be their interest, and cannot be presumed to have been their intention, to clog and embarrass its execution by withholding the most appropriate means. . . . It is, then, the subject of fair inquiry, how far such means may be employed.

The government which has a right to do an act, and has imposed on it the duty of performing that act, must, according to the dictates of reason, be allowed to select the means.

* * *

But the constitution of the United States has not left the right of Congress to employ the necessary means, for the execution of the powers conferred on the government, to general reasoning. To its enumeration of powers is added that of making "all laws which shall be necessary and proper, for carrying into execution the foregoing powers, and all other powers vested by this constitution, in the government of the United States, or in any department [or officer] thereof."

The counsel for the state of Maryland have urged various arguments, to prove that this clause . . . is really restrictive of the general right, which might otherwise be implied, of selecting means for executing the enumerated powers.

. . . [Maryland argues that] Congress is not empowered by it to make all laws, which may have relation to the powers conferred on the government, but such only as may be "necessary and proper" for carrying them into execution. The word "necessary" is considered as controlling the whole sentence, and as limiting the right to pass laws for the execution of the granted powers, to such as are indispensable, and without which the power would be nugatory. That it excludes the choice of means, and leaves to Congress, in each case, that only which is most direct and simple.

Is it true, that this is the sense in which the word "necessary" is always used? . . . We think it does not. If reference be had to its use, in the common affairs of the world, or in approved authors, we find that it frequently imports no more than that one thing is convenient, or useful, or essential to another. To employ the means necessary to an end, is generally understood as employing any means calculated to produce the end, and not as being confined to those single means, without which the end would be entirely unattainable.

Let this be done in the case under consideration. The subject is the execution of those great powers on which the welfare of a nation essentially depends. It must have been the intention of those who gave these powers, to insure, as far as human prudence could insure, their beneficial execution. This could not be done by confiding the choice of means to such narrow limits as not to leave it in the power of Congress to adopt any which might be appropriate, and which were conducive to the end. This provision is made in a constitution intended to endure for ages to come, and consequently, to be adapted to the various crises of human affairs. To have prescribed the means by which government should, in all future time, execute its powers, would have been to change, entirely, the character of the instrument, and give it the properties of a legal code. It would have been an unwise attempt to provide, by immutable rules, for exigencies which, if foreseen at all, must have been seen dimly, and which can be best provided for as they occur. To have declared that the best means shall not be used, but those alone without which the power given would be nugatory, would have been to deprive the legislature of the capacity to avail itself of experience, to exercise its reason, and to accommodate its legislation to circumstances. If we apply this principle of construction to any of the powers of the government, we shall find it so pernicious in its operation that we shall be compelled to discard it.

* * *

We admit, as all must admit, that the powers of the government are limited, and that its limits are not to be transcended. But we think the sound construction of the constitution must allow to the national legislature that discretion, with respect to the means by which the powers it confers are to be carried into execution, which will enable that body to perform the high duties assigned to it, in the manner most beneficial to the people. Let the end be legitimate, let it be within the scope of the constitution, and all means which are appropriate, which are plainly adapted to that end, which are not prohibited, but consist with the letter and spirit of the constitution, are constitutional.

* * *

It being the opinion of the court that the act incorporating the bank is constitutional, and that the power of establishing a branch in the state of Maryland might be properly exercised by the bank itself, we proceed to inquire: Whether the state of Maryland may, without violating the constitution, tax that branch?

That the power of taxation is one of vital importance; that it is retained by the states; that it is not abridged by the grant of a similar power to the government of the Union; that it is to be concurrently exercised by the two governments; are truths which have never been denied. But, such is the paramount character of the constitution that its capacity to withdraw any subject from the action of even this power, is admitted. . . . [T]he paramount character [of the Constitution] would seem to restrain, as it certainly may restrain, a state from such other exercise of this power as is in its nature incompatible with, and repugnant to, the constitutional laws of the Union. A law, absolutely repugnant to another, as entirely repeals that other as if express terms of repeal were used.

* * *

This great principle is, that the constitution and the laws made in pursuance thereof are supreme; that they control the constitution and laws of the respective states, and cannot be controlled by them. From this, which may be almost termed an axiom, other propositions are adduced as corollaries, on the truth or error of which, and on their application to this case, the cause has been supposed to depend. These are, 1st. That a power to create implies a power to preserve. 2d. That a power to destroy, if wielded by a different hand, is hostile to, and incompatible with, these powers to create and to preserve. 3d. That where this repugnance exists, that authority which is supreme must control, not yield to that over which it is supreme.

... [T]axation is said to be an absolute power, which acknowledges no other limits than those expressly prescribed in the constitution, and like sovereign powers of every other description, is trusted to the discretion of those who use it. But the very terms of this argument admit that the sovereignty of the state, in the article of taxation itself, is subordinate to, and may be controlled by the constitution of the United States. How far it has been controlled by that instrument must be a question of construction. In making this construction, no principle not declared can be admissible, which would defeat the legitimate operations of a supreme government.

* * *

All subjects over which the sovereign power of a state extends, are objects of taxation; but those over which it does not extend, are, upon the soundest principles, exempt from taxation.... The sovereignty of a state extends to everything which exists by its own authority, or is introduced by its permission; but does it extend to those means which are employed by Congress to carry into execution—powers conferred on that body by the people of the United States? We think it demonstrable that it does not. Those powers are not given by the people of a single state. They are given by the people of the United States, to a government whose laws, made in pursuance of the constitution, are declared to be supreme. Consequently, the people of a single state cannot confer a sovereignty which will extend over them.

If we apply the principle for which the state of Maryland contends, to the constitution generally, we shall find it capable of changing totally the character of that instrument. We shall find it capable of arresting all the measures of the government, and of prostrating it at the foot of the states. The American people have declared their constitution, and the laws made in pursuance thereof, to be supreme; but this principle would transfer the supremacy, in fact, to the states. If the controlling power of the states be established; if their supremacy as to taxation be acknowledged; what is to restrain their exercising this control in any shape they may please to give it? Their sovereignty is not confined to taxation. That is not the only mode in which it might be displayed. The question is, in truth, a question of supremacy; and if the right of the states to tax the means employed by the general government be conceded, the declaration that the constitution, and the laws made in pursuance thereof, shall be the supreme law of the land, is empty and unmeaning declamation.

* * *

We are unanimously of opinion, that the law passed by the legislature of Maryland, imposing a tax on the Bank of the United States, is unconstitutional and void. This opinion does not deprive the states of any resources which they originally possessed. It does not extend to a tax paid by the real property of the bank, in common with other real property within the state, nor to a tax imposed on the interest which the citizens of Maryland may hold in this institution, in common with other property of the same description throughout the state. But this is a tax on the operations of the bank, and is, consequently, a tax on the operation of an instrument employed by the government of the Union to carry its powers into execution. Such a tax must be unconstitutional.

Reversed.

Brown v. Board of Education of Topeka, Kansas (1954)

Brown v. Board of Education *(1954) was a momentous opinion, invalidating the system of segregation that had been established under* Plessy v. Ferguson *(1896). However, the constitutional pronouncement only marked the beginning of the struggle for racial equality, as federal courts got more and more deeply involved in trying to prod recalcitrant state and local governments into taking steps to end racial inequalities.*

The Brown case involved appeals from several states. In each case, the plaintiffs had been denied access to public schools designated only for white children under a variety of state laws. They challenged the Plessy v. Ferguson *(1896) "separate but equal" doctrine, contending that segregated schools were by their nature unequal.*

Chief Justice Warren first discussed the history of the Fourteenth Amendment's equal protection clause, finding it too inconclusive to be of assistance in determining how the Fourteenth Amendment should be applied to the question of public education.

Chief Justice Warren writing for the majority.

. . . The doctrine of "separate but equal" did not make its appearance in this Court until 1896, in the case of *Plessy v. Ferguson,* involving not education but transportation. American courts have since labored with the doctrine for over a half a century. In this Court, there have been six cases involving the "separate but equal" doctrine in the field of public education.

* * *

In the instant cases, [the question of the application of the separate but equal doctrine to public education] is directly presented. Here, . . . there are findings below that the Negro and white schools involved have been equalized, or are being equalized, with respect to buildings, curricula, qualifications and salaries of teachers, and other "tangible" factors. Our decision, therefore, cannot turn on merely a comparison of these tangible factors in the Negro and white schools involved in each of the cases. We must look instead to the effect of segregation itself on public education.

In approaching this problem, we cannot turn the clock back to 1868 when the [Fourteenth] Amendment was adopted, or even to 1896 when *Plessy v. Ferguson* was written. We must consider public education in the light of its full development and its present place in American life throughout the Nation. Only in this way can it be determined if segregation in public schools deprives these plaintiffs of the equal protection of the laws.

Today, education is perhaps the most important function of state and local governments. Compulsory school attendance laws and the great expenditures for education both demonstrate our recognition of the importance of education to our democratic society. It is required in the performance of our most basic responsibilities, even service in the armed forces. It is the very foundation of good citizenship. Today it is a principal instrument in awakening the child to cultural values, in preparing him for later professional training, and in helping him to adjust normally to his environment. In these days, it is doubtful that any child may reasonably be expected to succeed in life if he is denied the opportunity of an education. Such an opportunity, where the state has undertaken to provide it, is a right which must be made available to all on equal terms.

We come then to the question presented: Does segregation of children in public schools solely on the basis of race, even though the physical facilities and other "tangible" factors may be equal, deprive the children of the minority group of equal educational opportunities? We believe that it does.

In *Sweatt v. Painter*, in finding that a segregated law school for Negroes could not provide them equal educational opportunities, this Court relied in large part on "those qualities which are incapable of objective measurement but which make for greatness in a law school." In *McLaurin v. Oklahoma State Regents*, the Court, in requiring that a Negro admitted to a white graduate school be treated like all other students, again resorted to intangible considerations: ". . . his ability to study, to engage in discussions and exchange views with other students, and, in general, to learn his profession." Such considerations apply with added force to children in grade and high schools. To separate them from others of similar age and qualifications solely because of their race generates a feeling of inferiority as to their status in the community that may affect their hearts and minds in a way unlikely ever to be undone. The effect of this separation on their educational opportunities was well stated by a finding in the Kansas case by a court which nevertheless felt compelled to rule against the Negro plaintiffs:

"Segregation of white and colored children in public schools has a detrimental effect upon the colored children. The impact is greater when it has the sanction of the law; for the policy of separating the races is usually interpreted as denoting the inferiority of the Negro group. A sense of inferiority affects the motivation of a child to learn. Segregation with the sanction of law, therefore, has a tendency to [retard] the educational and mental development of Negro children and to deprive them of some of the benefits they would receive in a racial[ly] integrated school system." Whatever may have been the extent of psychological knowledge at the time of *Plessy v. Ferguson,* this finding is amply supported by modern authority. Any language in *Plessy v. Ferguson* contrary to this finding is rejected.

We conclude that in the field of public education the doctrine of "separate but equal" has no place. Separate educational facilities are inherently unequal. Therefore, we hold that the plaintiffs and others similarly situated for whom the actions have been brought are, by reason of the segregation complained of, deprived of the equal protection of the laws guaranteed by the Fourteenth Amendment. This disposition makes unnecessary any discussion whether such segregation also violates the Due Process Clause of the Fourteenth Amendment.

Because these are class actions, because of the wide applicability of this decision, and because of the great variety of local conditions, the formulation of decrees in these cases presents problems of considerable complexity. On reargument, the consideration of appropriate relief was necessarily subordinated to the primary question—the constitutionality of segregation in public education. We have now announced that such segregation is a denial of the equal protection of the laws.

Roe v. Wade (1973)

One of the most significant changes in constitutional interpretation in the last four decades has been the Court's willingness to look beyond the explicit language of the Bill of Rights to find unenumerated rights, such as the right to privacy. In discovering such rights, the Court has engaged in what is known as substantive due process analysis—defining and articulating fundamental rights—distinct from its efforts to define the scope of procedural due process, when it decides what procedures the state and federal governments must follow to be fair in their treatment of citizens. The Court's move into the substantive due process area has generated much of the political discussion over the proper role of the Court in constitutional interpretation.

The case that has been the focal point for this debate is Roe v. Wade, *the 1973 case that held that a woman's right to privacy protected her decision to have an abortion. The right to privacy in matters relating to contraception and childbearing had been recognized in the 1965 decision of* Griswold v. Connecticut, *and was extended in subsequent decisions culminating in* Roe. *The theoretical issue of concern here relates back to the incorporation issue: Should the Supreme Court be able to prohibit the states not only from violating the express guarantees contained in the Bill of Rights, but its implied guarantees as well?*

Texas law prohibited abortions except for "the purpose of saving the life of the mother." The plaintiff challenged the constitutionality of the statute, claiming that it infringed upon her substantive due process right to privacy.

Justice Blackmun delivered the opinion of the Court.

. . . [We] forthwith acknowledge our awareness of the sensitive and emotional nature of the abortion controversy, of the vigorous opposing views, and the deep and seemingly absolute convictions that the subject inspires. One's philosophy, one's experiences, one's exposure to the raw edges of human existence, one's religious training, one's attitudes toward life and family and their values, and the moral standards one establishes and seeks to observe, are all likely to affect one's thinking [about] abortion. In addition, population growth, pollution, poverty, and racial overtones tend to complicate and not to simplify the problem. Our task, of course, is to resolve the issue by constitutional measurement, free of emotion and of predilection. We seek earnestly to do this, and, because we do, we have inquired into, and in this opinion place some emphasis upon, medical and medical-legal history and what that history reveals about man's attitudes toward the abortion procedure over the centuries.

* * *

[The Court here reviewed ancient and contemporary attitudes toward abortion, observing that restrictive laws date primarily from the late nineteenth century. The Court also reviewed the possible state interests in restricting abortions, including discouraging illicit sexual conduct, limiting access to a hazardous medical procedure, and the states' general interests in protecting fetal life. The Court addressed only the third interest as a current legitimate interest of the state.]

. . . The Constitution does not explicitly mention any right of privacy. In a line of decisions, however, . . . the Court has recognized that a right of personal privacy, or a guarantee of certain areas or zones of privacy, does exist under the Constitution. . . . This right of privacy, whether it be founded in the Fourteenth Amendment's concept of personal liberty and restrictions upon state action, as we feel it is, or, as the District Court determined, in the Ninth Amendment's reservation of rights to the people, is broad enough to encompass a woman's decision whether or not to terminate her pregnancy. The detriment that the State would impose upon the pregnant woman by denying this choice altogether is apparent. Specific and direct harm medically diagnosable even in early pregnancy may be involved. Maternity, or additional offspring, may force upon the woman a distressful life and future. Psychological harm may be imminent. Mental and physical health may be taxed by child care. There is also the distress, for all concerned, associated with the unwanted child, and there is the problem of bringing a child into a family already unable, psychologically and otherwise, to care for it. In other cases, as in this one, the additional difficulties and continuing stigma of unwed motherhood may be involved. All these are factors the woman and her responsible physician necessarily will consider in consultation.

On the basis of elements such as these, appellants and some amici [friends of the Court] argue that the woman's right is absolute and that she is entitled to terminate her pregnancy at whatever time, in whatever way, and for whatever reason she alone chooses. With this we do not agree. Appellants' arguments that Texas either has no valid interest at all in regulating the abortion decision, or no interest strong enough to support any limitation upon the woman's sole determination, is unpersuasive. The Court's decisions recognizing a right of privacy also acknowledge that some state regulation in areas protected by that right is appropriate. As noted above, a State may properly assert important interests in safeguarding health, in maintaining medical standards, and in protecting potential life. At some point in pregnancy, these respective interests become sufficiently compelling to sustain regulation of the factors that govern the abortion decision. The privacy right involved, therefore, cannot be said to be absolute. In fact, it is not clear to us that the claim asserted by some amici that one has an unlimited right to do with one's body as one pleases bears a close relationship to the right of privacy previously articulated in the Court's decisions.

* * *

We therefore conclude that the right of personal privacy includes the abortion decision, but that this right is not unqualified and must be considered against state interests in regulation.

Where certain "fundamental rights" are involved, the Court has held that regulation limiting these rights may be justified only by a "compelling state interest," and that legislative enactments must be narrowly drawn to express only the legitimate state interests at stake.

. . . The District Court held that the appellee failed to meet his burden of demonstrating that the Texas statute's infringement upon Roe's rights was necessary to support a compelling state interest. . . . Appellee argues that the State's determination to recognize and protect prenatal life from and after conception constitutes a compelling state interest. As noted above, we do not agree fully with either formulation.

The appellee and certain amici argue that the fetus is a "person" within the language and meaning of the Fourteenth Amendment. In support of this they outline at length and in detail the well-known facts of fetal development. If this suggestion of personhood is established, the appellant's case, of course, collapses, for the fetus' right to life is then guaranteed specifically by the Amendment. The appellant conceded as much on reargument. On the other hand, the appellee conceded on reargument that no case could be cited that holds that a fetus is a person within the meaning of the Fourteenth Amendment.

The Constitution does not define "person" in so many words. Section 1 of the Fourteenth Amendment contains three references to "person." The first, in defining "citizens," speaks of "persons born or naturalized in the United States." The word also appears both in the Due Process Clause and in the Equal Protection Clause. "Person" is used in other places in the Constitution. . . . But in nearly all these instances, the use of the word is such that it has application only postnatally. None indicates, with any assurance, that it has any possible pre-natal application.

All this, together with our observation, that throughout the major portion of the 19th century prevailing legal abortion practices were far freer than they are today, persuades us that the word "person," as used in the Fourteenth Amendment, does not include the unborn.

. . . The pregnant woman cannot be isolated in her privacy. She carries an embryo and, later, a fetus, if one accepts the medical definitions of the developing young in the human uterus. . . . The situation therefore is inherently different from marital intimacy, or bedroom possession of obscene material, or marriage, or procreation, or education, with which [earlier cases defining the right to privacy] were concerned. As we have intimated above, it is reasonable and appropriate for a State to decide that at some point in time another interest, that of health of the mother or that of potential human life, becomes significantly involved. The woman's privacy is no longer sole and any right of privacy she possesses must be measured accordingly.

Texas urges that, apart from the Fourteenth Amendment, life begins at conception and is present throughout pregnancy, and that, therefore, the State has a compelling interest in protecting that life from and after conception. We need not resolve the difficult question of when life begins. When those trained in the respective disciplines of medicine, philosophy, and theology are unable to arrive at any consensus, the judiciary, at this point in the development of man's knowledge, is not in a position to speculate as to the answer.

. . . In view of all this, we do not agree that, by adopting one theory of life, Texas may override the rights of the pregnant woman that are at stake. We repeat, however, that the State does have an important and legitimate interest in preserving and protecting the health of the pregnant woman, whether she be a resident of the State or a nonresident who seeks medical consultation and treatment there, and that it has still *another* important and legitimate interest in protecting the potentiality of human life. These interests are separate and distinct. Each grows in substantiality as the woman approaches term and, at a point during pregnancy, each becomes "compelling."

With respect to the State's important and legitimate interest in the health of the mother, the "compelling" point, in the light of present medical knowledge, is at approximately the end of the first trimester. This is so because of the now established medical fact . . . that until the end of the first trimester mortality in abortion is less than mortality in normal childbirth. It follows that, from and after this point, a State may regulate the abortion procedure to the extent that the regulation reasonably relates to the preservation and protection of maternal health. Examples of permissible state regulation in this area are requirements as to the qualifications of the person who is to perform the abortion; as to the licensure of that person; as to the facility in which the procedure is to be performed, that is, whether it must be a hospital or may be a clinic or some other place of less-than-hospital status; as to the licensing of the facility; and the like.

This means, on the other hand, that, for the period of pregnancy prior to this "compelling" point, the attending physician, in consultation with his patient, is free to determine, without regulation by the State, that in his medical judgment the patient's pregnancy should be terminated. If that decision is reached, the judgment may be effectuated by an abortion free of interference by the State.

With respect to the State's important and legitimate interest in potential life, the "compelling" point is at viability. This is so because the fetus then presumably has the capability of meaningful life outside the mother's womb. State regulation protective of fetal life after viability thus has both logical and biological justifications. If the State is interested in protecting fetal life after viability, it may go so far as to proscribe abortion during that period except when it is necessary to preserve the life or health of the mother.

Measured against these standards, the Texas Penal Code, in restricting legal abortions to those "procured or attempted by medical advice for the purpose of saving the life of the mother," sweeps too broadly. The statute makes no distinction between abortions performed early in pregnancy and those performed later, and it limits to a single reason, "saving" the mother's life, the legal justification for the procedure. The statute, therefore, cannot survive the constitutional attack made upon it here.

* * *

Reversed.

United States v. Nixon (1974)

The Supreme Court has had few occasions to rule on the constitutional limits of executive authority. The Court is understandably reluctant to articulate the boundaries of presidential and legislative power, given the Court's own somewhat ambiguous institutional authority. In the case that follows, however, the Court looked at one of the ways in which the Constitution circumscribes the exercise of presidential prerogative.

United States v. Nixon *(1974) involves claims to executive authority. President Richard Nixon was implicated in a conspiracy to cover up a burglary of the Democratic Party Headquarters at the Watergate Hotel in Washington, D.C., during the 1972 re-election campaign. The Special Prosecutor assigned to investigate the break-in and file appropriate criminal charges asked the trial court to order the President to disclose a number of documents and tapes related to the cover-up in order to determine the scope of the President's involvement. The President produced edited versions of some of the materials, but refused to comply with most of the trial court's order, asserting that he was entitled to withhold the information under a claim of "executive privilege."*

CHIEF JUSTICE BURGER delivered the opinion of the Court.

In the District Court, the President's counsel argued that the court lacked jurisdiction to issue the subpoena because the matter was an intra-branch dispute between a subordinate and superior officer of the Executive Branch and hence not subject to judicial resolution. That argument has been renewed in this Court with emphasis on the contention that the dispute does not present a "case" or "controversy" which can be adjudicated in the federal courts. The President's counsel argues that the federal courts should not intrude into areas committed to the other branches of Government. He views the present dispute as essentially a "jurisdictional" dispute within the Executive Branch which he analogizes to a dispute between two congressional committees. Since the Executive Branch has exclusive authority and absolute discretion to decide whether to prosecute a case, it is contended that a President's decision is final in determining what evidence is to be used in a given criminal case.

. . . Although his counsel concedes the President has delegated certain specific powers to the Special Prosecutor, he has not "waived nor delegated to the Special Prosecutor the President's duty to claim privilege as to all materials which fall within the President's inherent authority to refuse to disclose to any executive officer." The Special Prosecutor's demand for the items therefore presents, in the view of the President's counsel, a political question since it involves a "textually demonstrable" grant of power under Art. II. . . .

The demands of and the resistance to the subpoena present an obvious controversy in the ordinary sense, but that alone is not sufficient to meet constitutional standards. In the constitutional sense, controversy means more than disagreement and conflict; rather it means the kind of controversy courts traditionally resolve. Here at issue is the production or nonproduction of specified evidence deemed by the Special Prosecutor to be relevant and admissible in a pending criminal case. It is sought by one official of the Government within the scope of his express authority; it is resisted by the Chief Executive on the ground of his duty to preserve the confidentiality of the communications of the President. Whatever the correct answer on the merits, these issues are "of a type which are traditionally justiciable."

* * *

. . . We turn to the claim that the subpoena should be quashed because it demands "confidential conversations between a President and his close advisors that it would be inconsistent with the public interest to produce." The first contention is a broad claim that the separation of powers doctrine precludes judicial review of a President's claim of privilege. The second contention is that if he does not prevail on the claim of absolute privilege, the court should hold as a matter of constitutional law that the privilege prevails over the subpoena. . . .

* * *

[*The Court discussed its authority to interpret the Constitution, concluding that it had full power to adjudicate a claim of executive privilege.*]

In support of his claim of absolute privilege, the President's counsel urges two grounds one of which is common to all governments and one of which is peculiar to our system of separation of powers. The first ground is the valid need for protection of communications between high government officials and those who advise and assist them in the performance of their manifold duties; the importance of this confidentiality is too plain to require further discussion. Human experience teaches that those who expect public dissemination of their remarks may well temper candor with a concern for appearances and for their own interests to the detriment of the decisionmaking process. Whatever the nature of the privilege of confidentiality of presidential communications in the exercise of Art. II powers the privilege can be said to derive from the supremacy of each branch within its own assigned area of constitutional duties. Certain powers and privileges flow from the nature of enumerated powers; the protection of the confidentiality of presidential communications has similar constitutional underpinnings.

The second ground asserted by the President's counsel in support of the claim of absolute privilege rests on the doctrine of separation of powers. Here it is argued that the independence of the Executive Branch within its own sphere, insulates a president from a judicial subpoena in an ongoing criminal prosecution, and thereby protects confidential presidential communications.

However, neither the doctrine of separation of powers, nor the need for confidentiality of high level communications, without more, can sustain an absolute, unqualified presidential privilege of immunity from judicial process under all circumstances. The President's need for complete candor and objectivity from advisers calls for great deference from the courts. However, when the privilege depends solely on the broad, undifferentiated claim of public interest in the confidentiality of such conversations, a confrontation with other values arises. Absent a claim of need to protect military, diplomatic or sensitive national security secrets, we find it difficult to accept the argument that even the very important interest in confidentiality of presidential communications is significantly diminished by production of such material for *in camera* inspection with all the protection that a district court will be obliged to provide.

The impediment that an absolute, unqualified privilege would place in the way of the primary constitutional duty of the judicial branch to do justice in criminal prosecutions would plainly conflict with the function of the courts under Art. III. In designing the structure of our Government and dividing and allocating the sovereign power among three coequal branches, the Framers of the Constitution sought to provide a comprehensive system, but the separate powers were not intended to operate with absolute independence. To read the Art. II powers of the President as providing an absolute privilege as against a subpoena essential to enforcement of criminal statutes on no more than a generalized claim of the public interest in confidentiality of nonmilitary and nondiplomatic discussions would upset the constitutional balance of "a workable government" and gravely impair the role of the court under Art. III.

Since we conclude that the legitimate needs of the judicial process may outweigh presidential privilege, it is necessary to resolve those competing interests in a manner that preserves the essential functions of each branch. The rights and indeed the duty to resolve that question does not free the judiciary from according high respect to the representations made on behalf of the President. The expectation of a President to the confidentiality of his conversations and correspondence, like the claim of confidentiality of judicial deliberations, for example, has all the values to which we accord deference for the privacy of all citizens and added to those values the necessity for protection of the public interest in his responsibilities against the inroads of such a privilege on the fair administration of criminal justice. The interest in preserving confidentiality is weighty indeed and entitled to great respect. However we cannot conclude that advisers will be moved to temper the candor of their remarks by the infrequent occasions of disclosure because of the possibility that such conversations will be called for in the context of a criminal prosecution.

On the other hand, the allowance of the privilege to withhold evidence that is demonstrably relevant in a criminal trial would cut deeply into the guarantee of due process of law and gravely impair the basic function of the courts. A President's acknowleged need for confidentiality in the communications of his office is general in nature, whereas the constitutional need for production of relevant evidence in a criminal proceeding is specific and central to the fair adjudication of a particular criminal case in the administration of justice. Without access to specific facts a criminal prosecution may be totally frustrated. The President's broad interest in confidentiality of communications will not be vitiated by disclosure of a limited number of conversations preliminarily shown to have some bearing on the pending criminal cases.

We conclude that when the ground for asserting privilege as to subpoenaed materials sought for use in a criminal trial is based only on the generalized interest in confidentiality, it cannot prevail over the fundamental demand of due process of law in the fair administration of criminal justice. The generalized assertion of privilege must yield to the demonstrated, specific need for evidence in a pending criminal trial.

* * *

In this case the President challenges a subpoena served on him as a third party requiring the production of materials for use in a criminal prosecution on the claim that he has a privilege against disclosure of confidential communications. He does not place his claim of privilege on the ground they are military or diplomatic secrets. As to these areas of Art. II duties the courts have traditionally shown the utmost deference to presidential responsibilities. No case of the Court, however, has extended this high degree of deference to a President's generalized interest in confidentiality. Nowhere in the Constitution, as we have noted earlier, is there any explicit reference to a privilege of confidentiality; yet to the extent this interest relates to the effective discharge of a President's powers, it is constitutionally based.

* * *

[*The Court distinguished this case from cases involving claims against the president while acting in an official capacity.*]

Mr. Chief Justice Marshall sitting as a trial judge in the *Burr* case was extraordinarily careful to point out that: "[I]n no case of this kind would a Court be required to proceed against the President as against an ordinary individual." Marshall's statement cannot be read to mean in any sense that a President is above the law, but relates to the singularly unique role under Art. II of a President's communications and activities, related to the performance of duties under that Article. Moreover, a President's communications and activities encompass a vastly wider range of sensitive material than would be true of any "ordinary individual." It is therefore necessary in the public interest to afford presidential confidentiality the greatest protection consistent with the fair administration of justice. The need for confidentiality even as to idle conversations with associates in which casual reference might be made concerning political leaders within the country or foreign statesmen is too obvious to call for further treatment. We have no doubt that the District Judge will at all times accord the presidential records that high degree of deference suggested in *United States v. Burr*, and will discharge his responsibility to see to it that until released to the Special Prosecutor no *in camera* [private] material is revealed to anyone. This burden applies with even greater force to excised material; once the decision is made to excise, the material is restored to its privileged status and should be returned under seal to its lawful custodian.

Affirmed.

United States v. Lopez (1995)

How far does Congress's authority extend with respect to the states? Since the 1930s, when a liberalization of Supreme Court doctrine cleared the way for an expansion of federal authority, Congress has relied on a loose interpretation of the Commerce Clause to justify extensive involvement in state and local affairs. (Congress can also shape what states do, for example, by placing conditions upon the receipt of federal funds). In 1990, Congress enacted the Gun-Free School Zones Act, making possession of a firearm in designated school zones a federal crime. When Alfonso Lopez, Jr., was convicted of violating the act, his lawyer challenged the constitutionality of the law, arguing that it was "invalid as beyond the power of Congress under the Commerce Clause." In a striking reversal of interpretation, the Supreme Court agreed and declared the law invalid, holding that banning guns in schools was too far removed from any effect on interstate commerce to warrant federal intervention. Critics of the decision argued that the Court's reasoning might invalidate a large body of federal crime and drug legislation that relies on the connection between regulated activity and interstate commerce. Supporters maintained that the decision marked a new era of judicial respect for federalism and state autonomy.

Chief Justice Rehnquist delivered the opinion of the Court.

In the Gun-Free School Zones Act of 1990, Congress made it a federal offense "for any individual knowingly to possess a firearm at a place that the individual knows, or has reasonable cause to believe, is a school zone." The Act neither regulates a commercial activity nor contains a requirement that the possession be connected in any way to interstate commerce. We hold that the Act exceeds the authority of "Congress to regulate Commerce . . . among the several States. . . ." (U.S. Constitution Art. I, 8, cl. 3).

On March 10, 1992, respondent, who was then a 12th-grade student, arrived at Edison High School in San Antonio, Texas, carrying a concealed .38 caliber handgun and five bullets. Acting upon an anonymous tip, school authorities confronted respondent, who admitted that he was carrying the weapon. He was arrested and charged under Texas law with firearm possession on school premises. The next day, the state charges were dismissed after federal agents charged respondent by complaint with violating the Gun-Free School Zones Act of 1990.

A federal grand jury indicted respondent on one count of knowing possession of a firearm at a school zone, in violation of 922(q) [the relevant section of the Act of 1990]. Respondent moved to dismiss his federal indictment on the ground that 922(q) "is unconstitutional as it is beyond the power of Congress to legislate control over our public schools." The District Court denied the motion, concluding that 922(q) "is a constitutional exercise of Congress' well-defined power to regulate activities in and affecting commerce, and the 'business' of elementary, middle and high schools . . . affects interstate commerce." Respondent waived his right to a jury trial. The District Court conducted a bench trial, found him guilty of violating 922(q), and sentenced him to six months' imprisonment and two years' supervised release.

On appeal, respondent challenged his conviction based on his claim that 922(q) exceeded Congress' power to legislate under the Commerce Clause. The Court of Appeals for the Fifth Circuit agreed and reversed respondent's conviction. It held that, in light of what it characterized as insufficient congressional findings and legislative history, "in the full reach of its terms, is invalid as beyond the power of Congress under the Commerce Clause." Because of the importance of the issue, we granted *certiorari* and we now affirm.

We start with first principles. The Constitution creates a Federal Government of enumerated powers. As James Madison wrote, "[t]he powers delegated by the proposed Constitution to the federal government are few and defined. Those which are to remain in the State governments are numerous and indefinite." (*The Federalist*, No. 45). This constitutionally mandated division of authority was adopted by the Framers to ensure protection of our fundamental liberties. Just as the separation and independence of the coordinate branches of the Federal Government serves to prevent the accumulation of excessive power in any one branch, a healthy balance of power between the States and the Federal Government will reduce the risk of tyranny and abuse from either front.

[*For the next several pages Rehnquist reviews the evolution of interpretations of the Commerce Clause, starting with* Gibbons v. Ogden *(1824). This case established the relatively narrow interpretation of the Commerce Clause in which the Court prevented* states *from interfering with interstate commerce. Very rarely did cases concern Congress's power. The 1887 Interstate Commerce Act and the 1890 Sherman Antitrust Act expanded Congress's power to regulate intrastate commerce "where the interstate and intrastate aspects of commerce were so mingled together that full regulation of interstate commerce required incidental regulation of intrastate commerce," arguing that the Commerce Clause authorized such regulation. Several New Deal era cases,* NLRB v. Jones & Laughlin Steel Corp. *(1937),* United States v. Darby *(1941), and* Wickard v. Filburn *(1942) broadened the interpretation of the Commerce Clause.*]

Jones & Laughlin Steel, *Darby*, and *Wickard* ushered in an era of Commerce Clause jurisprudence that greatly expanded the previously defined authority of Congress under that Clause. In part, this was a recognition of the great changes that had occurred in the way business was carried on in this country. Enterprises that had once been local or at most regional in nature had become national in scope. But the doctrinal change also reflected a view that earlier Commerce Clause cases artificially had constrained the authority of Congress to regulate interstate commerce.

But even these modern-era precedents which have expanded congressional power under the Commerce Clause confirm that this power is subject to outer limits. In *Jones & Laughlin Steel*, the Court warned that the scope of the interstate commerce power "must be considered in the light of our dual system of government and may not be extended so as to embrace effects upon interstate commerce so indirect and remote that to embrace them, in view of our complex society, would effectually obliterate the distinction between what is national and what is local and create a completely centralized government." Since that time, the Court has heeded that warning and undertaken to decide whether a rational basis existed for concluding that a regulated activity sufficiently affected interstate commerce.

* * *

Consistent with this structure, we have identified three broad categories of activity that Congress may regulate under its commerce power. First, Congress may regulate the use of the channels of interstate commerce. Second, Congress is empowered to regulate and protect the instrumentalities of interstate commerce, or persons or things in interstate commerce, even though the threat may come only from intrastate activities. Finally, Congress' commerce authority includes the power to regulate those activities having a substantial relation to interstate commerce, those activities that substantially affect interstate commerce.

Within this final category, admittedly, our case law has not been clear whether an activity must *affect* or *substantially affect* interstate commerce in order to be within Congress' power to regulate it under the Commerce Clause. We conclude, consistent with the great weight of our case law, that the proper test requires an analysis of whether the regulated activity *substantially affects* interstate commerce.

We now turn to consider the power of Congress, in the light of this framework, to enact 922(q) [The Gun-Free School Zones Act]. The first two categories of authority may be quickly disposed of: 922(q) is not a regulation of the use of the channels of interstate commerce, nor is it an attempt to prohibit the interstate transportation of a commodity through the channels of commerce; nor can 922(q) be justified as a regulation by which Congress has sought to protect an instrumentality of interstate commerce or a thing in interstate commerce. Thus, if 922(q) is to be sustained, it must be under the third category as a regulation of an activity that substantially affects interstate commerce.

First, we have upheld a wide variety of congressional Acts regulating intrastate economic activity where we have concluded that the activity substantially affected interstate commerce. Examples include the regulation of intrastate coal mining; intrastate extortionate credit transactions, restaurants utilizing substantial interstate supplies, inns and hotels catering to interstate guests, and production and consumption of home-grown wheat. These examples are by no means exhaustive, but the pattern is clear. Where economic activity substantially affects interstate commerce, legislation regulating that activity will be sustained.

Even *Wickard*, which is perhaps the most far reaching example of Commerce Clause authority over intrastate activity, involved economic activity in a way that the possession of a gun in a school zone does not. Roscoe Filburn operated a small farm in Ohio, on which, in the year involved, he raised 23 acres of wheat. It was his practice to sow winter wheat in the fall, and after harvesting it in July to sell a portion of the crop, to feed part of it to poultry and livestock on the farm, to use some in making flour for home consumption, and to keep the remainder for seeding future crops. The Secretary of Agriculture assessed a penalty against him under the Agricultural Adjustment Act of 1938 because he harvested about 12 acres more wheat than his allotment under the Act permitted. The Act was designed to regulate the volume of wheat moving in interstate and foreign commerce in order to avoid surpluses and shortages, and concomitant fluctuation in wheat prices, which had previously obtained. The Court said, in an opinion sustaining the application of the Act to Filburn's activity, "One of the primary purposes of the Act in question was to increase the market price of wheat and to that end to limit the volume thereof that could affect the market. It can hardly be denied that a factor of such volume and variability as home-consumed wheat would have a substantial influence on price and market conditions. This may arise because being in marketable condition such wheat overhangs the market and, if induced by rising prices, tends to flow into the market and check price increases. But if we assume that it is never marketed, it supplies a need of the man who grew it which would otherwise be reflected by purchases in the open market. Home-grown wheat in this sense competes with wheat in commerce" (317 U.S., at 128).

Section 922(q) is a criminal statute that by its terms has nothing to do with *commerce* or any sort of economic enterprise, however broadly one might define those terms. Section 922(q) is not an essential part of a larger regulation of economic activity, in which the regulatory scheme could be undercut unless the intra-state activity were regulated. It cannot, therefore, be sustained under our cases upholding regulations of activities that arise out of or are connected with a commercial transaction, which viewed in the aggregate, substantially affects interstate commerce.

Second, 922(q) contains no jurisdictional element which would ensure, through case-by-case inquiry, that the firearm possession in question affects interstate commerce. . . . 922(q) has no express jurisdictional element which might limit its reach to a discrete set of firearm possessions that additionally have an explicit connection with or effect on interstate commerce.

* * *

The Government's essential contention, in fine, is that we may determine here that 922(q) is valid because possession of a firearm in a local school zone does indeed substantially affect interstate commerce. The Government argues that possession of a firearm in a school zone may result in violent crime and that violent crime can be expected to affect the functioning of the national economy in two ways. First, the costs of violent crime are substantial, and, through the mechanism of insurance, those costs are spread throughout the population. Second, violent crime reduces the willingness of individuals to travel to areas within the country that are perceived to be unsafe. The Government also argues that the presence of guns in schools poses a substantial threat to the educational process by threatening the learning environment. A handicapped educational process, in turn, will result in a less productive citizenry. That, in turn, would have an adverse effect on the Nation's economic well-being. As a result, the Government argues that Congress could rationally have concluded that 922(q) substantially affects interstate commerce.

We pause to consider the implications of the Government's arguments. The Government admits, under its "costs of crime" reasoning, that Congress could regulate not only all violent crime, but all activities that might lead to violent crime, regardless of how tenuously they relate to interstate commerce. Similarly, under the Government's "national productivity" reasoning, Congress could regulate any activity that it found was related to the economic productivity of individual citizens: family law (including marriage, divorce, and child custody), for example. Under the theories that the Government presents in support of 922(q), it is difficult to perceive any limitation on federal power, even in areas such as criminal law enforcement or education where States historically have been sovereign. Thus, if we were to accept the Government's arguments, we are hard-pressed to posit any activity by an individual that Congress is without power to regulate.

Although Justice Breyer argues that acceptance of the Government's rationales would not authorize a general federal police power, he is unable to identify any activity that the States may regulate but Congress may not. Justice Breyer posits that there might be some limitations on Congress' commerce power such as family law or certain aspects of education. These suggested limitations, when viewed in light of the dissent's expansive analysis, are devoid of substance.

Justice Breyer focuses, for the most part, on the threat that firearm possession in and near schools poses to the educational process and the potential economic consequences flowing from that threat. Specifically, the dissent reasons that (1) gun-related violence is a serious problem; (2) that problem, in turn, has an adverse effect on classroom learning; and (3) that adverse effect on classroom learning, in turn, represents a substantial threat to trade and commerce. This analysis would be equally applicable, if not more so, to subjects such as family law and direct regulation of education.

For instance, if Congress can, pursuant to its Commerce Clause power, regulate activities that adversely affect the learning environment, then, a fortiori, it also can regulate the educational process directly. Congress could determine that a school's curriculum has a "significant" effect on the extent of classroom learning. As a result, Congress could mandate a federal curriculum for local elementary and secondary schools because what is taught in local schools has a significant "effect on classroom learning," and that, in turn, has a substantial effect on interstate commerce.

Justice Breyer rejects our reading of precedent and argues that "Congress . . . could rationally conclude that schools fall on the commercial side of the line." Again, Justice Breyer's rationale lacks any real limits because, depending on the level of generality, any activity can be looked upon as commercial. Under the dissent's rationale, Congress could just as easily look at child rearing as "fall[ing] on the commercial side of the line" because it provides a "valuable service" namely, to equip [children] with the skills they need to survive in life and, more specifically, in the workplace. We do not doubt that Congress has authority under the Commerce Clause to regulate numerous commercial activities that substantially affect interstate commerce and also affect the educational process. That authority, though broad, does not include the authority to regulate each and every aspect of local schools.

Admittedly, a determination whether an intrastate activity is commercial or noncommercial may in some cases result in legal uncertainty. But, so long as Congress' authority is limited to those powers enumerated in the Constitution, and so long as those enumerated powers are interpreted as having judicially enforceable outer limits, congressional legislation under the Commerce Clause always will engender "legal uncertainty." As Chief Justice Marshall stated in *McCulloch v. Maryland,* (1819), "The [federal] government is acknowledged by all to be one of enumerated powers. The principle, that it can exercise only the powers granted to it . . . is now universally admitted. But the question respecting the extent of the powers actually granted, is perpetually arising, and will probably continue to arise, as long as our system shall exist." The Constitution mandates this uncertainty by withholding from Congress a plenary police power that would authorize enactment of every type of legislation. Congress has operated within this framework of legal uncertainty ever since this Court determined that it was the judiciary's duty "to say what the law is." Any possible benefit from eliminating this "legal uncertainty" would be at the expense of the Constitution's system of enumerated powers.

* * *

These are not precise formulations, and in the nature of things they cannot be. But we think they point the way to a correct decision of this case. The possession of a gun in a local school zone is in no sense an economic activity that might, through repetition elsewhere, substantially affect any sort of interstate commerce. Respondent was a local student at a local school; there is no indication that he had recently moved in interstate commerce, and there is no requirement that his possession of the firearm have any concrete tie to interstate commerce.

To uphold the Government's contentions here, we would have to pile inference upon inference in a manner that would bid fair to convert congressional authority under the Commerce Clause to a general police power of the sort retained by the States. Admittedly, some of our prior cases have taken long steps down that road, giving great deference to congressional action. The broad language in these opinions has suggested the possibility of additional expansion, but we decline here to proceed any further. To do so would require us to conclude that the Constitution's enumeration of powers does not presuppose something not enumerated, and that there never will be a distinction between what is truly national and what is truly local. This we are unwilling to do.

For the foregoing reasons the judgment of the Court of Appeals is Affirmed.

Obergefell v. Hodges (2015)

In this landmark ruling on same-sex marriage, the Supreme Court decided that the Fourteenth Amendment requires states to permit two people of the same sex to marry and to recognize a marriage between two people of the same sex when their marriage was performed in another state. Justice Kennedy wrote for the majority that "marriage is a keystone of our social order" and "[t]here is no difference between same- and opposite-sex couples with respect to this principle." The decision was 5–4, with separate dissents from the Court's four most conservative members (Roberts, Scalia, Alito, and Thomas).

Supporters of same-sex marriage accumulated an impressive series of wins in the Fourth, Seventh, Ninth, and Tenth Circuits, but a Sixth Circuit ruling upheld state laws in Michigan, Kentucky, Ohio, and Tennessee that defined marriage as a union between one man and one woman. With this conflict between the lower courts, the stage was set for the Court's historic decision.

JUSTICE KENNEDY delivered the opinion of the Court.

The Constitution promises liberty to all within its reach, a liberty that includes certain specific rights that allow persons, within a lawful realm, to define and express their identity. The petitioners in these cases seek to find that liberty by marrying someone of the same sex and having their marriages deemed lawful on the same terms and conditions as marriages between persons of the opposite sex. * * *

[*What follows is from the syllabus of the decision; internal citations to other cases are omitted and the page numbers refer to the pages in the slip opinion.*]

(a) Before turning to the governing principles and precedents, it is appropriate to note the history of the subject now before the Court.

(1) The history of marriage as a union between two persons of the opposite sex marks the beginning of these cases. To the respondents, it would demean a timeless institution if marriage were extended to same-sex couples. But the petitioners, far from seeking to devalue marriage, seek it for themselves because of their respect—and need—for its privileges and responsibilities, as illustrated by the petitioners' own experiences.

(2) The history of marriage is one of both continuity and change. Changes, such as the decline of arranged marriages and the abandonment of the law of coverture, have worked deep transformations in the structure of marriage, affecting aspects of marriage once viewed as essential. These new insights have strengthened, not weakened, the institution. Changed understandings of marriage are characteristic of a Nation where new dimensions of freedom become apparent to new generations.

This dynamic can be seen in the Nation's experience with gay and lesbian rights. Well into the 20th century, many States condemned same-sex intimacy as immoral, and homosexuality was treated as an illness. Later in the century, cultural and political developments allowed same-sex couples to lead more open and public lives. Extensive public and private dialogue followed, along with shifts in public attitudes. Questions about the legal treatment of gays and lesbians soon reached the courts, where they could be discussed in the formal discourse of the law. In 2003, this Court overruled its 1986 decision in *Bowers v. Hardwick*, which upheld a Georgia law that criminalized certain homosexual acts, concluding laws making same sex intimacy a crime "demea[n] the lives of homosexual persons" (*Lawrence v. Texas*). In 2012, the federal Defense of Marriage Act was also struck down (*United States v. Windsor*). Numerous same-sex marriage cases reaching the federal courts and state supreme courts have added to the dialogue. Pp. 6–10.

(b) The Fourteenth Amendment requires a State to license a marriage between two people of the same sex. Pp. 10–27.

(1) The fundamental liberties protected by the Fourteenth Amendment's Due Process Clause extend to certain personal choices central to individual dignity and autonomy, including intimate choices defining personal identity and beliefs. Courts must exercise reasoned judgment in identifying interests of the person so fundamental that the State must accord them its respect. History and tradition guide and discipline the inquiry but do not set its outer boundaries. When new insight reveals discord between the Constitution's central protections and a received legal stricture, a claim to liberty must be addressed.

Applying these tenets, the Court has long held the right to marry is protected by the Constitution. For example, *Loving v. Virginia* invalidated bans on interracial unions, and *Turner v. Safley* held that prisoners could not be denied the right to marry. To be sure, these cases presumed a relationship involving opposite-sex partners, as did *Baker v. Nelson*, a one-line summary decision issued in 1972, holding that the exclusion of same-sex couples from marriage did not present a substantial federal question. But other, more instructive precedents have expressed broader principles. In assessing whether the force and rationale of its cases apply to same-sex couples, the Court must respect the basic reasons why the right to marry has been long protected. This analysis compels the conclusion that same-sex couples may exercise the right to marry. Pp. 10–12.

(2) Four principles and traditions demonstrate that the reasons marriage is fundamental under the Constitution apply with equal force to same-sex couples. The first premise of this Court's relevant precedents is that the right to personal choice regarding marriage is inherent in the concept of individual autonomy. This abiding connection between marriage and liberty is why *Loving* invalidated interracial marriage bans under the Due Process Clause. Decisions about marriage are among the most intimate that an individual can make. This is true for all persons, whatever their sexual orientation.

A second principle in this Court's jurisprudence is that the right to marry is fundamental because it supports a two-person union unlike any other in its importance to the committed individuals. The intimate association protected by this right was central to *Griswold v. Connecticut,* which held the Constitution protects the right of married couples to use contraception and was acknowledged in *Turner.* Same-sex couples have the same right as opposite-sex couples to enjoy intimate association, a right extending beyond mere freedom from laws making same-sex intimacy a criminal offense.

A third basis for protecting the right to marry is that it safeguards children and families and thus draws meaning from related rights of childrearing, procreation, and education. Without the recognition, stability, and predictability marriage offers, children suffer the stigma of knowing their families are somehow lesser. They also suffer the significant material costs of being raised by unmarried parents, relegated to a more difficult and uncertain family life. The marriage laws at issue thus harm and humiliate the children of same-sex couples. This does not mean that the right to marry is less meaningful for those who do not or cannot have children. Precedent protects the right of a married couple not to procreate, so the right to marry cannot be conditioned on the capacity or commitment to procreate.

Finally, this Court's cases and the Nation's traditions make clear that marriage is a keystone of the Nation's social order. States have contributed to the fundamental character of marriage by placing it at the center of many facets of the legal and social order. There is no difference between same- and opposite-sex couples with respect to this principle, yet same-sex couples are denied the constellation of benefits that the States have linked to marriage and are consigned to an instability many opposite-sex couples would find intolerable. It is demeaning to lock same-sex couples out of a central institution of the Nation's society, for they too may aspire to the transcendent purposes of marriage.

The limitation of marriage to opposite-sex couples may long have seemed natural and just, but its inconsistency with the central meaning of the fundamental right to marry is now manifest. Pp. 12–18.

(3) The right of same-sex couples to marry is also derived from the Fourteenth Amendment's guarantee of equal protection. The Due Process Clause and the Equal Protection Clause are connected in a profound way. Rights implicit in liberty and rights secured by equal protection may rest on different precepts and are not always coextensive, yet each may be instructive as to the meaning and reach of the other. This dynamic is reflected in *Loving*, where the Court invoked both the Equal Protection Clause and the Due Process Clause; and in *Zablocki v. Redhail*, where the Court invalidated a law barring fathers delinquent on child-support payments from marrying. Indeed, recognizing that new insights and societal understandings can reveal unjustified inequality within fundamental institutions that once passed unnoticed and unchallenged, this Court has invoked equal protection principles to invalidate laws imposing sex-based inequality on marriage, and confirmed the relation between liberty and equality.

The Court has acknowledged the interlocking nature of these constitutional safeguards in the context of the legal treatment of gays and lesbians. This dynamic also applies to same-sex marriage. The challenged laws burden the liberty of same-sex couples, and they abridge central precepts of equality. The marriage laws at issue are in essence unequal: Same-sex couples are denied benefits afforded opposite-sex couples and are barred from exercising a fundamental right. Especially against a long history of disapproval of their relationships, this denial works a grave and continuing harm, serving to disrespect and subordinate gays and lesbians. Pp. 18–22.

(4) The right to marry is a fundamental right inherent in the liberty of the person, and under the Due Process and Equal Protection Clauses of the Fourteenth Amendment couples of the same-sex may not be deprived of that right and that liberty. Same-sex couples may exercise the fundamental right to marry. The State laws challenged by the petitioners in these cases are held invalid to the extent they exclude same-sex couples from civil marriage on the same terms and conditions as opposite-sex couples. Pp. 22–23.

(5) There may be an initial inclination to await further legislation, litigation, and debate, but referenda, legislative debates, and grassroots campaigns; studies and other writings; and extensive litigation in state and federal courts have led to an enhanced understanding of the issue. While the Constitution contemplates that democracy is the appropriate process for change, individuals who are harmed need not await legislative action before asserting a fundamental right. *Bowers*, in effect, upheld state action that denied gays and lesbians a fundamental right. Though it was eventually repudiated, men and women suffered pain and humiliation in the interim, and the effects of these injuries no doubt lingered long after *Bowers* was overruled. A ruling against same-sex couples would have the same effect and would be unjustified under the Fourteenth Amendment. The

petitioners' stories show the urgency of the issue they present to the Court, which has a duty to address these claims and answer these questions. Respondents' argument that allowing same-sex couples to wed will harm marriage as an institution rests on a counterintuitive view of opposite-sex couples' decisions about marriage and parenthood. Finally, the First Amendment ensures that religions, those who adhere to religious doctrines, and others have protection as they seek to teach the principles that are so fulfilling and so central to their lives and faiths. Pp. 23–27.

(c) The Fourteenth Amendment requires States to recognize same-sex marriages validly performed out of State. Since same-sex couples may now exercise the fundamental right to marry in all States, there is no lawful basis for a State to refuse to recognize a lawful same-sex marriage performed in another State on the ground of its same-sex character. Pp. 27–28.

772 F. 3d 388, reversed.

Acknowledgments

Greg Abbott: "Restoring the Rule of Law with States Leading the Way," by Governor Greg Abbott. Office of the Governor Press Release, January 8, 2016. Reprinted by permission of the Office of the Governor, State of Texas.

George J. Annas: From *The New England Journal of Medicine*, George J. Annas, "Jumping Frogs, Endangered Toads, and California's Medical-Marijuana Law," Vol. 353, Issue 21, pp. 2291-2296. Copyright © 2005 Massachusetts Medical Society. Reprinted with permission from Massachusetts Medical Society.

Yoni Appelbaum: "America's Fragile Constitution," *The Atlantic*, October 2015. © 2015 The Atlantic Media Co., as first published in The Atlantic Magazine. All rights reserved. Distributed by Tribune Content Agency, LLC.

Ronald Bailey: "Globalization is Good for You," Reason Magazine and Reason .com, June 2015. Reprinted by permission of the Reason Foundation.

Charles Beard: From *An Economic Interpretation of the Constitution of the United States* by Charles A. Beard. Copyright © 1913 and 1935 by Macmillan Publishing Co. Copyright renewed © 1941 by Charles A. Beard. Copyright renewed © 1963 by William Beard and Miriam B. Vagts. Reprinted with the permission of Free Press, a Division of Simon & Schuster, Inc. All rights reserved.

Peter Beinart: "Should the Poor be Allowed to Vote?" *The Atlantic*, October 22, 2014. © 2014 The Atlantic Media Co., as first published in The Atlantic Magazine. All rights reserved. Distributed by Tribune Content Agency, LLC.

Campaign Legal Center Staff: "Why Our Democracy Needs Disclosure," Campaign Legal Center Blog, August 18, 2011. Reprinted by permission of the Campaign Legal Center.

David Cole: "The Angry New Frontier: Gay Rights vs. Religious Liberty." From *The New York Review of Books*. Copyright © 2015 by David Cole. Reprinted by permission of The New York Review of Books.

Shikha Dalmia: "A State's Rights Approach to Immigration Reform," Reason Magazine and Reason.com, December 7, 2015. Reprinted by permission of the Reason Foundation.

Alexis de Tocqueville: "Political Association in the United States," pp. 189-195 from *Democracy in America* by Alexis de Tocqueville. Edited by J.P. Mayer and Max Lerner. Translated by George Lawrence. English translation copyright © 1965 by Harper & Row, Publishers, Inc. Reprinted by permission of HarperCollins Publishers.

Larry Diamond: "Ending the Presidential-Debate Duopoly," *The Atlantic*, May 8, 2015. © 2015 The Atlantic Media Co., as first published in The Atlantic Magazine. All rights reserved. Distributed by Tribune Content Agency, LLC.

The Economist: "Hamilton's heirs: Donald Trump's administration could deport millions of undocumented immigrants, using a system perfected under Barack Obama," *The Economist*, December 10, 2016. © The Economist Newspaper Limited, London 2016. Reprinted with permission; includes figure from "5 facts about illegal immigration in the U.S.," Pew Research Center, (November, 2016) http://www.pewresearch.org/fact-tank/2016/11/03/5-facts-about-illegal-immigration-in-the-u-s/. Reprinted with permission.

Chris Edwards: "Options for Federal Privatization and Reform Lessons from Abroad," *Cato Institute Policy Analysis*, No. 794, June 28, 2016. Reprinted by permission of the Cato Institute.

Daniel J. Elazar: "The Political Subcultures of the United States" from *The American Mosaic: The Impact of Space, Time, and Culture on American Politics* (Boulder, CO: Westview Press, 1994), pp. 229-36, 239-46. Reprinted by permission of the Estate of Daniel J. Elazar.

Richard F. Fenno, Jr.: "U.S. House Members in Their Constituencies: An Exploration," *The American Political Science Review*, Vol. 71, No. 3 (Sept., 1977). Copyright © 1977 American Political Science Association. Reprinted with the permission of Cambridge University Press.

Morris P. Fiorina: "The Decline of Collective Responsibility in American Politics," *Daedalus*, Vol. 109, No. 3, Summer 1980. © 1980 by the American Academy of Arts and Sciences. Reprinted by permission of MIT Press Journals.

John Fund: "Voter Fraud: We've Got Proof It's Easy," *National Review*, January 12, 2014. Copyright 2016 National Review. Used with permission.

George Gallup: "Polling the Public" from *A Guide to Public Opinion Polls* by George Gallup. © 1944 Princeton University Press, 1948 revised 2nd. Edition, 1975 renewed. Reprinted by permission of Princeton University Press.

William Galston: "Telling Americans to Vote, Or Else." From *The New York Times*, November 5, 2011. © 2011 *The New York Times*. All rights reserved. Used by permission and protected by the Copyright Laws of the United States. The printing, copying, redistribution, or retransmission of this Content without express written permission is prohibited.

Jon Gertner: "The Rise and Fall of the G.D.P." From *The New York Times*, May 16, 2010. © 2010 *The New York Times*. All rights reserved. Used by permission and protected by the Copyright Laws of the United States. The printing, copying, redistribution, or retransmission of this Content without express written permission is prohibited.

Allen C. Guelzo and James H. Hulme: "In Defense of the Electoral College," from *The Washington Post*, November 15, 2016. Reprinted by permission of Allen C. Guelzo, Gettysburg College and James H. Hulme. James H. Hulme is an attorney in private practice in Washington, D.C. He has been a partner with the law firm of Arent Fox LLP for thirty years.

Pratheepan Gulasekaram and Karthick Ramakrishnan: "Forget Border Walls and Mass Deportations: The Real Changes in Immigration Policy are Happening in the States," *The Washington Post, Monkey Cage*, September 24, 2015. Reprinted by permission of the authors.

Edmund Haislmaier, Nina Owcharenko, Robert Moffit, and Alyene Senger: "A Fresh Start for Health Care Reform," *Heritage Foundation Backgrounder* No. 2970, October 30, 2014. Reprinted by permission of The Heritage Foundation.

Tara Helfman: "The Religious-Liberty War." Reprinted from COMMENTARY [May/2015], by permission; copyright © 2016 by Commentary, Inc.

John R. Hibbing and Elizabeth Theiss-Morse: "Too Much of a Good Thing: More Representative Is Not Necessarily Better." *Political Science & Politics* (March 1998). Reprinted with the permission of the authors.

A. Barton Hinkle: "How to Fix the Economy, and Income Inequality, The Libertarian Way," Reason.com, August 10, 2015. Reprinted by permission of Richmond Times-Dispatch.

David C. John: "Providing Social Security Benefits in the Future." From *The Heritage Foundation Backgrounder,* No. 1735, March 25, 2004. Reprinted with the permission of The Heritage Foundation.

Jihii Jolly: "How Algorithms Decide the News You See." This article by Jihii Jolly originally appeared online in the *Columbia Journalism Review,* May 20, 2014, as part of a series on News Literacy. Reprinted by permission of the author.

Charles O. Jones: "Perspectives on the Presidency." From *The Presidency in a Separated System.* Copyright © 1994 by The Brookings Institution. Reprinted with the permission of The Brookings Institution, Washington, D.C.

Robert P. Jones, Daniel Cox, E.J. Dionne, and William A. Galston: "What it Means to Be an American: Attitudes in an Increasingly Diverse America Ten Years after 9/11," Governance Studies at Brookings Institution and Public Religion Research Institute, 2016. Reprinted by permission of Brookings Institution, Washington D.C. and Public Religion Research Institute.

Michael Kammen: "Introduction" by Michael Kammen, from *The Origins of the American Constitution: A Documentary History,* edited by Michael Kammen, copyright © 1986 by Michael Kammen. Used by permission of Viking Books, an imprint of Penguin Publishing Group, a division of Penguin Random House LLC.

V.O. Key, Jr.: "The Voice of a People: An Echo," reprinted by permission of the publisher from *The Responsible Electorate: Rationality in Presidential Voting, 1936-1960* by V.O. Key, Jr., with the assistance of Milton C. Cummings, Jr., pp. 1-8, Cambridge, Mass.: The Belknap Press of Harvard University Press, Copyright © 1966 by the President and Fellows of Harvard College.

Ezra Klein: "A Third Party Won't Fix What's Broken in American Politics," Vox .com, December 8, 2014. Reprinted by permission of Vox Media Inc.

Matt Levendusky: "Are Fox and MSNBC Polarizing America?" *The Washington Post, Monkey Cage,* February 3, 2014. Reprinted by permission of Matt Levendusky.

Sanford Levinson: Chapter 1, "The Ratification Referendum," from *Our Undemocratic Constitution: Where the Constitution Goes Wrong (And How We the People Can Correct It)* by Sanford Levinson, pp. 11-24. Copyright © 2006 by Oxford University Press, Inc. Reprinted with permission of Oxford University Press.

Theodore J. Lowi: "American Business, Public Policy, Case Studies, and Political Theory," *World Politics* Vol. 16, No. 4 (July 1964). Copyright © 1964 Trustees of Princeton University. Reprinted with the permission of Cambridge University Press.

David Mayhew: From *Congress: The Electoral Connection* (New Haven: Yale University Press, 1974). Copyright © 1974 by Yale University. Reprinted by permission of Yale University Press.

Louis Menand: "The Unpolitical Animal: How Political Science Understands Voters," *The New Yorker,* August 30, 2004. Copyright © Louis Menand. Reprinted by permission of the author.

Lorraine C. Minnite: "The Myth of Voter Fraud," by Lorraine C. Minnite. This article was originally published on BillMoyers.com, March 9, 2015. Copyright © 2015 Public Square Media, Inc. CC BY-ND 4.0 License.

Richard Morin: "Choice Words: If You Can't Understand Our Poll Questions, Then How Can We Understand Your Answers?" From *The Washington Post,* January 10, 1999, © 1999 The Washington Post. All rights reserved. Used by permission and protected by the Copyright Laws of the United States. The printing, copying, redistribution, or retransmission of the Material without express written permission is prohibited.

Richard Neustadt: "The Power to Persuade," from *Presidential Power: The Politics of Leadership from FDR to Carter,* 1st Edition, © 1980. Reprinted by permission of Pearson Education, Inc., New York, New York.

John Nichols: "Democracy Denied," *The Progressive,* December 2016/January 2017, pp. 15-18. Reprinted by permission of The Progressive.

David M. O'Brien: "The Court in American Life." From *Storm Center: The Supreme Court in American Politics,* Third Edition by David M. O'Brien. Copyright © 1993, 1990, 1986 by David M. O'Brien. Used by permission of W. W. Norton & Company, Inc.

Mancur Olson: "The Logic of Collective Action," from *Rise and Decline of Nations* (New Haven: Yale University Press, 1982). Copyright © 1982 by Yale University. Reprinted by permission of Yale University Press.

Walter Olson: "An Article V Constitutional Convention? Wrong Idea, Wrong Time," Cato Institute, January 5, 2016. Reprinted by permission of Walter Olson.

Paul E. Peterson: From *The Price of Federalism.* Copyright © 1995 by The Brookings Institution. Reprinted with the permission of The Brookings Institution, Washington, D.C.

Paul R. Pillar: "Welcome to Generation War," *The National Interest,* July/August 2016. Reprinted by permission of The National Interest.

Richard A. Posner: "In Defense of the Electoral College." From Slate, November 12, 2013. © 2012 The Slate Group. All rights reserved. Used by permission and protected by the Copyright Laws of the United States. The printing, copying, redistribution, or retransmission of the Material without express written permission is prohibited.

Markus Prior: Excerpts from "News vs. Entertainment: How Increasing Media Choice Widens Gaps in Political Knowledge and Turnout," *American Journal of Political Science,* July 2005, Vol. 49, Issue 3, pp. 577-592. Copyright © Midwest Political Science Association. Reprinted by permission of John Wiley & Sons, Inc.

Nicol C. Rae: "Be Careful What You Wish For: The Rise of Responsible Parties in American National Politics." Reproduced with permission of *Annual Review of Political Science.* Volume 10 © 2007 by Annual Reviews, www.annualreviews.org

Jonathan Rauch: "In Defense of Prejudice: Why Incendiary Speech Must be Protected." Copyright © 1995 Harper's Magazine. All rights reserved. Reproduced from the May issue by special permission.

Jon Riches: "The Victims of 'Dark Money' Disclosure: How Government Reporting Requirements Suppress Speech and Limit Charitable Giving," *Goldwater Institute Policy Report*, August 5, 2015, pp. 11-15. Reprinted by permission of the Goldwater Institute.

Gerald Rosenberg: Excerpts from *The Hollow Hope: Can Courts Bring About Social Change?* (University of Chicago Press, 1993). © 1991 by The University of Chicago. Reprinted by permission of the University of Chicago Press.

Antonin Scalia: "Constitutional Interpretation the Old Fashioned Way." Remarks at the Woodrow Wilson International Center for Scholars in Washington, D.C., March 14, 2005.

Michael Schudson: From *The Good Citizen: A History of American Civic Life* by Michael Schudson. Copyright © 1998 by Michael Schudson. Reprinted with the permission of Free Press, a Division of Simon & Schuster, Inc. All rights reserved.

John Sides: "Can Partisan Media Contribute to Healthy Politics?" *The Washington Post, Monkey Cage,* March 10, 2013. Reprinted by permission of John Sides.

Rogers M. Smith: "Beyond Tocqueville, Myrdal and Hartz: The Multiple Traditions in America," *The American Political Science Review,* Vol. 87, No. 3 (Sept., 1993). Copyright © 1993 American Political Science Association. Reprinted with the permission of Cambridge University Press.

George Soros: "The Age of Open Society." From *The New Era*. Reprinted with the permission of the author.

Matthew Spalding: "Congress' Constitutional Prerogative vs. Executive Branch Overreach," *The Daily Signal,* April 1, 2016. © 2016 The Daily Signal. Reprinted by permission of The Daily Signal.

David B. Truman: "The Alleged Mischiefs of Faction." From *The Governmental Process* (New York: Alfred A. Knopf, 1971). Reprinted with permission of Edwin M. Truman.

Steven M. Warshawsky: "What Does It Mean To Be An American?" *American Thinker,* July 2, 2007. Reprinted by permission of the author.

Janine R. Wedel: "Federalist No. 70: Where does the Public Service Begin and End?" *Public Administration Review,* December 2011, Vol. 71, Issue s1, pp. s118-s127. © American Society for Public Administration. Reprinted by permission of John Wiley & Sons, Inc.

George Will: "How Income Inequality Benefits Everybody." From *The Washington Post,* March 25, 2015, © 2015 The Washington Post. All rights reserved. Used by permission and protected by the Copyright Laws of the United States. The printing, copying, redistribution, or retransmission of the Material without express written permission is prohibited.

Ray Williams: "Why Income Inequality Threatens Democracy," *Psychology Today,* August 12, 2015. Reprinted by permission of the author.

James Q. Wilson: Excerpts from *Bureaucracy: What Government Agencies Do and Why They Do It*. Copyright © 1989 James Q. Wilson. Reprinted by permission of Basic Books, a member of the Perseus Books Group.